W9-ASX-416

From Slavery •

to Freedom

From Slavery to Freedom

A History of Negro Americans •

THIRD EDITION

• **John Hope Franklin**

Vintage Books

A Division of Random House · New York

TO **Aurelia**

Preface TO THE THIRD EDITION

Almost twenty years ago the first edition of this work appeared. Ten years ago I revised it and brought it up to date. Since that time the very pace at which events have moved has discouraged any effort to prepare a revision that would inevitably be out of date at the time of its publication. It seems fitting, nevertheless, to present a rather extensively revised edition on the occasion of the twentieth anniversary of the first edition.

I feel constrained to add that even the revolutionary developments of the last decade should not obscure the fact that this is essentially a history and not a contemporary tract. Therefore, these developments have been valuable for the historian not only in themselves but also in the new perspectives they provide as one looks at past, even remote events. These new perspectives are reflected in some of the revisions of the earlier parts of the book.

The revisions have been greatly facilitated by the generous and helpful criticisms and suggestions of my students, colleagues, and friends. Arthur Spingarn and August Meier have assisted me in correcting several serious errors; and Richard Fuke, my research assistant, has been a virtual collaborator in his critical reading of the text and in his valuable updating of much of the material. To these and all the others who have helped in countless ways I am deeply grateful.

Chicago, Illinois
July 4, 1966

JOHN HOPE FRANKLIN

Preface TO THE SECOND EDITION

The nine years that have elapsed since this work first appeared have been among the most momentous in the history of the American Negro. The postwar years witnessed vigorous efforts, not always successful, on the part of Negroes and many white Americans to elevate substantially the position of the Negro in American life. The 1954 decision of the Supreme Court in the school desegregation cases was the most dramatic and significant of the frontal attacks on segregation and discrimination, but by no means was it the only one. World attention, moreover, has been focused on the issue of race as never before, and the status of the Negro in the United States has been scrutinized with extreme care by peoples in many other parts of the world. This very scrutiny has had a most salutary effect. The task of the historian in tracing and properly evaluating the numerous developments that have taken place abounds in difficulties, but it nevertheless seems worthwhile at this point to take cognizance of some of the more significant trends.

If this edition is an improvement over the first edition, it is due largely to the able assistance of many persons. The reviewers of the first edition, letters from readers, and my own colleagues and students were not only generous in praise but helpful in pointing out errors and oversights. I am grateful to these careful readers for their thoughtful generosity, and I have taken into consideration their suggestions. The increased interest in the problems of the Negro has stimulated much research and writing in the field; the numerous books and articles on almost every aspect and period of Negro life and history have greatly increased my understanding of the matters with which this book deals. At many points the influence of these works is reflected. I can only hope that I have done violence neither to the diligent work of others nor to the dramatic events that have transpired.

Washington, D.C.
June 15, 1956

JOHN HOPE FRANKLIN

Preface TO THE FIRST EDITION

In the present work I have undertaken to bring together the essential facts in the history of the American Negro from his ancient African beginnings down to the present time. In doing so it was deemed unnecessary to relate the development of Negro life and history in other parts of the world except where there was a discernible connection with the history of the Negro in the United States. Thus only so much of African history was considered here as evolved in the area from which the vast majority of American Negroes came, and as much more as helped to shape Afro-American institutions in the Old World and the New. On the other hand, it was necessary to consider briefly the Negroes of the Caribbean and of Latin America, because their history belongs to the larger pattern of development of the Negro in the New World. For a similar reason, it was deemed desirable to give some attention to the Negroes of Canada, for they are in a large measure erstwhile citizens or residents of the United States.

I have made a conscious effort to write the history of the Negro in America with due regard for the forces at work which have affected his development. This has involved a continuous recognition of the main stream of American history and the relationship of the Negro to it. It has been necessary, therefore, to a considerable extent, to re-tell the story of the evolution of the people of the United States in order to place the Negro in his proper relationship and perspective. To have proceeded otherwise would have been to ignore the indisputable fact that historical forces are all pervasive and cut through the most rigid barriers of race and caste. It would have been impossible to trace the history of the Negro in America without remaining sensitive to the main currents in the emergence of American civilization.

While I have sought to interpret critically the forces and personalities that have shaped the history of the Negro in the United States, I have attempted to avoid a subjective and unscientific treatment of the subject. This procedure has involved the maintenance of a discreet balance between recognizing the deeds of outstanding persons and depicting the fortunes of the great mass of Negroes. To be sure there were times when dominant personalities forged to the front and assumed roles of responsibility and leadership; these individuals have been recognized. But the history of the Negro in America is essentially the story of the strivings of the nameless millions who have sought adjustment in a new and sometimes hostile world. This work is, therefore, a history of the Negro people, with a proper consideration for anonymous as well as outstanding people.

I have given considerable attention to the task of tracing the interaction of the Negro and the American environment. It can hardly be denied that the course of American history has been vitally affected by his presence. At the same time it must be admitted that the effect of acculturation on the Negro in the United States has been so marked that today he is as truly American as any member of other ethnic groups that make up the American population. That is not to say that the story of the Negro is one solely of achievement or of success. Too frequently the Negro's survival in America has depended on his capacity to adjust—indeed, to accommodate—himself to the dominant culture and the obstacles have at times been too great to permit him to make significant achievements in the usual sense of the word. The task here has been not to recite his achievements—though naturally some have been so outstanding as to warrant consideration—but to tell the story of the process by which the Negro has sought to cast his lot with an evolving American civilization.

The obligations which I am under for direct and indirect aid received in writing this book are numerous, and it is not possible for me to indicate every instance of assistance which co-operative persons have rendered. Without the researches of Carter G. Woodson, Charles H. Wesley, W. E. B. DuBois, Luther P. Jackson, and many other scholars who have contributed significant writings to the field, it would not have been possible for me to write this book. I am grateful to all these patient, careful scholars for the indispensable services they have performed for all students of American history. I am under special obligation to the Library of Congress which generously placed its many facilities at my disposal, and to the North Carolina College Library, the Stanford L. Warren Library, the Duke University Library, the New York Public Library, and the American Museum of Natural History for their kind assistance.

I am under obligation to the following publishers for their kind permission to make brief quotations from works published by them: The Columbia University Press: Lorenzo J. Greene, *The Negro in Colonial New England* and Sterling Spero and Abram L. Harris, *The Black Worker;* Harcourt, Brace and Company: Claude McKay, *Harlem Shadows;* The Macmillan Company: C. Vann Woodward, *Tom Watson, Agrarian Rebel;* The University of Michigan Press: Dwight L. Dumond, *The Antislavery Origins of the Civil War;* The Yale University Press: Bell I. Wiley, *Southern Negroes, 1861–1865;* and Doubleday and Company: R. R. Moton, *Finding a Way Out.*

To Abram L. Harris, C. Vann Woodward, Mrs. Arthur P. Chippey, Howard K. Beale, L. D. Reddick, Rayford W. Logan, Clement Eaton, Mrs. Dorothy Porter, and Arthur S. Link, I am grateful for helpful suggestions and numerous criticisms. Among my colleagues who have assisted me in this effort I am especially grateful to Joseph H. Taylor, Joseph S. Himes, W. Edward Farrison, Albert L. Turner, Charles A. Ray, Albert Manley, and Miss Helen G. Edmonds. President James E. Shepard kindly relieved me of my teaching duties so that I could complete the manuscript, and I am sincerely appreciative of his generosity. The dedication of the work to my wife expresses inadequately my deep gratitude to her for her sacrifices, co-operation, and enthusiastic support of my efforts in historical writing.

Durham, North Carolina　　　　　　　　　　JOHN HOPE FRANKLIN
April 4, 1947

Contents

Illustrations

From Slavery •
to Freedom

1 •

A Cradle of Civilization

Physical and Human Geography

● *Egypt was an especially attractive land. Its warm climate* was eminently suited for human beings who had not yet learned how to live with ease in colder areas. The great Nile, with its annual overflow, gave fertility to the valley through which it ran; and the abundant vegetation springing up from the rich soil and growing to maturity under the vital sun in a long season minimized the struggle for existence. There was just enough geographic protection to make invasion difficult, but not enough to foster isolation and stagnation. Protection, food, and warmth—these were the factors that made Egypt so attractive to the hordes who sought the security of its bosom and founded the civilization that was to be the basis for so many of the institutions of the Western world.

Long before the dawn of literary history, the peoples of the eastern Mediterranean world had begun to yield to the temptation of migrating into Egypt. From almost every direction they came. From the North came those who are commonly referred to as the Mediterranean race. From the East came the Semitic nomads, who represented in their own ancestry a constant intermingling of the racial groups of Western Asia. From the South came the black and brown tribes of Ethiopia, who saw in the Nile the highway over which they could join their fellows in the search for a better life. If one group was indigenous to the area, the others were there before any noticeable advancements in the direction of civilization were made. And the intermingling of these races was so extensive, and the fusion of their cultures was so complete that it is almost impossible to ascribe any feature of the civilization which emerged to any particular group. What happened was that before the culture and civilization of Egypt took shape there had come into being a new group of people, neither basically Mediterranean, Semitic, nor Ethiopian, but Egyptian—the sum total of the intermingling. This is not to say that racial stabilization was thus achieved. Migrations from all directions continued, and frequently the character and appearance of the Egyptian leaned toward that group whose infiltration was, for the moment, heaviest.

The picture that one can derive of the physical appearance of the Egyptian depends on the source of the description and the period for which the observation is made. Doubtless, many were "black and curly-haired" as Herodotus described them in the fifth century before Christ. Homer and other Greek writers regarded the Egyptians as black. The art pieces that have been recovered by archaeologists show a great variation in the appearance of the Egyptians, ranging from the Mediterranean type with features usually associated with Caucasians to the distinctly Negroid type with fleshy lips, broad noses, and woolly hair. The controversies that have raged among modern historians regarding the physical appearance of the Egyptians not only reflect the tendencies of many students to interpret facts as they desire, but they also bear witness to the fact that in all probability Egyptians were a decidedly mixed race with all the variable characteristics that such a group usually possesses.

If each of the racial groups that entered Egypt shared in the creation of a new ethnic group, they also shared in the development of the civilization that was to gain for Egypt the title, "A Cradle of Civilization." It would be impossible, as well as pointless, to ascribe to each group certain specific contributions, although students have tentatively agreed that the Semitic groups, for example, influenced the language of the area to a considerable degree. The contributions of each group should neither be minimized nor overrated. There is no conclusive evidence, as has been contended, that the "feat of building up the civilization of Egypt was chiefly that of the Mediterranean race." Doubtless, they contributed heavily, but the constant infiltration of Negroid peoples from the south and the domination by Negroes of the country's political life in its later stages of development cannot be regarded lightly in any final evaluation of the sources of culture and civilization in ancient Egypt.

A Civilization Emerges

The favorable geographic factors and the presence of diverse races who shared with each other their own peculiar cultural and social experiences gave to Egypt an advantage over many other lands and stimulated the early development of a civilization there. By the time of the New Stone Age the inhabitants of Egypt had settled down to a sedentary life of agriculture. There is much evidence to bear out the belief that they were cultivating wheat, millet, barley, and flax. They had also domesticated many animals, including goats, sheep, donkeys, and cattle. Shortly, they began to reclaim land and to develop a system of irrigation. Their resourcefulness and self-sufficiency are amply demonstrated in the high degree of skill which they achieved in weaving linen and other textiles, in making tools, and in building houses. As they entered the age of metal, they displayed exceptional skill in fashioning objects of art and implements in copper and bronze.

Even before 3000 B.C. there was a large industrial population in Egypt. Men were engaged in mining, metallurgy, brickmaking, masonry, carpentry, tanning, weaving, and shipbuilding. The rather clear-cut division of labor encouraged specialization and promoted efficiency in production. Craftsmen working in their own shops, on the estates of the great landlords, or in the royal workhouses produced works of such utility and beauty that any age would be proud to claim them.

Sculpture and painting are seldom highly developed except in areas where the social and cultural experience of a people has endured for a long period of time and where economic and political life make for both stability and freedom. It would be too much, therefore, to expect that Egyptian sculpture and painting were what modern critics would judge as advanced. They did, however, serve a useful purpose for Egyptians as religious and historical materials. The sculpture was hardly more than crudely cut outlines of subjects, while painting lacked perspective and shading. In architecture the Egyptians made remarkable advances in the precision-like constructions of houses, royal palaces, and pyramids. These works gave clear evidence of a thorough knowledge not only of architecture but physics, engineering, and geometry as well.

Egyptians, again drawing on the diverse experiences of their several forebears, organized the kind of political state that evolved from the simple to the complex, from the local city-states to a powerful national unit. As prosperity came to Egypt and as the inhabitants discerned the advantages in larger political units, small villages began to cooperate in order to bring about more effective methods of irrigation and to pool their resources for the general welfare. As cities began to unite, political organization shifted from a kinship to a territorial basis, and there came into existence the large city-states, generally called "nomes." As the rulers of nomes extended their influences to other areas, the process of national unification was well under way. By 4000 B.C. the nomes had become so unified as to form an upper and a lower kingdom. Gradually a complete system of government had evolved with powerful officials who maintained their position both by reason of heredity and military strength.

It was near the end of the fourth millennium B.C. that Egypt was unified under one ruler, the Pharaoh. There emerged a conception of him that at once strengthened his position and made possible the almost irrevocable cohesion of the country. He was regarded as the descendant of a god and therefore divine. He wielded absolute authority over the social, religious and economic life of his people. He was, moreover, the defender of the realm and the dispenser of justice. There were well-conceived notions of impartial justice, the administration of which was guaranteed by the Pharaoh. Under him was a hierarchy of officials, secular and religious, who executed his decrees and commands.

Just as there emerged a central political organization, there also evolved, in due time, a kind of national religion, at the head of which was, of course, the Pharaoh. The principal god of the country was the principal god of the city from which the Pharaoh came. Finally, the sun god, Ra, and later Amon-Ra, stood at the center of the Egyptian pantheon with many lesser deities playing subordinate roles. The elaborate hierarchy of priests administered the souls of the living and the dead. Intricate rites were performed in the temples and at the pyramids, the burial places of members of the royal family. The priests not only played an important role in systematizing and directing

Egyptian religious life, but also wielded considerable influence in secular life. Whenever the opportunity presented itself, the priests would ally themselves with members of the nobility to reduce the power of the Pharaoh and thereby enhance their own position. That the opportunity seldom came was due to the fact that the Pharaoh usually maintained a sufficiently firm hand to prevent the rise of any group that could successfully challenge his authority.

Ethiopian Domination

This whole development of Egyptian civilization took place in an atmosphere of change, manifested largely by the continuous migration into the land of peoples from the outside world. It was not invasion, that is, not until the Hyksos came in during the eighteenth century B.C., but rather a steady flow of peoples from all directions bringing additional experiences and elements of other cultures that improved that which Egypt had created. By the second millennium B.C. Egypt had already become the crossroads of civilization through which passed the peoples from Asia, Europe, and Ethiopia. Some remained temporarily, while others remained indefinitely, but all affected, and were affected by, the civilization which had emerged.

Not only was there a steady infiltration of black peoples from the South, but periodically great hordes of them would descend from the upper Nile valley and threaten the equilibrium of life which the peoples of Egypt had achieved. In the third millennium before Christ, one such incident occurred, when the Pharaoh experienced difficulty in repulsing the Negroes from the Nubian desert. Within less than a century, however, a Negro, Ra Nahesi, was on the throne. From time to time, after 1703 B.C. when a new empire was founded, Negroes occupied positions of responsibility and honor in the Egyptian government. Nefertari, the wife of Ahmose I, Egypt's great imperial leader, has been described as a Negro woman "of great beauty, strong personality, and remarkable administrative ability." As the co-founder of Egypt's Eighteenth Dynasty, she contributed a decidedly Negroid tint to her descendants who were to rule after Ahmose I.

During the Hyksos invasion (c. 1700–1580 B.C.) many Egyptians fled to the upper Nile valley and mingled freely with the

Negroes, Ethiopians, of that region; and the result was that Egyptians became more Negroid than ever before. This tendency toward mixing was, in all probability, extended in the imperial period when the Egyptian rulers established political control over a considerable portion of Ethiopia. The political domination and the resulting commercial intercourse made Ethiopia and her people an integral part of Egyptian culture. Indeed, the integration became so complete that by the first millennium before Christ Ethiopians were gaining a political ascendancy that shortly won for them the coveted positions at the head of the Egyptian government.

Complete control over the Egyptians was achieved in the eighth century before Christ by Piankhi, whose father had seized control of the upper Nile a few years earlier. Beginning about 741 B.C. Piankhi opened a campaign of conquest which resulted in the complete subjugation of Egypt. With his large contingent of trained soldiers and river navy he routed the Libyans who were threatening his position in the area below Thebes. One by one the cities of the Northern region, Heracleopolis, Memphis, Heliopolis, Mesed, fell before the might of this wily Ethiopian. When Piankhi returned to his capital, Napata, he had subdued sixteen princes and had made Egypt a dependency of Ethiopia. The domination continued for the better part of a century. Piankhi's brother, Shabaka, succeeded him in 710 B.C. He maintained peace throughout the land and sought to repel the Assyrians by negotiation. The succeeding Ethiopian Pharaohs, Shabataka and Taharka, experienced increased difficulty in resisting the Assyrians; and by 670 the Asiatic soldiers had driven the Ethiopians out of lower Egypt. Gradually Egypt's role in later history became more and more manifest, as now Asiatics then Europeans began to overrun her, crushing her political and social institutions, defiling her holy places, and making her the pawn of international intrigue and chicanery.

Egypt suffered no unusual cultural decline under the Ethiopian Pharaohs. Having played a part in the growth and development of the civilization of the North and having absorbed much of the culture of the Egyptians during centuries of continuous intercourse, they felt themselves a part of the civilization whose custodians they now were. The blacks from Nubia had helped to construct the great Sphinxes, pyramids, and public buildings of Egypt. They had helped to perfect the political organization of the country. With their imaginative genius they had played a part in the evolution of Egyptian religious institutions. Thus, it was not at all awkward for Piankhi to offer sacrifice to the Egyptian gods in all the cities he conquered and to appropriate all the available property for his own treasury and the sacred fortune of Amon, the Theban god which had attained prominence in Egyptian religion many centuries earlier.

The period of Ethiopian domination of Egypt witnessed an attempt at cultural and artistic revival under Shabaka, who built a magnificent chapel at Karnak, which required an expedition to the great quarries at Hammamat. He also restored the temple at Thebes, and sponsored the restoration of an ancient religious text in the temple of Ptah from which so much information regarding the history of Egypt has been derived. Despite the wars that plagued his reign, Taharka was able to improve the economic, cultural, and religious life of his domain. Buildings were constructed at Tanis, Memphis, and Thebes; and a great temple was begun at Karnak. Prosperity was so extensive and his control was so absolute that Taharka styled himself the "Emperor of the World."

After the Assyrian conquest of Egypt the Ethiopian rulers retired to their own land where they continued an uninterrupted rule for many centuries. At Napata and later at Meroe the Ethiopian kings ruled in splendor and reflected in their political and cultural institutions their long contact with Egypt. The Egyptian system of writing was adopted, and temples, pyramids, and baths, similar to those found in Egyptian cities, were constructed at Meroe, Napata, and other Ethiopian cities. By the beginning of the Christian Era, Ethiopia enjoyed a position of respectability independent of that of Egypt. Semites, Romans, and Egyptians began to migrate to the attractive land; and by the fourth century A.D., it was a Christian dependency of the Roman empire. This connection with a foreign power resulted in the opening up of Ethiopia to the outside world. It became the highway across which went not only Romans, but peoples from Eastern Europe and Arab tribes from beyond the Red Sea. Trade with Byzantium and India followed, and Ethiopia became a part of a great intercontinental cultural movement that extended from Britain to India.

When the militant religion of Mohammed began to sweep into Africa it was the Christian Ethiopians who repulsed them for more than two centuries. From their new capital at Dongola, the Ethiopian kings sent thousands of soldiers to resist the

Islamic invasions. When, finally, the fiery Mohammedans could no longer be repulsed, an agreement was reached whereby the Ethiopians were required to pay tribute to the Arabs, a practice which was maintained for six hundred years. Sporadic fighting broke out almost every year until the kingdom finally fell in the sixteenth century.

The coming of Greeks, Romans, and Arabs into Ethiopia in the Christian Era fixed on that land a character of change and fluctuation that was to deprive it of much of the culture that can be said to have been indigenous. It also awoke in the Nubians themselves a passion for migration, since they could no longer consider their own land as belonging to them. The result was that they began to migrate westward into the forests and deserts of the Sudan and finally on to the Atlantic, where they found civilizations already developed in Yoruba and Benin. Thus, the culture of Egypt and Ethiopia was extended to many other parts of Africa, and was fused with the indigenous cultures of those areas and with the other cultures that made their way to the western land. These various ingredients could still be distinguished in West Africa when Europeans began to make inroads at the end of the Middle Ages.

II •

Early Negro States of Africa

Ghana

● *When the Arabs swept into North and West Africa in the* seventh century they found a civilization that was already thousands of years old. Although the land from the Atlantic to the Nile had enjoyed limited contact with other civilized portions of the world for many centuries, there is substantial evidence that much of the culture which the Arabs found was indigenous to the area. Indeed many well developed political states had risen and fallen before any lasting contact was established between West Africa and the Near East. These states sprang up in more or less the same general region, from the Mediterranean southward to the Gulf of Guinea and from the Atlantic eastward almost to the Nile. Successively in this region rose the major states of Ghana, Melle, Songhay, and many lesser states.

The first West African state of which there is any record is Ghana, also known as Kumbi and Walata. Although its accurately recorded history does not antedate the fourth century, there is much evidence that Ghana's political and cultural history extends, perhaps, back into the pre-Christian era. By 300 A.D. at least forty-four kings had ruled in that land. It has been held by some that Ghana was founded and ruled by white men from the East. The available evidence tends to show, however, that there were white settlements in Ghana, but the black people were the real rulers to whom the Semitic and other non-Negroid groups paid tribute. When the earliest observations of Ghana were made, it was a confederacy of a series of settlements extending from the Senegal to the upper Niger. Its boundaries were not well defined, and doubtless they changed with the fortunes of the kingdom. The territory was divided into provinces of which there were several subdivisions, suggesting a rather high degree of political organization. Most of the public offices were hereditary, and the tendency was for the stratified social order to become solidified.

The records seem to bear out the view that most of the expansion of Ghana was not the result of military conquest and that the people were, on the whole, devoted to the pursuits of peace. They were an agricultural people, and enjoyed some prosperity until continuous droughts extended the desert to their principal farm lands. As long as they were able to carry on their farming, gardens and date groves dotted the countryside, and there was an abundance of sheep and cattle in the outlying areas. They were also a trading people, and their chief town, Kumbi-Kumbi, was an important commercial center during the Middle Ages. By the beginning of the tenth century the Mohammedan influence was pronounced. Kumbi-Kumbi had a native and an Arab section, and the people were gradually adhering to the religion of Islam. The prosperity that came in the wake of Arabian infiltration increased the power of Ghana, and its influence was extended in all directions. In the eleventh century, when the king had become Mohammedan, Ghana could boast of an army of 200,000 and a lucrative trade across the desert. From the Mohammedan countries came wheat, fruit, and sugar. From across the desert came caravans laden with textiles, brass, pearls, and salt. Ghana exchanged rubber, ivory, slaves, and gold for these commodities. The Tunka, or emperor, recognized the value of this commercial intercourse by imposing a tax on imports and exports and appointing a collector to look after his interests.

Under the Negro rulers of the Sisse dynasty, Ghana reached the height of its power. Tribes as far north as Tichit in present Mauretania paid tribute to the king of Ghana; while in the south its influence extended to the gold mines of the Falome and of the Bambuk whose yields supplied the coffers of the Sisse with the gold used in the trade with Moroccan caravans. In faraway Cairo and Bagdad, Ghana was the subject of discussion among commercial and religious groups.

The reign of Tenkamenin in the eleventh century is an appropriate point at which to observe the kingdom of Ghana. Tenkamenin reigned over a vast empire which, through the taxes and tributes collected by the provincial rulers, made him immensely wealthy. He lived in a fortified castle made beautiful by sculpture, pictures, and decorated windows of the royal artists. The royal grounds also contained temples in which native gods were worshipped, a prison in which political enemies were incarcerated, and the tombs of the preceding kings. The king, highly esteemed by all his subjects, held court in magnificent splendor. His personal attire consisted of robes made of the most elegant materials available, a turban decorated with jewels, and a gold collar and bracelets.

The king of Ghana personally administered justice to his subjects. Taking his seat under a large open-air pavilion, he welcomed his subjects who desired some royal favor. It was an awe-inspiring spectacle as Tenkamenin presided on such auspicious occasions. Ten horses, adorned with gold trappings surrounded the pavilion. Ten armed pages stood behind him, while the male members of the royal family, magnificently attired, stood to his right. The governors and imperial officials sat on the ground before the king. Trained mastiffs, with gold and silver collars and bells, guarded the doors of the pavilion. In this setting Tenkamenin sat in judgment of his subjects. After the court was opened with the beating of drums, the king bestowed honors on worthy subjects and punished those who had won his disfavor.

During Tenkamenin's reign the people of Ghana adhered to a religion based on a belief that every earthly object contained good or evil spirits that had to be satisfied if they were to prosper. The king, naturally, was at the head of the religion. In 1076, however, a fanatical band of Mohammedans called the Almoravides invaded Ghana and gradually brought the area under the influence of their religion. They captured the capital and killed all who would not accept their religion of Islam. The religious strife that ensued was enough to undermine the kingdom of Ghana. By the end of the eleventh century, Ghana entered a period of economic decline brought on by a series of droughts that dried up the important Wagadu and Bagana Rivers. Under such trying circumstances it fell easy prey to the waves of conquerors who swept in to destroy the kingdom in the twelfth and thirteenth centuries.

Melle

As Ghana began to decline another Negro kingdom in the west arose to supplant it and to exceed the heights which Ghana had reached. Melle, also called Mellestine and Mandingoland, began as a strongly organized kingdom about A.D. 1235, but the nucleus of its political organization dates back to the beginning of the seventh century. For the first four centuries, it was relatively insignificant and its mansas, or kings, had no prestige or influence. In the middle of the eleventh century the king of Melle, Baramendana Keita, was converted to Mohammedanism because he believed the Moslems responsible for the coming of the much needed rain. In gratitude for this act of Allah, Baramendana made a pilgrimage to Mecca. Although the natives continued to adhere to their own religion, the king was now in a position to strengthen himself through military and religious alliances with fellow followers of Islam. Kangaba, once a mere residence of a tribal chief, soon became the capital of a kingdom and, finally, the center of a veritable empire as the influence of the king of Melle spread in all directions. Trade relations were established with neighboring states and with distant Arab states; and the Mansa of Melle soon became the most powerful person of West Africa. One by one he disposed of the small states—Soso, Diara, Galam—that had attempted to build on the ruins of Ghana. No longer a vassal of anyone, he was the master to whom many vassals paid homage.

The credit for consolidating and strengthening the kingdom of Melle goes to Sundiata Keita who overran Sosa, the king of Soso, and leveled the former capital of Ghana in 1240. It was a later successor, however, variously called Gonga-Mussa and Kankan-Mussa, who carried the Mandingoes to new and glorious heights. This remarkable and semi-barbaric member of the Keita dynasty ruled from 1307 to 1332. Having an empire comprising most of what is now French-speaking West Africa he could devote his attention to the peaceful pursuits of encouraging the industry of his people and displaying the wealth of his kingdom. The people of Melle were predominantly agricultural, but a substantial number was engaged in weaving, construction, and mining. The fabulously rich mines of Bure were now at

their disposal and they served to enrich the already well supplied royal coffers.

The best information which the period affords on the level of
attainment of these native kingdoms comes from the accounts of
the royal pilgrimages to Mecca. The native kings, newly converted to the religion, were as ardent and pious as any Arabs of
their day. As good Moslems, they looked forward to showing
their devotion by making the traditional pilgrimage to Mecca.
Such a pilgrimage, moreover, was an excellent opportunity to
display the wealth of the kingdom and to attract trade. The
historic pilgrimage of Gonga-Mussa in 1324 exceeded all visits
to Mecca by previous royal personages from the West and was
to be matched by few, if any, in the years to come. A kind of
barbaric and "gilded age" splendor characterized the trip. The
entourage was composed of 60,000 persons, a large portion of
which constituted a military escort. No less than 12,000 were
servants, 500 of whom marched ahead of their king, each bearing a staff of pure gold. Books, baggage men, and royal secretaries there were in abundance. To finance the pilgrimage, the king
carried eighty camels to bear his more than 24,000 pounds of
gold. Gifts were lavished on the populace, and mosques were
built where they were needed. As the camels approached Mecca,
their burden was considerably lighter than it was when they left
Kangaba.

Since any such pilgrimage was a display of wealth and power
as well as a holy journey to kiss the black stone of Kaaba, there
was no need of proceeding directly to and from Mecca. Gonga-
Mussa first visited various parts of his kingdom to show his
subjects and vassals his tremendous wealth and to demonstrate
his benevolence. He then proceeded to Tuat, in the land of the
Berbers and after making a deep impression there he crossed
the desert, visited Cairo, and finally went to the holy places of
Mecca and Medina. He returned by way of Ghadames, in Trip-
oli, where he received many honors and from which point he
was accompanied to his kingdom by El-Momar, a descendant of
the founder of the dynasty of the Almohades. A more significant
visitor to return with Gonga-Mussa was Ibrahim-Es-Saheli, or
Abu Ishak, a distinguished Arabian poet and architect of a
Granada family. The two visitors were unimpressed with the
modest straw huts that were used in Melle for temples, whereupon Gonga-Mussa engaged his architect friend to supervise the

building of pretentious temples at Timbuktu, Jenne, Kangaba, and elsewhere. These structures added further splendor to the already well developed kingdom of Melle. For this improvement the king presented Es Saheli with 180 kilograms of gold.

When Gonga-Mussa died in 1332, Melle could boast of a political state as powerful and as well organized as any of that period. Traveling in the area a few years later, Ibn Batuta, the celebrated Arabian geographer, could report that he was greatly impressed by "the discipline of its officials and provincial governors, the excellent condition of public finance, and the luxury and the rigorous and complicated ceremonial of the royal receptions, and the respect accorded to the decisions of justice and to the authority of the sovereign." In the middle of the fourteenth century Europe was just beginning to feel the effects of her commercial revolution and her states had not yet achieved anything resembling national unity; but Mandingoland, under Gonga-Mussa and his successor, Suleiman, enjoyed a flourishing economy with good international trade relations and could point with pride to a stable government extending several hundred miles from the Atlantic to Lake Chad. The people adhered to a state religion which had international connections, and learning flourished in the many schools that had been established. It was not until the fifteenth century that the kingdom showed definite signs of decline and disintegration. The powerful blows of the Songhay, the attacks of the Mossi, and the inroads of the Portuguese combined to reduce the power of Melle. The decline did not go on indefinitely, however, and Melle continued to exist for many years as a small, semi-independent state.

Songhay

The Negro kingdom that was in a position to dispute the power of Melle by the fifteenth century was Songhay. The latter had experienced a long and checkered career as a kingdom. Beginning in the early eighth century at Gao, near the bend of the Niger, it had remained a small and relatively inconsequential kingdom for many years. By 1000 A.D. it had expanded to include other settlements on the Niger from Hukia to Timbuktu, but it got no farther at this time. In fact, it fell under the powerful influence of Melle, and for a time its rulers were vassals of Gonga-Mussa and his successors. Undaunted, the Songhay waited for the first opportunity to throw off the yoke of Melle and to assert their sovereignty. Gonga-Mussa, drunk with the enjoyment of his power, laid the foundation for the destruction of his empire at a later date. On his return from Mecca in 1325 he visited Gao, which his army had just subdued, and took two sons of the Songhay king as hostages. One of these young men accepted the education given him by Gonga-Mussa, but remained bitter and planned to escape and return to his people. After careful planning, he succeeded, and in 1355 founded the new and virile dynasty of the Sonnis. Seventeen kings reigned in this dynasty, the last being Sonni Ali, who raised the Songhay to the position of the most powerful kingdom in West Africa.

When Sonni Ali began his rule of the Songhay in 1464 most of West Africa was ripe for conquest. Mandingoland was declining, and the lesser states, though ambitious, had neither the leadership nor the resources necessary to achieve dominance. The hour of the Songhay had arrived. Sonni Ali conceived of a plan to conquer the entire Niger region by building a river navy that would seize control of both banks. By 1469 he had conquered the important town of Timbuktu, and proceeded to capture Jenne and other cities. Finally he attacked the kingdom of Melle and with its conquest the Songhay kingdom was catapulted into a position of primacy in West Africa. Because of his lack of enthusiasm for the religion of Islam, there was considerable opposition to the rise of Sonni Ali; but he was ruthless with his opponents who suffered death or exile at his hands. His years were filled with fighting; but when he died of drowning in the Niger in 1492 the kingdom of Songhay had been firmly established as the dominant power of West Africa.

The day of the Sonnis was over, however, and in 1493 the dynasty was overthrown by a Sarakelle general, Askia Mohammed, who became Songhay's most brilliant ruler. From 1493 to 1529 he devoted his energies to strengthening his empire, making his people prosperous, and encouraging learning. He recruited a professional army of slaves and prisoners of war and left his subjects to engage in farming and commerce. Native rulers, four viceroys, and Askia's brother, as chief lieutenant, maintained peace and administered the empire. In 1494 Omar and the army conquered all of Massini, while in subsequent years most of Mandingoland, Diara, Hausa, and many other West African kingdoms fell before the power of the Songhays. Finally, the empire of the Songhays was extended from the Atlantic to Tibeste and Borku and from the Berber country in the north to the Mossi and Benin states in the south. It was easily the largest and most powerful state in the history of West Africa.

To be sure, Askia Mohammed was an orthodox Mohammedan; but one does not get the impression that his pilgrimage to Mecca in 1497 was either for ostentatious display or merely to pay homage to Allah. This shrewd ruler wanted to improve his empire, and he knew that such a journey would prove profitable from many points of view. His retinue was composed primarily of scholars and officers of state, with a military escort numbering only fifteen hundred men. The gold, valued at $900,000, was less than one-fifth of the amount carried by Gonga-Mussa almost two centuries earlier. He and his followers conversed with doctors, mathematicians, scientists, and scholars and were doubtless benefited by these contacts. They learned much on how to improve the administration of the government, how to codify the laws of Songhay, how to foster industry and trade, and how to raise the intellectual level of the country. Even Askia Mohammed's investiture as Caliph of the Sudan may be interpreted as a move to strengthen his country. At a time when Spain and Portugal were disputing the control of the world before Pope Alexander VI and when Portuguese inroads into Africa were increasing steadily, it was a strategic move; for if the Songhays could consolidate all the strength of the Moslem world behind them, they could make a united stand against the Christian Europeans.

Upon his return from the East Askia Mohammed and his advisers instituted many of the reforms they had studied. Carefully chosen governors, called *Fari*, were assigned to rule over subdivisions of the empire. Chiefs, or *Noi*, were appointed to administer provinces and large cities. The army was reorganized on a more efficient basis. The laws of Mohammed and the Koran were the bases for administering justice. In the area of economic life, banking and credit were improved. A uniform system of weights and measures was established, and sales were inspected. Arabians and Negroes were encouraged to trade with other countries. The markets of Timbuktu and Gao were visited regularly by traders from Europe and Asia. With government cooperation all of Songhay became prosperous. Professor Alexander Chamberlain has observed: "In personal character, in administrative ability, in devotion to the welfare of his subjects, in open-mindedness towards foreign influences, and in wisdom in the adoption of non-Negro ideas and institutions, King Askia . . . was certainly the equal of the average European monarchs of the time and superior to many of them."

It was in the area of education that Askia made his most significant reforms. Schools were everywhere established and encouraged. Gao, Walata, Timbuktu, and Jenne became intellectual centers, at which were concentrated the most learned scholars of West Africa, and to which scholars from Asia and Europe came for consultation and study. White scholars like El-Akit and Negro scholars like Bagayogo, both juriconsults, were educated at Timbuktu, and in the sixteenth and seventeenth centuries a distinctly Sudanese literature was emerging. At the University of Sankore black and white youths studied grammar, geography, law, literature, and surgery, while in the mosques Askia and his subjects studied the religion of Islam in order that they could more effectively practice and promote it.

Civil wars, massacres, and unsuccessful military expeditions followed the reign of Askia, who was dethroned by his oldest son. Although there were brief periods of revival the empire was definitely declining. The Moors, recently expelled from Spain, viewed the Sudan covetously and began to push down across the desert in the effort to recoup the losses they had suffered at the hands of Ferdinand's armies. With Spanish renegades as their allies, the Moors overthrew the Askias and began to rule in Timbuktu.

Lesser States

Among the lesser states of West Africa was the empire of Wagadudu, commonly known as the Mossi States. It was founded near the middle of the eleventh century by an adventurer named Ubri. It was never a large state, occupying as it did the area south of the bend of the Niger; but its population was always dense, and its people had a fiercely independent spirit. For a time there were actually five states which comprised the loose confederation. Cohesion was greatest in time of emergency, and they managed to repel the attacks of Melle and Songhay and remained more or less independent down to the nineteenth century when France incorporated them into its African empire. The governors of the five states constituted the council of state and served as the chief ministers in the imperial organization. Working with them were eleven ministers ruling such departments as the army and finance. Beneath them was a hierarchy of officials which extended to the most insignificant local functionary.

The strength of the Mossi lay in their efficient political and military system. The emperor was absolute. His subordinates operated with carefully worked out and rigidly defined duties. Each morning the emperor received his ministers of state who reported on the affairs of the realm. In the evening the ruler dealt with matters concerning public order and criminal justice. The procedures of hearings and decisions bore striking resemblance to the practice of trial by jury. The emperor made periodic inspection tours through his realm, a practicable procedure because of its limited size. There was no standing army, but the political and social system was so organized as to make possible the calling up for military service of every able-bodied man on the briefest notice. The survival of the Mossi States in an area which was dominated by powerful empires such as Melle and Songhay is a testimonial to their efficiency and to their wise leadership.

The Afno or Hausa people are said to have had seven original states, Biram, Gober, Kano, Rano, Zaria, Katsena, and Daura. The Hausa States occupied roughly the area which today is known as Nigeria. In the fifteenth century these states were united under the authority of the kings of the Kebbi, an area to the west on the Niger. These sovereigns established no undisputed control, however. Each kingdom retained its identity, with Kano emerging into the limelight for a while, then yielding to Katsena, Gober, and so on. There was commerce with the other African states. A lively trade was maintained in fruit and dairy products. Katsena became a center of learning where law and theology were studied and where the language of the people was refined. It was not until the beginning of the nineteenth century, when Islam made noticeable inroads, that the Hausa States began to yield to outside influences.

To the east and west of Lake Chad resided the people of Kanem and Bornu respectively. These people were made up of a large number of tribes that had early been attracted to the region by the oases and the Lake. Some were white, while others were Negroid. As an organized state, Bornu-Kanem dates from about 1220 A.D., but instability characterized the government for the next two centuries. The copper mines around the lake brought prosperity to the people, and by the sixteenth century there was a semblance of order under Idris III (1573–1603). In the seventeenth and eighteenth centuries the Moslems attempted to subdue these people and convert them, but with only slight success, except among the ruling classes. Complete subjugation by outsiders was not achieved until 1900 when Bornu became a protectorate of Britain.

There is remarkably little available information concerning African states south of the equator. The absence of substantial physical barriers in some areas made possible the continuous infiltration of migratory tribes which hampered political stability. In other areas, the thick, almost impenetrable jungle militated against the evolution of the corporate state. This land of the Bantu, Bushmen, Hottentots, and Pygmies certainly had some political organizations, and there is considerable anthropological and archaeological evidence to sustain the view that in some areas there was an advanced culture. It is impossible, however, to trace with any degree of accuracy the political development of these peoples before their Europeanization. It is clear that none of them reached the size or influences of West African states such as Melle and Songhay.

From the mouth of the Niger around to the Cape of Good Hope, there were a number of states which flourished for a time before the sixteenth century. For example, there was the kingdom of the Brama which lay between Cape Lopez and the mouth of the Congo River, and about which practically nothing is known. The so-called "Empire of the Congo," founded in the fourteenth century, dominated the area between Setti-Carnuna in the north and Benguella to the south. Inland it reached as far as the upper Zambezi. With its capital at Banya, modern São Salvador, its kings experienced difficulty in maintaining control over the wily tribes of the Congo valley, and its boundaries shrank steadily in the seventeenth century.

South of the "Empire of the Congo" was a state near the present City of Mossamedes. Hottentots, Damara, and other tribes in the region constituted the population of the kingdom whose ruler was called the Mataman. In what is modern South Africa there was a large homogeneous state inhabited by the Bechuana, Basuto, Zulu, and Hottentot peoples. On the east coast the Matebelle and Makalaka peoples were incorporated in an ancient state which dated from the tenth century. Its instability was caused by frequent incursions by the Wazimba, a cannibalistic people living to the west. The remainder of the eastern coast fell early under the influence of the Moslems and became dependencies of various sultanates founded by the Arabs and Persians who gained control of East Africa. In the interior were the kingdoms of the Barotse, the Katanga, and Balubo, extending from the Zambezi to Lake Tanganyika. When historians, archaeologists, and anthropologists throw the light of their scholarship on these regions, perhaps there will be revealed a significant story of the political development of these obscure states.

III •

The African Way of Life

● *It is obviously impossible to make an unlimited number of* generalizations concerning the way of life in a continent so large as Africa, with so many variations in climate, physiography, and population. As in any other area, at any other time, Africa presents variations in degrees of civilization that run the entire gamut from the most primitive to remarkably advanced ones. At this point one can do little more than observe various aspects of the African way of life with a view to understanding more adequately the cultural heritage of these people who have come to claim the concern of Europeans and Americans in recent centuries. If the emphasis seems to be placed on the way of life in West Africa, it is because there seems to be merit in trying to secure as intimate an understanding as possible of the area in which the bulk of the people lived who became the black workers of the Americas.

Political Institutions

It is not without significance that wherever one observes the peoples of Africa he finds some form of political organization. They were not all highly organized kingdoms—to be sure, some were simple, isolated family states—but they all seem to indicate the normal capability and desire of establishing governments to solve the problems which every community of people encountered. The family state prevailed in areas where the territory was divided among a number of distinct families and where there was no inclination or desire on the part of these families to merge their resources to organize a stronger state. In such situations the chief of state was extremely powerful, because his political strength was supplemented by the strength which was his by virtue of being head of the family. In some instances, several such states, the constituents of whom enjoyed a common ancestry, came together to form a more powerful state known as the clan state. If it became possible to surmount the obstacles of tradition and clannishness, several groups could come together and form what has come to be known as the village state or tribe seat.

Village states flourished all through West Africa. The growth and prosperity of some prompted them to merge, voluntarily or by force, to form small kingdoms, the most popular form of government in Africa. These kingdoms, if they met with a favorable set of circumstances—able leadership, adequate resources, and strong military organization—could grow into federations or even "empires" such as those of Melle and Songhay. These various degrees of political organization were attained by the Negroes of Africa in their successive stages of development. Despite the fact that they existed at different times and at different places, it is remarkable to observe the same essential characteristics that seem to have prevailed in all of them.

The power to govern a state usually resided in a given family and was transmitted by it. Two other families, however, performed important functions in establishing a royal personage on the throne, the electing family and the enthroning family. The electing family could exercise a choice within the royal family. In this way the Africans recognized the stabilizing effect that a royal family might have on the political fortunes of the people. At the same time, they were practical enough to recognize the fact that the eldest son was not necessarily the ablest or most desirable and felt free to choose their ruler among any of the male members of the royal family. The new king could exercise no authority until he had been properly invested in office by persons so designated by the enthroning family. These practices had the effect of insuring to the people a more satisfactory monarch than automatic descent of authority might give them.

Each African king of any real importance had a group of

ministers and advisers. Indeed, in some states custom imposed on the king the obligation of appointing a given number of advisers and delegating real authority to them. Custom generally conferred each ministerial charge on a certain family. These ministers and other advisers and members of the nobility functioned as a kind of parliament that in some instances exercised substantial authority. It is interesting to observe that a peculiar African custom served to limit the authority of many kings. If the king did not belong to the family of the first person occupying the ground in his kingdom, he had no rights over the land. Any questions involving the land were settled by the descendants of the first occupants, which could conceivably be an insignificant subject of the king or even a prisoner of war. It seems that most kings were willing to conform to this ancient custom.

It is possible, however, to overemphasize the importance of the central political organization among the Africans. To be sure, the power of the kings, ministers, and subchiefs was considerable; but beneath this semblance of national unity was the strong attachment on the part of the individual to local authority and local loyalties. Each locality had its own "king," and in many matters of a purely local nature this royal personage exercised power that was indisputable. It was this concept of the division of authority—a kind of dichotomy of sovereignty— that kept the great kings sensitive to the possibility of conflict within their realm. Few powerful kings of the great empires and kingdoms ever achieved so much authority as to destroy completely the feeling of local rulers that they enjoyed a degree of sovereignty themselves. Stability could be achieved only through extensive military organization and a carefully organized central government. That this stability was frequently achieved is a testimonial to the wisdom, strength, and not infrequent ruthlessness of the native kingdoms.

Economic Life

It would be fallacious to assume that Africans were either primarily nomadic or simply agricultural. There exists in Africa such a diversity of physical environments that it would be impossible for people though similar in racial characteristics to evolve identical ways of life in different parts of the continent.

Essentially an agricultural people, the natives of Africa displayed a remarkable degree of specialization within this ancient economic pursuit. The African concept of land ownership stemmed from the importance of agriculture in the natives' way of life. The land was considered so important to the entire community that it belonged not to individuals but to the collective community comprised of the first occupants of the soil. One of the most important local dignitaries was the "master of the ground" who was at the same time the grand priest of the local religion and the administrator of the soil. The importance of this official can be clearly seen, it may be recalled, in the fact that not even the political ruler could make any disposition of land without the consent of the "master of the ground." Individuals or groups of persons could obtain the right to use a given parcel of land, but such permission did not carry with it the right of alienation or any other form of disposition. When use was not made of the land, it reverted to the collective domain.

Whether the land was held individually or collectively—and it seems that both practices prevailed—the tillers of the soil devoted all their energies to the cultivation of their crops. Soil was cleared by chopping down trees and burning the underbrush. The ashes were used to fertilize the ground which was in turn prepared for planting by large spades with short handles. Seeds or sprouts were planted in mounds or embankments which had been carefully prepared. Frequent weeding was necessary, especially in new ground, in order to prevent the young plants from being choked. It is not possible to list all the agricultural products of the African farm. They vary in different places, of course. Most frequently seen were farms on which millet, wheat, rice, cassava, cotton, fruits, and vegetables were grown. Dotting the countryside were towers from which watchmen drove away birds and other grain-eating animals. Harvest time was a particularly busy period during which grain was harvested, threshed, milled, and stored, while other fruit and grain were made into fermented drinks, and cotton was manufactured into thread and cloth.

Domestic animals were a part of almost every native farm; but in some areas the rural people devoted most of their attention to the grazing of sheep and cattle and the raising of chickens and other fowls. In Northeastern Africa some tribes were known for their great skill in the breeding and care of cattle, while in the East many villages ascribed so much importance to the raising of cattle that wealth was measured in terms of heads of cattle. The Bantu and Hottentots engaged in large-scale cattle, goat, and sheep raising.

Perhaps the most significant area of economic activity, from the point of view of the modern student, was artisanry. Even among the so-called backward tribes, natives were skilled along many lines. Among many people, there was a remarkable knowledge of basketry, textile weaving, pottery, woodwork, and metallurgy. The Pygmies manufactured bark cloth and fiber baskets. The Hottentots devoted much time and attention to making clothing from textiles, skins, and furs. The Ashantis of the Gold Coast wove rugs and carpets and turned and glazed pottery with considerable skill. In many parts of the Sudan there was extensive manufacturing of wooden ware, tools, and implements.

The use of iron was developed very early in the economy of Africa. From Ethiopia to the Atlantic, there is much evidence of adroitness in the manufacture and use of iron. Indeed, many careful students of primitive civilizations credit the Negroes of Africa with the discovery of iron. Boas insists that Africans were using iron when European and Asiatic peoples were still in the stone age. The simple processes which Africans were found to have used and the early date at which they began to make iron suggest that it was the natives of Africa, and not the Hittites, that first discovered the use of iron. Africa exported iron for many years, and blacksmiths and other workers in iron were found in many parts of Africa. With simple bellows and a charcoal fire, the native blacksmith smelted his ore and forged implements such as knives, saws, and axes. Natives worked also in silver, gold, copper, and bronze. In Benin, bronze and copper implements and art objects demonstrated great skill on the part of the smiths, while many tribes, including those of Yoruba, Melle, and Jenne devoted attention to the making of ornamental objects from silver and gold.

The interest of early Africa in the outside world can best be seen in the great attention that was given to commerce. The tendency of tribes to specialize in some phase of economic activity made it necessary that they maintain commercial intercourse with other tribes and with other countries in order to secure the things which they did not produce. Some villages, for example, specialized in fishing; others concentrated their talents on metallurgy; while others made weapons, utensils, and so on.

In tribes where such specialization was practiced tradesmen travelled from place to place to barter and to purchase. Upon returning they were laden with goods which they sold to their fellows. Some tradesmen from the West Coast went as far north as the Mediterranean and as far east as Egypt, where they exchanged their goods with the wares of tradesmen from other parts of the world. It is to be recalled that the travels of the kings and emperors did much to stimulate this international traffic. Africa was, therefore, never a series of isolated self-sufficient communities, but an area which had far-flung interests that were based on agriculture, industry, and commerce. The effect of such contacts on the culture was immeasurable. It can only be said here that these routes of commerce were the highways over which civilization as well as goods travelled and that Africa gave much of her own civilization to others and received a good deal in return.

Social Organization

As among other peoples, the family was the basis of social organization in early Africa. At the basis even of economic and political life in Africa was the family with its inestimable influence over its individual members. Although the eldest male was usually the head of the family, there was the widespread practice of tracing relationships through the mother instead of the father. In areas where this latter practice was followed, children belonged solely to the family of the mother, her eldest brother exercising the paternal rights and assuming all responsibility for the children's lives and actions. In tribes which admitted only female relationship, the chief of the family was the brother of the mother on her mother's side. In tribes which did not follow this practice, the chief was the real father. With either group, those persons forming the family comprised all the living descendants of the same ancestor, female among the matriarchal system and male among the patriarchal system.

Nowhere was the wife considered a member of her husband's family. After marriage she continued to be a part of her own family. Since her family continued to manifest a real interest in her welfare, the bride's husband was expected to pay her family an indemnity, a compensation for taking away a member of the family and a guarantee for good treatment. This indemnity was not a purchase price, as has frequently been believed. The woman did not legally belong to her husband, but to her own family. Naturally, the amount of the indemnity varied both with tribal practice and with the position of the bridegroom. Indeed, in some tribes the tradition was maintained by a mere token payment out of respect for an ancient practice which once had real significance in intertribal relationships.

Although polygamy was permitted virtually in every region, it was nowhere universally practiced. In marriage, the practice was for the chief of the family to defray the expenses involved in the first marriage of a male member of the family. For the second wife, however, the husband had to meet all the expenses. It was this practice that forced all except the well-to-do to be monogamous. Religion played a part in determining the number of wives a man could have. The native religions did not limit the number. When the Moslems made inroads into the tribes of Africa, they forbade adherents to take more than four wives. Wherever the Christians established a foothold among the natives they insisted on monogamy altogether. Where polygamy was practiced, it does not appear to have produced many evils, because of its limited extent. As a matter of fact, the division of household duties in a polygamous family had the effect of reducing the duties and responsibilities of each wife, a highly desirable condition from the point of view of the wives if the husband was without servants or slaves. The rights of each wife were so carefully defined and the duties of the husband were so clear-cut that there was seldom friction as a result of the polygamous relationship.

The clan, the enlarged family, was composed of all the families which claimed a common ancestor. The clan would develop in the same community or area, but as it became larger and as some families found opportunities elsewhere it would separate, and one or more families would go to some other area to live. Unless the separation resulted from a violent quarrel or fight the departing families regarded themselves as still being attached to the clan. Once the unity was broken by separation, however, the clan tended to disintegrate for the reason that cooperation in war, economic activities, and religious life was no longer practicable. In the course of time the traditions and practices of the clan tended to become obscure and unimportant under the strain that separation imposed upon them. Consequently, little more than the common name bound members of the same clan together; and new environments and new linguistic influences had the effect of causing the clan names to be changed or modified. In such instances, members of the same clan living in different places would have no way of recognizing each other.

Early in its development, Africa showed signs of social stratification in its many tribes. At the top was the nobility, "the good men," who could prove that they descended from free men. Since they could claim the name of a respected clan, they had a right to the places and positions of respect in the social order. Next was the great mass of workers, largely serfs, who found it difficult or impossible to raise a genealogical tree that would bear careful scrutiny. Although they might carry a perfectly good clan name, they could not prove their right to it and therefore were not able to qualify for a position in the upper class. At the bottom of the social structure were those persons who enjoyed no political or social rights. They were slaves, war captives, disgraced or degraded persons, and those living beyond the pale of the law. It must be added that the social structure had an economic base, and wealth tended to be concentrated in the upper class. Families, moreover, not individuals, constituted the several classes. Since families wielded economic power, through their politically important positions or through the domination of certain crafts and other economic pursuits, they had a way of influencing the nature of the social order. Work in itself did not elevate or debase a family, but the nature of the work did. There was a rather definite respectability attached to certain types of work, and the graduation toward debasement was equally as definite. The working of the soil was the most noble of all pursuits. Following in close order were cattle-raising, hunting, fishing, construction, navigation, commerce, gold mining, and the processing of commodities such as soap, oil, and beer. There were variations from tribe to tribe, but everywhere there was the tendency to dignify or to degrade families on the basis of the types of work in which they were engaged.

It must not be assumed that persons in the lower levels of the social order were not respected or accorded any privileges. All persons were regarded as necessary to society and were respected for what they contributed to society. They were accorded numerous privileges because their acknowledged skills earned for them the privileges of movement from one place to another and entrance into groups that otherwise would be closed to them.

Nor is it to be assumed that there was absolute rigidity in the social structure of tribal Africa. As among other peoples, tact, special knowledge, wealth, or good fortune tended to create a fluidity in African society. By taste, a member of a mining family might choose to farm; and although his new occupation did not of itself elevate him from the lower social position of his family, in due time he could gain so much respect and admiration as a farmer that he would be regarded as a legitimate member of the class of noble tillers of the soil. As in almost every society in the world, power and wealth could, in many instances, be substituted for nobility of origin.

Slavery was an important feature of African social and economic life. The institution was widespread and was perhaps as old as African society itself. Slaves were predominantly persons captured in war and could be sold or kept by the persons who captured them. Slaves were usually regarded as the property of the chief of the tribe or the head of the family. In law, slaves were chattel property, but in practice they often became trusted associates of their masters and enjoyed virtual freedom. Some, however, were sold and exported from the country, while others were sacrificed by kings in the worship of their royal ancestors. The children of slaves could not be sold and thus constituted an integral and inalienable part of the family property. Enjoying such security it was not uncommon for the children of slaves to be favored with manumission at the hands of their masters.

Religion

Certainly down to the period of the many European incursions into Africa the vast majority of the natives engaged in religious practices that were indigenous to the continent. To describe these religions as fetishes is to place upon them a connotation that is at once inaccurate and incomplete. To be sure, there were symbols of superstition which may be described as fetishes, but these were only outward manifestations of certain religious beliefs and, like symbols in other religions, they did not indicate the specific character of the religion. The religion of the early Africans can most accurately be described as ancestor worship. The Africans believed that the spirits of their forefathers had unlimited power over their lives. In this, as in almost every aspect of African life, the kinship group was important. It was devoutly believed that the spirit that dwelled in a relative was deified upon death, the spirit continuing to live and taking an active interest in the family of the deceased. The spirits of early ancestors had been free to wield an influence for such a long time that they were much more powerful than the spirits of the more recently deceased; hence, the devout worship and the complete deification of the early ancestors. Not only were the spirits of deceased members of the family worshipped, but a similar high regard was held for the spirits which dwelt in the family land, the trees and rocks in the community of the kinship group, and the sky above the community.

Because of the family character of African religions, the priests of the religions were the patriarchs of the families. They were the oldest living members of the descendants of the initial ancestor, and had therefore inherited the earthly prerogatives of their predecessors. Thus, they had dominion over the family grounds, waters, and atmosphere. It was the family patriarch who entered into communication with the souls of his ancestors and the natural forces in his immediate vicinity. He was therefore authorized to conduct the ceremonies of worship. The temples of worship could be any structure set aside for that purpose. They contained holy objects, such as the bones of the dead, consecrated pieces of wood, rock or metal, and statuettes representing objects to be worshipped. Bells or rattles were used to invoke the spirits and the worshippers. The blood of victims, chickens, sheep, goats, or human beings, was offered as sacrifices to appease the gods. There was never a universal practice of sacrificing human beings in Africa, but in some areas prisoners and captives were sacrificed in worship of the various deities. Libations of palm wine, beer, or some other fermented drink were offered in some forms of worship. In addition to offerings, sacrifices and libations, prayers and songs were other manifestations of adoration.

It was only natural that in a society such as that found in Africa there would be considerable reliance on the magical power of amulets, talismans, and the like. Anything that helped to explain and answer the imponderables was a welcome addition to tribal practices. Magic was, therefore, practiced on a great scale. By resorting to ill-defined powers, known only to him, the magician of Africa invented techniques and created rites which were designed to secure for individuals the specific ends which they desired. Where religion was a collective attempt to secure satisfaction for the kinship group, magic was an individual attempt to achieve certain satisfactions on the part of a particular person. Even in areas where animistic worship prevailed, belief in magic was widespread. Many natives had great confidence in the efficiency of magical practices; and it may be that this blind reliance on the divination of sorcerers was responsible, in part, for the retardation of the civilization of Africa. The practice of casting magical spells and the use of powders intended to influence action certainly were not conducive to developing the resourcefulness and ingenuity on which civilizations move forward.

The elaborateness of funeral rites all over the continent attests to the regard which the natives had for the idea that the spirit of the dead played an important part in the life of the kinship group. The funeral was the climax of life, and costly and extensive rituals were sacred obligations of the survivors. The dead were generally buried in the ground either beneath huts where they lived or in cemeteries. Burial often took place within a few days after death, but at times the family would delay interment for several weeks or longer. The grave was not completely closed until every member of the family had had an opportunity to present offerings and to participate in some rite incident to interment. Nothing more clearly demonstrates the cohesiveness of the African family than the ceremonies and customs which were practiced on the occasion of the death and burial of a member.

In all probability the influence of the religion of Mohammed on the African way of life has been greatly exaggerated. This is certainly true for the period before the fourteenth century. Moslems crossed from Arabia over into Egypt in the seventh century. In the following century they swept across North Africa where they met with notable success, but progress was slow below the Sahara in the land of the blacks. It will be recalled that the kingdoms of Ghana, Melle, and Songhay accepted Islam quite reluctantly, while other groups rejected it altogether. Some Negro kings accepted Mohammedanism for what seemed to be economic and political reasons; but frequently their subjects held tenaciously to their tribal religious practices. Moslems were never able, for example, to win over all the people of Melle, Hausa, Yoruba, and Susu. The commercial opportunities offered by the Moslems were especially attractive. It must also be added that despite the proselytizing character of

Mohammedanism, Negroes were accepted as social equals by the followers of the Prophet and were given an opportunity to enjoy the advantages of education and of cultural advancement which the religion offered. Even as a slave, the Negro Mohammedan was considered as a brother. Doubtless these features were as important to Negroes as the purely ritualistic features of the new religion. Even so, numberless Negroes summarily rejected Islam in preference for the cults and rituals which were historically a part of their way of life.

Christianity became entrenched in North Africa early. It was there when Mohammedanism made its appearance in the seventh century, and these two great faiths engaged in a life and death struggle for the control of that area. In West Africa, where the Negro population was especially dense and from which the great bulk of slaves were secured, Christianity was practically unknown until the Portuguese and Spaniards began to plant missions in the area in the sixteenth century. It was a strange religion, this Christianity, which taught equality and brotherhood and at the same time introduced on a large scale the practice of tearing the natives from their homes and transporting them to a distant land to become slaves. If the natives were slow to accept Christianity, it was not only because they were attached to their particular forms of tribal worship but also because they did not have the superhuman capacity to reconcile in their own minds the contradictory character of the new religion.

The Arts

In some areas of art the Africans attained a high degree of expression. In carvings and sculptures of wood, stone and ivory, their work displayed an originality both in technique and subject matter that marked them clearly as a people with an abundant capacity for aesthetic expression. There was, of course, a great degree of variation from place to place in the level of expression attained, but hardly any tribe, however primitive, failed to show some inclination toward the use of certain art forms. In Benin the bronze and brass works of roses, doorplates, and metal vases reflect great skill in the use of this difficult medium. In Yoruba the delicacy of form seen in the terra cotta pieces is a testimonial to the rare artistry which these people possessed. The statuettes of persons and animals widely used by African tribes in religious rites serve as a reminder that almost everywhere some persons concerned themselves with artistic activities so as to supply the temples with the icons and other symbols needed in their worship. From Timbuktu to the Congo there was considerable work in gold, silver, glass, clay, and the like; and it cannot be denied that many of these pieces bear witness to the fact that Negro African art was not only indigenous but also worthy of the name.

In the manufacture and construction of items to be sold or used, the Negroes of Africa enhanced their beauty and value by decorating them in various ways. Ornamented and glazed pottery, delicately carved spoons and knives, golden jewels of filigree, and elegantly woven mats, cloth, and tapestries are outstanding examples of the application of art in industry. In the construction of houses, royal palaces, and temples this same proclivity toward ornamentation can be seen. As Moslem architects and scientists came into the region south of the desert a marked improvement in the symmetry and beauty of West African architecture can be seen. It must be added, however, that there is abundant evidence to support the view that many basic elements of beauty in African architecture were evident before the incursion of the Moslems.

An important element in aesthetic expression in Africa is music. Among the principal musical instruments developed in Africa were the xylophone, violins, guitars, zithers, harps, and flutes. The most frequently used musical form was, of course, the song, with or without instrumental accompaniment. The songs were usually antiphonal and were characterized by highly developed rhythms. It must not be assumed that the musical forms were simple or easy. Some songs and other forms were quite complex with respect to scale, rhythm, and general organization. There was also great variation in the types of African musical forms, ranging from lullabies and dance songs to work songs and sacred melodies. Too frequently the people of the Western world confuse the music of Africa, much of which contains melodic though brief phrases, with the dance of Africa with its extensive use of drums as rhythmic accompaniment. The sound effects provided for the dances were not considered as music, nor can the observer consider them as such. There were many forms of the African dance. Some were for recreational or social purposes, while others performed ritualistic or religious functions. Both music forms and dance forms were regarded by Africans as integral parts of their culture.

The wide variety of spoken languages found in Africa always constituted a barrier to the development of literary forms. Not only were there the several great groups of languages, but an infinite number of languages and dialects within each group. From the Atlantic to Abyssinia, through the heart of the continent, the languages of the Sudanic group are spoken; and there are at least two hundred and sixty-four of them. In the southern half of Africa one hundred and eighty-two Bantu languages are spoken. The Bushmen tribes speak languages which fall into three groups, central, southern, and northern; and each of these in turn is divided into a larger number. There are at least ten Semitic dialects, ranging from the Arabic spoken in North Africa to the Berber dialects heard in the Great Desert. Besides, there are many tribal dialects and languages which have no apparent relationship with the principal language groups. Among these are the languages of Suto, Ruanda, and Banda. Thus, where there is so much heterogeneity in the spoken language, even within a relatively small area, one can readily

ART PIECES FROM AFRICA. The camwood boxes from Mangbetulan, The Congo (formerly Belgian), are excellent examples of the way in which natives of that region have for centuries combined art with utility. The bronze pieces from Benin reflect the rare artistic skill for which the people of West Africa have become noted. Courtesy American Museum of Natural History, New York.

see the almost insurmountable difficulties involved in the evolution of adequate literary forms as media of articulation.

In early Africa few of the languages were reduced to writing. The literature was, therefore, predominantly oral, and there was an abundance of it. Handed down principally through the kinship group, the oral literature was composed of supernatural tales, moral tales, proverbs, epic poems, satires, love songs, funeral pieces, and comic tales. Some individuals, griots, made a specialty of collecting these bits of oral literature and purveying them before kings as well as ordinary families. They sang, told stories, and recited poetry. They kept in their memories the history, law, and traditions of their people and were themselves living dictionaries who occasionally performed invaluable services to their communities. The use of Arabic by educated Moslem Negroes after the fourteenth century was rather extensive and made possible the reduction of some of the oral literature to permanent form. Examples of this are the *Tarikh-es-Soudan*, a history of the Sudan, written by Es-Sadi and *Tarikh-El-Fettach*, written by Kati, a Sudanese. Some African scholars even sought to adapt the Arabic alphabet to the writing of one of the African languages by adding diacritical marks to represent sounds that do not exist in the Arabic. This extremely difficult feat made possible the more extensive use of Arabic in developing a written literature among the natives.

Such was the way of life in Africa down to the end of the sixteenth century. It was at this stage of development when Europeans began to make incursions for the purpose of engaging in the trade in men. It was by no means a simple way of life which the white men found. The basic problems of existence had been solved. Almost everywhere there were stable political, economic, and social institutions. Whether the states were great empires such as that of Songhay or mere political entities such as Katsena of the Hausa States, they were elaborately organized with limited monarchies and a myriad of public officials. Well-defined concepts of law and order prevailed, and even if there was considerable rivalry and strife among states a remarkable degree of order prevailed within the several governments. Citizens seemed to take their responsibilities and loyalties seriously. The Negroes of Africa were on the whole well disciplined, and records of rebellions and revolutions are rare indeed. This does not mean that all rulers were benevolent or that all their subjects were completely free from oppression. It does mean that a relatively satisfactory balance had been achieved between the people and their government. Usurpers and pretenders did emerge, to be sure, and at times they created considerable chaos in their respective states, but perhaps these situations were no worse than the strife and chaos in the states of Europe during the late medieval and the early modern period.

There was usually enough stability within the African States and among them to make possible a healthy economic development. In some respects Africa was behind other areas of the world in economic organization, but it must be recalled that there were many evidences of a successful encounter with the forces of nature in the struggle for existence. Nor was there merely the uncreative dependence on the bountiful goodness of the soil and climate for the necessaries of life. The extensive division of labor and the widespread practice of specialization in occupations display a versatility and variety of talents and tastes that were a remarkable achievement for peoples in their early stages of development. The interest in commerce and the realization of the economic importance of contact with the European and Asiatic worlds reveal a maturity in economic concepts that was as advanced as those of any contemporary states in other parts of the world.

Nothing is more impressive in the social institutions of Africa than the cohesive influence of the family. The immediate family, the clan, and the tribe undergird every aspect of life. The rule of discipline enforced in the family is responsible in large measure for the stability that has been observed in various aspects of life. The hold which the patriarch has over the members of the family and the influence which he wields are largely responsible for the stability which is characteristic of the area. The deep loyalty and attachment of the individual to the family approaches reverence and, indeed, is the basis for most of the religious practices, in which ancestor worship plays such an important part. The religions of Africa were a product of an environment in which the population lived close to nature. These sacred rites were manifestations of a people who were in desperate search for answers to the imponderables. Their gods functioned intimately in their daily lives, and the adherents demanded effective, practical demonstrations of their deistical power in terms of better crops and victory over warring enemies. If Africans displayed a measure of religious skepticism in their willingness to accept new tribal gods or even new religions from the outside world, it was because they failed to see why additional gods would not give them greater opportunities for success in their undertakings.

These people who, of necessity, had to devote most of their energies and attention to the important problems of existence did not neglect the aesthetic aspects of life. Everywhere one can find evidences of pronounced proclivities to artistic expressions. Whether in painting, sculpture, or carving there is a delicate sensitivity and an appreciation of the beautiful that reflect a basic regard for the finer things of life. Even in the industrial arts and crafts Africans took the time to beautify their products by applying to them the best of their artistic talents and knowledge. The song and dance played important parts in their social life. With stringed and rhythm instruments they made merry with their friends, worshipped their gods, and buried their dead. Nor is their aesthetic proclivity absent from the literary activities of the African people. As in every other endeavor, the literary activities of Africans were tied up closely with their everyday life. Their oral literature, made up of tales, proverbs, epics, histories, and laws, served as educational devices, sources of amusement, and guides for the administration of government and the conduct of religious ceremonies. If their written literature was limited it was certainly not for a want of literary interests but rather because of the technical obstacles in the way of developing written languages. The extant treatises, largely in Arabic, show that when a written language was mastered the resulting works were worthy of serious comparison with their contemporaries in other parts of the world.

The Transplantation of African Culture

Students of Africa and America have discussed for many years the question of the extent to which this culture of Africa was transplanted and preserved in the New World. Of course, a considerable number of students formerly contended that nothing existed in Africa that approached civilization and there was, therefore, nothing for the Africans to bring with them. As evidence to the contrary began to pile up, that position was no longer tenable. The questions still remained as to whether Africans continued to be African except in color and whether any substantial elements of Africa became a part of the general acculturative process taking place in America. Sociologists like E. B. Reuter and Robert E. Park have failed to see anything in Negro life today which can be traced to the African background; while historians and anthropologists like Carter G. Woodson and Melville J. Herskovits insist that the African cultural heritage can still be seen in many aspects of American life today. Although the controversy continues it seems that it is possible to make a tentative statement with regard to this important problem.

Although there was so much dispersion of the Negro population in the New World that it was impossible for Negroes to wield any political influence as a group, there persisted among them as individuals such a deep appreciation of the function of the State that obedience to law and patriotism for their new country were not at all difficult for them. It is to be remembered, furthermore, that the Negro slaves came from a complex social and economic life; and they were not overwhelmed or overawed by their New World experiences. Despite the heterogeneity in many aspects of African life, there were sufficient common experiences for Negroes in the New World to cooperate in the fashioning of new customs and traditions which reflected this African background. To be sure, there were at least two acculturative processes, going on side by side in the New World. As Africans of different experiences lived together, there was the interaction of the various African cultures which produced a somewhat different set of customs and practices which manifestly had their roots deep in the African experiences. At the same time, there was the interaction of African and Western cultures which doubtless changed the culture patterns of both groups. It is to be remembered that European institutions did not exist everywhere with the same degree of fixity, and where the European practices were relatively weak the opportunities for African survivals were correspondingly strengthened.

In the cultural conflict which proceeded in the New World following the introduction of Negroes, the acculturative process varied in different places and under different circumstances. In some places it was all but stymied where there was sufficient consensus of experience among the Africans to take the Western culture and reinterpret it almost wholly in terms of their own experiences. In other places, such as Brazil and some Caribbean islands, successful revolts made possible the transplantation of an African way of life to a considerable degree. Elsewhere, one can observe the process going on in a normal or gradual way, but with at least some survival of African culture an obvious fact. When it comes to measuring or evaluating the persistence of African culture in the New World the problem becomes much more difficult. In the language one can see it in such words as yam, goober, canoe, and banjo. In literature one can observe it in the folk tales that have been preserved in recent years by American writers. In religion there are the divinations and various cult practices, some of which can be traced to the African background. In work, in play, in social organization and aesthetic manifestations there are evidences of Africanisms.

The survival of varying degrees of African culture in America does not suggest that there has been only a limited adjustment of the Negro to the New World situation. To the contrary, it merely points up the fact that he came out of an experience that was sufficiently intrenched to make possible the persistence of some customs and traditions. There is some validity in the view that in the conflict of cultures only those practices will survive whose value and superiority give them the strength and tenacity to do so. African survivals in America also suggest a pronounced resiliency of African institutions. There had been sufficient intertribal and interstate intercourse to give Africans the important experience of adopting many of the practices of those with whom they came in contact, while at the same time retaining much of their earlier way of life. After all, perhaps the survival of Africanisms in the New World was as great as it was because of the refusal of the members of the dominant group in America to extend, without reservations, their own culture to the Negroes whom they brought over.

IV •

The Slave Trade

European and Asian Interests

● *When the Christians of Western Europe began to turn their* attention to the trade in men in the fifteenth and sixteenth centuries, they were not introducing a new practice among human beings. Although they displayed much originality in approach and technique, they were engaging in a pursuit that had been the concern of men for countless centuries. As a matter of fact, slavery was widespread during the earliest known history of Africa as well as of other continents. Doubtless there was cruelty and oppression in African slavery as there was anywhere that the institution developed. At least in some portions of Africa there was no racial basis of slavery. The Egyptians enslaved whatever peoples they captured. At times they were Semitic, at times Mediterranean, and at other times they were blacks from Ethiopia. Slavery in the Greek and Roman empires is well known. In both periods the traffic in men from Western Asia and North Africa brought a continuous stream of slaves to perform the personal services and to till the fields for the master class. Neither in Greece nor Rome was menial service regarded as degrading. The opportunities for education and cultural advancement were, therefore, opened up to the slaves. It was not unusual to find in this class persons possessing a degree of intelligence and training not usually associated with slaves.

When the Mohammedans invaded Africa, they contributed

greatly to the development of the institution of Negro slavery by seizing Negro women for their harems and Negro men for military and menial service. By purchase as well as by conquest, the Moslems recruited Negro slaves and shipped them off to Arabia, Persia, or some other land of Islam. As Negro kings and princes embraced the Mohammedan faith, they cooperated with the Arabians in the exportation of human cargo. Long before the extensive development of the slave trade in the hands of Europeans, many of the basic practices of the international slave trade had already been established. It is to be noted, however, that slavery among the Mohammedans was not an institution which was used primarily for the production of goods from which wealth could be derived. There were no extensive cotton, tobacco, and sugar cane fields in Arabia, Persia, and Egypt. Slaves in these lands were essentially servants, and the extent of the demand for them depended in a large measure on the wealth of the potential masters. Slavery was, therefore, a manifestation of wealth, and the institution showed little of the harshness and severity that it possessed in areas where it was itself the foundation on which wealth was built. It should be added, moreover, that slaves who were converted to Islam were regarded as brothers. Although this did not release them from their duties as bondmen, it did have the effect of elevating their standing and enhancing their dignity among their fellows. While in the face of continued enslavement this was of doubtful value, it could have been viewed by slaves of a later and a more ruthless system as a substantial straw to which to clutch.

It was the forces let loose by the Renaissance and the Commercial Revolution that created the modern institution of slavery and the slave trade. The Renaissance gave to man a new kind of freedom—the freedom to pursue those ends which would be most beneficial to his soul and body. It developed into such a passionate search that it resulted in the destruction of long-established practices and beliefs and even in the destruction of the rights of others to pursue the same ends for their own benefit. It must never be overlooked that the concept of freedom which emerged in the modern world bordered on licentiousness and created a situation that approached anarchy. As DuBois has pointed out, it was the freedom to destroy freedom, the freedom of some to exploit the rights of others. It was, indeed, the concept of freedom with little or no social responsibility. If, then, a man was determined to be free, who was there to tell him that he was not entitled to enslave others?

Coupled with this new concept of freedom was the revitalized economic life of Europe brought forth by the Commercial Revolution. The breakdown of feudalism, the rise of towns, the heightened interest in commercial activities, and the new recognition of the strength and power of capital, all of which were essential elements of the Commercial Revolution, brought about a type of competition which was characterized by ruthless exploitation of any commodities that could be viewed as economic goods. The rise of powerful national states in Western Europe—Spain, France, Portugal, and, later, Holland—provided the political instrumentalities through which these new forces could be channeled. While the state acted as referee for the competitors within its borders, it also served to stimulate competition between its own merchants and traders and those of other countries. Thus, the states of Western Europe encouraged any methods employed by their citizens that would result in political and economic advantage over other states. The spirit of the Renaissance, with its sanction of ruthless freedom, and the practice of the Commercial Revolution, with its new techniques of exploitation, conspired to bring forth new approaches to the acquisition of wealth and power. Among these was the erection of the institution of modern slavery and the concomitant practice of importing and exporting slaves.

Doubtless, some of the Negroes of Africa who were sold to the East and North during the period of Mohammedan domination found their way into the markets of Western Europe. It was not until the end of the fourteenth century, however, that Europeans themselves began to bring slaves into Europe. Both Spanish and Portuguese sailors were exploring the coast of Africa in the wake of the great wave of expansionism that had swept over Europe. They went to the Canary Islands and to innumerable ports on the mainland as far as the Gulf of Guinea. Everywhere they made contacts with the natives and looked into the possibility of establishing trade relations with the natives. They carried Africans to Europe and made servants of them, feeling justified in doing so because the natives would thereby have the opportunity to cast off their heathenism and embrace the Christian religion. By the middle of the fifteenth century, Europeans were selling in their home markets many African commodities, among which were nuts, fruit, olive oil, gold, and Negro slaves.

Within a very few years, the slave trade became an accepted and profitable part of European commerce. Largely under the encouragement of Prince Henry, the sailors and merchants of Portugal early saw the economic advantages which the African slave trade afforded. Intrepid sailors, like the Venetian Cadamosto, attached themselves to the Portuguese court primarily because of the opportunities for wealth which the Guinea slave trade promised. By the time of the death of Prince Henry in 1460, seven or eight hundred slaves were being carried to Portugal annually.

The last half of the fifteenth century may be considered as the years of preparation in the history of the slave trade. Europeans, mainly Spaniards and Portuguese, were establishing orderly trade relations with the natives and were erecting forts and trading posts at which points they could carry on their business. It was the period in which Europeans were becoming accustomed to having Negroes do their work and were exploring the possibilities of finding new tasks for them. In Spain, for example, Negroes were seen in various places performing many tasks. Europeans were undertaking to settle among themselves the question of who should and who should not engage in the traffic; and the mad scramble for monopoly even before the close of the century is indicative of the importance with which they regarded the traffic. Finally, this was the period in which Europeans developed a rationalization for their deeds based on Christianity. Portuguese and Spaniards led Europeans in invoking the missionary zeal of Christianity to justify their activities on the African coast. If they were chaining Negroes together for the purpose of consigning them to a lifetime of enforced servitude, it was "a holy cause" in which they had the blessings of both their king and their Church.

There was never any profitable future for Negro slavery in Europe. Although Europe was undergoing drastic economic change in the fifteenth and sixteenth centuries, its new economic institutions did not utilize Negro slavery on a sufficiently large scale to make the trade excessively profitable. Banking houses, shipyards, mercantile establishments, and the homes of the newly rich could use only a limited number of slaves. To be sure, there were many new jobs to be performed, but the large white population which was dispossessed of land by the enclosure movement in England and on the continent was in search of employment. If there were jobs to be filled, these impecunious Europeans claimed them for themselves. But the new era in economic development ushered in some activities in which the Negro could perhaps be used. It was too much to expect that these activities would be confined to Europe as the international competition developed. The search for new trade routes, new lands, and new commodities provided the opportunities for the use of Negro slaves for which the Europeans had been looking. It was the New World with its vast natural resources and its undeveloped regions that could make slavery and the slave trade profitable, if indeed it could be profitable anywhere.

The Negro in the New World

From the very beginning of the Europeans' exploits in the New World, Negroes came as explorers, servants, and slaves. Even if Pedro Alonso Niño of the crew of Columbus was not a Negro as has been claimed, there were many Negroes who accompanied other European explorers to the New World. As early as 1501, Spain relinquished her earlier ban and permitted Negroes to go into the Spanish lands in the New World. Thirty Negroes, including Nuflo de Olano, were with Balboa when he discovered the Pacific Ocean. Cortés carried Negroes with him into Mexico, and one of them planted and harvested the first wheat crop in the New World. Two Negroes accompanied Velas in 1520. When Alvarado went to Quito, he carried two hundred Negroes with him. They were with Pizarro on his Peruvian expedition and carried him to the Cathedral after he was murdered. The Negroes in the expeditions of Almagro and Valdivia saved their Spanish masters from the Indians in 1525.

As the Spanish and Portuguese explorers moved into the interior of North America, Negroes assisted in the undertakings. They were with Alarcón and Coronado in the Conquest of New Mexico. They accompanied Narváez on his expedition of 1527 and were with Cabeza de Vaca in the exploration of the southwestern part of the present United States. One of the outstanding Negro explorers was Estevanico, who opened up New Mexico and Arizona for the Spaniards. Little Stephen, as Estevanico was known among his fellows, proceeded into the interior and sent back wooden crosses to indicate his progress. When his crosses increased in size until they were as tall as a man, the Spaniards realized that the Negro explorer had experienced great success. Indians brought news of Little Stephen's approach to the fabulous seven cities about which so much had been heard. Shortly after Stephen entered the city, the Indians killed him, believing him to be an imposter when he said that he was the emissary of two white men. Although Estevanico was murdered he prepared the way for the conquest of the Southwest by the Spaniards.

Negroes were with the French in their explorations of the New World. In the Canadian expeditions, Negroes were with the Jesuit missionaries. When the great conquest of the Mississippi Valley was undertaken by the French in the seventeenth century, Negroes constituted a substantial portion of the pioneers who settled in the region. Negroes, however, did not accompany the English on their explorations in the New World. It is not without ironical significance that Negroes were thus extensively engaged in the task of opening the New World for European exploitation. These pioneering efforts of this early period revealed the possibilities which the Western hemisphere held for the new economic life of Europe. They paved the way toward discovering the enormous wealth that lay in the extensive cultivation and exportation of staple crops to Europe. If Negroes helped to raise the curtain on the drama of economic life in the New World, they were to play an even more important part in the exploitation of its resources, once here; and once fastened to a lifetime status of slavery, they became an integral part of the economic life of the old world and of the new.

When the countries of Europe undertook to develop the New World, they were interested primarily in the exploitation of America's natural resources. Labor was, obviously, necessary, and the cheaper the better. It was only natural that Indians, readily available, would be the first to be used. The Europeans displayed excessive inhumanity in the employment of Indian slaves in the mines of Haiti, while the work in the fields of the Caribbean almost exterminated them. The great susceptibility of Indians to the diseases carried by Europeans and the simple economic background of the Indians which did not prepare them for the disciplined regime of the plantation system all but eliminated them as workers in the economic system which the Europeans established. Nowhere was Indian slavery profitable. Even if it had been, it would have been insufficient for the robust agricultural life that the European colonies were fostering in the seventeenth century. Other sources of labor supply would have to be tapped if the agricultural development in the

New World was not to be retarded by the insufficiency of workers. The search for acceptable workers in large quantities became a major preoccupation of the English and Spanish colonists in the seventeenth century.

Although Negroes were in Europe in considerable numbers in the seventeenth century and although they had been in the New World at least since 1501, the European imperialists did not at first regard them as a solution to their labor problems when the Indians proved inefficient and inadequate. To be sure, Negroes were being employed but the colonists and their Old World sponsors were extremely slow in recognizing them as the best possible labor force for the tasks in the New World. Before they made this recognition, they resorted to the poor whites of Europe. In the first half of the seventeenth century, these landless, penniless whites were brought over to do the work of clearing the forests and cultivating the fields. When the supply of those who voluntarily indentured themselves for a period of years proved insufficient, the English resorted to more desperate means. They raided the prisons of England in search of workers and, as Benjamin Franklin was to say later, dumped "upon the New World . . . the outcasts of the Old." Their desperation is clearly seen in the emergence of the widespread practice of kidnapping children, women, and drunken men; and Dr. Eric Williams has indicated that the horrors these people experienced in the trip to the New World equaled those experienced by any group before or after. In the English colonies many landlords sought to reduce these servants to the status of slaves. Only gradually did servants achieve a position of respectability in the colonies.

England came to realize that white servants were unsatisfactory. There was the fear that white servants in the colonies might become more interested in industry than agriculture to the detriment of England. Even with all the means used to recruit workers the supply was still insufficient as the tobacco, rice, and indigo plantations displayed an almost insatiable appetite for laborers. The terms of service of indentured people were the source of constant irritation for all concerned. Not only did the servants chafe under the requirement of remaining until their indenture had expired, but many went so far as to sue masters and ship captains for illegal detention. Many of them ran away, and since others of their ilk were migrating into unsettled lands, it became increasingly difficult, as well as ex-

pensive, to apprehend them once they had gotten away. Englishmen began to ask themselves why they should concern themselves with white servants when Negroes presented so few of the
difficulties encountered with the whites. Because of their color,
Negroes could be easily apprehended. Negroes could be purchased outright and a master's labor supply would not be in a
state of constant fluctuation. Negroes, from a pagan land and
without exposure to the ethical ideals of Christianity, could be
handled with more rigid methods of discipline and could be
morally and spiritually degraded for the sake of stability on the
plantation. In the long run, Negro slaves were actually cheaper.
In a period when economic considerations were so vital, this
was especially important. Negro slavery, then, became a fixed
institution, a solution to one of the most difficult problems that
arose in the New World. With the supply of Negroes apparently
inexhaustible, there would be no more worries about labor.
European countries could look back with gratitude to the first of
their nationals who explored the coasts of Africa and brought
this black gold to Europe. It was the key to the solution of one
of America's most pressing problems. At the same time it
erected for Europeans one more of those important economic
institutions, the slave trade, perhaps the last major development
in the Commercial Revolution that was in itself a source of great
wealth for those who would engage in the traffic of human souls.

The Big Business of Trading in Men

When, in 1517, Bishop Las Casas advocated the encouragement
of immigration to the New World by permitting Spaniards to
import twelve Negroes each, the slave trade to the New World
was formally opened. Monopolies of the trade went to the highest bidders. Sometimes it was held by Dutch traders, at other
times by Portuguese, French, or English. As the West Indian
plantations grew in size and importance the slave trade became
a huge, profitable undertaking that was, in itself, a great
economic enterprise employing thousands of persons and involving a capital outlay of millions of dollars. By 1540 the
annual importation of Negro slaves into the West Indies was
estimated at 10,000. Even if the figure was not that high, there
can be no doubt that by the end of the century the business of
carrying slaves to the New World was a lively one.

Although Portugal was the first European country to engage

in the African slave trade, it did not become one of the principal countries to realize great profits from the trade. At a time when the other countries were granting monopolies to powerful, government-supported trading companies, Portugal elected to leave her trade in the hands of merchants who proved ineffective matches for their competitors from other countries. Not until 1692 did Portugal license the Portuguese Company of Cacheo. By that time several strong companies of other countries had so monopolized the slave trade that Portugal did not have an opportunity to garner more than the proverbial crumbs from the table. Spain had been excluded from Africa by the Papal arbitration of 1493 and was forced to content herself with granting the privilege of carrying slaves to her colonies, the much sought after Asiento, to various companies and individuals of other countries.

The trade in men that developed into such a big business in the seventeenth and eighteenth centuries was largely in the hands of Dutch, French, and English companies. After Holland extricated herself from the control of Spain in the late sixteenth century she launched upon a bold program of competing with the other European countries for a share in the wealth of the New World. The Dutch contented themselves with relatively small territorial possessions and concentrated all their energies on seizing control of the commercial routes to the New World. In 1621 the Dutch West India Company was organized with a monopoly both of the African trade and the trade with the Dutch colonies in the New World. Immediately the company challenged the claim of Portugal to exclusive trading privileges on the African coast, and by the middle of the century it had gained a substantial foothold on the coast. When England was preoccupied with civil wars at home, Holland was strengthening her position both in Africa and America. Dutch slavers could be seen in the ports of almost all the American colonies in the seventeenth century. They brought the first Negroes to several French islands, including Martinique and Guadeloupe. On occasion they even carried Negroes to the Spanish islands, much against the will of their erstwhile subjector.

With the reorganization of the Dutch West India Company in 1675, Holland sought to recapture some of the African slave trade that had been slipping away from her. Her wars with France and England had left her considerably weakened, however, and never again did she achieve the dominance in the trade that she had formerly held. Many independent Dutch traders sought wealth in Africa, a situation which the Company tried to obviate by offering licenses to such persons. By her aggressiveness in the eighteenth century, Holland encountered new difficulties with other countries. Her traders pushed into sections of Africa that were admittedly under French influence, while on the Guinea coast her seizure of certain positions caused much concern in England. In the West Indies and in South America Holland used her holdings as centers for the distribution of slaves throughout the New World. Although the end of the century brought a noticeable decline in Dutch influence both in Africa and the New World, this did not take place until after Dutch traders had reaped a bountiful harvest from the trade in men.

In the sixteenth century the French made no attempt to establish permanent holdings on the African coast. By the middle of the century, however, the merchants of Rouen and other Norman towns were carrying on a lively trade with Africa, and in the seventeenth century organized efforts were made to secure a share in the slave trade. In 1634 a group of Norman merchants secured a patent from the government to carry on slave trading in Africa. In the latter year Colbert organized the French Company of the West Indies which bought out the smaller groups in Africa and began in earnest to promote France's interests in the slave trade. These efforts were none too successful, however, and in 1673 the Company of the Senegal was formed. Lack of capital and, perhaps, poor management sent this organization into bankruptcy by 1681. There were other efforts, such as the second Company of the Senegal, the Company of Guinea, and the Royal Company of the Senegal, but none of them met with marked success. At the opening of the eighteenth century, the French had just enough holdings in Africa, along the Senegal and in the Congo region, to excite the jealousy and concern of England. The century-long struggle between the countries had repercussions in Africa, and their slave trading posts were constantly changing hands in the Seven Years' War and in the American War for Independence. The measure of success which attended the French efforts in the Angola and Congo regions somewhat balanced the dismal failures that conflict with England brought them in the region north of the Equator.

Long before Sir John Hawkins inaugurated the English slave

trade, merchants of that country had become interested both in the trade of Africa and of the New World. Before the end of the reign of Henry VIII traders from Britain were developing relationships along the Guinea coast and along the Brazilian coast. Gold, ivory, and spice were the principal commodities in the English trade until 1562 when Elizabeth's John Hawkins broke the fiction of Portugal's monopoly in Africa and Spain's monopoly in the Americas by carrying slaves from Portuguese Africa to Spanish America. It was the seventeenth century, however, that brought the first substantial profits to Englishmen who engaged in the slave trade. In 1618 James I chartered the Company of Adventurers of London trading into parts of Africa which had control over the trade on the west coast. Under this company the first English trading post in West Africa was built. But its trading expeditions were dismal failures, and Dutch traders for many years furnished the English colonies with a majority of the slaves they purchased. In 1631 Charles I granted a group of traders a 31-year monopoly of the trade in Guinea, Benin, and Angola. Although little is known of the activities of this company, the complaints of its creditors and the attention given to the idea of organizing another company to supplant it seem to suggest that it was experiencing difficulty as a going concern.

Many individuals and organizations, including the powerful East India Company, manifested an interest in the African slave trade by the middle of the seventeenth century. The increased needs of the flourishing English colonies in the New World and the chaotic political conditions at home which held out the hope to almost any group that perchance it might rise in favor stimulated concern as well as investments in the slave trade. The relative stability which the Restoration brought ushered in a period of renewed activity which was crowned with eminent success. In 1672 the king chartered the Royal African Company, the reorganized group which had held the monopoly for a decade. For almost a half century this company dominated the English slave trade and, indeed, became the most important single group in the world engaging in the human traffic. It jealously guarded the monopoly which the king had granted it, and at the same time it attempted to drive the French and the Dutch out of West Africa. The growing number of independent traders in England bitterly fought the company's exclusive right to enjoy the African trade. While some wrote against it in the

English press and bitterly denounced it in the House of Commons, others disregarded the monopoly and pushed into the dark continent to share in its rape. The pressure of both groups resulted in the company's loss of its monopoly in 1698. Though it continued to trade in men its margin of profits declined. In 1731 it gave up the slave trade and centered its attention on ivory and gold dust.

Greater success attended England's efforts to control the west coast than the Royal African Company experienced in its efforts at national monopoly. The decisive defeats of the Dutch by the British and by the French in the late seventeenth century had the effect of enhancing England's prestige in Africa. The blow which France sustained in the War of the Spanish Succession resulted in England's securing the Asiento—the exclusive right to carry slaves to the Spanish colonies for thirty years. With her colonies in the Caribbean and on the mainland paying handsome dividends with their bountiful productivity, England's commerce came to dominate the entire world. With a strengthened navy and almost unlimited resources in capital for investment, England could now undertake to satisfy not only the growing demand of her own colonies for slaves but the demands of other colonies in the New World as well.

During the Seven Years' War England carried more than ten thousand slaves to Cuba and approximately forty thousand to Guadeloupe. By 1788 two-thirds of all the slaves brought by England to the New World were sold in foreign colonies. Naturally the planters in the English colonies objected to their competitors in the New World being furnished with slaves by British traders. It was not fair, they felt, and it was certainly contrary to England's mercantilist theory which fostered intra-imperialistic cooperation against her rivals. What the planters did not realize, perhaps, was that the slave trade had itself become an important factor in England's economic life. If England's colonies were the foundation of her economic system, certainly in the eighteenth century the slave trade became an important cornerstone.

The Machinery of the Slave Trade

Since England came to dominate the slave trade, it is to be expected that the machinery for prosecuting the traffic was to a large extent the product of her ingenuity. England certainly had no monopoly on the development of slave trading practices, but her extensive interests and her great success marked her as the country to be emulated. It is for this reason that one almost invariably associates these practices with England. The techniques of trading in slaves were developed after years of trials and failures. By the eighteenth century all countries trading in Africa had specified methods of procedure in handling the traffic. Trading posts, or factories, on the coast were the indispensable bases of operation. Once they had been established, and the more the better, trading could proceed. Ships laden with European goods either brought traders out or furnished those already there with goods with which to trade. Cotton textiles of all descriptions, utensils of brass, pewter, and ivory boxes of beads of many sizes and shapes, guns and gunpowder, spirits—whiskey, brandy, and rum—and a variety of foodstuffs were some of the more important items to be exchanged for slaves. The value of the cargo varied with the size of the ship and the time of the trading. A typical cargo would seem to be that of the *King Solomon* which, in 1720, had an inventory of £4,250 worth of goods when it left London for Cape Castle on the west coast. At each trading post were stationed a number of factors, slave traders, who maintained friendly relations with the natives in order to procure slaves. These factors represented their king and their company of the merchants who sent them there. The posts, often bulging with European goods, were well fortified and were guarded by soldiers. There were dangers of interlopers, traders from competing countries, and natives who might develop an inclination to secure the goods they desired without trading for them.

Upon arrival at a trading post in Africa the trader was ready to establish his contacts both with the officials at the post and with the natives who assisted in securing the desired slaves. The usual procedure was to go to the chief of the tribe and to make arrangements with him and to secure "permission" to trade on his domain. The chief, after being properly persuaded with gifts, then appointed various assistants who were at the disposal of the trader. Chief among these was the caboceer who assumed the responsibility of gathering up the natives to be sold—at prices previously agreed upon between the trader and the chief. The trading proceeded apace once the captives had been brought before the trader for inspection. It was necessary for the trader to consult with his physician and other advisers concerning purchases. Frequently, the prospective slaves had been so cleanly shaven and soaked in palm oil that it was most difficult to ascertain their ages or physical condition. The prices, of course, varied greatly depending on the age of the slave, the period of the trading, and the location of the post. Many transactions were mere barter, but there are accounts which reveal that in the middle of the eighteenth century £20 sterling was a typical price to pay for a healthy young man at Cape Castle or some other important post on the Guinea coast.

It must not be supposed that trading in slaves involved the simple procedure of sailing into a port, loading up with slaves, and sailing away. In addition to the various courtesy visits and negotiations which protocol required and which the traders were inclined to follow in order to keep the native leaders in good humor, it was frequently difficult to find enough "likely" slaves to fill a ship of considerable size. Frequently, traders had to remain at one place for two or three weeks before enough slaves were rounded up to make the negotiations worth while. It was not unusual for a ship to be compelled to put in at four or five places in order to purchase as many as five hundred slaves. The interior frequently had to be scoured and much coercion used to secure enough slaves to meet the demands of the traders. While the extent of the interior search is open to some question, there can be little doubt that the supply of slaves was not furnished from the immediate vicinity of the posts.

Another delay came in disposing of the cargo which had been brought from Europe and in provisioning the ship with supplies needed for the voyage to America. Experience taught the traders what to carry, but at times they carried goods which were not especially desired at the places where they were able to purchase their slaves and, thus, were forced to carry them all the way back to England if the permanent post officials could not be persuaded to take them. At the post and from natives the traders obtained supplies for the western voyage across the Atlantic. Indian corn, kidney beans, yams, fruit, coconuts, and plantains (dried bananas) were the principal foodstuffs secured. In addition sundry medicines, including the Malagetta (similar to the Indian pepper), were stocked in order that the physician might administer to the slaves who were almost certain to become ill en route.

There can be no doubt that the natives offered stiff resistance to their capture, sale. and transportation to the unknown New

World. Fierce wars broke out between tribes when the members of one sought to capture members of another to sell them to the traders. Slaves brought to the post for sale were always chained, for the caboceers and slave captains very early learned that without such safeguards the slaves would make their escape. Guards were employed to chaperone the slaves out to the ship and see to it that they were held there until the ship was ready to set sail. One trader remarked that the Negroes were "so wilful and loth to leave their own country, that they have often leap'd out of the canoes, boat and ship, into the sea, and kept under water till they were drowned," to avoid being taken up by their captors. At the first opportunity, if indeed it ever presented itself, many would leap off the ship into the mouths of hungry sharks to prevent enslavement in the New World.

One-Way Passage

The voyage to the Americas, popularly referred to as the "Middle Passage," was a veritable nightmare. Overcrowding was most common. There are records of ships as small as ninety tons carrying a complement of 390 slaves in addition to crew and provisions. The practice of overcrowding slaves became so common that the British Parliament felt compelled to specify that not more than five slaves should be carried for every three tons of the burden of a ship of 200 tons. This regulation, like so many others, was not enforced. More slaves meant greater profits, and few traders could resist the temptation to wedge in a few more. There was hardly standing, lying, or sitting room. Chained together by twos, hands and feet, the slaves had no room in which to move about and no freedom to exercise their bodies even in the slightest.

It was doubtless the crowded conditions on the vessels that so greatly increased the incidence of disease and epidemics during the voyage to America. Smallpox was one of the dread diseases of the period, and one experienced observer remarked that few ships that carried slaves escaped without it. Perhaps even more deadly than smallpox was flux, a malady from which the whites on board the slave ships were apparently spared. Beginning with pains in the head and back, chills, fever, and nausea, this disease baffled both Negroes and whites, and most frequently it was fatal. "Hunger strikes" at times aggravated unfavorable

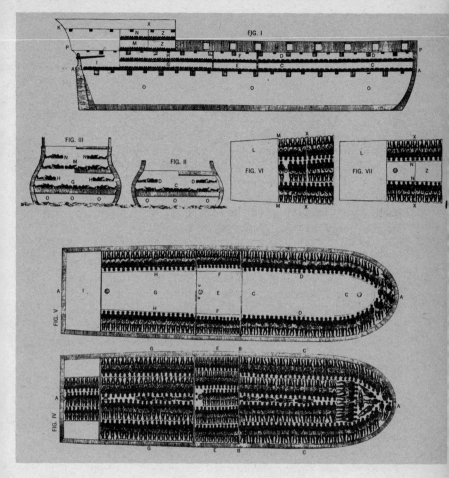

THE PLAN OF THE BROOKES. A) *lower deck;* B) *lower deck; breadth;*
C) *men's room;* D) *platforms, men's room;* E) *boys' room;* F) *platforms,*
boys' room; G) *women's room;* H) *platforms, women's room;* I) *gun room;*
K) *quarter-deck;* L) *cabin;* M) *half-deck;* N) *platforms, half-deck;* O)
hold; P) *upper deck.* Fig. I) *lengthwise cross section;* II) *breadthwise*
cross section of men's section; III) *breadthwise cross section of women's*
section; IV) *lower deck, with platforms;* V) *lower deck, without platforms;*
VI) *half-deck, with platforms;* VII) *half-deck, without platforms. The* Brookes,
a 320-ton vessel, was one of the eighteen slave-trading ships examined by a
committee before making recommendations to the English Parliament for
the regulation of such vessels in 1788. The abolitionists claimed that the
Brookes, *built to accommodate 451 persons, carried as many as 609 slaves on*
one of her voyages. From a pamphlet by Thomas Clarkson, London, 1839.

health conditions and induced illnesses where previously there had been none. The filth and stench caused by close quarters and illness brought on more illness and the mortality rate was increased accordingly. Perhaps not more than half the slaves shipped from Africa ever became effective workers in the New World. Many of those that had not died of disease or committed suicide by jumping overboard were permanently disabled by the ravages of some dread disease or·by maiming which often resulted from the struggle against the chains. Small wonder that one trader who arrived at Barbados with 372 of his original 700 slaves was moved to remark: "No gold-finders can endure so much noisome slavery as they do who carry Negroes; for those have some respite and satisfaction, but we endure twice the misery; and yet by the mortality our voyages are ruin'd and we pine and fret ourselves to death, to think that we should undergo so much misery, and take so much pains to so little purpose."

It may be reasonably doubted that the situation was as unfavorable as the above trader pictured it. To be sure, there were difficulties of many kinds, not the least of which was the great mortality among the white men themselves who were associated with the trade. Even with the great expenses attached to the trade and the extensive loss sustained in the mortality of slaves in transit, the slave trade was still one of the most important sources of European wealth in the seventeenth and eighteenth centuries. In the late eighteenth century, it was possible for a ship captain to make a commission of £360 on the sale of 307 slaves and for the trader to earn £465 on the same sale. It was not unusual for a ship carrying 250 slaves to net as much as £7,000 on one voyage. Profits of 100 per cent were not uncommon for Liverpool merchants. Perhaps those engaged in the trade did undergo much misery, but if they were seeking profits (and who among them had other motives?) it hardly seems accurate for one of them to add that they took "so much pains to so little purpose."

It is not possible to give an accurate figure of the number of slaves imported into the New World from Africa. In eleven years, from 1783 through 1793, Liverpool traders alone were responsible for the importation of 303,737, while in the following eleven years they were certainly responsible for as many. While the closing years of the eighteenth century represented the peak in the slave trade, the preceding two centuries show a steady increase leading to the apogee reached in the 1790's. It has been

estimated by Dunbar that 900,000 were imported in the sixteenth century, 2,750,000 in the seventeenth, 7,000,000 in the
eighteenth, and 4,000,000 in the nineteenth. These figures,
among the most conservative estimates, may not be accurate. It
cannot be denied, however, that the total number of Africans
removed from their native land ran far into the millions. When
one considers the great numbers that must have been killed
while resisting capture, the additional numbers that died during
the middle passage, and the millions that were successfully
brought to the Americas the aggregate approaches staggering
proportions. These figures, five, ten, or fifteen millions, are
themselves a testimonial to the fabulous profits that must have
been realized in such a sordid business, to the ruthlessness with
which the traders must have prosecuted it, and to the tremendous demands being made by New World settlers for laborers.

It is more difficult to measure the effect of such an activity on
African life than it is to estimate the number of natives removed. The expatriation of millions of Negroes from the continent of Africa in less than four centuries constitutes one of the
most far-reaching and drastic social revolutions in the annals of
history. It is to be remembered that the traders would have none
but the best available natives. They demanded the healthiest,
the largest, the youngest, the ablest, and those that were the
most advanced culturally. It is to be remembered, moreover,
that the vast majority of the slaving was carried on in the area
of West Africa where civilization had reached its highest point
on the continent, with the possible exception of Egypt. The
removal of the flower of African manhood left the continent
impotent, stultified, and dazed. The encouragement which Europeans gave them to fight among themselves, with explosive
weapons donated by the Europeans, further debilitated them
and removed the last vestige of opportunity to recover from the
body blow which the slave trade had dealt them. Africa, which
culturally was within some measurable distance from Europe at
the beginning of the fifteenth century, received the worst possible influence from her Christian neighbors to the north, and
under these adverse circumstances she began a recession that in
time was to be accelerated by the imperialistic enslavement that
was to be thrust upon her in the nineteenth century.

V •

Seasoning in the Islands

Colonial Enterprise in the Caribbean

● *The slave trade became a tremendously important factor in* European economic life primarily because of the developments in the New World. The trade in men would have remained inconsequential if it had been confined to the importation of a few servants into Europe. Its great growth came as the colonies in the New World grew and manifested a pressing need for labor to do the job of clearing the land and tilling the fields. It is, therefore, no mere accident that the seventeenth century which witnessed the first important advances in the slave trade also saw the growth of European interest in colonizing and developing the economic life of the New World. The Caribbean was the scene of the first serious effort to develop a lucrative agricultural economy in the New World. It was to the islands in that area that important complements of slaves were sent in the seventeenth century.

The rivalry between European countries for the control of the islands in the seventeenth century presaged the more intense rivalry that was to characterize the struggle for hegemony on the mainland the following century. Spain, of course, had prior claim to the islands, thanks to the explorations of her sailors in the fifteenth century and the papal arrangement of 1493. The Spaniards took advantage of this position by channeling their energies and capital into the development of their insular possessions, the most important of which were Cuba, Puerto Rico,

Hispaniola, and Jamaica. Although they were to lose some of these and other islands in various conflicts, they nevertheless made the most of them by producing staple crops with slave labor. Early in the sixteenth century large consignments of slaves were sent to the Spanish islands. In 1518, for example, the king of Spain granted a trader the right to ship 4,000 Negroes to the Spanish islands. By 1540 the annual importation had reached approximately 10,000. It must be remembered, moreover, that there was already developing an illicit trade the size of which there was no way of determining.

The breaking of the Spanish monopoly in the Caribbean is closely connected with the slave trade. What the English first sought was an opportunity to share in the Caribbean trade which, during the early years of Elizabeth's reign, already gave promise of being decidedly profitable. When Spain rejected this bid, the English, led both in thought and action by John Hawkins, decided that the monopoly could be broken only by force. Thereupon, Hawkins planned to carry slaves to the New World with the hope that the colonists' desire for them would be sufficient to overcome their respect for the royal ban on unlicensed trade. The pattern which he set in selling slaves and other African goods at Hispaniola in 1563 was eagerly followed by other and less scrupulous English imitators, who were summarily arrested and punished by the Spanish officials in the island. Spain's stern policy of resistance to English encroachment led to the employment of harsh measures against Hawkins and other traders who sought to share in the trade in 1569. Although for the moment Spain had checked the encroachment, it was at best only temporary. It was only a matter of time before she would have to yield valuable ground in regard both to the commercial and the territorial monopoly which she had enjoyed.

In the seventeenth century Spain lost all claim to exclusive control over the islands in the Caribbean. Denmark, Holland, France, and England acquired territory in the area. The Dutch buccaneers were entrenched in Curaçao, St. Eustatius, and Tobago by 1640, and the Dutch West India Company, supported enthusiastically by its government, was promoting the slave trade in these and foreign islands. At about the same time the French Company of the Islands of America settled Guadeloupe, Martinique, and Marie Galante. In the fifties, St. Lucia and Grenada were acquired by France. The English secured control of St. Christopher in 1623, Barbados in 1625, and in the thirties they added Nevis, Antigua, and Montserrat to their possessions. In 1655 they won one of the great prizes of the Caribbean by driving the Spaniards out of Jamaica. In 1671 the Danes acquired St. Thomas. Spanish monopoly had indeed been broken, and the West Indies had become not only a pawn in European diplomacy but an important source of revenue as each country sought to develop its insular possessions with whatever resources it could command. African slavery proved to be invaluable in this development.

The Plantation System

Negroes were first used on the tobacco plantations of the Caribbean islands. By 1639, however, the European markets had become so glutted with the weed that the price decreased sharply, and a great loss was sustained by the West Indian planters. Some of them turned to cotton and indigo, neither of which proved to be as profitable as they had hoped. Some heeded the suggestions of the Dutch merchant traders who suggested that they try sugar. A few went to Brazil to study at first hand the highly successful methods which the Portuguese had employed there for three generations. It appeared to be a good opportunity, and with capital borrowed from Dutch and English merchants, West Indian planters began to cultivate sugar cane. The results surpassed their greatest expectations, and plans for the extension of the cultivation were immediately undertaken. The problem of labor became acute. The whites were both insufficient in number and unsatisfactory in conduct. The planters turned more and more to the use of Negro slaves, and thus in the middle of the seventeenth century the importation of Negroes into the Caribbean islands began in earnest.

In 1640 there were only a few hundred Negroes in Barbados. By 1645, after the new sugar plantations had demonstrated their profitableness, there were 6,000 Negro slaves there; and by the middle of the century the Negro population had increased to 20,000. Between 4,000 and 5,000 Negroes of good quality were delivered to the island in the sixties, and they found a ready market among the sugar planters. By the end of the century Barbados had a Negro population of upwards of 80,000. A similar growth of the Negro population took place in many of the other Caribbean islands in the seventeenth century. The momentum of importation was so great by the end of the century that in the next hundred years, when the demand for slaves in the islands was declining, importation was continued and in most places it even increased. By 1763 there were 60,000 Negro slaves that had been imported into Cuba. In the next three decades they were introduced at a much more rapid rate. Through a system of granting special licenses to importers Spain was able to bring into Cuba as many as 17,000 Negroes in a single year in the seventies. Between 1763 and 1790, about 41,000 were brought in, while between 1791 and 1825 no less than 320,000 were delivered in Havana alone. Jamaica, Nevis, Montserrat, St. Christopher, St. Vincent, St. Lucia experienced proportionately similar increases.

The tendency to overpopulate the islands of the Caribbean arose from several important factors. Of course, many slaves that were brought into the islands were to be re-exported, a matter which will be discussed later. Furthermore, there seemed to be no substantial increase in the Negro population of the islands as a result of births. The death rate was so extraordinarily high that it raises the question of the treatment of slaves. In one year, for example, 2,656 Negroes were born in St. Vincent, but in the same year there were 4,205 deaths. On one plantation in Jamaica more than half of the children died in infancy, while miscarriages were high in number. Some authorities have attributed the high mortality rate to improper food and the ravages of disease. Doubtless these conditions were present; but the view of many masters that slaves were cheaper to purchase then to breed and the consequent imposition of undue labor on men and women of all conditions and ages apparently caused more deaths than anything else.

There were few evidences of humanitarianism on the plantations of the West Indies. Slavery was essentially, almost exclusively, an economic institution. Slaves were being extensively used for the sole purpose of producing sugar and other staple crops. The revenue from these crops was enhancing the prestige and increasing the wealth of European countries. Through the use of slaves to produce the rich crops the islands became the favorites of their mother countries. For example, the islands were "of immense importance to the grandeur and prosperity of England." If the importation of more slaves meant a larger measure of prosperity—and it seemed so to the island planters—they were imported with little regard for consequences other than those purely of an economic nature. There was, consequently, no effort to develop or foster those institutions that might have had the effect of at least softening the horrors of West Indian slavery. Indeed, in so many instances those persons intimately responsible for the conduct of affairs in the islands were not residents of the islands.

It was this absentee landlordism that constituted one of the most important factors in the development of practices that were manifestly destructive of health and life among the slaves. Some English landlords pleaded that the climate of the sugar colonies was "so inconvenient for an English constitution that no man will chuse to live there, much less will any man chuse to settle there, without the hopes of at least supporting his family in a more handsome manner, or saving more money than he can do by any business he can expect in England, or in our plantations upon the continent of America." The islands were, therefore, regarded not as a place of residence but merely as a source of wealth. There was complete disregard for any considerations that might bring a modicum of civilization to the area. If a planter came out to the Caribbean, he regarded it as a temporary sojourn. Soon he would return to his home country, and with the wealth he had amassed he would buy an estate and live like a gentleman. Why, then, should he interest himself in schools, churches, and laws that would improve conditions of life for everyone?

In the islands absentee landlordism had a most deleterious effect on the institution of slavery. Left in the hands of overseers, the slaves became the victims of disinterested persons whose only concern was to produce wealth for their employers. To the absent landlords, things were going well in the islands if revenues were increasing. This simple criterion for measuring successful management left much to be desired in the way of human relationships in the islands. The overseers proceeded to make the plantations prosperous by seeking to increase productivity. The result was the evolution of practices in mistreating slaves that have few counterparts in the history of the institution.

Since Negro slaves were constantly being brought in from Africa, overseers found it necessary to develop a practice of "breaking in" the newcomers. In some areas they were distributed among the "seasoned" or veteran slaves, whose duty it was to teach the newly-arrived slaves the ways of life in the New World. In other places they were kept apart and supervised by a special staff of guardians and inspectors who were experienced in breaking in Negroes who might offer resistance to adjusting in their new environment. In either case the mortality rate was exceptionally high, with estimates of deaths running to as much as 30 per cent in a seasoning period of three or four years. Old and new diseases, change of climate and food, exposure incurred in running away, suicide, and excessive flogging were among the main causes of the high mortality rate among the newcomers.

In the West Indies slaves were sent to the farms at daybreak and labored all day except for the thirty-minute period for breakfast and a two-hour period in the hottest portion of the day, which was frequently the time set aside for doing lighter chores. At harvest time the workday was much longer, sometimes eighteen hours. Twelve hours were spent by half the group at the boiling house and they were followed by the other half who spent an equal amount of time there.

Both groups had five or six hours of additional work cutting and bringing cane to the mill, caring for the animals, cutting grass, and hauling water. The driver or overseer did not distinguish between men and women in work requirements or in applying the lash for dereliction of duty. Women maintained the same hours as men did in the fields and at the mills. The investigations made by the British Parliament in 1790–91 brought out the fact that pregnant women were forced to labor up to the time of childbirth and that a month was the maximum amount of time allowed for recovery from childbearing. Pregnant women were lashed severely when they were unable to keep pace with the other workers. Women who paused in the fields to care for their babies whom they carried on their backs were lashed with cart whips for idling away their time.

Food was, on the whole, insufficient for slaves, engaged as they were in such arduous labor. The planters did not often encourage any type of diversified agriculture which would have provided food for the workers. Where this was done at all, slaves were given small plots of land sometimes far from their houses which they could cultivate in spare moments. The time for such activities was usually Sundays, but they were so fatigued by the labor of the week that they were hardly capable of working at all on the traditional rest day. In Barbados, where planters had the reputation of providing for their slaves better than the planters of other islands, slaves were generally ill fed. On one plantation each adult slave was given a pint of grain and half of a herring (not infrequently rotten) for twenty-four hours. In the famous investigation of 1790–91 no plantation was found where a slave received more than nine pints of corn and one pound of salt per week. Fish of the least desirable grades were imported from the New England colonies; and where this was done the planter acquired a reputation for his great benevolence.

The Caribbean Black Codes

Perhaps it was the slave codes and their enforcement that did more than anything else to carry forward the process of "seasoning" the slaves in the islands. On many islands the Negro population outnumbered the whites. For example, as early as 1673 there were 10,000 Negroes in Jamaica and only 8,000 whites. In 1724 there were 32,000 Negroes and 14,000 whites. At the end of the century the population of St. Christopher was over 20,000, "well nigh twenty times that of the white population." It was the preponderance of Negroes over whites that promoted the enactment of a slave code of excessive severity. The influence of the planters in England made possible the passage, in 1667, of the "Act to regulate the Negroes on the British Plantations." It referred to the Negroes in the Caribbean as "of wild, barbarous, and savage nature to be controlled only with strict severity." Slaves were not to leave the plantation without a pass; they were not to be away on Sunday under any circumstances, and they were not allowed to carry any weapons. If a slave struck a Christian, he was to be severely whipped, and for the second offense he was to be branded on the face with a hot iron. If the owner accidentally whipped a slave to death, he was not subject to fine or imprisonment. The other European countries had similar laws, but there seemed to have been considerable variation in enforcement. While the well-known French "Code Noir" was relatively humane, it became the agency of great brutality in the hands of some French colonials. When Ogé and his associates were found guilty of conspiring to revolt in the last decade of the eighteenth century all were cruelly executed. "Their arms, thighs, legs, and backbones were broken with clubs on a scaffold. They were fastened round a wheel in such a manner that their face was turned upward to receive the full glare of the sun." The judge ordered that "Here they are to remain for so long as it shall please God to preserve them alive," after which their heads were to be cut off and exposed on tall poles.

One important ingredient in the seasoning process was the overseer's lash. A typical one was made of plaited cowhide. In the hands of a stern overseer it could draw blood through the breeches of a slave. One visitor in Jamaica fell ill at his first sight of a common flogging. At times the floggings were so severe as to inflict wounds so large that a man's finger could be inserted in them. Another favorite type of punishment was to suspend the slave to a tree by ropes and tie iron weights around his neck and waist. Still another was to crop the slave's ears and to break the bones of his limbs. If these punishments would seem to shorten life and to reduce efficiency it must be remembered that Negroes were being brought in at an increasing rate down past the opening of the nineteenth century and there was, consequently, no great inclination to preserve life. Furthermore, it was extremely important in a society where Negroes outnumbered whites that the Negroes be continuously impressed with the superior strength of the whites and their willingness to exercise it in all its fury whenever necessary.

If cruel treatment was designed to prevent uprisings and running away, it was eminently unsuccessful. On almost every island there is record of some serious revolt against the plantation system, and everywhere there is evidence of constant running away. When the British took possession of Jamaica in the middle of the seventeenth century, most of the Negro slaves promptly escaped to the mountains and were frequently joined by other fugitives. These runaways, called Maroons, continuously harassed the planters by stealing, trading with slaves, and enticing them to run away. By 1730 these ex-slaves, under Cudgo, their powerful leader, had terrorized the whites to such an extent that England was compelled to send out two additional regiments to protect them.

Haiti also had its Maroons as early as 1620, and the outlawed colony grew to such proportions that the Colonial government recognized it in 1784. The Maroons kept in constant touch with the slaves and incited many to revolt. It is conceded that they were largely responsible for the Haitian uprisings of 1679,

1691, and 1704. In the middle of the eighteenth century the recalcitrant Negroes of Haiti found a peerless leader in Macandal, a native African, who announced that he was the Black Messiah sent to drive the whites from the island. He decried the fact that the whites had taken the island from the Indians and prophesied that one day it would be in the hands of the blacks. In 1758 he carefully laid his plans for the coup d'état. The water of Le Cap was to be poisoned, and when the whites were in convulsions the Negroes, under the leadership of Macandal and his Maroons, were to seize control. By accident, the plot was discovered, and the fear-stricken planters hunted down Macandal and executed him. At the time of his execution he warned his enemies and comforted his friends by telling them that one day he would return, more terrible than before. Many Negroes, and perhaps some whites, were later to believe that Toussaint L'Ouverture was the reincarnation of Macandal.

Even in the small Danish islands there are records of resentment to the seasoning process. The lack of sufficient food drove many slaves to steal and to refuse to work. In 1726 the officials executed seventeen of the leading offenders, but this did not quiet the slaves. The situation became increasingly worse, and in 1733 the Governor of St. Thomas issued a drastic decree providing for severe punishments of slave offenders by burning, whipping, and hanging. Two months later the Danish Islands experienced their worst uprising, which occurred on St. John. Negroes carrying wood entered one of the forts of the Danish West India Company and murdered the guard by stabbing him. Another group of slaves attacked six soldiers and killed five of them. Having captured the garrison, they raised the flag and fired three shots from the cannon, the signal for a general uprising on all the plantations on the island. The leading magistrate was one of the first victims. With flintlocks, pistols, and cane-knives the Negroes went about the bloody business of murdering all the whites they could find. Only after several days of terror was the uprising brought under control by the captain of the militia. It was the same everywhere—conspiracies, uprisings, bloodshed. The seeds of cruelty reaped a bountiful harvest of murder and bloodshed. It can hardly be said that the stern measures employed by the officials, planters, and overseers in the islands were satisfactory seasoning processes. Much more effective was the seasoning that only time could give. As the years passed and as the slave learned his duties he performed them, albeit reluctantly. Time also proved that he could adjust to the climate and food of the New World. Although his term of service in the islands was by no means satisfactory, he was regarded as seasoned within three or four years and was viewed by mainland planters as much more desirable than the raw Negroes fresh from the wilds of Africa.

Decline in the Islands

Slaves were being constantly exported from the islands, especially from the British islands. In an effort to capture the slave trade with foreign islands, British traders first brought the slaves into some British island and then quietly re-exported them to Cuba, Puerto Rico, or some other foreign island. While it is not possible to estimate the number of Negroes carried into Cuba from the British islands, it is quite clear that this was Cuba's most important source of slaves. Jamaica alone sent more than 10,000 slaves there in 1756. Of the 90,331 Negroes imported into the British West Indies between 1784 and 1787, some 19,964 were re-exported; but it is not possible to determine whether they went to French, Spanish, or Portuguese markets, to other British islands, or to the mainland. Miss Elizabeth Donnan says, "occasional items, such as the statement that, in 1763, 180 negroes were carried from St. Croix, ten of them sold at Monte Christi, the rest sent to Cape François, show that negroes were being carried from island to island for sale, and an accumulation of such items might give us much information concerning the commercial relations among the islands."

As the prosperity of the West Indies declined in the early eighteenth century and as the attention of Europe became more focused on the continent of North America, more slaves were doubtless exported from the islands to the mainland. The demand for slaves in the mainland colonies was steadily increasing, and a decided preference for slaves seasoned in the colonies was manifested. In 1764 several shipments of slaves were made from the West Indies to South Carolina. They came from St. Christopher, Antigua, Barbados, and even Havana. Although the islands could not satisfy the growing demand for slaves on the mainland, they sent some of their surplus yearly, as the records amply testify. Indeed, re-exportation itself became a lucrative business in which many persons were engaged. On the islands of St. Christopher, Barbados, and Jamaica there were firms that carried on a regular business of re-exporting Negroes to other islands and to the mainland. In the colonies many firms did business direct with traders in the islands.

The cost of producing sugar increased as the soil exhaustion manifested itself after a century of intensive cultivation. The price of slaves, moreover, was increasing as the demand for them increased on the mainland. White society was so completely without resourceful and imaginative leadership that it was not able to discover areas of economic activity which would compensate for the losses it was sustaining in the older activities. Desperate efforts were made both in Europe and in the island colonies to encourage whites to migrate to the Caribbean. Some islands required planters to import proportionate numbers of whites for all the slaves they brought; but many planters found it easier to pay the fines. With a surplus of slaves on their hands, the residents of the West Indies were willing to sell many of them to the mainland colonies.

The increasing exportation of Negroes from the West Indies is a clear manifestation of social and economic debility. After several centuries of European occupation, religious institutions were still weak, and vice and immorality of all kinds flourished. Education was at an especially low ebb, and ignorance prevailed even among the whites. The ineffectiveness of the law showed itself in its inability to prevent running away, insurrections, and wholesale miscegenation. In sending many of its slaves to the mainland, the West Indies served notice to the world that they had yielded the long-held economic primacy in the New World to the mainland.

VI •

Servitude and Slavery
in the Southern Colonies

The Beginnings in Virginia

● *The twenty Negroes that were left at Jamestown in 1619 by* the captain of a Dutch frigate were the beginning of the involuntary importation of human beings into the mainland that was not to stop until more than two hundred years later. Their arrival did not solve the labor problem that had already begun to plague the infant colony. So insensible were the Virginians to the unlimited possibilities of Negro labor that nothing resembling a spirited importation of Negroes began until the last quarter of the seventeenth century. To be sure, the colonists viewed the introduction of Negroes as just another aspect of the many-sided economic problem they faced and gave little attention either to the status of the newly arrived blacks or to their place in the evolving colony. There can be little doubt that the earliest Negroes in Virginia occupied a position similar to that of the white servants in the colony. They were listed as servants in the census enumerations of 1623 and 1624; and as late as 1651 some Negroes whose period of service had expired were being assigned land in much the same way that it was being done for white servants. The records of Virginia contain many indentures of Negro servants during the forty-year period following their introduction; and during the same period there are records of free Negroes in the colony.

It seemed that Virginia was willing to exhaust every possibility in her effort to solve her labor problem before finally resorting to Negro slavery. As she experimented with various practices, she encountered the same difficulties that her insular colleagues had experienced. Indian servitude and slavery were abject failures, and the attempts proved fruitless and wasteful. The white servants were found to be unsatisfactory on two counts. There was no possibility that the supply would satisfy the demand in a country where there was so much work to be done. There was, moreover, the disturbing factor of having to replace indentured servants every few years as their period of service expired. This was a most unsatisfactory feature that applied to Indian and Negro servants as well as to white servants. The answer to this vexing problem appeared to be the perpetual servitude of Negroes, whose supply seemed inexhaustible and who apparently presented none of the problems that white servants presented. If they ran away they were easily detected because of their color. If they proved ungovernable they could be chastised with less qualms and with greater severity than in the case of whites, because the Negroes represented heathen people who could not claim the immunities accorded to Christians. By the middle of the seventeenth century Virginians realized the possibilities that lay in the exploitation of black labor; and all that was needed was the legislative sanction to give validity to the practice that was already developing.

There was no statutory recognition of slavery in Virginia until 1661. Steps in that direction had earlier been taken by modifying the definition of the condition of persons legally recognized as servants. Most of the Negroes brought into Virginia after 1640 had no indentures or contracts and could not look forward to freedom after a specified term of service. Some others that were brought in enjoyed the dubious distinction of having contracts providing that they were "servants for life" or "perpetual servants." This was the result of vigorous efforts, extending over a generation, to lengthen and renew terms of indenture so as to provide for continuous service. When legislative recognition finally came in Virginia it did not reduce to the status of slaves those Negroes that were already free. The initial laws and those of succeeding years were designed to secure for the whites the title to Negroes so that they could be held in perpetual servitude. It appeared to be the only solution to the problem of labor, and these colonists were not inclined to shrink from the enslavement of a people if such a procedure was to have a salutary effect on the economic life of the colony.

The Negro population of Virginia grew slowly during the first two generations. In the years immediately following the initial arrival there were few if any Negroes imported into the colony. In 1625 there were only twenty-three Negroes in Virginia, and by the middle of the century only 300 Negroes were to be found in the colony. The increased interest of Englishmen in the slave trade during the Restoration and the establishment of the powerful Royal African Company doubtless had the effect of stimulating the importation of slaves into the mainland colonies. In the last quarter of the seventeenth century slave importations into Virginia increased so sharply that some inhabitants began to entertain doubts concerning the advisability of flooding the country with ungovernable and irascible Negroes so recently removed from a barbaric land. At the close of the century they were being brought in at a rate of more than one thousand per year, and the very size of the importations emphasized to the Virginians the dangers of a large Negro population. By 1708 there were 12,000 Negro tithables as compared to 18,000 whites. The monopoly of the slave trade which England secured in the Treaty of Utrecht was doubtless responsible for much of the increase after 1713. In 1715 there were 23,000 Negroes in the colony when the white population numbered 72,500. By 1756 there were 120,156 Negroes and 173,316 whites. In many counties Negroes outnumbered whites, and only on the frontier were the Negroes of such small numbers as not to cause any alarm.

Virginia appeared unable to prevent the disturbing increase of Negroes within her borders. To be sure, these newly arrived workers solved the labor problem, but many colonists came to feel that this was too costly a price to pay for the solution. The dire and irremediable social consequences that flowed from the infiltration of Negroes were creating problems which taxed the resourcefulness of the colonists fully as much as the labor shortage had done. The mixture of the races was especially disturbing as were the rumors, real and fancied, of conspiracies of rebellion. These fears had much to do with the enactment of laws placing heavy duties on the importation of slaves. When the slave traders awoke to the fact that the duties were for the purpose of discouraging importation, they vigorously and successfully opposed these devices and continued to bring slaves into the colony in larger and larger numbers. The fight that ensued between the colonial assembly on the one hand and the slave trading interests on the other shows the importance which both sides attached to the institution. While there were no moral principles invoked, the struggle clearly emphasizes the conflict in the minds of Virginians over the value of Negroes in the economic life of the colony over against their threat to social stability. It shows, moreover, the power of the slave trading interests in eighteenth century England.

Virginia had real reason to fear the Negro population, for as early as 1663 the slaves gave evidence of being restive under their yoke and began conspiring to rebel against their masters. In the following decades there was open discontent among the slaves in several sections of the colony. In 1687 a plot was uncovered in the Northern Neck in which the slaves, during a mass funeral, had planned to kill all the whites in the vicinity in a desperate bid for freedom. By 1694 lawlessness among the slaves had become so widespread that Governor Andros complained that there was insufficient enforcement of the code.

The growth of the Negro population and the fears of uprisings which the white population entertained had the effect of bringing forth a body of laws that were designed to keep the Negroes under control. Before the end of the seventeenth century the slave code of Virginia was well established. No slave was allowed to leave the plantation presumably on an errand for his master without the written permission of his master. Slaves wandering about without such permits were to be taken up and returned to their masters. Slaves found guilty of murder or rape were to be hanged, and their masters were to be compensated by the colony. For robbing a house or a store a slave was given sixty lashes by the sheriff, placed in the ·pillory with his ears nailed to the posts for a half hour, and then his ears were severed from his head. For petty offenses slaves were whipped, maimed, or branded. These and other features of the code demonstrate the extent to which slaves had become a pressing problem by the end of the colony's first century of existence. The pattern which the pioneers set was to be followed in subsequent years, as the institution became more deeply entrenched and as fears regarding the reaction of Negroes to their status increased. Before the end of the colonial period Virginia', like her neighbors, had become an armed camp in which masters figuratively kept their guns cocked and trained on the slaves in order to keep them docile and tractable and in which the assembly, the courts, and the custodians of the law worked for the maintenance of peace and order among the black workers.

Colonial Maryland's Slaves

Although there was no statutory recognition of slavery in Maryland until 1663, there was no long period in which the status of the Negro was doubtful, as in the case of Virginia. The date of the initial introduction of Negroes into the colony is uncertain, but certainly within the first decade Negroes were landed and were immediately reduced to slavery. There was reference to slaves in some proposed legislation in 1638, and by 1641 no less a person than the governor of the colony owned a number of slaves. The settlers of Maryland were under no delusions regarding their function in the economic life in the New World, and if Negro slaves would enhance their opportunities neither the Catholic zealots nor the contentious Protestants would hesitate to use them.

During the early years of the colony the Negro population grew slowly not so much from disinterest in slavery on the part of the settlers as from the unavailability of Negroes in large numbers. There were sufficient Negroes in the colony by 1663, however, for the colony to turn its attention to them and through a series of enactments to give statutory recognition to the institution of slavery. So sweeping was one of the laws that it undertook to reduce to slavery all Negroes in the colony and to enslave all that were to be born regardless of the status of their mothers. This departure from the custom that had been established under the Roman imperial system was somewhat rectified in 1681 when the law provided that children born of white servant women and Negroes were free. As the free Negro population increased the practice developed of giving to the child the status of his mother.

During the Restoration period several acts were passed to encourage the importation of slaves into Maryland. One of these was the Act of 1671 which contended that conversion of slaves to Christianity did not affect their status. Masters who had been confused over the matter of purchasing heathens and subjecting them to continuous toil without the benefit of religious instruction could now import them and convert them without fear of their emancipation. The Negro population began to increase by several hundred each year. In 1700 three hundred Negroes were brought into Patuxent Bay. In 1708 the governor reported that six or seven hundred had been imported during the preceding ten months. In the following years both the white and Negro population increased rapidly, but the per cent of Negro increase was greater. By 1750 there were about 100,000 whites as compared with about 40,000 Negroes, while in 1790 the white population of 200,000 was about twice that of the Negroes in Maryland at that time.

It seems that the duties levied on the importation of Negroes were more for the purpose of raising revenue than of discouraging the traffic in human beings. The duty was levied early and was only one part of a revenue bill which laid duties on many items including Irish servants and liquor. By the middle of the eighteenth century, however, some opposition to the unlimited importation of slaves was developing. During the French and Indian War some citizens expressed the fear that the importation of slaves would increase because Negroes were not subject to military service as white laborers were. Finally, during the War for Independence the sentiment against the unrestricted importation of slaves became so strong that prohibitive duties were laid on such importations and remained in force until the foreign slave trade was outlawed.

Although there was little if any organized resistance to slavery on the part of Negroes during Maryland's colonial period, there was considerable opposition on the part of individuals. In several instances Negro women killed their masters, not infrequently by poisoning them. In 1742 seven Negroes were executed for the murder of their master. Other slaves struck at the institution by burning tobacco houses and residences of white masters and by stealing rum, tobacco, meat, and other items of great value. Such acts of depredation could hardly be tolerated if the whites of Maryland were to maintain their position of effective dominance over the Negroes.

Just as everywhere else, the increase in the number of Negroes in Maryland and their proclivity to lawlessness called forth the enactment of stringent laws designed to keep order among the blacks. In 1659 laws were passed covering the return and treatment of fugitive slaves. A few years later statutes were enacted which forbade slaves to deal in stolen goods and liquor. Special laws were passed providing for the punishment of slaves and free Negroes guilty of murder, arson, larceny, association with whites, insolence, and the like. The punishments ranged from death and branding to whipping. By the end of the colonial period, Maryland had a well-developed slave code that was the result of her experiences and those of her neighbors.

The laws were stringent and the enforcement was rigorous; but there is some reason to believe that leniency was, on occasion, meted out by the administering officials. There are many examples on record of clemency, and one is inclined to believe that such a policy was rather commonplace. In 1762 the governor reprieved a Negro convicted of a felony and ordered the sheriff to set him free on the condition that if he caused any trouble he would be called to his former sentence. In 1766 a slave was convicted of breaking into his master's store in St. Mary's County. The master sought his pardon on the grounds that he had himself confessed and that he was not a chronic offender. He even persuaded the magistrate to plead with the governor for clemency. In a striking document the magistrate said, "I am not fond of having rogues escape punishment, but on the contrary should rather choose they should suffer as examples to others, particularly Negroes, among whom villainy and roguery is but too common. Yet on this occasion I must hope your Excellency will grant what is desired." This leniency may have arisen out of a sense of realization that justice was not impartial where the Negro was concerned; or it may have stemmed from a feeling that the Negro was an irresponsible person in the body politic. There is little evidence that suggests that the colonists of Maryland felt that the Negro crimes were the natural result of the existence which the whites had forced upon their black subordinates.

There is a real possibility that Negroes in Maryland were factors in the religious strife in that colony. From its very beginning in 1634 Maryland had witnessed an intense rivalry between the Catholics, favored by the ruling Calverts, and the Protestants who were heartened by the Puritan ascendancy in England. In 1689 there were rumors that the Catholics were plotting against the government of Maryland. Indians were suspected of collusion with the Catholics, and the Negroes of some of the southern counties were also watched with suspicious eyes. This doubtless led to the law of 1695 which prevented frequent meetings of Negroes. In the eighteenth century when some Maryland colonists hoped for a Jacobite succession in

England, those opposed to it continued to keep under surveillance all the Catholics, Indians, and Negroes to be certain that they did not conspire to commit some devilish act. No effective rebellion ever materialized during the colonial period, but Negroes enjoyed the distinction of being suspected of belonging to an international clique conspiring to overthrow the government of Maryland and handing it over to the French, the Indians, or the English Catholics, or all three.

The Carolinas

The Carolina colonists never debated either the question of bringing Negroes into the colony or what their status should be upon arrival. There can be no doubt that the founders of the colony had observed the value of slaves in the economic development of the other colonies. Not only were they interested in the use of slaves in the solution of their labor problem, but they had a material interest in the slave trade. Four of the proprietors of the colony were members of the Royal African Company and doubtless looked forward to realizing profits both in the traffic and in the employment of Negro slaves. With slavery so firmly established in several of the English colonies and with a vast grant of some of the best lands for the cultivation of staple crops in the New World, the proprietors had good reason to believe that plantation slavery would be the basis for a healthy economic life in Carolina. Small wonder, then, that slavery was established even before the colony was settled. In his "Fundamental Constitutions," John Locke said that "every freeman of Carolina shall have absolute power and authority over his negro slaves, of what opinion or religion soever." Not only was slavery thereby sanctioned, but its existence was protected against any presumed jeopardy to which conversion might expose it. In no other colony did slavery begin more auspiciously, nor was there anywhere any greater prospect for its success.

The proprietors early sought to encourage the importation of Negro slaves into the colony. In 1663 they offered to the original settlers twenty acres for every Negro man slave and ten acres for every Negro woman slave brought into the colony in the first year, or ten and five acres respectively for every man or woman slave brought in within the first five years. Although there are no available estimates of the Negro population of

Carolina before the early eighteenth century, legislation as well as the remarks of colonial leaders indicate that Negroes were in the colony from the beginning. In 1708 the Negro and white population was almost equal, with 4,100 Negroes and 4,080 whites. By 1715 the Negroes led the whites with 10,500 to 6,250. In 1724 there were three times as many Negroes as whites, while in 1765, the Negro population was 90,000, while the whites numbered only 40,000. These figures eloquently reflect both the impetus which slavery early received from the encouraging legislation of the Restoration and the effective cooperation between the traders and the planters.

This tremendous increase in Negroes filled many white South Carolinians with apprehension. No other colony experienced quite the threat that sheer numbers brought to South Carolina; and the colony did not wait for any demonstrations of the Negroes' ungovernable temper to erect a slave code that became a model for the mainland in severity and scope. Beginning in 1686 the colonial legislature passed laws to insure the domination of white masters over their slaves that Locke's Constitutions had promised. The first law forbade Negroes to engage in any kind of trade and further provided that they should not leave their master's place between sunset and sunrise without a note of explanation from the master. White persons who encountered a slave violating this act were authorized to chastise and correct him and send him home. The law was strengthened in 1722 when justices were authorized to search Negroes for guns, swords, "and other offensive weapons" and to take them unless the Negro could produce a permit less than a month old authorizing him to carry such a weapon. Not more than one Negro on a plantation was to be permitted to have possession of a gun. Patrols were given full authority to search Negroes and to whip those who were deemed to be dangerous to peace and order. Murder, burglary, robbery, arson, and running away were, of course, capital crimes. For lighter offenses such as stealing hogs and chickens, slaves were to be branded with the letter "R" on the right cheek. Chronic offenders in these categories were to suffer death.

While the Carolina colonists were enthusiastically in favor of Negro slavery, they feared that the flood gates that had been opened by unlimited importation would prove disastrous in the long run, and that not even the stringent code could keep the Negroes under control. Consequently they began to pass laws looking toward decreasing the disparity in the ratio of the white and Negro population. In 1716 a law was enacted requiring each planter to have one white servant for every ten Negro slaves, and a bounty of £25 was offered for every white servant brought into the colony. In 1719 a duty of £10 per head was levied on all Negroes imported from Africa and £30 on all Negroes imported from the islands. In 1722 a duty of £50 was laid on Negroes brought from other colonies, for South Carolina did not want to have in her borders any Negroes that were deported from other colonies because of ill behavior.

Some Carolinians with a keener eye on the economic consequences to the colony of large slave importations than on the prosperity that the traffic brought to the traders feared that the trade would result in economic disaster. In 1738 one writer opined:

> I cannot avoid observing that altho'h a few Negroes annually imported into the province might be of Advantage to most people, yet such large importation to 2,600 or 2,800 every year is not only a loss to many, but in the end may prove the Ruin of the Province, as it most certainly does that of many industrious Planters who unwarily engage in buying more than they have occasion or are able to pay for.

Thus, before the middle of the eighteenth century the rice planters of Carolina were running the dangerous risk of overinvesting in slaves and of thereby destroying the economic gains they had made.

South Carolina did not begin too soon to be apprehensive over the influx of Negroes. Although the code sought to establish complete control over them and although the import duties sought to discourage planters from bringing them in, there were enough to cause serious trouble as early as 1711. In that year they were described by the provincial legislature as keeping the inhabitants in "great fear and terror." In 1720 several slaves were burned alive and still others banished because of implication in a revolt near Charleston. Ten years later a serious outbreak was suppressed in the same area. In 1739 there were three uprisings in the colony. The most serious was the so-called Cato conspiracy which began about twenty miles west of Charleston on a plantation at Stono. The slaves killed two guards in a warehouse and secured arms and ammunition and proceeded to escape toward Florida and freedom. Joined by other Negroes, they marched to the beating of two drums and killed all whites that interfered. Soon the alarm spread among the whites, many of whom armed themselves and pursued the rebels. After several encounters all but ten were captured or killed. In this incident about thirty whites and forty-four Negroes lost their lives.

In June, 1740, a plot involving roughly two hundred Negroes in the Charleston area was uncovered. On the appointed day one hundred and fifty unarmed Negroes were attacked. Fifty were captured and hanged at the rate of ten per day. In the same year a fire swept through the city, doing great damage. Slaves were immediately suspected and at least two were executed, one of whom is said to have confessed.

These disturbances led to a thorough revision of the slave code. More stringent provisions were enacted against the assembling of slaves and against other situations which might lead to insurrections. The selling of liquor to slaves was prohibited. Owners were warned against undue cruelty to slaves which might incite them to revolt. Owners were prohibited from working slaves more than fifteen hours per day between March 25 and September 25 and more than fourteen hours per day between September 25 and March 25. The last provisions were a tacit admission that slaves could be driven to revolt. What the Carolinians realized all too late was that slaves were not as tractable as they believed and that the danger of having so large a slave population in their midst was more real than fancied.

If conditions were at all ameliorated among the Carolina slaves, it was the result of the efforts of the Society for the Propagation of the Gospel in Foreign Parts. The SPG sought to raise the level of living both among the whites and the Negroes, with considerable success in some instances. The missionaries of the organization urged upon the masters the importance of conversion among their slaves, thereby insisting, though indirectly, on the importance of the personality of the slave. They also suggested that slaves should be given time to study the Scriptures and to learn to read and write. In several instances they taught slaves themselves and in one notable instance they fostered the establishment of a school for Negroes in Charleston in which the teachers were Negro slaves owned by the Society. While these were significant ameliorations, they were also evidences of acceptance of the basic idea of enslavement, and with the religious sanction which the SPG gave to slavery, the planters felt more secure than ever in their belief in the righteousness of the institution.

By 1700 the northern portion of the Carolina colony was evolving a history that was in some respects separate and distinct from that of the southern portion. Even before 1700 men of small means began to leave Virginia and settle in the unoccupied lands of the Albemarle Sound. The stream of settlers increased in the eighteenth century, and the newcomers filled in the northern and central portion of the colony. The Cape Fear region gradually attracted settlers, and finally Scotch and Irish, Germans, and others filled in the Piedmont back country. The Negro population was small during these early years, for the more affluent Carolinians were occupying the rich lands in the region of the Ashley and Cooper Rivers. Final separation from South Carolina came in 1729, at which time the population of North Carolina was about 6,000 Negroes and 30,000 whites. No great stimuli to importation were present, and as late as 1756 there were only 19,000 Negroes in a total population of 79,000.

Down to the separation of the colonies North Carolina and South Carolina shared the same slave code. In 1741 North Carolina passed an act entitled "An Act Concerning Servants and Slaves" that constituted the basis of her colonial slave codes. It was concerned primarily with the procedure by which slave offenders were to be tried. Two justices and four slaveowners were to sit in judgment of a slave before the court and to direct the punishment of guilty parties according to their discretion. By the law slaves were not permitted to own property, to carry arms, or to move about without permission. Other clauses provided for the punishment of slave thieves, insolent slaves, and those who transacted business with whites.

The presence of Quakers in North Carolina had a salutary effect upon the conditions among slaves in the colony. They urged the establishment of regular meetings for slaves, and Quaker slaveholders were enjoined to use their Negroes well. Before the end of the colonial period there was some sentiment among the Quakers to discourage members to purchase slaves and finally, in 1770, the organization described the slave trade as "an iniquitous practice" and sought its prohibition. Members of the SPG also sought to improve conditions among Negroes as well as Indians and, as in South Carolina, encouraged masters to permit their slaves to attend religious services.

It is interesting to note that there was no real slave insurrection in North Carolina during the colonial period. The fact that the slave population was relatively small and that there was little impersonality on the North Carolina plantation was doubtless responsible for this peaceful situation. The early dispersion of the population and the impecunious state of many of the inhabitants discouraged extensive slaveholding. In comparison with her neighbors, North Carolina presented a picture of remarkable calm in the period before the War for Independence.

Georgia Adopts Slavery

Georgia is unique among the English colonies in three of the restrictions which the trustees placed on the settlers. There were to be no free land titles, no alcoholic beverages, and no Negro slaves. But Georgia was a unique colony anyway. It was to be settled by Englishmen who were released from prison to come to the New World, and this factor had much to do with the policy which the founding fathers established. The trustees were particularly determined to keep slavery out of the colony. They reasoned that the colonists would be too poor to purchase slaves, and it would be demoralizing if some had slaves and some did not. The social experiment of rehabilitation, moreover, would be rendered ineffective if the settlers devoted their time to overseeing Negro slaves and protecting them from the clutches of the conspiring Spaniards instead of themselves engaging in the honest pursuits of husbandry. Furthermore, Georgia was to provide England with silks, oils, dyes, and drugs. There really would be nothing for Negro slaves to do. Finally, if Georgia held slaves, it could not perform its proposed function of serving as something of a "no slave's land" between slaveholding South Carolina and disaffected Spanish Florida.

These were logical and unanswerable reasons and perhaps would have been acceptable except for the fact that the settlers of Georgia were normally imitative and envious persons. It was too much to expect that they should have been content without slaves when their neighbors to the north were well stocked with black laborers to do the hard work of clearing the fields and planting and harvesting the crops. The great social experiment had hardly begun before signs of discontent grew into agitation and then into formal requests for permission to import Negro slaves into Georgia. The first petition in 1738 was rejected and the colonists were remonstrated for their discontent. They could have been told to follow the examples of the industrious Germans at Ebenezer who neither had slaves nor wanted them. The examples set by the South Carolinians were more impressive, however, and the Georgia colonists did not cease their agitation. They smarted under their remonstrance, abandoned their plantations, and went sulking off to Savannah to organize themselves as "The Malcontents" and to lead a lawless and riotous existence. In 1741 they again sought relief but again their plea was rejected; whereupon they began to hire slaves on 100-year terms from South Carolina planters, so intent were they upon having slave labor to do their work.

Thanks to the agitation of men like the Reverend George Whitefield and his friend, James Habersham, the third petition in 1749 brought about a repeal of the hated prohibition against Negroes in 1750. The ratio of male Negroes to white servants was fixed at four to one. The repeal law sought to regulate the development of the institution of slavery by requiring an inspection of incoming Negroes by health officers, by insisting on the sanctity of Negro marriages, and by providing that Negroes were to be tried according to the laws of England. The supporters of a free colony, including Oglethorpe, had fought gallantly but in vain. The issue had finally resolved itself into one of choosing between disastrous economic consequences of a general strike which the settlers were intent upon carrying out and the socially malodorous institution of slavery which would nullify some of the aims of the founding fathers. In choosing the former, the trustees of Georgia removed her from the status of an anomalous colony to one that was in step with her neighbors.

Georgians had no excuse now. Alcoholic drinks had been granted them in 1742. In 1750 they had secured both the much desired free land titles *and* Negro slaves. If strong drink, unencumbered possession of the land, and Negro slaves to do their work constituted their formula for success, they had it. Upon the enactment of the law permitting slavery to exist in Georgia, numerous slaveholding families of South Carolina began to move southward across the Savannah River. In one year alone, 1752, more than one thousand Negroes were brought in. By 1760, when there were 6,000 whites in the colony, there were 3,000 Negroes. Six years later there were 10,000 whites and 8,000 Negroes. In the last estimate before the War for Independence, in 1773, the white population had increased to

18,000 while the Negro population of 15,000 represented an almost 100 per cent increase in the preceding seven years.

The slave code of Georgia was adopted as a whole in 1755. It was not the result of experiences with Negroes in Georgia. Rather, it was a full-grown body of laws which reflected the experiences of a state—South Carolina—which had gone through the horrors of insurrection and the nightmare of being outnumbered by the slave population. The guarantees which the trustees sought to give the slaves in the law which repealed the slave prohibition tended to disappear before the onslaught of one of America's most stringent codes on the subject of slavery. Not more than seven slaves were allowed to be out together unless some white person was with them. Between Saturday evening and Monday morning, not even those slaves who had permits to possess arms were allowed to carry them on their person. Slaves were not to have possession of canoes, horses, cattle, etc. Under no conditions were Negroes to be taught to read and write. A gesture toward protecting the health of the slave was made in the provision which stated that no slave was to work more than sixteen hours out of twenty-four.

The institution of slavery was not blighted by insurrection during Georgia's brief colonial period. It is reasonable to believe, however, that it suffered considerably from depletion by runaways who were attracted by the freedom offered by the governor of Spanish Florida. This was an eventuality which all must have realized before slavery was introduced into Georgia, and perhaps the colonists were realistic and philosophical about it. At any rate, Georgians had no great fear of insurrections, as is shown by their subjection of slaves to military service. Although very few were actually armed, many of them were called up to work on fortifications and other military installations. If there had been the grave fear that other colonies entertained, the slaves would doubtless have been excluded from military service altogether. Perhaps the service which Spanish Florida rendered as a place of escape for the more discontented among the Negroes made possible the paradoxical practice of using Negroes as militiamen in the colonial period.

General Characteristics

In all the southern colonies slavery grew slowly in the seventeenth century. This was the result of the efforts of the colonists to test other labor systems before resorting to Negro slavery, or the economic instability of the colonial situation which discouraged new economic ventures, or the reluctance to populate the country where so many whites had resolved to live permanently with a race of people believed to be incapable of assimilation. When, finally, the stream of slaves to the mainland began to flow uninterruptedly, it was as much the result of stimulation on the part of the Royal African Company as it was the clamor for slaves on the part of the colonists. The victory of England over France in 1713, the securing of the prized Asiento, and the new Whig commercial policy eliminated every possible obstruction in the way of a flourishing slave economy in the southern colonies. The tobacco of Virginia, North Carolina, and Maryland, and the rice and indigo of South Carolina and Georgia, all grown with slave labor, enabled the Mother Country to smile on the southern colonies and point to them as the pride of the empire, the kind of exemplary children of which any mother would be proud.

It was in the southern colonies that the problem of labor was most serious, and it was in these colonies that the process of rationalizing the institution went farthest. To the southern colonist, slavery was first an economic institution inaugurated for the purpose of solving an aggravating economic problem. With Indian and white labor, both unsatisfactory and insufficient, the only solution lay in the establishment of Negro slavery. This solution was made by Virginia and subscribed to by the others with the exception of Georgia, as they were created.

While the earliest justification offered by Europeans for the recognition of Negro slavery was the salvation of souls, this seems to have been of secondary importance to the colonists in the New World. There were no strong evangelical churches at the outset, and the furtherance of Christianity was viewed by the majority with considerable indifference. The early view that Christianization opened the way to freedom served to diminish what zeal there might have been, and officers of the church and state had difficulty in persuading planters that Christianity had no manumitting powers. The statement by the Virginia Assembly in 1667 is typical of this effort: "Baptisme doth not alter the condition of the person as to his bondage or freedom. . . ." Gradually the doctrine that freedom was inherent in Christianity began to wane in popularity and was supplanted by a point of view that was in itself a rationalization of the institution. This view was that slavery was good in that it brought heathens into contact with Christianity and led to the salvation of their souls. Masters, far from discouraging the Christianization of slaves, should cooperate with the agents of the church and the result would be the creation of a more obedient servile class. The heathenism of the Africans thus became one of the important justifications for slavery.

Another turn began to develop in the thinking of the colonists that was to form one of the most powerful rationalizations of the institution in the nineteenth century. Even in the rationalization that stemmed from the newly discovered evangelical zeal of the colonists there was a racial basis. If it was justifiable to enslave heathens because they had not been exposed to Christianity the attention must be centered on Negroes, since other important servants came from Christian lands. There began to evolve, therefore, the idea that it was the Negro that was the barbarian and the *race* needed the humanizing influences that contact with Western civilization would give it. It was not difficult to generalize from this position that the Negro was a fit subject for enslavement. By nature, temperament, pigmentation, and civilization—or the lack of it—the Negro's natural lot was slavery, the colonists reasoned. Though this rationalization found its most eloquent supporters in the period of stress and strain preceding the Civil War, it had its inception in the colonial period in the southern colonies.

From the beginning to the end of the colonial period the southern colonies remained essentially frontier communities and this condition placed an indelible mark upon the institution of slavery. No colonist could speak of the Indian problem without revealing some anxiety and feeling, and in some parts of the region the danger was very real indeed. There was, moreover, the lawlessness which every frontier situation bred. While the communities on the coast may have outlived the worst aspects of this legal chaos, by the end of the period none could escape the influence of its existence in the back yard of all the colonies. Finally, there was the reckless wastefulness which the existence of rich, available lands encouraged. For the institution of slavery this meant that planters always feared collusion between Indians and Negroes and that the latter could find freedom among the groups of Indians that were always lurking near the plantation. There was, further, the tendency of every planter to regard himself as the supreme source of law in his own bailiwick and the creator of his own slave code. With little or no regard for the law that was created in the colonial assembly or in London the planter made of the institution of slavery whatever he desired it to be. The wastefulness which characterized his treatment of the land was likely to characterize his treatment of the slaves. With no discernible threat to the supply of land or slaves, he was likely to be ruthless, reckless, and extravagant in the use of both. While this is by no means an exhaustive description of the effects of the frontier environment, it is enough to suggest that its effects on slavery were permanent and far-reaching.

VII •

Experimenting in
the Middle Colonies

New York and New Jersey

● *It is usually conceded that the middle colonies were more*
interested in slaves as commodities of commerce than as laborers. Negroes were, nevertheless, important workers in this region during the entire colonial period. The introduction of
Negroes into New Netherland is not as clearly a matter of
record as their first appearance in Jamestown, but one can be
certain that the Dutch did not long neglect their own colony.
Indeed, the West India Company, which was so instrumental in
fostering the Dutch interests in the slave trade, owned large
plantations in New Netherland and soon these areas were cultivated largely with the labor of Negro slaves. As early as 1628,
less than twenty years after their first settlements, the Dutch
were concerned about the conduct of the "irascible slaves from
Angola." In the following year the directors of the West India
Company indicated their intention of using Negroes on their
plantation. In 1638 the Director-General of New Netherland
could report that the largest farm owned by the company was
"cultivated by the blacks."

It was an unromantic, patriarchal type of slavery which the
Dutch established in their colony. Down to 1664 there was a
small but steady importation of black workers from Angola and
Brazil. They were concentrated primarily on the farms in the
Hudson River Valley, enjoying fairly humane treatment and
receiving many considerations as to their personal rights. There

were few laws to circumscribe their movements, and manumission was not an uncommon reward for long or meritorious services. Celebrations at Christmas, New Year's, and Pentecost—which the Negroes called "Pinkster"—lightened their yoke considerably. In this stage of their economic development the Dutch seemed to be so preoccupied with the commercial aspects that they neglected to institute a rigid system of slavery with all the trappings of a harsh slave code. Though the demand for slaves always exceeded the supply in New Netherland, the number that the Dutch imported never grew to such proportions as to cause serious difficulty during the period of their domination.

As soon as the English captured New Netherland and renamed it New York in 1664, it became clear that slavery would become one of the very important economic institutions of the colony. The new Royal African Company was interested in extending slavery to as many areas as possible so that it would have a profitable market for its precious cargoes. The Restoration leaders of England were, moreover, ready to send Negroes in large numbers in the hope that New York, with its excellent harbor, would provide many commodities for the imperial trade. The Law of 1665 recognized the existence of slavery where persons had willingly sold themselves into bondage, and in the statute of 1684 slavery was recognized as a legitimate institution in the province of New York.

The Negro population of New York grew as English vessels landed a larger and larger number of Negroes at the port each year. Between 1701 and 1726 the colony imported 1,573 from the West Indies and 802 from Africa. New York City merchants competed with English traders for the profits from the trade, and the result was that in the eighteenth century the Negro population increased substantially. In 1698 there were only 2,170 Negroes in a total population of 18,067. In 1723 the census listed 6,171 slaves in the colony. By 1771 the Negro population had increased to 19,883 in a total population of 168,007.

Although the English permitted some of the Dutch customs and practices to remain, they instituted regulations regarding Negroes similar to those that prevailed in their other colonies. There had been some early gestures toward humanitarianism. In 1688 Governor Andros was instructed to prohibit any cruel treatment against the slaves which colonists might be inclined to practice and to use his influence in seeing that they were instructed in religious matters. Again, in 1702, Queen Anne instructed the officials in the colony to "take especial care, that the . . . Province may have a constant and sufficient supply of merchantable Negroes, at moderate prices" and that a "law be passed for the restraining of any inhuman severity." The people were also urged to find the best means to "facilitate and encourage the conversion of Negroes and Indians to the Christian religion." These were mere gestures, however, for in the same year the colony enacted a law for regulating slaves that had unduly severe features. The law forbade any citizens to trade with Negro slaves and put an end to all meetings of more than three slaves. Penalties for concealing slaves and for slaves convicted of stealing were as severe as those imposed by any other colony. A "common whipper" was appointed to carry out the sentences of the courts.

As the years passed, New York rounded out her slave code. In 1706 the colonial legislature enacted a law stating that baptism of a slave did not provide any grounds for that slave's claim to freedom. It further provided that no slave would at any time be admitted as a witness in a case involving a freeman. In 1705, during Queen Anne's War, the assembly enacted a law which provided that any slaves caught travelling forty miles above Albany—presumably bound for Canada—would be executed upon the oath of two credible witnesses. This was not merely a military measure, for in 1715—after the war was over—it was re-enacted for an indefinite period. In 1710 New York City passed an ordinance forbidding Negroes from appearing "in the streets after nightfall without a lantern with a lighted candle in it."

These laws were apparently insufficient to restrain the Negroes of New York from disorderly conduct. They early displayed a sullenness and a defiance of authority that were to cause considerable trouble in the colony. In 1696 when the mayor of New York ordered a group of slaves to disperse, they refused. When he threatened to strike some of them and to take them into custody, one of the slaves "assaulted the mayor on the face." The following day the general sessions court sentenced him to "be by the public whipper forthwith Carryed to the public whipping Post . . . and then to be stripped Naked from the middle upwards and then . . . be tyed to the tale of a Carte . . . and . . . be drawn round this City . . . till he Return to the said whipping post and at the Corner of every street shall Receive Eleaven lashes upon his body." Despite the law against it, Negroes were often meeting on Sundays, frequenting public taverns and ale houses, and playing on the streets. Nor was there an absence of violence in their conduct. In 1708 a Negro woman and an Indian man were burned at the stake for murdering their master, mistress, and five children.

The ungovernable temper of New York's Negroes flared up into a fully organized insurrection in the spring of 1712. About twenty-seven slaves armed with guns, knives, and hatchets, met in an orchard near the center of the town. At the appointed time one of them set fire to an outhouse of his master. As whites hurried to the burning building the Negroes shot them, killing nine and wounding five or six. The militia was called out to pursue the Negroes who fled into the woods. The next day sentries were posted to prevent any escape from Manhattan. When the Negroes were captured, six had committed suicide. One man shot his wife first and then himself, while the others had cut their own throats. Twenty-one were executed: some, including a woman, were hanged; one was suspended in chains alive without food or drink until he was dead; some were burned, one of whom was to be consumed by a slow fire for eight or ten hours; one was broken on the wheel, his head and quarters being placed at the Queen's disposal.

The nightmare of insurrection so aroused New Yorkers that they felt compelled to strengthen their slave code. The severe provisions of the earlier laws were re-enacted and new measures were enacted to provide for more effective enforcement. The number of slave crimes punishable by death was increased to include the willful burning of barns, outhouses, stables, stacks of corn or hay, or residences, the conspiracy to kill non-slave subjects of Queen Anne, or the murdering of any Negro, Indian, or mulatto slave. In 1722 slaves found guilty of gambling were to be sentenced to a public whipping. New Yorkers were especially apprehensive over what in the way of a conspiracy might eventuate from a slave funeral. In 1722 the city required that all dead slaves had to be buried before sunset. In 1731 the number of slaves at a burial was restricted to twelve, besides the grave digger and the corpse bearers.

In 1741 the hysteria resulting from the fear of a slave uprising plunged the city of New York into the greatest orgy of Negro persecutions that appeared anywhere during the colonial period. The winter had been unusually severe, and the city's two thousand Negroes had been among the hardest hit. The war between England and Spain had brought serious danger to New York, always one of the dearest prizes in the New World when old world adversaries were struggling. This situation distressed most of the 10,000 whites in the city who feared that the Negro population would, perchance, prove to be of assistance to the Spaniards if they dared to enter the port. Almost anything could have thrown the city into a panic. The series of incidents that did take place were especially inflammable in such a tense atmosphere.

On the night of February 28, 1741, the house of Robert Hogg, local merchant, was entered and money and linen were taken. Suspicion was directed to two white men, John Hughson and John Romme, who were known to have received stolen goods from Negroes. Some of the goods were found near Romme's home. Meanwhile a series of fires broke out, at times several of them going simultaneously. They became so numerous, and so many things were missing after each fire, that the citizens knew that they were not accidental. Panic gripped the town in a flash. Then it happened: the emergence of the rumor that Negroes and poor whites were conspiring to destroy law and order in the city and seize control. The city council offered generous rewards for information leading to the arrest of the conspirators: £100 to a white person, £45 to free Negroes, Indians, or mulattoes, and £20 and freedom to slaves. The informer was to be pardoned for any connection he might have had with the conspiracy.

Mary Burton, an indentured servant in the home of Hughson, came forward to claim the reward by making a series of revelations, as sensational as they were inaccurate. She said that three Negroes, Caesar, Prince, and Cuffee, frequently met at Hughson's and had evolved a plan to burn the town, kill all the white people, and establish a monarchy with Hughson as king and Caesar as governor. This surpassed the wildest imaginations of the whites. As the testimony was gathered many others, including a Catholic priest, were indicted and brought to trial. Little irrefutable evidence was introduced by the prosecution, but the public, the jury, and the judges were so completely caught up in the excitement of the moment that convictions were not to be denied. An impartial trial was impossible, and contradictions as well as falsifications are obvious in the "confessions" and other testimony that were presented. In the minds of New Yorkers the conspiracy of a great Negro insurrection had taken shape, and vengeance must be swift and complete.

In the trials 154 Negroes and 25 whites were prosecuted. Convictions were secured in the case of 101 Negroes, of whom eighteen were hanged, thirteen burned alive, and seventy banished. Four white people, two of whom were women, were also hanged. "At the rate of two every week, one hanged and one burned alive, the victims were executed amid prayers, imprecations and shrieks of agony. The hauling of wood to the stake and the preparations of the gallows kept the inhabitants in a state of great excitement. All business was suspended, and every face wore a terrible look." The city, exhausted by the prolonged excitement, gradually settled down late in the year and began the argument concerning the extent of the so-called Negro plot that has lasted to this day. There were no more serious outbursts in the colonial period. The citizens, perhaps, had outdone themselves and realized it. The growing supply of white labor, moreover, had the effect of reducing both the necessity and the fear of Negroes. By the time of the Revolution New York had begun to recognize the moral and economic undesirability of the institution of slavery.

Despite the fact that New Jersey had the largest slave population of any northern colony except New York its Negro history contains no exciting chapters during the colonial period. The early Swedish and Dutch settlers were indifferent to slavery and imported few black workers into their colony. It was the English who, as in the case of New York, encouraged the growth of slavery in New Jersey. At the beginning of English rule in 1664 each settler who accompanied the first governor was offered seventy-five acres for every servant or slave brought into the colony. The inhabitants in the eastern portion of the colony were especially interested in slavery, while in the western portion, the colonists, under the influence of the Pennsylvania Quakers after 1680, remained indifferent. After the two areas were united in 1702, the importation of slaves into all parts of the colony was encouraged, and laws to regulate that portion of the population were enacted. Harsher penalties were substituted for the mild punishments for slave infractions in the seventeenth century. Whipping, branding, castration, and death were to be invoked for petty theft, grand larceny, rape, and murder respectively. Slavery in New Jersey had become orthodox in every respect.

In the eighteenth century, the Negro population of New Jersey grew steadily. In 1726 there were 2,581 Negroes in a total population of 32,422. In 1738 there were 3,981 Negroes and 43,388 whites in the colony. By 1745 the Negro population had increased to 4,606, while the whites had increased to 56,797. After the middle of the century the Negro population grew so rapidly that by 1790 there were 11,423 slaves and 2,762 free Negroes. From time to time the concern over the growth of the Negro population was reflected in the laws of the colony. In 1713 the slave code was strengthened and a law was passed to prevent the acquisition of real property by any Negro. In the same year a duty of £10 was imposed on all slaves brought into the colony between 1716 and 1723 in the hope that colonists would be encouraged to import white servants for the "better peopling of the country." In 1762 the duty was reimposed for the reason that both New York and Pennsylvania had such imposts.

The Negroes of New Jersey, preoccupied with their duties of farming, mining, lumbering, and maritime work, did not appear very restive under their yoke. In 1741 two Negroes were burned at the stake for allegedly setting fire to seven barns in Hackensack, but there seemed to be no panic such as that which swept New York in the same year. Doubtless, the work of the Society for the Propagation of the Gospel and the Society of Friends did much to improve the lot of slaves and thereby to allay unrest among them. As early as 1709 the SPG expressed an interest in training the poor children of New Jersey, and in 1712 the Society's first schoolmaster arrived. While the activities of this organization did not extend to an opposition to slavery, the instruction of Negroes and the solicitude for their care can be regarded as having had a salutary effect.

It was the Quakers who performed the greatest service for New Jersey Negroes during the colonial period. As a part of the Philadelphia Yearly Meeting, they were in contact with the staunchest supporters of freedom. John Woolman, of Mount Holly, New Jersey, began in 1743 his long and persistent opposition to slavery that brought many New Jersey citizens over to his views. By 1758 Quakers were opposed not only to the importation and purchase of slaves but to the retention of those already possessed. They were also actively engaged in the establishment of schools for Negro children. Thanks to the growth of humanitarian sentiment in New Jersey during the Revolutionary period, the early nineteenth century was to witness the rapid disintegration of the institution of slavery.

Pennsylvania and Delaware

Long before William Penn received his grant of land from Charles II, Negroes were living in the area that later was to be named Pennsylvania. In 1639 the Dutch were sentencing convicts to terms in the South River settlement where Negroes were working. In 1662 the Dutch West India Company agreed to furnish as many as fifty Negroes to be used as workers on the lowlands near the Delaware River. When Penn settled his colony there were Negroes in the Philadelphia area, and a few years later, in 1687, they were living in and near Chester.

The growth of the Negro population in Pennsylvania was at an uncertain rate during the entire colonial period. Perhaps in no other English colony were the forces for and against slavery so pronounced as in Penn's colony. Early in its history strong objections to slavery were raised on moral and ethical grounds. In 1688 the Germantown Quakers issued their celebrated protest, and in 1693 George Keith remonstrated Pennsylvanians for holding men in perpetual bondage. There was, moreover, an important economic consideration. The white artisans, shopkeepers, and small farmers did not feel any special need for slaves and were opposed to their presence, because of the disadvantage which the non-slaveholders suffered in competition with those who held slaves. These two considerations—moral and economic—strengthened each other and produced a strong opposition to the growth of slavery. The Royal African Company, however, was anxious to send slaves into the colony because it appeared to be a good market for black labor. The company therefore used its influence to create a favorable sentiment for slavery in the colony. There were some residents of Pennsylvania, of course, who were not only willing but anxious to have slaves. Even William Penn, in 1685, expressed the view that Negro slaves were better than white servants since the former could be held for life.

The struggle over the question of Negro slavery is graphically illustrated by the import duty legislation and by the slave population statistics. As early as 1700 a duty of twenty shillings was laid on every Negro brought into the colony, and in 1705 the duty was doubled. In 1712 the assembly passed a law preventing the importation of slaves altogether, but, of course, the Royal African Company had enough influence in England to see that the law was disallowed. Even so, the slave trade in Pennsylvania declined. In 1715 Pennsylvania imposed a duty of £5 on each slave imported. The law was disallowed, but in 1722 the duty was reimposed. In 1729 the duty was reduced to £2 where it remained for a generation. Although most colonies were importing an increasing number of Negro slaves, Pennsylvania's importation was declining and her white servant population was increasing. By 1750 the importation of Negroes had almost ceased. In 1761 the duty was raised to £10 where it remained until 1780 when importation was forbidden altogether.

Meanwhile, the Negro population was growing slowly. In 1721 it was estimated as being between 2,500 and 5,000. In 1741 Oldmixon estimated the Negro population to be about 3,600. In 1751 it was widely believed that there were 6,000 Negroes in Philadelphia and a total of 11,000 in the entire colony. This is perhaps a very generous estimate, for in 1780 a careful estimate placed the slaves at 6,000. In 1790 there were 10,274 Negroes, of whom 3,737 were slaves and 6,537 were free. Pennsylvania never had the slave population of which her neighbors, New Jersey and New York, could boast. The opponents to the institution, the most powerful in colonial America, had succeeded in keeping the numbers down.

Before 1700 the legal status of Negroes was vague. To be sure, there was *de facto* slavery, but it had no legal basis, and in many ways slaves and indentured servants enjoyed similar positions. In 1700, however, slaves were recognized as such and laws were passed to distinguish them from other persons. They were not to be tried in regular courts but in a special court before two justices and six freeholders. Murder, burglary, and rape were to be punished by death; attempted rape by castration; and robbing and stealing by whipping. In 1726 racial intermarriages were forbidden. Negroes could not go more than ten miles from their master's place without a pass. They were not to be out after 9 o'clock in the evening and not more than four were ever to meet together. After 1726 there were only minor revisions of the slave code.

Almost all contemporary observers regarded slavery in Pennsylvania as a mild institution. Hector St. John de Crèvecœur asserted that the slaves had about as much liberty as their masters and frequently were a part of the household. Another, Peter Kalm, remarked about the ample food and clothing which the slaves of Pennsylvania had. Few Pennsylvanians held more than one or two slaves and frequently slave and master worked together on the small farms or in the small shops. Despite the laws Negroes moved about freely, visiting each other at will, and enjoying a social life of their own. Some ran away when the opportunity presented itself, but at no time during the colonial period did the slaves of Pennsylvania conspire to rebel against their masters.

The mildness of slavery in Pennsylvania was by no means satisfactory to the humanitarians of the colony. Some were constantly trying to improve conditions among the slaves, while others were attempting to abolish the institution altogether. Quakers took seriously the admonition of George Fox that owners were to give their slaves religious instruction and teach them the Gospels. In 1700 Penn was instrumental in getting a Monthly Meeting established for the Negroes. Many colonists were teaching the slaves and free Negroes. In 1722 one person offered to teach "his poor Brethren the Negroes to read the Holy Scriptures . . . without any Manner of Expence to their respective Masters or Mistresses." By the middle of the century numerous classes in the rudiments were being held for Negroes. Many Germans from the beginning discountenanced slaveholding and sought to bring it to an end. English Quakers shifted their position from opposing importation to opposing the institution altogether. These groups were the nucleus for an anti-slavery movement in the colony which had much to do with the decline of importation, the deterioration of slavery, and the growth of the free Negro population.

As a part of Pennsylvania down to 1703, Delaware's history is inextricably woven with that of its larger neighbor. Just as in Pennsylvania, slavery existed in the colony long before its formal organization. As early as 1636 slavery existed on the right bank of the Delaware. The Dutch and the English were importing slaves into the area in the middle of the century. The early laws of Pennsylvania applied to Delaware, and these acts were in force until 1721 when the first separate law was enacted. By the act a special court, similar to that of Pennsylvania, was set up to handle the cases of slaves. It forbade meetings among slaves, banned the carrying of arms by slaves, and prohibited fornication and adultery among the blacks. As the free Negro population increased the colony sought, in 1767, to restrain manumission by requiring the master to post a bond of £60 as a guarantee of the slave's good conduct and independence. The laws of Delaware prevented neither the growth of slavery nor of free Negroes. Without a substantial number of Quakers or other opponents of slavery, Delaware drifted away from her mother colony and became more and more identified in interests with her southern neighbors.

The Failure of Slavery

As an economic institution slavery in the middle colonies had failed, for the most part, before the end of the colonial period. The predominantly commercial and industrial nature of the economic life of the region did not encourage any large scale employment of slave labor, and many of the slaves that were cleared through the New York and Pennsylvania ports were later sent into the southern colonies. Except for limited areas on the Hudson and Delaware Rivers there were no farms that welcomed large consignments of slaves. The meticulous care with which the Dutch, Swedes, and Germans cultivated their farms did not lend itself to the extensive use of slaves, and when one couples these factors with the considerable antipathy for the institution on moral grounds he can well understand why slavery was not a success in the middle colonies.

A study of the region affords an opportunity to make an interesting contrast in the process of acculturation. In New York where there was only an economic interest in Negroes and a concerted effort to destroy every vestige of satisfactory social intercourse, there was fear, antagonism, and violence on both sides. The Negroes, feeling completely frustrated under the series of intolerable acts the colony passed and without an opportunity for wholesome living in the ghetto where they lived with the lowest elements of the white population, failed to respect law and order and to accept the conventions of morality and respectability which the community had established.

In Pennsylvania, on the other hand, there was an interest in the Negro population that went beyond the realm of economics.

There was considerable respect for the Negro as a human being, which led to an early movement for manumission. Even those to whom the institution was acceptable shrank from the wholesale and indiscriminate enslavement of black people simply because it was possible. Pennsylvania was not only free from violence and interracial bloodshed, but the Negroes made strides toward genuine accommodation to their new environment. The lines of communication between the Negroes and the whites were not altogether closed, and the former gained much through these contacts. Schools and churches were a part of the lives of Negroes. The institution of marriage was respected and the Negro family achieved a stability unlike that in most English colonies. If the picture in Pennsylvania was more favorable it was because these German and Quaker colonists permitted the acculturative process to go on without any stifling interference and with some degree of encouragement.

VIII •

Puritan Masters

Importance of the Slave Trade

● *There has never been any satisfactory verification of the* report that Samuel Maverick, pioneer merchant of the Bay Colony, owned two slaves as early as 1624. Agreement is general, however, that by 1638 the Negro had been introduced into New England. In that year Captain William Pierce sailed the Salem ship *Desire* into the Boston harbor and unloaded, among other things, salt, tobacco, cotton, and Negroes. From that time on, Negroes are mentioned in the records of the New England colonies with increasing frequency. In 1639, three years after Hartford was settled, a Negro is said to have murdered his Dutch master. In the following decade Negroes were used in the construction of houses and forts in New Haven and New Hampshire. By the middle of the century the refugees at Providence had found it desirable to employ Negroes to help in the establishment of their colony.

The status of these first Negroes is not at all certain. In all probability the first were, as in the case of Virginia, servants bound to masters for a definite number of years. The desirability of a permanent labor force led to the establishment of slavery by custom before it was firmly entrenched by legal recognition. In 1641 Massachusetts enacted her justly famous "Body of Liberties" which provided that there should never be any bond slavery in the colony, "unless it be lawfull Captives taken in just warres, and such strangers as willingly sell them-

selves or are sold to us." Despite the fact that apologists for the
Puritan colony have contended that the Body of Liberties was a
proscription against slavery, there seems to be no prohibition of
the institution in the document. While specific legal recognition
awaited legislation dealing with the problems created by slavery,
the law of 1641 was as explicit an approval of the institution as
energetic traders in human chattel could desire. They only had
to take care to see that the slaves they brought in were taken in
wars, or that the slaves either willingly sold themselves or were
sold to them by someone else. It was in the last quarter of the
seventeenth century that the colonies of New England extended
legal recognition to slavery. Long before that time it was firmly
established in the economic and social life of the region.

The importance to New England of slavery and the slave
trade is emphasized by the energy with which the Puritans
entered into the business of enslaving. In this activity they
disregarded altogether the views of their leaders that the Bible
Commonwealth must be kept pure of foreign or disbelieving
groups if it was to survive. The economic consideration was
powerful indeed, and the Puritans simply ran the risk of rendering their utopia ineffective by bringing in Negroes. The arrival
of the local ship *Desire* with Negroes in 1638 opened up a new
opportunity for the procurement of workers and for the traffic of
a commodity of prime commercial importance. From that time
until the War for Independence, New England ships were important in the development of the slave trade. They brought
slaves from Africa to the West Indies and to the mainland, and
brought many West Indian commodities to the mainland.

It was difficult for the New England slave traders, with fewer
ships and smaller resources to compete with the powerful trading companies of Europe. Not infrequently they were driven
from the Guinea coast before they could secure a cargo of slaves
and were forced, at times, to ply their trade on the East African
coast. That, in part, accounts for the presence in America of
some of the slaves from Madagascar and its neighboring lands.
The New England traders were not to be outdone, however.
They fought energetically for a place in the slave trading business, and before the end of the eighteenth century their efforts
were generously rewarded. The Anglo-Dutch wars checked the
power of Holland in West Africa and in the New World. In
1696, moreover, the slave trading monopoly of the English
Royal African Company was broken and it became fairly safe

for the New England slave traders to seek slaves in West Africa. When England secured the *Asiento* in 1713 the new responsibility of importing 4,800 slaves into Spanish America each year was so great that New England merchants were welcomed into the trade as an integral part of the Mother Country's program to maintain commercial hegemony in Africa and the New World.

The first half of the eighteenth century was the golden age of the New England slave trade. New Englanders entered with zest in the formation of the lucrative triangular trade that carried their ships to Africa, thence to the West Indies, and back to the North American mainland. Massachusetts was the leading slave trading colony of New England, with Rhode Island, Connecticut, and New Hampshire following in that order. Towns such as Boston, Newport, Salem, Providence, and New London bustled with activity as outgoing ships were loaded with rum, fish, dairy products, and many other goods, and as Negroes, molasses, and sugar were unloaded from the incoming ships. While it is true that the vast majority of the slaves taken from Africa by New England traders were left in the West Indies or some southern colony on the mainland, there was sufficient demand on the part of the Puritan masters to cause some of them to be brought to New England. Too frequently, however, it was the weaker slaves that were brought to New England; for the demand for able-bodied field hands was so strong in the plantation colonies and the price was so high that the New England merchants could not resist the temptation to sell them there. On occasion traders took pride in announcing in Boston or Newport the arrival of a cargo of "lusty strong" or "well-limbed" Negroes for local sale.

Two New England colonies saw fit to place a duty on imported Negroes. In 1705 Massachusetts imposed a levy of £4 per person, and in 1711 Rhode Island imposed a levy of £3 for each Negro brought in. These duties were hardly for the purpose of discouraging the trade. Doubtless they were primarily for revenue. There is no indication that the importations were decreased even slightly after the enactments. Down to the War for Independence New England merchants regarded the slave trade as vital to their economic life and the very heart of the highly profitable triangular trade. It is significant that one of the main objections which the New England colonists offered to the Sugar Act of 1764 was that the new duty of three pence on foreign molasses (designed to prevent smuggling) hurt the slave trade and was therefore unacceptable.

The Growth of Slavery

It has been estimated that in 1700 when the total population of the New England colonies was approximately 90,000, there were not more than one thousand Negroes in the region. The eighteenth century witnessed a substantial increase in the Negro population. Massachusetts, with the largest and busiest city in the colonies, led the other New England colonies in the early part of the century in the number of Negroes. In 1715 its Negro population was estimated at 2,000. In 1735, when the white population of Massachusetts was 141,400, there were 2,600 Negroes. By 1764 there were 5,235 Negroes as against 218,950 whites. In 1776 the Negro population was 5,249, while the white population was 343,845. Connecticut was second in the early part of the century and took the lead from Massachusetts just before the War for Independence. In 1715 Connecticut's Negro population was roughly estimated at 1,500. In 1730 her Negro population was estimated at 700, while it was reported that there were approximately 37,300 whites. By 1756 there were 3,587 Negroes and 128,212 whites in the colony. On the eve of the War for Independence in 1774, Connecticut had 6,464 Negroes and 191,392 whites. The largest percentage of Negroes was to be found in Rhode Island. In 1708 there were 426 Negroes and 6,755 whites. In 1749 the Negro population was 3,077, while that of the whites was 28,439. By 1774 there were 3,761 Negroes and 54,435 whites in Rhode Island. New Hampshire was never able to boast of many Negroes. In 1700 there were only 150 in the colony, and by 1773, when the white population was 71,418, there were only 674 Negroes there.

These figures have little significance in themselves. The total number of Negroes was never as much as 20,000 in colonial New England, and only one colony, Rhode Island, had a Negro population that was as much as 5 per cent of the total population. In relation to the social and economic life of the region, however, even the meager Negro population of New Hampshire has real significance. Here were the most fervently religious colonists in America who not only fostered the slave trade as no other group in the New World but who also countenanced the existence of slavery in their midst. No plantation agriculture created a pressing demand for labor as in the southern colonies or even in the middle colonies. In a region where religion played an important part in the political and social life of the people, slavery loomed large as an economic factor in the growth and development of the colonies. Puritanism did not prevent its adherents from becoming masters of other human beings.

It was not too difficult for New Englanders to justify the enslavement of Negroes. They complained of a shortage of labor and saw in slavery an answer to their needs. It must be recalled, however, that New Englanders benefited more than any other colonists, from the great migration from Europe in the seventeenth century, and the region remained among the most densely populated areas in colonial America down to the separation from England. The Puritans, moreover, sought to justify slavery on spiritual grounds. Negroes were a cursed people, and enslavement was a proper method to bring them within the reach of God's grace. Here, it must be remembered that Puritans were not overly zealous in extending their religious views to others, preferring, for the most part, to content themselves in the enjoyment of their special position of religious enlightenment and in keeping it free from unorthodoxy and heresy. These economic and religious grounds, specious though they might have been, were enough to create an atmosphere in which the institution could exist and in which anti-slavery sentiment had real difficulty in growing.

New England slavery needed little legal recognition for its growth and development. The codes did not emerge until late in the seventeenth century, although slavery actually existed long before the middle of the century. In 1670 Massachusetts passed a law providing that the children of slaves could be sold into bondage, and ten years later it began to enact measures restricting the movement of Negroes. A law of 1680 forbade Negroes to board ships in Massachusetts ports without permits. In 1693 that colony forbade whites to trade with Negroes. Connecticut, in 1660, barred Negroes from military service. In 1690 it restrained Negroes from going beyond the limits of the town without a pass. Most of the New England colonies prohibited Negroes from being on the streets at night. Connecticut led in this restriction with its law of 1690, followed by Massachusetts with similar legislation in 1703. It was, of course, illegal in all the colonies of the region for whites to sell liquor to Negroes, and in 1750 Rhode Island went so far as to forbid the sale of cider to them. Common, also, in the New England slave code were provisions against whites entertaining slaves and laws forbidding Negroes to strike or defame white persons. By the end of the first quarter of the eighteenth century the New England colonies had enacted the most important provisions of their slave codes, and only slight revisions and amplifications were necessary in the remainder of the period. The codes were not nearly as harsh as those of the southern colonies or even the middle colonies. There were few capital crimes and little branding and maiming. The usual form of punishment was the lash which, admittedly, was generously used both by masters and by colonial officials.

Since the New England colonies consisted primarily of towns and since enforcement of the codes was consequently difficult, the slaves of Puritan masters did not feel the merciless oppression that their fellows experienced in the colonies south of them. It was frequently necessary to teach the slave to read and write so that he could do his assigned task more effectively. Since many were used as porters, clerks, and messengers, it would have been difficult to enforce curfew laws even if the Puritan masters had wanted to do so. Many slaves worked *with* and not simply *for* their masters, and there resulted a familiarity that softened the institution and rendered ineffective many of the laws that had been enacted to control the slaves. The number of slaves remained relatively small throughout the period, and there was no distressing fear of insurrection such as that which plagued the slaveholders in other parts of English America. It can be said with some confidence that if Puritans failed to display humanitarianism by holding slaves they demonstrated it in the enactment of their codes and in the treatment of their slaves.

The mildness of slavery in New England was not satisfactory to all the slaves. Freedom was preferable to slavery, and many ran away to secure it. There was no New England colony that was free of the anxiety concerning runaway slaves. Some slaves fled to the West Indies, while others sought freedom in other mainland colonies. The New England Negro, moreover, felt little responsibility for obedience to law, and, as a result, he frequently disregarded the law in his efforts to retaliate against his master and at the same time to secure his freedom. In addition to the regular crimes, of which others in the community were guilty, the slaves burned homes, barns, and ships in protest against their enslavement. In 1749, for example, a

Negro girl attempted to blow up her master's house in Boston by dropping a live coal in a cask of gunpowder. She succeeded in shattering the house and seriously injuring herself. Negroes frequently attacked whites and in some instances killed them. In Middletown, Connecticut, a slave almost escaped punishment for mutilating his master's son, because there was no law covering such a crime. The officials finally decided that the old Semitic law—*lex talionis*—could be invoked in this instance. In 1695 a slave was sentenced to be whipped for putting arsenic in his mistress' milk. In Massachusetts, in 1689, a Negro who was charged with murdering a white man escaped although he was held in chains.

Negroes even plotted to rebel against the institution of slavery. Although the New England insurrections were neither as large nor as successful as some in the other colonies, they reveal the same kind of unrest and dissatisfaction that motivated the larger uprisings. As early as 1658 the Negroes and Indians of Hartford made a break for their freedom by destroying several houses of their masters. In 1690 a plot was uncovered in which the Negroes and Indians of Newbury, Massachusetts, were to have the assistance of some of the whites. In 1741 a Negro man and woman conspired to burn Charlestown, Massachusetts. The man, a boatswain, viewed every white man as his enemy and looked forward to bringing an end to the wretched institution. In 1723 a series of fires broke out in Boston, and it was supposed that they were started by Negroes in an effort to create a chaotic situation and force an overthrow of slavery. Within one week in April, 1723, ten or twelve fires were reported, and several Negro suspects were arrested. The Reverend Joseph Sewall found it desirable to preach on the matter the following Sunday, and the governor issued a proclamation offering a reward for the apprehension and arrest of the guilty persons. Meanwhile, the selectmen of Boston passed an emergency law requiring slaves to remain off the streets and to refrain from "idling or lurking together." The alarm in Boston did not reach a fever pitch, but it was deemed sensible to take some precautionary measures.

Ameliorative Factors

There was too much respect for learning in New England for the Negroes to fail to benefit from the intellectual activities which such a respect fostered. Puritans undertook, with some degree of earnestness, to convert their slaves, and the ability to read the Bible was deemed necessary for true adherence to the Puritan faith. In 1674 John Eliot, who had done so much in improving life among the Indians, turned his attention to the matter of instructing Negroes. He invited masters within a radius of two or three miles to send their slaves to him for instruction once each week. His early death prevented the execution of this beneficent undertaking. Cotton Mather, busy as he was with his writing and teaching, took time to instruct Negroes. In 1717 he began his evening school for Indians and Negroes which, unfortunately, remained open only a few months. In 1728 Nathaniel Pigott announced that he was opening a school for the "Instruction of Negroes in Reading, Catechizing and Writing," but there is no record of its success or failure.

In the early eighteenth century, after the disintegration of the Puritan theocracy, other religious groups entered the New England field and extended their services to Negroes. Not only did the New England Quakers question the right to hold persons in perpetual bondage, but they advocated the education of young Negroes. The Society for the Propagation of the Gospel furnished schoolmasters to teach slave children, and at times white and Negro children were taught together. In 1762 the Associates of Dr. Bray maintained a school for Negroes in Newport, Rhode Island, with thirty in attendance. In addition to these organized efforts, instruction was given by many individual white persons. The result was that the New England Negro was the best trained and the most articulate of all the Negroes in the New World.

Many of the Negroes of New England were able to understand the ramifications of the Puritan faith because of their training. Thus the Reverend Stoughton's Negro woman was baptized in Dorchester in 1641 not only because of "true godliness" but because of "sound knowledge" as well. Frequently, it was not quite so easy to embrace the Christian religion if a New England slave desired to do so, because of the objections which some of the masters had to conversion. Some feared that Christian slaves would take too much time out for Scriptural study and church attendance and, therefore, their economic value would be diminished. Others felt that upon conversion slaves would regard themselves as the equals of the whites and would refuse to obey orders. Another apprehension, generally held throughout the colonies, was that baptism conferred freedom on the slave. Still another objection, which was peculiar to New England, was that baptism would place the franchise in the hands of slaves, since church membership was the basis for exercising the franchise. By the early eighteenth century these fears had been allayed in various ways, and the conversion of slaves began in earnest. Perhaps the competition which resulted from the appearance of Anglicans and Quakers in New England accounts for the spirited activity among Negroes. The fervent religious spirit which the Great Awakening evoked must not be overlooked in seeking an explanation for the speedy conversion of Negroes in this period. A majority of the Negroes, of course, became Congregationalists, but many embraced the Anglican Church as a result of the work of the SPG. Some joined the Society of Friends. Despite these and other efforts, however, Dr. Lorenzo Greene, the authority on the Negro in New England, asserts that "most of the Negroes in New England, as in other colonies, were still infidels" at the end of the Colonial period.

Much more stable and perhaps more important in the life of the New England Negro than the church was the institution of marriage. It was extended to the Negro without reservation and it had the effect of creating a greater sense of responsibility on the part of the Negro than any other single force. Negroes, both slave and free, were required to marry in New England just as any other persons. They had to publish the banns two weeks before the ceremony and appear before a magistrate to cele-brate the rites as the law required. Here was a civil contract which Puritan New England regarded so highly in their moral conduct that even those persons not generally regarded as capa-ble of making a contract were required to observe the law. Negroes seemed to have taken pride in conforming to this law and the innumerable records of the performance of the rites for Negro couples, or Negro-Indian couples, or Negro-white couples bear testimony to the willingness of the Negro to abide by the law when he was not put to serious disadvantage.

Unlike the other sections New England forbade any kind of recreational activity on Sunday, and this worked a serious hard-ship on the slaves who were busy with their work on the other days of the week. There was no inordinate infraction of the rule of keeping the Sabbath Day holy, and most slaves seemed to content themselves with fun and frolic which the observance of special days brought to all the people. Although Negroes were early barred from military service in the colonies they enjoyed the training days as much as any portion of the population. When the governor of the colony was inaugurated, Negroes were permitted to attend and enjoy the festivities. New England Negroes also "elected" their own "governors," and inaugurated their ruler with much pomp and fanfare. In some colonies, such as Massachusetts, the "election" was the occasion of a week's vacation given to the slaves by their masters. Not only did masters permit slaves to use their horses and carriages but, in some instances the master whose slave was "elected" financed the inauguration. This led Mr. E. R. Potter of Rhode Island to declare to his slave, "Governor" John, that one of them would have to quit politics or both would be ruined. "Governor" John retired to private life.

The "election" of John Anderson to the "Governorship" of Connecticut in 1776 created a furore in the colony. Anderson was the slave of Governor Phillip Skene, a British officer on parole for implication in a Negro plot. It was feared that Skene had sought the elevation of his slave in order that the latter might do what he failed to accomplish. The Connecticut officials decided to investigate the "election." Skene denied any implication in the plot. Anderson admitted that he had spent $25 to have himself appointed by the retiring "Governor," but asserted that his master had nothing to do with it and that as "Governor" he planned no insurrection. The British may not have been implicated, but it is interesting to note that the expenses of a dance for Anderson shortly after his "inauguration" were borne by two British army officers to the extent of fifty shillings.

The Negroes of New England seemed to have been free to associate with each other and with peaceful Indians. The houses of some free Negroes became the rendezvous for Negroes to dance, play games, and tell stories. Slaves like Lucy Terry of Deerfield, Massachusetts, and Senegambia of Rhode Island had a seemingly limitless store of tales about Africa and other faraway places that filled many an hour with excitement and pleasure. There was, moreover, ample opportunity for association with whites, for hardly a house or church raising, an apple paring, or a corn husking took place without the presence of at least a portion of the slave population. On Guy Fawkes Day, Dr. Greene says that "Negroes joined in the boisterous crowds that surged through the streets of Boston, much to the annoyance of pedestrians."

The Negro in New England was unique in colonial America. He was not subjected to the harsh codes or the severe treatment which his fellows received in the colonies south of the region. Yet during the colonial period the masters held a firm hand on the institution as it existed and turned a deaf ear to the proponents of freedom until the revolutionary period. Shrewd businessmen that they were, the Puritan masters had few qualms concerning the enslavement of their darker brothers. But they were keen enough, also, not to glut their home markets with Negroes and thereby bring on themselves the nightmares of fears of insurrections which the other colonists experienced. With the supply of Negroes well under control the slaveholders of New England could afford to indulge a system of slavery that had many of the characteristics of servitude and some of the features of a free society.

IX •

Latin America's Bondmen

Spanish Slavery on the Mainland

● *In 1501 the government at Madrid authorized the introduc-*
tion of Negroes from Africa to make up for the deficiency in
Indian labor which the Spaniards had been using in the New
World. The condition that only such Negroes should be taken as
had been born under the power of Christian masters was shortly
overlooked as the demand for Negro workers increased. They
were being brought into Cuba in such large numbers by 1506
that the Spanish government was moved to prohibit their further importation, for fear of an uprising among the slaves. For a
decade the importation of Negroes slowed to a trickle, and the
extensive use of Indians was resumed. Bishop Bartholomé de
Las Casas, together with his Dominican colleagues, vigorously
protested the harsh treatment of the Indians and proposed that
the hardier Negroes of West Africa should be used to replace
the Indians in the mines and on the plantations. In the following
year, 1516, Charles II issued licenses to several Flemish traders
to carry Negroes into the Spanish colonies. In 1517 the ban
against the use of Negroes was removed, with the stipulation
that one-third of those imported should be women. By the time
that Cortés launched his conquest of Mexico Negroes were in all
the Spanish island colonies and were being rapidly introduced
into the mainland.

In the early years of the Spanish colonies the slave trade was
viewed as unchristian and illegal. To overcome this dual disfa-

vor, it was necessary for traders to secure special permission—
the Asiento—to bring slaves into the Spanish colonies. This
made it relatively easy for the crown to subject the traffic in
Negroes to rigid control. Since the contracts or permits were
monopolistic, the holders were required to pay a tax to the
crown on each slave brought in. The crown reserved the right to
revoke the Asiento if the traders did not make accurate reports
on the numbers of Negroes imported or if the Negroes were not
healthy or otherwise undesirable as workers. Whether the
Asiento was held by private persons or companies, by Spaniards
or foreigners, the crown could use its power to grant it as an
effective diplomatic and economic weapon to enhance its influence in both hemispheres.

The Asiento changed hands rather frequently. Flemish traders had it in 1516. In 1528 the German merchants Eynger and
Sayller had it. Later in the century Flemish and Portuguese
companies enjoyed the privilege. At times it was divided among
a number of traders. The scramble for it was always great
because of the opportunity of the monopolists to bring into the
Spanish colonies all forms of unauthorized goods from Europe,
Africa, and elsewhere. Despite the political and economic implications of the Asiento and despite the preoccupation of many of
the traders with other matters, the practice did make possible
the importation into the Spanish colonies the millions of
Negroes that were to constitute a considerable portion of the
laboring force in Spanish America.

It would be erroneous to assume that the slave traders in
Spanish America confined their activities to the insular possessions. Almost from the beginning slaves were carried to Mexico,
Panama, Colombia, Peru, and Argentina, and from these points
were dispersed in all directions—wherever the Spaniards were
pushing back the wilderness and creating a New World civilization. Only the line of supply directly from Africa or from the
Caribbean entrepôts were officially recognized, but smugglers
and interlopers were not averse to bringing Negroes from English, French, or Dutch colonies or from other points when it was
economically profitable to do so. By these various routes of
commerce more than 60,000 Negroes entered Mexico during
the first century of conquest. In the following century the increase was even greater. While the islands and the adjacent
continent possessed a limited capacity to absorb slaves, the
Mexican market was the veritable paradise of the traders. The

Jesuit Father Andrés de Rivas estimated that three or four thousand entered the country each year. Gonzalo Aguirre Beltrán, the Mexican historian, asserts that a conservative estimate for the seventeenth century would place the figure at 120,000 slaves. In the eighteenth and early nineteenth centuries the importation declined sharply, with no more than 20,000 slaves entering the viceroyalty of New Spain during that period. When Baron Alexander von Humboldt visited the country in 1793 he said that there were only 10,000 slaves. Certainly 200,000 had entered the country, but the majority had become mixed with the whites and Indians so extensively that they were no longer recognizable as a distinct element in the population by the end of the eighteenth century.

During the colonial period Central America was, largely, a part of the viceroyalty of New Spain, and no separate figures are available for the importation of slaves into that region. It is known, however, that in the eighteenth and nineteenth centuries the British introduced numerous slaves into Belize and on the Mosquito coast (in modern Honduras and Nicaragua). Negroes in Central America perhaps were a small, but important segment of the population. They were imported into Guatemala as early as 1524, when the Spaniards occupied the land. In the 1620's Thomas Gage, the English Catholic explorer, noticed a considerable number of Negroes on the southern coast working on the indigo plantations and the large cattle *haciendas* that abounded in the country. While the number was never as large as 10,000 they were a considerable source of trouble to the Spanish authorities. Runaways would band themselves together in the woods of Sierra de las Minas and with their bows and arrows would harass the countryside for miles around. The entire force of Guatemala City found it impossible to subdue them. Some Negroes became free and themselves became substantial citizens. One such freedman became an extensive landowner and herdsman. Although he made a great profit from the dairy products which he sold in Guatemala City, the authorities felt that perhaps some hidden treasure was the real source of his wealth. He periodically denied this, and until his death he stood as a living example of what the Negro was able to accomplish in Central America.

Perhaps the largest concentration of Negroes in continental Spanish America was to be found in the Viceroyalty of New Granada, comprising the modern states of Panama, Colombia,

Venezuela, and Ecuador. The ports along the Caribbean early became entrepôts of Negro slaves and points from which they were distributed to the interior. Panama, Caracas, and Cartagena were among the largest slave markets in the New World. While Negroes were concentrated on the Caribbean and Pacific coasts there were many in the interior areas, such as the Magdalena Valley. They were engaged in placer gold mining, the cultivation of plantations of cacao, sugar, and tobacco, and in domestic service in the cities. By the time that accurate census figures for the area became available, Negroes were of considerable numbers. In the Audiencia of Santa Fé—present Panama and Colombia—there were, in 1810, approximately 210,000 Negroes and mulattoes, slave and free, in a total population of 1,400,000. In the Captaincy General of Caracas—present Venezuela—Negroes and mulattoes numbered 493,000 in 1810, while the total population was 900,000. About the same time, the Presidency of Quito—present Ecuador—had 50,000 Negroes in a total population of 600,000.

One of the most striking features of the dispersion of Negroes in Spanish America is the presence of large numbers on the Pacific coast in the colonial period. As Romero has pointed out, "the slave trade in the Spanish South American colonies followed well-established lines from north to south and from south to north, the two currents converging on Peru." The Viceroyalty of Peru—roughly present Chile and Peru—was, thus, an area of concentration of Negroes. Lima not only received a great share for her own exploitation but served as a market from which Andean planters and herdsmen could purchase black workers. Some were sent into this remote viceroyalty from Panama and Cartegena, while others were sent directly from Africa around Cape Horn. In 1622 the viceroy reported the presence of 30,000 Negroes in his domain, with 22,000 at Lima. Toward the end of the seventeenth century Melchor Liñán y Cisneros said that Negroes existed in great numbers. In the middle of the following century one observer declared that the Negroes were many, but it was impossible to ascertain the exact numbers as the owners feared that the government would use the figures as the basis for a new tax.

When the first trustworthy census was taken in 1791 the population of Peru was approximately one and one-quarter millions. Of that number, 40,000 were Negroes and 135,000 were whites. The remainder were Indians, *mestizos*, and *castas*.

Negroes constituted 25 per cent of the population of Lima. At about the same time the population of Chile was approximately 500,000, of which 30,000 were Negroes and mulattoes. These figures do not tell the entire story of the Negro population in the Viceroyalty of Peru. Accurate statistics were always difficult to secure, because owners, fearing additional taxation, hid their slaves when census takers came around. The rapid absorption of the Negro race in the total population, moreover, made it difficult to measure the impact of the Negro population upon the area into which they were sent.

The absence of a considerable Negro population in modern Uruguay and Argentina does not mean that Spain neglected to furnish these colonies with African slaves. Instead, it is suggestive of the remarkable biological and cultural fusion that has taken place. Montevideo and Buenos Aires were major ports of entry for the slave traders during colonial days. While there are no figures available for the total Negro population of the Viceroyalty of La Plata during the colonial period, there can be no doubt that there was a large Negro population, especially in the area of the estuary of the Rio de la Plata. A contemporary estimated that in 1805 about 2,500 slaves were being imported annually. In 1803 the Negro population of Montevideo was 1,040 out of a total of 4,726. There is every indication that Buenos Aires also had a substantial Negro population. As late as 1827 there were seven African societies in the Argentine capital. The disappearance of the Negro population in the southern part of South America is an eloquent testimony of the complete absorption of a people by the tremendous migration of Europeans which occurred in the last century.

Adjustment in the New World

As in other areas where slavery existed, the Negro in Spanish America was primarily an agricultural worker. On vast estates, which were so characteristic a feature of rural life, Negro slaves cultivated the cacao, maize, tobacco and other indigenous crops, and cared for the many fruits, vegetables, and other products which the Spaniards introduced. They were also used on the large ranches that flourished in the Plata region and elsewhere. They worked in the mines as helpers and as scouts. In the urban communities they were employed in a number of tasks. Many were held for ostentation, for social prestige, while others worked in the homes, shops, and docks. Some urban homes were workshops where slaves produced various articles for the market. In port cities owners frequently hired their slaves out for long periods, thus escaping the responsibility of caring for and controlling them.

While the slaves were a source of profit they were also a source of constant trouble. Living as they did in small, crowded huts and subsisting on coarse fare they frequently became restive and sought to break the chains of slavery. As the numbers increased the fears that had been entertained of an uprising were seen to be well founded. In 1550 the slaves of Santa Marta, Colombia, committed great atrocities and burned the city. Five years later a Negro calling himself "king" led a violent insurrection that was subdued only by the strenuous exertions of the authorities. It was outbreaks of this kind that brought forth a series of laws and royal decrees that were designed to preserve order among the slaves. As early as 1536 Negroes had been forbidden on the streets of Lima at night, except when accompanying their masters. First offenders were to be given one hundred lashes; second offenders were to suffer brutal mutilation. Any Spaniard meeting a Negro at night might take away his arms, and if the Negro resisted he could be killed. Slaves who ran away for as long as six days were to be mutilated. If they remained away for a longer period, they might be killed. For the minor crime of stealing corn, Negroes were to be given one hundred lashes for the first offense and mutilation for the second.

The Viceroyalty of Peru was especially anxious that Negroes would have little or no opportunity for social intercourse or recreation. The severest rules were enacted to prevent Indians and Negroes from living together. Negroes were not to wear fine clothing, silk, or jewels. They could not buy wine or *chicha*. They were not permitted to ride on horseback. Unruly Negroes were to be hunted down. If they could not be taken they could be killed; and in order to receive the reward for their capture one needed only to present the head of the outlaw at the *cabildo* or city council. When Negroes died their remains could not be taken away in a coffin.

The royal decree of 1798 provides one of the best opportunities available to observe the way in which the mother country sought to control slavery in the colonies. In order that they might be baptized, all slaves were to be instructed in the principles of the Catholic religion. Masters were not permitted to work their slaves on Sunday and on certain feast days (approximately thirty). On feast days the slaves could enjoy moderate amusements provided that there were no excessive eating and drinking, that the sexes were kept apart, and the slaves were in their respective places by nightfall.

Masters were required to feed and clothe their slaves and the wives and children of slaves even if they were free. Slaves between seventeen and sixty were to be assigned tasks suited to their age, sex, and strength. Sick slaves were to be supported and cared for, and dead slaves were to be buried at the owners' expense. Owners were to guarantee the well-being of any manumitted slaves. Owners could whip slaves up to twenty-five lashes and could punish them by imprisoning them and putting them in chains or stocks. If a slave committed a crime against his master or his family he was to be tried as a free person. If a master was found guilty of violating these regulations he was to be fined $50 for the first offense, $100 for the second offense, and $200 for the third.

As in most matters the control of slaves in the Spanish colonies was assumed to be an administrative matter that could be handled at Madrid. It need not be added that the slave codes emanating from the Spanish capital were, for the most part, ineffective. Neither his Catholic Majesty nor the Council of the Indies knew enough about the operation of the peculiar institution to deal intelligently with it. Thus, many of the rules governing slaves were altogether impracticable. Perhaps even more serious was the delay in handling problems that was inherent in the system. When, for example, the king and the council got around to issuing the famous order of 1798 for the control of slaves, the slaveholders in America had already faced the problem and had evolved practices that had become well established.

Slavery in colonial Spanish America was not as harsh as the institution in English America. To be sure, there was severity in many of the laws and cruelty on the part of many of the slaveholders. There was also marked unrest on the part of many of the slaves. Several influences, however, mitigated the harshness of the institution. One of these was the influence of the Catholic Church. While Las Casas was responsible for the introduction of Negroes on a commercial basis, his Dominican order, the Society of Jesus, and other similar agencies did much to foster the religious and secular instruction of the slaves and to reduce the evils of the institution. Another influence was the wide area over which a relatively small number of slaves was dispersed. From the Rio Grande to Cape Horn was no mere island, as in the case of Hispaniola, or a mere section as in the case of the Atlantic seaboard colonies of English America. There was more *lebensraum* in which both the master and the slave could assert themselves. Except in cities like Lima and, perhaps, Cartagena, the slaves presented no serious problem in sheer numbers; and, therefore, the fear of insurrection, although it existed, was not so great as to tax the ingenuity of the Spaniards to become inhumanly severe. Finally, there was generally a greater respect for Negroes as human beings than there was in English America. The willingness of Spaniards to intermarry with Negroes is ample proof of this. It may have been the absence of large numbers of white women and the transitory nature of Spanish colonial institutions that encouraged the practice. But the fact remains that there existed all through Spanish America an inclination to merge the blood of the Spaniard with the blood of the Negro—on a respectable basis—that, in the long run, had a profound effect on the institution of slavery itself.

The Growth of Brazil's Negro Population

It was only natural that the Portuguese, the first to sense the importance of African slave labor, would undertake to populate their new world empire with Negroes. Although they made extensive use of Indian labor throughout the sixteenth century, they introduced Africans into Brazil as early as 1538, when the first shipment of Negroes from the Guinea coast reached Bahia. It was the introduction of sugar into the colony about 1540 that stimulated the importation of Negro slaves, and after that time the slave trade continued unabated. It was during the period of Spanish control, 1580–1640, that the slave trade to Brazil increased with great rapidity. In 1585 there were 14,000 slaves in the colony out of a population of 57,000. Toward the end of the century there occurred a veritable deluge of slaves from Guinea, São Thome, Mozambique, and other parts of Africa. Though there was a tendency for them to be concentrated in Pernambuco, Bahia, and Rio de Janeiro, they fanned out in various directions as the sugar and coffee plantations were developed in the fertile interior valleys.

There were five centers of distribution from which Negroes were distributed into the various parts of Brazil. First, there were Bahia and Sergipe from which they were taken to the plantations and to domestic service on the coast. Secondly, from Rio de Janeiro and São Paulo they were taken to the cane fields and coffee plantations or were kept to work in the capital. Thirdly, Minas Geraes sent the greater portion of her slaves to the gold mines such as those of Goyaz. The fourth point of distribution was at Pernambuco, which supplied the sugar-producing provinces of the Northeast. Finally, from Maranhão and Pará slaves were sent to the cotton plantations of the North. In the seventeenth century it was estimated that more than 44,000 Negroes were imported annually, while the following century witnessed an annual importation of no less than 55,000 blacks. The estimates of the number of Negroes imported into Brazil vary widely. While the Brazilian historian, Calogeras, insists that at least eighteen millions were brought into the country, his fellow countryman, Ramos, asserts that not more than five million Negroes actually arrived in Brazil. Whatever the total figures may be, it is clear that between 1538 and 1828 Negroes were imported in such large numbers that persons with Negro blood still constitute a considerable portion of the population.

In 1798 the first reliable estimate of the population listed 406,000 free Negroes and 1,582,000 slaves in a total population of 3,250,000. By 1818 the total population had risen to 3,817,000 in which there were 1,930,000 Negro slaves and 585,000 freedmen. Thus, it can be seen that in that twenty-year period Negroes were largely responsible for the increase in the total population. In 1830 they constituted 28.6 per cent of the population. In 1847, in a total population of 7,360,000, including 800,000 civilized Indians, there were 3,120,000 Negro slaves, 1,100,000 free persons of color, and 180,000 free native Africans. In the year of the emancipation of Brazil's slaves, there were only 18,496 freemen and 723,419 slaves. The decline in the numbers in both groups merely emphasizes the rapidity with which the amalgamation of the races occurred in Brazil.

Negro Labor

There were three distinct groups of slaves in colonial Brazil. There were the urban slaves, most of whom worked as servants in the town homes of planters, in shops at the docks, and in numerous other capacities. Their lot was, on the whole, not difficult. Some were specially skilled in arts and crafts, and performed invaluable services in helping to improve living conditions in the urban areas. Others were kept in the homes to render personal service to their masters and mistresses. There was a tendency for the urban owner to maintain too large a staff of personal servants, a practice which led one mistress to assert that she had nine lazy servants for whom there was not enough employment. Some owners solved this problem by sending their slaves out to find work wherever possible. These free lancers, *negros de ganho*, often stood on street corners ready to assist shoppers with their packages or went from house to house offering their services to persons who did not have servants. At times they were led by a chief or a captain who acted as their spokesman. Many were able to earn fairly good wages because of their special skills and their ability to read and write. With the opportunity to hire out their own services some slaves not only made money for their masters but also earned enough for themselves to purchase their own freedom in due time.

With the discovery of gold in the seventeenth century, large numbers of Negroes were employed in the mines. The simultaneous decline in the sugar economy caused many planters either to sell or hire their slaves to prospectors and mine owners. Negroes began migrating into the interior near Goyaz, Corumba, and the Plateau of Matto Grosso. Some of them were not employed in the mines, but demonstrated their aptitudes and abilities in other ways. They became iron workers, shoemakers, and even architects and sculptors.

The vast majority of Negroes—perhaps five-sixths—was always employed on the great sugar, coffee, cotton, and cacao plantations. It was these farm workers who fared the worst in Brazil. They worked from sunrise to sunset and were supervised, for the most part, by white stewards who, with whips in their hands—*bacalhaus*—threatened, intimidated, and tortured the slaves into performing their work. As in the Spanish colonies there were laws which sought to protect the slave from cruel masters and overseers, but the difficulty in enforcing such statutes made them largely ineffective. The invention of the instruments of torture must have taxed the ingenuity of those in command. There was the *tronco* made of wood or iron, by which the slaves' ankles were fastened in one place for several days and the *libambo* which did the same thing to the arms. The *novenas* and *trezenas* were devices by which a slave was tied, face down, and beaten for nine or thirteen consecutive nights.

Life among the Slaves

There were some mitigating features of Brazil's institution of slavery. Since there was no law against the teaching of slaves to read and write, many of them became proficient in the use of the language. The law required that slaves be baptized within at least one year after their arrival in the country. After this rite was performed, slaves were expected to attend mass and confession regularly. In thus recognizing that slaves possessed souls the Church in Brazil elevated the Negro to a position he seldom enjoyed in the English colonies. In the second place, the manumission of slaves was actually encouraged in Brazil. Faithful nurses were often set free. There was a general custom that when a Negro mother gave birth to ten children she was to be set free. The clergy urged pious communicants to manumit their slaves at death if not sooner. There are perhaps no records of the refusal to emancipate a slave who was able to purchase his freedom. Finally, there is general agreement that in the colonial period Brazilians felt little, if any, color prejudice. Negroes were given many opportunities for advancement, and free Negroes enjoyed all the rights and privileges before the law that white persons enjoyed.

The treatment of the Brazilian Negro was not good enough, however, to induce complete satisfaction on his part. From the very beginning he registered his resentment against the institution by running away, and the owners were often frantic over the financial loss which they sustained by slaves running away. Sometimes the runaways gathered together in organized groups which the Portuguese called *quilombos*. It was these organized groups that caused so much trouble in the thickly settled areas. In 1607 the governor of Bahia complained of an insurrection among the runaway Hausa Negroes. In 1650 the slaves of Rio de Janeiro organized and caused the officials much trouble. Throughout the seventeenth and eighteenth centuries Negroes were running away and organizing resistance groups against their owners and the law enforcement officials. Numerous decrees and royal orders were issued to strengthen the hand of the whites against the *quilombos*. Captured fugitives were to be branded with an "F"—for *fugão*—and their ears were to be slashed. Chronic offenders were to receive severe whippings such as those given in the *novenas* and *trezenas*.

Resistance in Brazil

Perhaps the most desperate bid of the Negro for freedom in the New World occurred in Brazil in the seventeenth century. It was the establishment of the Republic of Palmares, a Negro state in Alagoas in northeastern Brazil between 1630 and 1697. Fleeing from the towns and plantations between Bahia and Pernambuco, the Negroes penetrated the heavy forests and settled rustic communities in the Rio Mundahu Valley. In the early years there were two settlements, the greater Palmares with six or seven thousand inhabitants and the lesser Palmares with five thousand or less. The first settlements were virtually destroyed in 1644 by the Dutch who were attempting to occupy that section of Brazil. The towns were almost immediately rebuilt and lasted until 1676 when the Portuguese Captain Fernão Carrilho and his men leveled a great portion of the republic, which was larger than the first one. The nephew of the deposed Negro leader, however, refused to surrender to the Portuguese and reopened hostilities, thus establishing the third republic which lasted until 1696. In that year Governor Bernardo Viera de Mello organized an army of seven thousand men and set out to destroy Palmares. The walled city was besieged in the face of a desperate defense. It was a slow and bitter battle. The audacity, resourcefulness, and courage of the defenders have caused the siege to be described as the "Black Troy." Finally, in 1697, the superior Portuguese soldiers entered the city only to see the leader and his principal assistants hurl themselves from the rocky promontory to certain death. This refusal to surrender caused one anonymous Portuguese chronicler to remark, "Valor mixed with brutal fury, it revealed a spectacle to our army which inspired the profoundest awe."

Palmares was a remarkable political and economic achievement for the fugitive slaves of Brazil. From a handful of fugitive slaves from nearby communities it grew into a complex political organism of many settlements of which Cerca Real do Macaco was the capital. The king lived there and was assisted by a minister of justice, guards, and many military and civil servants. A crude system of law was devised in which murder, robbery, and adultery were punishable by death. At first the economic problems of Palmares were solved by marauding, but gradually a more responsible system was worked out. The Negroes began to trade with the inhabitants of nearby towns. They carried their agricultural products such as beans, cane, and bananas into the villages and exchanged them for utensils, arms, and ammunition. Each community of huts was a veritable fortress designed specifically for defense. The 20,000 inhabitants of Palmares represented an interesting fusion of African elements with Western culture to meet the demands of a new experience brought on by dissatisfaction with subjugation.

After the destruction of Palmares Negro insurrections continued. In the eighteenth century several serious outbreaks occurred. In 1756 the Negroes planned an attack on their masters when they were attending Good Friday Mass. When the plot was discovered the slaves fled into the forests and perhaps contented themselves with organizing another *quilombo* which had become common in the previous century. In 1757 there were so many communities of fugitives in the region of Sapuchay that the governor ordered an expedition to march against them and destroy them lest they become insurrectionary. It took a squadron of 400 men six months to bring these settlements under control. In 1772 the Negroes of São Thomé and San José de Maranhão joined with the Indians to attack the whites in the area. They were subdued only after a very costly campaign.

Between 1807 and 1835 the great city insurrections of the Moslem Negroes occurred in Bahia. These were not mere slave uprisings. To be sure, they resented their status as slaves; but more than that they had learned to be proud of their Mohammedan heritage in the Sudan and were carrying on the kind of holy war that they and their forebears had waged in Africa. In their Moslem temples and in their secret societies they plotted against Negroes who would not join them as well as the whites for whom they harbored a fierce hatred. In 1807, 1809, 1813, and 1816 there were outbreaks in Bahia. In 1813, for example, the

Negroes arose one morning at four o'clock, burned the homes of whites as well as their own slave quarters, and killed thirteen whites. They died rather than surrender. In January, 1835, the officials heard of plans of a great uprising. Every precaution, including a search of the Negro quarters, was taken in order to prevent the uprising. At one place the searching officials were fired on and were overcome. The Negroes then unsuccessfully stormed the jail of Ajuda and moved on to fire on several soldiers guarding the *Largo do Teatro*. One soldier was killed at the artillery barracks. Then they attacked several other police and army posts killing several Negroes and whites. The uprising was not put down until after the entire city of Bahia had been thoroughly terrified and many persons killed and wounded. The best testimonial to the bravery and courage of the captured Negro leaders is the fact that instead of being hanged as common criminals they were shot with full military honors. Though slavery lasted in Brazil longer than anywhere else in the New World, the Negroes never tired of registering the kind of resentment that the Hausa Negroes of Bahia showed in 1835.

X •

That All Men May Be Free

Slavery and the Revolutionary Philosophy

● *By the middle of the eighteenth century, slavery in the* United States was an integral part of a maturing economic system. There had been protests against the slave trade, some colonies had imposed almost prohibitive import duties, and some religious groups, notably the Quakers, had questioned the right of one man to hold another in bondage. There had been, however, no frontal attack upon the institution, and even in the northern colonies, where there was no extensive use of slaves, the majority of the articulate colonists paid little attention to slavery. Their preoccupation with economic and political relations with England doubtless accounted for the widespread indifference with which they regarded slavery. The colonial problems were so urgent that little time was left in which the colonists could concern themselves over humanitarian matters. If there could be assurance that Negroes would neither conspire to rebel nor offer aid and comfort to the French or the Indians, there seemed to be little reason to be concerned over their condition.

This general attitude prevailed down to the end of the French and Indian War in 1763. This significant year marked not only the beginning of a new colonial policy for England but also ushered in a new approach, on the part of the colonists, to the problem of slavery. There was, moreover, a discernible connection between the two developments. As the colonists saw in

England's new colonial policy a threat to the economic and political freedom that they had enjoyed for several generations, they also seemed to realize a marked inconsistency in their position as oppressed colonists *and* slaveholders. John Woolman, the New Jersey Quaker, and Anthony Benezet, the Philadelphia Huguenot, had already begun their antislavery activities in the middle colonies, and others, such as Benjamin Franklin and Benjamin Rush, had joined in the work to free the slaves; but there had been no dramatic denunciation of the institution by any outstanding political leader in the colonies. The resurrection of the hated Navigation Acts and the imposition of new regulations like the Sugar Act of 1764 brought forth eloquent defenses of the position of the colonists. One act of Parliament had, as James Otis declared, "set people a-thinking in six months, more than they had done in their whole lives before." They began to think of their dual role as oppressed and oppressor. Almost overnight the grave but quiet efforts of Benezet and Woolman bore fruit, as colonial leaders began to denounce not only England's new imperial policy but slavery and the slave trade as well.

The Whig policy of *Quieta non Movere* lent itself to the flow of ideas across the Atlantic as much as it winked at the clandestine flow of commerce in numerous directions. There is little reason to believe that the colonists were unaware of the revolutionary literature flowing from the pens of such French thinkers as Rousseau. There were enough revolutionary ideas in England, however, to inspire a movement against the proscribing policy of the mother country. Long before 1776 most Americans viewed John Locke's treatises on government as political gospel, and upon occasions such as that which presented itself after 1763, they used these works to bolster their arguments. If Locke could justify the Revolution of 1688, certainly the same line of reasoning could justify the colonial action of the 1760's and 1770's.

It was almost natural for the colonists to link the problem of Negro slavery to their fight against England. The struggle of Negroes to secure their freedom was growing. When James Otis was penning his eloquent protest on the *Rights of the British Colonies* in which he affirmed the Negro's inalienable right to freedom, Negroes themselves were petitioning the General Court of Massachusetts for their freedom on the grounds that it was their natural right. The incident in Boston in March, 1770 must have greatly impressed many of the colonists of the incongruity of their position. The presence of British soldiers in Boston excited the indignation of the people and many wondered what could be done about it. The decision was made by a group, described by defense counsel John Adams at the trial of the British soldiers, as "a motley rabble of saucy boys, Negroes and mulattoes, Irish Teagues and outlandish Jack Tars." Led by Crispus Attucks, a runaway slave, and shouting, "The way to get rid of these soldiers is to attack the main guard," they rushed into King Street to protest by action. They were fired upon by several men of Captain Preston's company. Attucks was the first to fall; two others were killed instantly; and two others later died from wounds.

Attucks could hardly be described as a saucy boy. Nor was he deserving of the other harsh things John Adams had to say about those who fell in the Boston Massacre. He was more than forty-seven years old and had made his living during the twenty years after he ran away from his Framingham master by working on ships plying out of Boston harbor. As a seaman he probably felt keenly the restrictions which England's new navigation acts imposed. He now undertook to make the protest in a form that England would understand. Attucks's martyrdom is significant not as the first life to be offered in the struggle against England. Indeed, there ensued almost five years of peace during which time it appeared as though Samuel Adams and his group would not get their war after all. The significance of Attucks's death seems to lie in the dramatic connection which it pointed out between the struggle against England and the status of Negroes in America. Here was a fugitive slave who, with his bare hands, was willing to resist England to the point of giving his life. It was a remarkable thing, the colonists reasoned, to have their fight for freedom waged by one who was not as free as they.

In the years that followed the Boston Massacre, the colonists, as though pricked by conscience, almost always spoke against slavery and England at the same time. In 1773 the Reverend Isaac Skillman went so far as to assert that in conformity with the laws of nature, slaves should rebel against their masters. In 1774 the faithful Abigail Adams wrote her husband: "It always appeared a most iniquitous scheme to me to fight ourselves for what we are daily robbing and plundering from those who have as good a right to freedom as we have." About the same time Thomas Jefferson wrote "A Summary View of the Rights of British America" in which he said that the abolition of slavery was the great object of desire in the colonies, but that it had become increasingly difficult because Britain had consistently blocked all colonial efforts to put an end to the slave trade.

In their thinking some colonists had thus moved from the position of acceptance of the institution of slavery to the position that it was inconsistent with their fight with England and finally to the view that England was responsible for the continuation of slavery. This view was translated into action in the fall of 1774 when the Continental Congress passed an agreement not to import any slaves after December 1, 1775. Georgia, the only colony not present, adopted a similar measure in July, 1775. These can hardly be regarded as anti-slavery measures, however. It must be remembered that there was general resentment against England's "Intolerable Acts" passed earlier in the year, and that these, like many other enactments of the first Continental Congress, were retaliatory measures of a temporary nature.

The test of the colonists' regard for slavery came in their reaction to the Declaration of Independence submitted to the Continental Congress by Thomas Jefferson. The formulation of a general political philosophy to justify the drastic step the colonists were taking was generally acceptable, even to the proposition that all men, being created equal, were endowed with "certain unalienable Rights . . . Life, Liberty, and the pursuit of Happiness." Jefferson's specific charges against the king were harsh and uncompromising. Among them were the following:

He has waged cruel war against human nature itself, violating its most sacred rights of life and liberty in the persons of a distant people who never offended him, captivating and carrying them into slavery in another hemisphere, or to incur miserable death in their transportation thither. This piratical warfare, the opprobrium of *infidel* powers, is the warfare of the Christian king of Great Britain. Determined to keep open a market where MEN should be bought and sold, he has prostituted his negative for suppressing every legislative attempt to prohibit or to restrain this execrable commerce; and that this assemblage of horrors might want no fact of distinguished die, he is now exciting these very people to rise in arms among us, and to purchase that liberty of which he deprived them, by murdering the people upon whom *he* also obtruded them; thus paying off former crimes committed against the *liberties* of one people, with crimes which he urges them to commit against the *lives* of another.

These charges, described by John Adams as the "vehement phillipic against Negro slavery" were unacceptable to the Southern delegation at the Continental Congress and were stricken from the document.

The members of the Congress doubtless realized that Jefferson's bold accusations of the king in regard to slavery were at considerable variance with the truth. The slave trade had been carried on not only by British merchants but by the colonists as well, and in some colonies no effort had been made even to regulate it. There was, moreover, much favorable disposition to slavery in the southern colonies, an attitude shared by a larger number than the "few bold and persevering pro-slavery men" described by Mr. George Livermore. Those who favored slavery at all realized that if Jefferson's views prevailed in the Declaration of Independence, there would be no justification for the institution once the ties to England were completely cut. It would be better, therefore, to reject the strong language in which the complete responsibility was laid to the door of George III. In thus declining to accuse the king of perpetuating slavery and the slave trade the colonists contented themselves, in this respect, with engaging in what Rufus Choate later called "glittering generalities" and in connecting all too vaguely the status of the Negro with the philosophy of freedom for all men.

The silence of the Declaration of Independence on the matter of slavery and the slave trade was to make it equally difficult for the abolitionists and proslavery leaders to look to that document for support. Even if Jefferson did say that all men were created equal, it could not be forgotten that the anti-slavery passages of the Declaration were ruled out altogether. By endowing men with inalienable rights superior to those of positive law, it was, however, a standing invitation to insurrection which few could accept. The implications of the Declaration, however vague, were so powerful that Southern slave owners found it desirable to deny the self-evident truths which it expounded and were willing to do battle with the abolitionists during the period of strain and stress over just what the Declaration meant with regard to society in nineteenth century America.

Negroes Fighting for American Independence

From the beginning of hostilities in 1775 the question of arming the Negroes, slave and free, consistently plagued the patriots who, most of the time, had troubles enough without this aggravating situation. The fear of slave insurrections had caused the colonists to exclude Negroes from militia service even in Massachusetts and Connecticut in 1656 and 1660 respectively. Despite this exclusion, Negroes frequently participated in the wars against the French and the Indians, thus developing a tradition of military service that was alive at the time of the War for Independence. As early as the battles of Lexington and Concord in April, 1775, Negroes took up arms against the mother country, and their presence at subsequent battles in the spring and summer of that eventful year are an important part of the military history of the struggle.

In May, 1775, the Committee on Safety—commonly known as the Hancock and Warren Committee—took up the matter of the use of Negroes in the armed forces, and came to the significant conclusion that only freemen should be used, since the use of slaves would be "inconsistent with the principles that are to be supported." It is doubtful that this policy was adhered to, for evidently slaves, as well as free Negroes, fought in the Battle of Bunker Hill. Furthermore, many slaves were manumitted in order to serve in the army. Indeed, one of the outstanding heroes of the battle, Peter Salem, had, shortly before battle, been a slave in Framingham, Massachusetts. One story not thoroughly substantiated says that Salem won the admiration of his comrades in arms by shooting the British Major Pitcairn. Mounting the redoubt and shouting, "the day is ours," Pitcairn received the full force of Peter Salem's musket as he fired on the British leader who displayed more valor than judgment. The death of Pitcairn was a part of the moral victory won by the patriots on June 17, 1775.

Peter Salem was not the only Negro who succeeded in distinguishing himself at Bunker Hill. Another, Salem Poor, a soldier in a company and regiment made up largely of white men, won the praise of all his superiors who said that in the battle he "behaved like an experienced officer as well as an excellent soldier." In an official commendation presented to the Massachusetts General Court these military leaders said, "we would only beg leave to say, in the person of this said negro centres a brave and gallant soldier. The reward due to so great and distinguished a character, we submit to the Congress." While Peter Salem and Salem Poor stand out for their extraordinary feats of heroism, other Negroes were integrated into the companies of whites and performed services for which they were later commended. Among these were Caesar Brown of Westford, Massachusetts, who was killed in action; Barzillai Lew, a fifer and drummer; Titus Colburn and Alexander Ames of Andover; Prince Hall, later an abolitionist and Masonic leader; and many other Massachusetts Negroes: Cuff Hayes, Caesar Dickerson, Cato Tufts, Grant Cooper, and Sampson Talbert. While this is not an exhaustive list, it is indicative of the early use of Negroes in the War for Independence.

The Negro soldier had by no means won the right to fight for the independence of the United States. In the formulation of an over-all policy for military service shortly after General Washington took command, it was decided that the Negro's services were not needed. Out of the council of war which Washington held on July 9, 1775, an order was sent to recruiting officers that they were not to enlist "any deserter from the ministerial army, nor any stroller, negro, or vagabond, or person suspected of being an enemy to the liberty of America nor any under eighteen years of age." It was a rather strange expression of gratitude for the service which Negroes had rendered that Washington and the high command found it desirable to exclude them from enlistment.

The ban on enlistment obviously did not affect those Negroes already in the service, but within a few months a movement was afoot to rid the army of all Negroes. On September 26, 1775, Edward Rutledge of South Carolina moved in the Continental Congress to discharge all Negroes in the army. Although he was strongly supported by many of the Southern delegates, he lost his point. On October 8, however, a council of war composed of Washington, Major Generals Ward, Lee, and Putnam; and Brigadier Generals Thomas, Spencer, Heath, Sullivan, Greene, and Gates met and considered the use of Negroes. It was agreed unanimously to reject all slaves and, by a large majority, to reject Negroes altogether. Ten days later a group of civilians, among whom were Benjamin Franklin and Thomas Lynch, met with Washington and the deputy governors of Rhode Island and Connecticut to discuss plans for recruiting a new army. It was again agreed to reject Negroes altogether. On November 12, 1775, General Washington issued an order instructing recruiters not to enlist Negroes, boys unable to bear arms, or old men unable to endure the fatigues of campaign.

Thus, the new army under George Washington had settled the question of the Negro soldier by deciding not to permit any Negro, slave or free, to enlist. There is no indication that there would have been a change of policy had not the British made a political move which harassed the feeble Continental army almost as much as a significant military maneuver. On November 7, 1775, Lord Dunmore, the governor of Virginia, issued a proclamation that caused immediate concern among the patriots. In part, he said, "I do hereby . . . declare all indentured servants, Negroes, or others (appertaining to rebels) free, that are able and willing to bear arms, they joining his Majesty's troops, as soon as may be, for the more speedily reducing this Colony to a proper dignity." Had Washington known of this proclamation on November 12, he perhaps would not have issued his order prohibiting the enlistment of Negroes. As soon as he learned of Dunmore's designs he manifested great concern. During the month of December he was almost alarmed at what the consequences of the wholesale enlistment of Negroes in the British army might mean in Virginia. In a letter to Richard Henry Lee on the day after Christmas, Washington asserted that if Dunmore was not crushed before spring he would become the most formidable enemy to the cause of independence. His strength would increase "as a snowball, by rolling; and faster, if some expedient cannot be hit upon to convince the slaves and servants of the impotency of his design."

Washington had to act quickly. On December 31, he partially reversed his policy regarding the enlistment of Negroes and in a report to the President of the Congress said that he was permitting the enlistment of free Negroes. He said that the free Negroes who had served in the army were very much dissatisfied at being discarded. He further reported that it was feared that they would seek service in the British army if they were not permitted to serve with the Patriots. On January 16, 1776, Congress approved Washington's action of permitting free Negroes to enlist but made it clear that no others were to be received.

Virginians were alarmed. The hated Dunmore was openly soliciting support among their slaves. They felt constrained to counteract this bid with pleas and promises to the Negroes. On November 23, 1775, there appeared an article in the Williamsburg paper severely criticizing Dunmore's proclamation and pointing out to the Negroes that the British motives were entirely selfish. Negroes were urged not to join Dunmore's forces and were promised good treatment if they remained loyal to the Virginia patriots. On December 13, the committee of the Virginia Convention officially answered the Dunmore Proclamation. The Convention not only denounced the British for enticing their slaves away, but promised pardon to all slaves who returned to duty within ten days.

The alarm of the military high command and of Virginians was fully justified. Edmund Pendleton wrote Richard Henry Lee on November 27, 1775, that slaves were flocking to Dunmore in abundance. In March of the following year, Dunmore himself reported to the British Secretary of State that the enlistment of Negroes was proceeding very well, "and would have been in great forwardness, had not a fever crept in amongst them, which carried off a great many fine fellows." During the remainder of the war large numbers of Negroes escaped to the British lines, seeking the freedom which had eluded them during their stay in the colonies. Wherever the British armies went they attracted many Negroes, and Maryland, Virginia, and South Carolina were especially alarmed over the future of slavery regardless of the outcome of the war. As late as 1781 Richard Henry Lee could write his brother that two neighbors had lost "every slave they had in the world. . . . This has been the general case of all those who were near the enemy."

The presence of British troops in America and the existence of the war had an unsettling effect on slavery in general. Slaves ran away in large numbers even if they had no intention of reaching the British lines. Thomas Jefferson estimated that in 1778 alone more than 30,000 Virginia slaves ran away. Ramsey, the South Carolina historian, asserted that between 1775 and 1783 his state lost at least 25,000 Negroes. It has been estimated that during the war Georgia lost about 75 per cent of her 15,000 slaves. How effective the British were in utilizing this manpower is not at all clear. Here and there, such as at Ft. Cornwallis, there are accounts of Negroes serving in the British army. Perhaps their service was more valuable than has been believed; for in 1786, a corps of runaway Negroes that had been trained by the British during the siege of Savannah were still

calling themselves the "king of England's soldiers" and continued to harass the countryside of Georgia in an eighteenth century resistance movement.

The British bid for Negroes during the war had the effect of
liberalizing the policy of the colonists toward Negroes. Not only
did Washington order the enlistment of free Negroes, but most
of the states, either by specific legislation or merely by a reversal of policy, began to enlist both slaves and free Negroes. In
1776 a New York law permitted the substitution of Negroes for
whites who had been drafted. In the same year Virginia went so
far as to permit free mulattoes to serve as drummers, fifers, and
pioneers; and in the following year Virginia merely required
that all Negroes who enlisted should furnish a certificate of
freedom secured from a justice of the peace. In 1778 both
Rhode Island and Massachusetts permitted slaves to serve as
soldiers. In the same year North Carolina, in legislating against
fugitive slaves, made it clear that the penalties under the law
were not to be applied to liberated slaves in the service of North
Carolina or the United States.

Under the more liberal laws of the states, Negroes began to
enlist in the state and Continental armies in large numbers. In
1778 Massachusetts and Rhode Island felt that enough Negro
soldiers could be raised within their borders to form separate
regiments. Indeed, it appeared as though states were now vying
with each other in enlisting Negroes. New Hampshire offered
the same bounty to Negro soldiers that it was giving to whites,
and masters were given bounties as payment for the freedom of
their slaves. When the recruiting of white soldiers in Connecticut declined, a vigorous enlistment of Negroes began. New York
offered freedom to all slaves who should serve in the army for
three years, while owners were given a land bounty for their
slaves. Before the end of the war most states, as well as the
Continental Congress, were enlisting slaves with the understanding that they were to receive their freedom at the end of their
service.

Only two states, Georgia and South Carolina, continued to
oppose the enlistment of Negro soldiers. It was a source of
considerable embarrassment to Col. John Laurens, who, in
1778, was asked to raise several battalions of Negroes in his
native South Carolina. In 1779 Congress recommended that
3,000 Negroes be recruited in Georgia and South Carolina. The
Congress was to pay the owners not over $1,000 for each slave

recruited; and at the end of the war the slave was to be set free and given $50. Georgia and South Carolina were alarmed over the plan and summarily rejected it. Despite the several pleas of Laurens, neither state ever permitted such enlistment. By this time, Washington had so completely accepted the idea of Negroes as soldiers that he could write of South Carolina and Georgia, "That spirit of freedom which at the commencement of this contest would have gladly sacrificed everything to the attainment of its object, has long since subsided, and every selfish passion has taken its place." Even in these states, however, Negroes were running away—to fight with the British and win their own freedom or with the Patriots and win the freedom of their country as well as their own.

Of the 300,000 soldiers who served the cause of independence, approximately 5,000 were Negroes. Despite the fact that the bulk of the Negro population was in the South, the majority of the Negro soldiers were from the North. They served in every phase of the war and under every possible condition. Some volunteered, others were drafted, while still others were substituted for white draftees. There were only a few separate Negro fighting groups. In Massachusetts two Negro companies were formed, one under Major Samuel Lawrence and the other—the Bucks of America—under Middleton, a Negro commander. Connecticut put a Negro company in the field under the leadership of Captain David Humphreys, while the Rhode Island black company was under Col. Jeremiah Olney and later under Col. Christopher Greene. Some of these groups won the admiration and respect of their leaders and of the citizenry. Lawrence's company was described as a group "of whose courage, military discipline, and fidelity" their leader always spoke with respect. On one occasion his men rescued him after he was completely surrounded by the enemy.

The command of an all-Negro company was, at first, studiously avoided by most of the white officers. There was, therefore, some difficulty in securing a commander for the Connecticut company of Negroes. Finally, Captain Humphreys volunteered his services, and under his leadership the group so distinguished itself that thereafter the officers were said to have been as desirous of obtaining appointments in that company as they had previously been in avoiding them. In the Battle of Rhode Island, August 29, 1778, the Negro regiment under Col. Greene "distinguished itself by deeds of desperate valor." On three occasions they repulsed the Hessian soldiers who were charging down on them in order to gain a strategic position. In 1781, when Col. Greene was surprised and killed near Points Bridge, New York, his Negro soldiers heroically defended him until they were cut to pieces, and the enemy reached him over the dead bodies of his faithful men. One white veteran described them as "brave, hardy troops. They helped to gain our liberty and independence."

The vast majority of Negro soldiers served in fighting groups made up primarily of white men. The integration of them was so complete that one Hessian officer, Schloezer, declared that "no regiment is to be seen in which there are not Negroes in abundance: and among them are able-bodied, strong, and brave fellows." Not only were they in the regiments of the New England and Middle Atlantic states, but they were to be found fighting by the side of their white fellows in the Southern states. Hardly a military action between 1775 and 1781 was without some Negro participants. They were at Lexington, Concord, Ticonderoga, Bunker Hill, Long Island, White Plains, Trenton, Princeton, Bennington, Brandywine, Stillwater, Bemis Heights, Saratoga, Red Bank, Monmouth, Rhode Island, Savannah, Stony Point, Ft. Griswold, Eutaw Springs, and Yorktown.

As in any undertaking which involves large numbers of persons, most of the Negroes who served in the War for Independence will forever remain anonymous to posterity. There were some, however, who by their outstanding service won recognition from their contemporaries and a conspicuous place in the history of the War for Independence. Two Negroes, Prince Whipple and Oliver Cromwell, were with General Washington when he crossed the Delaware on Christmas Day, 1776. Tack Sisson, by crashing the door with his head, facilitated the capture of the British General Richard Prescott at Newport, Rhode Island, July 9, 1777. In the same year, Lemuel Haynes, who was later to become a distinguished minister in white churches, joined in the expedition to Ticonderoga to stop the inroads of Burgoyne's northern army. The victory of Anthony Wayne at Stony Point in 1779 was made possible by the spying of a Negro soldier by the name of Pompey. At the siege of Savannah in 1779, more than seven hundred Haitian free Negroes were with the French forces that helped save the day. Among the wounded soldiers was Christophe, who was later to play an important role in the liberation of Haiti.

There are many instances of Negroes serving in the Navy during the War for Independence. Having piloted vessels in the coastal waters before the war, their services were finally accepted during the dark days of the war. They were able and ordinary seamen, pilots, boatswain's mates, and gunner's mates. They were among the crews of the coastal galleys that defended Georgia, North Carolina, South Carolina, and Virginia. Dr. Luther P. Jackson has called attention to the service of Virginia Negroes in the Navy of the Revolution. He points out that Negro sailors fought on the *Patriot, Liberty, Tempest, Dragon, Diligence,* and many other vessels and indicates that some were enlisted for as many as ten or eleven years. In Connecticut and Massachusetts Negroes served in the Navy, such as the three black seamen who were on Captain David Porter's *Aurora* and a like number that were on the crew of the galley *Aurora.* When he was but fourteen years old, James Forten was a powder-boy on Stephen Decatur's *Royal Louis* and participated in the victory over several English vessels. Later, when he was captured and offered a home in England, he refused on the grounds that he felt that he should suffer the prisoner's lot in the cause of independence and to do less would to betray his country.

Negro patriots saw clearly the implications for their own future in their fight against England. They wanted human freedom as well as political independence. Even before Mrs. Adams pointed to the inconsistency of fighting for independence while adhering to slavery, Negroes spoke out. As early as 1766 Negroes were seeking their freedom in the courts and legislatures. In January 1773 a group of "many slaves" asked the General Court of Massachusetts to liberate them "from a State of Slavery." In 1774 a group of Negroes expressed their astonishment that the colonists could seek independence from Britain yet give no consideration to the slaves' pleas for freedom. Negroes made literally scores of such representations and, in so doing, contributed significantly to broadening the ideology of the struggle to include at least some human freedom as well as political independence.

The Movement to Manumit Negroes

By the end of the War for Independence the ideology of the struggle that had been so clearly defined and so loudly proclaimed at the outset had been dimmed and muffled by the grim and practical realities of the war. Only the perspective of a brief period was needed to realize that the aims of the leaders were more political than social. And yet, some forces had been set in motion that operated to effect a change in the status of persons that reached down even to the Negro. It is no mere coincidence that when the Battle of Lexington was fought the first anti-slavery society was just beginning to formulate its plans for action. This and similar organizations reflect the social implications of the revolutionary philosophy. So powerful did the philosophy act upon the minds of the people that almost every state enlisting slaves to serve in the army either freed them at the outset or promised manumission at the end of service. The records of the several states in the 1780's abound in deeds of manumission of Negro soldiers and their families. While the number is undeterminable, it is not difficult to conclude that hundreds, if not thousands, of slaves secured their freedom at the end of the war.

The freedom of some of the Negro soldiers did not go uncontested at the end of the war. Some masters sought to repossess their slaves who had fought for freedom from Britain; and General Washington found it necessary to authorize several courts of inquiry to establish the validity of such claims. Finally, some states resorted to the enactment of laws such as the one which Virginia passed in 1783 which granted freedom to all slaves "who served in the late war." A clear distinction was made, however, between those slaves who served in the army of the American states and those who merely ran away or who escaped to the British lines. Even General Washington expressed alarm at the news that Negroes were embarking with the British fleet at various American ports, and he asked a friend in New York to help him retrieve some of his own runaways whom he suspected of being in that vicinity.

Other evidences, beside the manumission of soldier-slaves, that the revolutionary philosophy was taking effect are seen in the activities of individuals immediately after the war. While no person as prominent as Thomas Jefferson took up the cudgel against slavery, numerous persons of considerable stature spoke out against the institution. Samuel Hopkins of Rhode Island, Ezra Stiles of Connecticut, and Jeremy Belknap were outstanding in the group of theologians who expressed anti-slavery views. In Virginia St. George Tucker's *Dissertation on Slavery* was

studied by the author's students at William and Mary and by
Virginia slave owners as well. Other anti-slavery educators were
Jedidiah Morse, the father of American geography, and William Rogers of the College of Philadelphia. Benjamin Franklin
and Benjamin Rush continued to speak out against slavery,
while the legal profession had outstanding spokesmen in Zephe-
miah Swift, Noah Webster, and Theodore Dwight.

Manumission and anti-slavery societies became more widespread after the war. The Quakers who had organized the first
society in 1775 were now joined by many other groups in this
and other organizations. In 1785 the New York Society for
Promoting the Manumission of Slaves was organized with John
Jay as president. In Delaware a similar society was set up in
1788, and by 1792 there were anti-slavery societies in every
state from Massachusetts to Virginia. Some sought to prevent
the slave trade, while others were concerned with the deportation of Negroes from the state. Most of them envisioned a
scheme, however remote, of complete abolition of slavery. Local
societies collected information on slavery and published reports
on the progress of emancipation. Others published orations and
addresses designed to arouse public sentiment against slavery.

The legislation against the slave trade, which began as a
measure to combat England's commercial domination before
the war, continued after hostilities were over. In 1783 Maryland
prohibited the traffic in Negroes. In 1786 North Carolina increased substantially the duty on every Negro imported. A duty
of £15, for example, was levied on a Negro between twelve and
thirty years of age imported directly from Africa. This law was
repealed in 1790. In 1787 South Carolina prohibited the importation of slaves for several years, an act which was renewed
from time to time until 1803 when it was repealed on the
grounds that it was unenforceable.

Even before the surrender at Yorktown, the state of Pennsylvania, in 1780, had made provisions for the gradual abolition of
slavery. The law provided that no Negro born after that date
should be held in bondage after he became twenty-eight years
old, and up to that time he was to be treated as an indentured
servant or an apprentice. The preamble clearly indicates the
influence of the Revolution. In recalling the struggle against
England, Pennsylvanians said that they felt they were called
upon to manifest the sincerity of their professions of freedom,

and to give substantial proof of gratitude, by extending a portion of their freedom to others, "who, though of a different color, are the work of the same Almighty hand." By 1783 the courts of Massachusetts had abolished slavery by asserting that the Constitution of 1780 discountenanced the institution by saying that "all men are born free and equal." In 1784 Connecticut and Rhode Island passed acts which abolished slavery gradually. Manumission acts were passed in New York in 1785 and in New Jersey in 1786, though effective legislation was not achieved in those states until 1799 and 1804 respectively. While the Northern states were thus eradicating the institution, some of the Southern states, such as Virginia and North Carolina, were enacting legislation which facilitated the efforts of slave owners to manumit their human chattel. Perhaps the high-water mark of the post-war anti-slavery movement was reached in 1787 when the Congress added to the Northwest Ordinance the provision that neither slavery nor involuntary servitude should exist in the territory covered by the Ordinance.

The Conservative Reaction

Despite the efforts of anti-slavery leaders to deal a death blow to slavery after the War for Independence they were unable to do so. Resistance to their abolitionist schemes hardened in the Southern states where so much capital was invested in slaves and where already a new economic importance was being attached to the institution. In the 1780's, moreover, there was the sobering fear that the social program that grew out of the struggle against Britain would get out of hand and uproot the very foundations of social and economic life in America. As the plain people began to demand liberal and democratic land laws, moratoriums on their debts, and greater guarantees of human rights, they challenged the authority by which the select few ruled the American state. To this "horrid vision of disorder" which the leaders conjured up must be added the loud insistence of the anti-slavery leaders for the destruction of property in human beings and the extension of liberty to all. Where would all this lead! The rebellion of Daniel Shays in Massachusetts suggested the answer: real revolution, pure and simple. The country's leaders had already planned their counter-attack in the calling of a convention to meet in Philadelphia in 1787 to stabilize and strengthen the government and to stem the tide of social revolution.

It was only natural that slavery should have become an important consideration in the Constitutional Convention. In the heated debates over representation in the Congress, the question arose as to how the slaves should be counted. Most of the Northern delegates could regard slaves in no light except as property and thus not deserving any representation. The Georgia and South Carolina delegates were loud in their demands that Negroes be counted equally with the whites. Gouverneur Morris declared that the people of Pennsylvania would revolt on being placed on an equal footing with slaves, while Rufus King of Massachusetts flayed slavery in a fiery speech and condemned any proposal that would recognize slavery in the Constitution. The three-fifths compromise that was finally written into the Constitution was perhaps satisfactory to no one, but it demonstrates clearly the strength of the proslavery interests at the Convention. It was inserted in Article I, Section 2, and reads as follows:

> Representatives and direct Taxes shall be apportioned among the several States which may be included within this Union, according to their respective Numbers, which shall be determined by adding to the whole Number of free Persons, including those bound to Service for a Term of Years, and excluding Indians not taxed, three fifths of all other persons.

It has been seen that several states had already acted to prohibit the slave trade. In 1787 the opponents of the traffic in human beings fervently hoped that the Constitutional Convention would act to stop this evil. To this end the Pennsylvania Abolition Society drafted a memorial imploring the Convention to make the slave trade a part of its deliberations and gave it to Benjamin Franklin to present. When it became obvious that the Convention would consider the problem in any case, it was decided not to present the memorial lest the suspicions of Southern members be aroused, thereby doing more harm than good. When the matter came before the Convention an argument ensued that was as fiery as any witnessed by the delegates. Young Charles Pinckney said that South Carolina could never accept a constitution that would prohibit the slave trade. Significantly, he added, "If the States be all left at liberty on this subject, South Carolina may perhaps by degrees do of herself what is wished, as Virginia and Maryland have already done." His cousin, General C. C. Pinckney, was more severe on Virginia and Maryland. He asserted that these states would gain by stopping importations. Virginia's slaves would rise in value, and it would be "unequal to require South Carolina and Georgia to Confederate on such unequal terms." The fear of rupture at this critical moment led the states of the North and upper South to compromise with the states of the lower South and to extend the slave trade for twenty years. The provision finally adopted in Article II, Section 9, reads:

> The Migration or Importation of such Persons as any of the States now existing shall think proper to admit, shall not be prohibited by the Congress prior to the Year one thousand eight hundred and eight, but a Tax or duty may be imposed on such Importation, not exceeding ten dollars for each Person.

It is significant that there was almost no opposition to the proposal that states give up fugitive slaves to their owners. The public obligation to return fugitive slaves, which had already been provided for in several Indian treaties between 1781 and 1786, was established in the Northwest Territory in 1787 in connection with the prohibition of slavery in that region. When the provision came before the Convention for consideration, it was late, August 28, and the delegates were already impatient to return to their homes. Too, the slave owners had already won such sweeping constitutional recognition of slavery that the question of fugitive slaves was an anticlimax to the great debates. When Roger Sherman of Connecticut asserted that he saw "no more propriety in the public seizing and surrendering a slave or servant, than a horse," he found no support even among his New England colleagues. Without serious challenge, therefore, the provision was inserted in Article IV, Section 2:

> No Person held to Service or Labour in one State, under the Laws thereof, escaping into another, shall, in Consequence of any Law or Regulation therein, be discharged from such Service or Labour, but shall be delivered up on Claim of the Party to whom such Service or Labour may be due.

When the delegates to the Constitutional Convention returned to their homes in September, 1787, they could look back on three months of political and economic wire-pulling that was to check effectively the trend toward social upheaval. Perhaps in no area had there been greater success than in the matter of checking the anti-slavery movement. Quakers and other groups could view the new document as devoid of guarantees of human liberties, and zealous reformers could regard the Constitution as a victory for reaction; but their objections were silenced by the effective organization for ratification that was in operation even before the Convention had adjourned. The fathers of the Constitution were dedicated to the proposition that "government should rest upon the dominion of property." For the Southern fathers this meant slaves, just as surely as it meant commerce and industry for the Northern fathers. In the protection of this property the Constitution had given recognition to the institution of human slavery, and it was to take seventy-five years to undo that which was accomplished in Philadelphia in 1787.

The adoption of the federal Constitution marks the end of an era not only in the political history of the United States but in the history of the American Negro as well. With British domination at an end and stable government established, Americans could no longer lay the onus for slavery at the door of the Mother Country. They proudly accepted the challenge and responsibility of their new political freedom by establishing the machinery and safeguards that insured the continued enslavement of the Negro. Ironically enough, America's freedom was the means of giving slavery itself a longer life than it was to have in the British empire. New factors on the horizon were about to usher in a new day for slavery as the old day passed away.

XI •

The Turn of the Century

The Negro Population in 1790

● *In the year following the inauguration of George Washington* as President of the United States, foreign observers could view with a critical eye the low level of culture in the new republic, but none could deny the happy prospect for permanence which stemmed from a continuously increasing population. There were nearly four million inhabitants in the United States, and the most casual observer could see signs of growth everywhere. Among these signs of growth was the Negro population which, in 1790, numbered slightly more than three-quarters of a million. Of course, the vast majority, almost 89 per cent, lived in the South Atlantic states where the plantation system was making the greatest demands for black labor. In 1790 Virginia had already taken the lead in Negro population which she was to hold during the entire slave period. Her 304,000 Negroes were almost three times the number held by South Carolina, her nearest rival. Most of the states in that region, however, presented a picture of an abundant Negro population. Only two, Georgia and Delaware, which no longer deserved to be classified with Pennsylvania, had less than 100,000 Negro residents. There were 641,691 slaves in the South Atlantic states and 32,048 free Negroes.

Considering their location and economic interests, the Middle Atlantic States of New York, New Jersey, and Pennsylvania had a substantial Negro population. Of the 50,000 Negroes in the region, approximately one-half of them lived in New York, while New Jersey followed with 14,000, and Pennsylvania occupied the last position with slightly more than 10,000. The decline of slavery in the region is revealed by the fact that by 1790 there were approximately 14,000 free Negroes, comprising about 28 per cent of the total Negro population. This figure is a silent tribute to the unobtrusive but effective work of the antislavery groups that made capital out of the revolutionary philosophy that was in vogue for a few years following the War for Independence.

By 1790 slavery in New England was dying rapidly. The 3,700 slaves in the region were a mere one-fourth of the total Negro population of more than 13,000. Indeed, some states, Vermont and Massachusetts, reported no slaves at all. Connecticut was holding on tenaciously to her slave population. Her 2,600 slaves were the bulk of the New England slave population. The time was not distant, however, when all the New England states would report that only free Negroes were within their borders.

Although neither Kentucky nor Tennessee had become states in 1790 they were being rapidly settled and were soon to qualify for statehood. Among the inhabitants who were being counted in the quest for the new status were the Negroes who had been taken thither by the Virginians and Carolinians who made their way across the mountains. In 1790 there were more than 12,000 slaves in Kentucky, while Tennessee had 3,400. Together these two prospective states could count only 475 free Negroes. The migration of slaves to these new regions set the pattern that became so well established in the nineteenth century.

It need not be added that the Negro population in 1790 was essentially rural. The concentration of Negroes in areas where there were few urban centers would naturally lead one to this conclusion. Even so, some cities and towns could point to a substantial black population. Among these was New York City, which was already known for her heterogeneous population. There were 3,252 Negroes, of whom 2,184 were slaves and 1,078 were free Negroes. Philadelphia had 1,630 Negroes, but only 210 of them were slaves. At the other extreme was Baltimore with 1,578 Negroes, of whom only 323 were free. Only one American city could boast that it had no slaves: All of Boston's 761 Negroes were free.

There was hardly any indication that the Negro population

would decline in the years following the first decennial census. Indeed, forces were already in operation to fasten slavery on the country with greater permanency and to increase, at least temporarily, the slave importations into the country. In 1790 the center of Negro population was twenty miles west-southwest of Petersburg, Dinwiddie County, Virginia. Growth and migration were to cause it to shift with every passing decade. And this phenomenon alone was enough to indicate that the Negro population was among the most thriving of any of the ethnic groups in America.

Slavery and the Industrial Revolution

In the years immediately following the Treaty of 1783 the areas where the slaves were concentrated experienced a severe depression. The tobacco plantations were plagued by two evils: soil exhaustion and a glutted market. Rice and indigo production brought little profit to the planters of these commodities. The price of slaves was declining, and there was some reason to believe that the institution would fall into complete deterioration. The planters, however, would not have it so; and they did everything they could to sustain their losses until a better day presented itself. For this better day they did not have long to wait. Already the system of producing cotton textiles was undergoing revolutionary changes in England; and with the inventions of spinning and weaving machinery, the manufacturing process was so cheapened that the demand for cotton goods was greatly stimulated. Before the end of the eighteenth century the work of Crompton, Hargreaves, Darby, Cort, and other such merchants, inventors, and manufacturers had been accomplished. The demand for cotton fiber to feed the newly developed machinery seemed insatiable; this at a time when the planters of the United States were in desperate need for some form of economic reorganization that would inject new life into the sluggish plantation system.

For many years the manufacturers of the world had regarded cotton as among the most satisfactory textile materials. Technological difficulties, however, had stood in the way of their becoming more extensively produced. Now that they could be spun and woven easily, the two-fold problem of discovering a variety that could be more easily separated from the seed and of inventing a machine to do this work was all that was left to be solved before cotton would become the world's greatest textile. As early as 1786 planters on the Georgia-Carolina coast began to experiment with growing a long, silky sea-island fiber that was quite superior to the green-seed, short-staple variety that had been cultivated on a small scale for many years. They found it highly satisfactory, and even without machinery to separate the seed from the fiber a greater quantity could be produced because of the ease with which the operation was effected. South Carolinians and Georgians began to plant larger cotton crops and to employ Negroes not only to cultivate the crops but to separate the fiber from the seeds as well. The area in which the sea-island cotton would grow was limited, however, and until some method was developed by which short-staple cotton, which could flourish in a variety of places, could be seeded there could be no wholesale expansion of cotton culture over the South.

The Southern planters confidently hoped that in the near future an invention would relieve them of their anxiety. In 1792 Georgia went so far as to appoint a commission to look into the possibilities of the invention of a cotton gin. In the following year a young Yankee school teacher, Eli Whitney, visited the South in search of a position. The talk concerning the difficulties of seeding cotton interested him greatly. He soon grasped the problem and set out to find a solution to it. Within a few days he had made a model which gave promise of being satisfactory. It was only a matter of weeks before the major mechanical difficulties had been mastered, and Whitney and his host, Phineas Miller, began to make plans for the commercial manufacture of cotton gins. Whitney failed to establish the monopoly over the manufacture of cotton gins which he hoped to do; but his failure simply meant that a larger number of these machines was available for the use of Southern planters at lower prices.

Within a few years after the invention of the cotton gin, the South was on its way to making the economic transition which the new development induced. Since the cultivation of cotton required no large capital many farmers, even the poorer ones, began to shift from the cultivation of rice, indigo, or tobacco to cotton. Production increased, new lands were cleared, and Negro labor could now be employed exclusively in the cultivation of the crop instead of in the tedious task of seeding cotton. Exports mounted rapidly, but England and the other manufacturing countries continued to receive, at high prices, all the cotton that the United States could furnish for many years. In the beginning, it seemed that all the Southern farmers would prosper under the stimulation of cotton cultivation. As the years passed, however, and as the more economically resourceful planters began to purchase more lands and more slaves, those without capital found themselves at a disadvantage and were forced to yield to those planters who were in a position to carry on large-scale cultivation.

The invention of the cotton gin and the extension of the area of cotton cultivation ushered in a period of economic change in the southern United States that, in degree, compared favorably with any changes in the history of agriculture. One of the most important manifestations of this change was the increased demand for Negro slaves. Not only was there now a great opportunity to use the slaves that many had kept against their better judgment, but there was the opportunity to use even more if they could be secured. Thus in the closing years of the eighteenth century and the opening years of the nineteenth century the importations of slaves into the United States continued to flourish. In 1803, for example, it was estimated that no less than 20,000 slaves were imported into Georgia and South Carolina. As though they were racing with time, the merchants of New England sought to supply the planters of the South with the precious human cargo, the importation of which was to be outlawed within a few years.

Trouble in the Caribbean

While the United States was making the effort to stabilize her political life and while the South was desperately attempting to salvage her economic system, there were rumblings not far off that disturbed both the political and economic equilibrium of the United States. When the French Revolution broke out in 1789 the Negroes in the French possessions looked toward the prospect of securing for themselves the same elements of freedom for which the Frenchmen at home were fighting. On the island of Saint Domingue, even the people on the eastern, or Spanish, end of the island sought the equality which the French Revolution promised. When the whites on the island gave signs of opposing the extension of these rights to Negroes, there occurred an uprising in August, 1791, which in its magnitude and intensity demonstrated the Negro's determination to secure freedom and equality. The Negroes so ruthlessly killed their white masters that the Assembly in France felt compelled to withdraw the rights which it had extended and to send troops to quell the disturbance. The Negroes were not awed by the appearance of soldiers from France, and there ensued a bitter struggle that lasted for more than two years. No semblance of order was restored until the French Republic issued a decree granting freedom to all slaves who supported its cause.

The intrepid leader of the Negro forces in Haiti was Toussaint L'Ouverture. An able and experienced soldier, he cast his lot with the forces of the Republic in 1794. For six years he was the dominant figure on the island, serving successively in higher military positions. By 1800 he was at the height of his power. Napoleon, however, regarded Toussaint as an obstacle to his plan to create a great French empire in the New World. With Louisiana in his hands and with Saint Domingue as a key point in the Caribbean area, he could dominate the entire Western hemisphere, or a substantial portion of it. He therefore dispatched a large army of 25,000 men under General LeClerc to subdue the island. Although the French were successful, by a series of tricks, in capturing Toussaint and carrying him back to France, they were not successful in subduing the island. Yellow fever and the bitter determination of the followers of Toussaint to be free conspired to defeat the aims of Napoleon.

The effect of these events on the course of American history was extremely important. Of Toussaint, Dr. DuBois said, "he rose to leadership through a bloody terror, which contrived a Negro 'problem' for the Western Hemisphere, intensified and defined the anti-slavery movement, became one of the causes, and probably the prime one, which led Napoleon to sell Louisiana for a song, and finally, through the interworking of all these effects, rendered more certain the final prohibition of the slave-trade by the United States in 1807." Americans were terrified at the news of what was happening in Haiti. For more than a decade beginning in 1791 many Americans were more concerned with events in Haiti than with the life and death struggle that was going on between France and England. Despite the fact that Southern states wanted more slaves they were afraid to import them. In 1792 South Carolina found it inexpedient to allow Negroes "from Africa, the West India Islands, or other places beyond the sea" to enter for two years. In 1794

North Carolina passed an act "to prevent further importation and bringing of slaves." Virginia and Maryland strengthened their non-importation laws. Though the Middle Atlantic and New England states did not seem as disturbed as their Southern neighbors over Haiti, there were attempts by Quakers and other humanitarian groups to take advantage of the situation and to strengthen various aspects of anti-slavery legislation. It would not be too much to say that the revolution in the West Indies did as much as anything else to discourage the importation of slaves into the United States.

As early as 1790 several organizations, including the yearly Meeting of Friends in New York and the Pennsylvania Abolition Society, presented memorials to the Congress requesting immediate legislation against the slave trade. The violent opposition of Southern representatives prevented decisive action. The anti-slavery organizations continued their activities during the succeeding years. The news from the Caribbean had the effect of hastening action by the Congress. In 1794 a bill seeking to prevent the slave trade to foreign ports and to prevent the fitting out of foreign vessels for the slave trade in the United States ports was passed by the Senate and the House. This was no victory for the anti-slavery forces in the United States. Instead, it merely represented the fear which many citizens entertained of the possibility that the revolution of the Haitian Negroes might spread to the United States.

Closely allied with the slave trade was the question of fugitive slaves. Negroes from the Caribbean had escaped into the United States during the conflict in Haiti. They were moving rather freely from place to place. Slaves were escaping from the plantations during this troubled period as they had always done. If these trends continued, it was within the realm of possibility that disaffected Negroes might attempt some desperate measures to overthrow the institution of slavery. It was deemed wise, therefore, to institute legislation to implement the constitutional provision for the rendition of fugitive slaves. In 1793 the first fugitive slave law was enacted. It empowered the master of an interstate fugitive to seize him wherever found, carry him before any federal or state magistrate in the vicinity, and obtain a certificate warranting his removal to the state from which he had fled. This law allowed no trial by jury and required conviction only on the oral testimony of the claimant or on an affidavit certified by a magistrate of the state from which the Negro was alleged to have fled. Various groups protested the passage of the act, but to no avail. Although it proved to be exceedingly difficult to enforce the measure, it remained a part of the federal law and thus, to many, a manifestation of national approval of the institution of slavery.

The purchase of Louisiana was also connected with the trouble in the Caribbean as well as with the institution of slavery in the United States. Louisiana had already become a center of sugar cane cultivation, whether it was in the hands of the French or the Spanish. Both these European groups lived in New Orleans and had spread up the river banks to cultivate the rich lands of the Mississippi delta. Negro slaves were introduced into these areas by the Creole planters; and by the late eighteenth century some were being brought into Louisiana from the Caribbean. The acquisition of Louisiana by France in 1800 greatly disturbed the United States, since in 1795 the new republic had negotiated a satisfactory arrangement with Spain for the navigation of the Mississippi River. In the attempt to insure continued navigation of the river for western farmers, the representatives of the United States were offered the whole of Louisiana, which, as is well known, the United States purchased in 1803. Perhaps several reasons caused Napoleon to decide to sell Louisiana. One important factor was his failure to hold Haiti and the consequent dark prospects which existed for his erecting a great empire in the New World with Louisiana and Haiti as important pivotal points. Thus it was the Negroes of Haiti that were, to a large degree, responsible for the acquisition of Louisiana by the United States. The purchase of this new land made possible the extension of cotton and sugar culture by the planters of the Southern United States and the greater entrenchment of slavery in the region.

The Closing of the Slave Trade

Despite the prohibitory state laws, the African slave trade to the United States continued to flourish during the first decade of the national government. The slave interests found themselves in a curious dilemma: They feared the wholesale importation of raw and unruly Negroes from Africa or the revolutionary and resourceful Negroes from the Caribbean. On the other hand, they were in desperate need of a larger number of slaves to cultivate the cotton that was now in such great demand. The practicality, if not the venality, of the merchants and planters compelled them to decide in favor of continued importation, hoping that the safeguards erected by the national and state governments would stem any tide of insurrection that might develop in the United States. In defiance of local laws, New England traders carried on a large traffic; while Southern planters were willing to receive slaves from whatever source possible.

Early in the nineteenth century anti-slavery groups resumed their efforts to secure stringent federal legislation against the slave trade. In January, 1800, the free Negroes of Philadelphia led the way by requesting Congress to revise the laws on the slave trade and on fugitives. When South Carolina reopened her ports to the trade in 1803, the anti-slavery forces began to press for action. Resolutions were introduced in the following Congress condemning the slave trade, but no conclusive steps were taken. In 1804 an attempt was made to prevent the importation of slaves into Louisiana, but the resolution presenting this matter received scant attention.

The question of the slave trade was brought dramatically before the country when in December, 1805, Senator Bradley of Vermont introduced a bill to prohibit the slave trade after January 1, 1808. After a second reading, consideration of the measure was postponed. In February, 1806, Representative Bidwell of Massachusetts introduced a similar measure, but nothing was done about it. In his message to the Congress, December 2, 1806, President Jefferson called the attention of the Congress to the approaching date on which the slave trade could be prohibited. He suggested that measures be taken to "prevent expeditions to Africa that could not be completed before January 1, 1808." On March 2, 1807, the law prohibiting the African slave trade was passed. Persons convicted of violating the act were to be fined and imprisoned. The fines ranged from $800 for knowingly buying illegally imported Negroes to $20,000 for equipping a slaver. The disposition of the imported Negroes was left to the legislatures of the states. Finally, coastwise trade of slaves was prohibited if it was carried on in vessels of less than forty tons. Every provision of the bill was vehemently debated by representatives of the slaveholding and non-slaveholding interests. Most of the voting was sectional in character; and there was open defiance, on the part of Southerners, of some of the provisions of the law.

Anti-slavery interests both in England and the United States rejoiced in the year 1807. England had outlawed the slave trade; and in the same year the United States had followed. There was little real reason for rejoicing in the United States, however, for from the beginning, the law went unenforced. Responsibility for the enforcement of the act fell first to the Secretary of the Treasury, then to the Secretary of the Navy. At times, even the Department of State was given some duties in connection with its enforcement. In the midst of such shifting of responsibility it is not surprising to find the law poorly enforced. Some Southern states reluctantly passed the supplementary acts disposing of illegally imported Africans, while others enacted no such legislation at all. Most of these supplementary laws provided for the sale of the Negroes, the proceeds to be paid into the public treasury and to the informer. Violations of the law were numerous. New England shipmasters, Middle Atlantic merchants, and Southern planters all disregarded the federal and state legislation when they found it expedient to do so. Those who had an unselfish interest in the closing of the slave trade could say, within a few years after 1808, that hardly anything had happened to the nefarious traffic except that it had been driven underground. The first underground railroad was not that carried on by the abolitionists to get the Negro slaves to freedom but the one carried on by merchants and others to introduce more Negroes into slavery.

The Search for Independence

The Industrial Revolution in England, the invention of the cotton gin, the extension of slavery into the new territories, and the persistence of the slave trade into the nineteenth century all had the effect of establishing slavery in the United States on a more permanent basis than ever before. As the nineteenth century opened, there seemed little prospect that slavery would ever cease to exist in the United States. The atmosphere in which Negroes lived, whether North or South, was charged with the permanent character of slavery in the United States. Even in the New England States, where laws were putting an end to the institution, the Negroes could not express much optimism or any great faith in the future for it is well known that New England merchants were still carrying slaves into the South and there was still no great moral indignation against the institution except in isolated areas and groups. Beginning with the Revolutionary period the Negro had to seek ways not only of participating in the struggle to secure independence for his country, but also to secure for himself a measure of independence in an atmosphere laden with subordination, subservience, and disrespect for his personality. This last was a most difficult task. It involved the search for independence on the part of individuals and the effort to forge separate institutions on the part of groups of persons. This phase of Negro life and history constituted a significant step in the history of adjustment and acculturation in America.

One of the first Negroes to make the search for a form of intellectual and spiritual independence was Jupiter Hammon, a slave on Long Island. Growing into manhood during the years when the Wesleyan revival was strong both in England and America, Hammon was greatly influenced by the writings of Charles Wesley and William Cowper. In 1761 he published "An Evening Thought. Salvation by Christ, with Penetential Cries." In 1778 he published a twenty-one stanza poem "To Miss Phillis Wheatley." Other poems and prose pieces appeared in the next two decades. In "An Address to the Negroes of the State of New York," published in 1787, Hammon showed that he felt it his personal duty to bear slavery patiently, but at the same time he expressed the view that it was an evil system and that young Negroes should be manumitted. He lived to see his master write a will ordering that certain of his slaves be set free at the age of twenty-eight, and in 1799, the year before his death, Hammon could rejoice that the State of New York enacted legislation looking to the gradual emancipation of all slaves within the state.

Perhaps the best known Negro of the period was Phillis Wheatley, born in Africa about 1753 and brought to America when still a little girl. In Boston she became the personal maid of Mrs. Susannah Wheatley and apparently received kindly treatment and an opportunity to cultivate her mind. She rapidly learned to read the Bible and developed an appreciation for history, astronomy, geography, and the Latin classics. In 1770 her first poem, "On the Death of Reverend George Whitefield," appeared. In 1773 she was manumitted and sent to England for her health. She met the Countess of Huntingdon, to whom one of her first poems was addressed and rapidly gained popularity. Before leaving England, arrangements were made to have her first book published, *Poems on Various Subjects, Religious and Moral.* Upon her return she composed "His Excellency General Washington," "Liberty and Peace," and numerous other poems before her death in 1784. Phillis Wheatley attempted to write lyric poetry. She was not concerned with the problems of the Negro or of the country. Even the poem to General Washington is largely impersonal, while her "Liberty and Peace" is only remotely connected with the struggle against England. Her writings are, perhaps, a good example of the search for independence through the method of escape, which was to become a favorite device of the Negro of a later century.

While Gustavus Vassa was not an American Negro, the narrative of his life was so frequently printed and read in America that he can be said to represent the growing independence of spirit which the Negro was manifesting at the end of the eighteenth century. Vassa was born in Benin in 1745. At the age of eleven he was kidnapped and taken to America. After working on a Virginia plantation he became the servant of a British naval officer. While in the service of a Philadelphia merchant he saved the money with which he purchased his freedom. Then he went to England where he made his home between his extensive journeys. He joined in the anti-slavery movement, and in 1790 he presented to Parliament a petition for the suppression of the slave trade. In 1789 he published, in two volumes, *The Interesting Narrative of the Life of Oloudah Equiano, or Gustavus Vassa.* It was immediately successful, and within five years eight editions had been issued. There can be no doubt of Vassa's resentment of slavery, for in his narrative he vigorously condemns Christians for their enslavement of Negroes. Only one who had achieved a measure of personal independence could have condemned slavery in the following language:

O, ye nominal Christians! might not an African ask you— Learned you this from your God, who says unto you, Do unto all men as you would men should do unto you? Is it not enough that we are torn from our country and friends, to toil for your luxury and lust of gain? Must every tender feeling be likewise sacrificed to your avarice? . . . Why are parents to lose their children, brothers their sisters, or husbands their wives? Surely, this is a new refinement in cruelty, which, while it has no advantage to atone for it, thus aggravates distress, and adds fresh horrors even to the wretchedness of slavery.

Perhaps the most accomplished Negro in the period immediately following the establishment of the national government was Benjamin Banneker. Born in 1731 in Maryland, of thrifty and industrious parents, Banneker attended a private school open to whites and Negroes near Baltimore and developed a keen interest in science and mathematics. While still a young man he astounded his family and neighbors by constructing a clock from wooden materials. This display of mechanical genius attracted the attention of George Ellicott, a Quaker, who had moved into the neighborhood to establish a flour mill. Banneker frequently visited the Ellicott mills during their construction; and his general knowledge of the mathematical and engineering problems drew him and Ellicott closer together. Soon, Ellicott began to lend Banneker books on mathematics and astronomy. Within a few weeks Banneker had not only mastered the material in the books, but had discovered several errors in the calculations of the authors. By 1789 he had become so proficient in astronomy as to predict a solar eclipse with considerable accuracy.

In 1791 Banneker began the issuing of his almanacs, a worthy undertaking which lasted until 1802. Among the prominent men attracted by this "Black Poor Richard" was James McHenry, later the Secretary of War in the cabinet of John Adams. Through McHenry, Banneker was able to establish a number of important connections with officials of the national government. McHenry said that Banneker's work "was begun and finished without the least information or assistance from any person, or from any other books." He added that this Negro was "fresh proof that the powers of the mind are disconnected with the color of the skin, or, in other words, a striking contradiction to Mr. Hume's doctrine, that the Negroes are naturally inferior to the whites, and unsusceptible of attainments in arts and sciences."

Banneker sent a manuscript copy of his first almanac to Thomas Jefferson, and in the accompanying letter he made a strong appeal for the exercise of a more liberal attitude toward the Negro. He pointed to his own achievements as proof that the "train of absurd and false ideas and opinions which so generally prevails with respect to the Negro should now be eradicated." Jefferson warmly praised the almanac and sent it to Condorcet, the secretary of the Academy of Sciences in Paris, for, as he told Banneker, he considered it "a document to which your whole race had a right for its justifications against the doubts which have been entertained of them."

The most distinguished honor that Banneker received was his appointment to serve with the commission to define the boundary line and lay out the streets of the District of Columbia. It was perhaps at the suggestion of his friend George Ellicott, himself a member of the commission, that Banneker's name was submitted to President Washington by Jefferson. When he arrived in the Federal Territory with Major L'Enfant and Ellicott, the Georgetown *Weekly Ledger* described him as "an Ethiopian whose abilities as surveyor and astronomer already prove that Mr. Jefferson's concluding that that race of men were void of mental endowment was without foundation." After his work with the commission, he returned to his home in Maryland and resumed the work on his almanacs and continued his astronomical investigations.

The disastrous wars of 1793 greatly disturbed Banneker, and he devoted considerable attention to devising means of putting an end to all wars. In his almanac in 1793 he carried a lengthy article by Dr. Benjamin Rush who pointed out that one of the objections to the new government was that it did not have an office in the President's cabinet "for promoting and preserving perpetual peace in our country." Rush proposed the establishment of a Secretary of Peace, "who shall be perfectly free from all the present absurd and vulgar prejudices of Europe upon the subject of government; let him be a genuine republican and a sincere Christian." There can be no doubt that Banneker published the article by Rush because he subscribed so enthusiastically to the views of Rush on the subject of peace. Banneker agreed that a program of education could foster the ideals of peace. As a man of peace he endorsed the suggestion by Rush that all militia drills, military dress, military titles, and the like should be eliminated. Perhaps few Americans during this period were more devoted to the cause of peace than Benjamin Rush and Benjamin Banneker. Banneker often opened the pages of his almanac to those who had constructive suggestions to make for the improvement of mankind. In this way he contributed to the development of the whole nation. His life was a search for independence through his concern with problems that transcended race and even nation.

Among the Negroes who were searching for economic independence and group self-respect during the post-revolutionary period, Paul Cuffe was one of the most outstanding. Very early in his life he developed an interest in commerce, and at sixteen years of age, in 1775, he secured employment on a whaling vessel. In the following year, during his second voyage, he was captured by the British and detained in New York for three months. During the war he and his brother refused to pay taxes in Massachusetts on the grounds that they were denied the franchise. Shortly thereafter Massachusetts passed a law allowing free Negroes liable to taxation all the privileges belonging to other citizens. In 1780 Cuffe began to build ships of his own and to engage in commerce. As profits mounted, he expanded his seagoing activities and built larger vessels. He began with a small open boat of less than ten tons. By 1806 he owned one large ship, two brigs, and several smaller vessels, besides considerable property in houses and land. After joining the Society of Friends he became deeply interested, along with many other Quakers, in the welfare of Negroes and wanted to engage in some activity that would improve their lot. In 1811 he went to Sierra Leone in his own vessel to investigate the possibilities of taking free Negroes back to Africa. The war with England in the following year prevented his carrying out his plans. In 1815, however, he took thirty-eight Negroes to Africa at an expense of three or four thousand dollars to himself. He learned, as colonizationists of a later day were to learn, that the expense of taking Negroes back to Africa was so great as to be prohibitive.

The individual strivings of Jupiter Hammon, Phillis Wheatley, Gustavus Vassa, Benjamin Banneker, and Paul Cuffe represent not only the effort of Negroes to secure a measure of independence for themselves in the post-revolutionary period, but they are examples of the movement of Americans toward intellectual and economic self-sufficiency that was so characteristic of the period. Indeed, it can be said that these Negro Americans were, in a sense, leading the way since they overcame both the degraded position of their race and the psychological and intellectual disadvantage which all Americans of the period suffered. Their search for independence was matched only by the efforts of groups of Negroes who found it necessary to forge separate institutions for their people during the same period.

In their efforts to elevate themselves intellectually in the post-revolutionary period, Negroes benefited from the general trend to establish and improve schools in the new republic. There was, also, the sentiment in favor of the education of Negroes which the various abolition and manumission societies expressed before the turn of the century. The New England and Middle Atlantic states were especially active in this area. Whites in Boston were teaching Negro children both privately and in public institutions. In 1798 a separate school for Negro children was established by a white teacher in the home of Primus Hall, a prominent Negro. Two years later the Negroes asked the City of Boston for a separate school, but the citizens refused to accede to the request. The Negroes established the school anyway, and employed two Harvard men as instructors. The school continued to flourish for many years. Finally, in 1820 the City of Boston opened an elementary school for Negro children.

One of the best known schools for Negroes during the period was the New York African Free School established by the Manumission Society in 1787. When it began it had forty students, the number never exceeding sixty in its first decade of existence. The opposition to the school was at first keen; but in 1800 interest in the school increased. New impetus for its continued growth came in 1810 when the state required masters to teach all slave children to read the Scriptures. By 1820 the institution was accommodating more than 500 Negro children.

New Jersey began educating her Negro children in 1777. By 1801 there had been short-lived schools set up in Burlington, Salem, and Trenton. In addition Quakers and other humanitarian groups were teaching Negro children privately. As early as 1774 the Quakers of Philadelphia established a school for Negro children, and after the war, thanks to funds provided by philanthropists like Anthony Benezet, the program was enlarged. In 1787 a school was built, and ten years later there were no less than seven schools for Negroes in Philadelphia. This interest in the development of Negro education continued down into the nineteenth century.

The interest in the South was not nearly as great. In 1801 a member of the Abolition Society of Wilmington, Delaware, held school for Negro children on the first day of each week and taught reading, writing, and arithmetic. In 1816 a school and library were established with a Negro teacher. A few years later an academy for the instruction of young Negro women was established. In Maryland plans were made late in the eighteenth century for the opening of an academy, but they never materialized. In Virginia, however, schools were set up in Richmond, Petersburg, and Norfolk. Quakers like Robert Pleasants offered land and money for the development of schools in Virginia and the Carolinas, but the insurrection of 1800 so frightened Southern planters that further expansion of the educational program was discouraged. In the nineteenth century Negroes in the Southern states had to content themselves, for the most part, with clandestine schools and private teachers.

It was perhaps in the area of religion that Negroes showed the most determined efforts to secure real independence in the post-revolutionary period. For a time, it seemed that the churches of the embryonic United States would insist upon complete integration of the Negro into the religious life of the nation and would spearhead the attack against the institution of slavery. In 1784, for example, the Methodists declared that slavery was "contrary to the golden laws of God" and gave their members twelve months to liberate their slaves. This position proved to be somewhat premature, however, as Virginia and other Southern states forced a suspension of the resolution. In 1789 the Baptists said that slavery was a "violent depredation of the rights of nature and inconsistent with a republican government." Gradually, however, they were forced by circumstances to recede from this position. After the war many churches accepted Negroes, but whites were afraid that too liberal a policy would be disastrous to the effective control of slavery. Negro ministers and church officials, it was thought, would exercise too much authority over their slave communicants and would, perhaps, cause trouble on the plantations.

The American churches were having their own troubles, and they found little time to devote any attention to the problems of the Negro. The Toryism of a great number of the Anglican clergy caused many Americans to insist upon church disestablishment. Every denomination, except Roman Catholicism, moreover, was busy organizing a wing of its church that would be entirely separate from its European sponsor; and even the Catholics of the United States were to be set apart and controlled by a special Prefect Apostolic. These preoccupations tended to crowd the problem of the Negro off the church scene and were, in part, the cause for the establishment of separate churches for Negroes.

During the War for Independence Negro Baptist churches began to spring up. George Liele, an industrious and resourceful Negro leader, founded a Baptist church in Savannah in 1779, before he finally left the country and settled in Jamaica. The work there was continued by his understudy, Andrew Bryan, who preached to whites as well as Negroes. At the end of the war the whites sought to close up the church by whipping the members and imprisoning Bryan; but his benevolent master supported him, and finally it became the nucleus for the organization of Negro Baptists in Georgia. Virginia Negroes organized Baptist churches such as the ones at Petersburg in 1776, Richmond in 1780, and at Williamsburg in 1785. In some of these efforts they had the cooperation of white ministers.

It was in Northern communities that Negroes went farthest along the line of establishing independent churches. The best example of this trend is the work of Richard Allen and his followers in Philadelphia. This prospective leader demonstrated his industry and determination by saving enough money with which to purchase himself from his Delaware master in 1777, the year in which he also was converted. Within a few years he was preaching and winning the favor of Bishop Asbury. In 1786 he moved to Philadelphia where he began to hold prayer meetings for his own people. His proposal to set up a separate place of worship for Negroes was opposed by whites and some Negroes. It was only after the officials of St. George Church, where he frequently preached, proposed to segregate the large number of Negroes who came to hear him that it became clear to him and to others that Negroes should have a separate church. The die was cast when, on one occasion, the officials pulled Allen, Absolom Jones, and William White from their knees during prayer. Allen immediately organized the independent Free African Society, with the help of Absolom Jones. Though Jones did not continue to cooperate with him, Allen was able to organize and dedicate the Bethel Church in 1794. In 1799 Bishop Asbury ordained him deacon, and later he was elevated to the status of an elder. His church became known as the Bethel African Methodist Episcopal Church.

Branches of the AME Church began to spring up in Baltimore, Wilmington, and various Pennsylvania and New Jersey towns; and a number of able persons, such as Daniel Coker, Nicholson Gilliard, and Morris Brown, came to Allen's aid. The church grew in strength until by 1816 it was possible to bind the churches together in a formal organization. The conference chose Daniel Coker as its bishop, but he resigned; and Allen was elected to fill the place. It adopted a book of discipline similar to that of the Wesleyans and was thus launched on a career that was to make the AME Church the leading organization among Negro Methodists. By 1820 there were 4,000 Negro Methodists in Philadelphia alone, while in the Baltimore district there were almost 2,000. The organization immediately spread as far west as Pittsburgh and as far south as Charleston. Only the strong opposition to Negro organizations, brought forth by the Vesey insurrection of 1822, served to check the growth of Negro Methodism in the Southern states.

The white Methodists of New York had much the same attitude toward their Negro fellows as those of Philadelphia. The result was a withdrawal of Negroes from the John Street Methodist Episcopal Church and the establishment of the African Methodist Episcopal Zion Church in 1796. Leading in this movement were Peter Williams, father of the first Negro priest in the Protestant Episcopal Church, James Varick, elected the first bishop in 1822, George Collins, and Christopher Rush. They could find no one in either the Episcopal or the Methodist church who would ordain and consecrate their elders, and finally they had to do it themselves. Overcoming schisms within and opposition without, the church was sufficiently stable by 1822 to elect a bishop and to set up a program of expansion.

The same trend toward independent organizations manifested itself among the Baptists. In 1809 thirteen Negro members of a white Baptist church in Philadelphia were dismissed to form a church of their own. Under the leadership of Rev. Burrows, a former slave, it became an important institution among the Negroes of that community. The Negro Baptists of Boston, under the leadership of Rev. Thomas Paul, organized their church in 1809. At about the same time he was assisting in organizing the church in New York that later came to be known as the Abyssinian Baptist Church. In each instance organization was brought about as a result of the separation of the Negroes from white congregations.

This establishment of separate houses of worship for Negroes, as inconsistent as it may seem with the teachings of the religion which they professed, gave the Negroes an unusual opportunity to develop leadership. Cut off as they were from participation in the political life of the community and enjoying only a very limited amount of educational opportunities, their religious institutions served as a training ground for many types of activities. Although Negroes frequently took the initiative in bringing about separation, it appears that such steps were not taken until it was obvious that they were not welcome in the white churches. This keen sensitivity to mistreatment and the consequent organization of separate and independent religious organizations of their own were to be the cause for the church occupying such an important place in Negro life in the nineteenth and twentieth centuries.

Not only were Negroes organizing separate churches but they were establishing other organizations of a benevolent and fraternal nature. On March 6, 1775 a British army lodge of Freemasons attached to a regiment under General Gage near Boston initiated fifteen Negroes, including Prince Hall, a young Negro who had come to the mainland from Barbados ten years earlier. Hall was a minister and a recognized leader and spokesman of his people. He and his Negro brothers sought permission from the Americans to establish a chapter of Negro Masons, but their plea was rejected. In 1784 they applied to the Grand Lodge of England, and a warrant was immediately granted. The organization was not perfected, however, until 1787 with Hall as the Master of African Lodge, No. 459 located in Boston. In 1792 a Negro Grand Lodge was organized, with Hall as Grand Master. Five years later he issued a license to thirteen Negroes who had been initiated in England and Ireland to set up a lodge in Philadelphia; and another was organized in Providence. Gradually, Negro Masonry spread over the land as three Grand Lodges were in existence by 1815. Although there was serious objection to Negro Masons in the beginning, white Masons were visiting the Negro lodges within a few years and cooperating in a number of ways.

In 1796 the African Society was organized by forty-four Negroes of Boston. It declared its objectives to be benevolent ones and asserted that it would take "no one into the Society who shall commit any injustice or outrage against the laws of their country." It is said that this and similar organizations did much to bind Negroes together and give them the experience of leadership and cooperation that was to mean much in a later day. They early sought integration into the political, social, and economic life of the nation. Having been generally rejected there was no alternative except to forge out of their limited background and training institutions of their own. It is significant, moreover, that in the case of these institutions, just as in the case of individuals, a considerable effort was made to share in the general development of the country and to contribute to its growth. The Negro's search for independence at the turn of the century was essentially, therefore, a struggle to achieve status in the evolving American civilization.

XII •

The Westward March

Frontier Influences

● *Even before the turn of the century there were unmistakable* evidences of profound economic and social changes taking place on the American scene. After 1800 the signs were much more discernible. Already there was talk about industrialization in the United States, and American businessmen looked at developments in England and Europe with envious eyes. Europeans were beginning to resume their migrations to the New World, once more hopeful about the bright future it held out for them. The land beyond the areas of settlement was beckoning new settlers and began to exercise an influence on American life that seemed to increase with every passing year. This land beyond, the frontier land, rapidly became an influence in the evolution of the institution of slavery and, therefore, in the history of the Negro in America.

In the early nineteenth century the United States could appraise its western lands as one of its most valuable assets, especially after the purchase of Louisiana. Although it would be years before this area would be settled, Americans and Europeans were rapidly moving into the area beyond the mountains. Young, adventurous men from the seaboard states and Scotch-Irish and Germans from the Old World pushed back the frontier and became a part of the new states that were added to the American union.

Many of the settlers in the New West were affiliated with

religions that emphasized equality and brotherly love, and those who were not ardent believers were without the means considered necessary to build a civilization based on slavery. Thus, a spirit of freedom was dominant on the frontier, but it was destined to be rendered unimportant and ineffective by the economic and social forces at work in the older states. Many of the residents of the seaboard states became attracted to the new lands because of their inability to adjust themselves in the old environment. Others found it impossible to satisfy their economic needs in the areas already settled, where competition was keen and where the better opportunities were in the hands of a relative few. Still others, many of whom belonged to the upper level of society, sought new lands on which to grow the cotton for which there was now such a great demand. Frequently this last group had resources, among which were sometimes slaves, with which to dominate the economic and social life of the frontier and to change the character of life there. The frontier, which had formerly been the haven to which the social malcontents escaped and to which the economic "ne'er do wells" retreated, now became the battleground on which the lovers of freedom fought those who sought to entrench the institution of slavery.

It was not possible for the lovers of freedom to win in their battle against the slaveholders. The Industrial Revolution and the invention of the cotton gin had already determined the course of events on the American frontier. The ideals of freedom succumbed before the powerful forces demanding slavery, and the attractive lands of the Southern Gulf states made the establishment of a cotton kingdom based on slavery an almost foregone inevitability. At first the frontiersmen fought the whole system of the East, but as the prospects of enrichment for all appeared, even the frontiersmen gradually gave their support to the institution.

Something may be said, moreover, of the manner in which the frontier influences may have assisted in the westward march of slavery. The sentiment in favor of freedom and democracy in the West came as much from a new type of settler—German, Scotch-Irish, etc.—as it did from a transformation of the character of the people who moved from the seaboard to the back country. The greater portion of the people who moved from the Atlantic coastal states were committed to the institution of slavery and, when possible, demonstrated this commitment by carrying slaves with them. If the spirit of freedom affected them at all, it was in the direction of confirming their right to control the lives of others and to engage in a ruthless exploitation of natural and human resources that was sanctioned by the frontier. The ideal of the West was not so much, as Professor Turner has suggested, the right of every man to rise to the full measure of his own stature as it was the right of every man to take advantage of every opportunity which presented itself to gain the ends he desired and to ignore the basic, ethical restraints which would have made some distinction between liberty and license. It is conceivable, therefore, that the frontier, with its attractive land and its spirit of ruthless freedom, may actually have encouraged the westward march of slavery in the early part of the nineteenth century.

The War of 1812

The westward march was not seriously checked by the diplomatic stress and strain of the early nineteenth century or by the war which culminated from it. Indeed, it may be said that the War of 1812 was, to some extent, a part of the expansionist program of those who were moving westward. There were the controversies over the impressment of American sailors by the British and the violation of neutral rights, but there was also the possibility that a war would result in the acquisition of new lands. If the newly acquired lands lay to the north they could attract Northern settlers who otherwise might go into the emerging cotton kingdom and obstruct the extension of slavery. If, perchance, the expansionists could acquire more lands in the Southwest it would help to satisfy the appetites of an economic system that was already showing signs of insatiability. In either case, a victorious war would encourage the extension of slavery, and the warhawks and expansionists knew it.

When war finally came in 1812, Negroes had an opportunity once more to serve their country. The number of Negroes who served, however, remained small, perhaps because the areas from which they naturally would have come—New England and the Middle Atlantic states—showed little enthusiasm for the war. There seemed to be no serious objections to the Negro's service in the armed forces of the United States, but there was little inclination to recruit Negroes. New York, however, in

1814, passed an act providing for the raising of two regiments of men of color. Each regiment was to consist of slightly more than one thousand men, who were to receive the same pay as other soldiers. If slaves enlisted with the permission of their masters they were to receive their freedom at the end of the war. Doubtless these Negro soldiers served faithfully, for in 1854 at the New York State Convention of the Soldiers of 1812, a resolution was passed asking the Congress to provide the officers, men, and their widows with a liberal annuity, "and that such provisions should extend to and include both the Indian and African race . . . who enlisted or served in that war, and who joined with the white man in defending our rights and maintaining our independence."

Scattered through the white units were Negroes who served largely in menial capacities. Some, however, fought gallantly; and the records indicate their heroism. One of the outstanding soldiers in the Battle of North Point was William Burleigh, a Philadelphia Negro. When the City of Washington was taken, Philadelphia and other Eastern cities were alarmed over the possibility of suffering the same fate. The Vigilance Committee of Philadelphia called on three leading Negro citizens, James Forten, Bishop Allen, and Absolom Jones, and asked that Negroes help erect adequate defenses for the city. More than 2,500 Negroes met in the State House yard, went to Grays Ferry, and worked almost continuously for two days, after which they received the praise of a grateful city. A battalion of Negroes was organized in Philadelphia and was on the verge of marching to the front when peace was announced.

A large number of Negroes were enrolled in the Navy, frequently without reference to race. It is estimated that at least one-tenth of the crews of the fleet on the Upper Lakes were Negroes. Captain Oliver H. Perry was not satisfied with the men, "blacks, soldiers, and boys," that were sent to him. Commodore Chauncey cautioned Perry that he should be proud of whatever he received and added that the fifty Negroes on his ship were among the best men he had. Later, after the Battle of Lake Erie, Perry gave unstinted praise to the Negro members of his crew and declared that "they seemed absolutely insensible to danger." Other naval officers spoke of the gallantry of Negro seamen. Nathaniel Shaler, the commander of the *Governor Tompkins,* said that the name of John Johnson, a Negro seaman on his ship, should be registered in the book of fame. As

Johnson lay dying after he had been struck by a twenty-four pound shot, he exclaimed, "Fire away my boys; no haul a color down." Another Negro, John Davis, who was struck in much the same way, begged Commander Shaler to be thrown overboard, saying he was only in the way of the others.

It was with General Andrew Jackson that Negroes performed their most effective services during the War of 1812. Jackson, in need of augmenting his forces in the autumn of 1814, called upon the free Negroes of Louisiana to answer the appeal of their country. He confessed that the policy of the United States in barring Negroes from the service had been a mistaken one. He promised that all Negroes who enlisted would receive the same pay and bounty as white soldiers and that although their officers would be white, their noncommissioned officers would be chosen from among them. Shortly before the battle of New Orleans, after several units of Negro soldiers had been recruited and had served in the preliminary campaigns, Jackson told them that in their performance they had surpassed his hopes. He told them that the President would be informed of their conduct and that the "voice of the representatives of the American nation shall applaud your valor, as your general now praises your ardor."

In the Battle of Chalmette Plains, commonly known as the Battle of New Orleans, the Negro soldiers occupied a position of strategic importance. They were very near Jackson's main forces—on the left bank of the Mississippi River, just at the right of the advancing left column of the British. One battalion, under Major Lacoste, was composed of men of color of New Orleans and numbered about two hundred and eighty. The other, under Major Daquin, was composed of Negroes from St. Domingo and numbered about one hundred and fifty. These Negro soldiers erected the cotton-bag defenses for Jackson and contributed substantially to the American victory. As the British, under General Pakenham, attempted to take Jackson's position by assault, the frontiersmen, Negroes, regular army men, and others opened up a counterattack from behind their breastworks that was disastrous for the British. The war had already ended, but this belated victory for the Americans was significant psychologically as well as from a military viewpoint.

All during the war Negroes, in search of freedom, went over to the British. As in the War for Independence the British promised freedom to all fugitive slaves. It is impossible to make any estimate of the number who escaped to the British lines, but

it is well-known that some were later living in the British West
Indies and in Canada. Some of those in the West Indies, however, had been sold into slavery. Many Negroes entered the war
on the side of America expecting to secure their freedom. Some
did, but others were actually sent back to their masters at the
end of the struggle. Thus, both sides betrayed, to some extent,
the Negroes who enlisted in the hope of getting their freedom.
The Treaty of Ghent provided for the mutual restoration of
properties. This applied to personal property—slaves—as much
as it applied to any territories that may have been won during
the war. Since the British had been selling fugitive slaves in the
West Indies the Americans sought indemnities for this and
other properties that were not restored by the British. It was not
until 1828, however, that the British finally acceded to the
demands of the United States and granted indemnities of more
than one million dollars.

Emergence of the Cotton Kingdom

The peace that settled over the United States in 1815 made
possible the acceleration of the westward movement of the population that was well under way before the war. The men of the
South and West, the most enthusiastic supporters of the war,
now felt that they had a right to move on to better lands. Many
of the Indian dangers had been allayed, and the demand for
cotton was increasing now that peace had come to the entire
world. The years immediately following the close of the war
witnessed an unparalleled movement of the population westward. Into the Gulf region went large numbers of settlers to
clear the rich lands and cultivate extensive crops of cotton.
Louisiana had already become a state in 1812, and the population continued to increase as cotton and sugar cane became
profitable crops of the slaveholding planters. Mississippi and
Alabama became states in 1817 and 1819 respectively. There
had been only about 40,000 people in this area in 1810, but by
1820 there were 200,000 inhabitants, and twenty years later the
population had almost reached the one million mark. The Negro
population had also grown rapidly. In 1820 there were only
75,000 Negroes in the Alabama-Mississippi region, while by
1840 almost half a million Negroes were in the area. The
increase of the white population, coupled with the tremendous

growth of the Negro population, which consisted largely of slaves, is essentially the story of the emergence of the cotton kingdom.

A considerable number of planters from the seaboard states moved into the cotton kingdom, realizing that only in the new area could slavery have a possibility of becoming profitable. Attempts to grow cotton in Virginia and North Carolina had not been altogether satisfactory. At the beginning of the century the southeastern states had grown most of the cotton. By 1821, however, the South Central states were producing over one-third of the cotton grown in the United States. By 1834 the coastal states produced 160 million pounds, while Alabama, Mississippi, Louisiana, and the other newly settled areas were dominating the production with 297½ million pounds. Small wonder that slaveholders were going into the cotton kingdom. In 1832 the Lynchburg *Virginian* complained that "the constant emigration to the great West of our most substantial citizens, the bone and sinew of the country . . . is the daily subject of complaint among our mercantile men and of which our naked streets and untenanted house are such emphatic evidence. . . ." Four years later a South Carolinian wrote: "The spirit of emigration is still rife in our community. From this cause we have lost many, and we are destined, we fear, to lose more, of our worthiest citizens."

As the income of the planters in the new lands grew to surprising immensity and as the word of the prosperity found its way back to the seaboard, the wave of migration increased. The demand for slaves increased and, naturally, the prices of slaves went up. This mad scramble for land in the west, slaves to cultivate the land, and for huge profits with which to expand were the ingredients that made the cotton kingdom one of the most dynamic areas of economic and social activity during the first half of the nineteenth century. The emergence of the cotton kingdom in which the work was carried on primarily by Negro slaves had the effect of committing the Gulf region to a regime of slavery and unifying the South, enjoying common peculiar interests, against any group or section that threatened to destroy these interests.

The acquisition of Florida in 1819, the settling of Missouri and its entrance into the Union as a slave state in 1821, and the movement which culminated in the acquisition of Texas in 1845 were, to a large extent, a result of the forces which the emergence of the cotton kingdom let loose. In order to safeguard slaveholders against the possibility of losing their slaves through their escape to Spanish soil, Florida was considered both desirable and necessary. The controversy over the entrance of Missouri demonstrated the determination of the South to secure, if possible, a political balance, and an equal determination on the part of the North to maintain political domination. The question of the Negro was consequently catapulted into national prominence, and the incident seems to be symbolic of the irrevocable commitment of the South to the institution of slavery. Nothing more clearly demonstrates the insatiable appetite of plantation slavery for new lands than the generation-long struggle for the acquisition of Texas. It was, perhaps, the high-water mark in the effort of the South to absorb all the lands into which the cotton kingdom could be extended.

Shortly before the beginning of the War of 1812 the men of the West expounded the doctrine that later came to be known as "Manifest Destiny." R. M. Johnson of Kentucky, for example, said that he would not die happy until all of Britain's North American possessions were incorporated into the United States. "The waters of the St. Lawrence and the Mississippi interlock in a number of places," he said, "and the great Disposer of Human Events intended those two rivers should belong to the same people." Points of view like this came more and more to be expressed by men of the slaveholding states, though many Northerners shared the same ideas on the matter. One of the most important motives for expansionism was declared to be to extend the area of freedom. The area of the United States must be extended so as to make possible the development of a great "empire for liberty" in the New World. It was rather strange, therefore, to hear this doctrine expounded by men who held slaves and who saw little incongruity in their position as slaveholders and their pronouncements in favor of extending freedom and democracy.

It may be safe to say that the extension of democracy was probably neither a primary motive of any of the Southern expansionists nor even a secondary motive of many of them. Their preoccupation was with extending the area not of freedom, but of slavery. It will be remembered that many of the Southern spokesmen called for the annexation of new areas as a means of defeating those who were antagonistic to the rights of Southern states. It must be admitted, however, that the slaveholders perhaps were blind to their inconsistency and seriously were concerned with the acquisition of areas in which the liberties of their section could remain inviolate. Indeed, the extension of slavery appeared necessary to the liberties of their section. Thus, Manifest Destiny became a platform from which the slaveholder could plead for an extension of the institution of slavery. The Southerner, in his thinking, had exempted the Negro from his religious and moral conceptions of freedom, and had evolved the new concept that the enslavement of the Negro was essential to his (the white man's) freedom. It is not too much to say, therefore, that Manifest Destiny, one of America's most dramatic shibboleths in the nineteenth century, contributed substantially to the extension of slavery in the generation immediately preceding the Civil War.

Negroes were not only moving involuntarily into the South Central states where slavery was deeply entrenched, but they were also moving voluntarily into the North Central states where presumably slavery would not exist. By 1830 there were more than 16,000 Negroes in Ohio, Indiana, Illinois, and Michigan; and although under the Northwest Ordinance slavery was not permitted, there were no less than 788 slaves in the region at the time of the fifth census. Some of these Negro migrants were runaway slaves, but others were free persons who were seeking greater opportunities, as were the white persons who moved into the North Central states after the War of 1812. An example of a fugitive slave moving into the region is William Trail who, in 1814, ran away from his Maryland master, and with the aid of a forged pass went to Indiana. Although he was pursued and captured on two occasions, he finally won his freedom through court action and settled down to become a prosperous landowning farmer in Union County, Indiana. An outstanding citizen of Cleveland after 1830 was John Melvin who moved to that community from Prince County, Virginia, where he was born of a slave father and free mother. Melvin, through a succession of jobs, amassed sufficient money to purchase a lake vessel and engage in the carrying trade. He helped to organize the First Baptist Church and so vigorously opposed the segregation of Negroes that the principle of free seating was adopted. He also assisted in organizing the first school for Negro children in Cleveland and sponsored the setting up of other such schools in Ohio. Thus, the same search for independence that characterized the efforts of Negroes in the seaboard states was to be found in the activities of Negroes in the newly settled states in the West.

The Domestic Slave Trade

One of the most important single factors augmenting the westward movement was the domestic slave trade. Although many migrants carried slaves with them, others, less financially able, did not. Once in the South Central states and having realized some profits from their early ventures, the ambitious farmers began to seek slaves. Perhaps the best sources of supply were the states of the Atlantic seaboard that had found it increasingly difficult to maintain the institution at a profitable level. In the economic reorganization that circumstances forced upon Maryland, Virginia, and the Carolinas, slave trading took its place along with diversified farming as solutions to the difficult problems of economic readjustment. Even before 1800 the domestic slave trade in Maryland and Virginia was well developed. States like South Carolina that forbade importations from Africa permitted their citizens to purchase slaves from other states, thereby stimulating the domestic traffic considerably. Gradually, the interstate trade became a profitable economic acivity, and the consequent rising value of slave property had the effect of destroying much of the anti-slavery sentiment in Maryland and Virginia after the turn of the century.

With the official closing of the African trade in 1808 the domestic trade became more profitable; and by 1815, about the time of the great movement of the population into the cotton kingdom, it had become a major economic activity in the country. Rapidly the machinery for handling the traffic developed, and before the very eyes of Americans there emerged an institution which served as a substitute, or a supplement, for the African trade and which was only slightly less obnoxious in its effects upon the social order. Many business firms that dealt in farm supplies and animals frequently carried a "line" of slaves. Auctioneers who disposed of real estate and personal property sold slaves along with their other commodities. Planters who were abandoning their farms or were undergoing some kind of retrenchment either passed the word around or advertised in the newspapers that they had slaves for sale. Benevolent organizations frequently sold slaves by lottery.

Almost every community in Maryland and Virginia had either traders or their agents who scoured the countryside in search for slaves whom they could purchase at the lowest possible price and sell in the cotton kingdom at the highest possible price. Firms like Woolfolk, Saunders, and Overly of Maryland, and Franklin and Armfield of Virginia developed the slave-trading business to a point where it greatly enriched the members of the firm. Although they were generally held in low esteem, they were tolerated because they performed a service that was 'of great importance both to the slaveholders and those wishing to acquire slaves. Benjamin Lundy called Austin Woolfolk a "monster in human shape." When Woolfolk retaliated by beating Lundy mercilessly the court fined him only one dollar, suggesting that the general disapproval of slave traders was rather superficial. The newspapers cooperated with the traders in many ways. Not only did they serve the traders as advertising media, but they often received orders and acted as intermediaries between seller and purchaser.

The slave traders were a ubiquitous lot. They could be seen at the general stores, the taverns, the county fairs, and on the plantations. Wherever they heard of the possibility of the sale of slaves they were there. When estates were to be probated or liquidated they sought out the persons and pressed them for whatever slaves were involved. Few salesmen today have the dual talent possessed by the slave traders of the ante-bellum period. They could convincingly argue that a Virginian no longer needed his slaves and with equal firmness could show a Mississippian where he needed at least ten new hands. Their advertisements are suggestive of twentieth century methods. In 1834 Franklin and Armfield announced that they would pay cash for five hundred Negroes and would offer higher prices "than any other purchaser who is now, or may hereafter come into the market." Small wonder that these tycoons were able to move thousands of slaves each year from an area where they were not desired to a section where there was a pressing demand for them.

Baltimore, Washington, Richmond, Norfolk, and Charleston were the principal trading centers in the older states, while Montgomery, Memphis, and New Orleans were the outstanding marts in the newer areas. Although Washington was not the largest slave market it was the most notorious down to 1850, when the slave trade in the District of Columbia was brought to a close. Interstate traders made the District of Columbia their headquarters and operated out of there in Maryland and Virginia. Alexandria, which was a part of the District of Columbia down to 1846, was, moreover, a good place from which to ship slaves by water or overland. The District was aptly called, therefore, "the very seat and center of the slave trade." Foreign vsitors to the nation's capital were puzzled at the sight of slave auction blocks, slave jails, and slave pens. Many of them, as well as many Americans, such as John Randolph of Roanoke, roundly condemned the practice of selling human beings in the capital of the world's most democratic nation. Washington was not alone, however, in possessing the various buildings and other symbols of the slave trade. Practically every city of the upper South and lower South had pens, jails, and other necessary accouterments for the effective prosecution of this profitable traffic. Who could deny, anyway, that jails were necessary? Were not some of the slaves unruly, indolent workers or, worse still, under suspicion as conspirators?

Some slaves were sold in the centers of the upper South and shipped to the cotton kingdom via the Atlantic Ocean. As far north as New York and Philadelphia slaves were loaded on cargo ships and sent into the lower South. Chesapeake ports such as Baltimore, Washington, and Norfolk, were especially important in the slave trading activity. New Orleans was, of course, the important port of entry and became the most important slave trading center of the lower South. Other slaves were sent overland, through Southwestern Virginia to Tennessee, thence into Alabama, Mississippi, and Louisiana. If they went by land, frequently they walked most of the way. When they reached the Ohio, Tennessee, or Mississippi Rivers they were placed on flatboats and shipped "down the river" like any other cargo. In most instances, whether by water or by land, they were carried in chains. More than one traveller was startled at the sight of migrating slaves who were either handcuffed or chained together or both. Always they were under the watchful chaperonage of the long-distance traders or their agents who saw to it that none escaped, lest the profits be therefore proportionally reduced.

There was always the fear on the part of all concerned that the supply of slaves would become exhausted while the demand was still great. One of the ways in which the slaveholders guarded against this distressing eventuality was the systematic breeding of slaves, one of the most fantastic manipulations of human development in the history of mankind. Despite the denials and apologies of many of the students of the history of American slavery, there seems to be no doubt that innumerable slaveholders deliberately undertook to increase the number of salable slaves by advantageously mating them and by encouraging prolificacy in every possible way. As early as 1796 a South Carolina slaveholder declared that the fifty slaves he was offering for sale were purchased for stock and breeding. In 1832 Thomas R. Dew admitted that Virginia was a "Negro raising state" and that she was able to export 6,000 per year because of breeding. Moncure Conway of Fredericksburg, Virginia, boldly asserted that "the chief pecuniary resource in the border states is the breeding of slaves; and I grieve to say that there is too much ground for the charges that general licentiousness among the slaves, for the purpose of a large increase, is compelled by some masters and encouraged by many." Experiments in slave rearing were carried on, albeit surreptitiously, in much the same way that efforts were made to discover new products that would grow on the exhausted soil. Slave rearing was another evidence of the desperation that gripped the upper South after it lost its economic leadership to the states of the cotton kingdom.

Slave breeding, strangely enough, was one of the most approved methods of increasing agricultural capital. The trader was castigated by the slaveholding gentry as being inhuman, vicious, and extremely venal; but slave breeding owners were far more common and much more highly esteemed in the community. One respectable Virginia planter boasted that his women were "uncommonly good breeders" and that he never heard of babies coming so fast as they did on his plantation. Of course, the very gratifying thing about it was that "every one of them . . . was worth two hundred dollars . . . the moment it drew breath." Indeed, breeding was so profitable that many slave girls became mothers at thirteen and fourteen years of age. At twenty some young women had given birth to as many as five children. Bounties and prizes were offered for great prolificacy, and in some instances freedom was granted to mothers who had enriched their masters to the extent of bearing them ten or fifteen children.

Since the domestic slave trade and slave breeding were essentially economic and not humanitarian activities, it is not surprising to find that in the sale of slaves there was the persistent practice of dividing families. Husbands were separated from their wives, and mothers were separated from their children. This is not to say that there was never any respect manifested for the slave family. Here and there one can find sufficient respect for basic human rights or ample sentimentality to prevent the separation of families; but it was not always good business to keep families together. Since people sold and bought slaves largely for economic reasons, they eschewed the civilities that would have frowned upon separation. The law of Louisiana forbade the separation of the mother from her child under ten years of age, and some other states discouraged the division of families. These laws, if enforced, would have done much to ameliorate the conditions of slavery; but they were almost wholly disregarded and were, therefore, entirely without effectiveness.

Few owners were sufficiently insensible to human decency to admit that they were willing to divide slave families by sale. As a matter of fact, families were frequently advertised as being for sale together, but they were not always sold together. Frequently slaves brought higher prices when sold separately. The large number of single slaves on the market bears testimony to the rather ruthless separation of families that went on during the slave period. Frederic Bancroft asserts that "the selling singly of young children privately and publicly was frequent and notorious." It was not unusual to see advertisements in which traders sought young Negroes from eight to twelve years of age. Some traders, moreover, announced that they made a specialty of buying and selling young children.

In justification of the separation of families it was argued that family ties among slaves were either extremely loose or non-existent and that slaves were, therefore, indifferent to separation. This does not at all seem to have been the case. In every coffle of slaves shipped into the cotton kingdom by land or by water the slaves were handcuffed or chained, and hard-boiled traders often admitted that youngsters or oldsters, as the case might be, were unwilling to leave their families. Even more eloquent a denial of the claims of masters that ties of slave families were weak was the advertisements for runaways. All too frequently the masters admitted that the fugitives had, perhaps, gone to a certain place where the slave was known to have had a wife, husband, or children. The frequency of such advertisements also belies the claim of many that slave families were hardly, if ever, separated.

The prices of slaves in the domestic trade reflected all the forces operating to create supply and demand. In the early nineteenth century, the prices of prime field hands were modest, ranging from $350 in Virginia to about $500 in Louisiana. Later, as the demand increased in the lower South the prices on both the Northern and Southern markets tended to rise. The high point of the number of slaves sold in the domestic market was reached just before the panic of 1837 when Virginia reported that in the previous year she had exported no less than 120,000 slaves into the lower South. After the panic, the slump both in prices and in demand became so pronounced that some traders were forced to return to Virginia and Maryland with their slaves and to sustain staggering losses. The forces which operated to increase slave prices in the last decade before the Civil War were largely political and social. In order to convince themselves and the abolitionists that slavery was a moral and economic good and to convince their neighbors of their affluence, planters continued to purchase all the slaves offered on the market. Prices skyrocketed, and by 1860 prime field hands were selling for $1,000 in Virginia and for $1,500 in New Orleans.

Closely allied with slave trading was the practice of slave hiring. Owners had various reasons for hiring out their slaves instead of selling. Some wanted to spread the income from the investment over a long period of time, others wanted to escape whatever stigma there might have been attached to being known as a slave seller, and still others wanted to keep the slaves either for the good of the latter or for the prestige that came from ownership. At any rate, there was almost always the opportunity to make a temporary disposition of slaves because of the demand for such servants. Some whites hired slaves because the purchase was, for the moment, beyond their means; others merely had a temporary need for the services of a slave and saw no need of purchasing him; still others reasoned that it was more economical in the long run to purchase services rather than titles, thereby escaping the responsibility that devolved on the owner during the slave's illness or old age.

Slaves were hired by the day, month, or by the year. The employer promised in the agreement to provide food, clothing, shelter, and medical care in addition to the stipulated wage. If the slave became ill or ran away the wage continued. If the slave died, the wage ceased but the person to whom the slave was hired usually was compelled to show that he was not in any way responsible for the slave's death. The annual contracts ran for fifty-one weeks, and did not cover the period from Christmas to New Year's Day. Hiring day was January 1 or some day early in the New Year. Some communities set aside a hiring day and gave all interested persons an opportunity to transact their business with great ease since the owners as well as the hirers would be able to find each other easily. On January 1, 1858, hiring day in Warrenton, Virginia, five hundred slaves were advertised as being for hire.

The business of hiring was almost as highly organized as slave trading. There were hiring agents who prepared the papers, collected the money, and performed other similar services. At times these agents were also slave traders. In some instances, however, they were men without the resources necessary to engage in slave trading. Interestingly enough, there was no stigma attached to the business of serving as a hiring agent, and in their advertisements the agents frequently proudly listed the names of their "patrons."

Slaves were hired to engage in all kinds of work, but it was usually customary to state the nature of work in the agreement. They were hired by small farmers who needed a few extra hands at harvest time. They also worked in the forests as wood-cutters and turpentine hands. Hired slaves could also be found in the factories, mines, on railroad construction jobs, and in canal digging. There were, of course, a considerable number in the towns serving as maids, porters, messengers, cooks, and the like. The rates of hire varied considerably depending on the skill of the slave as well as the supply. In 1800 a slave hand brought $100 per year in the lower South. By 1860 he brought $200 or more. Toward the end of the period a young blacksmith in Mississippi hired for $500, while several hands in Texas brought as much as $600.

Slave trading and hiring were thus essential parts of the economic and social fabric of the South. While practices which may have developed within the system were frowned upon, there was almost universal acceptance of the general principle of buying and selling human beings. To the owners of the upper South it meant the opportunity to dump on the market those persons who were a serious burden in the period of economic transition. By breeding slaves for the market, moreover, those same owners could go far in the direction of reconstituting themselves economically. To the traders it meant commissions and profits that ranged all the way from 5 to 30 per cent of the sale price of the slaves, no mean return on a short-term investment. The social stigma of slave trading reduced competition and consequently increased the opportunity for profits. To the planters of the lower South the domestic slave trade provided an opportunity to secure the supply of labor necessary for the development and cultivation of new lands. Without the slaves of the upper South they felt stymied and frustrated. With them their opportunities for amassing wealth and influence were considered almost limitless.

Persistence of the African Trade

As the demand for slaves increased in the nineteenth century and as prices went up, merchants and traders experienced a great temptation to engage in the African trade, although it had been closed by the federal legislation of 1807. The long, unprotected coast, the certain markets, and the prospect of huge profits were too much for American merchants and they yielded to the temptation. After the War of 1812 it was generally admitted that American capital, American ships, and American sailors were carrying on an extensive slave trade between Africa and the New World. England was distressed greatly, because she was committed to a program of eliminating the slave trade. In all her treaties with the new republics of Latin America England forced them to promise not to engage in the slave trade. But it was embarrassing to England to observe that her recent enemy, with whom she was now on friendly terms, persisted in winking at gross violations of her own laws. There was little that England could do except to bring the pressure of world opinion to bear on the United States, but the citizens of the latter country were not ashamed and did not even heed the words of their own leaders.

In 1839 President Van Buren asked for an amendment of the law against the African slave trade in order to preserve the "integrity and honor of our flag." In June 1841, President Tyler said that there was every reason to believe that the traffic was on the increase. Almost every year witnessed an appeal of the President or some public leader for a more rigid enforcement of the law, but nothing was done. The most flagrant violations could not be used to create opinion to bring action against those who were profiting from the trade; and in this instance, it was not a sectional profit. New York merchants as well as those of New Orleans were benefiting from the illicit traffic. In 1836 the consul at Havana reported that whole cargoes of slaves fresh from Africa were daily being shipped to Texas in American vessels and that more than one thousand had been sent within a few months. Two months later it was estimated that 15,000 Africans were annually taken into Texas. Bay Island, in the Gulf of Mexico, was a depot where at times as many as 16,000 Africans were on hand to be shipped to Florida, Texas, Louisiana, and other markets.

By 1854 those engaged in the African slave trade had become so bold as to advocate openly the official reopening of the trade. Between 1854 and 1860 every Southern commercial convention gave consideration to the proposition to reopen the trade. At the Montgomery convention of 1858 a furious debate was carried on over the problem. William L. Yancey, the Alabama "fire eater," argued, with considerable logic, that "if it is right to buy slaves in Virginia and carry them to New Orleans, why is it not right to buy them in Cuba, Brazil, or Africa and carry them there?" The following year, at Vicksburg, the convention voted favorably on a resolution recommending that "all laws, State or Federal, prohibiting the African slave trade, ought to be repealed." Only the states of the upper South, enjoying the profits reaped from the domestic slave trade, were opposed to reopening the African trade.

The law of 1807 was so weak and the enforcement so lax that a repeal was unnecessary to reopen the trade. When offenders were caught they were placed under bond, which they promptly forfeited. Sometimes the cases involving offenders were never brought before the courts. Thus, for all practical purposes the trade was open in the last decade before the Civil War, much to the distress of the Quakers and similar organizations. As the intersectional strife increased in intensity, importations into Southern ports became "bold, frequent, and notorious." Stephen A. Douglas asserted that more slaves were brought into the United States in 1859 than in any year when the trade was legal. He said that he had seen three hundred recently imported Negroes at Vicksburg and another large contingent at Memphis. Newly arrived Negroes were openly advertised for sale, and most of the cities of the South had depots where one could purchase newly arrived Africans if, for some reason, Negroes from the upper South were not desired. In doing everything possible to keep the African trade open, Southerners were merely seeking to secure themselves against the possibility that the domestic slave trade would eventually go into a state of desuetude. There was the possibility, moreover, that if they could increase the supply of slaves they would be able to secure them at lower prices.

Without slavery and the slave trade the westward movement on the Southern frontier would have been unsuccessful. It was the slaves, brought in either by the settlers or the traders, who transformed the Southern frontier from a wilderness to flourishing cotton and sugar plantations. It was the slaves, moreover, who represented one of the most substantial forms of capital to be found in the cotton kingdom. Frederick Jackson Turner, an historian of the frontier, always described the trader as having preceded the farmer. He was, of course, referring to the person who carried on barter with the Indians. In this instance, however, the trader *followed* the farmer. He was the person who brought the labor supply to the farmer. Although the order is, in this case, reversed, it would not be too much to say that the slave trader, with his black workers, had a more profound effect on the history of the Southern frontier than did the Indian trader, with his trinkets and fire water.

XIII •

That Peculiar Institution

Scope and Extent

● *Plantation slavery, as it developed in the cotton kingdom,* was something of an anomaly on the American frontier. Although slavery was almost as old as the permanent settlements in America, it did not come to occupy so much of the attention and energies of the settlers as to threaten almost all other forms of labor until the nineteenth century. The frontier had been a place where a man could make or lose a fortune largely by his own labors. The emergence of the great cotton plantation introduced a kind of exploitation of human and natural resources and fostered a type of discipline in the rural areas that created what could, at best, be called a peculiar situation. Indeed, every aspect of agricultural life in the Southern United States underwent a complete transformation as a result of the new economic and social forces let loose by the Industrial Revolution. And what the Industrial Revolution did to the capitalistic system, new lands and the prospects of wealth from cotton culture did to the system of slavery. Large scale operations were the order of the day. The farm became a plantation which in turn became a rural factory with the impersonality that large scale economic organizations usually possess. The face of the Southern frontier had been changed. Cotton and slavery were the great transforming forces.

One of the most rapidly growing elements in the population was the Negro. In 1790 there had been less than 700,000 slaves.

By 1830 there were more than two million. The South Atlantic
states, from Delaware to Florida, were still ahead in numbers,
with 1,300,000; while the states of the lower South, none of
which was in the Union in 1790, now had 604,000 Negro slaves.
At the last census enumeration before the Civil War, the Negro
slave population had grown to 3,953,760! The states of the
cotton kingdom had taken the lead, with 1,998,000 slaves
within their borders. Virginia was still ahead in the number of
slaves in a single state, but Alabama and Mississippi were
rapidly gaining ground. As a matter of fact, the slave population of all the states of the lower South was increasing rapidly,
while that of the upper South was either increasing very slowly
or, as in the case of Maryland, was actually declining. The
increase of the slave population to virtually four million persons
by 1860 is an eloquent testimony to the extent to which slavery
had become entrenched in the Southern states in the nineteenth
century.

The impression should not be conveyed that the white population of the South, numbering around eight million in 1860,
generally enjoyed the fruits of slave labor. There was a remarkable concentration of the slave population in the hands of a
relative few. In 1860 there were only 384,884 owners of Negro
slaves. Thus, fully three-fourths of the white people of the South
had neither slaves nor an immediate economic interest in the
maintenance of slavery or the plantation system. And yet, the
institution came to dominate the political and economic thinking of the entire South and to shape its social pattern for two
principal reasons. The great majority of the staple crops was
produced on plantations employing slave labor, thus giving the
owners an influence all out of proportion to their numbers.
Then, there was the hope on the part of most of the non-
slaveholders that they would some day become owners of slaves.
Consequently, they took on the habits and patterns of thought of
the slaveholders before they actually joined that select class.

While slaves were concentrated in the areas where the staple
crops were produced on a large scale, they were largely on what
might be considered small plantations. That is, the bulk of them
were owned by small farmers. It is not too generally known that
more than 200,000 owners in 1860 had five slaves or less. Fully
338,000 owners, or 88 per cent of all the owners of slaves in
1860, held less than twenty slaves. It is fairly generally conceded
that from thirty to sixty Negroes constituted the most profitable

agricultural unit. If that is true, there were few plantations in the South that had what might be considered a satisfactory working force. The concentration of 88 per cent of all the slaveholders in the small slave owning group is significant for several important reasons. In the first place, it emphasizes the fact that the influence of large owners must have been enormous, since they have been successful in impressing posterity with the erroneous conception that plantations on which there were large numbers of slaves were typical. In the second place, it brings out the fact that the majority of slaveholding was carried on by yeomen rather than gentry. Finally, in a study of the institution of slavery, there is a rather strong indication that some distinction should be made between the possession of one or two slaves and the possession of, say, fifty or more.

But it was the tremendous productivity of the large plantations that placed the large slaveholder in a position of great influence. By 1860 the Southern states were producing 5,387,000 bales of cotton annually. Four states, Mississippi, Alabama, Louisiana, and Georgia, produced more than 3,500,000 bales of this crop. It is no mere accident that these same states were also at the top of the list in the number of large slaveholders. Of the states having slaveholders with more than twenty slaves, Mississippi led, just as she did in productivity of cotton, followed by Alabama, Louisiana, and Georgia.

The Black Codes

After the colonies secured their independence and established their own governments they did not neglect the matter of slavery in the laws which they enacted. Where slavery was growing, as in the lower South in the late eighteenth and early nineteenth centuries, new and more stringent laws were enacted. All over the South, however, there emerged a body of laws generally regarded as the Black Codes which covered every aspect of the life of the slave. There were variations from state to state, but the general point of view was the same in most of such legislation. The point of view was that slaves were not persons but property; and laws should protect the ownership of such property, should protect the whites against any dangers that were likely to arise from the presence of large numbers of Negroes, and should maintain a position of due subordination on the part of the slaves in order that the optimum of discipline and work could be achieved.

The regulatory statutes were frankly repressive and the whites made no apologies for them. They represented merely the reduction to legal phraseology of the philosophy of the South with regard to the institution of slavery. A slave had no standing in the courts: he could not be a party to a suit at law; he could not offer testimony, except against another slave or a free Negro; and his irresponsibility meant that his oath was not binding. Thus, he could make no contract. The ownership of property was generally forbidden, though some states permitted slaves to have certain types of personal property. A slave could not strike a white person, even in self-defense; but the killing of a slave however malicious, was rarely regarded as murder. The rape of a female slave was regarded as a crime only because it involved trespassing on and destroying the property of another person.

The greater portion of the Black Codes involved the many restrictions placed on slaves to insure the maximum protection of the white population and to maintain discipline among the slaves. They were primarily negative. Slaves could not leave the plantation without authorization, and any white person finding a slave out without permission could take him up and turn him over to the public officials. They could not possess firearms, and, in Mississippi, they could not beat drums or blow horns. They could not hire themselves out or, in any other way, conduct themselves as free men. Their relationships with whites and free Negroes were to be kept at a minimum. They could not buy or sell any goods. They could not visit the homes of whites or free Negroes. They could not entertain such persons in their quarters. They were never to assemble unless a white person was present, and they were never to receive, possess, or transmit any incendiary literature calculated to incite insurrections.

Whenever there was an insurrection, or even rumors of one, it was usually the occasion for the enactment of more stringent laws to control the activities and movements of Negro slaves. For example, after the Vesey uprising in 1822 South Carolina enacted a law requiring the imprisonment of all Negro seamen during the stay of their vessel in port. The Nat Turner insurrection of 1831 and the simultaneous drive of the abolitionists against slavery brought forth the enactment of many new repressive measures in other parts of the South as well as in

Virginia and neighboring states. Long before the end of the slave period the Black Codes in all the Southern states had become so elaborate that there was hardly need for modification even when new threats arose to shake the foundations of the institution.

Ample machinery was set up to provide for the effective enforcement and execution of the Black Codes. In some states, slaves were tried in the regular courts for infractions of the law. In other states, specially constituted slave tribunals had the responsibility of examining evidence and judging the guilt or innocence of slaves. Some states required trials by juries composed of slaveholders, while others merely required the cognizance of one, two, or three justices of the peace. Most of the petty offenses were punishable by whipping, while the more serious ones were punishable by branding, imprisonment, or death. Arson, rape of a white woman, and conspiracy to rebel were capital crimes in all the slaveholding states. There was considerable reluctance to imprison a slave for a long period or to inflict the death penalty on him for the obvious reason that he represented an investment, and to deprive the owner of the slave's labor or life was to deprive the state of just that much wealth. Slaveholders were, therefore, extremely cautious about judging a slave offender hastily, because of the danger of losing their own slave through such a process at some later date. This is not to say that slaves enjoyed anything resembling due process of law or justice in any sense in which the term is applied to free persons. Since slaves were always regarded with suspicion and since some crimes were viewed as threats to the social order, they were frequently punished for crimes they did not commit and were helpless before a panic-stricken group of slaveholders who saw in the rumor of an insurrection the slow but certain undermining of their entire system.

One of the devices set up to enforce the Black Codes was the patrol, which has been aptly described as an adaptation of the militia to maintain the institution of slavery. Counties were usually divided into "beats" or areas of patrol, and free white men were called upon to serve for a stated period of time, one, three, or six months. These patrols were to apprehend Negroes out of place and return them to their masters or commit them to jail, to visit slave quarters and search for various kinds of weapons that might be used in an uprising, and to visit assemblies of Negroes where disorder might develop or where conspiracy might be planned. This proved so inconvenient to some citizens that they regularly paid the fines that were imposed for dereliction of duty. A corrupted form of the patrol system was the vigilance committees which came into existence during the emergencies created by uprisings or rumors of them. At such a time, it was not unusual for the committee to disregard all caution and prudence and kill any Negroes whom they would encounter in their search. Committees like these frequently ended up engaging in nothing except a lynching party.

Despite the elaborateness of the Black Codes both in the number of statutes and in the machinery of enforcement, there were innumerable infractions that went unpunished altogether. When times were quiet there was an inclination to disregard the laws and to permit slaves to conduct themselves in a manner which would be regarded as highly offensive during an emergency. There was the desire, moreover, on the part of every master to take all matters involving his slaves into his own hands and to mete out justice in his own way. The strong individualism that was bred on the frontier plantation and the planter's conception of himself as the source of law and justice had the effect of discouraging conformity to statutes even when they were passed in the interest of the plantation system. Slaveholders always had the feeling that they could handle their own slaves, if only something could be done about those on the neighboring plantation. Such a point of view was not conducive to the effective enforcement of the Black Codes.

Plantation Scene

One must not lose sight of the fact that the primary concern of the owner was to get work out of his slaves. And the work of slaves was primarily agricultural. It is estimated that only 400,000 slaves lived in towns and cities in 1850. This left approximately 2,800,000 to do the work on the farms and plantations. The great bulk of them, 1,800,000, were to be found on cotton plantations, while the remainder were primarily engaged in the cultivation of tobacco, rice, and sugar cane. The cotton plantation was, therefore, the typical locale of the Negro slave. It must be recalled that where there were few slaves on a plantation, as was the case in a vast majority of instances, the slaves and their owners worked together in the fields and were

compelled to engage in a variety of tasks. On the larger plantations, where organization was so elaborate as to resemble a
modern factory, there was extensive supervision by the owner or
his overseer or both; and there was considerable division of
labor among the slaves. The large plantation always had at least
two distinct groups of workers, the house servants and the field
hands. The former cared for the house, the yards and gardens,
cooked the meals, drove the carriages, and performed the other
services expected of personal servants. The favored ones frequently travelled with their owners and enjoyed other advantages in the way of food, clothing, and education or experience
which were generally denied workers in other categories.

Unfortunately, there are few records of the activities of slaves
on the smaller units. Therefore, a great deal has been made of
the existence of a large force of house servants because a
considerable number of large slaveholders kept diaries, journals, and other materials that have given a clear picture of their
activities. It is clear that in some of these instances there were
many more house servants than necessary. If a planter could
display a considerable number of house servants, he could convey the impression, frequently inaccurate, that he had great
affluence and lived in a state bordering on luxury. The house
servant group, moreover, tended to perpetuate and even to
increase itself. Once having served in a home, working in the
field was frowned upon and resisted with every resource at one's
disposal. House servants were even anxious to "work" their
children into the more desirable situation and to marry them off
to the children of other house servants. The result was that the
group increased in numbers beyond the point necessary to
maintain the average planter's home adequately.

What may be termed the productive work was done in the
fields by a force that constituted the principal group of slaves.
Where there were not enough slaves to have house servants as
well as field hands, the agricultural activities seldom suffered. In
such instances the slaves found it necessary to do the chores
around and in the house at times which ordinarily would have
been their own time. The cultivation of a crop was a demanding
responsibility, and the entire future of both slaves and owners
depended on the success with which this undertaking was handled. Except on rice plantations, where slaves were given a
specific assignment or "task" each day, the gang system was
used. Literally, gangs of slaves were taken to the field and put to

work under the supervision of the owner or the overseer. The leader instructed them concerning when to begin work, when to eat, and when to quit. Slaves under this system were wholly irresponsible and had little opportunity to develop initiative.

It was generally believed that one Negro was required for the successful cultivation of three acres of cotton. The planting, cultivation, and picking of the cotton required little skill, but a great deal of time. Men, women, and children could be used, though it is to be doubted if the very young and the very old were of any real value to the plantation. Aside from the duties in connection with raising the crop, there were other things to do, such as clearing land, burning underbrush, rolling logs, splitting rails, carrying water, mending fences, spreading ferti-lizer, breaking soil, and the like. Small wonder that many slaves worked not merely from sunrise to sunset, but frequently long after dark. During harvest time the hours were longest since the planter was anxious to harvest the crop before it would be seriously damaged by inclement weather. Under such circum-stances slaves were driven almost mercilessly. In 1830, for example, fourteen Mississippi slaves picked an average of 323 pounds of cotton in one day. It was conceded that if an adult slave picked 150 pounds in one day it was a satisfactory performance. On the Louisiana sugar cane plantations it was not unusual for slaves to work eighteen and twenty hours each day during the harvest season.

When there was not watchful supervision little was accom-plished in a system of slavery. Negro slaves felt no compulsion to extend themselves in their work unless the planter or overseer forced them. Their benefits would be the same, except on a few plantations where systems of rewards and bounties were devel-oped, whether they worked conscientiously or whether they shirked at every opportunity. There was a great deal of com-plaining about the idleness and laziness of slaves, but such was inherent in a system of forced labor. On one occasion George Washington said that his slave carpenters were notorious pid-dlers and not one even of his house servants was worthy of trust. If slaves felt overworked they frequently feigned illness or sim-ply walked off for a day or so or, perhaps, forever. The consist-ent evasion of work on the part of the slaves was one of the reasons why planters always felt in need of more slaves to increase the productivity of their plantations.

In the effort to get work out of slaves the lash was frequently

used. There was the general belief, born of a naive racial justification for the institution of slavery, that Negroes were a child-
like race and should be punished just as children were punished.
Some planters went so far as to specify the size and type of lash
to be used and the number of lashes to be given for specific
offenses. Almost none disclaimed whipping as an effective form
of punishment, and the excessive use of the lash was one of the
most flagrant abuses of the institution. Many slaves fled because
of the brutal beatings by their owner or the overseer.

The great majority of the plantations were managed by the
planters themselves. An overseer would not be needed unless
there were more than twenty slaves or unless the planter was an
absentee landlord. In many instances, moreover, the planters
worked in the fields and shared the same experiences of their
slaves. Under such conditions, there was likely to be less brutality on the part of management and more work on the part of the
laboring force than under other circumstances. Southern planters were at the center of the economic, social, and political life
of their community, and naturally had the feeling that they
should dominate the lives of their black property completely. If
they were inclined to be benevolent and understanding, the
slaves were fortunate indeed. If they were inclined to enjoy the
exercise of authority and the cruelty that authority frequently
fostered, then the slaves perhaps either looked forward to running away or being sold to a better owner. Perhaps the average
owner, difficult as it is to ascertain, is between the two. Doubtless he was stern, sensitive to economic consequences, and quite
conscious of his position as a member of the upper class.

It was on plantations where there were overseers that the
greatest amount of cruelty and brutality existed. Since overseers
came from a non-slaveholding and frequently landless group
they had no interest in the institution except of a most temporary nature. Too frequently they hated the system and directed
especial contempt toward the Negro, because they were of the
opinion that Negro slavery was responsible for their unfortunate
economic plight. They had the job of managing the entire
plantation in the absence of the planter, or if it was too large for
the planter to handle alone the overseer was delegated a considerable portion of the responsibility. In any event, his authority over the slaves was almost unlimited. The owners demanded
that the overseers get work out of the slaves and produce a
superior crop. With such a mandate the overseers were ruthless

and excessively cruel in their treatment of slaves. Frequently, fights grew out of attempts of overseers to punish slaves; and in several instances the overseers were run off the plantation by irate slaves. Before the planter had the opportunity to reprimand the overseer for his bestiality he had often done irreparable damage. It must be remembered, moreover, that unless his cruelty bordered on sensationalism, many planters were not concerned about it. On some plantations a Negro, called the driver, was selected to assist the owner or overseer in getting work out of the slaves. The other workers frequently resented this delegation of authority to one among them, and the driver was sometimes viewed by the slaves as a traitor, especially if he took his duties seriously.

The responsibility of providing the necessities of life for the slaves was a major one. The preoccupation with raising the staple crops was everywhere so great that insufficient attention was given to the very important matter of growing food. Consequently, many plantations were compelled to purchase foodstuffs and other supplies not only for the family of the planter but for the slaves as well. Professor Charles S. Sydnor has observed that few Mississippi planters raised enough food to supply their needs. A considerable amount of food, therefore, had to be brought in from other sections of the country. At any rate, the fare was not a particularly exciting one, the principal items being meal and meat. On some of the larger plantations there was a central kitchen where the food was prepared, but on the average plantation each slave was responsible for the preparation of his own food. He received a daily or weekly ration of meal and salt pork. For adult persons the weekly ration was about a peck of meal and three to four pounds of meat. This was, at times, supplemented with sweet potatoes, peas, rice, syrup, and fruit. Some slaves had their own gardens and chickens, but there was always the possibility of incurring the disfavor of the owner or overseer by spending too much time in this pursuit. A further supplement to one's own diet could be made by hunting and fishing whenever possible.

It would be too much to suppose that slaves always resisted the temptation to take food from the owner's larder if the opportunity presented itself. The difficulty there was that such supplies were locked up and except for a few house servants no Negroes had access to them. But the house servants, who usually ate the same food as the whites whether they were permitted to do so or not, were perhaps not inclined to take food unless some kind of cabal had been formed for the systematic depletion of the owner's food supply. The break in the monotony of the unattractive fare came on holidays like Christmas when the owner sometimes provided items such as cheese, coffee, and candy as a contribution to the festive spirit.

The filching of perishable items like food was simple when compared with any effort on the part of the slave to augment his supply of clothing. Some house servants were favored with the cast-off garments of their owners, but the average slave wore what was generally described as "Negro clothes." They consisted of jeans, linseys, kerseys, and osnaburgs for men and calico and homespun fabrics for the women. On some plantations Negro women spun and wove the cloth out of which they made their dresses. Shoes, called "Negro Brogans," were not provided except for the winter months. No more clothing was furnished than was absolutely necessary. Planters reasoned that perhaps slaves needed ample food in order to work efficiently, but they saw little connection between clothing and work. In a system as harshly materialistic as plantation slavery there was little or no inclination to indulge in any expenditures for slaves that were viewed as unnecessary for increased productivity.

Housing for slaves was especially poor. The small, rude huts were usually inadequate as well as uncomfortable. Windows and floors were almost unheard of. Frederick Olmsted was shocked when he viewed the slave cabins on some of the plantations he visited. He described them as small and dilapidated with no windows, unchinked walls, and practically without furnishings. One of the better ones had a bed, a chest, a wooden stool, some earthenware, and cooking vessels. Many cabins were wholly without beds, and slaves were compelled to sleep on quilts or blankets with only some straw or shucks between them and the earth. The inadequacy of space was, if possible, even worse than the absence of comforts and conveniences. One Mississippi planter had twenty-four huts, each measuring sixteen by fourteen feet, for his 150 slaves. Ulrich B. Phillips and others have defended the frightfully inadequate housing of slaves on the grounds, first, that the plantation was so close to the frontier that even few planters could boast of entirely satisfactory living accommodations and, secondly, that slaves were out of their cabins most of the time and, therefore, did not have a real need for greatly improved housing. In all fairness, these apologists could have added that these unfortunate living conditions go far to explain the crime, delinquency, and aversion to the "civilizing" tendencies of the plantation of which they so loudly accused the slaves.

Non-Agricultural Pursuits

In 1850 there were 400,000 slaves living in urban communities. It may be assumed that not only a majority of these were engaged in non-agricultural pursuits, but that their number was augmented by those plantation slaves whose owners hired them out to townspeople. There is no way of knowing how many such slaves were hired out, but there must have been thousands, especially in the period between the harvest and the new planting. It was in the non-agricultural pursuits that slaves displayed the greatest variety of talent and training. Many plantations had their slave carpenters, masons, and mechanics; but the skilled slaves were to be most frequently found in the towns. Indeed, a large number of the town slaves possessed some kind of skill. In the Charleston census of 1848, for example, there were more slave carpenters than there were free Negroes and whites. The same was true of slave coopers. In addition, there were slave tailors, shoemakers, cabinet makers, painters, plasterers, seamstresses, and the like. Many owners realized the wisdom of training their slaves in the trades, for their earning power would be greatly enhanced; and if the slave was ever offered for sale he would perhaps bring twice as much as a field hand of a similar age would bring.

The white artisans were violently opposed, for the most part, to the teaching of the trades to Negroes. One white skilled worker in Mississippi, for example, said that he would starve before he taught a slave his trade. Most of the planters and pro-slavery leaders advocated training the Negroes in special skills, not only because it increased their value but because if slave labor were more extensively used there would be a wider and more enthusiastic support of the system. If the towns as well as the plantations became completely dependent on slave labor, whatever indifference there was to the institution would be transformed into warm advocacy.

Only the most demagogic of the Negrophobes contended that it was not possible to train Negroes in artisanry. There were too many examples that belied such a contention. No state and few communities were without highly skilled Negro slaves, or slaves employed other than on the plantation. To be sure, the majority of Negroes in non-agricultural pursuits found work as domestic servants, porters, or common laborers in the towns. But there was a sufficient number of slave artisans to make it clear that they had the capacity to acquire skills. Frequently the advertisements of Negroes for sale or of runaways described slaves as a "first rate boot and shoe maker," an "experienced weaver and chair spinner," or an "excellent carpenter." In Virginia they were used in the mills, iron furnaces, and tobacco factories. The Saluda textile factory in South Carolina at one time employed ninety-eight slave operatives. They were also in the textile mills of Florida, Alabama, Mississippi, and Georgia. In Kentucky they were employed in the saltworks of Clay County and the iron and lead mines of Caldwell and Crittenden Counties. The Southern railroads also employed a considerable number of slaves to carry on the construction work. It is reported that in 1838 a corporation purchased 140 slaves at a cost of $159,000 to work on the construction of a railroad between Jackson and Brandon, Mississippi. For ten years a Negro was the engineer on the West Feliciana Railroad, one of the oldest in the Southern United States. Finally, slaves were frequently employed in river transportation and at docks. Despite Olmsted's observation that Irish workers were employed to unload boats on the Mississippi River because slaves were too valuable, slaves were extensively used in such work. They worked on the docks at New Orleans, Savannah, Charleston, Norfolk, and other Southern ports.

There were even slave inventors. In 1835 and 1836 one Henry Blair, designated in the records as a "colored man" of Maryland, received patents for two corn harvesters which he had developed. By 1858, however, the Attorney-General ruled that since a slave was not a citizen the government could not enter into an agreement with him by granting him a patent, nor could the slave assign the invention to his owner. Benjamin Montgomery, a slave owned by Jefferson Davis, invented a boat propeller toward the end of the slave period. Davis made an attempt to have it patented, but failed. This perhaps accounts for the passage of a law by the Confederate Congress in 1861 providing that if the owner took an oath that his slave had actually invented a device the patent would be issued to him. It was not until after the Civil War that Negroes were able to secure patents for their inventions without any difficulty.

Social Considerations

It has been assumed too frequently that slavery provided an idyllic existence not only for the owner but for his slaves as well. The fact is, however, that even for the planter, life was not always pleasant, and there was little in the way of recreation and other diversions to foster a zest for living either on the plantation or in the Southern towns. Life was so barren generally that it can hardly be described as "the good life" even under the most favorable circumstances; and the plantation with its inherent isolation and consequent social and cultural self-sufficiency frequently bordering on stagnancy tended to perpetuate the barrenness. For the slave there was little in the way of enjoyment and satisfaction during the moments or hours he was off his job. It must be remembered that, for the most part, the slave had no time he could call his own; and not infrequently he worked such long hours that periods of "free time" necessarily had to be used literally as periods of rest. Even if there was no work and even if an opportunity for diversion presented itself, the slave could never escape the fact that he was a slave and that his movements as well as his other activities were almost always under the most careful surveillance. If a slave found it possible to enjoy the periods when he was not on the job he either possessed a remarkable capacity for accommodation or he was totally ignorant of the depth of his degraded position.

Most slave children had the run of the plantation and played with the white children in and out of the "big house," in and out of the cabins, and through the yards without any inhibitions. When the Negroes reached the useful age, which was very early for some purposes, much of the playing was over. When they reached the social age, the interracial playing was over altogether, and they settled down to the existence that was the inevitable lot of the slave. There was almost nothing, of a day-to-day nature, for the slave to do in the way of recreation. If the plantation was near a stream it might be possible for slaves to make it through the woods and spend an hour or so fishing; but not infrequently this was for the specific purpose of supplementing the fare instead of for recreation. When the whites went hunting at night they usually carried some Negro men, but on a large plantation there were many who never got this opportunity. Races, fairs, militia muster, and election days were occasions for the relaxation of rules on the plantation. Some slaves were favored by being given permission to attend these events. Even if they did not go, there was an opportunity for them to sing, dance, and visit because of the festive spirit that such occasions brought to the plantation.

There were two periods to which slaves could look forward as periods of recreation and relaxation: the summer lay-by and Christmas. At the end of the cultivation period, there was a considerable reduction of duties, which gave slaves an opportunity either to work for themselves or to engage in some kind of recreation. The Christmas season brought a complete suspension of work, except the bare essentials such as cooking and washing, and for one week both town and plantation slaves had a period of merrymaking. On the Atlantic seaboard much of the festivities centered around the John Canoe celebration, a custom practiced in the Caribbean and perhaps in Africa in which the Negroes engaged in singing, dancing, drinking, and visiting the whites and asking for Christmas presents. Weddings, anniversaries, and the like, whether of the whites or the blacks, were other opportunities for merrymaking. Some planters even gave dances for their slaves. Doubtless these were exceptions. Few of the four million slaves in 1860 led anything except the most barren existence in which their only moments of pleasure were in the singing of a plaintive melody, the strumming of a banjo, the telling of a tale, or the playing of a game.

As long as proper precautions were taken there was little opposition to some form of religious activity among the slaves. Owners had reason to be suspicious if the emphasis was on instruction or if there were Negro leaders. Otherwise there was either support of a religious program for slaves or passive indifference. There were some Negro congregations on the larger plantations and in the towns. Richmond, Charleston, and Lexington, Kentucky, are examples of cities in which churches for slaves were located. One Mississippi planter erected a small Gothic church and paid a clergyman $1,500 to preach to him and his slaves. The number of Negro preachers was always considerable, and few plantations were without at least one black exhorter. When the abolitionists began their crusade against slavery the planters became more cautious with regard to Negro religious activities and undertook to control them more effectively. In most states Negro preachers were outlawed between 1830 and 1835, and thereafter Negro religious services were presided over by some white person. More and more, however, Negroes were required to attend the churches of their masters.

The invitation to Negroes to attend the white churches, the acceptance of which bordered on compulsion, did not represent a movement in the direction of increased brotherhood. Rather, it was the method the whites employed to keep a closer eye on the slaves. It was believed that too many of the conspiracies had been planned in religious gatherings and that such groups gave the abolitionists an opportunity to distribute incendiary ideas and literature. When Bishop Atkinson of North Carolina raised the question "Where are our Negroes," he not only implied that they were in churches other than the Episcopal Church but that they were beyond the restraining influence of the conservative element of the white society. When the slaves attended the churches of the planters they usually sat either in the gallery or in a special section. The earliest examples of the segregation of the Negro are to be found in practices in the churches. In one instance the white congregation developed the ingenious scheme of constructing a partition several feet high to separate the masters from the slaves.

In the states of the lower South the Baptist and Methodist denominations had the greatest influence on the plantation Negroes. These were the evangelical churches that moved with the population and adjusted their program to the needs of the people. The Methodist camp-meetings and the Baptist "protracted" meetings were opportunities not only for religious refreshing but for social intercourse as well. They were the most effective means of releasing the pent-up emotions that the barren life of the rural South created. Thus, whites attended in large numbers, and, as Gilbert Seldes has pointed out, they were "times of refreshing." Under such circumstances, whites and Negroes sang together, shouted together, and spent themselves emotionally together. It was the nearest thing to interracial religious fellowship that the South produced.

Once the planters were convinced that conversion did not have the effect of setting their slaves free they sought to use the church as an agency for maintaining the institution of slavery. Ministers were encouraged to instruct the slaves along the lines of obedience and subserviency. Bishops and high church officials were not above owning slaves and fostering the continuation of slavery. In Louisiana the Episcopal Bishop Polk owned four hundred slaves; and although he regularly gave them religious instruction, there is no indication that he attempted to set them free. The Presbyterians and Quakers seemed to have been the most liberal in their attitude toward Negroes, but they were not the large slaveholders. The latter were to be found in the Episcopal church on the Atlantic seaboard and in the Baptist and Methodist churches in the cotton kingdom. In the last three decades before the Civil War the church became one of the strongest allies of the pro-slavery element. Slaves who had found refuge and solace in the religious instructions of the white clergy had reason to believe that they were now trapped in by an enemy that had once befriended them.

FAMILY WORSHIP ON A SOUTH CAROLINA PLANTATION. This drawing, from the Illustrated London News *for December 5, 1863, was made by an English artist while visiting a plantation near Port Royal, South Carolina. The "state of almost patriarchal simplicity," which characterized the planter's position reflects the sympathetic attitude that many Englishmen had toward the Confederacy during the Civil War.*

Despite legal restrictions and despite contentions on the part of Southerners like John Calhoun that Negroes could not absorb educative experiences, Negro slaves were receiving education in various parts of the South. It is remarkable how generally the significant laws against the teaching of Negroes were disregarded. Planters became excited over the distribution of abolition literature in the South, but they gave little attention to preventing the training of slaves to read, which would have rendered abolition literature ineffective to a large extent. Indeed, some masters themselves taught their slaves. William Pease of Hardman County, Tennessee, was taught by his owners. There was one strange case in which a planter taught his slaves to spell and read but not to write. One planter in Northern Mississippi boasted that all twenty of his slaves could read and that they purchased their own books. The case of Frederick Douglass having been taught by his mistress is perhaps the best known instance of an owner teaching a slave. In some cases, even when masters were opposed to their slaves receiving instruction, the children of masters would teach slaves to read and write. There are records of hirers and even overseers giving instruction to slaves.

The instruction of one or two slaves, though a violation of the law, was not regarded as serious, and there was hardly any danger of prosecution. But the instruction of slaves in schools for that purpose was another thing. Even this was undertaken in various parts of the South. Naturally, more care had to be exercised in the selection of students and in the dissemination of information concerning the schools, but there were Negroes and whites who were willing to run the risk of legal prosecution and social disapprobation in order to teach slaves. Negro schools are known to have existed in Savannah, Georgia; Charleston, South Carolina; Fayetteville, New Bern, and Raleigh, North Carolina; Lexington and Louisville, Kentucky; Fredericksburg and Norfolk, Virginia; and others in Florida, Tennessee, and Louisiana. Francis Cardozo attended school in Charleston until he was twelve years of age. After searching for some time Frederika Bremer finally found one of the schools in Charleston and visited it. In 1847 there was a school for Negroes in Louisville, Kentucky, in which slaves were attending upon presenting permits from their masters.

There is no way of knowing the extent to which Negroes attended the schools of whites. In 1840 Negroes were permitted to attend school with white children in Wilmington, Delaware. There is an interesting account, though perhaps fictional, of one Julius Melbourn who was sent to a white academy near Raleigh, North Carolina, by his mistress and remained there until it was discovered that he was a Negro. Other mulattoes may well have had more success than did Melbourn. Nor is there any way of ascertaining with any degree of accuracy the extent of education among the slaves. Some Southern whites said that Negroes did not have the capacity to learn. Some Northern abolitionists said conditions in the South were so bad that almost no Negroes had the opportunity to learn. Amos Dresser believed that one out of every fifty slaves in the Southwest could read and write. C. G. Parsons estimated that about 5,000 of Georgia's 400,000 slaves were literate. Whatever the number was it represented a clear-cut step in the direction of Americanization and made, at least for some, the process of adjustment to freedom somewhat less difficult.

The slave family experienced great difficulty in maintaining itself on a stable basis in a system where so little opportunity for the expression of the slave was possible. Too seldom did the owner recognize the slave family as an institution worthy of respect, and frequently the blind forces inherent in the system operated to destroy it. Courtship and the normal relationships preliminary to marriage seldom existed. Only when the owner manifested some real interest in the religious and moral development of his slaves was there an effort to establish the slave family on a stable basis. There are instances where planters insisted on religious ceremonies to unite slave couples, and there is one case of a mistress insisting upon "passing" on all the suitors of her female slaves. One thing that distressed almost all slaveholders was the desire of slaves to marry persons on other plantations. Such a union, the planters knew, would involve one or the other of the slaves being away from his own plantation at various times and reducing his efficiency as a worker. Slaves were, therefore, encouraged to marry on the plantation, if at all possible; and when this was not possible masters sought either to purchase the spouse of his slave or sell his slave to the owner of the spouse.

The permanency of a slave marriage depended on the extent to which the couple had an opportunity to work and live together so that through common experiences they could be drawn closer together. There are numerous examples of the emergence of a stable slave family, especially where there were children to strengthen the bond and where they were not divided through sale. It has been well said by E. Franklin Frazier that the economic interests of the masters were often inimical to the family life of the slaves.

The bearing of children was frequently extremely hard for the slave women. Although having learned, by observing the white family unit, the basic elements of decency and self-respect the slave woman was frequently forced into cohabitation and pregnancy by the venality of her master and in such cases the family status was established on a very tenuous basis. She may have learned to care for her husband who had been forced upon her, but the likelihood was not very great. Nor did she have much opportunity to develop any real attachment for her children. Little time off was given for child bearing, and, of course, child rearing was a haphazard arrangement in which the mother, just as everyone else, was relieved of any responsibility. Just the same, the slave mother did what she could to stabilize her family and to keep them together. They fiercely resisted the division by sale. J. W. Loguen's mother, for example, had to be tied to a loom when her children were taken from her to be sold; and Josiah Henson's mother looked on "in an agony of grief" as she saw her children sold one by one.

Sir Charles Lyell said that "one of the most serious evils of slavery is its tendency to blight domestic happiness; and the anxiety of parents for their sons, and constant fear of licentious intercourse with slaves is painfully great." This "evil" not only blighted the happiness in the white family but was one of the powerful forces operating to destroy the slave family altogether. The extensive miscegenation which went on during the slave period was largely the result of people living and working together at common tasks and the subjection of Negro women to the whims and desires of white men. There was some race mixture that resulted from the association of Negro men and white women, but this was only a small percent of the total. Despite all the laws against the intermingling of the races, the practice continued; and its persistence is another example of the refusal of the members of the dominant group to abide by the laws which they themselves created.

In cities like Charleston, Mobile, and New Orleans there was widespread intermixture. In New Orleans the practice of young white men maintaining young Negro women in a state of concubinage became so generally practiced as almost to gain social acceptability. Some relationships were the result of physical compulsion on the part of the white man, and if resistance was offered it was frequently beaten back in the most vicious manner. Many slave women carried scars to their graves which had been inflicted by their owners or other whites when resistance was offered to their advances. Other slave women did not resist, either because of futility, the prestige that such a relationship would bring, or because of the material advantages that might accrue from it. Children born of such unions were slaves; and the result of such extensive mixing was that by 1850 there were 246,000 mulatto slaves out of a total slave population of 3,200,000. By 1860 there were 411,000 mulatto slaves out of a total slave population of 3,900,000.

The reactions of white fathers to their Negro progeny was varied. Some had no feeling for them at all and sold them, when the opportunity presented itself, just as they would sell any other slave. Not infrequently they were encouraged in this by their wives who resented the presence of Negro children by their husbands. Other fathers, however, developed a great fondness for their Negro children and emancipated them and provided for them. Frequently old, repentant men atoned for their youthful waywardness by freeing their mulatto children and giving them land and money. Few, however, bestowed as much as John Stewart of Petersburg, who left to his "natural colored daughter" a house and a lot and all of his money which amounted to $19,500.

The Slave's Reaction to His Status

Owners of slaves almost always sought to convey the impression that their human chattel was docile, tractable, and happy. This effort became a part of their defense of the institution, and they went to the extreme in this representation. Frequently, also, the anti-slavery forces contended that the slaves were easily controlled and that was the explanation for their exploitation by their owners. Each group in its own way, therefore, was inclined to overstate the case and to refuse to make a realistic appraisal of the slave's true reaction to his status as a slave. There is no reason to conclude that the personality of the slave was permanently impaired by his engaging in duplicity in the slave-master relationships. It must be remembered that some of the manifestations of the slave were superficial and were for the purpose of misleading his owner regarding his real feeling. In the process of adjustment he developed innumerable techniques to escape work as well as punishment, and in innumerable instances he was successful. Any understanding of his reaction to his slave status must be approached with the realization that the Negro at times was possessed of a dual personality: he was one person at one time and quite a different person at another time.

It cannot be denied that as old as the institution of slavery was, human beings had not, by the nineteenth century, brought themselves to the point where they could be subjected to it without protest and resistance. Resistance has been found wherever the institution of slavery existed, and Negro slavery in the United States was no exception. Too frequently, there were misunderstanding, suspicion, and hatred which were mutually shared by master and slave. Indeed, they were natural enemies, and on many occasions they conducted themselves as such. There are numerous examples of kindness and understanding on the part of the owner as well as docility—which may be more accurately described as accommodation—and tractability on the part of the slave. But this was an unnatural relationship and was not, by the nature of things, inherent in the system.

The brutality which apparently was inherent in a system of human exploitation existed in every community where slavery was established. The wastefulness and extravagance of the plantation system made no exception of human resources. Slaves were for economic gain, and if beating them would increase their efficiency—and this was generally believed—then, the rod and lash should not be spared. Far from being a civilizing force, moreover, the plantation bred indecency in human relations; and the slave was the immediate victim of the barbarity of the system which exploited the sex of the women and the work of everyone. Finally, the psychological situation which was created by the master-slave relationship stimulated terrorism and brutality because the master felt secure in his position and because he frequently interpreted his role as calling for that type of conduct. Many masters as well as slaves got the reputation of being "bad," and their prevalence did nothing to relieve the tension which everywhere seemed to be mounting as the institution developed.

The laws that were for the purpose of protecting the slaves

were few and were seldom enforced. It was almost impossible to secure a conviction of a master who mistreated his slave. Knowing that, the master was inclined to take the law into his own hands. Overseers were generally known for their brutality, and the accounts of abuse and mistreatment on their part as well as on the part of hirers are numerous. Masters and mistresses were, perhaps, almost as guilty. In 1827 a Georgia grand jury brought in a true bill of manslaughter against a slaveowner for beating his slave to death, but he was acquitted. Several years later Thomas Sorrell of the same state was found guilty of killing one of his slaves with an axe, but the jury recommended him to the mercy of the court. In Kentucky a Mrs. Maxwell had a wide reputation for beating her slaves on the face as well as the body, women as well as men. There is, also, the shocking account of Mrs. Alpheus Lewis who burned her slave girl around the neck with hot tongs. Drunken masters had little regard for their slaves, the most sensational example of which is the Kentucky owner who dismembered his slave and threw him piece by piece into the fire. One Mississippi master dragged from the bed a slave whom he suspected of theft and inflicted over one thousand lashes on him. Repeated descriptions of runaways contain phrases such as "large scar on hip," "no marks except those on his back," "much scarred with the whip," and "will no doubt show the marks of a recent whipping;" they suggest a type of brutality that doubtless contributed toward the slave's decision to abscond.

To the demonstrations of brutality as well as to the very institution of slavery itself the Negro reacted in various ways. Thanks to the religion of his master he could be philosophical about the whole thing and escape through ritual and song. His emphasis on otherworldliness in his songs certainly suggested grim dissatisfaction with his worldly status. "Dere's a Great Camp Meetin' in de Promised Land," "Look Away in de Heaven, Lord," "Fo' My Soul's Goin' to Heaven Jes' Sho's You Born," and "Heaven, Heaven, Everybody Talkin' 'Bout Heaven Ain't Goin' There" are only a few of the songs which slaves sang in the hope that their burdens would be relieved in the next world. As long as he was in this world he had to make the most of the unfavorable situation by loafing on the job, feigning illness in the fields and on the auction block, and engaging in an elaborate program of sabotage. The slave was so hard on the farming tools that special ones were developed for him. He drove the animals with a cruelty that suggested revenge, and he was so ruthless in his destruction of the crops that the most careful supervision was necessary to insure their survival until harvest time. He burned forests, barns, and homes to the extent that members of the patrol were frequently fearful of leaving home lest they be visited with revenge in the form of the destruction of their property by fire.

Self-mutilation and suicide were popular forms of resistance to slavery. Slaves cut off their toes, hands, and mutilated themselves in other ways so as to render themselves ineffective as workers. One Kentucky slave carpenter, for example, cut off one of his hands and the fingers of the other when he learned that he was to be sold down the river. There are several instances of slaves having shot themselves in the hand or foot, especially upon being recovered after running away. The number of suicides seems relatively large, and certainly they were widespread. Slaves fresh from Africa committed suicide in great numbers. In 1807 two boatloads of newly arrived Negroes in Charleston starved themselves to death. When his slave woman was found dead by her own hanging in 1829, a Georgia planter was amazed since he saw no reason why she should want to take her own life. When two Louisiana slaves were returned to their master after having been stolen in 1858 they unbound themselves and drowned themselves in the bayou. One of the South's wealthiest planters, Charles Manigault, lost a slave by a similar act when the overseer threatened him with punishment. Sometimes slave mothers killed their own children to prevent them from growing up in slavery.

Much more disturbing to the South were the numerous instances of slaves doing violence to the master class. Poisoning was always feared, and perhaps some planters felt a real need for an official taster. As early as 1761 the Charleston *Gazette* remarked that the "Negroes have begun the hellish act of poisoning." Arsenic and other similar compounds were used. Where they were not available slaves are known to have resorted to mixing ground glass in the gravy for their masters' table. Numerous slaves were convicted for murdering their masters and overseers, but some escaped. In 1797 a Screven County, Georgia, planter was killed by his newly imported African slaves. Another Georgia master was killed by his slave who stabbed him sixteen times. The slave was later burned alive. The slave of William Pearce of Florida killed his master with an axe when Pearce sought to punish him. One Mrs. Carolina Turner of Kentucky was choked to death by a slave whom she was flogging. Though the citizenry had long complained of Mrs. Turner's merciless brutality in dealing with her slaves, her killer was summarily hanged for his deed. The times that overseers and masters were killed by slaves in the woods or fields were exceedingly numerous, as the careful reading of almost any Southern newspaper will reveal.

Every Southern community raised its annual crop of runaway slaves. There was both federal and state legislation to aid in their recovery, but many slaves escaped forever. The practice of running away became so widespread that every state sought to strengthen its patrol and its other safeguards, but to little avail. Hardly a newspaper went to press without several advertisements of runaways, and sometimes there were several columns of such advertisement. The following is a typical advertisement:

> Absconded from the Forest Plantation of the late William Dunbar, on Sunday the 7th instant, a very handsome Mulattress called Harriet, about 13 years old, with straight dark hair and dark eyes. This girl was lately in New Orleans, and is known to have seen there a man whom she claims as her father and who does now or did lately live on the Mississippi, a little above the mouth of the Caffalaya. It is highly probable some plan has been concerted for the girl's escape. . . .

Long before the Underground Railroad was an effective antislavery device (see Chapter XV) slaves were running away: men, women, and children, singly, in pairs, or in groups. At times they went so far as to organize themselves into groups called "Maroons" and to live in communities, on the order of Palmares in Brazil. The forests, mountains, and swamps of the Southern states were their favorite locations, and they proved to be troublesome to the masters who sought to maintain strict order on their plantations.

Some slaves disguised themselves or armed themselves with free passes in their effort to escape. Others simply walked off, apparently hoping that fate would be kind and assist in their permanent escape. Some were inveterate runaways such as the North Carolina woman who had fled from her master's plantation no less than sixteen times. Others were not as daring, and gave up after one unsuccessful attempt. While there is no way of even approximating the number of runaways, it is obvious that fleeing from the institution was one of the most effective means of resistance that slaves discovered. It represented the continuous fight that slaves carried on against their masters.

The most sensational and desperate reaction of Negroes to their status as slaves was the conspiracy to revolt. To the Negroes who could summon the nerve to strike for their freedom in a group, it was what might be termed "carrying the fight to the enemy" in the hope that it would end, once and for all, the degradation of human enslavement. To the whites it was a mad, sinister act of desperate savages, in league with the devil, who could not appreciate the benign influences of the institution and who would dare shed the blood of their benefactors. Inherent in revolts was bloodshed on both sides. The Negroes accepted this as the price of liberty, while the whites were panic-stricken at the very thought of it. Even rumors of insurrections struck terror in the hearts of the slaveholders and called forth the most vigorous efforts to guard against the dreaded eventuality.

Revolts, or conspiracies to revolt, persisted down to 1865. They began with the institution and did not end until slavery was abolished. It can, therefore, be said that they were a part of the institution, a kind of bitterness that the whites had to take along with the sweetness of slavery. As the country was turning to Jeffersonian Republicanism at the beginning of the nineteenth century, many people believed that a new day had arrived for the common man. Some Negroes, however, felt that they would have to force their new day by breaking away from slavery. In Henrico County, Virginia, they resolved to revolt against the institution under the leadership of Gabriel Prosser and Jack Bowler. For months they planned the desperate move, gathering clubs, swords, and the like for the appointed day. On August 30, 1800, over one thousand slaves met six miles outside of Richmond and began to march on the city, but a violent storm almost routed the insurgents. Two slaves had already informed the whites, and Governor Monroe, acting promptly, called out more than six hundred troops and notified every militia commander in the state. In due time scores of slaves were arrested, thirty-five were executed, four having escaped, one of whom committed suicide. Gabriel was captured in late September, and after he refused to talk to anyone he too was executed.

The whites speculated extravagantly over the number of

slaves involved in this major uprising. The estimates ran all the way from 2,000 to 50,000. The large numbers, together with the total disregard the slaves seemed to have for their own lives, caused the whites to shudder. The "high ground" which they took in maintaining silence added to the stark terror of the whole situation. When one was asked what he had to say, he calmly replied:

> I have nothing more to offer than what General Washington would have had to offer, had he been taken by the British officers and put to trial by them. I have ventured my life in endeavouring to obtain the liberty of my countrymen, and am a willing sacrifice to their cause; and I beg, as a favour, that I may be immediately led to execution. I know that you have predetermined to shed my blood, why then all this mockery of a trial?

The unrest among the slaves, even in Virginia, continued into the following year, and plots were reported in Petersburg and Norfolk and in various places in North Carolina. The latter state became so excited that many slaves were lashed, branded, and cropped, and at least fifteen were hanged for alleged implication in conspiracies. In the following years before the war with England there were reports of insurrection up and down the Atlantic seaboard. Conspiracy had crossed the mountains, for in 1810 a plot was uncovered in Lexington, Kentucky. The following year, more than four hundred rebellious slaves in Louisiana had to be put down by federal and state troops. At least seventy-five slaves lost their lives in the encounter and in the trials that followed. There was another uprising in New Orleans in the following year.

Following the War of 1812 the efforts of slaves to revolt continued. In Virginia, in 1815, one George Boxley decided to attempt to free the slaves. He made elaborate plans, but a slave woman betrayed the plans of the conspirators. Although Boxley himself escaped, six slaves were hanged and another six were banished. When the revolutions of Latin America and Europe broke out, Americans could not restrain themselves in their praise and support of the fighters for liberty. The South joined in the loud hosannas, while the slaves watched the movements for the emancipation of the slaves in Latin America and the Caribbean. Perhaps all these developments had something to do with what was the most elaborate, though not the most effective, conspiracy of the period: the Denmark Vesey insurrection.

Vesey had purchased his freedom in 1800 and for a score of years had made a respectable living as a carpenter in Charleston, South Carolina. He was a sensitive, liberty-loving person and was not satisfied in the enjoyment of his own relatively comfortable existence. He believed in equality for everyone and resolved to do something for his slave brothers. Over a period of several years he carefully plotted his revolt and chose his assistants. Together they made and collected their weapons: 250 pike heads and bayonets and 300 daggers. Vesey also sought assistance from St. Domingo. He set the second Sunday in July, 1822, for the day of the revolt; and when the word leaked out, he moved it up one month, but his assistants who were scattered for miles around Charleston did not all get the word. Meanwhile, the whites were well aware of what was going on and began to round up the suspects. At least 139 Negroes were arrested, forty-seven of whom were condemned. Even four white men were fined and imprisoned for encouraging the Negroes in their work. The estimates of the number of Negroes involved in the plot ran as high as 9,000.

The following decade saw the entire South apprehensive over possible uprisings. The revival of the anti-slavery movement and the publication of such incendiary material as David Walker's *Appeal* put the South's nerves on edge. Several revolts were reported on Louisiana plantations in 1829; and in 1830 a number of citizens of North Carolina asked their legislature for aid because their slaves had become "almost uncountroulable." The panic of the twenties culminated in 1831 with the insurrection of Nat Turner. This Southampton County, Virginia, slave was a mystical, rebellious person who had on one occasion run away and then decided to return to his master. Perhaps already he had begun to feel that he had been selected by some divine power to deliver his people from slavery.

Upon the occasion of the solar eclipse in February, 1831, Turner decided that the time had come for him to lead his people out of bondage. He selected the Fourth of July as the day, but when he became ill he postponed the revolt until he saw another sign. On August 13, when the sun turned a "peculiar greenish blue" he called the revolt for August 21. He and his followers began by killing Turner's master, Joseph Travis, and his family. In rapid succession other families fell before the blows of the Negroes. Within twenty-four hours sixty whites had been killed, and the revolt was spreading rapidly when the main group of Negroes were met and overpowered by state and federal troops. More than one hundred slaves were killed in the encounter and thirteen slaves and three free Negroes were immediately hanged. Turner was captured on October 30, and within less than two weeks, on November 11, he was executed.

The South was completely dazed by the Southampton uprising. The situation was grossly exaggerated in many communities. Some reports were that whites had been murdered by the hundreds in Virginia. Small wonder that several states felt it necessary to call special sessions of the legislature to consider the emergency. Most states strengthened their Black Codes, and citizens literally remained awake nights waiting for the Negroes to make another break. But the uprisings continued. In 1835 several slaves of Monroe County, Georgia, were hanged and whipped to death because of implication in a conspiracy. In the following decade there were several uprisings in Alabama, Louisiana, and Mississippi. In 1853 a serious revolt in New Orleans involving 2,500 slaves was aborted by the informing of a free Negro. In 1856 the Maroons in Bladen and Robeson Counties, North Carolina, "went on the warpath" and terrorized the countryside. Down to and throughout the Civil War, slaves demonstrated their violent antipathy for slavery by continuing to rise against it.

One little-known sidelight of slave revolts is the encouragement and assistance which white persons gave to the Negroes. Two Frenchmen were said to have been involved in Gabriel's plot. In 1802 a Virginia slave confessed that some white men had promised to help him secure arms and ammunition for an uprising. It will be recalled that four white men were convicted of encouraging Denmark Vesey's uprising. In Mississippi, in 1835, twenty-one "bleached and unbleached" conspirators were hanged. In the same year white men in Georgia were involved in a plot, and two whites were hanged in Louisiana for helping to plan an uprising. There were always reports that whites, whose names were most difficult to obtain, were assisting in some way with the Negro plots. It is not at all strange that some whites sought to encourage the revolts. When one considers the large number of whites in the South who could have traced their economic and social plight directly to slavery, he is surprised to find that there was not a larger number of whites who attempted to wipe out the institution of slavery.

XIV •

Quasi-Free Negroes

American Anomaly

● *With the prohibition of slavery in several Northern states*
and with programs for gradual emancipation in others before
the end of the eighteenth century, it was only natural that free
Negroes would, in due time, become a substantial element in the
population. It is also to be remembered that slavery had been
excluded from the Northwest Territory, though it persisted
there for several decades after 1787. There had been some free
Negroes during the entire colonial period; but for the most part
they were inconsiderable in number and inconsequential in
influence. The Revolution, with its philosophy of equalitarianism, had done much to increase the number of free Negroes, not
only in the North but in the South too, where many masters put
into practice the teachings of Jefferson. But in the South the
existence of a large group of free Negroes proved to be a source
of constant embarrassment to the slaveholders, for it tended to
undermine the very foundation on which slavery was built. The
perpetuation of relations existing between the whites and the
Negroes of the South was conditioned upon the indisputable
control of the latter by the former. Free Negroes, regardless of
what their rights were theoretically, could not be an exception.
It became necessary, therefore, for the Southerners to carry on
a campaign of vilification against the free Negroes in order to
"keep them in their place." In the heat of this campaign one

antagonist went so far as to describe free Negroes as "an incubus upon the land."

Despite Southern opposition to the presence of free Negroes, white persons themselves were frequently responsible for the increase. Masters, stricken by conscience, impelled by affection, or yielding to the temptation to evade responsibility, manumitted their slaves in large numbers until legislation either discouraged or prevented them altogether from doing so. Many slaves were freed by their masters through deeds of manumission. In some instances the manumitted were children of a master by one of his slaves. Others were manumitted through wills, like the slaves of John Randolph, numbering more than 400, who were set free upon his death in 1833. There were stipulations in some wills that the slaves should be set free upon reaching a certain age or upon the death of the testator's heirs. Either individual owners or the state manumitted slaves occasionally for meritorious services. The slave who saved the Georgia capitol from destruction by fire was set free in 1834. Pierre Chastang of Mobile was bought and freed by popular subscription because of his outstanding services in the War of 1812 and in the yellow fever epidemic of 1819.

Enterprising slaves were able to amass sufficient capital to purchase themselves, especially if their masters were willing to cooperate. There are several examples of masters who set up programs of self-hire for slaves who looked forward to purchasing themselves. Some slaves, regardless of their masters' point of view, saved enough money to purchase their freedom. Lunsford Lane of Raleigh, for example, spent his spare time making pipes, raising chickens, and engaging in other tasks in order to realize his ambition of becoming free. One could not always trust an owner who promised freedom upon the payment of a certain amount of money, as one of Lane's friends found out after he had given his owner $800 and had to run away. Thousands of free Negroes in the North and South secured their freedom by running away.

As their numbers increased by these various methods of obtaining freedom, they also multiplied through the natural excess of births over deaths. Children born of free Negro mothers were also free; and as the free Negro family achieved a degree of stability, children became an important factor in adding to their numbers. There was some increase, moreover, from the birth of mulatto children to white mothers. The prac-

Know all Men by these presents
that I Ebenezer Rothwell of St Georges
hundred and County of Newcastle and state
of Delaware. do for divers good Causes and
Reasons to me well known ~~myself~~
~~known~~ me hereunto moving do
Manumit Enfrancise and set at liberty
My Negro Man Isaac now my proper
Aged about twenty years when he the
Said Isaac shall have arived to the full
age of thirty ~~two~~ years — and I do for my
self my heirs Exrs admrs or assigns manumit
enfrancise and set at liberty my afsd.
Negro Man Isaac when he shall have
arived as aforesaid to afsd. age of thirty
two — years in witness whereof I have
hereunto set my hand and seal this
first day of April Anno. Domini. one
thousand Eight. Hundred
Witness present
Thomas Rothwell   Ebenr Rothwell Seal

DEED OF MANUMISSION. *Ebenezer Rothwell of Newcastle County, Delaware, promised to set free his 20-year-old slave, Isaac, when he reached the age of 32. Other popular forms of emancipation were by will and by legislative act. Original ms. Moorland Collection, Howard University.*

tice of white women mixing with Negro men was fairly wide-spread during the colonial period and had not entirely ceased by 1865.

There were 59,000 free Negroes in the United States at the time of the first decennial census in 1790. Slightly more than 27,000 were in the Northern states, and 32,000 in the Southern. In the next decade they increased approximately 82 per cent, and in the following decade by 71 per cent. After 1810 the rate of increase fell sharply, a trend that continued down to 1860. This decline was due largely to legal difficulties which masters encountered in trying to manumit slaves and to the opposition of those who viewed their increase with great alarm. Many states required Negroes to leave the state upon being manumitted. By 1830 there were 319,000 free Negroes in the United States, and thirty years later the number had climbed to 488,000, of whom 44 per cent lived in the South Atlantic states, and 46 per cent in the North. The remainder were to be found in the South Central states and the West. Maryland led all other states with 83,900 free Negroes in 1860, a figure only slightly smaller than the slave population. Virginia was next, with 58,000, followed closely by Pennsylvania with 56,000, her entire Negro population.

By 1860 free Negroes were concentrated in six areas: the tidewater counties of Virginia and Maryland; the Piedmont region of Virginia and North Carolina; the Southern cities of Baltimore, Washington, Charleston, Mobile, and New Orleans; the Northern cities of Boston, New York, Cincinnati, and Philadelphia; isolated areas in the old Northwest like Cass County, Michigan, Hammond County, Indiana, and Wilberforce, Ohio; and communities in which Negroes had mixed freely with Indians, such as those in Massachusetts, North Carolina, and Florida. Free Negroes were inclined to be urban. In 1860 there were 25,600 in Baltimore, 22,000 in Philadelphia, 12,500 in New York, 10,600 in New Orleans, and 3,200 in Charleston. The greater opportunities, both economic and social, doubtless accounted for their tendency to concentrate in cities.

Wherever free Negroes found themselves, they lived somewhat precariously upon the sufferance of the whites. Their legal status was fairly high during the colonial period and was strengthened somewhat during the revolutionary period. After that time, however, their status deteriorated, until toward the end of the slave period the distinction between slaves and free

Negroes had diminished to a point that in some instances was hardly discernible. Free Negroes found it especially difficult to maintain their freedom. A white person could claim, however fraudulently, that a Negro was a slave, and there was very little the Negro could do about it. There was, moreover, the danger of his being kidnapped, as often happened. The chances of being reduced to servitude or slavery by the courts were also great. A large majority of free Negroes lived in daily fear of losing what freedom they had. One slip or ignorance of the law would send them back into the ranks of slaves. Several states required registration, such as Virginia, Tennessee, Georgia, and Mississippi. Florida, Georgia, and several other states compelled free Negroes to have white guardians. All Southern states required them to have passes; and if one was caught without a certificate of freedom, he was presumed to be a slave.

The controls which the state and the community exercised over the free Negro mounted year by year. One especially annoying regulation limited his free movement. In no Southern state could he move about as he wished, and in some Northern communities it was dangerous to try, lest he be thought a fugitive slave. North Carolina prohibited free Negroes from going beyond the county adjoining the one in which they resided. Most seaboard states, as well as Alabama, Mississippi, and Louisiana, forbade free Negro sailors to leave their ships in port. As early as 1793 Virginia barred free Negroes from entering the state, and by 1835 most of the Southern and several Northern states had restricted or prohibited free Negro immigration. Penalties for violations of these laws were severe. In Georgia, for example, the offending free Negro was to be fined $100, and failing to pay it—which could be expected—he was to be sold into slavery. There were also laws against free Negroes leaving the state for any length of time, such as 60 or 90 days, and returning.

There was a mass of legislation designed to insure the white community against any threats or dangers from the free Negroes. Virginia, Maryland, and North Carolina were among the states forbidding free Negroes to possess or carry arms without a license. This permit was issued annually, and only to free Negroes whose conduct was above reproach. By 1835 the right of assembly had been taken away from almost all free Negroes in the South. They could not hold church services without the presence of a licensed and respectable white minister.

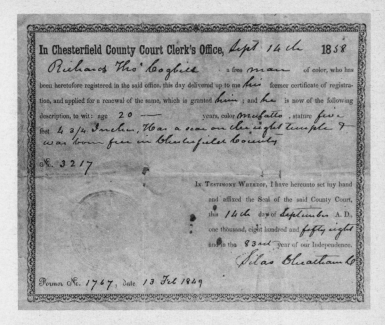

In Chesterfield County Court Clerk's Office, *Sept 14th* 1858

Richard Thos Coghill a free *man* of color, who has been heretofore registered in the said office, this day delivered up to me *his* former certificate of registration, and applied for a renewal of the same, which is granted *him*; and *he* is now of the following description, to wit: age *20* years, color *mulatto*, stature *five feet 4 3/4 Inches, Has a scar on the right temple & was born free in Chesterfield County*

No. *3217*

IN TESTIMONY WHEREOF, I have hereunto set my hand and affixed the Seal of the said County Court, this *14th* day of *September* A. D., one thousand, eight hundred and *fifty eight* and in the *83rd* year of our Independence.

Silas Cheatham C

Former No. *1767*, date *13 Feb 1849*

CERTIFICATE OF FREEDOM. Most communities required free Negroes to carry such a certificate on their person at all times. Not all of them provided printed forms such as this one, which was issued by the court clerk of Chesterfield County, Virginia. Original ms. Moorland Collection, Howard University.

Benevolent societies and similar organizations were not allowed to convene. In Maryland, free Negroes could not have "lyceums, lodges, fire companies, or literary, dramatic, social, moral, or charitable societies." In many communities the contact with slaves was kept at a minimum, and laws against entertaining slaves or visiting them were among those most strenuously enforced.

A number of proscriptions made it especially difficult for free Negroes to make a living. In 1805 Maryland prohibited free Negroes from selling corn, wheat, or tobacco without license. In 1829 Georgia made it illegal for free Negroes to be employed as typesetters. Two years later North Carolina required all Negro traders and peddlers to be licensed, while South Carolina forbade the employment of free Negroes as clerks. A large number of states made it illegal for Negroes either to purchase or to sell alcoholic beverages. A Georgia free Negro could not make purchases on credit without the permission of his guardian.

Despite these restrictions every state required free Negroes to work and their means of support had to be visible. As early as 1725 Pennsylvania had set the pattern by ordaining that "if any free negroe, fit to work, shall neglect so to do and loiter and misspend his or her time . . . any two Magistrates . . . are . . . impowered and required to bind out to service, such negroe, from year to year, as to them may seem meet." Other states passed similar laws during the national period, some going so far as to require free Negroes to post bonds as security against becoming public charges. Not only were adult free Negroes hired or bound out, but their children were taken and placed in the care of white persons. Illegitimate children, whose parents had violated some law or were without means of supporting them, were apprenticed out to be taught a trade and morally disciplined.

In some states the constitutions written during the revolutionary period did not exclude free Negroes from voting. They voted to a considerable extent in Maryland, North Carolina, New York, and Pennsylvania for several years. All Southern states entering the Union after 1789, except Tennessee, excluded Negroes from the franchise. Shortly after the beginning of the nineteenth century, as the campaign to reduce the free Negro's status got under way, states both North and South began to disfranchise him. Maryland's free Negroes lost the ballot in 1810. Those in Tennessee were disfranchised in 1834, followed by North Carolina the next year. Even Pennsylvania confined the privilege to white males in 1838, and Indiana in 1851. New York set up a property qualification of $250 and a residence requirement of three years for free Negro suffrage in her constitution of 1823. In states that did not disfranchise the Negro, his political influence was taken lightly and there was no extensive voting on his part anywhere after 1830.

Despite these significant reductions of status the free Negro was expected to bear the burdens that other citizens bore, and in some instances he was expected to do even more. In Pensacola, Florida, he had to pay a tax of $2 for putting on entertainments. In Baltimore, in 1859, he paid school taxes of $500, but his children were not allowed to attend these public-supported schools. In other places he was expected to pay school taxes, although his children were denied permission to attend. In general he was barred from serving in the state militia, except as a musician or a servant. Two significant exceptions were the

New York law of 1814 raising two regiments of Negroes and the Louisiana laws of 1812 authorizing a militia corps of free men of color and, in Natchitoches, a police corps of free Negroes.

The right to own and dispose of property was generally conceded to free Negroes. When Texas was a republic there was some question as to whether free Negroes could own land there, but their right had at least been partially recognized by the time Texas entered the Union in 1845. Only Georgia, in 1818, forbade free Negroes to own any real estate or slaves; but the following year the act was repealed, except for Savannah, Augusta, and Darien.

In courts of law the testimony of free Negroes was not admissible in cases where white persons were parties. Perhaps the clearest example of the disesteem in which the free Negro was held was the general policy of permitting slaves, viewed as wholly irresponsible before the law, to testify against free Negroes. In practice, however, the courts were fairly lenient to free Negroes. Indeed, from the courts, especially the higher ones, they received the greatest protection. In rejecting the claims of a white person that a Negro should be thrown out of court because he had not proved that he was free, the Maryland Court of Appeals said that, in pleading, he did not have to prove his freedom. A justice of the North Carolina Supreme Court went so far as to say that a free Negro could strike a white man in self-defense: "A free negro, however lowly his condition, is in the 'peace of the State,' and to deprive him of this right would be to put him on the footing of an outlaw."

Slaveholding states had a rather unusual way of demonstrating their interest in the welfare of free Negroes. Since the life of a free Negro was especially difficult, legislators were of the opinion that this class of persons should be given the opportunity to choose their masters and re-enslave themselves. In 1857 Tennessee enacted a law to facilitate re-enslavement. In the following year Texas enacted such a law, and in 1859 and 1860 respectively Louisiana and Maryland passed similar legislation. Several other states, including North Carolina, seriously considered such statutes, but for various reasons failed to enact them. Perhaps Arkansas went farthest: in 1859 the legislature passed an act to remove free Negroes and mulattoes by compelling those who remained in the state at the end of a year to choose masters "who must give bond not to allow such negroes to act as free."

Economic and Social Development

It was only natural that the free Negro should experience great difficulty in achieving anything resembling economic stability and independence. There was, first of all, the considerable psychological adjustment that had to be made in the transition from enslavement to freedom for all except those who were born free. The success and rapidity of this transition frequently depended upon the responsibility a person had been able to assume while still a slave. Another difficulty, almost insurmountable in some places, was the strong opposition of many white workers to Negroes, especially in the artisan class. Whites sought legislation barring them from certain trades; failing in this, they frequently resorted to intimidation and violence in order to eliminate the competition of free Negroes. Finally, there was the legislation which restricted the movements of free Negroes, barred them from certain occupations, and placed them at a disadvantage in other ways. The vast majority were without any special skills and had to content themselves with being agricultural workers or, in urban communities, common laborers. Thanks to the apprenticing system established in some states and to the practice of training many slaves as artisans, a considerable number of free Negroes possessed skills which enabled them to achieve a degree of economic independence and affluence before the Civil War.

Despite the strong opposition of white workers, urban free Negroes followed their trades if they had any. Even the unskilled found some kind of work to do, because they were concentrated in those areas that were losing white workers to the West, and in the shortage that prevailed even the labor of the despised Negro was welcomed. In Charleston, Dr. Charles H. Wesley found free Negroes engaged in more than fifty occupations, many of them requiring a high degree of skill. They worked in the building trades, made clothing and foods, operated machines, and piloted ships. There were more than 70 occupations in North Carolina in which free Negroes engaged. Among those working in Baltimore in 1860 were several confectioners, druggists, and grocers. Though there were only slightly more than two thousand free Negroes in Boston in 1860, they were scattered among nearly one hundred occupations, including paper-hanging, engraving, quarrying, photography, and tailoring. They also practised the professions of the ministry, teaching, law, and dentistry. Practically the same thing can be said for those in New York City and, to a less extent, in Cincinnati. In Philadelphia, in 1859, Negroes engaged in more than 130 occupations, all of which involved the exercise of skills. Even in the deep South there were free Negroes working in occupations and professions that would have disturbed those who were opposed to their progress, and surprised those who were convinced of their improvidence. In Atlanta, for example, Roderick Badger was practicing dentistry in 1859. In New Orleans there were teachers, jewelers, architects, and lithographers in 1860. Almost every community had its free Negro carpenters, barbers, cabinet makers, and brickmasons; many had shopkeepers, salesmen, and clerks, even where it was in violation of the law.

Aid given by organizations such as the Society of Friends, the Pennsylvania Society for the Abolition of Slavery, and the North Carolina Manumission Society helped free Negroes get a start, and this assistance frequently amounted to enough for them to acquire their first piece of property, usually personal. It will be remembered, moreover, that masters sometimes gave slaves real and personal property as well as their freedom. One benevolent master in Baltimore gave his manumitted slave a house and lot worth more than $12,000 in 1859. Several gave free Negroes as much as one hundred acres of land. Others sold them land at a nominal price. From these benevolences and from their own efforts, free Negroes gradually accumulated property. As early as 1800 those in Philadelphia owned nearly 100 houses and lots. By 1837, in New York City, they owned $1,400,000 worth of taxable real estate and had $600,000 on deposit in savings banks. In Cincinnati, free Negro property was valued at more than $500,000. These evidences of economic stability caused one European observer to describe them as "shrewd and sensible blacks. Some have amassed fortunes; and several conduct their businesses with considerable ability and integrity."

Free Negroes in the Southern states also accumulated property at a comparatively rapid rate. In Maryland they paid taxes on more than one million dollars of real property in 1860, and twelve owned property valued in excess of $5,000. Dr. Luther P. Jackson has found that in Virginia free Negroes in 1860 owned more than sixty thousand acres of farm land and their city real estate was valued at $463,000. In North Carolina they owned $480,000 worth of real property and $564,000 worth of personal property in 1860. In Charleston, 352 free Negroes paid taxes in 1859 on property valued in excess of $778,000. Tennessee's free Negroes owned about $750,000 worth of real and personal property in 1860. The affluence of a large number of free Negroes of New Orleans is well known. They owned more than $15,000,000 worth of property in 1860. Small wonder that in the preceding year the *Daily Picayune* was moved to describe them as "a sober, industrious, and moral class, far advanced in education and civilization."

The extent of slaveholding among free Negroes has been a matter of only recent concern to the student of history. The majority of Negro owners of slaves had some personal interest in their property. Frequently the husband purchased his wife or vice versa; or the slaves were the children of a free father who had purchased his wife; or they were other relatives or friends who had been rescued from the worst features of the institution by some affluent free Negro. There were instances, however, in which free Negroes had a real economic interest in the institution of slavery and held slaves in order to improve their economic status. This was true of Cyprian Ricard, who purchased an estate with 91 slaves in Louisiana, and of Charles Rogues and Marie Metoyer who had 47 and 58 slaves respectively. In the Charleston area, as well as around New Orleans, there were several free Negroes who had slaves in such great numbers as to indicate an economic interest in the institution. Free Negroes, on occasion, also employed white people to work for them. Thomas Day, North Carolina's best known cabinet maker, employed a white journeyman for several years. Jim Dungey, a free Negro wagoner of Nashville, Tennessee, had labor-management problems of his own, for in October, 1859, the *Republican Banner* reported that he "got into a fight with a white man in his employ."

Individual cases of affluence among free Negroes are numerous, and only a few will be cited. Solomon Humphries of Macon, Georgia, was a leading grocer in the city; before his death he accumulated property worth more than $20,000, including several slaves. Jehu Jones, proprietor of one of Charleston's best hotels, amassed a fortune of more than $40,000. James Forten, who had started out as an errand boy around the docks of Philadelphia, became a sailmaker and accumulated a fortune of more than $100,000. Thomy Lafon, the tycoon of New Orleans, was worth half a million dollars at his death. He had contributed so much to the development of the city that the state legislature ordered a bust of Lafon to be carved and set up in some public institution in New Orleans. Lafon, Forten, and the others, however, were not typical free Negroes. Much closer to the average was James Boon, a North Carolina artisan who, despite his excellence as a carpenter, spent most of his time trying to remain solvent and whose property, what little there was, was in the hands of his creditors more than his own.

In the beginning little social distinction was made in America on account of race. As the racial justification for slavery developed, there began to creep into the mores of American society a distinction between Negroes and whites. One of its first manifestations was the passage of laws against intermarriage. More and more, however, the real distinction came to be that between whites and those Negroes who had some claim to freedom. In the nineteenth century, as the slaveholding class found it necessary to establish safeguards for effective control of the free Negro, a veritable wall was erected around him, and he found it necessary to develop his own life and his own institutions. There existed between him and the rest of the world a minimum of communication, and even this communication steadily decreased.

The free Negro family evolved as a result of three lines of social relations: marriage within the group; marriage to slaves; and relations, legal or clandestine, with whites and Indians. The free Negro was not always subjected to the social controls which affected the rest of society. As a result, the relations out of which the free Negro family sprang were frequently adjudged immoral and uncivilized according to prevailing social conventions. When free Negroes married one another, however, they usually secured licenses and went through a civil or religious ceremony. The marriage of a free Negro to a slave, which could not be effected without consent of the slave's owner, was more frequently a rather informal union, for which no license was secured. Relations with white people were equally informal and consisted of a free Negro "taking up" with a white person or, as in New Orleans, a well-to-do white man maintaining a free Negro woman under a system of *placage* or concubinage. These relations, together with the manumission of free Negro children by white fathers, accounted for the 159,000 mulatto free Negroes in the United States in 1850.

There was little in the way of organized recreation for the free Negro. His pleasures came from the rather simple experiences of visiting, singing, or attending meetings of organizations to which he belonged. There was considerable drinking, though hardly as much as many of the whites thought. Gambling among themselves, with slaves, or with whites, all of which were criminal offenses, was another recreation for free Negroes. In urban areas they enjoyed the dances given by various societies and benevolent organizations. Cake-walks and balls were events in Baltimore to which many free Negroes looked forward. The best known of the dances were the quadroon balls in New Orleans and a few other Southern cities. These can hardly be called recreation for free Negroes, however, since only white men attended. The quadroons were either young women whom white men were keeping as concubines or those who were eligible for such relations. It was a source of pleasure and profit for the quadroons who attended. Only New York Negroes could boast of an "African Theater," which flourished for several years after it was founded in 1821.

Free Negroes held in high esteem their fraternal organizations and benevolent societies. The Masons continued to flourish during the generation immediately preceding the Civil War. In Maryland, for example, they had grown to the point by 1845 where it became desirable to form the First Colored Grand Lodge, and two years later another was set up. In 1843, under the leadership of Peter Ogden, a group of free Negroes organized the Grand United Order of Odd Fellows, which became one of the major Negro fraternal organizations. Negroes found it desirable to bind themselves together for social and cultural uplift, economic advancement, and mutualized relief. Thus, a large number of benevolent societies sprang into existence, some of which were secret. In Baltimore, there was one as early in 1821, composed of young free Negro men, and by 1835 there were 35. The Friendship Benevolent Society for Social Relief, the Star in the East Association, and the Daughters of Jerusalem were some of the more prominent organizations with substantial savings accounts in Baltimore banks. In other cities there were benevolent associations of mechanics, coachmen, caulkers, and other workers, suggesting that Negroes were organizing themselves into unions at about the same time as the whites. In the deep South these organizations were frowned upon by most whites and were outlawed altogether in many communities. They persisted, however, in some places. As late as 1860 they were being organized in New Orleans, where the Band Society, with a motto of "Love, Union, Peace," had by-laws requiring its members "to go about once in a while and see one another in love" and to wear the society's regalia on special occasions.

Important to the free Negro, as to the slave, was the church. Religious services offered opportunities for social intercourse as well as spiritual uplift. The independent church movement of the North continued to grow. The African Methodist Episcopal Zion Church increased its membership and extended its areas of operation. As Negroes moved West they founded churches of these sects, and maintained their connections with parent organizations. The African Methodist Episcopal Church began, in 1847, the publication of a weekly magazine, *The Christian Herald*, which was changed to *The Christian Recorder* in 1852. By maintaining national organizations the Negro Methodists were able to make their influence felt through important institutions in American life.

More free Negroes belonged to Baptist churches, but their influence was not as great as that of the Methodists because their churches were decentralized. Where a Negro Baptist church was associated with other churches, it was usually with white churches in the same area rather than with Negro churches elsewhere. While this was an important step in Americanization, it left Negro Baptists without much force among Negroes. There were strong Baptist churches in many Northern cities, including Philadelphia, New York, and Boston, and in some towns in the West, such as Cleveland, Cincinnati, Detroit, and Chicago.

The South generally proscribed Negro religious life between 1820 and 1860. Although the African Methodist Episcopal Church had made considerable headway in Charleston, for example, the organization was crushed by the weight of public opinion in 1822. Whites generally believed that Negro Methodists were implicated in the Denmark Vesey plot. Realizing the futility of trying to carry on against such odds, the Reverend Morris Brown, who later became a bishop, led his flock to the North. Other free Negro preachers in the South experienced even greater hardships. Although John Chavis was one of North

Carolina's most beloved Presbyterian ministers, he was not allowed to preach after 1831. Henry Evans, who organized the first Methodist Church in Fayetteville, North Carolina, would doubtless have been evicted from his post had he been living in 1831. Ralph Freeman, a well-known Baptist minister, was so determined to preach after 1831 that the Pee Dee Baptist Association of North Carolina felt compelled to publish a notice warning him to "refrain from making evening appointments of his own." White Episcopalians and Presbyterians solved the problem of free Negroes by admitting them to worship, usually in segregated sections of their churches. As an effective institution among free Negroes, the church declined before the outbreak of the Civil War.

One unique service that Negro religious leaders rendered was that of ministering to whites. Lemuel Haynes, the Revolutionary soldier, had set the example by his long service to white congregations in several Northern towns. Others were Samuel Ringgold Ward, pastor of a white congregation in Cortlandville, New York, and Henry Highland Garnet, who served a white church in Troy, New York. Many Southern Negro ministers, such as Freeman, Evans, and Chavis, preached to white congregations before the proscription laws of the twenties and thirties.

In Northern communities the opportunities for Negroes to secure an education widened in the nineteenth century. In many places, however, separate schools were maintained. Boston established them for Negro children in 1820, followed closely by other Massachusetts towns. Anti-slavery sentiment soon attacked the practice, and by 1855 both Boston and New Bedford permitted Negro children to attend white public schools. Rhode Island and Connecticut maintained separate schools, but in the last decade before the Civil War, larger funds were given to them. Not until 1824 did the New York Common Council begin to support African Free Schools. (See Chapter XI.) The city took them over altogether in 1834. Although some communities in the state permitted Negro children to attend white schools, the legislature made it clear in 1841 that any district could establish separate schools. New Jersey also maintained them for Negro children. The citizens of Pennsylvania continued to give both public and private support to their Negro schools as they increased in number, particularly in the western part of the state.

In the West, as more and more Negroes migrated, the citizens were faced with the problem of education too. Ohio excluded Negroes from public schools by law in 1829, and twenty years later provided for separate schools, but never appropriated enough funds to set up anything creditable. Citizens of Indiana and Illinois were equally indifferent. Michigan and Wisconsin adopted more democratic policies, but most Negroes in the West had to wait until after the Civil War before they were able to be educated in considerable numbers at public expense.

Free Negroes in the South experienced far greater difficulty. Public interest in education was extremely low. Since the responsibility for educating youth was largely a private one, the free Negro, who would not have benefited directly from public education, did not receive even the indirect benefits of contact with a more intelligent white populace. There was, moreover, very strong sentiment against educating free Negroes, because they were likely to imbibe seditious and incendiary doctrines through their reading. All the Southern states made it very difficult for them to secure an education by passing laws making it unlawful to instruct free Negroes. A surprisingly large number of them nevertheless learned at least the fundamentals. In Baltimore, for example, there were almost 200 adult Negroes studying in 1820. Five years later a day and night school was being maintained where many subjects were taught, including Latin and French. The Bethel Charity School, founded by Daniel Coker in 1816 as a part of the enlarged program of the African Methodist Episcopal Church, continued to flourish for a number of years. There were several other schools for free Negroes in Maryland.

Shortly after the settlement of the District of Columbia, several white teachers, including Henry Potter and one Mrs. Haley, taught Negro children. Later, Mrs. Maria Billings established a school in Georgetown. In 1807 several free Negroes, among them George Bell, Nicholas Franklin, and Moses Liverpool, built the first Negro schoolhouse in the District of Columbia. It was not until 1824, however, that there was a Negro teacher, John Adams, in the District. Then Negro schools began to increase in number and within a few years some of the best were to be found in Washington. Negro students came there from Maryland and Virginia to study under Negro teachers.

Free Negroes of Virginia and North Carolina received private instruction from whites and other free Negroes, but very little in schools. For almost thirty years John Chavis of Raleigh,

North Carolina, maintained a school in which he taught whites during the day and free Negroes in the evening, but after 1831 he confined his teaching to white children. The Negroes of Fredericksburg, Virginia, sought permission from the state legislature in 1838 to send their children to school out of the state, but their plea was summarily rejected. There is plenty of evidence, however, that many free Negroes in Virginia and North Carolina towns were being educated right down to the Civil War. In South Carolina their best opportunity to secure an education was provided in Charleston. As early as 1810 they had organized the Minor Society to school orphans, and other free Negroes also attended. In Florida some free Negroes sent their children away to school, while others hired teachers to instruct them, as in St. Augustine and Pensacola. New Orleans had several schools for free Negroes. The *Ecole des Orphelins Indigents*, set up in 1840, was generously supported by such wealthy free Negroes as Thomy Lafon, Madame Couvent, and Aristide Mary, who bequeathed it $5,000. Some Negroes went to France for an education, as did Edward Dede, who studied music in Paris.

From all this educational activity a more intelligent free Negro citizenry emerged. There is little doubt that free Negroes were eager to secure an education. Of 2,038 in Boston in 1850, almost 1,500 were in school. There were 1,400 at school in Baltimore and 1,000 in New Orleans. In the states and territories as a whole 32,629 Negroes were in school in 1860. In every community free Negroes were studying, with an apparent belief that education would solve some of their problems. Where opportunities did not exist, they sought to create them and gave enthusiastic support to their institutions. Just as Lafon and Madame Couvent set examples of philanthropy in New Orleans, so did free Negroes in other parts of the country. In several communities they organized Phoenix Societies with the special object of promoting the improvement of "Morals, literature and the mechanic arts. . . ." The "Mental Feast," a social feature, survived 30 years later in the interior towns of Pennsylvania and the West. It was a sign that Negroes were part of the great awakening that swept American education in the generation preceding the Civil War.

They also made a start in higher education. John Russwurm graduated from Bowdoin College in 1826, and before the Civil War Negroes were attending Oberlin, Franklin, and Rutland

Colleges, the Harvard Medical and other schools. The doors of several institutions that were to become colleges for Negroes opened during this period. In 1851 a young white woman of New York, Myrtilla Miner, went to Washington to establish an academy for Negro girls. So much opposition developed that the school was maintained only with difficulty. At the outbreak of the Civil War, it was still a small institution, but the idea had already been conceived for the college in Washington which long bore her name. In 1839 plans were made for an Institute for Colored Youth in Philadelphia. The school was incorporated in 1842, and began to flourish ten years later under the leadership of Charles L. Reason of New York. A bequest of $300,000 by the Rev. Charles Avery led to the establishment in 1849 of a college for Negroes that bore the benefactor's name in Allegheny City, Pennsylvania. With enough funds and an efficient faculty of both races this college flourished.

Two denominational institutions founded during the period that have continued to grow are Lincoln University in Pennsylvania and Wilberforce in Ohio. Lincoln, beginning as Ashmun Institute under Presbyterian sponsorship, was incorporated in 1854 and admitted its first students two years later. In 1855 the Cincinnati Conference of the Methodist Episcopal Church decided to raise money to establish a Negro college, which was incorporated the following year as Wilberforce University. Its early students were mainly the mulatto children of Southern planters. After a brief suspension at the beginning of the Civil War, it was reopened under the sponsorship of the African Methodist Episcopal Church.

One of the outstanding educational achievements of Negroes during this period was the appointment of several to the faculty of a white college. Charles L. Reason, William G. Allen, and George B. Vashon each held for a time the Professorship in Belle Lettres at Central College in McGrawville, New York. It was said that these teachers wore "the Professor's mantle gracefully, giving proof of good scholarship and manly character."

Negroes became much more articulate in ante-bellum years than they had been during the previous century. There emerged poets, playwrights, historians, newspaper editors, and others who expressed the Negro point of view to the world. In North Carolina, George Moses Horton, who was virtually free, wrote poems that were widely read. In 1829 he published a volume entitled *The Hope of Liberty*, and for the next 30 years wrote for students at the University of North Carolina and for various newspapers. Unfortunately, his interest in poetry diminished as he took to drink; perhaps he realized that for him there was no hope of liberty. Daniel A. Payne, who had a brilliant career as a bishop in the African Methodist Episcopal Church, published in 1850 a small volume, *Pleasures and Other Miscellaneous Poems.* Though they reveal little imagination, a critic said that "with his love of order and precision he had a sense of versification . . ." Frances Harper, whose *Poems on Miscellaneous Subjects* appeared in 1854, made her most significant contributions after the Civil War. The cultural life of Negroes in New Orleans was best represented by a group of seventeen poets, who issued in 1845 a book of poems entitled *Les Cenelles.* The editor, Armand Lanusse, and several contributors had lived or studied in France; and their work clearly shows the influence of Lamartine and Béranger.

The largest and perhaps most significant group of Negro writers were ex-slaves—fugitive or manumitted—who told the story of their experiences in "narratives." Frequently they were inspired and assisted by abolitionists who desired to use their writings as arguments against slavery. Some narratives, however, were the work solely of ex-slaves who had received the rudiments of an education. Because of their subjects, most of these have a dramatic quality that the imagination alone would have difficulty in achieving; though there is no reason to believe that all of the hair-raising episodes occurred just as they were told. Among Negroes who published their narratives between 1840 and 1860 were William Wells Brown (1842), Lunsford Lane (1842), Moses Grandy (1844), Frederick Douglass (1845), Lewis Clarke (1846), Julius Melbourne (1847), Henry Bibb (1849), J. W. C. Pennington (1850), Solomon Northup (1853), Austin Steward (1857), and J. W. Loguen (1859). Many more narratives were published during and after the Civil War. Despite their subjectivity, they are an important source for the study of slavery in America.

Some of these writers made other contributions. William Wells Brown described his foreign travels vividly in *Three Years in Europe* (1852) and was the first Negro to write a play, *The Escape; or a Leap to Freedom,* which appeared in 1858. J. W. C. Pennington, even before he published his narrative, had written a *Textbook of the Origin and History of the Colored People* (1841). A more capable historian, however, was

THE NARRATIVE OF FRED-
ERICK DOUGLASS. This is
one of many slave narratives
written in the ante-bellum period. Douglass wrote two other
autobiographies: My Bondage
and My Freedom (1855) and
The Life and Times of Frederick
Douglass (1881).

NARRATIVE

OF THE

LIFE

OF

FREDERICK DOUGLASS,

AN

AMERICAN SLAVE.

WRITTEN BY HIMSELF.

BOSTON:
PUBLISHED AT THE ANTI-SLAVERY OFFICE.
No. 25 CORNHILL
1845.

William C. Nell, whose *Services of Colored Americans in the
Wars of 1776 and 1812* first appeared in 1852. Three years
later it was issued in a substantially revised edition under the
title of *The Colored Patriots of the American Revolution with
Sketches of Several Distinguished Colored Persons to which Is
Added a Brief Survey of the Condition and Prospects of Colored Americans.* Nell was not alone in studying the condition of
Negro Americans. Martin R. Delany, a leading Negro physician who had studied at the Harvard Medical School, published
in 1852 *The Condition, Elevation, Emigration and Destiny of
the Colored People of the United States.* Seven installments of
his novel, *Blake; or the Huts of America,* appeared in the
Anglo-African Magazine in 1859. Similar books on the condition of Negroes indicated that they were becoming introspective and self-critical, an unmistakable sign of maturity and adjustment. In a class by itself, perhaps, was the work of Dr.
James McCune Smith of New York. In 1846 this graduate of
the medical college at the University of Glasgow published a
paper entitled, "Influence of Climate on Longevity, with Special Reference to Life Insurance."

Most of the Negro newspapers were concerned mainly with
the anti-slavery crusade. Best known were the first Negro paper,
Freedom's Journal, started by Samuel Cornish and John Russwurm in 1827, and *The North Star,* first published by Frederick Douglass in 1847. With its name changed in 1850 to
Frederick Douglass' Paper, for several years it enjoyed wide

circulation. Other short-lived papers were *The Mystery* (Pitts-
burgh, 1843); *The Colored Man's Journal* (New York, 1851);
The Mirror of the Times (San Francisco, 1855); and *The
Anglo-African* (New York, 1859).

The Struggle in the North and West

For thirty years before the Civil War, Negroes were migrating
North and West from the South. Not only were slaves running
away, but free Negroes were looking toward the North Star in
the hope of finding greater opportunities and better treatment.
They went to cities in the Northeast in large numbers, and also
to the Old Northwest along with white immigrants from Europe.
Between 1850 and 1860, for example, Michigan's Negro population jumped from 2,500 to 6,700; Iowa's more than tripled;
and California's increased from 962 to 4,086. The reaction to
this wholesale Negro migration was not pleasant. Northern
whites had shown no unusual hostility to Negroes who were
already in their midst, but they did not welcome the crude,
rough type which came from the South. Indeed, they hoped to
keep the West free not only of slavery but of the Negro as well.

Racial animosity grew in both the North and West, and in
many instances manifested itself in physical violence. In Philadelphia, in 1819, three white women stoned a Negro woman to
death. A few years later, the citizens adopted a policy of driving
Negroes away from Independence Square on the Fourth of July,
since they were considered not to have had any part in establishing the nation. In 1831 the people of New Haven, Connecticut,
became alarmed over the abolitionist proposal of Simeon Joce-
lyn to establish a Negro college, and resolved to oppose it with
all their resources. It will be remembered that when John Randolph's manumitted slaves were taken to Ohio, German settlers
opposed their presence so vigorously that Randolph's executor
had to find another place for them to settle. More than one
interracial fight on the California mining frontier grew out of
white resentment at Negroes being there.

Sometimes violence reached the proportions of riots. In 1830
a mob drove eight Negroes out of Portsmouth, Ohio. For three
days, in 1829, bands of white ruffians in Cincinnati took the law
in their own hands and ran out of the city those Negroes who

did not have the bonds required by law. More than a thousand found it advisable to leave. Negroes were also victims of the riot that occurred when the pro-slavery element of Cincinnati destroyed the office in which James G. Birney had published *The Philanthropist*, an anti-slavery newspaper. Defenseless Negroes were attacked in their homes, and many left the city. The fugitive slave riot of 1841 also involved many Negroes who were in no way connected with harboring fugitives.

In New York there were riots in Utica, Palmyra, and New York City in 1834 and 1839. The most serious anti-Negro outbreaks, however, took place in Pennsylvania. On August 12, 1834, a mob of whites marched down into the Negro section of Philadelphia and committed numerous acts of violence. The following day they wrecked the African Presbyterian Church, burned homes, and mercilessly beat up several Negroes. This reign of terror entered its third day before the police put an end to it. Similar uprisings occurred in 1835 and 1842. By the latter year a large number of whites were out of work, because of the severe depression, and when Negroes were celebrating the abolition of slavery in the West Indies, the unemployed broke up their parade, attacked scores of them, and burned the New African Hall and Presbyterian Church. State troops had to be called to assist the police in quieting the city. In 1839 there had been an outbreak in Pittsburgh during which the whites did considerable damage to the Negro section of the city by burning and pulling down dwelling houses.

The South enjoyed playing up Northern hostility to the Negro. When an observer said that in New York and Philadelphia the Negroes were noted chiefly for their "aversion to labor and proneness to villainy," he was quoted extensively in the Southern press. Southerners recounted with pleasure how a Georgia Negro returned after attempting to live in Ohio and Canada for two years, learning to dislike each place thoroughly. They also told of the Louisiana Negroes who suffered so much in New York City that they begged visiting Southerners to carry them back with them. When a North Carolina free Negro remarked that he had been kicked about and abused so much in Cincinnati that he would like to return, a Greensboro paper not only reported the incident, but reprinted the article five years later as though it had just happened.

There can be no doubt that many Negroes were sorely mistreated in the North and West. Observers like Fanny Kemble and Frederick L. Olmsted mentioned incidents in their writings. Miss Kemble said of Northern Negroes, "They are not slaves indeed, but they are pariahs, debarred from every fellowship save with their own despised race. . . . All hands are extended to thrust them out, all fingers point at their dusky skin, all tongues . . . have learned to turn the very name of their race into an insult and a reproach." Olmsted seems to have believed the Louisiana Negro who told him that Negroes could associate with whites more easily in the South than in the North. This Negro preferred to live South because he was more likely to be insulted in the North. Such points of views delighted slaveholders and confirmed their belief that slavery was better than freedom for the Negro.

Southerners did not seem to realize, however, that for the Negro the essential difference between the South and the North and West was that in the latter sections he had more of the law on his side and could therefore resist encroachments on his rights. Northern Negroes could organize and fight for what they believed to be their rights, and there was a substantial group of white citizens who gave them both moral and material support. In 1830 a convention of Negroes, with delegates from New York, Pennsylvania, Maryland, Delaware, and Virginia, met in Philadelphia "to devise ways and means for the bettering of our condition." James Forten, John B. Vashon, John T. Hilton, Samuel Cornish, and other leaders were present. They considered raising funds to establish a Negro college and to encourage Negroes to migrate to Canada. Many were opposed to these measures as unsound solutions to their problems, and indeed there were some who opposed the idea of a Negro convention at all.

For several years, however, these conventions met regularly, and the Negroes came to be joined by such leading white citizens as Arthur Tappan, John Rankin, and William Lloyd Garrison. In 1847, meeting at Troy, several delegates, including William C. Nell, urged that Negro students should seek admission to white colleges. Nell believed that diligent and outstanding Negro students would win the respect of enemies and convert them into friends. In 1850 a convention at Columbus, Ohio, resolved to resist all forms of oppression, promote universal education, and encourage Negroes to aspire to mechanical, agricultural, and professional pursuits.

In the decade preceding the Civil War, there were more

Negro conventions than ever before. They met in Rochester, Cleveland, New York, Philadelphia, and other cities. One of the most important, held at Rochester in 1853, saw the formation of a National Council of Colored People. A stirring memorial, signed by Frederick Douglass among others, was issued to the American people, asserting that "with the exception of the Jews, under the whole heavens, there is not to be found a people pursued with a more relentless prejudice and persecution, than are the free colored people of the United States." After reciting various ways in which they had been mistreated and humiliated, the memorial declared that no other race could have made more progress "in the midst of such an universal and stringent disparagement. It would humble the proudest, crush the energies of the strongest, and retard the progress of the swiftest. In view of our circumstances, we can, without boasting, thank God, and take courage, having placed ourselves where we may fairly challenge comparison with more highly favored men."

There were also conventions of special groups of Negroes. In 1848 the Citizens Union of Pennsylvania was organized to fight for first-class citizenship for Negroes. In 1850 the American League of Colored Laborers was formed in New York to promote cooperation among their fellows and to foster the education of young Negroes in agriculture, the mechanical arts, and commerce. In 1857 a convention called at Philadelphia concerned itself largely with denouncing the Dred Scott Decision.

These conventions were significant because they showed that the Negro population, a disadvantaged minority, resorted to the same techniques that were later employed by the Southern whites when they came to see that they were a hopeless minority too.

Colonization

The problem of what to do with Negroes who would not "adjust" to American life was an old one. It arose shortly after the arrival of the first Negroes in America. Banishment was an early punishment for the crimes of both whites and Negroes. As the number of free Negroes increased, it came to be felt that they must be sent out of the country if property in slaves was to be secure. Certainly there could be no complete discipline of slaves as long as free Negroes were in their midst. Even Northern communities felt that emancipation and concessions of equality were insufficient, because the two races could not always live together in harmony. The prevailing point of view was aptly summed up by J. C. Galloway of North Carolina who said, "It is impossible for us to be happy, if, after manumission, they are to remain among us."

As early as 1714 a "Native American," believed to be a resident of New Jersey, had proposed sending Negroes back to Africa. The idea did not die. Just after the War for Independence, Dr. Samuel Hopkins and the Reverend Ezra Stiles discussed the possibility of putting it into practice. In 1777 a Virginia legislative committee, headed by Thomas Jefferson, had set forth a plan of gradual emancipation and exportation. Several organizations for manumission, such as the Connecticut Emancipation Society, had as one of their objectives the colonization of free Negroes. Perhaps nothing brought colonization before the country more dramatically than the carrying of thirty-eight Negroes to Africa in 1815 by Paul Cuffe, at his own expense. His act suggested what might be done if more people, or even the government, became interested. It suggested, too, that Negroes themselves were interested in leaving the United States.

Within two years after Cuffe's voyage, the American Colonization Society was organized, with Justice Bushrod Washington as president and Henry Clay and John Randolph of Roanoke among its prominent members. Immediately plans were made to establish a Negro colony in Africa, with the aid of federal and state governments, and to educate public opinion to support the project. Agents were sent out to raise funds and to interest free Negroes in emigrating to Liberia, whose capital was honored with the name of President Monroe. Soon, thousands of dollars flowed into the Society for the purchasing and chartering of ships to transport Negroes. By 1832 more than a dozen legislatures had given official approval to the Society—even slaveholding states like Maryland, Virginia, and Kentucky. North Carolina, Mississippi, and other states had local colonization societies. At first, only free Negroes were transported to Africa. After 1827 some slaves who were manumitted expressly for this purpose were carried to Liberia. By 1830 the Society had settled 1,420 Negroes in the colony.

The Society's first ten years were its best. In 1831 the abolitionists, led by Garrison, once a friend of colonization, turned upon the scheme. Arthur Tappan, Gerrit Smith, and James G. Birney joined in the attack. Many auxiliary societies, desiring greater autonomy, seceded from the parent organization, which became insolvent in 1834. In Liberia, where the cost of living was high and the colony's affairs were mismanaged, many settlers were unhappy. Dark days thus descended upon the American Colonization Society, but it managed to struggle along for several years before it fell into complete desuetude in the decade before the Civil War.

Although the American Colonization Society comprised the largest group of persons interested in deporting the Negro, there were other groups and individuals no less interested. Southern newspapers, for example, did what they could to banish free Negroes. One Mississippi paper ran an advertisement of how pleasant a place Haiti would be for Negroes emigrating from the United States. Indeed, the Haitians were anxious to attract free Negroes to their island. A North Carolina newspaper urged free Negroes to solve their problems by emigration. It was suggested that they should go to Canada, Mexico, South America, or the American West. Few whites, however, supported the idea that free Negroes should move West after the great white migration began at the close of the War of 1812.

Despite all the schemes to deport free Negroes out of the United States, not fifteen thousand migrated. The American Colonization Society was responsible for most of them— approximately 12,000. To places other than Liberia there was less than a trickle of immigration. For several reasons all these schemes failed. In the first place, it was not economically practical to send to Africa or anywhere else such large numbers of Negroes as there were in the United States. The cost of transporting and maintaining several hundred thousand persons would run far into the millions if not billions of dollars; and there were not enough supporters of the idea to give it anything like a fair chance of success. In the second place, those who did support it were such a heterogeneous lot that in the long run they could not develop a program agreeable to all. Some advocates of colonization hoped to see an end to slavery and a return of all Negroes to their native land. They felt that whites were obligated to Negroes to this extent. Others supported the schemes because of their conviction that Negroes were basically incapable of adjusting themselves to Western civilization and would be better off in their original habitat. Still others saw in colonization an opportunity to carry Christianity and civilization to Africa. Slaveholders hoped, of course, to drain off the free Negro population, thereby giving greater security to the institution of slavery. Motives so incongruous as these doomed colonization. The attitude of Negroes themselves had a great deal to do with its failure.

Shortly after the formation of the American Colonization Society a group of free Negroes had met in Richmond and mildly approved of the idea of colonization; but they preferred to live elsewhere in the United States, possibly in the Missouri River Valley, rather than in Africa. Farther South, free Negroes who were weary of fighting a hopeless battle resigned themselves to colonization. The great majority of Negroes who went to Africa were from the slaveholding states. In the North, however, there was almost universal opposition to colonization, particularly in Africa. Three thousand Negroes of Philadelphia, led by Richard Allen and James Forten, met in 1817 and registered their objections to colonization, urging the "Humane and Benevolent Inhabitants of Philadelphia," to reject the scheme altogether. They branded it as an "outrage, having no other object in view than the benefit of the slaveholding interests of the country."

Within ten years opposition on the part of Negroes had risen to fever pitch. Meetings were held in Baltimore, Boston, New York, Hartford, New Haven, Pittsburgh, and many other cities. New York Negroes referred to the supporters of colonization as "men of mistaken views," while those of Lyme, Connecticut, described colonization as "one of the wildest projects ever patronized by enlightened men."

Every Negro convention opposed colonization, and their leaders spoke and wrote against the scheme. Martin R. Delany was especially hostile to the American Colonization Society, which he described as "anti-Christian in its character and misanthropic in its pretended sympathies." He denounced the leaders as "arrant hypocrites" who were conducting an organization that was obviously "one of Negro's worst enemies." The main motive of colonization, he claimed, was to eliminate Negroes from the United States, and for that purpose a government had been set up in Africa which was "not independent—but a poor miserable mockery—a burlesque on a government."

But not all Northern Negroes were opposed to colonization. Even Martin Delany thought that Negroes would prosper in

Central and South America, and upon one occasion he described these places as their future home in the New World. He also thought that Canada West (Upper Canada) would be a satisfactory home if it were not annexed to the United States. Such an eventuality, he said, would mean that the "fate of the colored man, however free before, is doomed, doomed, forever doomed." Several outstanding ministers supported colonization on the ground that it would extend Christianity to heathen lands. Among them were Alexander Crummell, who went to Africa in the interest of Christianity and colonization, and Daniel A. Payne, who spoke in their behalf on several occasions. Lott Cary and Colin Teague went to Liberia in 1821 under the auspices of the Richmond African Baptist Missionary Society and the General Baptist Missionary Convention. While Cary showed no enthusiasm for the policies of the American Colonization Society, he labored among the African settlers until his death in 1828. But colonization itself was doomed: the Negro was as permanent a fixture as there was in America.

Thus Negroes went through the terrible ordeal of moving toward freedom. It cannot be said even of the most fortunate that they were entirely free. They suffered indignities and insults, legal disabilities and economic privations, violent physical and verbal calumniations. Their reactions, even when sober and considered, were the reactions of a frustrated, stricken people. The mistreatment of free Negroes was not sectional. At best the situation in the North was tolerable only in a relative sense: it was better than in the South. Small wonder there was so much despair. Small wonder, too, that in the South a few free Negroes became slaves again. Too few of them saw that in the growing intersectional strife between North and South there was opportunity for the down-trodden and hope for the faint-hearted.

XV •

Slavery and Intersectional Strife

The North Attacks

● *The anti-slavery sentiment generated by the humanitarian* philosophy of the eighteenth century never completely died out in America. To be sure, there was a period of quiescence as the South found new opportunities for the profitable employment of slaves and as the North became concerned with her own economic and political problems. But some people continued to oppose slavery as an institution, and long before militant abolitionists appeared on the scene around 1830 the most convincing arguments against slavery had already been developed. Soon after the War of 1812 sectionalism was apparent as the North swung to manufacturing; and the South, still wedded to an agrarian civilization, came to see clearly that the interests of the two sections were becoming antagonistic. Indeed, the industrial development of the North changed the point of view of this section; as people there were brought closer together, they sought through cooperation to solve their pressing problems. In the South, however, the plantation system tended to preserve frontier independence: there was no communal life, no civic responsibility, and no interest in various programs for the improvement of mankind. The contest over Missouri, moreover, crystallized the sectional conflict and emphasized the importance of slavery as a national issue.

Anti-slavery sentiment in the North increased almost daily after 1815, as more ministers, editors, and other leaders of public opinion spoke out against the evils of the institution. Several years passed before almost all these critics were confined to the North. In 1817 Charles Osborn published *The Philanthropist,* an anti-slavery paper, in Ohio, but two years later he moved to Tennessee and published the *Manumission Intelligencer.* In 1820 Elihu Embree was publishing the *Emancipator* in Jonesboro, Tennessee, while William Swaim was expressing the opposition of Quakers to slavery in his *Patriot,* published at Greensboro, North Carolina. In 1821 the itinerant Benjamin Lundy began editing the *Genius of Universal Emancipation,* in which he set forth a complete program for the emancipation and colonization of Negroes. Although he lacked the emotional fervor of later abolitionists, he was not without courage and devotion to the cause of freeing the slaves.

Within ten years after the beginning of Lundy's work, three events indicated that the age of the militant abolitionists had arrived. These events were the publication of David Walker's *Appeal,* the appearance of William Lloyd Garrison's *The Liberator,* and the insurrection of Nat Turner, which many thought was inspired by the activities of men like Garrison. David Walker was a North Carolina free Negro who had moved to Boston, where he engaged in selling second-hand clothes. His bitter hatred for slavery was not diminished by his leaving the South. If anything, it was increased. In September, 1829, his essay appeared: *Walker's Appeal in Four Articles Together with a Preamble to the Colored Citizens of the World But in Particular and very Expressly to those of the United States of America.* It was one of the most vigorous denunciations of slavery ever to be printed in the United States. In unmistakable language he called upon Negroes to rise up and throw off the yoke of slavery:

> Are we men!! I ask you . . . are we MEN? Did our creator make us to be slaves to dust and ashes like ourselves? Are they not dying worms as well as we? . . . How we could be so *submissive* to a gang of men, whom we cannot tell whether they are as good as ourselves or not, I never conceive. . . . America is more our country than it is the whites—we have enriched it with our *blood and tears.* The greatest riches in all America have arisen from our blood and tears: And they will drive us from our property and homes, which we have earned with our blood.

Walker closed his appeal by quoting the Declaration of Independence to show that Negroes were justified in resisting, with force if necessary, the oppression of white masters. A startled country read the words of this Negro who called for militant action.

In January, 1831, the first issue of Garrison's *Liberator* appeared. Garrison had served his novitiate as Lundy's assistant on the *Genius of Universal Emancipation* and in jail for libelous words against a ship captain who had transported slaves to New Orleans. He was done with gradualism as a means of emancipating slaves; he had shifted from supporting colonization to opposing it. In the first issue of his newspaper he also invoked the Declaration of Independence, claiming that the Negro was as much entitled to "life, liberty and the pursuit of happiness" as the white man. Immediate and unconditional abolition of slavery was, from his point of view, the only solution. He laid down his challenge to slavery in most dramatic language when he said:

> I *will be* as harsh as truth, and as uncompromising as justice. On this subject, I do not wish to think, to speak, or write, with moderation. . . . I am in earnest—I will not equivocate—I will not excuse—I will not retreat a single inch—AND I WILL BE HEARD.

Thus Garrison became the most articulate spokesman of militant abolition. For a whole generation he was one of the most important forces working for the freedom of slaves. It was an auspicious beginning for an exciting career. Small wonder that people in the South connected the "incendiary" writings of Walker and Garrison with the insurrections of Nat Turner and of others. These three events heralded a new approach to the problem of slavery in America.

The militant anti-slavery movement that had developed by 1831 was, in itself, a powerful religious crusade—part of the larger humanitarian movement sweeping Europe and the northern United States. It stemmed from the growing popular concern for the welfare of underprivileged persons which manifested itself in the anti-slavery movement, the crusade for better working conditions in England, and the search for a better life in America. It was closely connected, in many respects, with movements for peace, women's rights, temperance, and other reform programs that developed simultaneously. In the West, it was connected with the Great Revival, of which Charles G.

Finney was the dominant figure, emphasizing the importance of being useful and thus releasing a powerful impulse toward social reform. The young converts joined Finney's Holy Band, and if the abolition of slavery was a way of serving God, they were anxious to enter into the movement wholeheartedly.

The abolitionists worked out in time an elaborate argument against the perpetuation of slavery. In the first place, they insisted that it was contrary to the teachings of Christianity, since Jesus taught the doctrine of universal brotherhood and one of the cardinal principles of Christianity was that all men were created in the image of God. James G. Birney's *Letter to the Ministers and Elders* (1834) and Theodore Weld's *The Bible Against Slavery* (1837) carried these religious arguments against slavery to their conclusion. In the second place, the abolitionists contended that slavery was contrary to the fundamental principles of the American way of life, which valued freedom as an inalienable right for the individual. Slaves were denied this right: they had no freedom in seeking employment, no religious freedom, no marriage or family rights, no legal protection, and few opportunities to secure an education. They also contended that slavery was economically unsound, because the workers could not be expected to be efficient and there was such a waste of physical and human resources in the plantation economy. The culture and civilization of the South suffered, moreover, for the master-slave relationship did not produce a gentility of spirit, but brought out instead the baser aspects of the nature of both. Theodore Weld expressed this view succinctly, pointing out that domination of one person by another is essentially uncivilized, when he said, "Arbitrary power is to the mind what alcohol is to the body; it intoxicates." Finally, the abolitionists condemned slavery as a menace to the peace and safety of the country. The South was becoming an armed camp, where the whites lived in constant fear of a widespread uprising of slaves, and this fear generated violence and was the cause of bloodshed.

Although the anti-slavery forces had for years believed that colonization was one way of relieving the country of its dreaded Negro problem, militant abolitionists were, on the whole, unalterably opposed to colonization. They were suspicious of it because of the support it received from slaveholders, who could not be interested in putting an end to slavery as an institution. Abolitionists felt, as the great majority of Negroes did, that colonization was primarily for the purpose of draining off the free Negro population in order to make slavery even more secure. Garrison said that the American Colonization Society had "inflicted a great injury upon the free and slave population; first by strengthening the prejudices of the people; secondly, by discouraging the education of those who are free—thirdly, by inducing passage of severe legislative enactments—and, finally, by lulling the whole country into a deep sleep." Even more vigorous denunciations appeared in his *Thoughts on Colonization,* published in 1832.

With principles of their own, not necessarily equalitarian, the abolitionists were now ready to organize and to wipe out the institution of slavery. In 1831 the New England Anti-Slavery Society was formed. Beginning with a small group of fifteen, Garrison imbued his followers with the idea of immediate emancipation. As their numbers grew, they became more radical and vociferous, the very voice of Garrison. Some, especially in New York and Philadelphia, were from the beginning opposed to Garrison's radical views. Encouraged by the abolition of slavery in the British empire, this moderate group did much to bring about the organization of the American Anti-Slavery Society in Philadelphia in 1833. Arthur Tappan, wealthy New York merchant, was the first president. Other important leaders were Theodore Weld, James G. Birney, William Goodell, Joshua Leavitt, Elizur Wright, Samuel May, and Beriah Green, most of whom had been active in local anti-slavery societies. The organization was dominated by Garrison, however, and when it issued a declaration of sentiments he was successful in getting his views incorporated in the document. A publicity program was drawn up and carried out largely by the New York group. Four periodicals were published: *Human Rights, Anti-Slavery Record, Emancipator,* and *Slave's Friend.* Pamphlets were distributed throughout the North and, when possible, in the South. Through its many agents, local units were organized and money was raised to further the program of emancipation. In 1836 there were seventy lecturers in the field, drawn largely from the ministry, theological seminaries, and colleges.

In the West the anti-slavery movement had become a crusade by 1830. Most of the leaders who left the South went West: James G. Birney came from Alabama to Kentucky and thence to Ohio. Levi Coffin left North Carolina and carried on his abolition activities in Indiana. Later, these men were joined by others who had found the atmosphere of their home communities peculiarly hostile to anti-slavery ideas. After Theodore Dwight Weld arrived at the Lane Theological Seminary in Cincinnati, the students there were encouraged to discuss the problem of slavery; and the free and open debates won many people, including Southerners, to the cause of abolition. The students put their views into practice by going out into the community to organize groups to assist the Negro; and they instructed Negro youth and participated in the dangerous activities of the Underground Railroad. When the students withdrew from Lane rather than submit to a conservative administration, they went in large numbers to Oberlin College, where a theological department was established with funds provided by such anti-slavery philanthropists as Arthur and Lewis Tappan of New York. From that time on Oberlin became an important center of anti-slavery activity. Western Reserve was another college from which students went forth imbued with anti-slavery ideas. Perhaps at no other time in American history have the colleges played such an important part in a program of social reform.

The zealous Garrison was impatient even with a national organization like the American Anti-Slavery Society, all of whose members were committed to a crusade for the immediate abolition of slavery. They did not press hard enough; they were unwilling to concede equality to women as leaders of the movement; and they hesitated to criticize the churches for not taking an unequivocal stand. In 1839 Garrison and his followers decided to seize control of the national organization. At a convention the following year Garrisonians were elected to the important offices and women were given places of responsibility. The New York group, opposed to this bid of Garrison for power, organized under Lewis Tappan the American and Foreign Anti-Slavery Society. It was friendly to the churches and sought to end slavery by moral suasion; it believed that political action was necessary to overcome constitutional and legal obstructions to emancipation.

The members of this new society became the nucleus of the Liberty Party which was organized in 1840. In two successive presidential campaigns they nominated James Birney, but at the peak of their strength in 1844 he polled only 60,000 votes. The dismal results proved conclusively that, although millions of people were opposed to slavery, a political party had to offer more than an anti-slavery platform in order to win their support. The Republican Party was to demonstrate in the next decade that it had learned this lesson.

By 1840, when the energies of the abolitionists were split into two national bodies, effective work was done by state and local organizations. They maintained agents in the field, published newspapers, and distributed anti-slavery literature throughout the country. Garrison remained strong to the end in New England. Among his followers he could list John Greenleaf Whittier, the poet of abolition; Wendell Phillips, "abolition's golden trumpet;" and women like Lucretia Mott, Lydia Maria Child, and Maria Weston Chapman. In the border states and the West, however, Birney and Weld were strong, and unlike Garrison they continued to counsel moderation and to insist upon political action.

While "Garrisonism" met more opposition than other forms of abolition, there was always much sentiment, even in the North, against any kind of anti-slavery agitation. David M. Reese, for example, called the American Anti-Slavery Society the "purest of all humbugs;" and Bishop John H. Hopkins of New Hampshire opposed it because he was convinced that Negroes were better off as slaves than as free men. The opposition to abolition frequently became violent. Elijah P. Lovejoy was run out of St. Louis for criticizing the leniency of a judge in the trial of persons accused of burning a Negro alive. Later, in Alton, Illinois, he was killed when a mob destroyed for the fourth time the press on which he printed the *Alton Observer*. In Cincinnati a mob destroyed James Birney's press in 1836, and he barely escaped with his life.

Anti-slavery lecturers often found it difficult to rent halls in which to speak. Even if they succeeded, they could not be certain that their program would go off as planned, for many a meeting was broken up by mobs. Even women who supported the anti-slavery crusade were in danger of having insults and indignities heaped upon them. When Prudence Crandall, a Quaker teacher, admitted a Negro to her school in Canterbury, Connecticut, white patrons boycotted it. After she decided to open a school for Negro girls, with the aid of abolitionists like Garrison and Lewis Tappan, the citizens showed that they would not stand for it. They broke windows, insulted Miss Crandall, and had her arrested for violating a state law which forbade the teaching of Negroes who were not residents of the state.

Abolitionists could expect little help or protection from the federal government. As early as 1828 they submitted a petition to Congress to abolish slavery in the District of Columbia, but nothing was done about it. As petitions began pouring in against slavery, the House of Representatives adopted a rule in 1836 providing that such petitions were to be received and laid on the table. This "gag rule," as abolitionists dubbed it, was vigorously opposed by men like John Quincy Adams of Massachusetts and Joshua Giddings of Ohio, but it was not rescinded until 1845. As long as it stood, abolitionists complained that the sacred right of petitioning the legislature for a redress of grievances was being denied.

It was the countenancing of violence by abolitionists that won them the enmity of many law-abiding citizens and rendered utterly hopeless their schemes to obtain government support. Convinced that slaveholders had the law of the land on their side, the abolitionists resorted to the principle of a "higher law" which they felt justified them in circumventing or breaking the law. Garrison and his followers openly praised the violence of the Nat Turner insurrection. In 1839 Jabez Hammond of New York said that only force would end slavery and that Negro military schools should be set up in Canada and Mexico. When slaves revolted aboard the *Creole* on its voyage from Hampton Roads to New Orleans, Representative Joshua Giddings not only opposed treating the slaves as common criminals but even praised them for seeking freedom. The House of Representatives, shocked by his open defiance of the law, censured Giddings. Forthwith he resigned, went home to Ohio, and was immediately returned to Congress by his anti-slavery constituency. The redoubtable Giddings later praised other Negroes and whites for seeking to abolish slavery, and finally the House became accustomed to his tirades against the institution. By 1850 the philosophy of force was so integral a part of abolitionist doctrine that many viewed it as a movement in the direction of anarchy.

Black Abolitionists

The whites were not alone in their opposition to slavery. From the beginning the Negro, who suffered most from the subjugation of his race, gave enthusiastic support to abolition. Indeed, strong abolitionist doctrine was preached by Negroes long before Garrison was born. Before the War for Independence, slaves in Massachusetts brought actions against their masters for the freedom which they regarded as their inalienable right. During and after the Revolutionary War, Negroes sought the abolition of slavery by petitioning the state and federal governments to outlaw the slave trade and to embark upon a program of general emancipation. Prince Hall, Benjamin Banneker, Absolom Jones, and Richard Allen issued strong denunciations of slavery before 1800, and organizations like the Free African Society of Philadelphia passed resolutions calling for its abolition. In the nineteenth century Negroes organized anti-slavery societies. By 1830 they had fifty groups, one that was very active in New Haven, and several in Boston, New York, and Philadelphia. One of the strongest was located in New York and named after the famous English anti-slavery leader, Thomas Clarkson.

The year 1829 was especially significant for black abolitionists. Out of Boston there came David Walker's *Appeal,* a blast against slavery, and out of Raleigh, North Carolina, the protest of George Moses Horton in his *Hope of Liberty.* Horton cried out,

> Bid Slavery hide her haggard face,
> And Barbarism fly:
> I scorn to see the said disgrace
> In which enslaved I lie.

It was in 1829, too, that Robert A. Young published his *Ethiopian Manifesto, issued in defence of the black man's rights, in the scale of universal freedom.* He prophesied, like Walker, that from the Negroes there would arise a messiah with the strength to liberate his people. Young did not create as much alarm as Walker, although he advocated measures fully as drastic to end slavery.

When the period of militant abolitionism began, Negroes were ready to join whites in fighting the hated institution. They organized their first national convention in the year before the publication of Garrison's *Liberator,* and issued strong denunciations of colonization and slavery which left no doubt in the minds of America where they stood. The eagerness of black abolitionists to join the movement for liberation is demonstrated by their reaction to the appearance of the *Liberator.* Most of the twenty-five subscribers to the first issue were

Negroes, and one enthusiastic, affluent black abolitionist sent Garrison a gift of $50. Such contributions helped to make possible his first trip to England.

Negroes were especially active in organizing the American Anti-Slavery Society. Members whose duty it was to draw up the Declaration of intentions met in Philadelphia at the home of a Negro, Frederick A. Hinton. Six Negro leaders served on the first board of managers: Peter Williams, Robert Purvis, George B. Vashon, Abraham Shadd, and James McCrummell. These Negro "Founding Fathers" were men of many interests and talents. For example, Purvis, born in Charleston of a well-to-do white father who generously provided for him, had attended Amherst College and was active in many local causes, including the Underground Railroad. Vashon, a graduate of Oberlin College, was a poet, lawyer, and teacher. At most of the annual meetings there were Negro delegates who spoke out frequently. When the American and Foreign Anti-Slavery Society was organized, Negroes were no less active in that body. Among those who joined in promoting the organization that was committed to political action were Christopher Rush, Samuel Cornish, Charles B. Ray, and James W. C. Pennington.

To local and regional anti-slavery organizations, which carried the burden of work, Negroes gave their time, energy, and money. The first presiding officer of the Philadelphia Female Anti-Slavery Society was a local dentist, Dr. James McCrummell. Frederick Douglass was elected president of the New England Anti-Slavery Society in 1847. Vigilance committees, set up to raise funds to help slaves escaping to freedom, were frequently dominated by Negroes. In 1835 David Ruggles became secretary of the New York committee and remained active until his eyesight failed him. In Philadelphia, Robert Purvis had charge of the first vigilance committee, which was headed several years later by William Still.

Negroes were prominent in the abolition movement as agents and speakers for the various societies. Several were full-time employees of local or national bodies. Among the better known agents were Frederick Douglass, Theodore S. Wright, William Jones, Charles Lenox Remond and his sister Sarah, Frances E. W. Harper, Henry Foster, Lunsford Lane, Henry Highland Garnet, Charles Gardner, Andrew Harris, Abraham Shadd, David Nickens, James Bradley, and William Wells Brown. A notable black abolitionist was Isabella, better known as Sojourner Truth. From New York she traveled through New England and the West, moving audiences by her quaint speech, and a deep, resonant voice, and the hatred for slavery which she expressed with a strange, religious mysticism.

White abolitionists took great pride in introducing Negro agents to doubting audiences to demonstrate what Negroes could do if given opportunity. They were among the best speakers. On one occasion, after Douglass had electrified his audience with his remarkable eloquence, Garrison rose to his feet and flung out the question, "Is this a man or a thing?" Henry Highland Garnet spoke with a "terrible pride," and William Wells Brown made a favorable impression wherever he went. Small wonder that many of these speakers were encouraged to carry the message of American abolition to Europe. More than a score of the black abolitionists went to England, Scotland, France, and Germany; among them were Douglass, Brown, Remond, Pennington, Garnet, Nathaniel Paul, Ellen and William Craft, Samuel Ringgold Ward, Sarah Parker Remond, and Alexander Crummell. Almost everywhere they were received with enthusiasm and were instrumental in linking up the humanitarian movement in Europe with various reform movements on this side of the Atlantic.

Black abolitionists wrote as well as spoke for the emancipation of Negroes. Most of the Negro newspapers founded before the Civil War were abolitionist sheets. Perhaps the outstanding journalist was Samuel Cornish, who with John Russwurm had established the first Negro newspaper, *Freedom's Journal*, in 1827. Two years later, Cornish began his second venture, *Rights of All*, an extremely radical but short-lived paper. In 1836 he published the *Weekly Advocate*, and in the following year, with the help of Charles B. Ray and Phillip A. Bell, he edited the *Colored American*. Other black abolitionist newspapers were the *National Watchman*, edited by William G. Allen and Henry Highland Garnet, the *Mirror of Liberty*, a quarterly issued by David Ruggles, and of course the *North Star* of Frederick Douglass.

Douglass was the outstanding black abolitionist. A fugitive slave, he was first introduced to the movement when, in 1841, he attended an anti-slavery convention in Nantucket, Massachusetts. After speaking there he was employed by several societies and rapidly became one of the best known orators in the United States, lecturing in the North and East, and even in England.

The narrative of his life was published in 1845. Two years later he started the *North Star,* an incident which led to his break with Garrison, previously one of his chief sponsors. Douglass was active in Negro conventions, the Underground Railroad, and many other efforts to improve the conditions of his race. He was endowed with the physical attributes of an orator: a magnificent, tall body, a head crowned with a mass of hair, deep-set, flashing eyes, a firm chin, and a rich, melodious voice. Few anti-slavery leaders did so much to carry the case of the slave to the people of the United States and Europe in the generation before the Civil War.

In their militant bitterness the black abolitionists equaled and sometimes surpassed their white brethren. David Walker was by no means alone in demanding violence. In 1844 the Rev. Moses Dickson established in Cincinnati an "order of Twelve of the Knights and Daughters of Tabor" to help overthrow slavery. Two years later he organized the Knights of Liberty in St. Louis. In 1843 Henry Highland Garnet made an address to the Buffalo Convention of Colored Citizens that shocked even many abolitionists: "Brethren, arise, arise! Strike for your lives and liberties. Now is the day and the hour. Let every slave throughout the land do this and the days of slavery are numbered. Rather die freemen than live to be slaves. . . . Awake, Awake, millions of voices are calling you! Let your motto be resistance; no oppressed people have secured their liberty without resistance." Although many Negroes viewed his utterances with alarm, by 1854 the Negro conventions were ready for violence. A resolution adopted at that time declared that "those who, without crime, are outlawed by any Government can owe no allegiance to its enactments [and] . . . we advise all oppressed to adopt the motto, 'Liberty or Death.' " Indeed, the Negroes had become as ardent in their "Garrisonism" as any follower of the high priest of abolitionism.

The Underground Railroad

Perhaps nothing did more to intensify the strife between North and South, and to emphasize in a most dramatic way the determination of abolitionists to destroy slavery in their own way, than the Underground Railroad. Slaves who ran away were irritating and troublesome enough, and the South had been plagued with them from the earliest days of slavery. But when free Negroes and whites, fired with an almost fanatical zeal, undertook systematically to wreak havoc on an institution that meant so much to the social and economic life of a people, it was almost too much to bear. It was this organized effort to undermine slavery, this manifestation of the workings of the "higher law," that put such a strain on intersectional relations and sent antagonists and protagonists of slavery scurrying head-long into the 1850's determined to have their uncompromising way.

The origin of the Underground Railroad goes back into the eighteenth century. Perhaps there were people to help fugitives as early as there were runaway slaves. By the end of the War for Independence, however, organized resistance seemed to be taking shape. At least George Washington thought so when he complained in 1786 of a slave, escaping from Alexandria to Philadelphia, "whom a society of Quakers, formed for such purposes, have attempted to liberate." By the following year Isaac T. Hopper had settled in Philadelphia, and though still in his 'teens he began to develop a program for the systematic assistance of slaves escaping from the South. Within a few years they were being helped in a number of towns in Pennsylvania and New Jersey. Slowly these anti-slavery operations spread in various directions.

Henrietta Buckmaster gives 1804 as the year of "incorporation" of the Underground Railroad. It was then that General Thomas Boude, an officer during the Revolution, purchased a slave, Stephen Smith, and brought him home to Columbia, Pennsylvania, followed by Smith's mother, who escaped and came to find her son. The Boudes took her in. Within a few weeks the woman who owned Smith's mother arrived and demanded her property. Not only did the Boudes refuse to surrender the slave, but the town supported them. The people of Columbia resolved to champion the cause of fugitives. By 1815 this sentiment was expressed in Ohio. And by 1819 underground methods were used to spirit slaves out of North Carolina. Even before the period of militant abolitionism the movement that was to be known as the Underground Railroad had grown into a widespread institution.

The name "Underground Railroad" was probably coined shortly after 1831 when steam railroads became popular. There are several versions of how the movement got its name. A plausible one concerns a slave, Tice Davids, who escaped from his Kentucky master in 1831 and got across the Ohio River. Although the master was in hot pursuit, he lost all trace of the slave after crossing the river, and was so confounded that he declared the slave must have "gone off on an underground road." That was entirely possible, for by 1831 there were plenty of "underground" roads on the Ohio River, and they had stations, conductors, and means of conveyance. From that time, which coincided exactly with the emergence of Garrison and his militant followers, down to the outbreak of the Civil War, the Underground Railroad operated in flagrant violation of the federal fugitive slave laws. It was the most eloquent defiance of slaveholders that abolitionists could make.

In the case of anything so full of adventure and danger as the Underground Railroad, it is difficult to separate fiction from fact. There are stories of breath-taking escapes and exciting experiences that would be quite incredible save for unquestionable verification by reliable sources. After the Railroad had developed an efficient organization, there was a generality of practice that makes possible a brief description of its operation. All, or almost all, of the operations took place at night, for that was the only time when the fugitive and his helpers felt even partially secure. Slaves prepared to make their escape by taking supplies from their masters and, if it was felt necessary, by disguising themselves. Those of fair complexion frequently passed as white persons and sometimes posed as their own masters. Darker ones posed as servants on their way to meet their owners. There are several cases on record where fugitives were provided at crucial moments with white babies in order to make their claims of being nurses appear more convincing. At times men posed as women and women as men.

In the early days of the Underground Railroad most of the fugitives were men and they usually traveled on foot. Later, when the traffic was heavy and women and children were fleeing from the South, escorts were used and vehicles provided. The conductors carried their human cargo in covered wagons, closed carriages, and farm wagons specially equipped with closed compartments. Negroes were sometimes put in boxes and shipped as freight by rail or boat. Thus Henry Box Brown was shipped from Richmond to Philadelphia by the Adams Express Company. When traveling by land—and at night—conductors and fugitives were guided by the North Star, by tributaries of the Ohio or other rivers, and by mountain chains. On cloudy nights, when there were no other means of finding directions, they even resorted to feeling the moss on tree trunks and moving north upon discovering it.

Since travel was almost exclusively at night, it was necessary to have stations rather close together, from ten to twenty miles apart, where fugitives could rest, eat, and wait for the next night's journey. During the day they were hidden in barns, in the attics of homes, and in other out-of-the-way places. Meanwhile, the word was passed to succeeding stations, by what was called "the grape vine telegraph," that fugitives were on their way. One ambiguous message mailed by a conductor to the next stationmaster in 1859 gave much more information than a casual glance revealed. It read: "By to-morrow evening's mail, you will receive two volumes of 'The Irrepressible Conflict' bound in black. After perusal, please forward and oblige."

All Underground Railroad lines led North. They began on various plantations in the South and ran vaguely—and dangerously—up rivers and valleys, and across mountains to some point on the Ohio or upper Mississippi River in the West, and to

RESURRECTION OF HENRY BOX BROWN. Among the many ways by which slaves escaped to the North was shipment as merchandise. Brown was shipped from Richmond to Philadelphia, a trip requiring 26 hours. The white men in the drawing are J. M. McKim, Professor C. D. Cleveland, and Lewis Thompson; the Negro is William Still. From William Still, The Underground Railroad.

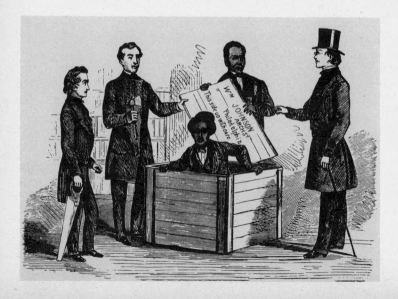

points in Pennsylvania and New Jersey in the East. Once the North had been reached the route was much clearer, though traversed with only slightly less danger, for planters, traders, and sheriffs pursued fugitives relentlessly and resorted to the most desperate means to recover them.

Even if the Underground Railroad did not need papers of incorporation, it needed capital. The fugitives required food and clothing, and frequently there were unexpected expenses such as boarding a train in order to evade a pursuing owner, or displaying affluence to convey the impression that one had been free long enough to accumulate wealth. Quakers and similar groups raised funds to carry on the work. The vigilance committees of Philadelphia and New York solicited money. Philanthropists contributed, as did the conductors and other "officials" of the Railroad. Harriet Tubman, one of the greatest of all conductors, would take several months off whenever she was running low in funds and hire herself out as a domestic servant in order to raise money for conveying slaves to freedom.

The Underground Railroad did not seem to suffer for want of operators. Professor Wilbur H. Siebert has catalogued more than 3,200 active workers; and there is every reason to believe that there were many more who will remain forever anonymous. Outstanding among the white workers was Levi Coffin, a Quaker and so-called "President" of the Underground Railroad. His home in Newport, Indiana, was on three important routes. His strategic location as well as his phenomenal zeal made it possible for him to help more than 3,000 slaves escape. Calvin Fairbanks, who had learned to hate slavery as a student at Oberlin College, began to travel in the South in 1837 on the dangerous business of freeing slaves. In Kentucky he engaged in a regular business of transporting slaves across the Ohio River. On one occasion, with a teacher from Vermont known as Miss Webster, he helped three slaves escape by their posing as her servants. It was said that not one of his fugitives was ever recaptured, though he spent many years in jail for his work.

In many respects the most daring white conductor on the Underground Railroad was John Fairfield. Son of a Virginia slaveholding family, he would have nothing to do with the institution and decided to live in a free state. Before going North, he helped a slave who was his friend escape to Canada. News of his exploit spread: not only did the whites of his community seek to find and arrest him, but the Negroes sought his aid to escape. He could not refuse them, and thus began his career as a conductor on the Underground Railroad. He delivered slaves "on order." Negroes in the North and in Canada would give him money and a description of their friends or relatives and he would deliver them. At times he conveyed as many as fifteen. He posed as a slaveholder, a Negro trader, or a peddler of eggs and poultry in Louisiana, Alabama, Mississippi, Tennessee, and Kentucky in order to gain the confidence of slaveholders. He was so convincing in each role that he was seldom suspected of being implicated in a slave's escape. Negroes he did not carry to Canada he delivered to Levi Coffin, who arranged the rest of their journey. His greatest triumph was in conveying 28 slaves to freedom by organizing them into a funeral procession. He suffered in his work from privations and exposure, and one time he was shot, but he persevered in his missions of freedom down to his death in 1860, when he was believed to have been killed in an insurrection of slaves in Tennessee. John Brown, dashing from Missouri with twelve slaves and later attacking Harpers Ferry in an attempt at insurrection, has received more notice from historians, but Fairfield was as effective a fighter of slavery as any man who lived before the Civil War.

There were many Negro "officials" on the Underground Railroad. Jane Lewis of New Lebanon, Ohio, rowed fugitives regularly across the Ohio River. John Parker, who purchased himself for $2,000, was in league with John Rankin and other white workers on the Railroad. Josiah Henson, born a slave, escaped with his wife and two children to Canada, learned to read and write, and returned South often to assist slaves in their escape. Once he went to Kentucky by a circuitous route through New York, Pennsylvania, and Ohio in order to avoid suspicion. He took thirty refugees out of Kentucky and led them to Toledo within a period of two weeks. Elijah Anderson has been called the "general superintendent" of the Underground Railroad in northwestern Ohio. From 1850 until his death seven years later in the Kentucky state prison, he worked arduously in behalf of fugitive slaves. By 1855 he had led more than a thousand to freedom. John Mason, himself a fugitive slave from Kentucky, was one of the most astute conductors. According to William Mitchell, a Negro missionary in Canada, Mason brought 265 slaves to his home in the course of nineteen months. On one occasion he was captured and sold back into slavery, but again

THE NEGRO EXODUS—the old style and the new. In the exodus of 1879 thousands of Negroes left the farms and towns of the South in search of a better life. Their departure greatly contrasted with the manner in which Negroes left the region in the period before 1865. From Harper's Weekly, May 1, 1880.

he made good his escape. In all he delivered about 1,300 slaves into free territory.

Easily the most outstanding Negro conductor on the Underground Railroad was Harriet Tubman. Although frail of body and suffering from recurrent spells of dizziness, she not only escaped from slavery herself, but conveyed many others to freedom, including her sister, her two children, and her aged mother and father. She is said to have gone South nineteen times and to have emancipated more than 300 slaves. Unable to read or to write, she nevertheless displayed remarkable ingenuity in the management of her runaway caravans. She preferred to start the journey on Saturday night, so that she could be well on her way before the owners had an opportunity the following Monday to advertise the escape of their slaves. She tolerated no cowardice and threatened to kill any slave who wished to turn back. Well known in Philadelphia, New York, and Boston, where she frequently delivered the escaped slaves, she preferred to carry them all the way to Canada after the passage of the Fugitive Slave Law in 1850, explaining that she could not trust Uncle Sam with her people any longer.

The very nature of the institution prevents any accurate estimate of the number of slaves who found freedom by the Underground Railroad. Governor Quitman of Mississippi declared that between 1810 and 1850 the South lost 100,000 slaves valued at more than thirty million dollars. This is a much larger figure than the census gives for Negroes in the North who were born in slaveholding states, but Professor Siebert believes that it is fairly accurate. He is certain, for example, that approximately 40,000 passed through Ohio alone.

The Underground Railroad intensified the resentment which the South felt toward outside interference. It was not realized that the Railroad ran inside the South. Not only Northerners participated in its management, but Southern whites and Negroes were among its most valuable engineers and conductors, and all the "passengers" were Negroes desperately anxious to get away from the peculiar institution of the South.

The South Strikes Back

Despite the fact that there was considerable Southern sentiment against slavery during the colonial and early national periods, the institution always had its defenders. Almost from the beginning no attack on slavery went unanswered. When Judge Samuel Sewall wrote The Selling of Joseph, John Saffin answered his attack on slavery with an enthusiastic rebuttal in 1701. Persons of no less stature than George Whitefield, the great evangelist, and his friend James Habersham sprang to the defense of slavery in the middle of the eighteenth century. When there was some doubt regarding the future of slavery under the new national government, most of the Southern delegates made it clear that they would tolerate no interference with the institution. From the time that Jefferson's Notes on Virginia were made public, Southern leaders did not hesitate to use his work to strengthen their contention that Negroes were by nature an inferior race and therefore should be enslaved. Some Southerners conceded that slavery was a political evil; but almost none agreed with anti-slavery antagonists that it was also a great moral evil.

In the early nineteenth century the question of slavery was overshadowed by other problems of a political and economic nature. Our foreign relations were strained, and our energies were directed toward trying to stay out of the Napoleonic wars in Europe. Our preoccupation with becoming more self-sufficient economically caused the North to turn its attention to shipping and, later, manufacturing; while the South made the transition from a tobacco and rice slave economy to one in which cotton was dominant. It would not be accurate, however, to describe sectional attitudes toward slavery during this period as altogether indifferent. As some people continued to attack slavery, its defenders spoke up, gradually developing the classic defense that was to be reiterated with so much feeling in the period ahead.

Even before the great debate over the admission of Missouri, the anti-slavery movement had assumed something of a sectional character. Emancipation of the slaves in Northern states had proceeded at a time when the institution was becoming more deeply entrenched in the South with the development of the cotton kingdom. The emigration of the majority of anti-slavery men and women from the slave states, moreover, deprived the South of an opportunity to hear the other side of the argument from its neighbors. Professor Dwight L. Dumond insists that this migration deprived the South of men and women "whose combined intelligence, moral courage, and Christian benevolence would have gone far toward modifying the harsher features of slavery, toward preventing so great a unanimity of opinion in that section in support of slavery as a positive good, and toward keeping alive the spirit of free discussion." Later, as anti-slavery men withdrew from the colonization movement and organized militant anti-slavery societies, the South found that it could no longer give any countenance to the enemies of slavery in its midst. The debate over Missouri, the insurrection of Denmark Vesey, and the increased activity of the abolitionists all convinced the men of the South that they must give more attention to the defense of their institution. When the call went out for defenders, they were sufficient both in number and in zeal. They began to strike back at their Northern traducers, blow for blow.

Southerners were now determined not to apologize for slavery. They stopped thinking of it as possessing any undesirable aspects. They evolved the idea, and clung to it with ferocious tenacity, that slavery was a positive good. In 1826 Edward Brown brought out his *Notes on the Origin and Necessity of Slavery*, which drew heavily from a pamphlet published the previous year by Whitemarsh B. Seabrook. Brown declared that "slavery has ever been the stepping ladder by which countries have passed from barbarism to civilization. . . . It appears . . . to be the only state capable of bringing the love of independence and of ease, inherent in man, to the discipline and shelter necessary to his physical wants. . . ." A few months later Dr. Thomas Cooper of South Carolina published his first pro-slavery pamphlet. One by one, Southern educators and ministers joined in the defense of slavery; and the war of words was on.

The pro-slavery argument was based on a theory of the racial inferiority and biological inequality of the Negro. There were four main postulates of the theory. In the first place, it was contended that slave labor was absolutely essential to the economic development and prosperity of the South. Governor Hammond of South Carolina expressed this point of view clearly: "In all social systems there must be a class to do the menial duties, to perform the drudgery of life. . . . Its requisites are vigor, docility, fidelity. Such a class you must have or you would not have that other class which leads progress, civilization, and refinement. It constitutes the very mud-sill of society and of political government; and you might as well attempt to build a house in the air, as to build either the one or the other, except on this mud-sill."

In the second place, it was asserted that the Negro race was inferior and destined to occupy a subordinate position. In his *Southern Institutes*, George S. Sawyer stated forcefully this point of view:

> The social, moral, and political, as well as the physical history of the negro race bears strong testimony against them; it furnishes the most undeniable proof of their mental inferiority. In no age or condition has the real negro shown a capacity to throw off the chains of barbarism and brutality that have long bound down the nations of that race; or to rise above the common cloud of darkness that still broods over them.

Dr. John H. Van Evrie, Dr. Joseph Clark Nott, and many others published works in which they subscribed to an ethnological justification of Negro slavery.

Another argument of pro-slavery leaders was that through the ages the church had sanctioned slavery as a means of converting the heathen to Christian civilization. There was, of course, some conflict between the theory that the Negro was incapable of improvement and the notion that he could be civilized and Christianized in slavery; but little attention was paid to this conflict, and each argument was used where it would do the most good. The Rev. James Henley Thornwell, Bishop Stephen Elliott, and Dr. B. M. Palmer were only three among many Southern religious leaders who held fast to this point of view and expressed it in their sermons and writings. With many Northern religious leaders holding to opposite points of view, an intersectional clash of denominations was inevitable. Thus fifteen years before the Civil War the Baptists, Methodists, and Presbyterians had each split into two groups.

Finally, the pro-slavery argument ran, the white race had not degenerated because of slavery but had developed a unique and high degree of culture. George Fitzhugh, Beverly Tucker, and others claimed that a society in which everyone was free was a failure, and that the South had solved its problems by acknowledging the fact that culture and civilization could advance only if slaves were available to do the work.

This war of words became so bitter, and the atmosphere in the South so tense, that free inquiry and free speech disappeared there. People with points of view at variance with the accepted pro-slavery creed were run out of the South. The colleges became a hotbed of secession, and every agency in the community was employed to defend slavery. Even men of letters, like William Gilmore Simms, in keeping with their thinking or with a feeling of necessity, wrote pro-slavery essays, poems, and songs. In words the South struck back with a vengeance.

The South loved action too well, however, to let the conflict remain on an academic level. It was a practical matter too: the vociferous anti-slavery preachers must be silenced if they were not to do irreparable damage to Southern institutions. In October, 1831, the Georgia legislature offered $4,000 for the arrest of Garrison. There was a price of $12,000 on the head of Arthur Tappan in Macon, and $20,000 in New Orleans. The vigilance committee of South Carolina offered $1,500 for the arrest of any person distributing the *Liberator* or Walker's *Appeal*. Most of the leading participants in the abolition movement and the activities of the Underground Railroad could boast that they were officially wanted in the South.

Pushing their program of resistance a step further, Southern leaders were resolved to keep the writings of the abolitionists out of their communities, by force if necessary. They worked up such popular resentment to the circulation of abolitionist literature in the South that citizens took the matter in their own hands. In July, 1835, a group in Charleston broke into the post office, seized anti-slavery newspapers, and made a bonfire out of them in the public square. Many other cities followed this example. When it appeared that the federal government would not punish them for their actions, Southern postmasters of their own accord began to take abolitionist literature out of the mails.

People living in the South, whether natives or from the North, found it desirable to speak with extreme caution on the question of slavery. One white man was lashed in Petersburg, Virginia, and ordered to leave the town for expressing the view that "black men have, in the abstract, a right to their freedom." A Georgian who subscribed to the *Liberator* was dragged from his home by a mob, tarred and feathered, set afire, ducked in the river, and then tied to a post and whipped. Amos Dresser, a former student at Lane Seminary, went into Tennessee to sell Bibles. When it could not be proved in court that he was spreading abolitionist doctrine, a mob lashed him one midnight in a public square, with the hearty approval of several thousand onlookers. Whites who associated with Negroes on any basis that suggested equality were severely dealt with. Several, for example, were murdered in Georgia and South Carolina for the "crime" of mixing with Negroes in public.

Pro-slavery leaders even carried the fight into enemy territory. They not only went North in pursuit of their runaway slaves, but they sought to spread pro-slavery doctrine and to spy on abolitionists. A Kentucky slaveholder, dressed in the garb of a Quaker, went into Indiana to get information on the Underground Railroad. Because he knew so little about Quaker speech and customs, he was soon discovered. Another went so far as to pose as an anti-slavery lecturer; visiting several communities in Indiana and Ohio, he discovered that fugitives were hiding out and notified the masters, who promptly came and claimed their property. He was in a community, however, that was hostile to slavery and the citizens insisted that the slaves be given a hearing. In court it was decided that the masters' claims were invalid, and the slaves were set free.

In the decade before the Civil War intersectional strife reached a new peak. There were division and dissension among the abolitionists with regard to policy, but there was more unity than ever among pro-slavery leaders. In both sections the war of words had failed to bring satisfactory results. In the North the practical abolitionists resolved to destroy slavery by perfecting the Underground Railroad and delivering slaves into free territory. In the South the practical pro-slavery leaders resolved to keep the institution of slavery inviolate by destroying every vestige of thought that was at variance with it. If conformity involved burning books or newspapers, spying on the enemy in order to be able to counter-attack him successfully, or even killing Negroes or whites, then in a situation where so much was at stake it simply had to be done.

Stress and Strain in the Fifties

Perhaps no decade in the history of the United States has been so filled with tense and crucial moments as the ten years leading to the Civil War; and closely connected with the majority of these crises was the problem of slavery. The period was ushered in by the controversy over slavery in the newly acquired territory in the Southwest. With the discovery of gold in California in 1848 and with the rapid peopling of many areas in the Mexican Cession, a policy had to be decided upon. Some leaders held that the new territory should be divided into slave and free sections as in the Missouri Compromise. The abolitionists, of course, and many others in the North, wanted a total exclusion of slavery from the territories, a point of view expressed in the Wilmot Proviso. Still others were of the opinion that the question should be decided by the people themselves who lived in the new territories, an approach to the problem which was popularized by Stephen A. Douglas. Finally, there were those who insisted that slavery could not be legally excluded anywhere, a view vigorously advanced by John C. Calhoun. The question of fugitive slaves, moreover, was very much alive. Southern owners had never had too much luck in recovering them. In 1842, in the case of *Prigg v. Pennsylvania*, the Supreme Court ruled that state officials were not required to assist in the return of fugitives, and the decision did much to render ineffective all efforts to recover slaves.

In 1850 these questions were thoroughly aired in Congress, and a desperate effort was made to work out a solution that would diminish intersectional strife. After considerable debate by Clay, Calhoun, Douglas, Seward, and Chase, an agreement was reached which provided that (1) California should enter the Union as a free state; (2) the other territories would be organized without mention of slavery; (3) Texas should cede certain lands to New Mexico, and be compensated; (4) slave-holders would be better protected by a stringent fugitive slave law; and (5) there should be no slave trade in the District of Columbia. The Compromise of 1850 was by no means satisfactory to all, and Georgia, Mississippi, Alabama, and South Carolina seriously considered secession. Southerners said they would remain in the Union only as long as there was strict adherence to the compromise, especially in enforcing the fugitive slave act.

It soon became clear that neither section was seriously reconciled to the Compromise of 1850 as a final settlement of the slavery question. Militant abolitionists were still determined to assist runaways, and new federal legislation could not deter them. In 1851 they went so far as to rescue a slave, Shadrach, from a United States marshal in Boston who was preparing to return him to his owner. It was the zeal of the slaveholders that especially irritated the abolitionists. With the new law against fugitives, the slaveholders put on an intensive man-hunt, determined to drive back into slavery even those fugitives who had lived as free men for years. For example, they seized Jerry McHenry, who had lived in Syracuse for several years and was regarded as a substantial citizen; but members of the Liberty party convening there were led by Gerrit Smith and William Seward to rescue McHenry and send him on his way. These are merely two examples of what came to be open defiance of the law on the part of the militant abolitionists. Their attitude convinced the South that the North was not willing to abide by the Compromise of 1850.

The appearance of *Uncle Tom's Cabin* in 1852 increased the strain on intersectional relations. This novel by Mrs. Harriet Beecher Stowe sold more than 300,000 copies in the first year of its publication and was soon dramatized in theatres throughout the North. Its story of abject cruelty on the part of masters and overseers, its description of the privations and suffering of slaves, and its complete condemnation of Southern civilization won countless thousands over to abolition and left Southern leaders busy denying the truth of the novel. The damage had been done, however, and when Southerners counted their losses from this one blow, they found them to be staggering indeed.

The sectional truce brought about by the Compromise of 1850 was at an end, but if it needed a legislative act to destroy it, the Kansas-Nebraska Act of 1854 was precisely the thing. Introduced into the Senate by Stephen A. Douglas of Illinois, the act provided that Kansas and Nebraska should be organized as territories and that the question of slavery should be decided by the territorial legislatures. Whatever the motives of Douglas may have been, the passage of the act precipitated a desperate struggle between North and South for the control of Kansas. The Missouri Compromise had been in effect repealed, and those forces that mustered the greatest strength in Kansas could win it. In the ensuing years abolitionist and pro-slavery factions fought and bled for Kansas; the land became a preliminary battleground of the Civil War. No longer was there much semblance of intersectional peace. Although the climate of Kansas would have prevented any extensive development of plantation slavery there, the principle was important to both sides, and they conducted themselves accordingly.

The Kansas-Nebraska Act persuaded many anti-slavery leaders that political action was necessary to combat the relentless drive of the pro-slavery forces to extend slavery. Northern Whigs, Free Soilers, and Democrats who had fought the passage of the Act came together, and out of their discussions arose the Republican Party. This new political organization, unalterably anti-slavery in its point of view, profited by the mistake of earlier anti-slavery parties and evolved a program broad enough to attract voters who were indifferent to slavery. Southerners, meanwhile, sought to counteract this new party by demanding further extension of slavery and the re-opening of the African slave trade.

The significance of these trends had hardly become apparent when the Supreme Court, in 1857, handed down a decision in the case of *Scott v. Sanford* that had the effect of widening the breach between North and South. Dred Scott was a Missouri slave whose master had first taken him to live in free Illinois and subsequently to a fort in the northern part of the Louisiana purchase, where slavery had been excluded by the Missouri

Compromise. Upon his return to Missouri, Scott sued for his freedom on the ground that residence on free soil had liberated him. The majority of the Court held that Scott was not a citizen and therefore could not bring suit in the courts. Chief Justice Roger B. Taney, speaking for the Court, added that since the Missouri Compromise was unconstitutional, masters could take their slaves anywhere in the territories and retain title in them. The decision was a clear-cut victory for the South, but the North viewed it with genuine alarm. With the highest court in the land openly preaching pro-slavery doctrine, there was little hope that anything short of a most drastic political or social revolution would bring an end to slavery. All abolitionists were not as optimistic as Frederick Douglass, but they hoped with him that "The Supreme Court . . . [was] not the only power in this world. We, the abolitionists and colored people, should meet this decision, unlooked for and monstrous as it appears, in a cheerful spirit. This very attempt to blot out forever the hopes of an enslaved people may be one necessary link in the chain of events preparatory to the complete overthrow of the whole slave system."

Indeed, only two more links were needed to bring on the bitter war which gave freedom to the slaves: one was the raid of John Brown and the other was a Republican victory at the polls in 1860. Brown had worked in the cause of freedom for many years. He had done his part to aid the anti-slavery forces in Kansas, and he had worked on the Underground Railroad out of Missouri. By 1859 he was anxious to strike a more significant blow for the freedom of slaves. He traveled through the North raising money and talking with white and Negro abolitionists. Finally, he laid his plans to attack slaveholders and liberate their slaves. On Sunday night, October 16, with a small band of less than 50 men he seized the federal arsenal at Harpers Ferry, Virginia, in the hope of securing sufficient ammunition to carry on a large-scale operation against the Virginia slaveholders. Immediately the countryside was alerted, and both federal and state governments dispatched troops which overwhelmed Brown and his men. Among those with Brown were several Negroes, including Lewis Sheridan Leary, Dangerfield Newby, John Anthony Copeland, Shields Green, and Osborn Perry Anderson. Leary and Newby were killed; Copeland and Green were hanged; and Anderson escaped.

The effect of this raid on the South was electrifying. It made slaveholders think that the abolitionists would stop at nothing to wipe out slavery. No one felt secure, because there were rumors of other insurrections to come, and widespread complaint that slaves were insolent because they knew their day of liberation was near. The whole South was put on a semi-war footing, with troops drilling regularly as far south as Georgia and with increasing demands for arms and ammunition by the militia commanders of most states.

On December 2, 1859, John Brown was hanged, but not before he had dazzled the country by his words and his conduct after the trial. He told a reporter of the *New York Herald,* "I pity the poor in bondage that have none to help them; that is why I am here; not to gratify any personal animosity, revenge or vindictive spirit. It is my sympathy with the oppressed and wronged, that are as good as you and as precious in the sight of God. . . . You may dispose of me easily, but this question is still to be settled—the negro question—the end of that is not yet." Upon hearing his sentence he calmly said, "Now, if it is deemed necessary that I should forfeit my life for the furtherance of the ends of justice, and mingle my blood further with the blood of my children and with the blood of millions in this slave country whose rights are disregarded by wicked, cruel, and unjust enactments, I say, let it be done."

Some people said that Brown was a madman, but few who saw him and listened to him thought so. Governor Wise of Virginia said, "They are themselves mistaken who take him to be a madman. . . . He is a man of clear head, of courage, of fortitude and simple ingenuousness." He terrified the South and captivated the North by his deed. Many had died fighting for freedom, but none had done it so heroically or at such a propitious moment. The crusade against slavery now had a martyr, and nothing wins followers to a cause like a martyr. Literally thousands of people who had been indifferent were now persuaded that slavery must be abolished. There can be no doubt that many voted the Republican ticket in 1860 because of this conviction.

When it became clear that the Republican candidate would stand on an anti-slavery platform, the South began once more to utter threats of secession. But with the nomination of Abraham Lincoln, instead of a pronounced abolitionist like Seward of New York or Chase of Ohio, it was the abolitionists who were worried. They were not sure how far Lincoln would go to put an

270 · FROM SLAVERY TO FREEDOM

end to slavery. And yet, as Professor Dumond has pointed out, his words and deeds for twenty years had clearly been anti-slavery. He had said many times that slavery was hostile to the poor man. During his one term in Congress he had done what he could to keep the territories free, so that poor people could feel secure there. He had said that the Negro should be protected in his civil right to the enjoyment of the fruits of his own labor, and he had vigorously denounced the Dred Scott decision. Nevertheless, Garrison, Phillips, Sumner, and other abolition-ists were skeptical of him because he was not one of them.

Lincoln's election, which many Democrats conceded after they split into factions at the Charleston and Baltimore conven-tions, marked the elevation to power of a party whose philoso-phy was, from the Southern point of view, revolutionary and destructive. There was no place in the Union for states unaltera-bly committed to the maintenance and extension of slavery. The November election returns which gave victory to the Republi-cans were the signal for calling conventions in the South to take the step that fire-eaters and pro-slavery leaders had already decided upon.

It was in an atmosphere of slavery that the weapons for waging the Civil War were sharpened. It was the question of slavery that sundered the sections and forced them to settle the question by a bloody war. The humanitarian reform movement would have proceeded apace had there been no slaves, for temperance, women's rights, and the like would have received generous support in communities where there was a tendency to assume civic responsibility. It was the question of slavery, how-ever, that intensified the reform crusade and brought the coun-try to the impasse of 1860. Without slavery, the question of the extent of federal authority in the territories would have re-mained academic, and could have been debated openly and peaceably. Without slavery the South would have remained a land where freedom of thought could command respect and where all institutions would not feel compelled to pursue a course of action prescribed by the planting aristocracy. Just as the anti-slavery movement had its roots deep in the liberal philosophy of the Revolutionary period, so intersectional strife and the Civil War itself had their roots in the question of the future of the Negro in the United States.

XVI •

Civil War

Uncertain Federal Policy

● *When President-elect Lincoln arrived in Washington late in* February, 1861, the nation he was to administer during the next four years was rapidly falling apart before his very eyes. Already seven states in the lower South had seceded, and there was talk of the same momentous step in each of the other slave states. Even before his inauguration Lincoln conceived his most important and difficult task was stemming the tide of national disintegration. In his carefully worded Inaugural he condemned the Southern citizens—not states—who were in insurrection, and thus he may have won friends in the doubtful border states; but his words were hardly encouraging to abolitionists who felt that the time for words was over. Action was needed in their opinion to bring an end to an institution against which the Republican Party had taken a stand during the election campaign. But Lincoln had to move cautiously lest he offend the eight slave states that still remained in the Union. No amount of caution, however, could maintain peace indefinitely without surrendering the authority of the federal government in the South. When the time came to defend Fort Sumter, Lincoln acted promptly; but the defense of the Fort cost him four more slave states and plunged the country into Civil War.

Even if there had not been the problem of keeping the remaining slave states—Delaware, Maryland, Kentucky, and Missouri—in the Union, there were still many people in the North who would have recoiled from a war against slavery or for abolition. Lincoln not only had to mollify the border slave states, but also avoid any policy offensive to thousands throughout the North who had grown weary of the abolition movement. He could hope in the meantime to soften the attacks which abolitionists were bound to make on him by giving ground to them on less dangerous matters.

When Negroes rushed to offer their services to the Union, they were rejected. In almost every town of any size there were large numbers of Negroes who sought service in the Union army; failing to be enlisted, they bided their time and did whatever they could to assist. In New York they formed a military club and drilled regularly until the police stopped them. Several Philadelphia Negroes offered to go South and organize slave revolts, but this was unthinkable. In the nation's capital, they made repeated requests of the War Department to be received into the army. At a meeting in Boston they passed a resolution urging the government to enlist them: "Our feelings urge us to say to our countrymen that we are ready to stand by and defend our Government as the equals of its white defenders; to do so with 'our lives, our fortunes, and our sacred honor,' for the sake of freedom, and as good citizens; and we ask you to modify your laws, that we may enlist,—that full scope may be given to the patriotic feelings burning in the colored man's breast."

The abolitionists began to wonder if they had supported the wrong candidate in Lincoln. They were filled with even greater despair when they observed the vacillating policy adopted by the government with reference to slaves who escaped to the federal lines. Indeed, there was no policy; for each commander used his own discretion. In the spring of 1861, Negroes sought refuge within the federal lines near Fortress Monroe in Virginia. When General Butler learned that the slaves had been employed in erecting Confederate defenses, he immediately declared that they were "contraband of war" and should not be returned to their owners. Instead, they were put to work for the Union forces. For several months it was not at all clear that the authorities in Washington would endorse his action, and several replies of the War Department to his requests for a clarification of policy were evasive. Later, when he was transferred to Louisiana, he found the conditions there quite different from those in Virginia; instead of declaring runaway Negroes contraband, he ordered them to be returned to their masters.

In June, 1861, several military officers spoke out in favor of returning all fugitives. In the West, General Halleck adopted this policy. But the lack of any uniform policy is clearly indicated by two developments in July, 1861. On July 9 the House of Representatives passed a resolution declaring it was no part of the duty of federal troops to capture or return fugitive slaves. One week later, General Winfield Scott wrote Brigadier General McDowell, in the name of President Lincoln, asking him to allow owners of fugitive slaves in Virginia to cross the Potomac and recover slaves who had taken refuge in Union lines. Small wonder that there was so much dissatisfaction among the abolitionists with regard to federal policy. Phillips, Sumner, and Garrison openly attacked the government and demanded a more forthright stand for fugitives and emancipation. It was not until the Confiscation Act of August 6, 1861, that anything resembling uniform treatment was applied to fugitives by the federal government. The act provided that any property used by the owner's consent and with his knowledge in aiding or abetting insurrection against the United States was the lawful subject of prize and capture wherever found. When the property consisted of slaves, they were to be forever free.

As the Union armies pushed into the South and occupied vast stretches of land, Negroes poured into the Union lines by the thousands. Yet federal policy for their relief and employment was hardly more clear-cut than it had been when the legality of receiving them at all was doubtful. Again each commanding officer seemed to use his own discretion. In West Tennessee, General Grant found it necessary to appoint John Eaton to take charge of all fugitives in his area in November, 1862. A special camp was set up for Negroes at Grand Junction, Tennessee, where Eaton supervised the hiring out of these ex-slaves, leased abandoned plantations to whites who hired them, and saw to it that they were paid for their work. In Louisiana, General Benjamin Butler leased Negroes to loyal planters who paid the ex-slaves ten dollars a month. It was most difficult to secure the cooperation of soldiers and officers who did not want to appear as if they were serving Negroes. The transition period for the Negroes was extremely difficult, and because of the confused and changing federal policy, they endured at times both hunger and exposure. While they did not suffer any cruel punishment, there were many instances of unfair treatment, a most perplexing problem to the officers whose principal responsibility it was to take the war to the enemy.

In December, 1862, Rufus Saxton, commanding the Department of the South, sought to reduce the confusion in the employment and relief of fugitives by issuing an order for a general plan to be followed everywhere. Abandoned lands were to be used for the benefit of ex-slaves. Negro families were allotted two acres for each working hand; they were to plant corn and potatoes for their own use, with tools to be furnished by the government, and plowing to be done by those assigned to that task. All Negroes were required to raise a certain amount of cotton for government use. In many areas superintendents of Negro affairs were appointed, whose duties were to take a census of the Negro population, see that they were employed and had the necessaries of life, take charge of land set aside by the government for their use, and protect those who had hired themselves out to white employers. Some superintendents, like the Reverend Horace James of the North Carolina area, performed their duties conscientiously; others did not show much interest in the problems of Negroes.

Relief was almost always difficult because of the small amount of land available for the use of Negroes. In his report in 1864 the Reverend James said, "We control indeed a broad area of navigable waters, and command the approaches from the sea, but have scarcely room enough on land to spread our tents upon." The government was selling much of the land to private parties for non-payment of taxes. Eastern capitalists and philanthropists bought most of the available land in South Carolina; and frequently, though not always, these new owners had little interest in the plight of the Negroes.

Another difficulty arose out of the fact that the Treasury contested the right of the War Department to administer Negro affairs. Although the Secretary of War desired the Treasury to control all confiscated property, except that used by the military, officers in the field were of the opinion that they could best handle everything. While the controversy raged during 1863 and 1864, Negroes suffered for want of any coordinated supervision. In his message to the Confederate Congress in the fall of 1863, President Davis excoriated Northern conduct of Negro affairs. After describing the starvation and suffering among

Negroes in contraband camps, he said that "there is little hazard in predicting that in all localities where the enemy have gained a temporary foothold, the negroes, who under our care increased sixfold in number . . . will have been reduced by mortality during the war to not more than one-half their previous number." While his criticism was by no means objective, it must be admitted that there was much suffering and death among the Negroes. In 1864 a Union official admitted that mortality in the Negro camps was "frightful" and that "most competent judges place it at not less than twenty-five percent in the last two years."

The federal policy for relief of freedmen developed so slowly that private persons, both Negro and white, undertook to supplement it. As early as February, 1862, meetings were held in Boston, New York, and other Northern cities for the express purpose of rendering more effective aid to Southern Negroes. On February 22, the National Freedmen's Relief Association was organized in New York, and soon thereafter the Contraband Relief Association in Cincinnati, which later changed its name to the Western Freedmen's Aid Commission. During this period the Friends Association for the Relief of Colored Freedmen was established in Philadelphia, and a group of Chicago citizens formed the Northwestern Freedmen's Aid Commission. In 1865 all were united in the American Freedmen's Aid Commission. Religious organizations, such as the United States Christian Commission and the American Missionary Association, joined in the relief of Negroes. Collections were taken up, clothing and food solicited, and agents went South to minister to the needs of ex-slaves.

A significant contribution of private agencies toward the adjustment of Negroes to their new status was in education. Although the federal government had no policy in this matter, it was not averse to cooperating with philanthropic organizations. Their work in educating Negroes began in 1861 when Lewis Tappan, treasurer of the American Missionary Association, wrote General Butler to offer the services of his organization. Butler welcomed such aid, and the Reverend L. C. Lockwood was sent to him to develop a program. On September 15, 1861, he opened a Sunday School for Negroes in the home of ex-President Tyler, and two days later the first day school, with Mary S. Peake as the teacher. Within a few months the American Missionary Association had established schools for Negroes at Hampton, Norfolk, Portsmouth, Newport News, and on several plantations. By 1864 more than 3,000 Negroes were at school with 52 teachers, of whom at least five were Negroes. They were paid by the associations, but the government furnished them with subsistence.

Several schools were established in Washington for refugees, and the freedmen's relief associations of Boston and Philadelphia supplied them with teachers. In North Carolina, the chaplains of Northern regiments took an early interest in the education of Negroes, and later the American Missionary Association and the relief organizations extended their program into this area. The first day schools were set up in July, 1863. One year later there were schools at Beaufort, Washington, Plymouth, Morehead, and other places, with 3,000 students and 66 teachers. Evening schools were also established for adults. General Butler took great interest in this work and sponsored the erection of a large building at Hampton to accommodate 800 students.

The New England Freedman's Aid Society started Negro education in South Carolina in 1862, when 31 men and women arrived as teachers. Schools were established on the larger plantations and in the towns, and by June, 1863, it was estimated that 5,000 Negroes were at school. Gradually Negro education was extended to most areas occupied by Union troops. In 1863 General Banks established a system of public education in the Department of the Gulf; and a Board of Education for Freedmen supervised their schools. By the end of the next year 95 schools had been set up in the Department, with 162 teachers, of whom 130 were Southerners and several were Negroes. There were 9,571 students in day schools, and another 2,000 attended evening schools.

The enthusiasm of Northerners for Negro education was tremendous. In the last year of the war at least 1,000 young Northern men and women were teaching and caring for ex-slaves. They brought with them slates, pencils, spelling books, readers, blackboards, and chalk. While they met strong opposition from a majority of the Southern whites, there were some who not only favored but contributed to the success of Negro schools. All through the South were to be found native whites teaching Negroes before the close of the war.

Some Negroes established schools for their own people. In Natchez, for example, three schools were started during the war by Negro women. In Savannah, Negroes could boast not only of two large schools which they had founded, but also of a Negro board of education to determine their policies. Most Negro schools had poor facilities, inadequate supplies, and insufficient teachers, but Negroes attended them in larger and larger numbers. The people responsible for establishing these schools—Northerners and Southerners, whites and Negroes—made a most significant contribution to the adjustment of Negroes coming out of slavery.

The opposition of the government early in the war to using Negro soldiers evoked unfavorable criticism from the abolitionists. There was considerable agitation for arming the Negroes. Garrison and Phillips believed that it was cruel to deprive Negro citizens of the opportunity to fight for the freedom of their brothers. White Northerners who were not abolitionists objected to fighting for the Negro's freedom when the Negro himself was not fighting. There were many, however, including some of the soldiers, who did not want the Negro to wear the uniform of the Union, feeling that it should be reserved for those whose citizenship was unquestioned. Lincoln feared that the border states would take exception to a policy of arming Negroes and that it would seriously alienate support in the North. He therefore gave no serious consideration to arming Negroes until the spring of 1862; and then it was forced on him.

As a result of considerable pressure from officers in the field, the acting Secretary of War authorized General Thomas W. Sherman in October, 1861, to "employ fugitive slaves in such services as they may be fitted for . . . with such organization as you may deem most beneficial to the service; this, however, not being a general arming of them for military service." While Sherman did not take advantage of this authorization to arm some slaves, his successor, David Hunter, sent out a call in May, 1862, for Negroes to serve in the army. Within a few months enough Negroes had responded for the "First South Carolina Volunteer Regiment" to be activated, but almost immediately Hunter was forced to disband the group, and the men were sent home unpaid and dissatisfied. In the autumn of 1862, however, Lincoln permitted the enlistment of some Negroes. General B. F. Butler mustered a whole regiment of free Negroes in Louisiana, and Hunter's South Carolina regiment was reorganized by General Saxton. In December, General Augustus Chetlain assumed control of Negro volunteering in Tennessee, and thereafter, as Professor Shannon has pointed out, the program was definitely considered a successful venture.

Machinery for recruiting Negro soldiers in the South was set up in the spring of 1863 by Adjutant General Lorenzo Thomas, who was sent to the Mississippi Valley to put it into operation. A special bureau was established in his office for the "conduct of all matters referring to the organization of Negro troops." Recruiting agents were selected and stations established in Maryland, Tennessee, Missouri, and at other strategic points. All able-bodies Negroes were eligible for military employment. Where loyal masters consented to the enlistment of their slaves, the masters were to receive $300 for each one. If sufficient recruits were not obtained in an area within thirty days, slaves were to be taken without consent of loyal owners. Although two years had elapsed before the federal government adopted a clear-cut policy regarding Negro soldiers, it demonstrated that when the circumstances were favorable, it could pursue a policy vigorous enough to satisfy even the most rabid abolitionists.

These months of vacillation on the treatment of runaway slaves, the relief of Negroes, and their military service had a disquieting effect on the status of the Negro during the Civil War. If the federal government would not take a stand to uphold him, he could expect little from private citizens. White reformers joined with such Negro leaders as Douglass, Langston, Remond, and Brown in fighting for his recognition, but they achieved small results. Newspapers in the North opposed to the Lincoln administration complained that the government had plunged the country into a costly war to help the undeserving Negro. The Philadelphia *Age* said that abolitionists had brought on the war to fulfill their "ebony ideals," ignoring the interests of millions of free white men. The editors of these papers strove to create an unfavorable public opinion of the Negro, and not infrequently they succeeded. They headlined any news of the rape of white women by Negro men and insisted that abolitionists were encouraging miscegenation. This sensational and irresponsible journalism had the desired effect: hostility toward Negroes actually increased in many Northern communities during the war.

Such hostility was most clearly shown by white workers of the North. They feared that emancipation of the slaves would cause a general exodus of Negroes to the North and that the ensuing competition for work would depress wages and create unemployment. White laborers in many places sought to raise their wages by striking, but the willingness of employers to use Negro strike-breakers convinced them that competition with Negro workers had already materialized. The result was that fights and riots occurred where Negroes sought work. In New York, in 1862, a group of Negro women and children who worked in a tobacco factory were mobbed. The use of Negro workers on the Camden and Amboy Railroad in New Jersey caused considerable agitation and threats of reprisals by unemployed whites. Longshoremen in Chicago, Detroit, Cleveland, Buffalo, New York, and Boston fought Negro workers whenever they were brought on the job.

The New York draft riots of 1863 were closely connected with the competition between whites and Negroes for work. Shortly before the riots began 3,000 longshoremen went on strike for higher wages. Negroes, with police protection, took their places. When the government began drafting these unemployed whites, they looked upon it as adding insult to injury: they had been displaced on their jobs by Negroes and were now being sent off to fight in a war to set more Negroes free. Consequently, they resisted conscription to the point of violence. During the riots in July, many Negro homes and business places were burned; and freedmen's associations, organized to help in the relief of Southern Negroes, found it necessary to aid Negroes in New York. To the end of the war this hostility to the Negro persisted and out of it grew the discriminatory policies adopted by many Northern cities in the twentieth century. Perhaps it is not too much to suggest that there was a discernible correlation between the uncertainty of federal policy and the hostile attitude of many white citizens in the North toward their darker fellows.

Moving Toward Freedom

From the very beginning of the war there had been speculation as to whether or when the slaves would be emancipated. Northern Democrats were opposed and said unequivocally that slavery was the best status for the Negro. The abolitionists supported the Republicans in 1860 principally because their platform was anti-slavery; and they demanded that the party fulfill its pledge by setting the slaves free. Lincoln had to move cautiously, however, for constitutional, political, and military reasons. His views on emancipation were well known. As early as 1849 he had introduced a bill in Congress for the gradual emancipation of slaves in the District of Columbia, and in the ensuing decade he announced his position on several occasions. For the abolitionists, gradual emancipation was bad enough, but not even to take definite steps in that direction was unforgivable.

The whole matter caused Lincoln grave concern. As he evolved his plan of emancipation, he was viewed all the more unfavorably because he felt it necessary to restrain enthusiastic officers who emancipated slaves without his authorization. In 1861 General John C. Frémont proclaimed military emancipation in Missouri, but Lincoln had to modify his action in keeping with the Confiscation Act. In 1862 General David Hunter proclaimed that slaves in Georgia, Florida, and South Carolina were to be forever free. When Lincoln learned of this order ten days later, he immediately issued a proclamation nullifying it and reminding slaveholders that they could still adopt his plan of compensated emancipation.

President Lincoln was going ahead with this plan for the solution of the problem of the Negro in America. He hoped to achieve emancipation by compensating the owners for their human property; and then he looked forward to colonizing the Negroes in some other part of the world. In the fall of 1861 he attempted an experiment with compensated emancipation in Delaware. He interested his friends there and urged them to propose it to the Delaware legislature. He went so far as to write a draft of the bill, which provided for gradual emancipation, and another which provided that the federal government would share the expenses of compensating masters for their slaves. Although these bills were much discussed, there was too much opposition to introduce them.

More definite steps in the direction of emancipation were taken in the spring of 1862. In a special message to Congress, President Lincoln recommended that a resolution be passed announcing that the United States would cooperate with any state adopting a plan of gradual emancipation together with satisfactory compensation of the owners. He urged the congressional delegations from Delaware, Maryland, West Virginia, Kentucky, and Missouri to support his policy. They opposed it, however, because their constituents were unwilling to give up their slaves. A joint resolution introduced by Roscoe Conkling nevertheless passed both houses and was approved by the President on April 10, 1862. The abolitionists were furious; they felt that Southern slaveholders should not be paid to surrender property they did not rightfully possess. Wendell Phillips, speaking in Cincinnati before a crowd hostile to his views, criticized the administration, declaring that the right hand of Southern aristocracy was Negro slavery and the left hand the ignorant white man. All over the North the abolitionists denounced Lincoln's plan of compensated emancipation.

Another of Lincoln's recommendations, which became law in April, 1862, provided for the emancipation of slaves in the District of Columbia. There would be compensation, of course, not exceeding $300 for each slave. A significant feature was the provision of $100,000 for the voluntary emigration of freedmen to Haiti and Liberia. Negro colonization seemed almost as important to Lincoln as emancipation. In August, 1862, he called a group of prominent free Negroes to the White House and urged them to support colonization. He told them, "Your race suffer greatly, many of them, by living among us, while ours suffer from your presence. In a word we suffer on each side. If this is admitted, it affords a reason why we should be separated." Perhaps some of them pledged their support, for in his second annual message he was able to say that many free Negroes had asked to be colonized. Largely at Lincoln's suggestion, the State Department made inquiries of South American governments and of some insular and African governments concerning the possibility of colonizing American Negroes. Only two replies were entirely satisfactory to Lincoln; they suggested that Negro colonies be established in Panama and on the Ile à Vache, an island in the Caribbean. Down to the end of the war Lincoln held out hope for colonizing at least some of the Negroes who were being set free.

From June, 1862, the policy of the government toward emancipation took shape rapidly. On June 19, the President signed a bill abolishing slavery in the territories. On July 17, a measure became law setting free all slaves coming from disloyal masters into Union-held territory. Lincoln again called together Congressmen from the border slave states and told them that since slavery would be destroyed if the war lasted long enough, they should accept his plan of compensated emancipation. His plea fell on deaf ears. Having gone as far as he had, however,

Lincoln considered emancipating by proclamation all slaves in rebellious states, an idea which he discussed with his Secretaries of State and Navy, Seward and Welles.

For two days, July 21 and 22, the Cabinet debated the draft of an emancipation proclamation which Lincoln read to them. Rebels were to be warned of the penalties of the Confiscation Act, reminded of the possibility of emancipating their slaves and receiving compensation, and all slaves in their possession on January 1, 1863, were to be set free. Only two cabinet members, Seward and Chase, agreed even in part with Lincoln's proposed proclamation; and Seward strongly advised him not to issue it until the military situation became more favorable. Apparently there was some hope, based on rumor, that the President would issue the proclamation in August; when it was not forthcoming, advocates of emancipation were sorely disappointed. Horace Greeley, writing in the *New York Tribune*, urged Lincoln to proclaim emancipation. Anti-slavery delegations called upon him. Interestingly enough, the President told one delegation that he could not free slaves under the Constitution, because it could not be enforced in the rebel states. Any proclamation would be about as effective, from Lincoln's point of view, "as the Pope's bull against the comet."

It was the Union victory at Antietam on September 17, 1862, that caused Lincoln to act. Five days later he issued a preliminary Proclamation. In this document he revived the possibility of compensated emancipation and said that he would continue to encourage the voluntary colonization of Negroes "upon this continent or elsewhere." The time had come, however, when more direct action was needed; so he proclaimed that on January 1, 1863, "all persons held as slaves within any State, or designated part of the State, the people whereof shall be in rebellion against the United States, shall be then, thenceforward, and forever free."

The general reaction in the North was unfavorable. Many whites felt that the war was no longer to save the Union but to free the Negro, and some soldiers resigned rather than participate in such a struggle. The Peace Democrats accused the administration of wasting the lives of white citizens in a costly abolition war. Abolitionists hesitated to condemn the Proclamation, since it was better than nothing; but to them it seemed at best very poor compensation for all the struggles and sacrifices they had made for more than a generation. Furthermore, what if the war should end and there were no rebellious States on the first of January, 1863? The prospect sent cold shivers through every ardent abolitionist. The real reaction was seen at the November elections. Although the Republicans maintained a majority in Congress, the Democrats won in many Northern communities and gained substantially in both House and Senate.

The preliminary Proclamation, despite this critical reaction, captured the imagination of workingmen in many parts of the world who viewed it as a great humanitarian document, and whenever slaves learned of it they laid down their tools and took on the mantle of their newly-found freedom. By the end of December, 1862, the suspense attending the final Proclamation was so great that even before it was read it had assumed the significance of one of the great documents of all times. On December 31 watch meetings were held by Negroes and whites in many parts of the country at which prayers of thanksgiving were offered for the deliverance of the Negro. At Tremont Temple in Boston, Frederick Douglass, William Wells Brown, William Lloyd Garrison, Harriet Beecher Stowe, Charles B. Ray, and other fighters for freedom heard on January 1 the words that emancipated more than three-fourths of the slaves. President Lincoln set free all slaves except those in states or parts of states not in rebellion against the United States at that time. These exceptions, in addition to the four loyal slave states, were thirteen parishes of Louisiana, including the city of New Orleans, the forty-eight counties of Virginia which had become West Virginia, and seven counties in eastern Virginia, including the cities of Norfolk and Portsmouth.

Lincoln left no doubt of his justification for the Emancipation Proclamation. Twice he mentioned the military necessity of pursuing this course. He described it as a "fit and necessary war measure" for suppressing the rebellion which he could take by virtue of the power vested in him as Commander-in-Chief of the Army and Navy. In the last paragraph of the Proclamation he said that it was "sincerely believed to be an act of justice, warranted by the Constitution upon military necessity." He counseled the slaves, however, to abstain from all violence except in self-defense and to work faithfully for reasonable wages.

If the Proclamation of Emancipation was essentially a war measure, it had the desired effect of creating confusion in the South and depriving the Confederacy of much of its valuable laboring force. If it was a diplomatic document, it succeeded in rallying to the Northern cause thousands of English and European laborers who were anxious to see workers gain their freedom throughout the world. If it was a humanitarian document, it gave hope to millions of Negroes that a better day lay ahead, and it renewed the faith of thousands of crusaders who had fought long to win freedom in America.

During the war years Negroes had moved significantly in the direction of freedom. Many of them were among the first, however, to realize that it had not been achieved. Even after the Proclamation was issued there were more than 800,000 slaves in the border states untouched by it, to say nothing of the hundreds of thousands if not millions in the Confederacy who were not even to hear about the Proclamation until months later. Political and economic freedom, moreover, the Negroes had neither in the South nor in the North. Their leaders were concerned about these matters. The National Convention of Colored Men, which met at Syracuse in October, 1864, discussed the questions of employment, enfranchisement, and the extension of freedom. If Negroes had no answers to these questions, it was because of the complexity and magnitude of the problems involved in adjusting more than four million people to a new climate of freedom.

Confederate Policy

One of the greatest anxieties of the South at the beginning of the war was the conduct of slaves. The reaction of the slave to his status involved not only the security of the white civilian population, but also the maintenance of a stable economic system without which there was no hope of prosecuting the war successfully. The owners took no chances. It was all right to talk about the love of slaves for their masters during times of peace; but in war idle talk and wishful thinking were not the stuff of victories. There was widespread sentiment for much closer control of the slaves. Patrol laws all over the Confederacy were strengthened. Instead of bi-weekly patrols, Florida in 1861 required them to make their rounds once a week, and even more often "when informed by a creditable citizen of evidence of insubordination or threatened outbreak, or insurrection of slaves." In 1862 Georgia cancelled exemptions from patrol duty, and Louisiana imposed a fine of ten dollars or twenty-four hours' imprisonment for failure to perform it.

The fears of Southerners appeared to be fully justified. Ordinary emergencies might not excite the slave, but gradually he became aware that in this war his freedom was at stake. To be sure, there were slaves who remained on the plantation, worked faithfully for their masters, and protected their mistresses, but, as Professor Bell I. Wiley has pointed out, "these acts of loyalty, in the light of contemporary evidence, must be considered as exceptional." The most widespread form of disloyalty was desertion. It could hardly be called running away in the sense that it was before the war. Between 1861 and 1865 Negroes simply walked off plantations, and when the Union forces came close, they went to their lines and got food and clothing. In Arkansas, according to Professor Staples, "whenever federal forces appeared, most of the able-bodied adult Negroes left their owners and sought refuge within the Union lines." Almost the entire slave population of the Shirley plantation in Virginia deserted to the Union lines. In August, 1862, a Confederate general estimated that Negroes worth at least a million dollars were escaping to the federals in North Carolina.

Confederate and state officials sought to halt the wholesale exodus of slaves by having planters engage in what was called "running the Negroes." When an area was threatened with invasion by federal troops, the planters would remove their slaves to safety, usually in the interior. More than two thousand were transferred from Washington and Tyrell Counties to the interior of North Carolina in the autumn of 1862. It was an interesting sight to see planters moving with "black capital," sometimes on foot, sometimes by wagon or cart, but always in haste. Not all Negroes were amenable to the idea of "refugeeing," at least not with their masters, and at times they openly resisted them and went off in the opposite direction—toward Union troops.

Slaves were often insolent toward the whites, especially when their lands were being invaded by the Union armies. In 1862 a Mississippi citizen wrote the governor that "there is greatly needed in this county a company of mounted rangers . . . to keep the Negroes in awe, who are getting quite impudent. Our proximity to the enemy has had a perceptible influence on them." The situation became so disturbing in Georgia that a bill was introduced in the legislature "to punish slaves and free persons of color for abusive and insulting language to white persons." The Richmond *Enquirer* reported that a coachman, upon learning that he was free, "went straightly to his master's chamber, dressed himself in his best clothes, put on his best watch and chain, took his stick, and returning to the parlor where his master was, insolently informed him that he might for the future drive his own coach." A North Carolina citizen summed up the prevailing white point of view in 1864: "Our Negroes are beginning to show that they understand the state of affairs, and insolence and insubordination are quite common."

As the war entered its more desperate stages, many slaves refused to work or to submit to punishment. A South Carolina planter complained in 1862 that "we have had hard work to get along this season, the Negroes are unwilling to do any work, no matter what it is." Another exasperated planter said, "*I wish every negro would leave the place* as they will do only what pleases them, go out in the morning when it suits them, come in when they please, etc." Some Louisiana slaves demanded wages for their labor. In Texas, a slave cursed his master "all to pieces" when the latter attempted to punish him. Relations became so strained in some areas of the South that masters and mistresses stopped trying to punish their slaves, lest they resort to desperate reprisals.

Other acts of slave disloyalty were giving information and guidance to federal troops, seizing the master's property upon arrival of these troops and helping to destroy it, and inflicting bodily harm upon white civilians. Most Southerners lived in constant fear of slave uprisings during the war, especially after the Emancipation Proclamation. Rumors of uprisings became common, and slaveholders were so terrified at the prospect of bloody insurrections that they frequently appealed to Union troops for protection.

One of the main objections of Southerners to conscription was that it would drain off the white male population and encourage Negroes to revolt. In 1864 the Richmond *Whig* said, "Take away all, or nearly all the vigorous whites, and leave the negro to the feeble control of women, children, and old men, and the danger is that famine will be superadded to insurrection." In several Alabama and Georgia towns Negroes were hanged for plotting insurrection; many were committed to jail for implication in these plots. The number of actual insurrections was relatively small because of the fact that Negroes secured their freedom without committing violence. The practice in the South, moreover, was to act summarily in the case of persons suspected of insurrection in order to discourage any large-scale revolt.

Since Southern agriculture had been based on staple crops, there was great difficulty in making the transition to a war-time economy that would provide the food necessary for the fighting forces. In most places cotton acreage was forcibly reduced by law, and there was a wholesale conversion of land to corn, wheat, and other cereal grains. The laboring force was the greatest problem. The supervision of Negroes, who knew little about grain production and were not interested in it, fell into the hands of women, disabled white men, and faithful Negroes.

Slaves were employed not only on farms but in factories as well. The iron works of Virginia and Alabama used them throughout the struggle. In 1862 the famous Tredegar works advertised for 1,000 slaves. In the iron works they cut wood for charcoal, hauled iron to shipping points, and engaged in more skilled types of labor. In 1864 there were 4,301 Negroes and 2,518 whites in the iron mines of the Confederate states east of the Mississippi. Slaves were also to be found mining coal and working in salt factories.

Confederate and state governments relied on slave and free Negro labor to do much of the hard work involved in prosecuting the war. Slave laborers were secured by contracts with the masters, by hiring them for short periods, and by impressment. By the fall of 1862 the labor shortage was so acute in the South that most states had authorized the impressment of slaves. In 1863 a desperate Confederate government passed a general impressment law, and one year later voted to impress 20,000 slaves. Down to the close of the war President Davis constantly urged that more slaves be impressed. The results were not at all gratifying. In the first place, the owners of slaves did not like the principle of impressment, by which their property could be seized at a price set by the government. Consequently, they simply refused to cooperate in many instances. The slaves did not like impressment, because to work for military authorities was vastly more strenuous than what they were accustomed to do for their own masters, if they chose to work at all. With master *and* slave opposed to impressment, there was little chance for its success.

Even without it the Confederate and state governments were able to secure the services of thousands of slaves who performed many important tasks. Most of the cooks in the Confederate army were slaves; and the government recognized their value to the morale and physical fitness of the soldiers by designating four cooks for each company and providing that each one should receive $15 a month as well as clothing. There were also slave teamsters, mechanics, hospital attendants, ambulance drivers, and common laborers. Much of the work in the construction of fortifications was done by Negroes. As Union armies invaded the South, tearing up railroads and wrecking bridges, gangs of slave and free Negro workers repaired them. They were also extensively employed in the manufacture of powder and arms. Of 400 workers at the naval arsenal in Selma, Alabama, 310 were Negroes in 1865.

Affluent Confederates took their Negro body servants to war with them. These workers kept the quarters clean, washed clothes, groomed uniforms, polished swords, buckles, and spurs, ran errands, secured rations, cut hair, and groomed the animals. Some even took part in the fighting. In November, 1861, it was reported that one servant "fought manfully" and killed four Union soldiers. As the fighting grew desperate, and rations shorter, most servants were sent home. The Confederate soldiers had come to realize that outside medieval romances there was no place for body servants on the field of battle.

It was one thing to have Negroes performing all types of work, even with the army, and quite another to put weapons of war in their hands. Some Southerners had wanted to arm Negroes from the beginning, and local authorities had permitted free Negroes to enroll for military service. In 1861 the Tennessee legislature authorized the governor to enlist in the state militia all free Negroes between fifteen and fifty years of age. Memphis went so far as to open a recruiting office for them. Public opinion, however, was generally against arming Negroes. There was, of course, the fear that they would turn on their masters. To accept Negroes for military service, moreover, would be an acknowledgment of their equality with whites. When a company of sixty free Negroes presented themselves for service at Richmond in 1861, they were thanked and sent home. A company of free Negroes in New Orleans was allowed to parade, but not to go into battle.

Despite the stern opposition of Southern leaders to enlisting Negroes, agitation in favor of it continued throughout the war. After reverses in the autumn of 1863 the debate increased, and the Alabama legislature recommended arming a large number of slaves. In 1864 General Patrick Cleburne proposed to officers in the Army of Tennessee that they organize a large force of slaves and promise them freedom at the end of the war. This proposal, coming from a high army official, provoked considerable discussion; and President Davis, fearing that it did the Confederate cause no good, ordered it to be stopped. Discussion continued, however, and at a meeting of the governors of North and South Carolina, Georgia, Alabama, and Mississippi, in October, 1864, a resolution was adopted suggesting the use of slaves as soldiers. Davis was still opposed to the proposition. In his message to the Confederate Congress the following month he said as much, but added: "Should the alternative ever be presented of subjugation or of the employment of the slave as a soldier, there seems no reason to doubt what should then be our decision."

The Congress in the winter of 1864–65 openly debated arming the slaves. A representative from Mississippi deplored any suggestion that slaves should be armed, and cried out, "God forbid that this Trojan horse should be introduced among us." The outspoken editor of the Charleston *Mercury* declared that South Carolina would no longer be interested in prosecuting the war if slaves were armed.

A bill was introduced in the Confederate Senate in 1865 providing for the enlistment of 200,000 Negroes and their emancipation if they remained loyal through the war. Advocates of the measure sought the approval of General Robert E. Lee. The South's most respected soldier said that the measure was not only expedient but necessary; that the Negro would make an efficient soldier; and that those who served should be freed at the end of the war. On March 13, 1865, a bill was signed by President Davis which authorized him to call on each state for her quota of 300,000 additional troops, irrespective of color, on condition that the slaves recruited from any state should not exceed 25 per cent of the able-bodied male slave population between eighteen and forty-five. Immediately recruiting officers were appointed to enroll Negroes for the Confederate army.

The enlistment of Negroes was very slow in the West. A Mississippian wrote his governor that the Negroes were fleeing to avoid conscription. Enlistment went better on the eastern seaboard, where officers resorted to dances and parades to work up enthusiasm among Negroes for the Confederate cause. It was too late, however, for the Confederacy had already been destroyed by the onslaught of the Union forces and by its own internal strife and disorganization. There are unconfirmed reports that some Negro troops saw action on the side of the Confederacy, but if true, their number was very small. Had the Confederacy reached a decision to use Negro troops two years earlier, a considerable force might have been enlisted. But in view of so much slave disloyalty, there is little reason to believe that Negroes would have fought effectively for the Confederate cause.

Negro Soldiers

When Negroes were finally permitted to enlist in the Union army, they did so with alacrity and enthusiasm. In the North leading Negroes like Frederick Douglass acted as recruiting agents. Rallies were held at which speakers urged Negroes to enlist, and in Boston, New York, and Philadelphia they went to the recruiting stations in large numbers. In the South too there were many who enlisted, but not all saw the necessity of fighting when they were winning their freedom without it. Negro enlistment was, however, a notable success: more than 186,000 had enrolled in the Union army by the end of the war. From the seceded states came 93,000, and from the border slave states, 40,000. The remainder, approximately 52,000, were from free states. It is possible that the total figure was larger, for some contemporaries insisted that many mulattoes served in white regiments without being designated as Negroes.

Negro troops were organized into régiments of light and heavy artillery, cavalry, infantry, and engineers. To distinguish them from white soldiers, they were called "United States Colored Troops," and for the most part they were led by white officers with some Negro non-commissioned officers. At first it was difficult to secure white officers for the Negro outfits, because regular army men were generally opposed to having Negroes in the service. Joseph T. Wilson says that West Pointers were especially averse to the idea of commanding these troops, and ostracized their fellows who undertook the task. There were those, however, who enthusiastically assumed the responsibility and made such a reputation for themselves and their men that it was not difficult to secure white officers for Negro outfits toward the close of the war. Among those who were outstanding as leaders were Colonel Thomas Wentworth Higginson of the First South Carolina Volunteers, Colonel Robert Gould Shaw of the Fifty-Fourth Massachusetts Regiment, and General N. P. Banks, who for a time had the First and Third Louisiana Native Guards under his command.

No considerable number of Negroes held commissions in the Union army. Two regiments of General Butler's *Corps d'Afrique* were entirely staffed by Negro officers, including Major F. E. Dumas and Captain P. B. S. Pinchback. An independent battery at Lawrence, Kansas, was led by Captain H. Ford Douglass and First Lieutenant W. D. Matthews. The One Hundred and Fourth Regiment had two Negro officers, Major Martin R. Delany and Captain O. S. B. Wall. Among the Negro surgeons who received commissions were Alexander T. Augusta of the Seventh Regiment, and John V. DeGrasse of the Thirty-Fifth. Charles B. Purvis, Alpheus Tucker, John Rapier, William Ellis, Anderson Abbott, and William Powell were hospital surgeons at Washington. Among the Negro chaplains with commissions were Henry M. Turner, William Hunter, James Underdue, William Warring, Samuel Harrison, William Jackson, and John R. Bowles.

At the beginning there was discrimination in the pay of white and Negro soldiers. The Enlistment Act of July 17, 1862, provided that whites with the rank of private should receive $13 a month and $3.50 for clothing, but Negroes of the same rank were to receive only $7 and $3 respectively. Negro soldiers and their white officers objected vigorously to this discrimination. The Fifty-Fourth Massachusetts Regiment served a year without pay rather than accept discriminatory wages, and went into battle in Florida in 1864 singing "Three cheers for Massachusetts and seven dollars a month." In the Third South Carolina Regiment, Sergeant William Walker was shot, by order of court martial, for "leading the company to stack arms before their captain's tent, on the avowed ground that they were released from duty by the refusal of the government to fulfill its share of the contract." After many protests the War Department, beginning in 1864, paid Negroes as much as whites.

Negroes performed all kinds of services in the Union army. Organized into raiding parties, they were sent through Confederate lines to destroy fortifications and supplies. Since they knew the Southern countryside better than most white soldiers, and could pass themselves off as just another Negro slave, they were extensively used as spies and scouts. White officers relied upon information secured by Negro spies. Harriet Tubman was a spy for Union troops at many points on the eastern seaboard.

Negro soldiers built fortifications along the coasts and up the rivers. They were engaged so much in menial tasks, instead of fighting, that their officers made numerous complaints. One said that he would rather carry his rifle in the ranks of fighting men than be overseer to black laborers. In 1864 Adjutant General Lorenzo Thomas took notice of the situation and issued an order that there should be no excessive impositions upon Negro troops and "that they will be only required to take their fair share of fatigue duty with white troops. This is necessary to prepare them for the higher duties of conflicts with the enemies."

The "higher duties of conflicts" had already begun, for Negroes saw action against Confederate forces as early as the fall of 1862. Hardly a battle was fought to the end of the war in which some Negro troops did not meet the enemy. They saw action, according to George Washington Williams, in more than 250 skirmishes. In the Battle of Port Hudson, eight Negro infantry regiments fought.

Naturally the Confederacy was outraged by the Northern use of Negro troops. The question immediately arose as to whether they should be treated as soldiers of the enemy or slaves in insurrection. The vast majority of Southerners viewed Negro soldiers as rebellious slaves and insisted that they should be treated as such. In 1862 President Davis ordered that all Negro slaves captured in arms were to be delivered to the state from which they came, to be dealt with according to state laws. Union officials insisted that captured Negroes should be treated as prisoners of war, but the Confederates never accepted that point of view until 1864, when the Southern government agreed.

Some captured Negroes, perhaps not many, were sold into slavery. Others were killed. The Confederate Secretary of War countenanced the killing of some Negro prisoners in order to make an example of them. In 1864 a Confederate officer, Col. W. P. Shingler, told his subordinates not to report the capture of any more Negroes. The worst case was the Fort Pillow affair. On April 12, 1864, the Fort fell to Confederate forces under command of General Nathan B. Forrest. Negroes who were there were not permitted to surrender; they were shot, and some were burned alive. Yet many Negro troops were captured and held by the South. In 1863 General Butler reported that 3,000 Negro troops were prisoners of the Confederates. Late in 1864 nearly 1,000 Negro prisoners worked on Confederate fortifications at Mobile.

Negroes saw action in every theater of operation during the Civil War. They were at Milliken's Bend in Louisiana, Olustee in Florida, Vicksburg in Mississippi, and at the siege of Savannah. They fought in Arkansas, Kentucky, Tennessee, and North Carolina. They played a part in the reduction of Petersburg and were at Appomattox Court House, April 9, 1865. Congress awarded a medal to Decatur Dorsey for gallantry while acting as color-sergeant of the Thirty-Ninth United States Colored Troops at Petersburg on July 30, 1864. Private James Gardner, of the Thirty-Sixth, received a medal for rushing in advance of his brigade to shoot a Confederate officer leading his men into action. Four men of the Fifty-Fourth Massachusetts Infantry earned the Gilmore Medal for gallantry in the assault on Fort Wagner, in which their commanding officer, Colonel Robert Gould Shaw, lost his life. Major-General Gilmore issued the following order to commend Negro soldiers under his command for a daring exploit:

On March 7, 1865, a party of Colored soldiers and scouts, thirty in number . . . left Jacksonville, Florida, and penetrated into the interior through Marion County. They rescued ninety-one Negroes from slavery, captured four white prisoners, two wagons, and twenty-four horses and mules; destroyed a sugar-mill and a distillery . . . and burned the bridge over the Oclawaha River. When returning they were attacked by a band of over fifty cavalry, whom they defeated and drove off with a loss of more than thirty to the rebels. . . . This expedition, planned and executed by Colored men under the command of a Colored non-commissioned officer, reflects credit upon the brave participants and their leader.

Testimonies similar to this were given by Major-Generals E. R. S. Canby, Godfry Weitzel, James G. Blunt, S. A. Hurlbut, Alfred H. Terry, and W. F. Smith, as well as by men of other ranks. The most significant thing about their words of praise is that they bear witness to the fact that Negro soldiers did what they could to save the Union and secure their freedom.

More than 38,000 Negro soldiers lost their lives in the Civil War. It has been estimated that their rate of mortality was nearly 40 per cent greater than among white troops. In the Fifth United States Colored Heavy Artillery, for example, 829 men died, the largest number of deaths in any outfit in the Union army. The Sixty-Fifth Colored Infantry lost more than 600 men from disease alone. The high mortality rate among Negroes is to be explained by several unfavorable conditions. Among them were excessive fatigue details, poor equipment, bad medical care, the recklessness and haste with which Negroes were sent into battle, and the "no quarter" policy with which Confederates fought them. It is impossible to estimate the number of Negroes who died at the hands of their enemy, but it must have run into thousands. There can be no doubt, therefore, that Negroes contributed heavily to the victory of Union forces in the second great war for freedom.

Victory!

The surrender of the Confederate army in 1865 meant victory not only for the powerful military forces of the North but also for an indestructible Union. Once and for all the question of whether states had a right to secede from the Union was settled. The question of the exact relation of a state to the federal government could arise again, but all states were bound henceforth to recognize the superior sovereignty of the federal government.

The surrender of the Confederacy was also a personal victory for President Lincoln and his policies. It was he who evolved the theory that the states had not seceded, but that rebellious citizens had gotten out of hand. Now he could use this theory, magnanimous as it was, to hasten binding up the nation's wounds. Almost as long as any man in public life, Lincoln had spoken out against slavery. Now he could view with satisfaction its abolition, which began with his war proclamations and ended with the adoption of the Thirteenth Amendment late in 1865.

The end of the war marked a victory for the abolitionists. At no time in the nation's history had a "pressure group" done so much to shape public opinion and then to move opinion to action. For a generation they had labored untiringly, suffering abuse and even bodily harm. With them, however, it was a moral crusade and they were blind to personal indignities and insensible to suffering. More effectively than ever before in our history they had roused the nation's conscience to its sins and misdeeds. Down to the present day Americans still feel the effects of the morality in human relations which was the creed of abolitionists.

For the Negro, Lee's surrender was a victory. At last he achieved what human beings everywhere have always wanted —freedom. The end of the war brought to a close a period of enslavement which had lasted for almost two hundred and fifty years. The desire for freedom had been kept alive through the centuries by relatively few Negroes who demonstrated by their conduct that freedom and the right to it transcended racial lines. The victory was won, in part, by their struggles through the centuries as well as by their services in the final battles.

Paradoxically, the end of the war was also a victory for the South. To be sure, it had suffered military reverses and lost much. But it had been delivered from the domination of an institution that had stifled its economic development and rendered completely ineffective its intellectual life. Opportunities for extensive development in new areas of economic activity had hardly existed in the South; and because it was sensitive to criticism of slavery, the region had expelled both freedom of speech and the talents which flourish only in freedom. It was a great day for the South when, at last, it could be realistic in economic life, and its churches, schools, and writers could face the truth and express it as they saw it. At least no system of slavery any longer demanded that they do otherwise.

The end of the war was, moreover, the beginning of a new era in the history of the United States. The economic revolution ushered in by the tremendous forces let loose in war was to transform every phase of American life and to create new problems and injustices for reformers to solve. In the new era the Republicans would have to find a new faith for their party, and the abolitionists new social ills to eradicate. The Negroes would have to perfect their freedom in a society that was changing so rapidly that adjustment would be difficult even for the best educated of them. For all Americans, perhaps the greatest problem which arose out of the Civil War and its economic aftermath was to find a way to retain freedom, the desire for which had become almost an obsession, and yet at the same time to enjoy security, which was becoming more precarious in the new economic order. As Negro and white people set out to find the perfect balance between freedom and security in post-Civil War America, democracy faced a new test.

XVII •

The Effort to Attain Peace

Reconstruction and the Nation

● *In few periods of our history has the whole fabric of* American life been altered so drastically as during the Civil War and the period immediately following it. To be sure, there were the social and economic changes that stemmed from the emancipation of four million Negroes in the South, but these changes were so completely interwoven with other consequences of the war as to make them wholly inseparable. Although the South, for example, did not experience great industrial development during the war, the North did; and the forces let loose were so powerful that they affected the entire course of so-called Reconstruction. The political changes that began with the secession of the Southern states concerned the whole nation; but the economic transformation brought on by numerous changes in production and distribution demanded the attention of every practical-minded man in the United States.

It must be remembered, as Professor Howard K. Beale has pointed out, that there is no way of understanding Reconstruction unless an attempt is made to study it in its setting. It is not a history of "Negro rule," as many historians have dubbed the period of Radical Reconstruction, nor is it Southern history, however much students in the past have approached it from a regional point of view. It is an integral part of the national history, and one may find an explanation for strange events in Alabama not only in the activities of people in that state, but in the movements and transactions of men in Boston, or New York, or Philadelphia. From 1865 to the end of the century the United States was picking up the threads of her social, political, and economic life, so abruptly cut in 1861, and attempting to tie them together in a new pattern as a result of the war. South Carolina's political life after 1865 was affected by more than the presence of Negroes in the state legislature or in other positions of public trust. It was affected, as well, by the dynamic changes of economic reconstruction. Reconstruction in 1865 was, indeed, nation-wide.

Southerners who travelled in the North after the Civil War were amazed at the changes that a few years had wrought in the economic life of the section. The pressing military needs, the extensive inflation of the Union currency, and the stimulating effect of protective tariff legislation had all conspired to industrialize the North. Steel factories were producing much more than what was needed for the prosecution of war; railroads were rapidly connecting the North and West in one large community. Hundreds of technological developments made possible the production of commodities, the conception of which would have unduly strained the imagination two decades earlier. New forms of economic organization emerged whose possibilities for expansion over the nation and the world were almost unlimited, and whose leaders were filled with a desperate anxiety to create monopoly and reap huge profits. Northerners were as anxious to sell to ex-Confederates as they were to have customers in the North. The most discerning Southerners must have seen that the new order of things was the result of the triumph of industrialism over the agrarian way of life. The new and old bustling cities were symbols of the triumph, while the wasted and abandoned lands of the South signified the defeat of the old agrarianism. The Southerner could also see that if his section was not careful it would suffer economic and psychological conquest by the North as completely as on the battlefield.

Politics were much disturbed in the period after the Civil War, and the problem of the reorganization of the seceded states was only part of the unsettled state of political affairs. During the war the President had exercised many powers that would not be tolerated in peace, and even before the war's end Congress signified by its choleric temper that it was anxious to restore the balance of the three branches of government. From the point of view of many men in Congress, the pendulum had to swing back, and not even a Lincoln should obstruct the delicate operations of constitutional government. The unexpected accession to the Presidency of Andrew Johnson merely complicated matters and made the Congress more determined than ever to have a full share in governing the country. The fear of Republicans that they would lose political control, the pressure of new industrialists for favorable legislation, and conflicting philosophies of Reconstruction are all considerations that cannot be overlooked in studying the politics of the period.

The political chaos that followed in the wake of war carried with it the inherent element of corruption. There was an extravagance about war-time spending that encouraged corruption, and the beneficiaries of graft and bribery had no intention of retiring from their pursuits at the end of the war. Indeed, many war-time profiteers kept within the bounds of respectability, but in the post-war period respectability was no longer desirable because of its restraining influence. As the more able men went into industry and other economic activities, incompetent people, the easy prey of cunning industrialists and unscrupulous politicians, took over the management of political affairs. Sound economic and political reconstruction became all the more difficult, and the United States surpassed other countries in corruption during the post-war years.

One cannot dismiss the problem of American political intelligence after the Civil War merely by observing that there were four million Negroes who were without any experience in public affairs. To these must be added the millions of Europeans who poured into the country in every post-war decade and who muddied the political waters considerably. Many of them had not participated in any kind of government, and most of them had no understanding of the workings of representative government. The vast majority, moreover, came from countries where a strange language, poor education, and a low standard of living made adjustment in the new world even more difficult. They were, of course, exposed to venal and corrupt politicians and frequently became unwitting accessories to the crimes of corrupt governments. The towns were attracting millions of people from the country. Although they were, for the most part, American citizens, they were so ignorant of the ways of urban communities that they fell victims to scheming city politicians. All these elements added to the political chaos of Reconstruction and made it more difficult.

The immediate problems of Reconstruction were numerous. One of the most important was the rebuilding of the war-torn South and the restoration of her economic life on the basis of free labor. At the end of the war there was no civil authority in the Carolinas, Georgia, Florida, Alabama, Mississippi, and Texas. Many despondent Southerners abandoned their farms or left the South altogether. Others, willing to start over again, did not know where to begin. The countryside had been devastated by the Union armies. Public buildings and private homes had been burned. The lands had deteriorated under poor cultivation or none at all, and titles to lands and crops in many areas were in dispute. Everywhere there was suffering from starvation and disease. Many Negroes, homeless and without jobs, wandered from place to place, much to the disgust and fear of the whites. The mental aberrations of the whites were disturbing: they had difficulty in thinking of the Negro as a free man, and this problem of reconciling themselves to his new status loomed larger and larger before their vision, blinding them to an objective consideration of other pressing problems.

The needs of the South were great, both in number and variety. There was the important problem of finding a way to restore the seceded states to their places in the Union. It was not as simple as welcoming a prodigal back into the family. Precautions must be taken to make sure that the state governments did not fall into the hands of irreconcilable ex-Confederates who might undo the accomplishments of the war. Involved in this problem were the questions of how much punishment the leaders of the Confederate states should suffer, and whether their states had, indeed, seceded at all. Tedious as the problem was, it appeared that it might soon be solved, and that the United States would once more be truly united.

Inseparably connected with the problems of rebuilding the South and bringing it back into the Union was the question of the Negro. There was no dispute over the fact that he was in dire need, but there was serious doubt who could best serve his needs. There was no question of his status as a free man, but conflict arose over the possible distinctions between him and a white man. Even more serious was the problem of whether his status should be settled and his condition improved before the Southern states were permitted to return to the Union.

A barrier to the solution of these pressing post-war troubles was the legacy of hate which those in whose hands the future of the country rested had inherited from a generation of bitter intersectional strife. Perhaps this animosity was the most grievous wound to heal, for it lay deep in the hearts of both Northerners and Southerners, and none knew how to attend it. There was no hope of solving any problem until a new spirit of conciliation and good will could be created. In this intangible and elusive area lay the key to intersectional peace.

Thus Reconstruction was essentially a national, not a sectional or racial problem. The major obstacles in the way of a satisfactory settlement grew out of developments that were for the most part national. With the perspective of one hundred years it becomes increasingly clear today that few crises in the history of the United States have so urgently demanded national action. Almost as obvious is the fact that the problem of Reconstruction was essentially the problem of the emergence of a nation moving painfully toward greater economic and political democracy.

Conflicting Policies

Lincoln early saw the need for a policy of dealing with the states of the South as they capitulated to the Union army and of handling the large number of Negroes who came under the control of the United States before the end of the war. Since he had insisted on waging war on the basis that it was a rebellion of Southern citizens rather than a revolt of the states, he could deal with citizens of the Confederacy on the assumption that they had misled their state governments. It was the function of the President, he believed, to undertake whatever measures were necessary to reorganize the states in the South. As states capitulated, Lincoln appointed military governors who had complete power until civil authority could be established. In December, 1863, he outlined to Congress his comprehensive plan for reconstruction and issued a proclamation containing its essential features.

Acting on the assumption that Reconstruction was an executive problem, President Lincoln extended general amnesty to the people of the South, except certain high Confederate civil and military officials, and called on them to swear allegiance to the United States. When as many as one-tenth of the people of a state as had cast votes in the election of 1860 complied with the proclamation, a government could be established that would be recognized by the President. Although his proclamation was generally well received and the Southern states proceeded to reconstruct themselves under its provisions, some members of Congress were of the opinion that the President was too lenient, and that Reconstruction was a matter to be handled by Congress. They enacted their own measure, the Wade-Davis bill, which disfranchised a larger number of ex-Confederates, delayed action until a majority of the whites had qualified as loyal voters, and required greater assurances of loyalty from the reconstructed governments. The President refused to sign the bill, but granted that it was one way for a state to reorganize if it chose to do so.

As far as the Negro was concerned, Lincoln realized that there must be a satisfactory settlement of his status if peace was to be secured in the South. It will be recalled that all during the war he entertained the hope that a substantial number of Negroes would choose to emigrate from the United States and that he sought congressional cooperation in encouraging Negroes to do so. It must have become obvious to him that the problem could not be solved in this way, and he was faced with having to reach some solution based on the Negro's continued presence in the United States and in the South. He permitted the establishment of a number of departments of Negro affairs which assumed responsibility for administering to the needs of Negroes in the early years of the war. Gradually, the work of these departments was taken over by the Freedmen's Bureau.

Concerning the recognition of the Negro as a full citizen, Lincoln was of the opinion that with education the Negro would qualify for it, at least on a restricted basis. In 1864 he wrote to Governor Hahn of Louisiana asking "whether some of the colored people may not be let in [to the elective franchise] as, for instance, the very intelligent, and especially those who have fought gallantly in our ranks." Doubtless he was disappointed when the new legislature met in the fall of 1864 and failed to extend the franchise to any of the Negroes of Louisiana, despite the fact that many of them were persons of considerable intellectual and economic achievement.

Some evidence of a conflict between the President and Congress over the policy of reconstructing the South was visible before the death of Lincoln in April, 1865. Shortly after Andrew Johnson took the oath of office as President, he made it clear that he would follow essentially the plan of reconstruction outlined by Lincoln. There were some indications that he might go beyond it. When Charles Sumner, the ardent protagonist of Negro rights, conferred with Johnson shortly after he became President, Johnson assured him that they were agreed on Negro suffrage. In his proclamation of May, 1865, he called for complete abolition of slavery, repudiation of the Confederate war debts, nullification of the ordinances of secession, and the disqualification of the people Lincoln had disfranchised as well as all Southerners worth $20,000 or more. He appointed provisional governors in the Southern states; and legislatures, based on white suffrage, were called to modify their constitutions in harmony with that of the United States.

Through 1865 and 1866 the states of the South gradually assumed the responsibility of governing their people. The greatest concern of Southerners was the problem of controlling the Negro. There were all sorts of ugly rumors of a general uprising in which Negroes would take vengeance on whites and dispossess them of their property. Most Southern whites, although willing to concede the end of slavery even to the point of voting for the adoption of the Thirteenth Amendment, were convinced that laws should be speedily enacted to curb the Negroes and to insure their role as a laboring force in the South. These laws bore a remarkable resemblance to the ante-bellum Black Codes and can hardly be described as measures which respected the rights of Negroes as free men. Several of them undertook to limit the areas in which Negroes could purchase or rent property. Vagrancy laws imposed heavy penalities that were designed to force all Negroes to work whether they wanted to or not. The control of the Negro permitted to white employers was about as great as that which slaveholders had exercised. If a Negro quite his job, he could be arrested and imprisoned for breach of contract. Negroes were not allowed to testify in court except in cases involving their race. Numerous fines were imposed for seditious speeches, insulting gestures or acts, absence from work, violating curfew, and the possession of firearms. There was, of course, no enfranchisement of Negroes and no indication that in the future they could look forward to full citizenship and participation in a democracy.

As it became clear to Northern protagonists of the Negro that the Reconstruction policy of President Johnson sanctioned white home rule in the South in ways strikingly similar to those which existed before the Civil War, they became furious. Friends of the Negro refused to tolerate a policy that would nullify the gains made during the war. Abolitionists, roused again to their crusade, demanded that the Negro be enfranchised and a harsher policy adopted toward the South. Practical Republicans, fearful of the political consequences of a South dominated by Democrats, became convinced that Negro suffrage in the South would aid in the continued growth of the Republican party. Industrialists, with an eye on markets and cheap labor in the South, were fearful that the old agrarian system would be resurrected by the Democrats. These groups began to pool their interests in order to modify substantially the Johnson policy of Reconstruction.

When Congress met in December, 1865, it was determined to take charge of Reconstruction. If there had been any doubt as to the direction in which the South was moving, it was dispelled by the character of the representatives sent to Congress. One had been vice-president of the Confederacy, four Confederate generals, five Confederate colonels, six Confederate cabinet officers, and fifty-eight members of the Confederate Congress. Although none could take the oath of office, their election indicated that the South stood solidly behind its defeated leaders. Thaddeus Stevens, wily Republican leader and vigorous supporter of a stern policy toward the South, was exasperated. He proposed that Congress assume control of Reconstruction, asserting that the President's policy had been essentially provisional. Congress adopted a Stevens resolution creating the Joint Committee on Reconstruction to inquire into the condition of the Southern States and to make recommendations for a new policy.

In two bills, one to strengthen the Freedmen's Bureau and extend its life and the other to guarantee civil rights to Negroes, Congress sought to exercise its influence in behalf of the Negroes. President Johnson vetoed the Freedmen's Bureau bill on the grounds that it was unconstitutional and proposed to do more for Negroes than had ever been done for whites. The attempt to over-ride the veto failed. He likewise vetoed the Civil Rights bill and declared that Negroes were not yet ready for the privileges and equalities of citizens. Johnson's veto of these two bills, his condemnation of the proposed Fourteenth Amendment, and his attack on Stevens, Sumner, and other Northern leaders, put Congress in an angry mood. Consequently, on April 9, 1866, it passed the Civil Rights bill over his veto.

The fight between President and Congress was now in the open. Both believed that they could muster strength enough to have their way. Johnson was so confident of his influence that he decided to carry the fight to the people and call on them to return men to Congress in the fall of 1866 who would support his program. His conduct during the well-known "swing around the circle" was so unbecoming and his utterances so indiscreet that the entire country was outraged. He was soundly repudiated at the polls when the nation elected to Congress an overwhelming majority to oppose him and his Reconstruction program.

The rejection of the Fourteenth Amendment by the Southern states, their enactment of Black Codes, the widespread disorder in the South, and President Johnson's growing obstinacy persuaded many people that the South had to be dealt with harshly. Consequently, the Joint Committee presented to Congress a measure that ultimately was the basis of the Reconstruction Act of 1867. Through this measure the ex-Confederate states, except Tennessee where reconstruction was moving satisfactorily, were divided into five military districts in which martial law was to prevail. On the basis of universal suffrage a convention in each state was to draw up a new constitution acceptable to Congress. No state was to be admitted until it ratified the Fourteenth Amendment. The former rebels who could not take the iron-clad oath were of course disfranchised. President Johnson vetoed the bill, contending that it was unconstitutional, unfair to the states that had been reorganized, and that the Negroes, not having asked to vote, did not even understand what the franchise was. Congress over-rode the veto and proceeded to enact · other measures in the new program of Reconstruction.

The victory of Congress over the President was complete. It had enfranchised Negroes in the District of Columbia, put the Freedmen's Bureau on a firm footing, carried forward its program of reconstructing the South through stern and severe treatment, and laid plans for subordination of the Presidency by removal of its incumbent. The victory of Congress marked not only the beginning of a harsh policy toward the South; it also signified the triumph of a coalition of interest—crusaders, politicians, and industrialists—all of whom hoped to gain something substantial through Congressional Reconstruction. It produced new conflicts, more bitter than preceding ones, and created so much confusion and chaos in almost every aspect of life that many of the problems would persist for more than a century.

Relief and Rehabilitation

In the closing months of the war and afterwards the South suffered acutely. The abandoned lands, the want of food and clothing, the thousands of displaced persons, and the absence of organized civil authority to cope with the emergency merely suggest the nature of the suffering. The extent of it among both Negroes and whites can scarcely be imagined. Negroes were distressed not only because they lacked the necessaries of life but also because they genuinely feared, especially after the death of President Lincoln, that they would gradually slip back into a condition hardly better than that of slaves. In the summer and fall of 1865 they held several conventions, all looking toward an improvement of their conditions. A Negro convention in Nashville protested seating the Tennessee delegation to Congress because the legislature had not passed just laws for Negroes. It also demanded that Congress recognize Negro citizenship. A group of 120, meeting in Raleigh, North Carolina, declared that they wanted fair wages, education for their children, and repeal of the discriminatory laws passed by the state legislature. Mississippi Negroes protested against reactionary policies in their state and asked Congress to extend the franchise to Negroes. It was the same thing in Charleston and Mobile: Negroes were demanding suffrage, the abolition of Black Codes, and measures for the relief of suffering.

While the pleas of Negroes were largely ignored in the South, there were Northerners who worked to relieve their distress. Private organizations had taken up this work during the war, and considerable pressure was applied to Congress as early as 1863 to assume responsibility for the welfare of needy whites and Negroes in the South. Military commanders did whatever they could or wanted to do with regard to relief.

The need, however, was for a comprehensive and unified service for freedmen. It was not until March, 1865, that the Bureau of Refugees, Freedmen, and Abandoned Lands, better known as the Freedmen's Bureau, was established. With officials in each of the Southern states, the Bureau aided refugees and freedmen by furnishing supplies and medical services, establishing schools, supervising contracts between freedmen and their employers, and managing confiscated or abandoned lands, leasing and selling some of them to freedmen.

The atmosphere in which the Freedmen's Bureau worked was one of hostility. Many Northerners looked upon it as an expensive agency, the existence of which could not be justified in times of peace. In the South the opposition to the Bureau was vehement. There was serious objection to federal interference with the relations between the worker and his employer. It was believed, moreover, that the Bureau had a political program for enfranchising the Negro and establishing a strong Republican party in the South.

There can be no doubt that the Freedmen's Bureau relieved much suffering among Negroes and whites. Between 1865 and 1869, for example, the Bureau issued twenty-one million rations, approximately five million going to whites and fifteen million to Negroes. By 1867 there were 46 hospitals under the Bureau staffed with physicians, surgeons, and nurses. The medical department spent over two million dollars to improve the health of freedmen, and treated more than 450,000 cases of illness. The death rate among freedmen was reduced, and sanitary conditions were improved.

The Bureau undertook to resettle many people who had been displaced during the war. Because of the urgent need for labor to cultivate the land, free transportation was furnished freedmen to leave congested areas and to become self-supporting. By 1870 more than 30,000 persons had been moved. Although abandoned and confiscated lands were generally restored to their owners under the amnesty proclamations of Lincoln and Johnson, the Bureau distributed some land to freedmen. Colonies of infirm, destitute, and vagrant Negroes were set up in several states. Small parcels of land were first allotted and then leased to them for management and cultivation.

The Bureau sought to protect the Negro in his freedom to choose his own employer and to work at a fair wage. Both parties were required to live up to their contract. Agents of the Bureau consulted with planters and freedmen, urging the former to be fair in their dealings, and instructing the latter in the necessity of working to provide for their families and to achieve independence and security. Thousands of Negroes returned to work under conditions more satisfactory than those which had existed before the Bureau supervised their relations with employers. General Oliver Otis Howard reported that "in a single state not less than fifty thousand such [labor] contracts were drawn." Paul S. Peirce has estimated that in the South as a whole there must have been several hundred thousand contracts.

When it was felt that the interest of Negroes could not be safely entrusted to local courts, the Bureau organized freedmen's courts and boards of arbitration. They had civil and criminal jurisdiction over minor cases where one or both parties were freedmen. Frequently an expression of the Bureau's interest was sufficient to secure justice for freedmen in the regular courts. In Maryland, for example, the case of a white physician who assaulted a Negro without provocation was carried by the Bureau agent to the state supreme court, which admitted the Negro's testimony and convicted the physician.

The Bureau achieved its greatest success in education. It set up or supervised all kinds of schools: day, night, Sunday, and industrial schools, as well as colleges. It cooperated closely with philanthropic and religious organizations in the North in the establishment of many institutions. Among the schools founded in this period which received aid from the Bureau were Howard University, Hampton Institute, St. Augustine's College, Atlanta University, Fisk University, Storer College, and Biddle Memorial Institute (now Johnson C. Smith University). The American Missionary Association, the Baptists, Methodists, Presbyterians, and Episcopalians were all active in establishing schools. Education was promoted so vigorously that by 1867 schools had been set up in "the remotest counties of each of the confederate states."

Teachers came down from the North in large numbers. Besides Edmund Ware at Atlanta, Samuel C. Armstrong at Hampton, and Erastus M. Cravath at Fisk, there were hundreds whose services were not as widely known. In 1869 there were 9,503 teachers in the freedmen's schools of the South. Although some were Southerners, a majority of the whites came from the North. The number of Negro teachers was growing; and gradually they took over supervision of some schools.

By 1870, when the educational work of the Bureau stopped, there were 247,333 pupils in 4,329 schools. Reports from all quarters "showed a marked increase in attendance, and advance in scholarship, and a record of punctuality and regularity which compared favorably with the schools in the north." The Bureau had spent more than five million dollars in schooling Negroes.

The shortcomings in their education arose not from a want of zeal on the part of teachers but from ignorance of the needs of Negroes and from the necessary preoccupation of students with the problem of survival in a hostile world.

Despite Southern hostility to the Bureau, and the inefficiency of many officials, it performed a vastly important task during Reconstruction. As a relief agency it deserves to be ranked with the great efforts of recent depressions and wars. It demonstrated that the government could administer an extensive program of relief and rehabilitation, and suggested a way in which the nation could grapple with its pressing social problems. To be sure, there was corruption and inefficiency, but not enough to prevent the Bureau from achieving a notable success in ministering to human welfare.

Another agency that offered both spiritual and material relief during Reconstruction was the Negro church. The end of the war led to the expansion of independent churches among Negroes. There were no longer Southern laws to silence Negro preachers and proscribe their separate organizations. Negroes began to withdraw from white churches once they had secured their freedom, and consequently the Negro church grew rapidly after the war. In 1865 Negro members of the white Primitive Baptist Churches of the South established a separate organization called the Colored Primitive Baptists in America. In 1869 the General Assembly of the Cumberland Presbyterian Church organized its Negro members in the Colored Cumberland Presbyterian Church. One of the most important separate churches emerged in the Colored Methodist Episcopal. By 1870, when the Negroes had organized five conferences, the first general conference was held, and white bishops came to consecrate W. H. Miles and R. H. Vanderhorst as the first Negro bishops, to be followed three years later by L. H. Holsey, J. A. Beebe, and Isaac Lane.

The older Negro churches entered a new stage of growth. The African Methodist Episcopal Church, which had only 20,000 members in 1856, boasted 75,000 ten years later. In 1876 its membership exceeded 200,000, and its influence and material possessions had increased in proportion. The Baptists likewise enjoyed phenomenal growth. Local churches sprang up overnight under the ministry of unlettered but inspired preachers. In 1866 the Negro Baptists of North Carolina organized the first state convention. Within a few years every Southern state had a large Negro Baptist organization. Their total membership increased from 150,000 in 1850 to 500,000 in 1870. As the first social institution fully controlled by Negroes in America, the churches gave them an opportunity to develop qualities of leadership, and it is no coincidence that many outstanding Negroes have been ministers. Bishop H. M. Turner of Georgia, the Rev. R. H. Cain of South Carolina, and Bishop J. W. Hood of North Carolina were a few of the political leaders who gained much of their experience in the Negro church.

Economic Adjustment

It was one thing to provide temporary relief for freedmen, and another to guide them along the road to economic stability and independence. The release from bondage of four million persons had serious implications for the economic structure of the South at a time when it could least afford to be disturbed. To be sure, many Negroes would not work because they were exhilarated by their new liberty, or scorned low wages and lacked confidence in their employers. But many were active and all were potential competitors in the labor market. To white workers the situation was extremely disturbing. The white planter, however, in an effort to re-establish himself, was anxious to secure labor at the lowest possible price; and if in his own mind he conceded the right of the Negro to be free, he was seldom able to realize that the Negro also had a right to refuse work. Many prospective employers therefore sought to force the Negro to work. The Black Codes were, in many instances, formulated with this specific end in view.

The Black Codes represented the effort of the South to solve problems created by the presence of freedmen, as the Freedmen's Bureau represented the efforts of the federal government to achieve the same end. The establishment of the Freedmen's Bureau and of Radical Reconstruction governments did not mean that the Black Codes had failed, but rather that political power over the South had been transferred to Washington. In the final analysis, neither the Black Codes nor Radical Reconstruction solved the economic problems of freedmen. What solution there was, however unsatisfactory, came by negotiations between the white employer and Negro worker, in some instances under the supervision of the Freedmen's Bureau. Because the federal government failed to give the Negroes much land, they slowly returned to the farms and resumed work under circumstances hardly more favorable than before the war. The Negro agricultural worker found himself at the mercy of the white planter. Labor contracts drawn up to bind both parties were frequently disregarded, employers failing to pay stipulated wages and workers failing to perform tasks outlined in their contracts.

Once the Negro was back on the farm as a worker, he was paid either in monthly wages or a share of the crop. Plantation wages ranged from $9 to $15 a month for men and from $5 to $10 for women, in addition to food, shelter, and fuel. Where the sharecropping system prevailed, freedmen were allowed from a quarter to half of the cotton and corn; they were also provided with a house, fuel, and in some cases with food. There was every opportunity for the contracting parties not to live up to their word; good faith was the only effective way to keep agreements. It need not be added that where hatred and bitterness prevailed, as in so many parts of the South, relations between employer and worker often militated against efficient production.

There can be no question that the majority of Negroes worked, despite Southern doubts of their efficiency as free workers. They had no other choice but to cast their lot with their former masters and assist them in restoring economic stability to the rural South. By 1870 the cotton kingdom had retrieved much of its losses, and by 1875 the white South had come to realize that cheap free labor could be the basis for a profitable agricultural system. The cotton crop of 1870 had not reached the level of production achieved just before the war, but by 1880 the South was producing more cotton than ever. While the sugar crop recovered more slowly, its continued improvement was marked. Thus Negro farm workers contributed greatly to the economic recovery of the South. As free workers, however, they gained but little. The wages paid to freedmen in 1867 were lower than those that had been paid to hired slaves. In the sharecropping system the cost of maintenance was so great that at the end of the year the freedman was indebted to his employer for most of what he made, and sometimes it was more than he made. The South generally recovered much more rapidly than the freedman.

Many freedmen had received the impression that abandoned and confiscated lands were to be distributed to them in lots of forty acres by January, 1866. This impression stemmed from the Confederate apprehension during the war that the Union government planned to seize their land and convey it to ex-slaves, and from the bill creating the Freedmen's Bureau which gave tacit encouragement to such a plan. Although nothing came of it, the federal government sought to encourage the dispersion of population from congested centers by opening public lands in Alabama, Mississippi, Louisiana, Arkansas, and Florida to all settlers regardless of race. Eighty acres were available for the head of each family. Within a year freedmen secured homesteads in Florida covering 160,960 acres, and in Arkansas they occupied 116 out of 243 homesteads. By 1874 the Negroes of Georgia owned more than 350,000 acres of land. "Forty acres and a mule" as a gift of the government had not been realized, but wherever possible the Negroes were acquiring land in their effort to achieve economic security.

Neither white nor Negro Southerners were aware of the revolutionary implications of the industrial changes taking place. While the South was preoccupied with the restoration of an agricultural regime, the rest of the country responded to the quickened pace of living ushered in by industrialization. Most Negroes remained in rural areas, but a considerable number joined their brothers in the urban centers of both North and South. They migrated to these cities not because they knew of their industrial development, but because of a repugnance to plantation life, which they still associated with slavery. The war was hardly over before the sharp cleavage between the white and Negro worker became apparent. White artisans and factory hands were keenly aware of the same threat to their security that had embittered the landless whites of the South before the war. Negro blacksmiths, bricklayers, pilots, cabinetmakers, painters, and other skilled workers met stern opposition from white artisans wherever they sought employment. In many instances the opposition broke out in violence, in the North as well as in the South.

The use made of Negro labor had the effect of making it more difficult for black workers to achieve security and respectability in the world of labor. Manufacturers and entrepreneurs did not hesitate to employ Negroes in order to undermine white labor unions. In 1867, for example, Negro ship caulkers were brought from Portsmouth, Virginia, to Boston to defeat the white workers' efforts to secure an eight-hour day. Operators of iron and cotton mills and railroad builders all looked South for cheap labor, even if it meant the displacement of workers of a much higher standard of living. The deliberate degradation of Negro labor by white employers in all sections of the country made it impossible for Negro and white workers to join hands or to present a solid front to management.

On the whole Negroes were not welcomed into labor organizations in the post-war period. Some local unions admitted them, like the carpenters and joiners of Boston in 1866, but other locals would not. The locals, moreover, prevented the national unions from adopting a non-descriminatory policy on the ground that local autonomy must be preserved. When the National Labor Union was organized in Baltimore in 1866, Negroes were invited to cooperate in the general movement, but it was made clear that if they were to be regarded as trustworthy they must be taught the true principles of labor reform. It looked as though Negroes were to be effectively barred from the white labor movement, and as a result a group of Negro workers met in December, 1869, to organize the National Negro Labor Union. During the next few years this organization sought affiliation with white labor, but without much success. Local Negro organizations advanced the cause of the black worker. But white workers did everything possible to retard the growth of a Negro labor movement, and Negro leaders too frequently sought to use their organizations for political purposes. Until after 1880 the Negro worker remained involuntarily outside the organized labor movement. In the meantime, as a victim of ruthless and unscrupulous employers, he acquired the reputation of being a strike breaker and one who worked for lower wages than whites. This reputation was to follow him for several generations after the Civil War.

Since Reconstruction was a period in which efforts were made by citizens everywhere to achieve economic independence through various forms of business enterprise, the Negro did likewise. Lack of capital was an obstacle to his success in business. In 1865 the Negroes of Baltimore organized the Chesapeake and Marine Railway and Dry Dock Company, capitalized at $40,000 with the stock divided into 8,000 shares. At the end of five years the company purchased a shipyard and was apparently prospering; but profits began to decline in 1877, and in 1883 the company went out of existence. In Savannah, Negroes invested $50,000 in a business venture which proved worthless. They also failed in an effort to run a land and lumber enterprise in which they had invested $40,000. There were other groups and individuals who sought to make a living by opening shops, but many of them failed, for they had no knowledge of how to operate a business, and those who knew how were caught in the depression following the panic of 1873.

One effort to assist the freedman in his economic adjustment was the encouragement given him to save his money. There had been several experiments with savings banks for Negroes during the war. After the allotment system was developed, many soldiers saved regularly in banks established for that purpose. Outstanding were the Free Labor Bank set up by General Banks at New Orleans, and another established by General Butler at Norfolk. Towards the end of the war, the Negro was given an opportunity to go on saving in the Freedmen's Savings and Trust Company, which was created by the federal government in 1865. The business of the organization, with William Booth as president, was confined to the Negro race, and two-thirds of the deposits were to be invested in securities of the United States.

On April 4, 1865, the headquarters of the Freedmen's Bank was opened in New York. Within the next few months branches were started in Washington, New Orleans, Nashville, Vicksburg, Louisville, and Memphis. By 1872 there were 34 branches, with only the New York and Philadelphia offices in the North, and by 1874 the deposits in all branches totaled $3,299, 201.

But unmistakable evidences of failure were apparent: there was inaccurate bookkeeping, and some of the cashiers were incompetent. There had been almost no Negro employees at the beginning, but gradually they were hired. Some proved able to perform their tasks, but not all. Political influence was used to secure loans. At a time when his business was tottering, Jay Cooke borrowed $500,000 at only 5 per cent interest, and Henry Cooke together with other financiers unloaded bad loans on the Bank. After the big financial houses failed in 1873, there was a run on the Bank, and many speculating officials resigned, leaving Negroes to take the blame. In March, 1874, Frederick Douglass was made president, but the Bank was already a failure, although neither he nor the public were aware of the fact. When he realized the truth, he resorted to desperate means to save the Bank, using his own money and appealing to the Senate Finance Committee for more. The Bank was placed in liquidation by Congress so that it could be reorganized, but it was too late. Confidence in the Bank had been completely shattered, and on June 28, 1874, it closed. Thousands of Negro depositors suffered losses they could ill afford. Negro leaders, some of whom were blameless, were castigated by their fellows, while the Cookes and others who benefited most escaped without public censure.

Perhaps the greatest failure of Reconstruction was economic. At the end of the period both white and Negro workers in the South were suffering from want and privation. In the North, where their lot was substantially better, they had not yet learned to cope with the powerful industrialists who were using political agencies as their most reliable allies and bribing officials with greater regularity than they paid their employees. While the white leaders of the South were preoccupied with questions of Negro suffrage and civil rights, Northern financiers and industrialists took advantage of the opportunity to impose their economic control on the South, and much of it has endured to the present day. The inability of the Negro to solve his problems was not altogether to his discredit. It was merely a symptom of the complexity of the new industrial America which baffled even the most astute of its citizens.

Political Currents

The Reconstruction Act of 1867 imposed on the South a regime more difficult to bear than defeat. The great majority of Southerners were to be disfranchised; Negroes and their allies, loyal whites and those from the North who apparently had come to stay, were to enjoy the ballot. Constitutional conventions were to be called for the express purpose of eradicating the last vestiges of the old order. From the Southern point of view all power was to be placed in the hands of those least qualified to control their destiny. Two years of white home rule were discredited because it was said that Southerners had tried to turn the clock back to the years before the war. Southerners thought the clock was now being turned back to the days of barbarism.

The constitutional conventions called in pursuance of the Reconstruction Act all contained Negro members. Only in South Carolina did they make up a majority of delegates, and in Louisiana they were equal to the whites, each race having 49 delegates. In some states the ratio of Negroes was small, as in Texas where there were only nine out of 90 members of the convention. In most states the Negroes constituted only a respectable minority of the delegates. In six states native white Southerners were in the majority. Some Negro members had been slaves, but others had always been free, and among them were emigrants from the North. Some Negroes were of considerable intellectual stature. In Florida it was generally conceded that Jonathan Gibbs was "the most cultured member of the convention." They were, for the most part, men of moderation. Typical of the magnanimity of the Negroes are the words of Beverly Nash before the constitutional convention of South Carolina:

> I believe, my friends and fellow-citizens, we are not prepared for this suffrage. But we can learn. Give a man tools and let him commence to use them, and in time he will learn a trade. So it is with voting. We may not understand it at the start, but in time we shall learn to do our duty. . . . We recognize the Southern white man as the true friend of the black man. . . . In these public affairs we must unite with our white fellow-citizens. They tell us that they have been disfranchised, yet we tell the North that we shall never let the halls of Congress be silent until we remove that disability.

A generous appraisal of the personnel of a Negro delegation was that made by the Charleston *Daily News:* "Beyond all question, the best men in the convention are the colored members. Considering the influences under which they were called together, and their imperfect acquaintance with parliamentary law, they have displayed, for the most part, remarkable moderation and dignity. . . . They have assembled neither to pull wires like some, nor to make money like others; but to legislate for the welfare of the race to which they belong."

The state constitutions drawn up in 1867 and 1868 were the most progressive the South had ever known. Most of them abolished property qualifications for voting and holding office; some of them abolished imprisonment for debt. All of them abolished slavery, and several sought to eliminate race distinctions in the possession or inheritance of property. Although the planters of Louisiana thought their constitution was the "work of the lowest and most corrupt body of men ever assembled in the South," the laws codified on the basis of this constitution, together with laws adopted later in three codes, remain even today the basic law of the state. In every state the ballot was extended to all male residents, except for certain classes of Confederates; and it is significant that some Negroes, like Nash of South Carolina and Pinchback of Louisiana, were vigorously opposed to any disqualification of Confederates.

The conservative elements of the South almost unanimously denounced the new constitutions and fought to defeat their ratification. When they gained power at the end of Reconstruction, however, they seemed anxious to rewrite only those clauses of the constitutions which had enfranchised Negroes. Florida finally adopted a new constitution in 1885, Mississippi in 1890, South Carolina in 1895, and Virginia in 1902. Like those written soon after the overthrow of Reconstruction, they were remarkably similar to the documents that had been so roundly condemned. Victors in the campaigns for white supremacy were wise enough to retain the public school systems, the modernized machinery of local government, and other measures in the Reconstruction constitutions which pointed toward a more progressive South.

During Reconstruction, Negroes held public offices in the

THE FIRST MIXED JURY IN THE UNITED STATES. This group of men was impanelled to serve on a jury to try Jefferson Davis, the president of the Confederacy. Although he had been held in prison since his capture, he was released without trial shortly after the impanelling had been made. Courtesy Howard University Library.

Southern states. They sat in the legislatures and assisted in enacting laws that have won both the praise and the condemnation of bitter partisans. It was in South Carolina that they wielded the greatest influence. In the first legislature there were eighty-seven Negroes and forty whites. From the outset, however, the whites controlled the state senate, and in 1874 the lower house as well. At all times there was a white governor. It can be said, therefore, that at no time were Negroes in control of South Carolina. There were two Negro lieutenant-governors, Alonzo J. Ransier in 1870 and Richard H. Gleaves in 1872. Samuel J. Lee was speaker of the house in 1872, and Robert B. Elliott in 1874. Francis L. Cardozo, an accomplished Negro who had been educated at the University of Glasgow and in London, was secretary of state from 1868 to 1872 and treasurer from 1872 to 1876. He was regarded by friends and enemies, says A. A. Taylor, as one of the best educated men in South Carolina, regardless of color.

The Negroes of Mississippi were not as largely represented in their new government. In the first Reconstruction legislature there were forty Negro members, some of whom had been slaves. In 1873 Negroes held three significant positions: A. K. Davis was lieutenant-governor; James Hill, secretary of state, and T. W. Cardozo, superintendent of education. On the whole, Negroes took little part in legislation, but a few were chairmen of important legislative committees. In 1872 John R. Lynch was speaker of the house, and at the end of the session a white Democrat praised him "for his dignity, impartiality, and courtesy as a presiding officer."

Between 1868 and 1896 Louisiana had 133 Negro legislators, of whom 38 were senators and 95 were representatives. At no time did they approach control of public affairs. Three Negroes, Oscar J. Dunn, P. B. S. Pinchback, and C. C. Antoine, served as lieutenant-governors; and Pinchback was acting governor for forty-three days in the winter of 1873, when Henry C. Warmoth was removed from office. While Negroes were not in control, they sought to improve political conditions. Oscar J. Dunn, for example, led the fight against corruption and extravagance.

Negroes were not significant in the leadership of Alabama during Reconstruction. They were, to be sure, in both houses of the legislature, but not in sufficient numbers to secure positions of power. They helped adopt the Fourteenth and Fifteenth Amendments, however, and put a state system of schools into operation. Although Negroes were elected to the first Reconstruction legislature of Georgia, they had difficulty in securing and retaining their seats. In September, 1868, the legislature declared that all Negro members were ineligible, and not until almost a year later, when the state supreme court declared them eligible, were they able to regain their seats. The Negro members introduced many bills on education, the jury system, city government reform, and woman suffrage. Two able Negro legislators, Jefferson Long and H. M. Turner, sought better wages for Negro workers, but got little support from their colleagues, who in many instances supported the industrialists seeking to exploit all forms of natural and human resources.

In Florida, Negro members of the Reconstruction government were primarily interested in relief, education, and suffrage. In Jonathan Gibbs, superintendent of public instruction from 1872 to 1874, they had an able leader, a champion of equal rights. H. S. Harmon led the fight for a satisfactory school law. With other Negro legislators he supported a homestead law and such measures as would provide greater economic security for the mass of citizens. North Carolina Negroes helped to inaugurate a system of public schools. An outstanding worker in the field of education was the Rev. J. W. Hood who had helped write the constitution of 1868. The struggle between the old regime and the invading capitalists was so bitter as to obscure any consideration for Negroes. They participated in this fight not so much as Negroes but as persons materially interested in one side or the other.

Very few Negroes held office in the new government of Virginia. Twenty-seven sat in the first legislature, and others served in minor posts Negroes were never powerful enough to determine any policy of the government except, as A. A. Taylor says, on a few occasions where they held the balance between militant factions. So far as the exercise of influence is concerned, the same thing can be said of Negroes in Tennessee, Arkansas, and Texas.

An important way in which the Negro participated in politics was by election to Congress. Between 1869 and 1901 two Negroes served in the Senate and twenty in the House of Representatives. The two Senators were Hiram R. Revels and Blanche K. Bruce, both representing Mississippi. Revels was a North Carolina free Negro who had migrated to Indiana, Ohio, and Illinois, receiving his education at a seminary in Ohio and at

Knox College in Illinois. By the time of the Civil War he had been ordained a minister in the African Methodist Episcopal Church and had taught school in several places. During the war he recruited Negroes for the Union army, founded a school for freedmen in St. Louis, and joined the army as chaplain of a Negro regiment in Mississippi. After the war he settled in Natchez, and became prominent in state politics. In 1870 he was elected to the United States Senate to fill the seat previously occupied by Jefferson Davis. He favored the removal of all disqualifications on ex-Confederates and worked diligently in the interest of his state. He admitted that during his year in the Senate he received fair treatment even in the matter of patronage.

In 1874 Blanche K. Bruce was elected to the Senate, the only Negro to be elected to a full term until the election of Edward Brooke, Republican from Massachusetts, in 1966. He had been born a slave in Virginia. When the war came, he escaped from St. Louis to Hannibal, Missouri, and established a school for Negroes. After the war he studied in the North for several years. In 1869 he went to Mississippi, entered politics, and worked up through a succession of offices from tax collector to sheriff and superintendent of schools. In the Senate he usually voted with his party and introduced a number of bills to improve the conditions of Negroes. When P. B. S. Pinchback was denied a seat in the Senate, to which he had been elected from Louisiana, Bruce spoke for him in vain. He succeeded in having some pension bills passed, but his chief work was with the committees on Manufactures, Education and Labor, as well as Pensions. As chairman of the select committee on the Freedmen's Bank, he conducted a thorough investigation of the causes for its failure. His wide range of interests as a lawmaker is seen in the introduction of bills on the Geneva award for the Alabama claims, another for aid to education and railroad construction, and one for the reimbursement of depositors in the Freedmen's Bank.

Of the 20 Negroes who served in the lower House, South Carolina sent the largest number, eight, and North Carolina followed with four. Alabama sent three; Georgia, Mississippi, Florida, Louisiana, and Virginia, one. It was in the Forty-first Congress, in 1869, that Negroes, three of them, first made their appearance in the federal legislature. In the next Congress there were five. The peak was reached in the Forty-third and Forty-fourth Congresses when seven sat in the House of Representa--

tives. In length of service J. H. Rainey and Robert Smalls, both of South Carolina, led with five consecutive terms for each. John R. Lynch of Mississippi and J. T. Walls of Florida both served three terms, and six others served two terms.

Most of the Negroes in Congress had some experience in public service before going to Washington, as delegates to constitutional conventions, state senators and representatives, and as state or local officials. While they were chiefly concerned with civil rights and education, their efforts were not by any means confined to problems of the Negro. Many fought for local improvements such as new public buildings and appropriations for rivers and harbors. Several, like Walls of Florida and Lynch of Mississippi, promoted protective tariffs for home products. Walls was also interested in the recognition of Cuba. Hyman of North Carolina advanced a program for relief of the Indians, and Nash of Louisiana uttered a plea for intersectional peace.

Concerning the work of Negro members of Congress, the white historian, James Ford Rhodes, wrote: "They left no mark on the legislation of their time; none of them, in comparison with their white associates, attained the least distinction." It must be remembered, however, that if few measures introduced by Negroes were enacted into law, there were other ways in which as members of Congress they served effectively. Many bills which they introduced were deemed unworthy of serious consideration, but this was true of a majority of bills presented to Congress. Others died a natural death on the tortuous road from one house to the other and to the President's desk. None of the Negro members enjoyed the prestige of being chairmen of important committees and had great difficulty in winning the respect even of colleagues in their own party. At a time when Congress could count among its members men affiliated with the most scandalous and corrupt deals in the history of the country, it was not without significance that a former Congressman and ex-Confederate general, Roger A. Pryor, was moved to say in 1873: "We have not yet heard that a Negro congressman was in any way implicated in the Credit Mobilier scandal." To James G. Blaine, who knew most of them, "the colored men who took seats in both Senate and House did not appear ignorant or helpless. They were as a rule studious, earnest, ambitious men, whose public conduct . . . would be honorable to any race."

More important than the men, white or black, who held office during Reconstruction were the forces operating to influence their actions. Negroes, to be sure, were members of Congress, lieutenant-governors, sheriffs, prosecuting attorneys, and recorders of deeds, but at no time was there Negro rule anywhere in the South. Indeed, it can be said with some reason that there was no carpetbag rule as the term is commonly understood. The South, as well as the North, was subject to the most dynamic political and economic currents that had ever stirred American life. Economic revolution, not Reconstruction, determined the pattern of public action after 1865. Tariff legislation was more important than civil rights; railroad subsidies were more important than the suffrage. The industrialists of the North, who had come to control the Republican party, wanted a satisfactory settlement of the Southern problem in order to hasten the exploitation of Southern resources and to capture Southern markets. When the Radical program served their purposes, they cooperated, as in the period when they sought favorable consideration from the Southern legislatures; but when the program failed to bring peace and order, thereby postponing prosperity, they helped to restore home rule to the South.

It is significant that Northern industrialists were active in the South throughout Reconstruction. As Horace Mann Bond points out, William D. Kelly and other Northern capitalists were so anxious to exploit the rich resources and cheap labor of Alabama that they used their influence to bring about a hasty, if not satisfactory, reconstruction of the state. Iron and railroad interests were powerful in Alabama and many Northern capitalists worked behind the scenes, manipulating the actors on the Reconstruction stage. In 1867, for example, the legislature granted $12,000 a mile to companies building railroads and later increased this sum to $16,000. Between 1867 and 1871 the Louisville and Nashville Railroad and the Alabama and Chattanooga Railroad received $17,000,000 in endorsements and loans. These subsidies became part of the Reconstruction debt.

It has been estimated that of $305,000,000 owed by eleven Southern states in 1871, at least $100,000,000 of the debt consisted of contingent and prospective liabilities incurred by the issue of railroad bonds. Southerners and Northerners, Republicans and Democrats, had cooperated in lending the credit of these states to railroad investments. A survey of the Reconstruction debt shows clearly that Southern legislatures were not as extravagant in the purchase of whiskey and cigars for their members as in yielding to the pressure of Northern money interests for favorable and costly legislation. In addition, the expenses of carrying out legitimate programs for improved roads, public education, and other social services accounted for much of the Reconstruction debt.

The graft and corruption of the period were neither new nor peculiar to the South. Public office has been used for personal gain too frequently to ascribe the practice to any particular group, section, or period. The Southern land agents who stole public funds during Van Buren's day would qualify as excellent thieves today. The North descended to a new level of public immorality after the Civil War. Bribery and thievery were rampant in the South during Reconstruction, but doubtless they stemmed from the same forces that made the Tweed Ring in New York and numerous scandals in the Grant administration disgraces to the whole nation. Similar forces have created similar situations in the America of later days.

From a national point of view Reconstruction was a period in which the country moved steadily toward a more powerful position in the world economy, thereby making possible the exercise of tremendous influence on world affairs in succeeding years. The Fourteenth Amendment gave Americans their first clear-cut definition of citizenship and strengthened their position as individuals in a complex social order. It also gave corporations an opportunity to flourish under the broad interpretation that the Supreme Court soon put upon the Amendment. In the Fifteenth Amendment, a wider exercise of the franchise was guaranteed along with the removal of race as a disability. In the South, Reconstruction laid the foundations for more democratic living by sweeping away all qualifications for voting and holding office, and by establishing a system of universal free public education. In failing to provide adequate economic security for the freedmen, Reconstruction left them no alternative but to submit to their old masters, a submission that made easier the efforts of Southern whites to overthrow Reconstruction and restore a system based on white supremacy.

XVIII •

Losing the Peace

The Struggle for Domination

● *The war was hardly over before the victors found out that it* was easy to sit in Washington and proclaim peace by presidential decree or legislative enactment, but very difficult to establish peace in a country so recently torn apart by civil conflict. Despite the fact that General Grant was of the opinion that the South would accept the verdict of the battlefield, there were others who believed that the South was irreconcilable. Carl Schurz returned from a tour of the region with the verdict that the South had submitted only because it saw no alternative. He was alarmed at having found "no expression of hearty attachment to the great republic." To his horror treason was not odious in the South. The tragic dispersion of the Confederate troops at the end of the war contrasted miserably with the presence of Northern invaders—not only white soldiers but also Negro troops, in fact, far fewer than the former Confederates claimed—stationed at strategic points to maintain the peace. This was evidence of the North's conviction that the South was barbarous and that the spirit of slavery had "debased the Southern mind, destroyed liberty and law, and vitiated all white elements upon which a restored union might be erected." Each section was thoroughly convinced that the other was wicked and, under the circumstances, not to be trusted to do the right thing.

The Republicans, having the upper hand even in the early

years of Reconstruction, were determined to strengthen their position and perpetuate their power. They had an effective propaganda for these purposes. They could remind the country that it was the South which had treasonably fought to destroy the Union; that old slaveholders were only waiting for an opportunity to re-enslave the Negroes; and that the Republican party had saved the nation from complete ruin at the hands of Democrats, both North and South. The vulnerable position of the Democrats was summed up by Schurz: "There is no heavier burden for a political party to bear, than to have appeared unpatriotic in war." To be sure, the Democrats claimed they were men of peace and union, but it was a modest claim compared to the extravagant and righteous pretensions of the Republicans. Many Republicans, whatever their altruistic motives, were moved to adopt the cause of the Negro almost solely by considerations of political expediency and strategy. It would have been unnatural for them not to have strengthened their party by enfranchising the Negroes and enlisting them as loyal voters. It would have been equally unnatural for the Democrats, especially the Southern wing, to have abided this clever political maneuver.

The struggle of these two parties to dominate national politics shaped the history of Reconstruction and led to the final defeat of both in attaining peace. The Democrats generally opposed all Republican measures regardless of their merits. The Republicans, convinced of the perfidy if not downright treason of the Democrats, sought to create a coalition that was too self-centered to be either altruistic or effective. To each party must be ascribed some share of the guilt for their utter failure to establish peace between the sections and the races.

With Union troops in the South and an increasing number of federal officials, most of whom were loyal Republicans, the latter sought to build up a strong southern wing of their party. Many Freedmen's Bureau officials were interested not only in the welfare of the Negro but in the growth of the Republican party as well. Moreover, the missionary groups and teachers from the North, who saw in the Republican party an instrument by which the South could be saved from barbarism, supported it enthusiastically. It would be incorrect, however, to conclude that these groups were primarily political in their motives or activities. But the special agency that recruited Republicans, primarily among the Negroes, was the Union League.

The Union League of America was organized in the North during the war. It did an effective job in rallying support for the war wherever there was much opposition. Later it branched out into the South to protect the fruits of Northern victory. As a protective and benevolent society, it welcomed Negro members and catechized them on their political activity. As the Freedmen's Bureau and other Northern agencies grew in the South, the Union League became powerful, attracting a larger number of Negroes. With the establishment of Radical Reconstruction, the League became the spearhead for Southern Republicanism. Since Negroes were the most numerous enfranchised group, the League depended on them for the bulk of Republican strength.

By the fall of 1867 there were chapters of the League all over the South. South Carolina alone had 88, and it was said that almost every Negro in the state was enrolled. Ritual, secrecy, night meetings, and an avowed devotion to freedom and equal rights made the League especially attractive to Negroes. At elections they looked to their chapters for guidance on voting. If they had any doubt about the straight Republican ticket, the League had only to remind them that the party was the party of Abraham Lincoln and of deliverance. A vote for Democrats, they said, was a vote for the return of slavery. During most of Reconstruction the Union League and such smaller organizations as the Lincoln Brotherhood and the Red Strings delivered the Negro vote to the Republican party in national as well as state and local elections.

As long as Lincoln and Johnson permitted some Southern whites to participate in Reconstruction, the latter believed that they could handle the Negro and resurrect the Democratic party. Even when the presence of Negro troops outraged them, they could protest vigorously to the President, as Wade Hampton did in 1866, and expect quick relief. These white Southerners were determined to guide their own destiny and control the Negro. When Radical Reconstruction made this impossible, in 1867, they struck with fury and rage.

The violence which culminated in the Ku Klux movement did not arise solely, however, from the establishment of Radical Reconstruction with the consequent elimination of Southern men from public life. As early as 1866, when Southern leaders had almost complete charge of reconstruction, a kind of guerrilla warfare was carried on against both Negroes and whites who represented the Washington government in the South. The head of the Freedmen's Bureau in Georgia, for example, complained that bands of men calling themselves Regulators, Jayhawkers, and the Black Horse Cavalry were committing the "most fiendish and diabolical outrages on the freedmen" with the sympathy not only of the populace but of the reconstructed governments too. There were scores of these coercive organizations all over the South. They were formed as white protective societies, and while Southern leaders enacted the new Black Codes, they were engaged in "keeping the Negro in his place" and sniping at Northerners who had come South.

Secret societies grew and spread when it became apparent to Southerners that their control was to be broken by Radical Reconstruction. For ten years after 1867 there flourished the Knights of the White Camelia, the Constitutional Union Guards, the Pale Faces, the White Brotherhood, the Council of Safety, the '76 Association, and the Knights of the Ku Klux Klan. Among the numerous local organizations were the White League of Louisiana, the White Line of Mississippi, and the Rifle Clubs of South Carolina. Southerners expected to do by extra- or illegal means what had not been allowed by law: to exercise absolute control over the Negro, drive him and his fellows from power, and establish "White Supremacy." Radical Reconstruction was at all costs to be ended, and the tactics of terrorist groups were the first step of Southern leaders toward this end.

The Camelias and the Klan were the most powerful of the secret orders. Armed with guns, swords, or other weapons, their members patrolled some parts of the South day and night. Scattered Union troops proved wholly ineffectual in coping with them, for they were sworn to secrecy, disguised themselves and their deeds in many ways, and had the respect and support of the white community. They used intimidation, force, ostracism in business and society, bribery at the polls, arson, and even murder to accomplish their deeds. Depriving the Negro of political equality became, to them, a holy crusade in which a noble end justified any means. Negroes were run out of communities if they disobeyed orders to desist from voting; and the more resolute and therefore insubordinate blacks were whipped, maimed, and hanged. In 1871 several Negro officials in South Carolina were given fifteen days to resign and they were warned that if they failed, "then retributive justice will as surely be used as night follows day."

Local efforts to suppress the outlaw organizations were, on the whole, unsuccessful. In 1868 Alabama, for example, passed a law imposing heavy fines and long jail sentences on anyone caught away from home wearing a mask or committing such acts as destroying property and molesting people, but it was generally disregarded. Congress undertook to suppress the Klan and similar groups in a series of laws passed in 1870 and 1871. It was made a punishable crime for any person to prevent another from voting by bribery, force, or intimidation; and the President was authorized to use the land and naval forces to prevent it. In 1871 a second law was passed to strengthen the first. After an extensive investigation, members of Congress were convinced that the Klan was still active, and in April, 1871, enacted a law designed to put an end to the movement. The President was authorized to suspend the writ of habeas corpus in order to suppress "armed combinations." Acts of conspiracy were declared tantamount to rebellion and were to be punished accordingly. As a result, hundreds of arrests were made, and many persons were found guilty of conspiracy. In South Carolina alone, nearly a hundred were sentenced and fined one year.

The struggle between the organized Southern whites on the one hand, and the Union League, Freedmen's Bureau, federal troops, and Negroes on the other, was essentially a struggle for political control of the South. From the Northern point of view it was a question of whether the gains of the war were to be nullified by the rebels who had brought the nation to the brink of disaster in 1861. From the Southern point of view it was a question of home rule—a right which they would defend to the end—and of who should rule at home, which they felt was largely academic since Negroes were not qualified. As surely as the struggle between 1861 and 1865 was civil war, so was the conflict from 1865 to 1877, with all the more bitterness and hatred, but less bloodshed. The peace was being lost because of the vigorous efforts of both parties and sections to recruit their strength from the ruins of war. Peace could not prevail in such war-like circumstances.

The Overthrow of Reconstruction

Reconstruction did not end abruptly as the result of Congressional or Presidential action. Rather it came to a gradual end as restraints were relaxed and stringent legislation repealed. Just as Reconstruction began long before the war was over, so it drew to a close long before the final withdrawal of troops from Southern soil. As early as 1865 many Southerners had resumed their places at home as respected citizens of their communities, and they entered public affairs on taking the oath of allegiance. Even during Radical Reconstruction they continued to return to the fold and to aid in restoring home rule. In 1869 the ex-Confederates of Tennessee were enfranchised. Within a few months large numbers of Southerners in other states reclaimed their citizenship through individual acts of amnesty. In 1871 the "iron clad" oath, which Congress had imposed at the beginning of Radical Reconstruction to disqualify many ex-Confederates, was repealed. In the following year a general amnesty restored the franchise to all but about 600 ex-Confederate officials. It then became possible for the South to take up where it left off in 1861 and to govern itself.

The effect of pardoning Southerners was early seen in the revival of the Democratic party. In 1870 the border states began to go Democratic; and North Carolina and Virginia came under the control of Conservatives who outnumbered the Republican combination of Negroes, "Scalawags," and "Carpetbaggers." In the following year the Georgia Democrats returned to power. In other states controlled by Republicans, the Democrats won partial control, especially in the so-called white counties. In 1874 and 1875 they resumed the rule of Texas, Arkansas, and Alabama. All that Republicans could claim in the South by 1876 were South Carolina, Florida, and Louisiana. The cause of Democracy had gained so much momentum that the overthrow of Republicanism was regarded by many as a crusade.

It had looked as though the Civil War would break out anew as the Democrats resorted to every possible device to overthrow the Radicals. In 1875 Mississippi was on the verge of war. The Negro militia maintained by Governor Ames was especially offensive to the resurgent Democrats; and when the Governor ordered 100 copies of *Infantry Tactics*, presumably for the Negroes, the whites thought it time for a "protective" white militia to step forward. Both sides imported arms, paraded, and actually skirmished. Although Ames promised to disband the Negro militia, disorder and killings continued until the election, when the Democrats carried the state by more than 30,000, and within two months dissolved the Republican party. In Louisiana, the Conservatives organized "White Leagues" and apparently planned to overthrow the Radical government by violence as early as 1874. The Radicals tried to seize the arms of the White Leagues, an attempt which resulted in a riot in New Orleans, killing forty and wounding more than a hundred people. Intermittent warfare continued through the election of 1876; and there was no peace until President Hayes withdrew the federal troops the following year. In South Carolina, the "Red Shirts" dominated campaign meetings and openly carried arms as a measure of "protection" against radical "tyranny." Workingmen's Democratic Associations were organized, and whites were urged to employ only Democrats. Many sections of the state were in constant turmoil, particularly Edgefield County, where Ben Tillman was rapidly becoming a public figure.

The town of Hamburg, South Carolina, was the scene of one of the bloodiest race clashes. When Negro militia paraded on July 4, 1876, several Negroes were arrested on the charge of blocking traffic. When their trial was postponed a large number of armed white men, estimated at several hundred, came into town to see that justice was meted out to the Negro offenders. An ex-Confederate general ordered them to apologize and to surrender their arms, which the Negroes refused to do; heavier arms and more munitions were then imported by the whites. Gunfire followed. The Negroes tried to escape, but too late, and several were killed in the attempt, besides five who were killed after being captured. It was not until Wade Hampton succeeded Chamberlain as governor in 1877 that South Carolina had even a semblance of peace.

The overthrow of the Radicals was accomplished not only by Southerners returning to political action and restoring Conservative governments, but also by other circumstances favorable to the Southerners. Intimidation of the Negroes was effective. Even where there were no riots, the whites kept Negroes from the polls by terrorism and thus insured Democratic victory. After the official dissolution of the Ku Klux Klan in 1869, other methods of intimidation were employed to render the Negroes politically a cipher. Indeed, intimidation was most effective after 1870, although the Ku Klux Klan disclaimed all responsibility because of its increasing violence. The crops of Negroes were destroyed, their barns and houses burned, and they were whipped and lynched for voting Republican. The organized whites became bolder as they patrolled the polling places to guarantee "fair, peaceful, and Democratic" elections. Negroes more and more remained at home, and political power changed from Republican to Democratic hands.

Disclosures of corruption in the Republican governments served to hasten the overthrow of Radical Reconstruction. The case for the Democrats was strengthened considerably as they pointed to misgovernment through bribery, embezzlement, misappropriation of funds, and other corrupt practices. The federal government was unable to rush to the defense of Southern Republican governments, because it was having difficulty in purging itself of corruption. It did not matter that white Southerners had also been corrupt on occasion before the war or that the provisional governments under Johnson were extravagant and corrupt. The Democrats were not in power in 1874, and consequently had all the advantages which the "outs" usually enjoy in such cases. Corruption discredited Radical Reconstruction; and with the loss of conscientious but disillusioned supporters, complete "white" home rule could be restored in the South.

The North had grown weary of the crusade for the Negro. Perhaps Stevens, Sumner, Butler, and old anti-slavery leaders could have gone on with it, but younger people, with less zeal for the Negro, took their places. Loyal party men, they were practical politicians who cared more about industrial interests in the North and South than Radical governments in the South. The assumption of Republican leadership by men like Hayes, Blaine, Conkling, and Logan was a signal for the party to turn to more profitable and practical pursuits.

Not even the Supreme Court postponed the overthrow of Radical Reconstruction. As a matter of fact, its decisions had the effect of hastening the end of Reconstruction. In 1875 several indictments under the Enforcement Act of 1870 charged defendants with preventing Negroes from exercising their right to vote in elections. In *United States v. Reese* the Court held that the statute covered more offenses than were punishable under the terms of the Fifteenth Amendment and was, therefore, unconstitutional. In *United States v. Cruikshank* the Court declared that the Fifteenth Amendment guaranteed citizens not the right to vote but only a right not to be discriminated against by the states on account of race, color, or previous condition of servitude. Neither Negroes nor Republicans could expect much support from a Court that brushed aside the very laws with which they had hoped to implement the franchise amendment. So far as the Court was concerned, the South was free to settle its problems as best it could.

The campaign of 1876 was the great test for both parties. The Democrats were committed to a program to end Reconstruction in the South; the Republicans had not openly promised to do so, but there was at least one wing of the party that was willing to withdraw troops and leave the South to its own devices. In the three states that had not been "redeemed," South Carolina, Louisiana, and Florida, the election campaign approached civil war. The result was, in the case of the first two, a hotly disputed election with both sides claiming victory and establishing dual governments. The Presidency of the United States hung on the decision regarding their disputed votes. To break the impasse the Republicans promised not only to withdraw the troops but also to assist the South in its long-cherished ambition for federal subsidies for internal improvements and better representation in affairs in Washington. When Hayes thus became President, the South was soon assuaged in its grief by his prompt withdrawal of troops. At last the South could rule itself without Northern interference or Negro influence.

With troops out of the South and in a spirit of great concili-ation, Congress removed other restrictions. In 1878 the use of armed forces in elections was forbidden. In 1894 the appropria-tions for special federal marshals and supervisors of elections were cut off. In 1898 the last disabilities laid on disloyal and rebellious Southerners were removed in a final amnesty. Before the dawn of a new century there had been complete recognition in law of what the South had itself accomplished in fact even before the election of 1876.

The Movement for Disfranchisement

After the Democrats returned to power in the South, they con-fronted the problem of finding ways either to nullify the politi-cal strength of Negroes or to disfranchise them altogether. Com-plete disfranchisement by state legislation was viewed with some misgivings as long as the Fourteenth and Fifteenth Amendments remained a part of the fundamental law. Until it was feasible, the Democrats contented themselves with other methods—some extra-legal, others incorporated in state codes—of preventing the Negro's participation in politics. There continued to be intimidation on an extensive scale. Earlier it had been justified in order to wrest political control from the unworthy Republicans, both white and black; but once control was secured, it appeared irresponsible to the more sensitive Southerners to depend upon night riders and Red Shirts to maintain them in power. For many Southerners, however, violence was still the surest means of keeping the Negroes politically impotent, and in countless communities they were not allowed, under penalties of severe reprisals, to show their faces in town on election day.

Other devices, hardly more legal than violence and intimidation, had a more respectable appearance. Polling places were frequently set up far from Negro communities, and the more diligent Negroes failed to reach them upon finding roads blocked and ferries conveniently "out of repair" at election time. Polling places were sometimes changed without notifying Negro voters; or if they were notified, election officials thought nothing of making a last-minute decision not to change the place after all. Election laws were so imperfect that in many communities uniform ballots were not required, and officials winked at Democrats who made up several extra ballots to cast with the one given them. The practice of stuffing ballot boxes was widespread. Criminal manipulation of the counting gave point to the assertion of an enthusiastic Democrat that "the white and black Republicans may outvote us, but we can outcount them."

For what Negro votes were cast and counted, the white factions vied with each other. Dances and parties, with plenty of barbecue and whiskey, were held for Negro voters on election eve as a reminder that they should vote for their benefactors. Some planters brought their Negro workers to the polls, and "voted them like a senseless herd of cattle." At times Negro candidates were nominated by whites in order to divide the vote of the race, while the whites all voted for one of their own race. A few candidates sought Negro votes by advocating measures favorable to them. In 1882, when he was running for the Georgia legislature, Tom Watson won many Negro votes by demanding free Negro schools and condemning the convict lease system which was especially burdensome to Negroes.

334 · FROM SLAVERY TO FREEDOM

Where possible the legislatures, now controlled by zealous White Supremacy Democrats, helped to disfranchise Negroes. Areas with a heavy concentration of Negroes were divided by a system of gerrymandering which rendered the Negro vote ineffective. Poll tax requirements, elaborate and confusing election schemes, complicated balloting processes, and highly centralized election codes were all statutory techniques by which Negroes were disfranchised. Some states went the limit in establishing "legal" barriers to Negro suffrage. Virginia, for example, reapportioned or gerrymandered its voting districts five times within seventeen years in order to nullify Negro ballots. Petty larceny, of which countless Negroes were convicted, was added to the long list of suffrage disqualifications, and the poll tax was made a prerequisite for voting. The elaborate election code of 1894 required that registration and poll tax certificates be shown at the polls, that the names of candidates be printed on the ballot not by party but by office (an extremely confusing arrangement for semi-literate and illiterate voters), and that if others were waiting to vote, an elector must not remain in a booth more than two and a half minutes. Such requirements virtually disfranchised Virginia's illiterate voters, whether white or black.

South Carolina was most adroit in making voting difficult. The law of 1882 required that special ballots and boxes be placed in every polling place for each office on the ballot, and that voters must put their ballots in the correct boxes. No one was allowed to speak to a voter, and if he failed to find the correct box his vote was thrown out. South Carolina and Virginia were not alone in devising ingenious schemes to render the Negro vote ineffective. All the Southern states used some device or other. The result appeared so satisfactory on the whole that by 1889 Henry W. Grady could say, "The Negro as a political force has dropped out of serious consideration."

Strangely enough, however, the elimination of the Negro from the political picture created circumstances that brought him back into the picture again. By the 1880's the menace of black Republicanism had disappeared, and with it the great cohesive force among Southern whites. Almost immediately sharp class lines appeared, and irregularity in party voting cropped out. Now that Southern farmers did not fear "Negro rule," they were more concerned with their own plight and held the dominant white groups responsible for their impending ruin. The coalition of classes which had united only to oppose another race began to disintegrate, as the poor whites came to distrust the Bourbons for substantial economic and political reasons.

An agricultural depression, caused largely by the over-expansion and increased production of cotton, settled down on the South after 1870. The panic of 1873 was especially disastrous, because thousands of small farmers lost their land. In their distress they turned upon the money powers that foreclosed their mortgages, the railroads that charged excessive freight rates but received subsidies from the state and federal taxes, the corporations that sought higher tariffs and charged higher prices for farm machinery, and the government that steadily raised taxes. In the South, moreover, a significant change had taken place in the leadership of the Democratic party. It no longer followed solely the plantation aristocrats, with whom the small farmers felt that they had something in common; industrialists and merchants, whom the small farmers disliked intensely, had come forward and were assuming important roles in party politics. In some states they were the dominant figures. The radical farmers, who wanted regulation of railroads, state aid for agriculture, and higher taxes on corporations, did not take to these new leaders, and consequently wavered in their party regularity. The threat of a Negro balance of power did not frighten hungry farmers, whose unconcern about race alarmed loyal Democrats. Small wonder that Henry W. Grady deplored the defections he saw everywhere among the whites.

Radical agrarian organizations had flourished all over the United States after the Civil War. The National Grange, or Patrons of Husbandry, was attracting thousands of farmers by 1870, but it was kept within bounds in the South during Reconstruction because of the dangers of Negro-Radical rule. Prostrated by depression, however, the Southern farmers organized and adopted a radical program. By 1889 the Southern Farmers' Alliance had branches in every Southern state. Although they did not admit Negro members, they believed that Negroes should at least be lined up in a parallel organization. In 1886, therefore, the Colored Farmers' National Alliance and Cooperative Union came into existence. It grew rapidly. By 1891 it claimed more than a million members in twelve state organizations. There were local chapters wherever Negro farmers were

sufficiently numerous. After a national organization was perfected in 1888, there was for a time close cooperation between
the white and Negro groups. But when the Colored Farmers'
Alliance proposed to call a general strike of Negro cotton pick-
ers, Colonel Leonidas L. Polk, president of the National Farmers' Alliance, opposed it with the argument that Negroes were
attempting to better their condition at the expense of the whites.
He insisted that farmers should leave their cotton in the field
rather than pay more than fifty cents a hundred pounds to have
it picked.

As the program of radical agrarianism evolved during the last
two decades of the century, however, Negro and white farmers
in the South drifted closer together and white solidarity became
more difficult to maintain. Radical leaders like Tom Watson of
Georgia told the poor whites and Negroes that they were being
deliberately kept apart and fleeced. He called on them to stand
together and work for their common good. Along with other
leaders, he was at the time opposed to Negro disfranchisement
and looked forward to a coalition of Negro and white farmers to
drive the Bourbons from power. Then it would be possible to
adopt progressive laws especially beneficial to the poor man.
Professor C. Vann Woodward says that under the tutelage of
radical agrarian leaders the white masses of the South were
learning to regard the Negro as a political ally bound to them by
economic ties and a common destiny. "Never before or since
have the two races in the South come so close together as they
did during the Populist struggles."

The People's or Populist party was the political agency of
these resurgent farmers. In 1892 the Populists sought to win the
Negro vote in most of the Southern states, and in many instances resorted to desperate means to secure the franchise for
Negroes in communities where by custom and practice they had
been barred from voting for more than a decade. The Democrats, alarmed to desperation, made overtures to the Populists,
but to no avail. They then turned to the Negroes. In some
communities Negroes were forced to vote for Democrats by the
very people who had dared them to attempt such an exercise of
the "white man's prerogative" only a few years before. Negroes
were hauled to towns in wagons and voted repeatedly. In Augusta, Georgia, they were imported from South Carolina to vote
for the Democrats.

Many Negroes, however, stood by the Populists, who advocated political if not social equality. One of the most zealous advocates of Tom Watson in Georgia was a young Negro preacher, H. S. Doyle, who made sixty-three speeches for Watson in the face of numerous threats. Democrats resorted to violence. A Negro Populist in Dalton, Georgia, was murdered in his home. It is estimated that fifteen were killed in Georgia during the state elections of 1892. Riots also broke out in Virginia and North Carolina. If Negro rule meant chaos and disorder to the Democrats, the mere threat of it was enough for the Democrats to resort to violence themselves.

In some states there was a successful fusion between the newly organized Populists and the remnants of the old Republican organizations. In 1894 such a combination seized control of the North Carolina legislature. Immediately the Democratic election machinery was dismantled and voting was made easier, so that more Negroes could vote and make their influence felt once more. Negro office-holding soon became common in the eastern Black Belt of the state. The fusion legislature of 1895 named 300 Negro magistrates. Many counties had Negro deputy sheriffs, Wilmington had fourteen Negro police, and New Bern had both Negro policemen and aldermen. One prominent Negro, James H. Young, was made chief fertilizer inspector and a director of the state asylum for the blind; and another, John C. Dancy, was appointed collector of the Port of Wilmington.

White Conservatives who witnessed the political resurgence of the Negro in North Carolina, Georgia, and other Southern states, deeply resented his exercise of power when they were unable to control him. As the Negro returned to prominence, either as an elector or an election issue, sentiment against his participation in politics grew. The Democrats, failing to control the Negro vote, moaned dismally about the return of Black Republicanism. Even when they controlled him, they said that he made for corruption in politics. Although the Populists could on occasion have the Negro vote, apparently they preferred not to tamper with it because of the dangers involved. The election laws, as they stood, might actually be turned against poor, ignorant whites if the Democrats became vindictive and sought to disfranchise the Populists as well as their Negro allies. It was much better, therefore, to have clear-cut constitutional disfranchisement of the Negro and to leave the white groups to fight elections out among themselves. Where the Populists were unable to control the Negro vote, as in Georgia in 1894, they believed that the Democrats had never completely disfranchised the Negroes because their votes were needed if the Democrats were to stay in power. This belief led the defeated and disappointed Tom Watson to support a constitutional amendment excluding the Negro from the franchise—a complete reversal of his position in denouncing South Carolina for adopting such an amendment in 1895.

With the collapse of the agrarian revolt in 1896, the movement for complete disfranchisement of the Negro helped to reunite the white South. The poor, ignorant white farmers reverted to their old habits of thinking and acting, comforted in their poverty by Conservative assurances that Negro rule must be avoided at any cost. They might look back to the time in the 1890's when they were on the verge of joining their darker brothers to fight for a common cause. The poor whites could say with one of their leaders that the Negro question was an everlasting, overshadowing problem which served to hamper their progress and prevent them from becoming realistic in social, economic, and political matters.

The Triumph of White Supremacy

When it became evident that white factions would compete with one another for the Negro vote, and thus frequently give the Negro the balance of power, it was time for the complete disfranchisement of the Negro, the Fifteenth Amendment to the contrary notwithstanding. On this, most Southern whites were agreed. They differed only over the method of disfranchising Negroes. The view prevailed that none but people of property and intelligence were entitled to suffrage. As one writer put it, white Southerners believed that "no person should enjoy the suffrage unless he gives sufficient evidence of his permanent interest in and attachment to the community." And yet there were many who opposed such stringent disfranchisement because it would disqualify numerous whites. The poor whites were especially apprehensive. Some of them had been disfranchised by earlier measures; and when competition grew keen between rival white groups, the Conservatives actually barred radical whites from the polls and permitted their own Negro supporters to vote. More poor whites were bound to be disfranchised by any new measures. The sponsors of a stricter suffrage had to be certain that they did not contravene the Fifteenth Amendment. Despite the fact that the Supreme Court had refused to apply it in the Reese and Cruikshank cases, there was no guarantee that the Court would view so favorably any state action obviously designed to disfranchise a group because of its race.

These were the problems that had to be solved by state constitutional conventions when they undertook to write into their fundamental law a guarantee of White Supremacy. It was in Mississippi, where a majority of the population were Negroes, that the problem was first faced and solved. As early as 1886 sentiment was strong for constitutional revision; a convention met in 1890, for the primary purpose of disfranchising the Negro. A suffrage amendment was written which imposed a poll tax of two dollars, excluded voters convicted of bribery, burglary, theft, arson, perjury, murder, and bigamy, and also barred all who could not read any section of the state constitution, or understand it when read, or give a reasonable interpretation of it. Isaiah T. Montgomery, the only Negro delegate to the convention, said that the poll tax and education requirements would disfranchise 123,000 Negroes and only 11,000 whites. Before the convention Negro delegates from forty counties had met and protested to President Harrison their impending disfranchisement. Doubtless they would have fought ratification, but the Conservatives would run no risk of having their handiwork rejected; after the convention approved the constitution, it was promulgated and declared to be in effect.

South Carolina followed Mississippi by disfranchising the Negro in 1895. Ben Tillman had worked toward this goal after he was elected governor in 1890, but he was unable to obtain sufficient support for a constitutional convention until 1894. Tillman was then in the United States Senate, but he returned to the convention to serve as chairman of the Committee on Rights of Suffrage and thus to be certain that the Negro was effectively disfranchised. The clause, when adopted, called for two years' residence, a poll tax of one dollar, the ability to read and write the constitution or to own property worth $300, and the disqualification of convicts.

Negro delegates bitterly denounced this sweeping disfranchisement. In answer to Tillman's charge that Negroes had done nothing to demonstrate their capacity in government, Thomas E. Miller replied that they were largely responsible for

"the laws relative to finance, the building of penal and charitable institutions, and, greatest of all, the establishment of the
public school system." He declared that numerous reform laws
"touching every department of state, county, municipal and
town governments . . . stand as living witnesses [on the statute books of South Carolina] of the Negro's fitness to vote and
legislate upon the rights of mankind." James Wigg of Beaufort
County said, "The Negro . . . has a right to demand that in
accordance with his wealth, his intelligence and his services to
the state he be accorded an equal and exact share in its government. . . . You charge that the Negro is too ignorant to be
trusted with the suffrage. I answer that you have not, nor dare
you, make a purely educational test of the right to vote. You
say that he is a figurehead, an encumbrance to the state, that
he pays little or no taxes. I answer you, you have not, nor dare
you make a purely property test of the right to vote. . . . We
submit our cause to the judgment of an enlightened public
opinion and to the arbitrament of a Christian civilization."
Only two whites joined the six Negroes in voting against the
constitution of 1895.

The story was essentially the same in Louisiana in 1898 when
a new device, the "grandfather clause," was written into the
constitution. This called for an addition to the permanent registration list of the names of all male persons whose fathers and
grandfathers were qualified to vote on January 1, 1867. At that
time, of course, no Negroes were qualified to vote in Louisiana.
If any Negroes were to vote, they would have to comply with
educational and property requirements. Booker Washington attempted to prick the conscience of Louisiana Democrats by
writing them that he hoped the law would be so clear that "no
one clothed with state authority will be tempted to perjure and
degrade himself by putting one interpretation upon it for the
white man and another for the black man. . . ." Negroes led by
T. B. Stamps and D. W. Boatner appeared before the suffrage
committee and admitted that a qualified suffrage might remedy
demoralized conditions; but they pleaded for an honest test,
honestly administered.

By 1898 the pattern for the constitutional disfranchisement
of the Negro had been completely drawn. In subsequent years
other states followed the lead of Mississippi, South Carolina,
and Louisiana. By 1910 the Negro had been effectively disfranchised by constitutional provisions in North Carolina, Alabama,

Virginia, Georgia, and Oklahoma. The tension arising from campaigns for white suffrage sometimes flared up into violent race wars. In Wilmington, North Carolina, three white men were wounded, 11 Negroes killed and 25 wounded, in a riot in 1898. In Atlanta, there were four days of rioting after an election in 1906 in which disfranchisement was the main issue. Robbery, murder, and brutality were not uncommon during this period.

For the cause of White Supremacy the effect was most salutary. In 1896 there were 130,344 Negroes registered in Louisiana, constituting a majority in twenty-six parishes. In 1900, two years after the adoption of the new constitution, only 5,320 Negroes were on the registration books; and in no parish did they make up a majority of voters. Of 181,471 Negro males of voting age in Alabama in 1900, only 3,000 registered after the new constitutional provisions went into effect. On the floor of the Virginia convention Carter Glass had said that the delegates were elected "to discriminate to the very extremity of permissible action under the limitations of the Federal Constitution, with a view to the elimination of every Negro voter who can be gotten rid of, legally, without materially impairing the numerical strength of the white electorate." This was accomplished not only in Virginia, but in every state where such means were resorted to.

The South universally hailed the disfranchisement of the Negro as a constructive act of statesmanship. Negroes were viewed as aliens, whose ignorance, poverty, and racial inferiority were incompatible with logical and orderly processes of government. Southern whites said that the Negro had done nothing to warrant suffrage. But as he made progress in many walks of life, it became increasingly difficult to allege that he was naturally shiftless and incapable of advancement. The framers of the new suffrage laws, however, were committed to the complete and permanent disfranchisement of the Negro regardless of his progress. Their view was summed up by J. K. Vardaman of Mississippi: "I am just as opposed to Booker Washington as a voter, with all his Anglo-Saxon re-enforcements, as I am to the coconut-headed, chocolate-colored, typical little coon, Andy Dotson, who blacks my shoes every morning. Neither is fit to perform the supreme function of citizenship." Southerners would have to depend on the administration of the suffrage laws to keep Negroes disfranchised, for there were many who would gradually meet the most stringent constitutional qualifications. White Supremacy would require an abiding belief in racial inequality, re-enforced, perhaps, by hatred born of bitter memories.

Once the Negro was disfranchised, everything else necessary for White Supremacy could be done. With the emergence of white Democratic primaries, from which all Negroes were excluded by rules of the party, whites planned their strategy in caucuses, and the party itself became the government in the South. Whites solemnly resolved to keep the races completely separate, for there could be no normal relationships between them. Laws for racial segregation had made a brief appearance during Reconstruction, only to disappear by 1868. When the Conservatives resumed power, they revived the segregation of the races. Beginning in Tennessee in 1870, Southerners enacted laws against intermarriage of the races in every Southern state. Five years later, Tennessee adopted the first "Jim Crow" law and the rest of the South rapidly fell in line. Negroes and whites were separated on trains, in depots, and on wharves. Toward the end of the century the Negro was banned from white hotels, barber shops, restaurants, and theatres, after the Supreme Court in 1883 outlawed the Civil Rights Acts of 1875. By 1885 most Southern states had laws requiring separate schools. With the adoption of new constitutions the states firmly established the color line by the most stringent segregation of the races and in 1896 the Supreme Court upheld segregation in its "separate but equal" doctrine set forth in *Plessy v. Ferguson*.

It was a dear price that the whites of the South paid for this color line. Since all other issues were subordinated to the issue of the Negro, it became impossible to have free and open discussion of problems affecting all the people. There could be no two-party system, for the temptation to call upon the Negro to decide between opposing factions would be too great. Interest in politics waned to a point where only professionals, who skillfully deflected the interest from issues to races, were concerned with public life. The expense of maintaining a double system of schools and of other public institutions was high, but not too high for advocates of White Supremacy who kept the races apart in order to maintain things as they were.

Peace had not yet come to the South. The new century opened tragically with 214 lynchings in the first two years. Clashes between the races occurred almost daily, and the atmos-

phere of tension in which people of both races lived was conducive to little more than a struggle for mere survival, with a
feeble groping in the direction of progress. The law, the courts,
the schools, and almost every institution in the South favored
the white man. This was White Supremacy.

XIX •

Freedom South of the Border

The Abolition of Slavery

● *Despite the fact that the United States was the first country* in the Western hemisphere to enunciate the doctrine of the essential equality of all men, it was not the first to set Negro slaves free. In all fairness, however, it must be added that it was not the last; for legal freedom did not come to all the Negroes of the New World until Brazil emancipated her slaves in 1888. Haiti was the first of the New World countries to sweep slavery aside. Indeed, the fight for independence in the French island was so inextricably connected with the fight for human liberty that one could hardly be achieved without the other. When the French Revolution broke out, the island of St. Domingue had 30,000 whites, 24,000 free Negroes and mulattoes, and 452,000 slaves. By the time the French people were rising up against their autocratic rulers, slavery in the colonies had become an issue at home as well as abroad. In 1788 the Society of the Friends of the Black had been organized, with some of France's leading liberals—or radicals—such as Comte de Mirabeau, Jean Pierre Brissot, Etienne Clavière, and Lafayette as active members. One of the first things that the revolutionists demanded was the abolition of the slave trade; and sentiment against the institution gained momentum everywhere, except among a relatively small number of merchants and planters who had an immediate interest in its perpetuation.

In 1789 the free Negroes of St. Domingue petitioned the

National Assembly for their political rights and privileges. They were not seeking the emancipation of their brothers held in slavery, but their action stimulated the desire of the slaves to be free. Two years later the Assembly declared that all persons born of free parents were entitled to all privileges of French citizens, and when the governor of the island did not want to proclaim such a radical doctrine, civil strife developed, which threw many of the free Negroes on the same side with the slaves. The struggle that ensued was so embarrassing to France and the danger of invasion by Britain was so imminent that in August, 1793, France proclaimed universal freedom for everyone living under the French flag. In the following year the National Convention ratified the proclamation, thus marking the first time that a legislative assembly had decreed the abolition of human slavery.

Ten years of warfare followed before anything resembling peace came to the island. During that time the first strong Negro leader, Toussaint L'Ouverture, imposed a system of forced labor that was little better than the slavery from which the Negroes had just emerged. The colony was divided into districts, each under a general, and everyone was forced to work. Shirkers, it is said, were buried alive, sawed between two planks, or made to suffer death or punishment in other horrible manners. Leaders justified this on the grounds of expediency. It was necessary for everyone to work in order that Toussaint's army would have the resources with which to resist the attempt of Napoleon to subjugate the island and re-enslave the Negroes. Prosperity returned to the island, and by 1801 Toussaint was able to establish himself as governor-general for life with the power to name his successor.

The effort of Napoleon to subjugate the blacks on the island ended in abject failure, but not before Toussaint had been captured and the Negroes had become thoroughly aware of the possible consequences of the re-establishment of French rule. That is the principal reason why Dessalines and his assistants were able to rally sufficient support to defeat those French forces that were not ravaged by malaria and yellow fever. When the French army capitulated, one of the first acts of Dessalines was to proclaim the Independence of St. Domingue and to abolish slavery forever. On November 29, 1803, Dessalines, with his aides, Christophe and Clervaux, made clear the position of the people of this island with the following pronouncement:

The Independence of St. Domingue is proclaimed. Restored to our primitive dignity, we have asserted our rights; we swear never to yield them to any power on earth. The frightful veil of prejudice is torn to pieces. Be it so for ever! Woe be to them who would dare to put together its bloody tatters!

They called upon well-meaning landholders to return to the island and reclaim their possessions. They asserted that they would act as brothers to those who were interested in the development of the island,

But as for those who, intoxicated with foolish pride, interested slaves of a guilty pretension, are blinded so much as to believe themselves the essence of human nature and assert that they are destined by Heaven to be our masters and our tyrants, let them never come near the land of St. Domingue! . . . We have sworn not to listen with clemency to any who would dare to speak to us of slavery.

On January 1, 1804, chiefs of the armies of St. Domingue met and swore to "abjure forever allegiance to France, to die rather than live under her domination, and to fight to the last for the preservation of their independence." The name St. Domingue was discarded in favor of the name Haiti. The break with the past was complete. Independence and freedom had come.

Sentiment for abolishing the institution in the British possessions had stemmed from the general growth of humanitarianism in England in the middle of the eighteenth century. In 1772 Lord Mansfield made it clear in the Somerset case that slavery was too odious an institution to exist in England itself without specific legislation which sanctioned it. Although the decision was not applicable to the colonies, it encouraged those persons who were interested in abolishing slavery everywhere. Thomas Clarkson, William Wilberforce, and others organized, in 1787, the Society for Effecting the Abolition of the Slave Trade. Thanks to the pressure this organization was able to bring to bear and to favorable economic and military circumstances, the slave trade was closed in 1807. It was now possible for anti-slavery leaders to turn to exposing the evils of the system and agitating for its complete abolition. Innumerable religious and humanitarian institutions sprang up in the colonies and in England to carry on the fight against slavery. One of the outstanding anti-slavery organizations was the Society for the Mitigation and Gradual Abolition of Slavery throughout the British Dominions, which was founded in London in 1823 largely through the efforts of Thomas Fowell Buxton. Within a short time several hundred branch societies were in existence; but, unfortunately for the more zealous anti-slavery leaders, this society devoted most of its attention to programs for the amelioration of slavery rather than its abolition.

The fight against slavery spread to the British possessions themselves. By 1825 an active crusade against slavery was in progress; free Negroes of the islands participated enthusiastically in it. They suffered under many discriminatory measures themselves and concluded that they would not enjoy complete freedom until everyone was free. The citizens of Jamaica declared themselves "the firm and unbending opponents of the present system—the zealous advocates of a change from slave to free labour with a due regard to the rights of every one." The free Negroes of Antigua said that they were not only willing to further a program of amelioration of slavery but they also wanted to join in a movement to destroy the system altogether. Effective opposition was carried on in many quarters; by 1830 the abolition of slavery in the possessions was one of the most pressing of England's imperial problems.

The pressure brought on the British government by anti-slavery crusaders culminated in the enactment of a bill for the abolition of slavery in 1833. Slave owners were to be compensated in an amount not exceeding £20,000,000, to be contributed by the colonies according to the number and value of the slaves. A system of apprenticeship was established as a method of transition from slavery to freedom. The ex-slaves were to enjoy some rights as free men, but their work was to be carefully supervised by specific justices whose responsibility was to prepare the Negroes for freedom. Almost immediately it became apparent to anti-slavery leaders that the Negroes were not enjoying freedom, that excessive flogging of the freedmen was permitted, and that in many ways they were being exploited as much as when they were legally enslaved. Despite the fact that the West Indian proprietors defended the system and the British government said that there were insufficient grounds to alter the act of 1833, the movement for complete emancipation had surged forward with such strength that it was irresistible. By the end of 1838 the apprenticeship system had disappeared from most of the British colonies, and Negroes were allowed to enter a period of responsible freedom.

On the mainland, in Spanish and Portuguese America, the struggle for the abolition of slavery was related to the struggle for independence. Negroes, both slave and free, fought for the independence of the colonies from European control. During the wars for independence, uprisings of the slaves against the wealthy, loyal planting class contributed substantially to the weakening of the hold of the mother country on the colonies. For example, the revolt of the Negroes in Coro, Venezuela, was one of the forerunners of the revolutionary movement in that country. On other occasions, moreover, slaves fought along with their masters in their fight for independence. Negroes crossed the Andes with San Martin from Argentina to Chile and participated in several battles of liberation, including those of Chacabuco and Maipu. Negroes were with José Artigas in his campaigns to liberate Uruguay. Their participation in the numerous struggles of the Cubans against Spain in the nineteenth century made them the legatees of the tradition of freedom and independence in that country.

All through Latin America the sentiment against slavery increased as the sentiment for independence grew. Once independence was achieved the fight for the emancipation of the slaves entered a new and more intense stage, with gratifying results in some areas shortly after independence was secured. In Central America, where the five small countries had federated themselves into one nation, the liberal assembly passed an act in 1824 ending slavery in Central America. The bill was significant, not so much because it emancipated slaves in Central America—there were only about one thousand—but rather because it was the first emancipation measure passed by a legislative body in continental America. The Spanish law, Professor Herbert I. Priestley says, looked upon the institution of "actual legal slavery with something of a spirit of abhorrence." It was, therefore, easier for slaves to achieve their liberty by purchase or by manumission than in the English speaking colonies. The continuous amalgamation of the Negro, Indian, and white races in Latin America and the view of impermanency with which many planters regarded slavery contributed to the decline of the institution and served to hasten its legal proscription.

Mexico's President Guerrero issued an emancipation decree in that country in 1829, when the senate refused to pass an emancipation bill. It was primarily aimed at stopping the migration of slaveholding farmers from the United States into Texas.

Although it had very little effect upon either migration or slavery in Texas, it was successfully enforced in all other parts of Mexico. In the next few years the momentum of sentiment for emancipation increased. In 1831 Bolivia emancipated her slaves. In 1842 slaves of Uruguay were set free. Within a decade the movement for abolition had crystallized in other countries, Colombia and Argentina setting their slaves free in 1851 and 1853 respectively. In 1854 President José Gregório Monagas of Venezuela reminded his congress that Simón Bolívar, who had led the country to independence, had wished the slaves to be free. Accordingly a law was passed emancipating the slaves and providing for the compensation of their owners. In Peru President Ramon Castilla and the progressive newspaper *Comercio* led the fight which resulted in the abolition of slavery in 1855. By this year, practically all slaves in Spanish America had been set free except those of Cuba where emancipation was not effected until 1886. The great fight for freedom in the New World in the last half of the nineteenth century was to be waged in Brazil, where slavery was still deeply entrenched at the time of the ratification of the Thirteenth Amendment by the people of the United States.

Brazil, however, was not lacking in sentiment against the institution of slavery. In the eighteenth and nineteenth centuries public opinion had increasingly favored the curtailment and abolition of slavery. By the middle of the nineteenth century the sentiment was so strong that the army stopped capturing fugitive slaves and the *quilombos*, the fugitive slave communities, were no longer molested. The Negroes themselves were contributing to the destruction of the institution. There were a number of Negroes like Chico Rei, a powerful leader in the province of Minas Geraes, who bought as many slaves as he could afford and set them free. Among the Negro anti-slavery leaders was Luiz Gama, a brilliant lawyer and vigorous abolitionist; André Reboucas, who helped found several anti-slavery organizations; José de Patrocinio, who has been described as the "very heart and soul of the abolitionist campaign," and many others. By 1870 a number of anti-slavery societies had been organized, the most important being the *Sociedade Emancipadora dos Escravos* in Rio de Janeiro. The leading newspapers took up the fight; everywhere slave power was in full retreat.

The retreat of slave power was manifested officially in various legislative enactments and decrees that extended through most of the century. The slave trade had been effectively stopped before 1830. In 1831 all slaves of foreign origin living in Brazil were declared to be forever free; forty years later all children of slave mothers were declared to be free. By 1883 all slaves of Ceara, in the Northeast part of Brazil, were freed, and in the following year an emancipation proclamation was issued in the province of Amazonas. In 1885 an imperial law provided that all bondmen be liberated upon reaching the age of sixty years. The die was cast; and the government acknowledged it by enacting a law in May, 1888, which emancipated the 700,000 remaining Negro slaves. A five-day holiday was held to celebrate the historic event. The American minister stationed in Brazil confessed his astonishment "that what had led to a devasting struggle in the United States was the cause of merriment and rejoicing in Brazil."

There had been opposition, of course, to the emancipation of the Negroes all over Latin America. Those persons who had invested heavily in human chattel were unwilling to see their assets evaporate into thin air by legislative act or presidential decree. In some countries they were consoled by compensation which the legislatures provided for them, but in other countries there was no compensation. It cannot be said, therefore, that the peace that followed in the wake of emancipation south of the border came because the owners were compensated. The basic difference between the reaction of the slaveholders in the United States and those in other parts of the Western hemisphere seems to lie, at least in part, in the difference in attitudes toward the institution. In the United States the vigorous defense of slavery on religious and ethnological grounds went farthest. Only in the United States were slaveholders convinced that the difference between Negroes and whites was so fundamental that the former could never be regarded as anything except slaves. On the other hand, in most other countries of the New World integration of the Negro into the life of the community was a continuous process, resulting in an attitude toward the enslaved race far different from that held by Southerners in the United States. While opposing emancipation, most Latin American owners of slaves were willing to acknowledge the human depravity of slaveholding, and when it came to an end, few of them harbored feelings of bitterness. The acceptance of the Negro into the life of the community presented few new problems to the Latin American. To the Southerner in the United States it was inconceivable that there could be such an acceptance. If the people of the United States saw in freedom for the Negro the unfolding of the most tragic period in the history of the country, the people south of the border saw in it a new deliverance for all and another step toward the realization of complete human freedom.

Progress in the Caribbean

The emancipation of Negroes in the Caribbean settled few problems of an economic or social nature. The main features of the slave regime, the large plantations and an army of landless workers, persisted throughout the nineteenth century and down into the twentieth century. Only in Haiti was there a substantial change in the economic status of the black workers. Thanks to the policy of the military leaders who achieved independence, a redistribution of the land was effected, but the military clique kept the lion's share for themselves and gave the peasants small quantities of less desirable land. Some Haitian peasants own as little as one-fifth of an acre, and the average holding is between three and six acres. Without additional training and with no capital with which to purchase modern implements and machinery, the small farmers have continued to cultivate coffee and other staples in a most primitive manner. Their experience as slaves on plantations where only money crops were emphasized has prevented their realizing the importance of growing an adequate food supply; and they are, consequently, almost entirely dependent on their staple crops for money to purchase the necessaries of life. As "toutistes"—persons who must do everything for themselves—they have no resources other than the cooperation which their neighbors are willing to give. Thus, during the rush seasons Haitians hold *coumbites*, a cooperative enterprise similar to the American husking bee. In this way they help each other to clear fields, and plant and harvest crops. Even in the twentieth century when there is so little prospect for it, the peasant's great ambition is to be a large landowner; and while he continues to work hard to provide for his family in the meanwhile, this unrealistic approach undoubtedly has the effect of detracting from his efficiency in his day-to-day activities.

Emancipation in the British islands of the Caribbean was accompanied by no such social upheaval as occurred in the

French islands. After the collapse of the apprenticeship system, the Negro was on his own; but his only recourse was to the plantation where he had once been enslaved. There he worked for pitifully low wages, and only the more fortunate ones were able to rise above the status of agricultural workers. On some islands, such as Trinidad, Negro peasants rose rapidly to land ownership and some affluence as a result of cultivating cocoa. In most communities, however, various obstacles were put in the way of Negroes' acquiring land, a situation which perpetuated a large laboring class for the white plantation owners. Where the laborers realized that they had the advantages which come from a shortage of workers they capitalized on it and demanded higher wages; but this realization was all too infrequent.

Because of the poverty and lack of resources of the freedmen, an arrangement between the workers and the landowner evolved that was not unlike the system which developed in the Southern United States at the end of the slave regime. Planters housed their workers and supplied them with food and deducted these costs from the wages, if they were laborers, or from crop sales, if they had a sharecropping arrangement. In many communities the male laborers receive, even today, an average of twenty-five cents per day. In order to reduce the wages even more and to provide for a larger labor supply, planters on several of the islands have advocated the importation of farm laborers from the outside. In 1852 Jamaica worked out a program for bringing workers from Madeira, and in 1855 more than 200 were brought in from that island. At about the same time Jamaica and several other islands in the British group began to bring in Chinese and Indian workers from the Orient. So serious was the labor problem in the Caribbean that before 1860 efforts were made to persuade free Negroes in the United States to migrate there.

Some Negroes in all the Caribbean islands have found it possible to make a living in urban centers. In Havana, Cuba, for example, a considerable number of Negroes make their living as carpenters, tailors, domestic servants, and laundresses. Many of the members of the police force are Negroes, while a large number of others serve the public as bus conductors and railwaymen. During the nineteenth century a larger and larger number of Negroes in the British West Indies went into the professions, especially medicine and law. Dr. Eric Williams points out that on some islands Negroes dominate the lower ranks of the civil service bureaucracy; and it is not impossible for them to work up to the top. One of the most famous chief justices in the history of Barbados was a mulatto, Sir Conrad Reeves. In 1873 a Negro was the chief justice of Dominica; and several other islands have had high Negro officials.

The major economic problems of the Negroes in the Caribbean have yet to be solved. Some have sought to solve their difficulties by migrating to the United States. Others have attempted to improve conditions through cooperation and through the promotion of social legislation. Still others have tried to solve the problems through education and diversified occupational activities. In all probability these and many other methods will be employed before the islanders are relieved of their more pressing economic strains.

The economic plight of the Negroes of the Caribbean has kept the political waters troubled. Haiti, born of revolution, has continued in that tradition down to the present time. Dessalines, who inherited the authority of Toussaint, was overthrown and killed by his own men who sought a greater share of the wealth of the country. Upon his death in 1807 the country was torn by the strife between Henri Christophe, ruling the Northern part of the country, and Alexandre Pétion, ruling the Southern part. Like the Latin American countries on the mainland the government of Haiti was viewed by its citizens as something to be seized at the first opportunity and turned to the advantage of those who could effect the coup d'état. The result was that in this Negro republic of the New World no less than seventeen governments were overthrown in the century ending with the outbreak of World War I. With the franchise limited to a relative few the country is dominated politically, as well as socially and economically, by the mulatto elite. It must be added, however, that the country has received little stabilizing influence from stronger countries of Europe and America. As for the part of the United States, it is enough to say that the long period of disorder, debt, and political deterioration led to the occupation by the United States Marines in 1915 and the domination of the life of the country from that time to 1934. During that period a semblance of order was brought out of the financial chaos that had characterized the early history of the country.

In the British islands in the Caribbean the economic problems were tied up closely with political conditions. As the working classes sought better wages, land ownership, and improved living conditions, they turned to political action. Being without the franchise for the most part, they found it necessary to resort to violence. In 1865, for example, the Negroes of Jamaica carried on a rebellion which looked toward a more equitable distribution of the land and of political power. They were especially disaffected by the fact that out of a total population of 440,000 less than 2,000 had the right to vote. Fear and contempt drove the white governor to put down the rebellion with a most ruthless hand. More than 400 Negroes were shot, 1,000 of their houses were burned, and countless numbers were flogged without mercy. Many such uprisings occurred, but except for a gradual extension of the franchise and the amelioration of conditions here and there, they brought no substantial improvement.

Since World War II the leadership of the greater portion of the Negro population of the British West Indies has passed from the middle class to the working class, made up of agricultural and industrial laborers. Men like Uriah Butler of Trinidad and Alexander Bustamente of Jamaica organized labor unions among most of the workers of the islands, educated workers regarding their potential power and their rights, and secured concessions from employers by invoking strikes and other weapons of labor warfare. Everywhere in those years, there was increased discussion of the potential political power of the lower classes in the islands. This led to the gaining of independence by several colonies. The Federation of the West Indies, looking toward independence, came into existence in 1958, but was dissolved in 1962. Thereafter, certain individual members became independent: Jamaica (1962), Trinidad and Tobago (1962), and Barbados (1966). On the mainland British Guiana became the independent parliamentary state of Guyana in 1966.

The Negroes of Cuba have attempted to improve their condition through political action. The concern of workers led to the appointment of a Secretary for Negro affairs by the Cuban Confederation of Labor, an organization affiliated with the Third International. There were demands for the abolition of all racial discrimination in employment and for contracts providing that one-half of the employees of a given job must be Negro. The Cuban Confederation of Labor was largely responsible for the fact that in the elections of 1940 several Negro candidates ran for office on the Communist Party ticket. In Puerto Rico the economic and social depression weighed so heavily on the Negroes that there was room for little in the way of political action; and although a Nationalist party has sprung up demanding complete and unconditional independence, there is no evidence that Negroes have any special interest in it. In the Dominican Republic the dictatorship is so complete that the desires of any portion of the population cannot be described because there is no free articulation in that section of the Caribbean.

The poverty and the political weakness of the great majority of the Caribbean people have militated against the development of a strong educational system on any of the islands. Even after emancipation the education of Negroes was of slow growth largely because there was no assumption of responsibility by the public, and missionaries carried most of the burden of educating the blacks. Just as during the slave period the planters were opposed to anything resembling universal education for two important reasons: Enlightenment would breed discontent and make it impossible for the planters to exercise effective control over their workers. Much of the work, moreover, was done by children of school age, whom the employers did not want to spare in order that the younger generation could prepare themselves for a larger future. In the British islands in the Caribbean the educational curriculum was geared to the English pattern, with a generous sprinkling of Latin and Greek and with examinations prepared in England for persons faced with problems of which the English examiners knew little. Even had a larger number of Negroes attended school, it is doubted that they would have been greatly benefited in the effort to solve their immediate problems. As it is, however, hardly more than three-fifths of the children of school age are in school. One particular hardship in attendance is caused by the concentration of the majority of the schools in urban centers, while the vast majority of the Negroes live in the rural areas. After World War II there was much agitation for an extensive reorganization of education in the British West Indies that led to the establishment of a University to serve all the islands.

Although many of the schoolmasters of Cuba were Negroes, the education of Negroes in that island was early viewed with disfavor. In 1827 a free Negro was denied permission to open a school for Negro girls. When a Negro attempted to open a night school for his people in 1865 he was told that the teaching of

grammar, geography, history, drawing, and the like was prohibited to Negroes. When slavery was abolished in 1886 Negro
children were debarred from schools in the interior, and Havana, with a Negro population of 400,000, maintained only four
schools for the education of Negroes. In the twentieth century,
however, there has been a relaxation of the restrictions on the
education of Negroes, with the result that significant strides
have been made in recent years. There is no longer any segregation in Cuban schools, and the University of Havana with an
outstanding reputation has several Negro members on its faculty. The Dominican Republic and Puerto Rico both have universities which have provided personnel trained in medicine,
law, and teaching for the improvement of life in those countries.
In recent years, thanks to the efforts of the Department of State
of the United States, the Pan American Union, and the Organization of American States, serious efforts have been made to
improve the educational systems in several of these countries.

In the British West Indies few contributions to cultural and
intellectual life were made by the Negroes, largely because
the vast majority of the talented and trained Negroes left the
islands to live either in Europe or in the United States. John
Russwurm, Denmark Vesey, and Edward W. Blyden of the
nineteenth century and Claude McKay and Marcus Garvey of
the twentieth century are proof of the genius of the West Indian
Negro who has found his field of service away from home.
Cubans, however, have made more significant contributions in
their native land. Two of Cuba's greatest poets in the slave era
were Negroes, Placido, a free mulatto, and Manzano, a slave. By
the end of the nineteenth century a Negro Cuban pianist, Brin-
dis de Salas, was known in Europe and America as an outstanding virtuoso. Four of the 26 teachers at the art school at San
Alejandro in more recent years were Negroes. Nicholas Guillen,
a mulatto, is one of Cuba's outstanding poets of this century,
and his *West Indies Ltd* has been described as showing
a "Caribbean consciousness rare in the particularism of the
area." One of the best known Cuban painters is the late
mulatto Alberto Pena.

The French Islands have produced some outstanding personages who have enhanced the cultural life of their homes. Price
Mars, the distinguished sociologist, has done much to foster an
understanding of the social problems of Haiti through his serious studies, while Jacques Roumain has become one of the

Caribbean's foremost men of letters. Julien Raimond of the Island of St. Domingue went to Paris late in the eighteenth century and made significant contributions to the anti-slavery movement by contributing essays to magazines and publishing pamphlets and brochures urging the recognition of the rights of Negroes in the colonies. Melvil Bloncourt, of Guadeloupe, whose *La France Parlementaire* was banned by Louis Napoleon, was described by Jules Levallois of France to be "one of the men who best uphold our country's intellectual and philosophical tradition." Since 1900 Daniel Thaly of Martinique has published eight volumes of verse and has won the praise of many distinguished critics. There is, finally, René Maran of Martinique who has been an outstanding literary figure since the publication of his *La Maison du Bonheur* in 1909. The scene of much of his writing is French Equatorial Africa where he worked for more than ten years. His outstanding work is the African epic *Le Livre de la Brousse*. He has been hailed as much for his unwillingness to compromise with his principles as for his literary mastery.

Trends on the Mainland

The steady amalgamation of racial elements constituting the population of the Latin American republics on the mainland makes it exceedingly difficult for students of the history of the United States to bring the racial problems of the area South of the Rio Grande into the framework of the pattern of this country's problems. It will be recalled that this intermingling was a continuous process during the slave regime. (See Chapter IX.) If anything, it has been hastened since emancipation; in some countries—Argentina, for example—Negroes as a distinct ethnic element have disappeared almost altogether. With contempt for the process, William L. Scruggs said that in Colombia the fusion has produced a "mongrel race impossible of ethnologic classification"; while several others have described Latin America as the world's greatest racial hodgepodge.

Some distinct Negro groups, however, are still to be found in parts of Latin America. In various countries of Central America there are a considerable number of Negroes, while in Panama the population is primarily black, large numbers having been brought in during the construction of the canal. In Colombia

Negroes live in the low lying areas of the Caribbean, as well as on the Pacific coast. Brazil is primarily black in the equatorial regions of the North; and even in the South, where the white population is larger, there is a substantial number of Negroes. The typical Latin American is neither white nor Negro. Perhaps he is not even Indian. In all probability he is either a *mestizo* (a mixture of white and Indian), a *mulatto* (a mixture of white and Negro), or a *zambo* (a mixture of Indian and Negro). There is some truth, therefore, in the assertion that these mixtures defy conventional classification. A discussion of the Negro in Latin America is of necessity a discussion of zambos and mulattoes, as well as pure-blooded Negroes. Although zambos and mulattoes would be regarded as Negroes in the United States, this classification is not necessarily made in the republics to the south.

Since the winning of independence in Latin America meant not so much the overthrow of tyranny and oppression as it did the transfer of absolute control from Madrid to the fortress of some caudillo, there was no social and economic upheaval by which the masses of people benefited. Thus, as slavery came to an end, freedmen found themselves in no better position economically than they were before emancipation. The great majority of them remained on the great plantations and established a new relationship with their ex-masters, that of a free man working for an employer. There emerged a form of peonage in which the freedman found himself bound to his employer for long periods of time without many rights and with almost no responsibility as a free man. This is not to say that the freedmen were degraded in the way they were in the United States, but that they remained, for the most part, impoverished because of the exacting economic system which emerged and from which there was almost no escape. Small wonder that Charles E. Chapman has declared that in most countries south of the border the colored races are still enslaved.

The great majority of Negroes remained agricultural workers. Some, however, became landowners and amassed wealth of their own. Others left the rural areas and went to the cities in search of better opportunities. No racial proscriptions obstructed them, and, as a result, many were able to adjust themselves to a new type of living. When John L. Stephens visited the capital of Honduras in 1839 he found many Negroes employed as mahogany cutters. The soldiers were all black, and some of the jurors as well as a judge in the court were mulattoes. An observer in Peru in 1870 noticed that the army was made up almost exclusively of Indians, Negroes, and zambos, with Indians predominating in the infantry and Negroes predominating in the cavalry. In Colombia Negroes became small merchants, carpenters, masons, contractors, and professional politicians. Whatever limitations they suffered in the Latin American countries were social and political rather than racial.

The political instability that characterized the age of the caudillos and thereafter in Latin America certainly did not contribute to the quiet and progressive development of the Negro element in the population. It must be added, however, that the endless succession of revolutions did not take away from Negroes liberties guaranteed to free men in the early constitutions any more than unsettled conditions took them away from others. Indeed, quite frequently Negroes participated in revolutions either as soldiers in the national armies or as civilians working with the revolutionists. In almost every country there were Negroes such as those of Colombia who have been described as "vagabond politicians or professional revolutionists with no thought of making a living other than by holding office under the government." In many countries, however, Negroes participated in politics because of the normal desire to contribute to the development of their country. Some became legislators, such as Evaristo Ferreira de Veiga, an outstanding Negro journalist and politician of Brazil, who was elected a deputy from the province of Minas Geraes for three terms and from Rio de Janerio for one term. Nilo Peçanha of Brazil was a deputy of the Constituent Assembly for a number of years, and while vice-president of the republic became president upon the death of the President in 1909. The absence of a "color line" and the lack of racial restrictions in voting and participation made it possible for Negroes to enjoy equal political opportunities with persons of other ethnic groups.

As Negroes came more and more to be absorbed into the population and as their opportunities to participate fully in the cultural life of the community increased, Negro institutions, as such, tended to disappear. There are no Negro schools, no Negro churches, few Negro newspapers and periodicals, and few other agencies of group articulation and cohesion. Only the color of Negroes remains to give evidence of their presence, and only where some aspect of the African culture has persisted is there evidence of the presence of the Negro as a distinct cultural and intellectual force. The exception is, of course, Brazil, where the Negro population is sufficiently large to encourage the preservation of customs, culture, and the like through organized activity. In 1924 one of the first Negro journals in Brazil, *O Clarim d'Alvorada,* was founded. Five years later it sponsored the first congress of Negro youth to inspire the Brazilian Negro to "emulate his racial brethren elsewhere in the world, where the colored race is striving to attain higher standards of progress." In 1930 Negro women of São Paulo formed the *Centro Civico Palmares* and urged the Negroes of Brazil to join in a concerted drive to improve the "civil, moral, and intellectual condition of the black race." Perhaps the most significant organization to be established was the *Centro de Cultura Afro-Brasileira* which was founded in 1937 to give unity and intellectual stimulus to the Negroes of Brazil. It has undertaken a number of research projects relating to the condition of the Negro and has already begun to publish its results.

The size of Brazil's Negro population is largely responsible for the fact that it is possible to identify quite easily some of the persons of Negro ancestry who have contributed to the literary and artistic development of their country. In the imperial period Antonio Gonçalves Texeira e Sousa won a secure place in Brazilian intellectual life as a poet, novelist, and dramatist. In 1846 Antonio Gonçalves Dias published his *Primeiros cantos* which won the praise of European critics and secured for him a position as professor of Latin and Brazilian history at the Collegio Dom Pedro II. Many look upon him as the great pantheistic poet of Brazil. One of the most versatile Brazilians was the mulatto Tobias Barreto, lawyer, philosopher, and scientist. He earned his livelihood as professor of law at Recife, but he found time to write, among many other things, a book of poems, entitled *Dias e Noites.* As a sculptor Antonio Francisco Lisboa (popularly called Aleijadinho, because of his affliction with leprosy) made significant contributions, including the twelve prophets in the church of Nosso Senhor de Mattosinhos in Congonhas do Campo, and in other churches. Manoel Querino was both a painter and a scholar, for in addition to doing the canvas in São João Theatre in Bahia, he also wrote two treatises on the art of Bahia. Among musicians were Father José Mauricio, founder of the first school of music in Brazil in the late eighteenth century, and Francisco Braga, composer of the opera

"Jupyra," organizer of the *Sociadade de Concertos Symphonicos*, and professor of musical theory at the National Institute of Music.

Thus Negroes have become a basic element in the life of the republics of Latin America. They are co-partners with Indians and whites in the development of their countries. In many areas they are in the minority, but they do not constitute a minority problem in the sense that persons in the United States understand the term. They are among the best examples that can be found of what happens to peoples when acculturation is permitted to proceed without legal restrictions and racial inhibitions and prejudices.

XX •

Canadian Negroes

Slavery and Emancipation

● *Although the first slaves in Canada were Indians, soon after* the first permanent settlements were made Negro slavery was introduced. In 1628 the captain of a British vessel sold a native of Madagascar to a French settler at Quebec; and from that time on there was a small importation of Negroes into the colony. Later in the century there were complaints that Quebec was handicapped by the lack of labor, and in 1689, at the suggestion of the governor and intendant, Louis XIV gave his consent to the importation of slaves from the West Indies. Stimulated by the encouragement of a royal edict, merchants increased their importation of slaves, and within a few years Negroes were scattered from Quebec to the western trading posts, clearing forests, constructing forts, and performing various other tasks. When the English settled Halifax in 1749 they brought Negro slaves with them to aid in the construction of ships for fishing and shipping. Apparently the need was only temporary, for in 1751 the *Boston Evening Post* advertised ten strong Negro men for sale in Boston, who had just arrived from Halifax, where they worked as caulkers, sailmakers, and rope-makers.

By the middle of the eighteenth century a lively interest in Negro slaves had developed throughout Canada. They were being bought and sold in the markets of Quebec, Montreal, and other cities, and the newspapers carried advertisements of

Negroes for sale. Many of the practices in connection with Negro slaveholding developed without the official sanction of the French government. When the third general assembly met in Nova Scotia in 1762, however, English colonists immediately enacted laws recognizing the institution and manifested an interest in its perpetuation. Many public officials owned slaves, and in some instances even the clergy owned Negroes. Slaveholding was no more extensive than it was because of the relatively small number of settlers in the Northern country and because of the restricted use that could be made of slaves. Without plantations large numbers of slaves could hardly be employed profitably, and the cost of maintenance in a cold climate served to discourage overinvestment in human chattel. Some demand for them continued, however. In 1763 the first governor of the new colony of Quebec sent an urgent request to New York for a shipment of Negro slaves. He said that nothing could be done without a larger supply of labor and that "black slaves are certainly the only people to be depended upon."

Slaves began early to resent their status, and the sparse settlements and the difficulty in enforcing the law encouraged them to run away. The difficulties that masters were having with their slaves in 1709 prompted the French masters to secure a royal decree stating that all Indians and Negroes brought into the colony were to be the absolute property of those who bought them. The suggestion is clear that the masters would also have power to discipline their slaves. In 1734 a Negro woman was hanged for setting fire to the home of her mistress and running away. When the problem of slaves escaping from the British possessions to French colonies became acute during King George's War, the king of France, in 1745, decreed that all such fugitives were the property of the king and were to be sold for his benefit. So many slaves were claiming their freedom on specious grounds that it was necessary for the authorities to issue a decree stipulating that only those manumissions which were effected by notarial act would be considered valid.

When Canada fell to England during the French and Indian War, provision was made for Frenchmen to keep their slaves. The end of the war witnessed an increase in the number of slaves in Canada, for English settlers, coming into the province in substantial numbers, brought slaves with them. The number was further increased during and after the War for Independence, when loyalists, fleeing to Canada from the wrath of the patriots, brought their slaves. By the time machinery was set up for the administration of Canada, slavery had become a problem which the citizens of the colony were compelled to recognize and to solve.

The Constitutional Act of 1791 provided for two provinces, Upper and Lower Canada, each with a separate government. The provinces were to be governed by English law in criminal matters and by French law in civil matters. The implications for slavery were immediately apparent. Whereas under the French regime slaves enjoyed many of the rights of servants, they were now stripped of these rights. The English law made a clear distinction between servants and slaves, and the latter enjoyed no marital, parental, or proprietary rights. Despite this obvious retrogression, slavery in Upper Canada was doomed, because of the attitude of its first administrator. The first lieutenant-governor, Colonel James Simcoe, had been impressed with the arguments of abolition leaders of England and had learned to hate slavery almost as much as those whom he emulated. Immediately after taking office he began to condemn the mistreatment of Negroes and to attack the institution of slavery itself. In July, 1793, largely through the influence of Simcoe, the Parliament of Upper Canada passed a bill, the preamble of which stated that it was unjust for free people to encourage the introduction of slaves and that it was highly expedient to abolish slavery in the province. The act provided that no Negro slave could be brought into the province, and that every child born to a slave mother should be free upon reaching the age of twenty-five. Although an effort was made after Simcoe left the province to encourage slavery by permitting immigrants to bring slaves with them, the act incorporating these features failed to pass the legislative council. By 1800 slavery in Upper Canada was slowly dying.

In the first session of the Parliament of Lower Canada a bill was introduced to abolish slavery. After considerable discussion, however, the bill was tabled; legislative emancipation was not further considered until 1799. Although passage of a law similar to the one enacted by the legislature of Upper Canada seemed unlikely, opponents of slavery had reason to be encouraged by the hostility which the courts demonstrated toward the institution of slavery. In 1798 a slave named Charlotte ran away from her mistress, and when committed to prison by the magistrate she sought release on a writ of habeas corpus and was freed by the chief justice. When this action became known, many slaves renounced their servitude, and one recently purchased for £80 was tried by the Court of the King's Bench. Chief Justice Monk set the slave free and declared that he would free every Negro who should be committed to prison by the magistrates.

The courts also took the position, quite contrary to the prevailing view, that a Negro was free unless the master could prove his alleged ownership. In 1798 a Negro was released by the court on the grounds that the alleged master had not been able to establish the title to him to the satisfaction of the court. The courts struck a final blow to slavery in 1800 in a case involving the runaway slave of a loyalist. The court took the position that the Imperial Act of 1797, which repealed the provision for the sale of Negroes to answer a judgment, had revoked all laws concerning slavery. It therefore released the Negro in question. Although the act did not repeal all laws concerning slavery, the decision of the court had the effect of rendering slavery in Lower Canada completely innocuous. The slave could not be compelled to serve longer than he wanted to, and the burden of slavery was rather on the master, who had to support his slave, than on the slave, who was apparently free to leave his master at will. Not until the Imperial Act of 1833 did slavery technically come to an end in Lower Canada; but by 1800 it had no importance as an economic institution.

By the last decade of the eighteenth century slavery was becoming unpopular in the Maritime Provinces. Loyalists in Nova Scotia, New Brunswick, Prince Edward Island, and Cape Breton Island for several years had enjoyed the rations that the government provided on the basis of the number of slaves they held. When the practice was discontinued the sentiment against slavery increased. The view was stated clearly by one citizen who said, "Independent of political and moral considerations such a system is by no means suitable to a Colony like Nova Scotia, where there are few branches of business requiring a regular body of labourers, and where their clothing and provision is attended with so much expense." As early as 1787 the assembly rejected a clause dealing with Negro slaves in a bill for regulating servants, on the grounds that slavery did not exist in the province and ought not to be mentioned. Although the courts recognized the existence of slavery, both juries and judges became quite skillful in finding flaws in masters' titles to ownership. The courts so overwhelmingly favored the slaves that masters were moved in 1808 to seek some protection from the legislature. They sought the passage of an act to secure them their property and to indemnify them for losses. Such a bill was introduced, but it never became law.

All over Canada at the beginning of the nineteenth century, slavery was dying. Its demise was not the result of legislative enactment, except in the bill for gradual abolition in Upper Canada, but of a strong public opinion that was antagonistic to the institution. This opinion stemmed from the realization of the impracticability of slavery and from the influence of anti-slavery leaders in England and their disciples in Canada. The opinion was reflected in the increasing number of manumissions and in the consistent favoritism which the courts showed for the slaves. When the Imperial Act which ended slavery throughout the empire was passed in 1833, Canadians were so preoccupied with the problem of slavery in the United States that they took little notice of the law which was the first measure which definitely abolished slavery in their own country.

Fugitives' Haven

The migration of Negroes, slave and free, from the United States to Canada in the nineteenth century accounts for the great majority of Negroes that were to be found there. At the very beginning of the century a few fugitive slaves found their way into Canada. The War of 1812 in which Negro troops fought against Canadians provided an excellent opportunity for Negroes to learn more of Canada as a possible haven for fugitive slaves, and they began to go to Canada in larger numbers. Neither their masters nor the government of the United States could do very much about it, if the slaves were determined to seek freedom North of the border. Slaveholders early became distressed over the possibility of permanently losing their slaves by their going to Canada. They resorted to the practice of describing Canada in the most unfavorable light. Most of the misrepresentations centered about the climate, with emphasis on the fact that Negroes simply could not live in a land that abounded in snow during the entire year. One fugitive said that his master told him that nothing except black-eyed peas would grow in Canada. Another stated that his master in Virginia said that the Detroit River was over 3,000 miles wide and that few persons ever succeeded in crossing it. Negroes apparently did not believe these fantastic descriptions and continued to go to Canada.

Officials in the United States, pushed to action by the slave-holders, sought a satisfactory arrangement with the Canadian officials whereby fugitives could be returned. In 1819 the Attorney General of Upper Canada said that "since freedom of the person was the most important civil right protected by the law of England which the Province had adopted, the Negroes were entitled to personal freedom through residence in the country, and any attempt to infringe their rights would be resisted by the Courts." In 1826 the Canadian government told Americans that it was "utterly impossible for them to agree to a stipulation for the surrender of fugitive slaves." Although the United States asserted in 1828 that the "evil" of Negroes escaping to Canada was likely to disturb the friendly relations of the two countries, Canadian officials were adamant and continued to refuse to give any satisfaction in the matter. As a matter of fact, England, in 1827, agreed to pay indemnities to the United States rather than surrender the slaves and other property that had been taken in the War of 1812. The Executive Council of Lower Canada issued a statement in 1829 which seemed to invite fugitives, in open defiance of the United States. In part, it said: "The state of slavery is not recognized by the law of Canada, nor does the law admit that any man can be the proprietor of another. Every slave therefore who comes into the province is immediately free whether he has been brought in by violence or entered it of·his own accord." With the increasing hardships on slaves in the South, with the encouragement of the Canadian government, and with the effective organization of the Underground Railroad, migration into Canada increased markedly after 1830.

It was the passage of the Fugitive Slave Law of 1850 that stimulated the migration of Negroes into Canada more than anything else. A stringent law meant that the fugitives in the Northern states were no longer safe, and they sensed its significance immediately. Within a month after the passage of the law the great trek to Canada began. At the end of three months 3,000 Negroes were estimated to have entered Canada. They came from all parts of the North, even from New England. Out of one Baptist church in Buffalo more than 100 members fled across the border. At Rochester all but two of the 114 members of the Negro Baptist church left with their pastor. Nearly all of the waiters in the Pittsburgh hotels left for Canada, armed with pistols and bowie knives, "determined to die rather than be captured." Henry Bibb, the Negro leader and editor of the *Voice of the Fugitive*, reported that Negroes were pouring into Canada in a steady stream. Slaves escaping to the North hardly paused before going on to Canada. In 1851 two Negroes from North Carolina travelled for 101 days, but they did not stop until they reached Canada. The *Detroit Advertiser* reported regularly on the number of fugitives passing through the city; and on one occasion it noted that 70 fugitives from Tennessee had crossed the river into Canada.

Not all who fled the states left their property behind. Some brought horses, wagons, and various other kinds of personal property. Some had sufficient capital to purchase farms. Most of them, however, were destitute and looked to their fellows to give relief until they could make the adjustment. Many agencies on both sides of the border came to the rescue of the fugitives. The Canada Mission was organized in 1838 to help feed and clothe the refugees. One of the main functions of the Anti-Slavery Society of Canada, which was organized in 1851, was to raise money for the relief of fugitives. In its first year the ladies auxiliary in Toronto raised more than $900 for such purposes. Churches and benevolent organizations of Canada provided money, food, clothing, and shelter for the fugitives. In the United States the churches, anti-slavery societies, and numerous other agencies sent money and material for the relief of the Negroes. One citizen of Battle Creek, Michigan, donated 2,000 fruit trees, while many others made presentations equally as valuable.

The great majority of the Negroes settled in the southwestern part of the present province of Ontario, in Essex and Kent Counties. They also went to many other places, however. There were two important settlements in New Brunswick, at Willow Grove and on Lake Otnabog. Some went to urban centers such as Toronto, Hamilton, and Montreal. Others went to live among the Indians. Negro fugitives were to be found as far north as Owen Sound on the shores of the Georgian Bay.

Negroes congregated in communities where they could have the benefit of the assistance and resources of their fellows. They were, perhaps, encouraged by some of the benefactors who doubtless knew something of the experiments in community living in the United States and in Europe. Several colonies were organized, and some of them enjoyed a measure of success. One of the earliest was the Wilberforce settlement, about twelve miles from London, Ontario, which was settled by a group of Negroes from Cincinnati in 1830. When Benjamin Lundy visited the colony in 1832 it had grown considerably. Twenty-five of the 32 families had bought land totaling more than 2,000 acres, and they owned more than 100 head of cattle, swine, and horses. There were a gristmill, a sawmill, two schools, and two churches. The houses appeared to Lundy to be neat, clean, and comfortable. The settlement had undertaken to stabilize its program by organizing a board of managers and a staff of officers. The president was Austin Steward, the well-known fugitive slave of Rochester, New York, who worked in the colony from 1831 to 1837. Two agents were appointed to solicit money for the schools and churches. The Reverend Nathaniel Paul was sent to England, and Israel Lewis was authorized to collect funds in the United States. Neither of these persons turned over any money to the settlement, however. Before the end of the decade the Wilberforce Colony showed unmistakable signs of decline. Its settlers soon scattered to other parts of the province.

In 1842 the Reverend Hiram Wilson and his co-worker, Josiah Henson, established a British and American Manual Labor Institute for Negro children at Dresden. They purchased 300 acres of land and erected several buildings. As the school grew settlers were attracted there. Within ten years there were more than 500 settlers in the community. By 1855, however, it began to decline. When Benjamin Drew visited the settlement he noticed that the dilapidated sawmill had not been fired up for about two years. Henson went to England where he raised $1,000 for the assistance of the school and the community, but that was not enough to keep the projects going. He also carried several loads of lumber away to sell in order to raise money for the colony; but when he did not return when the settlers expected him they lost patience and vented their anger by tearing up the foundations of the mill. For all practical purposes the colony had completely disintegrated before the outbreak of the American Civil War.

Perhaps the most successful Negro settlement in Canada was the one at Buxton. It was controlled by the Elgin Association which was incorporated in 1850 by William King of Louisiana, who had emancipated his slaves and brought them to Canada for settlement. The charter stated that the association was for "the settlement and moral improvement of the colored population of Canada, for the purpose of purchasing crown or clergy reserve lands in the township of Raleigh and settling the same with colored families resident in Canada of approved moral character." Within three years 130 families had settled there, and many buildings had been erected, including a school, a church, a minister's house, a store, a two-story hotel, a pearl ash factory, and a blacksmith's shop. When the Reverend Samuel G. Howe visited the settlement in 1862 for the Freedmen's Inquiry Commission he found more than 1,000 Negroes living there enjoying a measure of economic independence and security. Many of the descendants of these settlers are still living in or near Buxton.

The Refugees' Home colony was the outgrowth of the idea of Henry Bibb, a fugitive slave from Shelby County, Kentucky. After the passage of the Fugitive Slave Bill of 1850 Bibb proposed the organization of a society to purchase 50,000 acres of land on which to settle the many Negroes pouring into Canada. In 1851 the Refugees' Home Society was organized in Detroit, and the canvass for funds was begun. In the same year the Canada Land Company began selling land to the Society. By 1853 the Society had purchased 1,328 acres, 600 of which had been taken up by settlers. Families began moving into the community, and a school was opened. Its successful years were few, and within a short period of time the Bibb project had declined.

The idea of settling Negroes in colonies was extremely popular down to the Civil War. Although Wilberforce, Dresden, Buxton, and Windsor were better known, they were by no means the only settlements. There were others at Lake Simcoe, Woolwich, Chatham Creek, and Amherstburg. The Reverend Howe was moved to criticize the colonies, although he admitted that they were, in some respects, successful. He said that the Negroes should not be systematically congregated in communities, for "experience shows that they do best when scattered about, and forming a small proportion of the whole community." He added that the discipline of the colonies had the effect of prolonging a dependence "which amounts almost to servitude; and does not convert them so surely to hardy, self-reliant men, as the rude struggle with actual difficulties, which they themselves have to face and to overcome, instead of doing so through an agent." The real test of the Negro's assimilation in Canada was to come in the period after the disintegration of the colonies, where, down to the Civil War, the majority of them lived.

The vast majority of Canadians welcomed the refugees and demonstrated their brotherly feelings in tangible ways. The official pronouncements of the governments, the assistance given by organizations such as the Anti-Slavery Society of Canada, and the participation of many Canadians in the activities of the Underground Railroad show that there was an honest desire on the part of Canadians to strike a decisive blow to slavery in the New World. Perhaps one of the most demonstrative acknowledgments that Canadians were sincerely friendly to the cause of the Negro was made by John Brown, who held a convention in Chatham in May, 1858, to draw up a new constitution for the United States and to make the initial plans which eventually resulted in the fateful attack on Harpers Ferry. In issuing invitations to persons to attend the convention Brown described the citizens of Chatham as the "true friends of freedom."

As the Negro population of Canada increased, resentment against the presence of the Negro grew. The Reverend James Proudfoot of London, Ontario, noticed the growth of anti-Negro feeling, but insisted that it was not a British feeling. Rather, it was a prejudice, he said, brought in by the many American whites who had migrated into the country. A citizen of Malden complained that the sentiment against the Negro arose from the fact that Negroes were beginning to look upon themselves *"as the equal of the whites!"* The Honorable George Brown, a Member of Parliament from Toronto, was amazed at the growth of prejudice in Upper Canada. He related the following incident to show how it had increased:

> When I was a candidate for Parliament in Upper Canada, 150 people signed a paper, saying that if I would agree to urge the passage of a law that the negro should be excluded from the common schools, and putting a head-tax upon those coming into the country, they would all vote for me; otherwise they would vote for my opponent. There were 150 men degraded enough to sign such a paper and send it to me.

The Negroes were quite aware of the growing sentiment against them. One Negro physician of London, Ontario, said,

"There is a mean prejudice here that is not to be found in the States, though the Northern States are pretty bad." A Negro minister living in St. Catherines complained of more prejudice in Canada than there was in Massachusetts, while another asserted, with a feeling of resignation, that "the law is the only thing that sustains us in this country." The Negroes, for the moment at least, had no thought of returning to the United States, despite their disappointment with Canada. It was perhaps some consolation to realize that the law was on their side. Abolitionists in the United States, moreover, encouraged them to remain in Canada in order that they could argue more convincingly that Negroes were assimilable if given a fair chance.

Even those Canadians who did not want the Negroes among them admitted that they were, on the whole, an industrious group. The Reverend Howe asked many Canadians if Negroes were beggars, and all of them answered in the negative, adding that the only thing that the Negroes asked for was work. Most of them were farmers, raising grain and vegetables and selling them in the markets of nearby towns. The farmers spent their spare time hunting and trapping with considerable success. Austin Steward tells of numerous instances in which the settlers living in the Wilberforce Colony walked a few miles outside the settlement, shot wolves, bears, and other animals, and sold them to fur traders. Many fugitives went to urban centers and worked in the hotels and taverns, as well as laboring independently as carpenters, plasterers, blacksmiths, and the like. In 1855 Benjamin Drew described the activity of the Negroes in one town in the following manner:

> At Chatham the fugitives are as thick as blackbirds in a cornfield. Here, indeed, more fully than anywhere else, the traveller realizes the extent of the American exodus. At every turn, he meets members of the African race, single or in groups; he sees them building and painting houses, working in mills, engaged in every handicraft employment; here he notices a street occupied by coloured shop-keepers and clerks. If he steps into the environs, he finds the blacks in every quarter busy upon their gardens and farms.

Not only were more workers needed on the farms, but the railroad companies were clamoring for more laborers. In 1851 2,500 Negroes were working on the Canada Railway for $10 per month and board. In the following year the Great Western Railway carried an advertisement in the *Voice of the Fugitive* stating that it needed 1,000 workers immediately. Henry Bibb, the editor, urged fugitives to come, saying that mechanics and professional men were urgently needed. Canada was no place for barbers, bootblacks, and table waiters, he added. Many Negroes, however, found employment and, in some cases, easier money in the field of personal service.

As Negroes settled themselves in towns or in rural areas, they began to acquire property. Some of them had brought personal effects with them; now they added to them. They were, moreover, acquiring land. Although the Canada Company, from which most Negroes purchased land, was reluctant to sell an unlimited amount of real estate to Negroes, settlers continued to acquire both farm and town land by various methods. In some instances white persons cooperated with them by purchasing land and then selling it to Negroes. At the beginning of the Civil War all of the 75 Negro families in London, Ontario, were paying taxes on real or personal property. In Malden 71 of the 550 taxpayers were Negroes; while in Chatham 134 of the 1,021 taxpayers were Negroes. The Reverend Samuel G. Howe was gratified to observe that the houses of the Negroes were superior to those of the Irish or other foreign immigrants of the laboring class and that they were tidily furnished with "curtains at the windows."

Canadian school laws permitted Negroes to send their children to common schools or, if they desired, to have their own separate schools provided out of their share of the school funds. One of the early manifestations of anti-Negro feeling in Canada was the interpretation which some officials put on the law that they could establish separate schools for Negro children and exclude them from the common schools. Some Negroes, moreover, believed that separate schools were more desirable because of the prejudices of the whites and because such institutions would give the Negroes an opportunity to develop leadership and intellectual independence. Even where there was an indifference toward the matter of separate schools it usually developed that most of the schools that Negroes attended were, for all practical purposes, separate schools, because they were located in Negro settlements.

Negro settlers everywhere evinced a strong desire to set up schools for their children. Mrs. Laura S. Haviland, the first teacher in the Dawn settlement, was surprised to discover the "keen desire for education among the refugees." One of the first tasks that the settlers undertook was the establishment of a school in the community. Indeed, in some instances, such as in the case of the Dawn Industrial Institute, the school preceded the settlement and attracted colonists to it. Mr. William King, who was the leader of the Elgin settlement at Buxton, was so keenly cognizant of the importance of education and established a school of such excellence that the white people of the surrounding area sent their children to it. John Scoble, a frequent visitor at Buxton, noticed that after white children were transferred to the Negro school and distributed through the various classes, without distinction, they studied quite harmoniously together. In attendance and efficiency it was generally agreed that there was little difference between Negro and white children of the same socio-economic status.

Since many Negro leaders in Canada were ministers, the religious life of the refugees was not neglected. Churches were erected, and attendance was regular, especially in the Sunday schools. Dr. Howe remarked that in Canada the religion of the Negroes was "less nasal and more practical" than among their race in the South. Negro religious leaders from the United States, such as the Reverend Samuel R. Ward and Bishop Morris Brown, showed their interest by visiting communities and ministering to the people. By 1840 the African Methodist Episcopal Church had enough congregations to prompt Bishop Brown to organize a Canadian conference at Toronto. The lack of education among Negro ministers distressed John Scoble, who described them as "woefully ignorant, thoroughly ignorant and much wanting the reputation of good manners and a holy life." The education of the younger generation had the effect of improving the religious leadership markedly.

Almost every observer was impressed with the moral conditions of the refugees. There seemed to have been an earnest desire for self-improvement and for the establishment of stable human relationships. Frequently, for example, one of the first things that many married slaves did upon arrival in Canada was to have their plantation union reaffirmed by the form of marriage legal in Canada. One observer remarked that the "respect paid to women by colored men . . . is one of the most hopeful signs of their race. . . ." There was also a noticeable manifestation of temperance and sobriety. The conscious effort for self-improvement led to the organization of a special society, The True Band, dedicated to that purpose. Beginning in Amherstburg in 1854, the organization spread rapidly, and within two years there were fourteen branches with some having as many as 600 members. The objectives of the leaders were the improvement of schools and the increase of school attendance, the abatement of race prejudice, the arbitration of disputes between Negroes, the raising of a fund to aid destitute fugitives, the suppression of begging in behalf of refugees by self-appointed agents, and the prevention of divisions within churches. Some of the branches made a special effort to put an end to the drinking of alcoholic beverages among their members. Excellent results were reported in some aspects of the program of the organization.

As citizens of their new home the refugees used their privilege of voting freely in common with the native citizens, allying themselves with the two regular parties of Canada, the Conservative and the Reform. In some communities Negroes were elected to office. They became pathmasters, school trustees, and councillors. It was believed by the Reverend William King that while whites would not interfere with the exercise of the franchise by the Negro, they would refuse to vote for one running for Parliament. A friend of the refugees, Dr. J. Wilson Moore, observed that Negroes served frequently on juries with their white neighbors, and also in the Canadian militia. In Hamilton it was common, said Austin Steward, to meet "every few rods, a colored man in uniform, with a sword at his side, marching in all the military pomp allowed to the white man in this *Free Republic* [The United States]." When the rebellion broke out in 1837 many Negroes volunteered their services. Some of them feared that the United States might take advantage of the internal chaos and make a bid for the control of Canada. Josiah Henson became the captain of the Second Company of the Essex Colored Volunteers. He and his men helped to defend Fort Malden (Amherstburg) from Christmas, 1837, to May, 1838. He asserted that the Negroes were willing and anxious to defend the government that had given them a home when they had fled from slavery. The Reverend J. W. Loguen was another who was in command of a Negro company in 1838.

The experience of the Negroes in Canada during the first six decades of the nineteenth century provides a good opportunity to study the process of acculturation while resistance to the process was at a minimum. While there were manifestations of prejudice against the Negroes, the law was a constant reminder to the whites that Negroes were to be treated as equals. Thus, with all the handicaps that a long period of enslavement provided, they went far in the direction of assimilating themselves and of becoming responsible Canadian citizens. The righteous indignation which the majority of Canadians had toward slavery and the influx of a considerable number of Negroes from the Northern part of the United States in the fifties made possible the more rapid adjustment and integration of the black population. Even when the glowing accounts of abolitionists of the success of Negroes in Canada are discounted, because of the subjectivity with which they approached the subject, there is still left a record of industry, independence, and cultural striving that leaves little doubt as to the assimilability of that portion of the population. If they were to fail in a later period, the factors operating outside their group were, perhaps, to have a great deal to do with it.

Recent Trends

The national repugnance to slavery on the part of Canada caused its citizens to welcome fugitives because each arrival made the institution of slavery more precarious in the Southern part of the United States. The overwhelming support which Canadians had given the anti-slavery movement caused them to view with satisfaction the election of Lincoln in 1860. Papers such as George Brown's powerful Toronto *Globe* adopted a strong pro-Northern tone in the early months of the war. During the conflict the United States bought huge supplies of grain and cattle from Canada, and it is estimated that more than 40,000 Canadians fought on the side of the Union. When there was no longer any slavery from which the Negro could flee, he ceased to find welcome and scarcely found toleration in Canada. Once the Civil War was over the sentiment that had developed against the Negro before the war, but which had not been generally expressed, became more and more obvious and manifested itself in widespread hostility to Negroes. Negroes who had been reluctant to admit that conditions were unfavorable to their growth and development now freely confessed that the situation was growing worse, as they saw a greater effort to exclude them from the schools, from gainful employment, and from the enjoyment of the privileges to which all Canadian citizens were entitled. The most eloquent admission of the new hostility was seen in the general exodus of Negroes to the United States in the decade following the war. It must be admitted that some of the Negroes who returned to the United States would have done so regardless of conditions in Canada, because they viewed their sojourn in Canada as temporary, pending the end of slavery in the United States. But the number of migrants to the United States would hardly have been as large as it was had there not existed the feeling of utter hopelessness regarding the situation in Canada.

The most conservative estimates of the Negro population of Canada in 1860 place the figure somewhere around 50,000. In 1871 the Negro population had fallen to 20,000. Ten years later it was approximately the same. At the beginning of the twentieth century it was approximately 17,000, while at the end of World War I it had increased slightly to about 18,000. Ontario, where the refugees were concentrated and where the largest number of Negroes were settled, lost the greatest number of Negroes. There were 13,435 Negroes in the province in 1871. By 1900 the figure had fallen to 8,900; and at the end of World War I there were only 7,000 Negroes there. Nova Scotia's Negro population tended to remain the same, around 6,000, as did New Brunswick's at 15,000. The province of Quebec showed some increase, with 148 Negroes in 1871, 280 in 1901, and 1,046 in 1921.

Today the Negro population of Canada is hardly one third of what it was at the end of the Civil War, and it can be divided into three groups. First, there are the Canadian-born Negroes, the descendants of those who went into the country from 90 to 100 or more years ago. They constitute the largest element and live principally in the rural settlements in Ontario and on the outskirts of the large towns and cities. Secondly, there are the Negroes from the United States who migrated into Canada during and after the Civil War to work on the construction of railroads, such as the Canadian Pacific, and to perform personal services in connection with the operation of the railroads. They live, for the most part, in the large terminal cities, and enjoy an income that affords them a standard of living considerably higher than that of the majority of Canadian Negroes. Finally, there are the Negroes from the West Indies who have come to Canada in search of employment. This migration was one of the phenomena of World War I and immediately thereafter. The majority of this group settled in the large cities. The number of Negroes who may enter Canada is very carefully controlled by the Department of Immigration and Colonization, whose minister said a few years ago, "So far as the Negro is concerned we have never encouraged his settlement in Canada, regardless of his occupation, although we have admitted and still admit a few coloured folk who are able to comply with existing immigration regulations." Between 1901 and 1929 the average annual immigration of Negroes into Canada was less than 100.

Those Negroes who chose to remain in Canada after the Civil War had difficulty in securing profitable employment. While there has been some tendency for them to move to the cities, a majority of the Negroes still live in rural areas or in small communities. Most of the Negroes of Nova Scotia have remained in small communities or in rural areas where they are largely employed as day laborers on the farms of whites rather than as operators of their own farms. A larger number in Kent and Essex Counties in Ontario own their farms, but the Deputy Minister of Agriculture in Ontario said a few years ago that they "do not, as a rule make very successful farmers, but there are, of course, exceptions." Early in the present century a colony of Negro farmers was settled in northwestern Saskatchewan, but only a few families remain at the present time. There are two small colonies in Alberta, one at Athabasca and one at Junkins, and several farmers have enjoyed considerable success. The majority of the farmers of Canada have not had access to rich or extensive lands, and they have not been able to purchase the machinery which is required for large-scale farming. Their success has, therefore, been limited, if, indeed, their situation can be described as successful at all.

In recent years Negroes have not played a significant part in the occupational or professional life of Canada. Both men and women find employment as barbers, tailors, seamstresses, saloon and shopkeepers, bootblacks, cafe attendants, and the like. In 1929 the majority of the Negro men in the cities were sleeping car and parlor-car porters. At that time the Canadian National Railways had 1,095 Negroes in its employ, while the Canadian Pacific had a number almost as large. Until 1918 the Canadian Pacific Railway had never used Negroes in its dining cars.

When Negroes were employed, the men whom they displaced demanded an investigation, claiming that the company's action was due to their joining the Brotherhood of American Railway Employees. The mediation board found no evidence of discrimination against union labor, and after the war white waiters were again employed in the place of Negroes.

The competition which has developed between Negroes and immigrant workers has caused many whites to attempt to exclude Negroes from membership in the trade unions. Although the Trades and Labour Congress of Canada has a policy of accepting all workers into membership irrespective of race, color, or religion, in many instances Negroes have been effectively excluded from membership. In some communities Negroes working as carpenters, blacksmiths, coopers, and stone masons have been called strike breakers because, having failed to secure membership in the labor union, they have had to make a living by selling their labor at the price that they could obtain. The influence of the American Federation of Labor, which has enjoyed increasing prestige in Canada in the twentieth century, has not helped in the Negro's quest for jobs, since the practice of many of its autonomous unions of excluding Negroes in the United States has spread to Canada. An increasing number of Negroes, however, has succeeded in finding employment as garage mechanics, street car motormen, conductors, and factory workers.

In some areas the Negro has lost ground during the present century. Before World War I most of the first class hotels in Canada employed Negro waiters. Within the last 40 years the picture has changed; and Henry Bibb's statement that ·"Canada is no place for Negro waiters" seems truer today than it was when he made it almost a century ago. In a similar manner there has been a decline in the number of businesses operated by Negroes. The pastor of a Negro church in St. John, New Brunswick, described the situation a few years ago:

> There was a time when the restaurant business was carried on largely by Negroes, and many names are remembered in this connection. Whetzell carried on a successful ice business, employing between ten and twelve men regularly in the summer, and many more at winter. Brackett operated a thriving dyeing business; whilst Walker as lawyer and Richardson, Cole and Henderson as teachers played their parts.

To-day, they have no regular work. Some do trucking, handling coal and garbage, and a few do longshore work, they do general labour work when they can secure same. A Jackson and a Leslie work at the barber trade, their customers being largely white. There are none in business professionally.

In other places perhaps the picture was not so dark as it was at St. John, but the tendency has been the same everywhere. There are a few Negro attorneys and physicians in cities like Halifax, Toronto, and Montreal, but only the Negro clergy can claim any considerable number in the professions. There are some teachers, of course, largely in the schools that are predominantly Negro; but the number is comparatively small. Considering the picture as a whole it would not seem too much to say that opportunities for Canadian Negroes have shrunk and that their economic position has rather steadily retrogressed in the present century.

The legal status of Negroes in Canada has not changed, but public opinion, rather than the law, actually determines the status of Negroes in Canada. They vote and apparently no attempt is made to interfere with their exercise of the franchise, possibly because the number is inconsequential. Theoretically they are entitled to the same privileges of movement and of location as other citizens, but it does not work out that way. It has been extremely difficult for Negroes to secure accommodations at the better hotels. Many cases have come before the courts regarding the attempt of theater owners to segregate Negroes or to deny them entrance altogether, and the courts have usually decided that the Negro was not entitled to more in the way of damages than the price of the ticket. There are no legal proscriptions of Negroes in regard to areas of residence, but the majority of Negroes live in groups or communities, perhaps because some of them prefer such an arrangement, but also because landlords and landowners refuse to rent or sell property to Negroes in certain areas because of the pressure of public opinion. Segregation is not found in the schools, but in some communities there is considerable hostility to Negroes attending; and because of the dark prospects for employment upon graduation a great many do not remain in school. Most of the universities have a few Negro students, but some of them warn Negro medical students that they may have difficulty in doing their clinical work. The difficulties which many Negroes experience in attempting to enjoy full citizenship in Canada led

Miss Ida Greaves to conclude that "The actual position appears to be that the Negro has exactly the same rights as anybody else until he tries to exercise them, then he can be quite legally constrained."

The widespread rejection of the Negro by the larger Canadian community since the American Civil War has led to the continuation and growth of organizations among Negroes which seek to enhance their spiritual and cultural life and which look toward the improvement of their social and economic well-being. Negro churches, for example, have continued to grow, especially the Baptist and Methodist denominations. In 1917 the Eureka Association was organized in Montreal to assist in the purchase and construction of homes for Negroes. There are no longer the True Bands, but within the present century the Elks, the National Association for the Advancement of Colored People, and the Universal Negro Improvement Association have flourished, with some favorable results. But the lot of the Canadian Negro in the twentieth century has not been, on the whole, a happy one. There is considerable validity for the following observation made by a recent student of the problem, even if there is no basis for the suggested solution:

> The hopes of the first generation of settlers have vanished, and no tangible basis of security has taken place. The most to which the Negroes of to-day can look forward is to recross the border over which their ancestors came so hopefully, the path to Canadian freedom has proved a cul-de-sac.

XXI •

Philanthropy and Self-Help

Northern Philanthropy and Negro Education

● *The end of Reconstruction brought little improvement in the* economic and social status of the Negro. Meanwhile, their political gains rapidly disappeared before the vigorous, all-out efforts of Southern whites to wipe them out altogether. Negroes could be certain of an improved status only in the field of education, for many of the schools that had been founded in the days immediately following the war were still flourishing. (See Chapter XVII.) Despite the opposition of many Southerners to Negro schools, there seemed to be a greater willingness to tolerate the growing educational institutions than any of the other agencies of Negroes to improve themselves. The pursuit of education, therefore, came to be one of the great preoccupations of Negroes; and enlightenment was viewed by many as the greatest single opportunity to escape the increasing proscriptions and indignities that a renascent South was heaping upon the Negroes. Small wonder that Negro children were sent to school by their parents at great inconvenience to themselves, and that Negro fathers and mothers made untold sacrifices in order to secure for their children a portion of the learning that they had been denied.

Coincident with the growth of Negro schools in the South was the emergence of a new stimulus for educational institutions in the form of philanthropy. As the Freedmen's Bureau withdrew, the only outside assistance which the economically weak Negro

schools had was the help which came from denominational
boards. The American Missionary Association continued its
work, administering the interesting experiment for the coeduca-
tion of the races at Berea College in Kentucky, as well as
financing and operating academies and colleges throughout the
South. The Freedmen's Aid Society of the Methodist Episcopal
Church had broadened its scope to include not only the supervision of secondary schools and colleges but also two medical
colleges and three theological schools by 1878. Baptists were
working effectively through their Home Mission Society, while
the Presbyterians, Episcopalians, and Catholics increased their
activities. Each of the major Negro denominations maintained
both secondary schools and colleges; and Negroes themselves
seemed to be increasingly interested in their schools.

To many the church organizations appeared, undoubtedly
incorrectly, to be interested primarily in strengthening their
denominations instead of centering their attention on improving
the status of Negroes. Consequently, the appearance of large
educational foundations, established for the most part by the
new group of wealthy Americans, stimulated a broadening of
the concept of education for Negroes in the South. These newly
rich Americans were by no means confining their interests to
Negroes, for the period between 1860 and 1900 witnessed the
founding of 260 institutions of higher learning, many of which
were primarily white institutions financed by wealthy philanthropists. Vanderbilt (1873), Johns Hopkins (1876), Leland
Stanford (1855), and the University of Chicago (1892) are
cases in point. It was an age of philanthropy, and Negro education benefited substantially. Between the end of the Civil War
and the beginning of World War I several large educational
foundations were established which worked directly to advance
Southern Negro education: the Peabody Education Fund, the
John F. Slater Fund, the General Education Board, the Anna
T. Jeanes Fund, the Julius Rosenwald Fund, and the Phelps-
Stokes Fund.

George Peabody, who had amassed a fortune as a merchant
and financier in England and America, founded not only the
Institute at Baltimore and the Museums at Harvard and Yale
which bear his name, but also established an Education Fund in
1867 "for the promotion and encouragement of intellectual,
moral, or industrial education among the young people of the
more destitute portions of the Southern and Southwestern

States." In two separate grants he gave almost two and one-half million dollars to be administered by a board of trustees that was empowered to use the interest and 40 per cent of the principal. After thirty years the trustees could distribute two-thirds of the fund "among such educational or literary institutions or for other educational purposes as they might determine." They were to promote common school education immediately and assist in the establishment of a permanent system of public education in the South. Between 1867 and 1914 the Fund provided more than three and one-half million dollars for the advancement of education in the South.

In 1882 John F. Slater, the textile industrialist of Norwich, Connecticut, founded the fund which bears his name. Stimulated by the success of the Peabody Education Fund, Slater gave one million dollars "for uplifting the lately emancipated population of the Southern states and their posterity, by conferring on them the blessings of Christian education." The board of trustees, headed by former President Rutherford B. Hayes, undertook immediately to assist twelve schools that were training Negro teachers. Between 1882 and 1911 the Fund assisted both private and church schools in their teacher-training programs and made donations to public schools where the need and the work justified it. A considerable portion of the Fund's resources was expended in the promotion of industrial and vocational training. In 1911 the Fund began its support of county training schools, and within a decade more than one hundred such institutions had been assisted. The program of expenditures for the Peabody and Slater Funds was administered largely by J. L. M. Curry, who was the general agent for both funds during the early days of their existence and adviser to the Southern Education Board, made up of most of the influential Northern philanthropists.

In 1902 John D. Rockefeller, who had been giving largely to Baptist schools and who had financed the establishment of the University of Chicago, pledged one million dollars to an agency that was being created to promote education without distinction of race, sex, or creed. In the following year the General Education Board was incorporated and set about to support various programs for the diffusion of knowledge over a wide range. Among its major objectives were the general improvement of higher education in the United States, the support of education in the South, and the assistance of private and public institutions for the education of Negroes. Between 1902 and 1909 Rockefeller gave 53 millions to the Board in four large gifts and empowered its trustees to dispose of the principal whenever they saw fit. The Board seemed especially interested in providing means for the preparation of teachers for Negro schools over the South and, consequently, gave generously to institutions which were undertaking the task.

In 1905 Miss Anna T. Jeanes, the Quaker daughter of a wealthy Philadelphia merchant, gave $200,000 to the General Education Board to help improve Negro rural schools in the South. The money was set aside for that purpose and named the Anna T. Jeanes Fund for the Assistance of Negro Rural Schools in the South. Two years later Miss Jeanes gave one million dollars for the enlargement of the program. Under the guidance of Dr. James H. Dillard, the Fund sought the appointment of teachers to do industrial work in the rural schools and special teachers to do extension work. County agents, whose function was to improve rural homes and schools and create public sentiment for better Negro schools, were also appointed. The Jeanes Fund paid the salaries of these special teachers; county officials gradually assumed part of the responsibility. The work of the Fund attracted additional contributions from several other philanthropic agencies.

In 1910, in accordance with the will of Mrs. Caroline Phelps-Stokes, the Fund bearing her name was established. From the beginning the Fund manifested a special though not an exclusive interest in Negro education. It gave considerable attention to the improvement of existing institutions of proved experience and assured stability, and made specialized studies of educational institutions and problems, the results of which would help plan future educational programs. As early as 1910 Mr. Julius Rosenwald became interested in the improvement of conditions among Negroes. In the following year he visited Tuskegee Institute and accepted a place on its Board of Trustees in 1912. His interest in rural Negro schools and active assistance is dated from this time. Beginning as a small donor of amounts of $5,000, he soon became a major contributor to the improvement of the educational facilities for Southern Negroes. (See Chapter XXVIII.)

One of the major differences between church philanthropy and the large educational foundations—aside from the much larger amounts of money at the disposal of the latter—was one of motive. While church philanthropy either served some recognized social need or supported agencies for the promotion of its own interests, the educational foundations usually were interested in stimulating the public to recognize certain existent needs as yet unfelt by society. These new agencies hoped to establish the principle of self-help for the individual as well as for the state. There can be little doubt that the interests of the Northern business men in the South were correlated with their efforts to improve Southern citizenry, both black and white. In 1882 Dexter Hawkins, a New York lawyer, argued that the development of education in the South would enable that section to bear a larger proportion of national taxes. In 1888 the Reverend A. D. Mayo asserted that Northern capital could be attracted and Southern resources properly developed only if the working masses were educated in skill and dependability. As Northern industrialists moved into the South and invested heavily in railroads, textile mills, and steel mills, they became increasingly aware of the need for a trained working force to operate the machines and perform the other tasks required in an industrialized economy. Thus, they were at least interested in the improvement of the common schools; some even contributed materially to the improvement of higher education. Critics have accused Northern philanthropists of seeking the education of Negroes as well as whites in order that one could be played off against the other in the competition for jobs. Regardless of the validity of this charge, both groups benefited substantially from their generosity.

There was the motive, moreover, which stemmed from the successful businessman's sense of noblesse oblige. The contributions of large foundations, as well as those of individuals like Robert C. Ogden, H. H. Rogers, Collis P. Huntington, Andrew Carnegie, and William Baldwin were motivated, at least in part, by their feeling that they should assume responsibility for bestowing what the economic system from which they had benefited failed to provide directly for social need. In much the same way that the feudal aristocracy developed a sense of obligation to the masses upon whose continued industry and contentment depended its prosperity, the industrialists of the United States had a feeling of duty toward those whose profits from the economic order were not so obvious.

The age of the philanthropists contributed substantially toward bringing about a new day for education in the South. By conditional grants and aid to those institutions that had proved their worth, philanthropists did much to stimulate self-help on the part of the individual, the institution, and the states of the South. Public education was greatly improved as the boards supplemented teachers' salaries, bought equipment, and built schools. There was general approval of Northern philanthropy when the white citizens of the South discovered that their bene-factors showed little or no interest in establishing racial equality or of upsetting white supremacy.

Although philanthropists effected a greater support of public education in the South, they did little to encourage the equitable distribution of public funds for the education of all Southern children. Perhaps the whites of the South took the position that if the philanthropists were going to educate the Negroes, the taxpayers' money could be used to educate the whites. Too, they were strongly of the opinion that since Negroes paid little in the way of taxes they were not entitled to very much support for their educational institutions. Thus, in 1898 Florida's per capita cost of education per school population was $5.92 for whites and $2.27 for Negroes. Two years later the citizens of Adams County, Mississippi, were spending $22.25 for the education of each white child and only $2 for the education of each Negro child. Negroes, of course, denied that they were not supporting their own institutions through taxation. At the Sixth Atlanta Conference for the Study of Negro Problems in 1901 it was reported that between 1870 and 1899 Negroes paid a total of $25,000,000 in direct school taxes, while the indirect taxes which they paid amounted to more than $45,000,000. It was also reported that Negroes had paid more than fifteen millions in tuition and fees to private institutions. With a strong asser-tion that Negroes had done much to help themselves in the generation following Reconstruction, the report concluded, "It is a conservative statement to say . . . that Amerian Negroes have in a generation paid directly forty millions of dollars in hard earned cash for educating their children."

The schools had done much to sustain themselves. The Jubi-lee Singers of Fisk University set an example for other institu-tions. The treasurer of the college, George L. White, conceived the idea that through the singing of a group of young Negroes, the hearts and hence the pockets of the Northern citizens could be reached. Therefore, with money borrowed from the teachers and the citizens of Nashville, White carried a group of students in 1875 to Oberlin, Ohio, where the National Council of Congregational Churches was meeting. The Council was captivated with the way in which the young Negroes sang the spirituals and work songs of their people and their fame spread rapidly. In the East they sang in many halls, under the sponsorship of Henry Ward Beecher of Brooklyn. Many engagements followed, and

JUBILEE HALL, FISK UNIVERSITY. Funds for construction of this building were raised primarily by students who traveled through the North and Europe. It is an example of self-help in the period following emancipation. Courtesy Alumni Office, Fisk University.

FOUNDERS LIBRARY, HOWARD UNIVERSITY. Built in 1937 at a cost of approximately $1,000,000, this structure might be regarded as a symbol of the ideal twentieth century American education. Scurlock Studio.

the money flowed in. Later they went to England, Germany, and other European countries and appeared before several royal audiences. Within seven years they had raised $150,000, a part of which was used in the construction of Jubilee Hall. Student quartets, speakers, and other groups went out from other schools. In some communities money was raised at fairs and demonstrations. In many ways, the schools were learning that they could contribute to their own continuation and growth through the resources of their educated students.

The results of the efforts to insure the education of Negroes were gratifying. In 1900 there were 28,560 Negro teachers. At the same time there were more than 1,500,000 Negro children in school. Thirty-four institutions for Negroes were reported as giving collegiate training, and a larger number of Negroes were being permitted to enter the universities and colleges of the North. There were four state colleges for Negroes, in Virginia, Arkansas, Georgia, and Delaware; other institutions, begun by private groups or individuals, were later to be taken over by the states. By 1900 more than 2,000 Negroes had graduated from institutions of higher learning, while more than 700 were in colleges at that time. The great educational awakening that pervaded the United States in the closing years of the nineteenth century and the opening years of the twentieth century was certainly as clearly manifested among Negroes as it was among the other ethnic groups in the population.

For Negroes, however, the problem of education was complicated in a way that it was not for any other group. There was the feeling on the part of most persons that the success or failure of the Negro in adjusting himself depended on the type of education to which he was exposed. There were those who felt that the amount of education which the Negro could or should receive was limited, perhaps to the rudiments. Others were of the opinion that the Negro should not be regarded as a group for which a special amount or kind of education should be provided. Still others contended that the Negro, at his present stage of development, could best serve himself and his country with a type of education which could most rapidly help him find an indispensable place in the American social order. Into the controversy stepped Booker T. Washington who for more than thirty years so completely dominated the scene as to stamp upon the period his own name and personality.

The Age of Booker T. Washington

Writing in 1903 Dr. W. E. B. DuBois said, "Easily the most striking thing in the history of the American Negro since 1876 is the ascendancy of Mr. Booker T. Washington." The ascendancy of this man is one of the most dramatic and significant episodes in the history of American education and of race relations. In 1872 Washington, a lad about sixteen years old, arrived at Hampton Institute, a school molded from the ideas of practical education of its founder, General Samuel Chapman Armstrong. Armstrong taught his students that labor was a "spiritual force, that physical work not only increased wage-earning capacity but promoted fidelity, accuracy, honesty, persistence, and intelligence." He emphasized the value of acquiring land and homes, vocations and skills. Washington drank deeply of Armstrong's teachings and, in time, became the most eloquent exponent of the ideals he enunciated. By the time that Washington graduated he was convinced that in order for Negroes to achieve success they must do some useful service that the world wanted. It was his great preoccupation from that point on to find out the ways in which his people could be most useful to the world.

When Washington went to Tuskegee in 1881, he found none of the equipment with which to develop an educational institution; and he found a white community hostile to the idea of a school for Negroes. He, therefore, set about the twofold task of securing the necessary resources with which to conduct a school and of conciliating the whites. It was an ideal situation in which to relate education to life. Students cooperated in doing all the necessary work at Tuskegee, constructing the buildings, producing and cooking the food, and performing innumerable other tasks. The community was given assurances in many ways that the students were there to serve and not to antagonize. Washington believed that Southern whites had to be convinced that the education of the Negroes was in the true interest of the South. The students provided many of the services and much of the produce that the white community needed, and hostility to the new school began to disappear. Washington counseled the Negroes to respect the law and to cooperate with white authorities in maintaining peace. In this way he won the good will of the ruling class.

As Washington saw the salutary effects which his program was having on the white South as well as on his Negro students, he became more and more certain that this was the pattern for strengthening the position of Negroes throughout the area. He became the apostle of a form of industrial education that he saw would not antagonize the South and that would, at the same time, carve out a place of service for Negroes in their communities. Certainly a program of training Negroes to become farmers, mechanics, and domestic servants would be more acceptable to Mississippi's J. K. Vardaman than the program of classical education advocated by many Northern educators. Earlier Vardaman had said, "What the North is sending South is not money but dynamite; this education is ruining our Negroes. They're demanding equality." Washington was not demanding that, and it pleased the Southern whites to hear him say at the Atlanta Exposition in 1895, "In all things that are purely social we can be as separate as the five fingers, yet one as the hand in all things essential to mutual progress." To his own people he uttered this admonition: "To those of my race who depend upon bettering their condition in a foreign land or who underestimate the importance of cultivating friendly relations with the Southern white man . . . I would say 'Cast down your bucket where you are'—cast it down in making friends in every manly way of the people of all races by whom we are surrounded. Cast it down in agriculture, mechanics, in commerce, in domestic service, and in the professions."

Washington never tired of urging Negroes to develop habits and skills that would win for them places in their Southern communities. Intelligent management of farms, ownership of land, habits of thrift, patience, and perseverance, and the cultivation of high morals and good manners were encouraged. He said that the Negro must learn that all races have got on their feet largely by laying an economic foundation and, in general, by beginning in a proper cultivation and ownership of the soil. He was greatly distressed by the mass movement of Negroes from the country to the city, and did what he could to persuade them to return. He did not deprecate the study of such subjects as science, mathematics, and history; but he indicated on many occasions that he regarded them as impractical. He said that he believed that "for years to come the education of the people of my race should be so directed that the greatest proportion of the mental strength of the masses will be brought to bear upon the

everyday practical things of life, upon something that is needed
to be done, and something which they will be permitted to do in
the community in which they reside."

The Washington doctrine of industrial education, or, more
properly, vocational education, for the great mass of Negroes
was hailed by whites in the North and in the South. Some
Northern whites, weary of racial and sectional conflicts, saw in
it a formula for peace in the South with the establishment of a
satisfactory economic and social equilibrium between the races.
Others, skeptical of the capacity of Negroes to become completely assimilated in a highly complex civilization, viewed it as
leading the Negro to his proper "place" in American life. Still
other Northerners, with an eye on markets and a labor supply in
the South, thought it would perhaps make possible the greater
economic development of the South. Southerners, on the other
hand, liked Washington's relative disinterest in political and
civil rights for Negroes. They liked the way in which he placed
confidence in the Southern whites regarding their good treatment of Negroes who proved themselves to be useful, law-
abiding citizens. They agreed with his advocacy of a type of
education which they believed would consign Negroes to an
inferior economic and social status in Southern life. Finally,
they admired the tact and diplomacy with which he conciliated
all groups, North and South. Only twice did he threaten his
position among the whites in the South. Speaking on one occasion in Chicago he lashed out at race prejudice and asserted that
it was eating away the vitals of the South. On another occasion
he visited the White House and had lunch with President Theodore Roosevelt, an incident that was regarded by most Southerners as a serious breach of racial etiquette. (See Chapter
XXIII.) After fourteen years of intimate association with Washington, J. L. M. Curry, a leading Southern educator, could say
that he had never once known the principal of Tuskegee to say
or to do an unwise thing. Curry did not know that Washington
was financing some of the earliest court cases against segregation.

Because of their intense interest in the immediate goals of
Washington, perhaps few whites saw that this leader looked
forward to the complete acceptance and integration of Negroes
in American life. On one occasion he said, "I would set no
limits to the attainments of the Negro in arts, in letters or
statesmanship, but I believe the surest way to reach those ends

is by laying the foundation in the little things of life that lie immediately about one's door. I plead for industrial education and development for the Negro not because I want to cramp him, but because I want to free him. I want to see him enter the all-powerful business and commercial world." He always advocated the entrance of the Negro into the professions and other fields; and, it will be recalled, that he urged Negroes to make friends with their white neighbors in every "manly" way. Washington believed that the Negro, starting with so little, would have to work up gradually before he could attain a position of power and respectability in the South. The whites, on the other hand, looking at Washington's program of expediency, frequently regarded it as the ultimate solution to the Negro problem and believed that the latter's place would be permanently fixed by the Washington formula.

As Washington's prestige grew to the point where he was regarded not only as the outstanding exponent of industrial education but the spokesman of the millions of Negroes, opposition among his own people increased. Of course, some of it was envy; but a relatively small group of men took serious exception both to the point of view of the Washington philosophy and to the techniques he employed in elevating his people. Foremost among the opponents was W. E. B. DuBois, a young Negro who was trained at Fisk, Harvard (where he received the degree of Doctor of Philosophy), and Berlin. Although born in Massachusetts, DuBois was teaching at Atlanta University; and the series of studies he was making of the conditions of Negroes in the South had furnished him with considerable first-hand information concerning the group for which he undertook to speak. In books, essays, and addresses DuBois opposed what he viewed as the narrow educational program of Washington, which was too predominantly economic in its objectives. His *Souls of Black Folk* (1903) contained several searchingly critical essays on Washington. He accused Washington of preaching a "gospel of Work and Money to such an extent as apparently almost completely to overshadow the higher aims of life." In an essay entitled "The Talented Tenth" DuBois said, "If we make money the object of man-training, we shall develop money-makers but not necessarily men; if we make technical skill the object of education, we may possess artisans but not, in nature, men. Men we shall have only as we make manhood the object of the work of the schools—intelligence, broad sympathy, knowledge of the

BOOKER T. WASHINGTON. This bust of the distinguished Negro educator was done by Richmond Barthe, one of America's leading sculptors. It is in the New York University Hall of Fame, to which Washington was elected in 1945, thus becoming the first Negro to be so honored. Courtesy Hall of Fame.

WILLIAM EDWARD BURGHARDT DuBOIS. This photograph of the eminent editor, author, and leader of his people was made by Carl Van Vechten, who has been interested in Negro life and culture for more than 30 years. Mr. Van Vechten says that the background of the photograph is "A Hindu design, a variation, indeed, of the swastika. It is well-known in the Orient. The significance in this case is that Dr. DuBois is interested in colored peoples everywhere." Used by permission of the Rose McClendon Memorial Collection of photographs of Celebrated Negroes by Carl Van Vechten at Howard University.

world that was and is, and of the relation of men to it—this is the curriculum of that Higher Education which must underlie true life." He especially denounced the manner in which Washington deprecated institutions of higher learning, and he insisted that neither the Negro common schools nor Tuskegee could remain open one day were it not for the teachers trained in Negro colleges or trained by their graduates.

DuBois did not approve of the manner in which Washington ignored or winked at the white South's reduction of the Negro's political and civil status. He believed that the extension of the "palm branch" to Southerners had resulted in the disfranchisement of the Negro and the legal creation of a distinct status of civil inferiority of the Negro. DuBois contended that it was not possible, under modern competitive methods, for Negro artisans, business men, and property owners to defend their rights and exist without the suffrage; while the counsel of silent submission to civic inferiority would sap the manhood of any race in the long run. He called Washington's Atlanta Exposition speech the "Atlanta Compromise," "the most notable thing in Mr. Washington's career," and conceded that it made him the most distinguished Southerner since Jefferson Davis. It also made him the leader of his people, not by their own choice, but because of the manner in which he was acclaimed by the whites in the North and in the South. He became "a compromiser between the South, the North, and the Negro" and was consulted whenever any matters arose affecting Negroes anywhere in the United States. As the most eloquent spokesman for a growing number of Negroes, DuBois was alarmed by the ultimate effect of Washington's leadership.

While there was much to be said for the position that Washington took (and DuBois admitted the importance of many of Washington's teachings), his doctrine contained some weaknesses that are perhaps more obvious today than they were sixty years ago. He accepted uncritically the dominant philosophy of American business when he insisted that everyone had his future in his own hands, "that success came to him who was worthy of it, and that the greater the obstacles, the greater the victory over them." It was a doctrine of triumphant commercialism, which was strengthened by his contact with Ogden, Huntington, and other wealthy American businessmen. The Negro Business League which Washington organized in 1900 to foster business and industry, was based on the philosophy that if a person could make a better article and sell it cheaper he could command the markets of the world; that if one produced something someone wanted the purchaser would not ask who the seller is. Add to this a generous amount of tact, good manners, resolute will, and a tireless capacity for hard work and success in business would be the reward. As Spero and Harris have pointed out, this philosophy was an adaptation of the theories of free competition and political individualism that had been taught by the school of classical political economy and was becoming more fictitious than ever by 1900. The spread of "vertical and horizontal combinations capitalized in hundreds of millions was discrediting the idea that a man of small capital could raise himself to affluence and power through hard work and thrift." Washington showed little understanding of these realities as he developed a program for the economic salvation of Negroes.

The particular type of industrial education which Washington emphasized, with much attention given to the development of a class of artisans, was outmoded at the time he enunciated it, by the increasing industrialization of the country. He did not seem to grasp fully the effect of the Industrial Revolution upon the tasks that had been performed by the hands of workers for centuries. To be sure, brickmasons, carpenters, blacksmiths, and the like would still be needed, but their tasks were being reduced to a minimum in the industrial age; many of the occupations which Washington was urging Negroes to enter were disappearing almost altogether. As training grounds for industrial workers, the curriculums and the institutions urged by Washington were not at all satisfactory. Neither Washington nor the industrial schools for Negroes took cognizance of the problems peculiar to the wage earner in modern industry. In speaking of organized labor Washington went so far as to say that the Negro did not like an "organization which seems to be founded on a sort of impersonal enmity to the man by whom he is employed." He therefore utterly failed to see the relation of the laboring class to the Industrial Revolution and counseled an approach to the labor problem that had the effect of perpetuating the master-slave tradition.

In counseling Negroes to remain in rural areas Washington not only failed to see that the advent of expensive farm machinery put the impoverished Negro farmer at a serious disadvantage, but also that the industrial urban community was infinitely more attractive to Negroes as well as to whites. There were, on the surface at least, innumerable economic opportunities in the city. Furthermore, the city offered incomparable advantages for cultural and intellectual growth. If Washington wished for his people educational and economic opportunities that would facilitate their assimilation and acceptance, the urban centers seemed to be, by far, the oases in the desert of despair. Indeed, it would seem that nothing represented more vividly the Negro's reflection of a typical American reaction than his inclination to move from the country to the city in the late nineteenth and early twentieth centuries.

Despite the fact that there were Negroes who vigorously opposed Washington's leadership and that there were some valid exceptions to his program for the salvation of the Negro, he was unquestionably the central figure—the dominant personality—in the history of the Negro down to his death in 1915. The vast majority of the Negroes acclaimed him as their leader and few whites ventured into the matter of race relations without his counsel. During his lifetime lynchings decreased only slightly, the Negro was effectively disfranchised, and the black workers were systematically excluded from the major labor organizations; but Washington's influence, sometimes for better and sometimes for worse, was so great that there is considerable justification in calling the period, "The Age of Booker T. Washington."

Struggles in the Economic Sphere

While Northern philanthropists contributed to the education of Negroes in ever increasing amounts and while the controversy raged over the most practicable and effective type of education for Negroes, the vast majority of the Negroes were facing the difficult task of making a living and were becoming more and more convinced that they would have to work out their own salvation in terms of the means at their immediate disposal. Since more than 75 per cent of the Negroes in the United States were still in the former Confederate states in 1880 and were primarily engaged in agricultural work, it appeared that most of them would be compelled to make some sort of economic adjustment on the farms. They were without capital with which to purchase land, and they continued to engage in the various forms of tenancy and sharecropping that had evolved during the Reconstruction. Indeed, large numbers were mere farm laborers with no more stake in agricultural production than their own labor for which they were paid scant wages. In 1902 farm workers in South Carolina were receiving $10.79 per month, while those of New York were receiving $26.13. While some were paid by the week or month, others were paid at the end of the season, a method resorted to in order to hold the workers on the farm until the crop was harvested.

It was difficult for Negroes to purchase desirable farm lands even if they had the capital. With the destruction of the institution of slavery, whites looked upon land as their only important capital investment; and they were reluctant to sell land to Negroes, whom they did not want to enjoy the power that came from the ownership of land in the South. The number of Negro farm owners remained small in the entire period before World War I. In 1890 Negroes owned 120,738 farms, while in 1910 they owned 218,972 farms. The acreage was always relatively small. For example, Negroes of Shelby County, Tennessee, owned 5,469 acres of farm land in 1910, while whites of the same county owned 195,020 acres. Before 1890 almost nothing had been done to educate Negroes in the use of modern agricultural methods, and, as a result, productivity was low and there was general ignorance of the problems of marketing crops and of purchasing supplies. Booker T. Washington sought to improve this situation in 1892 when he issued the first call for a conference of farmers at Tuskegee. In this and succeeding years Negroes from the surrounding countryside listened to discussions on "the evils of the mortgage system, the one-room cabin, buying on credit, the importance of owning a home and of putting money in the bank, how to build school-houses and prolong the school term, and to improve moral and religious conditions." Small tracts and circulars containing some essentials of farm improvement were distributed to the farmers, and from time to time the Institute mailed them others. After 1907, thanks to the contributions of the philanthropists and the cooperation of Southern boards of education, farm demonstration agents helped to improve conditions.

Despite the efforts of Negro farmers to adjust themselves to the rural economy, the farm ceased to be attractive to many. The return of ex-Confederates to power, intermittent agricultural depressions, unfair and, sometimes, cruel treatment by landlords and merchants, and rumors of rich opportunities in the cities and in other parts of the country stimulated an exodus of Negroes from the rural South that began as early as 1879. Thousands of Negroes left Mississippi, Louisiana, Alabama, and Georgia and went to the North and West. There was a veritable stampede to Kansas, with Henry Adams of Louisiana and "Pap" Singleton of Tennessee assuming the leadership. Adams claims to have organized 98,000 Negroes to go West. Perhaps he at least collected the names of that many persons who expressed a willingness to go. Singleton distributed a circular entitled, "The Advantage of Living in a Free State" and actually caused several thousand to leave. The Southern whites became visibly alarmed over the movement of the Negroes and the prospects of increases. Various methods were resorted to to keep Negroes on Southern plantations—the enforcement of vagrancy and labor contract laws, the enactment of legislation imposing penalties for enticing laborers away, and the establishment of systems of peonage by which Negroes were hired out by the county in order to pay the fine for a crime or to pay a debt. More tactful whites sought to persuade Negroes to remain by promising them good treatment and high wages.

Negro leaders were themselves in wide disagreement over whether or not Negroes should leave the South. Frederick Douglass opposed the exodus on the grounds that the government should protect citizens wherever they live and that emigration was no permanent remedy for the plight of the Negro. He feared that Negroes would become nomads and lose what strength a sedentary existence would give them in the South, where they were concentrated. Richard T. Greener, Harvard's first Negro graduate and a former professor at the University of South Carolina, insisted that the Negroes should migrate in order to put an end to the bad treatment they received at the hands of Southern whites. He declared that the exodus would not only carry the Negroes to better economic and educational opportunities, but would benefit those who remained in the South. Perhaps none of these persuasions had any telling effect. Forces rather than words decided the fate of the Negroes. Most of them had neither the resources nor the initiative to go to new areas. Those that did go were lured just as other rural Americans of the period. They simply could not resist the temptation to move into the industrial communities of the North and a few cities in the South and cast their lot with the new way of life.

400 · FROM SLAVERY TO FREEDOM

In the last two decades of the nineteenth century the South began to feel the impact of the economic revolution that had already enveloped the North. The iron industry was growing in Tennessee and Alabama, cloth was being manufactured in the Carolinas, and the business of transporting manufactured goods to the Southern consumer was becoming a major economic activity. The new opportunities were numerous, and blacks as well as whites attempted to take advantage of them. For the most part Negroes in the Southern towns experienced great difficulty in securing some of the benefits of the new economic activity. In 1891 only 196 industrial employers of the South were using 7,395 Negroes. Ten years later the number had increased substantially, and some were employed in cotton seed oil mills, saw mills, and furniture factories, and in foundries, machine shops, boiler works, and the like. By 1910 the Negro factory workers had increased to more than 350,000. The Southern urban Negro even found it difficult to render his customary personal services to city dwellers. Barbers met with foreign competition, while cooks and caterers were displaced by the palatial hotels which frequently did not hire Negroes. Everywhere there was sentiment against hiring Negroes in jobs that had even the semblance of respectability. Negroes living in cities in the South discovered that urban life could be almost as frustrating as rural life.

Negroes themselves had made some contributions toward the growing industrialization of America. Jan E. Matzeliger, a Negro of Dutch Guiana who had been an apprenticed cobbler in Philadelphia and in Lynn, Massachusetts, invented the shoe lasting machine. It was purchased by the United Shoe Machinery Company of Boston, and effectively reduced the cost of manufacturing shoes by more than 50 per cent. In 1884 John P. Parker invented a "screw for tobacco presses." He established the Ripley Foundry and Machine Company and made presses for many businesses. Elijah McCoy patented 50 different inventions relating principally to automatic lubricators for machines. Granville T. Woods, who began inventing in 1885, made significant contributions in the fields of electricity, steam boilers, and automatic air brakes. Several of his inventions were assigned to the General Electric Company, the Westinghouse Air Brake Company, and the American Bell Telephone Company.

The urban Negro laborer, both in the North and in the South, was essentially faced with the problem of obtaining membership in the labor unions that came more and more to dominate the industrial picture. Prejudice against the Negro worker and the refusal of numbers of whites to work with Negroes served to exclude many from membership. Other factors, however, blocked the Negro's entrance into the industrial scene through organized labor. Most of the Negroes lacked the skills prerequisite to membership in most of the craft unions. There were those, moreover, who insisted that the Negro was temperamentally unfit for skilled mechanical work. In 1893 the *Manufacturers Record* of Baltimore reported that in a study made of employers' reactions to Negro factory workers it was found that Negroes were unfit for manufacturing. Although these points of view were not based on conclusive proof, they persuaded some manufacturers that hiring Negro workers was unsound.

Among the large post-Civil War labor organizations only the Knights of Labor, which placed little emphasis on skills, showed any enthusiasm for securing Negro members. In 1885 the national convention proposed that a Negro organizer be appointed for each of the Southern states; and although the resolution was approved, no further action was taken on the matter. In the following year the secretary-treasurer rejoiced that Negroes were flocking to the Knights of Labor and manifesting a desire to be organized and educated. Some locals had Negro and white members, while others had separate organizations. Approximately 60,000 Negroes had become members of the Knights of Labor by 1886. This organization was losing ground, however, because of the infiltration of radical foreign elements and the Haymarket Square riots in 1886.

Meanwhile, the American Federation of Labor, a confederation of autonomous craft unions, was growing in influence. At first the American Federation of Labor took a positive stand against discrimination against Negroes. In 1890 the convention declared that it looked "with disfavor upon trade unions having provisions which exclude from membership persons on account of race or color," a resolution that was reiterated in 1893. The leaders, however, began to realize that this unequivocal stand on the race question was preventing the expansion of the organization, for some independent craft unions which would not accept Negro memberships refused to join.

In order to attract powerful organizations like the National Machinists Union, the American Federation of Labor allowed unions to enter if they did not openly exclude Negroes in their constitutions. The exclusion then was merely transferred from the constitution to the ritual, and members were pledged to present for membership only white workers. Many all-white labor unions joined the American Federation of Labor, and the membership grew rapidly. In order not to exclude Negroes altogether, the Federation began to charter locals composed solely of Negroes, but this was seldom done if such a move was not acceptable to the white workers of the same community. In the effective exclusion of Negroes from the strong labor organizations, either by constitution or by ritual, it became impossible for them to participate to any considerable degree in the great industrial activity that was taking place. Some efforts were made to organize independent Negro unions, such as the National Association of Afro-American Steam and Gas Engineers and Skilled Workers of Pittsburgh, but none of them was able to make any headway against the monopoly which the white labor unions had established in the various industries.

It was only natural that Negroes, observing the success of various individuals during the age of heroic business enterprise, should enter the fields of business and industry. Frustrated in their efforts to participate in the development of the businesses of the whites, they embarked on a program of "Negro business enterprise" in which they undertook to be their own producers and employers. Negro leaders, taking their cue from the almost hopeless plight of millions of Negroes in the South, urged their followers to escape poverty and achieve economic independence by entering business and manufacturing themselves. Speaking before the Fourth Atlanta University Conference in 1898, John Hope, a professor at the University, said that the Negro's plight was not due altogether to ignorance and incompetence, but at least in part to competition between the races for employment in new fields. He therefore called upon the Negro to escape the wage earning class and become his own employer. The Conference adopted resolutions declaring that "Negroes ought to enter into business life in increasing numbers" and that "The mass of Negroes must learn to patronize business enterprises conducted by their own race, even at some slight disadvantage. We must cooperate or we are lost." The Conference also called for the dissemination of information concerning the need for Negro businesses and the organization of local, state, and national Negro Business Men's Leagues.

By 1900 Booker T. Washington had concluded that Negro

business must be immediately stimulated. He called a group of
Negro businessmen together in Boston and organized the National Negro Business League. More than 400 delegates came
from 34 states and elected Washington as their first president.
Washington, believing that taxpaying Negroes of intelligence
and high character almost invariably were treated with respect
by the whites, urged that shiftless, idle, and useless Negroes be
transformed into valuable, law-abiding citizens. He also urged
that a larger number enter various business fields. In his *The
Negro in Business* he stated that he was gratified by the large
number of new business enterprises that sprang up during the
first year of the League's existence. Many local organizations
were formed, and by 1907 the national organization had 320
branches.

At the end of the century Negroes were engaged in innumerable types and sizes of businesses. They operated grocery stores,
general merchandise stores, and drug stores; they were restaurant keepers, caterers, confectioners, bakers, tailors, builders,
and contractors. Some operated shirt factories, cotton mills,
rubber goods shops, lumber mills, and carpet factories. There
were many cooperative businesses, such as the Bay Shore Hotel
Company of Hampton, Virginia; the Capital Trust Company of
Jacksonville, Florida; the South View Cemetery Association of
Atlanta, Georgia; and the Southern Stove Hollow-Ware and
Foundry Company of Chattanooga, Tennessee. The success of
some of the Negro business men, while failing to approach the
success of the whites during the same period, was significant.
One of the new, flourishing businesses was Madam C. J. Walker's establishment for making hair and skin preparations, the
first of a large number of such businesses to spring up in the
next fifty years. In 1898 there were two real estate agents in New
York City worth more than $150,000 each, and one in Cleve-
land had property valued at $100,000. A fish dealer in Concord,
North Carolina, was worth $25,000; while several builders,
contractors, and merchants were worth more than $10,000.
Large industries, the department stores, and the trusts were
making it daily more difficult for the small capitalist with slender resources, whether Negro or white; and it is not surprising
that each year witnessed the failure of many such enterprises.

In the field of banking Negroes made a special effort to
establish themselves firmly. In 1888 the Reverend W. W.
Browne organized in Richmond the first bank to be adminis-

tered solely by Negroes, the Savings Bank of the Grand Fountain United Order of True Reformers. Later in the same year the Capital Savings Bank of Washington was organized. In 1889 the Mutual Bank and Trust Company of Chattanooga was founded, followed by the establishment of the Alabama Penny Savings Bank of Birmingham. By 1914 approximately 55 Negro banks had been organized. Most of them were closely connected with fraternal insurance organizations or churches or both. Most of the banks were short-lived, however, for the reason that its Negro depositors and borrowers did not engage in trade, industry, and commerce in a sufficient volume to support them satisfactorily. Perhaps the real significance of the organization of these banks lies in the fact that they represent an effort on the part of Negroes to adopt the business ideals and social values of the rest of America and, thus, to assimilate themselves more completely.

Social and Cultural Growth

Socially and culturally it was more necessary for the Negro to maintain a separate existence than economically. Whites in the South and, to a considerable extent, in the North kept a discreet distance from the everyday lives of Negroes; and as the problems of migration and existence in a complex industrial society multiplied their difficulties, Negroes had to work out their own formulas for survival. An important agency for maintaining group cohesion and rendering self-help was the church. Although church membership was increasing, the organized religious bodies were going through a period that was as critical for blacks as for whites. The conservative element, devoting its attention to denouncing the sins of the young people and concerned largely with otherworldliness, was in control. Its leadership, however, was being effectively challenged by a rising progressive element, which refused to accept the crude notions of Biblical interpretation and the "grotesque vision of the hereafter" portrayed by the conservatives. Educated Negroes began to reject the church as the agency of salvation and turned their attention more and more to the problems at hand; they did not hesitate to register their impatience with their leaders. They demanded a change in management which would give them more influence in the church, and insisted upon changes in forms of worship that were more in keeping with their improved intellectual level. Frequently the progressives withdrew from Baptist and Methodist denominations and joined Congregational, Presbyterian, Episcopalian, and Catholic churches, some of which seemed to have a more flexible attitude toward the reforms upon which the progressives insisted.

Among Baptists there was not only the conflict between the progressives and conservatives, but also a struggle between whites and Negroes. In many localities whites undertook to control Negro Baptist associations and conventions, much to the distress of the Negro leaders. When Negroes were refused the privilege of participating in the management of the American Baptist Home Mission Society, the strife began. A serious breach developed when the American Baptist Publication Society, under pressure from Southern churchmen, refused to accept contributions of Negroes to Sunday school literature. In 1886 the Negroes organized the National Baptist Convention, in an attempt to reduce the influence of white national bodies among Negroes. Soon the National Baptist Publishing House, under R. H. Boyd, began to circulate Sunday school literature among Negroes. Some Negroes continued to use the materials of the white organization, while others used the materials issued by Boyd's house. The resulting strife and confusion lasted far into the twentieth century.

Despite the disagreement within the church, religious bodies continued, and even increased, their responsibility in ministering to the needs of their people. Even the conservatives yielded to the demands of more enlightened members that the church serve as an agency for the improvement of the social and moral conditions among Negroes. As before the Civil War, the church promoted education, largely by encouraging its members to become Bible readers. It also encouraged the formation of literary societies among its young people. The greatest evidence of its socialization, however, was its increasing functions as a welfare agency. Innumerable services were rendered to the community by the new institutional churches. Some worked in slums and jails, several established missions in the slums of both the North and South, while others established or supported homes for the aged and for orphans. In Atlanta, Dr. H. H. Proctor's Congregational church organized a day nursery, kindergarten, gymnasium, school of music, employment bureau, and Bible school. Dr. W. N. DeBerry of Springfield, Massachusetts, led his Congregational members in the establishment of a home for working girls in Amherst, a welfare league for women, handicraft clubs for boys and girls, an evening school of domestic training, and a free employment bureau. Churches in New York, Detroit, Chicago, St. Louis, and other cities engaged in similar activities. This progressive development served not only to contribute to the improvement of conditions in urban communities, but also to attract better trained young men to the ministry of the Negro churches.

Another manifestation of the Negro's struggles to become socially self-sufficient was the remarkable growth of fraternal orders and benefit associations. Masons and Odd Fellows maintained large Negro memberships; in addition, organizations like the Knights of Pythias and the Knights of Tabor competed for membership among Negro men. Other secret orders—the International Order of Good Samaritans, the Ancient Sons of Israel, the Grand United Order of True Reformers, and the Independent Order of St. Luke—offered insurance against sickness and death, aided widows and orphans of deceased members, and gave opportunities for social intercourse. Some were strong only in certain localities; others had memberships that extended over several states and owned the buildings which housed their main offices as well as other property which they rented to Negro businesses.

A variation of fraternal organizations, without the feature of secret rituals, was the beneficial and insurance societies which became numerous during the period. These organizations usually collected weekly dues ranging from 25 cents to 50 cents from their members. The Young Mutual Society of Augusta, Georgia, organized in 1886, and the Beneficial Association of Petersburg, Virginia, organized in 1893, are examples of local benefit societies. Larger in scope and membership was the Workers Mutual Aid Association of Virginia. By 1898, four years after its founding, it had a membership of more than 4,000. Although these societies imposed relatively exorbitant dues on their members, they served as important training grounds where Negroes could secure business experience, and they helped develop habits of self-help which seemed to be more imperative as the new century opened.

A logical outcome of the mutual benefit societies was the Negro insurance companies, which were more economic than social in their functions. In Washington, D.C., S. W. Rutherford severed his connections with the True Reformers and organized a society that finally became the National Benefit Life Insurance Company which remained the largest Negro organization of its kind for more than a generation. In Durham, North Carolina, John Merrick, who had been an extension worker of the True Reformers, was able to interest several influential citizens in organizing an insurance company. He, together with Dr. A. M. Moore, James E. Shepard, W. G. Pearson, and others in 1898 became charter members of the organization that later became known as the North Carolina Mutual Life Insurance Company. Its period of substantial growth dates from the following year when C. C. Spaulding was added to the board and the company was reorganized. In Atlanta, Georgia, A. F. Herndon secured control of the Atlanta Mutual Aid Association and reorganized it into the powerful Atlanta Life Insurance Company. These and similar businesses grew as some white companies became more and more reluctant to insure Negroes and as Negroes learned the values of purchasing various types of insurance.

While little surplus capital among Negroes could be channeled into philanthropic and charitable undertakings, a surprising amount of effort was devoted to helping the unfortunate and underprivileged. Orphanages, homes for the aged, hospitals, and sanitariums were established in many communities; some of them were maintained solely by Negroes. The Tennessee Orphanage and Industrial School at Nashville, the Carrie Steele Orphanage at Atlanta, Georgia, the Florence Crittenden Home of Atlanta for the rescue of fallen women, and the Pickford Tuberculosis Sanitarium of Southern Pines, North Carolina, for example, were supported exclusively or principally from funds raised among Negroes. Many organizations primarily for charitable purposes were founded. In 1895 the National Association of Colored Women was established. Living up to its motto, "Lifting As We Climb," the organization through its local clubs set up girls' homes, hospitals, and other social agencies. The Colored Women's League of Washington, organized in 1892, established a kindergarten and did considerable rescue work, while the Farmers' Improvement Society of Texas instituted in 1891 a program of benevolent activities that extended to 36 towns in the state. Both the Young Men's Christian Association and the Young Women's Christian Association were extending their activities to Negroes during the period.

While there were no conventions quite comparable to those of the period before the Civil War, the Negro problem was the subject of a number of conferences held toward the end of the century. It will be remembered that Booker T. Washington had two such projects in the annual Farmers' Conference that met at Tuskegee and the National Negro Business League. There was also the Lake Mohonk Conference on the Negro Question in 1890 at which prominent white citizens discussed the educational, religious, and economic problems affecting Negroes. No Negroes attended this conference. The Hampton Conference, conducted in part by Negroes, dealt with problems peculiar to the Negro, while the Capon Springs Conference undertook a similar task.

With the founding of the Afro-American League of the United States in 1890, Negro self-help efforts reached an important critical juncture. Under the leadership of T. Thomas Fortune more than a hundred Negroes from many parts of the country met in Chicago and pledged themselves to fight any and all forms of segregation and discrimination.

Another of these efforts was the Conferences on Negro Problems held annually at Atlanta University between 1896 and 1914 under the general direction of W. E. B. DuBois. Not only did Negroes come together to discuss their problems, but each year a study of some phase of Negro life was made. Guy B. Johnson regards these efforts as "the first real sociological research in the South," while DuBois has indicated that the 2,172 pages of the published reports formed a "current encyclopedia on the American Negro problems." Among the more valuable publications of the conference were *Some Efforts of Negroes for Social Betterment* (1898), *The Negro in Business* (1899), *The College-bred Negro* (1900), and *The Negro Common School* (1901). Several of the reports were enlarged and brought up to date at later conferences.

Thus in many ways the Negro was attempting to take his fate into his own hands and solve his problems as best he could. His techniques were those commonly known to Americans of all races. They were the use of agencies already in existence, such as the school and the church, and the establishment of new agencies such as mutual aid societies and business leagues. Small wonder that the editor of the Atlanta University publications could say in 1898:

> Compared with modern civilized groups the organization of action among American Negroes is extremely simple. . . . And

yet there are among them 23,000 churches, with unusually wide activities, and spending annually at least $10,000,000. There are thousands of secret societies with their insurance and social features, large numbers of beneficial societies . . . there is the slowly expanding seed of cooperative business efforts. . . . Finally there are the slowly evolving organs by which the group seeks to stop and minimize the anti-social deeds and accidents of its members. This is a picture of all human striving—unusually simple, . . . but strikingly human and worth further study and attention.

One result of the social and cultural strivings was the emergence of a substantial number of Negroes who gave numerous evidences of intellectual growth and of a satisfactory assimilation in American life. This growth was notably reflected in the literary activity of the period. In history and biography there was a tendency to portray heroic deeds and dramatic successes so generally characteristic of the writing of the time. In his *The Colored Cadet at West Point* (1889) Henry Ossian Flipper told of his experiences in becoming the first Negro to receive a commission from the United States Military Academy. In 1881 Frederick Douglass brought his colorful career up to date in *The Life and Times of Frederick Douglass,* which was enlarged in 1892. The outstanding piece of autobiographical writing was Booker T. Washington's *Up From Slavery* (1900), which has become one of the classics in American biography largely because of the prominence of the author. It is the type of success story that many Americans were telling. Other Negro leaders, such as Bishop Daniel A. Payne and John M. Langston, wrote their autobiographies during the period. Two of the better biographical studies were Sarah Bradford's *Harriet, the Moses of Her People* (1886), the life of Harriet Tubman, and Charles W. Chestnutt's *Frederick Douglass* (1899).

In 1872 William Still issued his *Underground Rail Road,* which, while hardly qualifying as a historical narrative, reflected the new interest of the Negro in his past. Numerous church histories, written principally by ministers and church officials, are more important as source materials than as authoritative studies. Joseph T. Wilson wrote several histories during the period, including *Emancipation; Its Course and Progress from 1481 B.C. to A.D. 1875* (1882) and *The Black Phalanx* (1888), a history of the Negro in the Civil War. Similar historians were John Wallace who wrote *Carpetbag Rule in Florida*

(1888) and E. A. Johnson, author of *A School History of the Negro Race in America* (1891). A much abler historian was George Washington Williams, a Pennsylvania Negro who had served as a soldier in the Civil War and had been educated in Massachusetts. In 1883 G. P. Putnam's Sons published in two volumes his *History of the Negro Race in America from 1619 to 1880*, the result of years of painstaking and laborious research. It was the first historical study by a Negro to be taken seriously by American scholars, and one newspaper hailed him as the "Negro Bancroft." Five years later Harper and Brothers brought out his *History of the Negro Troops in the Rebellion*. Booker T. Washington's *Story of the Negro* in two volumes (1909) made no improvement on the earlier work of Williams. In 1896 the first scientific historical monograph written by a Negro appeared. It was W. E. B. DuBois's *The Suppression of the African Slave Trade, 1638–1870*, which became the first work in the Harvard Historical Studies. It was a landmark in the intellectual growth of the American Negro and is still regarded favorably by serious students of history.

In economics, sociology, and political science, the writings of Negroes were generally neither as numerous nor as satisfactory as in the field of history. There were, of course, the Atlanta University studies written primarily by DuBois, to which reference has already been made. While serving as an assistant instructor at the University of Pennsylvania, DuBois gathered material on the Negro community of Philadelphia which appeared as *The Philadelphia Negro* in 1900. Booker T. Washington wrote numerous books in the fields of education, race relations, economics, and sociology. Some of the titles are *The Future of the American Negro* (1899), *The Education of the Negro* (1900), *Tuskegee and Its People* (1905), and *The Negro in Business* (1907). They were largely restatements of his position regarding the place of the Negro in American life. T. Thomas Fortune made several contributions to economics and political science, including *Black and White: Land, Labor and Politics in the South* (1884) and *The Negro in Politics* (1885). The former is in support of organized labor among Negroes, while the latter is a vigorous attack upon Frederick Douglass's assertion that for Negroes, "The Republican Party is the ship, all else is the ocean."

In the field of fiction some of the anti-slavery leaders were still writing short stories and sketches of life in the South. In

1880 William Wells Brown published his last book, *My Southern Home*. The writer who made the greatest impression during the period, however, was Charles W. Chesnutt, whose novels and short stories were widely read and generously praised. Between 1899 and 1905 four books written by him were favorably received because of their vivid portrayal of character and their quality as lively narratives. They were *The Conjure Woman, The House Behind the Cedars, The Marrow of Tradition*, and *The Colonel's Dream*. Of *The Conjure Woman* Vernon Loggins has said that such a sincere work of art was "positive evidence that Negro literature was coming of age."

While Paul Laurence Dunbar wrote several novels during his short life, including *The Uncalled* (1898) and *The Love of Landry* (1900), he is best known for his poems, which led William Dean Howells to describe him as the first American Negro "to feel the negro life aesthetically and express it lyrically." Few poets in America had been able to capture so completely the spirit of some aspect of American life and to distill it into such delightful verse. His *Oak and Ivy* (1893), *Majors and Minors* (1896), and *Lyrics of Lowly Life* (1896) have caused many critics to refer to him as the "poet laureate of the Negro race." His poems went through many editions, and before he died in 1906 he was one of America's famous men of letters. It was the enthusiastic acclaim of Dunbar that overshadowed the works of James Madison Bell, Albery A. Whitman, and Frances E. W. Harper, who ordinarily may have been regarded much more highly as poets of a race coming of age.

While Negro editors did not have the same battles to fight as Frederick Douglass and Samuel Cornish had, they were no less preoccupied with the problem of fighting for the greater integration of Negro citizens in American life. Magazines like *The Southern Workman*, published at Hampton after 1872, and the *AME Review*, which was begun in 1884, were concerned primarily with educational, literary, and religious matters; but the newspapers were fighting economic and political battles. In 1900 there were three Negro daily newspapers—at Norfolk, Virginia, Kansas City, Kansas, and Washington, D.C.—all of which were short-lived. At the same time there were approximately 150 weekly newspapers which were widely read among Negroes. Georgia and Texas had no less than 23 each, while North Carolina had 10. The others were scattered in 26 states. Some were widely read and provoked considerable discussion.

In Boston, in 1901, for example, George Forbes and Monroe Trotter began the publication of the *Guardian*, which fought the program of Booker T. Washington and demanded full and immediate equality for the Negro. The majority of the newspapers were uncompromising, and their titles suggest the temperament and spirit of the editors. Among them were the *San Antonio X-Ray*, the *Austin Searchlight*, the *Baltimore Crusader*, the *Columbus New Light*, and the *Albany Iconoclast*.

The end of the century found the Negro in a stronger position in that he had educational institutions in which to develop and social agencies by which he could improve his status. The help which he received from philanthropists did much to make his lot easier, but his experiences in the economic and social world of the whites convinced him more and more that the brunt of the burden of his development would have to be borne by him. He assumed this responsibility without hesitation, and in typically American fashion he sought a larger share of the blessings of liberty. But as he developed his own institutions and, to a considerable extent, his own cultural life, it became clearer that the American melting pot, so far as Negroes were concerned, was not boiling; it was hardly simmering.

XXII •

The Negro
and American Imperialism

The Extension of American Influence

● *One of the most far-reaching consequences of post-Civil War* reconstruction and the economic revolution which accompanied it was the recurrence of a strong American nationalism, which had temporarily given way to the sectional strife. Once again the American people looked upon themselves as the guardians of civilization in the New World and, consequently, desired to extend the blessings which they enjoyed to other peoples in the Americas. Once more a united people, the citizens of the United States felt compelled to wield the kind of influence in the New World that had characterized their policy from the time of the enunciation of the Monroe Doctrine in 1823. A bigger and better navy was viewed as necessary in order to protect the New World against the encroachments of the Old, and missionaries extended their activities to the islands of the Caribbean, to Latin America, and even to the Pacific world. This was more than nationalism. It was the manifestation of a national egoism that found its natural expression in the effort to fashion the New World in the image of the United States.

Such a point of view had its logical culmination in the disintegration of national isolation and the pursuance of an imperialism similar to that which was characteristic of a large number of European countries. It was with considerable interest that the United States observed the increased imperialistic activities of

France and England and of the newcomers in the field, Belgium, Italy, and Germany. David Livingstone, Cecil Rhodes, and Henry M. Stanley did much to dramatize the importance of Africa to an industrialized world, while Leopold of Belgium, Wilhelm of Germany, and Victoria of England became the political instrumentalities in whose names the Dark Continent was divided. In the winter of 1884–85 an international conference was held at Berlin to discuss the question of Africa. The great basin of the Congo was given to Leopold II of Belgium, and the conference paved the way for the acquisition of East Africa, Southwest Africa, Togoland, and Kamerun by Germany, a vast expanse of land from the Cape to Cairo by England, and a considerable portion of West Africa by France. By the end of the century Africa was effectively divided among the great powers of Europe, and they were looking for more fields to conquer. As Americans watched developments in Africa and in other parts of the world, they began to regard the activities of Europeans suspiciously and viewed some of these movements as inimical to their own interests.

The United States had not been wholly inactive in the field of imperialism during the post-Civil War period. As industrial production increased, American manufacturers began their search for new markets as well as for new sources of raw materials. The great industrialists, their pockets bulging with surplus capital, began to search for areas in which to invest their profits. Consequently, exports increased enormously; and foreign investments skyrocketed. As immigrants continued to come into the United States in larger numbers the land in the West was rapidly filled up, and as at other periods in its history, the United States felt the need for *Lebensraum*. A newly confident America was turning her eyes outward. Sectional strife was over, the economic revolution had surmounted its greatest obstacles, and the people were tired of the relatively unexciting question of the perfection of a national economy. The United States was ready to assume a role in world affairs. It was hoped that it would be a role commensurate with her bursting power and her boundless resources.

In some respects the territorial growth of the United States from the acquisition of Louisiana in 1803 may be regarded as an imperialistic development, but the lands west of the Alleghenies were contiguous to the United States and were populated by persons similar in cultural heritage to the majority of the early American settlers. Long before the end of the nineteenth century, however, the United States had become initiated into the fraternity of imperialistic powers by the purchase of Alaska from Russia in 1867. Although at first some serious opposition was raised to the acquisition of Russia's "iceberg," the objections soon melted before the intense fire of a new manifest destiny that was burning by the end of the reconstruction period.

Already the Hawaiian Islands were attracting the attention of many American traders. As more of them visited the islands they saw their value as the site for a naval base, a coaling station, and a cable landing. In 1875 sugar and other Hawaiian products were given free entry into the United States. In 1884 the United States leased Pearl Harbor on the island of Oahu as a naval station. With this added military protection American investors poured capital into the islands, so that by 1890 the American plantations there were worth more than 25 million dollars. Despite the fact that the Hawaiian people had racial and cultural heritages vastly different from those of any American groups, the sentiment for the annexation of the islands to the United States grew steadily. In 1893 the royal government of Hawaii was overthrown by a revolt inspired and carried out largely by American residents of the islands. The revolutionary government immediately negotiated a treaty of annexation which, unfortunately for the imperialists, had not been ratified by the Senate when President Harrison's term expired. Cleveland, in office for his second time, was such an ardent foe of imperialism that he withdrew the treaty from the Senate. It was only a temporary delay, however, for during the McKinley administration, in 1898, the Congress annexed the islands by joint resolution.

Another early object of American covetousness was the Samoan Islands. In 1872 an American naval officer secured permission from the natives to establish a coaling station at Pago Pago, much to the surprise and indignation of several European powers. In 1878 the arrangement was confirmed by treaty, and Germany and England made it clear that they desired the same privileges. After a decade of rivalry, Great Britain, the United States, and Germany agreed to divide the islands. The United States got the favored island of Tutuila, Germany took the remainder, and Great Britain was compensated with other Pacific islands that had been acquired by Germany. Meanwhile, the United States was acquiring jurisdiction over many other small islands in the Pacific, including Wake, Midway, Palmyra, and Howland. Before the end of the century, therefore, the United States had acquired an empire composed primarily of darker peoples—Polynesian, Japanese, Chinese, and others. In so doing, the leading power in the Western hemisphere was conforming to the prevailing pattern of imperialism that had swept the world: the injection of the spirit of industrialism into a program to dominate the backward areas of the world. Invariably, these backward peoples were dark; and frequently, they were Negroid. The United States was well on her way to the development of an empire of darker peoples.

It was in the Americas, of course, that the United States pursued its new imperialistic policy most vigorously. In this area the policy was most strongly based, thanks to the Monroe Doctrine; and while this cornerstone of American foreign policy had usually been employed to prevent European influence from taking hold in the New World, it was now used to advance the interests of the United States in the area south of the border. To be sure, the United States was still firm in her determination to keep Europe out of Latin America, as is seen in President Cleveland's insistence on arbitrating the boundary dispute between Venezuela and British Guiana in 1895; but the United States had also undertaken to settle disputes between Latin American nations. In 1876 the boundary dispute between Argentina and Paraguay was settled largely through the arbitration of the United States. In 1889 the first Pan-American Congress was organized by James G. Blaine, Harrison's secretary of State; this agency was dedicated to bringing the countries of the Americas closer together under the leadership of the United States. In numerous ways during the period the United States, through its increasing financial and political influence, not only led but dominated the New World, thereby bringing under its imperialistic influence millions of persons of Negro or mixed blood.

By the end of the Civil War Spain could claim only two islands, Cuba and Puerto Rico, of a vast New World empire that had once extended from the upper Mississippi River to Cape Horn. Her steady decline as a major imperial power had not left her chastened or any the wiser in her dealings with dependent peoples. In her two islands she pursued a policy that was no more enlightened than that which she had followed in the seventeenth century. She had remained unaffected by the new trends in imperialism; and England's gestures of conceding self-government, even to some of the more backward areas, apparently did not impress her at all. Repression and rigid control of every aspect of life in Cuba had inspired numerous revolts against Spain, and they were becoming more frequent and more intense by the middle of the nineteenth century. Between 1868 and 1878 there was a full-dress uprising of the Cubans against the mother country, with innumerable incidents of atrocity and brutality on both sides. The willingness of the United States to permit filibustering expeditions against the Spanish in Cuba to operate out of American ports indicated the growing disgust of the people of this country for the Spanish policy in the New World.

Toward the end of the century Cubans became more determined to have their independence. This determination happily coincided with the increasing interest of citizens of the United States which stemmed from their material investments in the island. By 1890 Americans had invested more than 50 million dollars in plantations and sugar refineries. When, therefore, the Cubans revolted once again in 1895 the United States became alarmed over the damage that was done to American fields and factories in the island. Their material interest was broadened into an humanitarian interest in the following year when Spain sent General Valeriano Weyler to put down the insurrection. With more determination than wisdom, Weyler ordered much of the rural population to be placed in concentration camps, since it was extremely difficult to separate the loyalists from the insurgents. The starvation and disease that followed took such a toll of Cuban lives that the American press dubbed the Spanish leader "Butcher" Weyler. In the province of Havana alone, for example, more than 50,000 persons died.

It was inconceivable to Americans that such brutality could exist so close to the center of freedom in the Western world. An outraged America, for the moment, forgot the heated presidential campaign, as well as the campaign to disfranchise Negroes in the South, in order to pour out its wrath against the inhumanity of Spain in Cuba. The so-called "yellow journals" fanned the flames of indignation in America to the point that the Congress recognized the belligerency of the Cubans, and only the firmness of Cleveland prevented the country from going further. With some encouragement from the United States the Cubans were

418 · FROM SLAVERY TO FREEDOM

more determined than ever to have their independence. Under the leadership of the mulatto general, Antonio Maceo and of Quintin Bandera, known as "The Black Thunderbolt," the insurgents carried on a campaign of systematic devastation that won greater support for them among the Americans. In January, 1898, the American battleship *Maine* was ordered to Havana to protect American life and property and to impress the Spaniards that the government of the United States was willing to take energetic action. No one gave credence to the expressed official statement that the visit of the battleship was merely a gesture of friendly courtesy. On February 15, 1898, an explosion of undetermined origin sank the *Maine* in the Havana harbor with a loss of more than 250 officers and men. The incident set off a train of events that culminated in war between the United States and Spain two months later. It was America's first international conflict in more than fifty years; and it was more than anything else a clear-cut demonstration of America's growing interest in affairs outside her own territorial limits.

Negroes in the Spanish-American War

From the beginning Negro Americans were involved in the war against Spain. Indeed, there were at least thirty on the *Maine* when it was blown up. Twenty-two were killed, four were injured, and four others escaped injury. The Negroes of the United States had already been inspired by the soldiery of Maceo and Bandera and regarded "Weylerism as the synonym of barbarous warfare." With the loss of life for twenty-two Negroes as well as the general indignation which they shared with the entire country, American Negroes were anxious to vindicate the honor of the United States and help bring independence and freedom to Cubans, whom they regarded as Negroes and mulattoes. When, therefore, the President called for 200,000 volunteers to supplement the inadequate regular army, Negroes were as enthusiastic about enlisting as any group in America.

Among the regular army that numbered only 28,000 troops in 1898, there were four Negro outfits, all of which had been used in actions against the Indians in the West. The Ninth Cavalry was in the Department of the Platte and the Tenth Cavalry was stationed at Assiniboine, Montana. The Twenty-fourth Infantry was at Fort Douglas, near Salt Lake City, Utah, and the Twenty-fifth Infantry was at Missoula, Montana. These organizations had been activitated shortly after the close of the Civil War and had performed numerous duties in the Indian wars and in border service. The Ninth Cavalry, for example, had served at Fort Lancaster, Texas, at Santa Fe, New Mexico, at Fort Riley, Kansas, and at Fort McKinney, Wyoming. When they, along with other Negro and white regulars, were called to service in the Spanish-American War they were ill-prepared both in equipment and training for action in a tropical theater.

Under the conditions of the first call for volunteers only the organized militia of the states was acceptable. This left the Negroes out almost altogether, for very few Negroes were in the Northern militias, while the Southern states barred them altogether. The Negroes of the North and West made frantic efforts "to beat through the stone wall and get into the war anyway." In many of the Northern communities volunteer regiments of Negroes were raised and their services were offered to the states; but under the law governing the National Guard such contingents could not be accepted. Some Negroes appealed to the President for permission to enter the service, but they were courteously referred to the War Department, where nothing was done. Under the pressure of necessity and of Negro leaders the Congress authorized the activation of ten regiments of Negro soldiers, but the War Department insisted that the staff and line officers above the rank of second lieutenant be white men. Only four regiments were recruited under this act, the Seventh, Eighth, Ninth, and Tenth United States Volunteers, and none saw active service except for a small amount of garrison duty in Cuba at the end of the war.

Besides the four Negro outfits in the regular army and the four outfits recruited under the special act of the Congress, numerous other Negro groups served in the war against Spain. Several states permitted Negroes to organize outfits and enter the service. There were the Third Alabama Infantry of Volunteers; the Third North Carolina Infantry, called out by Governor Russell; the Sixth Virginia Infantry; the Ninth Ohio Infantry; the Twenty-third Kansas Infantry; the Eighth Illinois Infantry; two companies of the Indiana Infantry; and several smaller groups. Company "L" of the Sixth Massachusetts Infantry was the only Negro company that was mustered in as an integral part of a white regiment. It had Negro officers and, having been created during the War for Independence as the "Bucks of

America," boasted that it was the oldest Negro military organization in America.

The question of Negro officers plagued the military leaders from the beginning. The majority of the white soldiers in the regular army regarded the Negro as unfit for leadership, and pointed to the fact that although there were four Negro outfits in the regular army there was only one Negro commissioned officer, West Pointer Charles Young. The President finally commissioned about 100 Negro second lieutenants in the volunteer service, while the majority of the Negro military organizations in the service of the states were officered by Negro men. The Third North Carolina Infantry had all Negro officers. The commanding officer was Colonel James H. Young, a prominent leader in the state; his immediate aides were Lieutenant Colonel C. S. Taylor and Major Andrew Walker. The Eighth Illinois was commanded by Colonel John R. Marshall; Charles Young was made a Brevet Major and placed in command of the Ninth Ohio. The Massachusetts Company had Negro officers, the ranking one of which was Captain William J. Williams. The Sixth Virginia was staffed with white officers, but some changes were made when several Negro soldiers resigned because they had enlisted with the understanding that they were to have Negro officers.

Six noncommissioned officers were commissioned as second lieutenants in the field, because they had "rendered particularly gallant and meritorious services in the face of enemy action—" Sergeants William Washington and John C. Proctor of the Ninth Cavalry and Sergeants William McBryar, Wyatt Hoffman, Macon Russell, and Andrew J. Smith of the Twenty-fifth Infantry. Among the other special commissions issued were those to two paymasters with the rank of major. Recipients were John R. Lynch, former Representative from Mississippi and former Fourth Auditor of the Treasury, and Richard R. Wright, President of the Agricultural and Mechanical College of Georgia. Two Negro ministers were commissioned as chaplains, the Reverend C. T. Walker of Georgia and the Reverend Richard Carroll of South Carolina. Dr. Arthur M. Brown was appointed Assistant Surgeon with the Tenth Cavalry, and from August 2 to October 8, 1898, he was the commanding officer of his outfit.

In the swift and decisive action that brought victory to the United States only the Negroes in the four regular outfits saw any considerable service. In June, 1898, these groups sailed out of various Southern ports for Cuba. The Twenty-fifth Infantry, for example, sailed on June 7 from Tampa, Florida, on a government transport. During the week that the men were delayed at Tampa they were not allowed to go ashore unless an officer carried an entire company ashore to bathe and exercise. Upon embarkation, the Twenty-fifth was assigned to the bottom deck where there was no light, except that which came through the small port holes and very little air. Whites and Negroes were not permitted to mingle with each other on board ship. When they disembarked at Daiquiri in Guantanamo Bay on June 22, the campaign for the reduction of the Spanish forces in Cuba began. The American forces were divided into three units: one moved directly on San Juan Hill, the stronghold of the Spanish forces; another took Siboney and then moved on El Caney; and a third took Las Guasimas on the road to San Juan and then moved up the Hill.

The Negro contingents saw action with the forces principally at El Caney, Las Guasimas, and San Juan Hill. On June 24 two battalions of the First Volunteer Cavalry (Theodore Roosevelt's Rough Riders) moved up the Santiago Road toward Las Guasimas, where they met the enemy. At a crucial moment in the fighting, several Negroes of the Ninth and Tenth Cavalries came up, knocked down the Spanish improvised fort, cut the barbed wire, and made an opening for the Rough Riders, who then routed the Spaniards. One Negro corporal who manned a Hotchkiss gun during the action was killed at his post. At El Caney, on June 30, the Twenty-fifth was ordered up to reinforce the Rough Riders. In this decisive action many of the Negro troops were under fire for the better part of the day, with strict orders not to return the enemy fire. In the three days of fighting most of the Negro regulars in Cuba saw action and won the praises of practically all of their officers.

It has been claimed by many that the Ninth and Tenth Cavalries saved the Rough Riders from complete annihilation at Las Guasimas. One Southern white officer said, "If it had not been for the Negro cavalry the Rough Riders would have been exterminated. I am not a Negro lover. My father fought with Mosby's Rangers, and I was born in the South, but the Negroes saved that fight, and the day will come when General Shafter will give them credit for their bravery." Another said, "I am a Southerner by birth, and I never thought much of the colored man. But, somehow, now I feel very differently toward them.

. . . I never saw such fighting as those Tenth Cavalry men did. They didn't seem to know what fear was, and their battle hymn was 'There'll be a hot time in the old town tonight.'" Even among those who did not claim that the Negroes saved the Rough Riders, the praise was generous. Lieutenant Thomas Roberts said, "I have naught but the highest praise for the swarthy warriors on the field of carnage. Led by brave men, they will go into the thickest of the fight, even to the wicked mouths of deadly cannon, unflinchingly." The *New York Mail and Express* said:

> All honor to the black troopers of the gallant Tenth: No more striking example of bravery and coolness has been shown since the destruction of the *Maine* than by the colored veterans of the Tenth Cavalry during the attack upon Caney on Saturday. By the side of the Rough Riders they followed their leader up the terrible hill from whose crest the desperate Spaniards poured down a deadly fire of shell and musketry. They never faltered. . . . Firing as they marched, their aim was splendid, their coolness was superb, and their courage aroused the admiration of their comrades. Their advance was greeted by loud cheers from the white regiments, and with an answering shout they pressed onward over the trenches they had taken, close in the pursuit of the retreating enemy. The war has not shown greater heroism.

The reaction of Theodore Roosevelt to the performance of Negro troops was varied, depending upon the occasion. When he made his farewell address to the rather incongruous group of Indians, ranchers, cowboys, college athletes, and Negroes that served under him, Roosevelt had words of unqualified praise for the Negro soldiers. "The Spaniards called them 'Smoked Yankees,'" he said, "but we found them to be an excellent breed of Yankees. I am sure that I speak the sentiments of officers and men in the assemblage when I say that between you and the other cavalry regiments there exists a tie which we trust will never be broken." When campaigning for the office of governor of New York in October, 1898, Roosevelt said, "As I heard one of the Rough Riders say after the charge at San Juan: 'Well, the Ninth and Tenth men are all right. They can drink out of our canteens.'" Roosevelt expressed the highest praise for the Negroes who charged up San Juan with his Rough Riders and concluded, "I don't think that any Rough Rider will ever forget the tie that binds us to the Ninth and Tenth Cavalry." Writing in *Scribner's Magazine* in April of the following year, Roosevelt said that the Negroes behaved well, but "They are, of course, peculiarly dependent on their white officers. . . . None of the white regulars of Rough Riders showed the slightest sign of weakening; but under the strain the colored infantrymen . . . began to get a little uneasy and to drift to the rear. . . ." Roosevelt said that he could not allow this and drew his revolver in order to halt the retreating Negroes. He said that he would shoot any man who went to the rear under any pretense whatever.

The explanation for this retreat was not given by Roosevelt, but was supplied by Sergeant Preston Holliday of the Tenth Cavalry writing in the *New York Age*, May 11, 1899. Sergeant Holliday said that the Negroes who were going to the rear had been ordered to do so by Lieutenant Fleming to bring up rations and entrenching tools and to carry the wounded men to safer places. Lieutenant Fleming at the time made the explanation to Colonel Roosevelt, and some of the Rough Riders told Roosevelt that he would not have to shoot the Negroes. The reply of the Negro men was, "We will stay with you, Colonel." On the following day, Roosevelt admitted that he had misunderstood the actions of the Negro soldiers and expressed regret at having spoken harshly to them. Negro soldiers and civilians were, therefore, keenly hurt when Roosevelt wrote unfavorably of Negro soldiers within less than a year after the fighting had ceased. They could be consoled, however, by the remarks of Major General Nelson A. Miles, the ranking officer of the United States Army, who said at a peace jubilee in October, 1898: "The white race was accompanied by the gallantry of the black as they swept over intrenched lines and later volunteered to succor the sick, nurse the dying and bury the dead in the hospitals and the Cuban camps." Major General Miles probably had in mind the manner in which almost 100 men of the Twenty-fourth Infantry answered the call for volunteer nurses when the yellow fever epidemic broke out.

The service which Negroes rendered in the Navy was relatively inconsequential because they were employed primarily in menial capacities. There are instances, however, of gallantry and heroism above and beyond the call of duty. There is the case, for example, of Elijah B. Tunnell, who was employed as a cabin cook on a torpedo boat, the *Winslow*. On May 11, 1898, the boat was under severe fire from Spanish batteries on shore in the harbor of Cardenas. Tunnell left his regular work and went on deck to assist in arranging for the *Winslow* to be towed away. A shell burst on the deck, which instantly killed him and three others. Doubtless during the course of the war there were numerous other displays of courage.

Negro soldiers served as occupation troops at the close of the war. Some Negro troops, including the Third North Carolina, served in the Pacific. The Twenty-third Kansas Infantry did garrison duty in Cuba and the Eighth Illinois, which did not arrive in Cuba until August, 1898, did garrison duty in the province of Santiago. When an editorial appeared in the *Washington Post* discrediting Negro troops with Negro officers, Major Charles Douglass, writing in the *Colored American* on August 17, 1898, pointed out that the Eighth Illinois had been selected to replace a disorderly white regiment. He said, in conclusion, "The generals at the front know the value of Negro troops, whether the quill-drivers in the rear do or not." During this tour of duty Colonel Marshall served, for a while, as governor of San Luis, while Major R. R. Jackson acted as mayor of El Paso, Cuba.

Citizens of the United States did not view with complete favor the arming of Negroes to fight in the war and to serve as troops of occupation. As troops passed through the South en route to ports of embarkation, they were frequently treated with contempt by Southerners who were preoccupied with the task of reducing the status of the Negro. At the end of the war, when the Third North Carolina Volunteers were moved from Macon, Georgia, the *Atlanta Journal* carried an editorial entitled, "A Happy Riddance." Among other things, the editor said that the army and the country were to be congratulated on mustering out the North Carolina Negroes, for "a tougher and more turbulent set of Negroes were probably never gotten together before. . . . While stationed in Macon several of its members were killed either by their own comrades in drunken brawls or by citizens in self-defense." He added that while passing through Atlanta these Negro soldiers tried to make trouble, but those who attempted to do so were "promptly clubbed into submission." Dr. Charles F. Meserve, the white president of Shaw University, visited the North Carolinians at their camp and had nothing but praise for them. He described Colonel James H. Young as possessing in "a marked degree a quality of leadership as important as it is rare" and said that the men were well-disciplined on and off the post. It seems that the attitude toward Negro soldiers depended, in a large measure, on the quarters from which the sentiments came.

America's Negro Empire

At the end of the Spanish-American War the United States could regard itself as one of the great powers of the world. The victory over imperialistic Spain was so quick and decisive that it was only natural for many to expect that the United States would supplant Spain as a leading imperial power. The Treaty of Paris by which peace was established between the two powers left little doubt as to the direction in which the United States was moving. The treaty provided that Spain was to relinquish all claim to sovereignty over Cuba. In lieu of a war indemnity Spain ceded to the United States the island of Puerto Rico and the other Spanish insular possessions in the West Indies. Upon the payment of twenty million dollars by the United States Spain was to relinquish the Philippines to the victor. Although it was not immediately clear just what disposition the United States would make of Cuba, it was quite evident that the island would remain under the political and economic domination of the United States for an indefinite period of time. Puerto Rico was, from the outset, to become a part of America's growing empire, one that was constituted almost wholly of backward peoples. The Philippines gave to the United States the foothold that it desired in the Orient. In the same year Germany gained control of the Shantung Peninsula, England secured Wei-hai-wei, France obtained Kwanchow Bay, and Port Arthur came under the control of Russia. If the United States were to wield any influence in the Orient, it needed a satisfactory base. The Philippines answered that need.

As the pattern of American imperialism became clearer at the end of the century one could discern certain unmistakable similarities between it and that which European countries were practicing at the same time. Whether it was American or European imperialism, the areas brought under control abounded in resources which would supply the needs of highly industrialized economic systems and in human beings that were potential consumers of commodities provided by the advanced countries. The areas were uniformly populated by so-called backward peoples, and in most cases they were darker peoples. In Africa they were, of course, black peoples. In the Orient they were yellow. In the American empire they were black, white, and yellow, or a mixture of them. In Cuba there were more than 600,000 Negroes and persons having Negro blood. In Puerto Rico there were more than 300,000 such persons. Even in Hawaii and the Philippines there were some Negroes, with the majority of the population in both cases composed primarily of darker peoples. When the United States acquired the Canal Zone in 1903 many Negroes lived in the vicinity, and many more were brought in from the Caribbean islands to work on the Panama Canal.

One of the most salient features of the American imperial problem is that the United States, unlike the other imperial powers, has a color problem at home and therefore must pursue a policy with regard to race that will not upset the racial equilibrium in the United States. For example, it must always be remembered that in dealing with matters concerning Puerto Rico, approximately one-third of the population is distinctly Negroid and that many so-called "white" Puerto Ricans have sufficient Negro blood in their veins to qualify them as Negroes in the United States. In 1900, when the first organic act of Puerto Rico was passed by the Congress of the United States, the Southern members of that body—and some Northern members, too—were concerned not only with the fact that the Puerto Ricans should be carefully supervised in the operation of their government but also that the Negroes of the island would not enjoy such political liberties as to inspire the Negroes of the United States to fight for greater political opportunities. The governor and all of the important officials were to be appointed by the President of the United States; and Americans were to outnumber Puerto Ricans on the important Executive Council. The second organic act of 1917 remodeled the local government to resemble one of the states of the United States. Two legislative houses were established, members of which were to be elected by universal male suffrage; and all Puerto Ricans were to enjoy American citizenship. The power of appointing all the major officials of the island, however, was reserved for the President of the United States.

The major efforts of the United States in Puerto Rico have been directed toward the improvement of health, education, and public works and toward the Americanization of Puerto Ricans. In all these areas there have been notable advancements, but the low economic level of the people, stemming largely from the concentration of the wealth in the hands of a few, has prevented greater improvement and has caused hundreds of thousands to migrate to the mainland. Since the American investors in the island have reaped considerable profits, especially in the cultivation of sugar, there is an inclination on the part of the cursory observer to view the period of American control as highly successful. The high mortality rate, the abject poverty of the masses of the people, and the cultural and social debility present on the island seem to indicate the need for a new imperial outlook that will foster a greater improvement for the people of the island. The effort of Puerto Ricans to break up the large plantations in order to redistribute the land and the unfavorable reaction of American investors suggest that any improvement that may come from such an arrangement will be slow indeed. If Puerto Rico is ever to become a state, it will, in all probability, have to enjoy a greater measure of prosperity than it has at present. Assurances that the Negroes of the island will not wield too much political influence will have to be made to some Americans who will have the opportunity to pass on its statehood.

A significant expansion of America's Negro empire came with the purchase of the Danish West Indies in 1917. All during the nineteenth century the United States manifested some interest in the islands. In 1867 the Secretary of State, William Seward, visited the islands and later negotiated a treaty for the purchase of St. Thomas and St. John Islands for $7,500,000. Although Denmark ratified the treaty, it failed to pass the Senate of the United States. During the Spanish-American War interest in the islands grew and the desire to purchase them was revived. In 1902 a treaty for their purchase was negotiated, but this time the Danish parliament rejected the proposition. The people of the islands were greatly disappointed, for as early as 1867 a majority of them had registered their desire to be annexed to the United States. Upon the outbreak of World War I the United States feared that Germany would seize the islands and use them as bases in the Caribbean. Thus, in June, 1915, the Secretary of State authorized the American Minister to Denmark to begin negotiations for the islands.

Denmark was willing to sell the islands, but the Danish Foreign Minister made it clear that financial arrangements should not be proposed that would lead to haggling or fail to give guarantees of the kind treatment of the inhabitants, the vast majority of which consisted of Negroes. The American minister replied that the people of the United States were "so well acquainted with the true character of the negroes that they could make them more content than the Europeans." In August, 1916, the treaty for the purchase of the islands for $25,000,000 was negotiated, and in January of the following year the ratifications of the two countries were exchanged. The Marines landed shortly after the purchase, and a military government was established which lasted down to 1931, when President Hoover signed an order creating a civil government for the Virgin Islands.

Although the islands were acquired largely because of their military and strategic value in the Caribbean, the United States felt some responsibility for the improvement of conditions there. With whites comprising less than 10 per cent of the small population of approximately 25,000, the problem of the islands has been viewed by the United States as essentially a Negro problem. In 1924, because of unrest in the islands, President Coolidge appointed a federal commission of five Negroes of the United States to investigate conditions. In its report the commission criticized particularly the tax laws and the judicial system. It recommended the passage of a new organic act "so as to authorize the adoption of a new code of laws based upon American ideals and calculated to insure an administration and enforcement of the laws in keeping with American practices." This recommendation began a series of proposals and discussions that has not ended yet. Only in more recent years have Americans been willing to concede that although the Virgin Islands may not soon qualify for statehood, its government should be one in which 90 per cent of the population should have an important part. In 1937 President Roosevelt appointed William Hastie, a distinguished American Negro attorney, as the federal judge of the islands. In 1946 President Truman appointed Mr. Hastie governor of the islands. The inhabitants regarded these appointments as an indication of a new and enlightened interest on the part of the government and the people of the United States. They have high hopes that in the near future there will be a noticeable improvement in their economic and social conditions.

America's Negro empire has been substantially enlarged through the manner in which the United States has wielded influence over independent nations whose population is predominantly Negro. In Santo Domingo, for example, the control which the United States has exercised in the present century has been so extensive as to constitute almost complete domination. After its separation from Haiti in 1884, this country, composed largely of Negroes and mulattoes, demonstrated a remarkable similarity to other Latin American nations in its inability to establish stable political and economic conditions. It, therefore, became vulnerable to United States "Dollar Diplomacy" which has brought one Latin American nation after another within its sphere of influence. In 1907 by a convention concluded between the United States and Santo Domingo it was agreed that an American citizen would be named the General Receiver of Customs with authority to deposit $100,000 each month toward the interest and sinking fund that was held in trust for all national creditors. It may be presumed, also, that the Receiver would exercise considerable authority over other phases of the country's economic life. In May, 1916, the United States landed Marines in Santo Domingo to preserve order, and within a few months civil government had disappeared altogether. Despite the vigorous protests of the Dominican minister at Washington, the Marines were kept in the island republic until 1924. By that time peace and order had been restored, and the commercial relationship between the United States and the Negro republic had become so intimate as to guarantee the domination of its economic life for an indefinite period.

Haiti's experience with the United States has been similar to that of the Dominican Republic. Within a year after the beginning of World War I the United States and Haiti negotiated and ratified a treaty which permitted the United States to have control over Haiti's finances and police for a period of ten years. This gave the United States a satisfactory pretext to dominate every phase of life in the second oldest republic in the New World. In 1917 the United States placed the country under complete military rule and forced the extension of the treaty of 1915 for another ten years. The nature of the intervention is clearly demonstrated by a telegram which an American sent to the Secretary of the Navy: "Next Thursday . . . unless otherwise directed, I will permit Congress to elect a president." Almost from the beginning the Haitians resented American occupation of their country, and it was necessary for the Marines to shoot more than 2,000 inhabitants in order to restore peace and order.

The widespread sympathy which Haitians elicited is clearly demonstrated by the fact that in 1922 a group of distinguished Americans including Felix Frankfurter, Zechariah Chafee, Jr., and Moorfield Storey, issued a booklet entitled, "The Seizure of Haiti by the United States, A Report of the Military Occupation of the Republic of Haiti and the History of the Treaty Forced upon Her." In this document the authors declared that the United States should immediately abrogate the treaty of 1915, "unconditionally and without qualifications" and that a new treaty should be negotiated that would be mutually satisfactory to both countries and "by methods that obtain between free and independent sovereign states." In 1924 Dantes Bellegarde, the Haitian delegate to the League of Nations, brought the matter to the attention of the League. Although the League refused to place the matter on its agenda for discussion it was a victory for Haiti that M. Bellegarde was permitted to place the question before the League at all. The agitation continued, and in 1934, after nineteen years of occupation, the American troops evacuated Haiti. Haiti had already become, for all practical purposes, a part of America's Negro empire.

From the outset Liberia was, of course, regarded by realists as a protectorate of the United States. Early in the twentieth century, however, a closer economic relationship between the two countries began to develop. In 1909, at the request of Liberia, the United States government sent three commissioners to Liberia to report on boundary disputes between that country and Great Britain and France, and to study conditions there, with a view to making recommendations. In the following year the United States expressed a willingness to help Liberia by taking charge of her finances, her military organization, and any boundary questions that might arise. During World War I American interest in Liberia increased. In 1921 the United States arranged a loan of $5,000,000 to Liberia, but the Congress would not approve the transaction. In 1927 the Liberian government entered into contract with the Firestone Rubber Company of Akron, Ohio, for a loan of $5,000,000 on the condition that Liberia would give to the company 2,000 acres of land for experimental purposes, that the company would be given the opportunity to lease-up to one million acres of rubber land, and that the company would construct a harbor at Monrovia out of its own funds and with its own engineers. These expenditures were later to be paid by the Liberian government.

With the government of the United States committed to a policy of protection and with a powerful American industrial organization actively participating in the economic life of the country, the United States could well boast that, like the powers of Europe, it had substantial interests in the dark continent.

American Negroes themselves played an important part in extending the Negro empire of the United States. From the end of Reconstruction down to the beginning of World War I American ministers to Haiti were largely Negroes, and they manifested a keen interest in the extension of American influence. John M. Langston, for example, went to Haiti as the official representative of the government of the United States in 1877 and interested himself in the political and economic conditions of the island. He was quite disturbed over the unsettled political scene and made many suggestions to his government on the ways in which trade relations could be improved. Both J. E. W. Thompson, who went out in 1885, and Frederick Douglass, who became the American minister in 1889, were very much concerned over the treatment of American vessels in Haitian ports. William F. Powell, who was the minister in 1897, vigorously fought discriminating taxes against foreign merchants, while Henry W. Furness, the last Negro minister, concerned himself primarily with seeking advantages for American merchants in the matters of tariffs and customs duties.

From 1871 down to the present time most of the American ministers to Liberia have been Negroes. Beginning in 1871 J. Milton Turner helped to establish closer commercial relations between Liberia and the United States. Several others, including John Henry Smyth, E. E. Smith, and Ernest W. Lyon, praised the resources of the country and sought to encourage Americans to help develop the commercial and economic life of Liberia. Lyon, for example, is credited with having had a great deal to do with the organization of the New York Liberia Steamship Line in 1905. To the extent that these Negro representatives of the American government sought to extend the economic influence of the United States in Haiti and Liberia they were enlarging the black empire of the United States.

Credit has always been given to the United States for having had a more enlightened imperial policy than any of the European powers. The efforts to improve the health, education, and general well-being of the backward peoples of the American empire have seemed to be genuine even if they have not been very successful. There has, perhaps, been too much influence wielded by industrialists and financiers who have solely material interests in the outlying areas. This great influence has led to a foreign policy characterized by "dollar diplomacy" in areas enjoying a semblance of independence and to a policy of neglect or maladministration in dependent areas. There has been too great an inclination, moreover, to exercise military authority over nations whose territorial integrity and sovereignty we are supposed to respect. In many instances it has been argued that the landing of Marines in Haiti, Santo Domingo, and other nations has been for purposes of security; but it is doubtless indicative of the anxiety of a nation having so recently entered the family of great powers, to demonstrate its strength. It may also be a manifestation of jealousy, born of fear, of the powers of Europe whose experience in the field serves to excite the suspicions of the United States. The specter of color in America's Negro empire hangs over the mother country like the sword of Damocles and reminds her always that her imperial policy must take cognizance of that fact. For an America that would like to boast of having the most enlightened policy in the world, the problem of color at home serves to check the liberalism of her policy in the empire.

XXIII •

Dawn of a New Century

Urban Problems

● *The new century was one of hope for almost everyone in* America. During the previous generation it had emerged as a highly industrialized nation with a productive capacity far beyond its own needs. Toward the end of the period the country acquired an empire which placed it in fair competition with the great powers of the world. It was confidently believed that the new era would bring prosperity and plenty to everyone. If there were any unfavorable signs on the horizon they were the seemingly natural inclination of business combinations to increase to unmanageable proportions and to exploit the people. There was, moreover, an increase of social and political problems in the city, as urban populations grew to unprecedented heights. Few people worried very much about these national ills, for they were considered as inherent pains of growth. Even so, several steps had been taken to ease the pains. The Interstate Commerce Act had been passed in 1887 to curb the railroads; the Sherman Antitrust Act had been passed in 1890 to check the growth of monopolies; and the industrialists themselves were vying with each other in pouring their money into educational and charitable enterprises. Americans thus faced the new century with resolution and optimism.

There were signs of hope even for the Negro American. Despite the fact that he was being disfranchised in the Southern states and was experiencing difficulties in the economic world, his hopes for the future soared with those of other Americans. One major reason for the new hope was the succession of Theodore Roosevelt to the Presidency in 1901. Negroes had been shocked by Roosevelt's article partially discrediting the service of the Negro soldier in the Spanish-American War. (See Chapter XXII.) He was not long in office, however, before he satisfied the majority of Negroes, at least temporarily, that he favored the equality of all men. When he had been President only a month he invited Booker T. Washington to the White House and dined with him during the course of the interview. Southerners were outraged. The Richmond *Dispatch* exclaimed: "That was a deliberate act . . . and may be taken as outlining his policy toward the Negro as a factor in Washington society. . . . With our long-matured views on the subject of social intercourse between blacks and whites, the least we can say now is that we deplore the President's taste, and we distrust his wisdom." Negroes all over the country were delighted at this signal recognition of their leader. The Washington *Bee* asserted, "The Southern Democrats hoped and expected to blarney the President so as to continue unrestrained in their wicked reign of terror and proscription against the coloured race. They are shocked, boiled, smitten, and exasperated. In one fell swoop Mr. Roosevelt has smashed to smithereens their fondest idol. They are fuming with dire imprecations against him, and all because he took a meal of victuals with a coloured gentleman who had been entertained by the nobility of England, and the best people of America."

The debate over the incident continued for many months, with the President taking no cognizance of the matter at all. Less than two years later he appointed an outstanding Negro citizen, William D. Crum, to the Collectorship of the Port of Charleston, South Carolina. Once more, Southern citizens attacked the President. In this instance the appointment of Crum set no precedent. Negroes had served in similar capacities at Wilmington, North Carolina, and Savannah, Georgia. The whites, however, had looked forward to the elimination of Negroes from office-holding in the South; but the ascendancy of Booker T. Washington caused them to fear that he was dictating the White House Southern policy. The Negro world was overcome with joy. Negroes promptly forgot that within nineteen months in 1899 and 1900 McKinley had appointed twice as many Negroes to federal positions as any previous President.

Roosevelt further pleased them by declaring that unless some valid reason other than color could be urged against Crum the appointment would stand. In a letter to a Charleston citizen he said that he would not close the door of hope to any American citizen, a statement which caused one Negro editor to say that Roosevelt's words were "full of hope for the Negro and deadly miasma for the Southern whites." When Crum was confirmed, the editor of the *Coloured American Magazine* said that the Negro "had witnessed his greatest political triumph in twenty years. . . . In this crusade against the confirmation of Crum, the South has greatly weakened the growing regard which the North has here of late entertained for it. . . . Under a general of less courage and honour than Roosevelt, history would read differently. It has been thoroughly established that the law recognises no man by the colour of his skin. . . ."

A third incident which heartened Negroes and led them to believe that they would flourish under Roosevelt's "Square Deal" was the resignation of the postmistress at Indianola, Mississippi. This Negro woman had been in office since Harrison's administration, but because of pressure of the white citizens of the town she resigned. The Post Office Department refused to accept her resignation, and when she would not serve, the post office was closed. Several months passed before the office was reopened with a white postmaster in charge. Meanwhile, Negroes warmly praised Roosevelt and referred to him as "our President—the first since Lincoln set us free."

Not until Roosevelt was far into what he called his second term did Negroes begin to understand that his friendship was neither systematic nor sustained. Before that time, however, they had come to realize that the new century had brought with it all the difficulties they had experienced in the previous one and had added some new ones of its own. In the search for better economic opportunities Negroes, like their white neighbors, continued to move into urban areas of both North and South. Negroes, compelled by the objections which rural poor whites registered to their presence, divorced themselves from the soil, as life became almost intolerable under dishonest merchants and cruel, unscrupulous landlords. They were being run out of many parts of Arkansas, for example; and even before Oklahoma became a state the white citizens of Lawton demanded that the Negroes leave within twenty-four hours.

Coincident with the rise of the city in American life was the rise of the Negro community within the city, a kind of *imperium in imperio* so far as the social aspects of their existence were concerned. In 1900 there were 72 cities with more than 5,000 Negroes. Washington had more than 86,000, Baltimore 79,000, and New Orleans 77,000; Philadelphia, New York, and Memphis each had more than 50,000. The Negro populations of these cities, as well as Louisville and Atlanta, were growing rapidly. Negroes outnumbered whites in Charleston, Savannah, Montgomery, Jacksonville, Shreveport, Vicksburg, Baton Rouge, and several other Southern cities. More than half of the Negro population of Missouri lived in towns and cities, while one-third of that of Kentucky lived in urban areas. If cities afforded larger opportunities, Negroes hoped to benefit from them.

Employment opportunities were fewer than the number of people coming to urban areas, and Negroes found great difficulty in securing anything except the more onerous and less attractive jobs. They continued to exist around the "ragged edge of industry" with organized labor evincing a pronounced feeling of hostility. (See Chapter XXI.) Only the Cigarmakers' International Union and the United Mine Workers of America seemed to welcome Negroes into membership, although some other unions had Negro members. Negro women easily found employment as household servants, and the more certain employment of women had the effect of attracting a larger number of women than men to the cities. Many white industrialists claimed that Negroes were inefficient, while others refused to hire them because of objections raised by white employees. Although the prospects of securing satisfactory employment were not great, Negroes continued to migrate to the cities, thereby jeopardizing the opportunities of those already there.

The problem of housing, common to all persons migrating to the city, was aggravated for Negroes by the determination of white citizens to segregate them in one section of the city. The exploitation by white landlords of the newly arrived Negroes was made easier, since the latter had little choice in selecting places of residence. Municipalities gave sanction to this practice by enacting segregation ordinances. The first group of these laws was passed by Louisville, Baltimore, Richmond, and Atlanta in 1912 and 1913. Blocks containing a majority of white people were to be designated as white blocks, and blocks containing a majority of Negroes were to be designated as Negro blocks. No Negroes could move into white blocks and vice versa. The extreme congestion which resulted from the restriction upon the choice of residence and the occupancy of small, unsanitary homes by large families led, naturally, to poor health and a high mortality rate.

All of the ills usually associated with maladjustment in urban life arose from the unfavorable conditions which existed among Negroes in American cities, both North and South. Juvenile delinquency became rampant as slum areas grew steadily worse and as too few corrective measures were taken by either public agencies or private individuals. The parks and playgrounds movement that was developing throughout the country early in the century did little for the Negro; and when he attempted to avail himself of the opportunity to use public recreational facilities, violence and bloodshed frequently resulted. Family disorganization and disintegration were a logical consequence of the innumerable difficulties which Negroes faced, and although the church was assuming a greater responsibility, problems increased far more rapidly than it could solve them. The century, which had opened with such a note of optimism, very early revealed overtones of despair that equaled, if they did not surpass, any which the Negro had experienced. Perhaps the systematic movement to disfranchise and to degrade the Negro was the trend, and the Washington-Roosevelt dinner and the Crum appointment merely an aberration. At least Negroes came to realize that the solution to their many pressing problems was not to be found in the White House. Perhaps in an individualistic society it was too much to expect that the problems could be solved by presidential fiat, or even by legislation.

Even as these urban problems became more aggravated as the years passed, Negroes found themselves attempting to cope with innumerable other problems that plagued the country at the opening of the century. The exploitation of the people by unscrupulous businesses was general; the struggle for survival in complex urban society was no respecter of races. The Negro experienced the difficulties common to all, together with the peculiar obstacles placed before him because of his color. The opening of the century witnessed, moreover, a vigorous assault on privilege and exploitation by a group of writers dubbed by Theodore Roosevelt as the "Muckrakers." They attacked slum conditions, huge business combinations, corruption in city government, dishonesty in the United States Senate, the malodorous operations of the railroads, and numerous other urgent conditions. An aroused public opinion was determined to eradicate these social ills and proceeded to press for legislation to effect these ends. One muckraker, Ray Stannard Baker, studied the problem of the Negro in American life, but his book, *Following the Color Line*, was hardly in the muckraking tradition. Baker, while not defending lynching, for example, sought to explain it in terms of the distrust of the Southern white man of

THE DESTRUCTION OF NEGRO SLUMS. These substandard homes were replaced by 480 units of public housing, called "Yamacrow Village," which were completed in March 1941, in Savannah, Georgia. Courtesy Federal Public Housing Authority.

his own judicial processes. While muckrakers usually advocated legislation to correct social ills, Baker counseled that time, patience, and education were the only solutions to the Negro problem. The Negroes could look neither to the White House nor to the muckrakers for substantial assistance. They had to grope toward a new solution to their old problems. Before this approach could be made, however, there had to be a more dramatic and violent manifestation of the problem, in order to impress both the Negroes and the whites with the urgency of the situation.

The Pattern of Violence

Violent manifestations of hostility to Negroes in the North and in the South were not new. They had persisted almost from the beginning of the Negro's presence in the New World. (See especially Chapters XIV and XVIII.) Many believed, however, that the new century would bring with it a new and more civilized approach to the solution of racial differences. Others, sensing the preoccupation of the United States with problems of empire, reasoned that the leading democracy of the New World could ill afford to continue the wanton lynching and murdering of members of one-tenth of its population. In the last sixteen years of the nineteenth century there had been more than 2,500 lynchings, the great majority of which were of Negroes, with Mississippi, Alabama, Georgia, and Louisiana leading the nation. In the year of the Spanish-American War there had been the violence and bloodshed of the Wilmington, North Carolina, riot. Some considered this as the dying gasps of a reign of terror. Few regarded these manifestations of violence as an inherent part of the industrial imperialism to which America was committed, in the ideology of which the subjection of the black man to caste control and wage slavery was an integral part. Whatever the motives were, all were soon to realize that for the Negro the new century meant more violence and more bloodshed, a kind of organized brigandage of life and property against which all America revolted whenever it was practiced by lawless immigrants from Europe.

In the very first year of the new century more than 100 Negroes were lynched, and before the outbreak of World War I the number for the century had soared to more than 1,100. To be sure, the South was far ahead of the rest of the country, but several Northern states, notably those in the Midwest, contributed to the perpetuation of this ancient practice of total disregard for the processes of the law. Although the impression was widely held that most of the Negroes lynched had been accused of committing rape on the bodies of white women, the records do not sustain this impression. In the first fourteen years of the twentieth century only 315 lynch victims were accused of rape or attempted rape, while more than 500 were accused of homicide and the others were accused of robbery, insulting white persons, and numerous other "offenses." Regardless of the alleged crime of the victim, lynching in the twentieth century continued to be an important part of the system of punishment in the United States. For Negroes the practice was one of the most disheartening revelations of the inadequacies of the protection which the country provided for its citizens.

It was the epidemic of race riots that swept the country early in the century that aroused the greatest anxiety and discomfort among the Negro population. Although lynchings were decreasing slightly, riots were perceptibly increasing; and their dramatic nature had the effect of emphasizing the insecurity of Negroes throughout the country. In August, 1904, the state of Georgia was rocked by the occurrences in the small town of Statesboro. Two Negroes were accused of the brutal murder of a white farmer, his wife, and three children. After two weeks of "safe keeping" in Savannah, the Negroes were brought back to Statesboro for trial. They were convicted and sentenced to be hanged. Meanwhile, the white citizens had worked themselves into a frenzy of race hatred. There was constant talk of the way in which Negroes were becoming insolent. Two Negro women were whipped for allegedly crowding two white girls off the sidewalk. When the sentence was passed on the Negroes a mob that had formed surged upstairs and forced itself into the courtroom, after overpowering a company of Savannah militia whose rifles were not loaded "in tender consideration for the feelings of the mob." The Negroes were dragged out and burned alive. This was the signal for wholesale terrorism. One Negro was severely whipped for riding a bicycle on the sidewalk, while another was lashed "on general principles." The Negro mother of a three-day old infant was beaten and kicked, and her husband was killed. Houses were wrecked, and countless terrified

Negroes left the county. Although there was talk of punishing the leaders of the mob, nothing was ever done.

The South's most sensational riot occurred in Atlanta in September, 1906. For months the city had been lashed into a fury of race hatred by loose talk and by the movement to disfranchise Negroes. (See Chapter XVIII.) An irresponsible press published articles that intensified the feeling against Negroes. One editor called for the revival of the Ku Klux Klan, while another went so far as to offer a reward for a "lynching bee" in Atlanta. On Saturday, September 22, newspapers told of four successive assaults on white women by Negroes. The country people, in town for the day, joined with the urban element in creating an outraged, panic-stricken mob. Whites began to attack every Negro they saw. Many innocent persons were beaten, others were dragged from cars and wagons.

The following day was quiet, but the rioting broke out again on Monday in Brownsville, a suburb of Atlanta. Negroes there had heard that their fellows in Atlanta were being slaughtered en masse. Some sought asylum in two Negro institutions in the neighborhood, Clark University and Gammon Theological Seminary. Others, who were determined to defend themselves to the end, collected their arms. When officers of the law came out they began rounding up Negroes and arresting them for being armed. One officer shot into a crowd of Negroes. The fire was returned, killing one officer and wounding another. The whites then threw discretion aside and set out upon a general destruction of Negro property and lives. Four Negroes, all of whom were substantial citizens, were killed, and many were injured. Dr. J. W. E. Bowen, the president of Gammon, was beaten over the head with a rifle butt by a police official. Houses of Negroes were looted and burned. For several days the city was paralyzed: factories were closed and all transportation stopped. Numerous Negroes sold their property and left. The whites confessed their shame and condemned the rioters. A group of responsible Negro and white citizens came together and organized the Atlanta Civic League to work for the improvement of social conditions and to prevent other riots. Nothing was done to the rioters. Despairing Negroes loudly protested, but no one listened. Even Roosevelt's "door of hope" was apparently being shut in their faces.

President Roosevelt's handling of the riot in Brownsville,

Texas, convinced many Negroes that appeal to him in their present plight was useless. In August, 1906, three companies of the Twenty-fifth Regiment, composed of Negroes, were involved in a riot in Brownsville, Texas; one citizen was killed, another wounded, and the chief of police was injured. Whites reported that Negroes had "shot up the town," and race passion was stirred to a fever pitch. Only the firm stand of the commander at Fort Brown prevented the riot from reaching more dire proportions. In November, on the basis of the report of an inspector who had said that the Negroes had murdered and maimed the citizens of Brownsville, President Roosevelt dismissed the entire battalion without honor and disqualified its members for service in either the military or the civil service of the United States. Negroes, who had always taken pride in the service of their soldiers, were outraged. Many whites protested, among whom was John Milholland, who through the Constitution League, carried on a relentless fight for the soldiers. Even Senator Tillman, doubtless in order to embarrass the President, called it an "executive lynching."

When the Congress met in December, Senator Joseph B. Foraker of Ohio insisted that a full and fair trial should have preceded such drastic punishment. On January 22 the Senate authorized a general investigation of the whole matter, the President having revoked the civil disability of the discharged soldiers a week earlier. After several months of study the majority of the Senate Committee upheld the President's contention as to the guilt of the accused soldiers. A stinging minority report written by Senator Foraker denounced the findings of the majority. The Ohio Senator did not give up the fight. In 1909 he succeeded in forcing through an act of Congress establishing a court of inquiry to pass on the cases of the discharged soldiers. It provided that all of the discharged soldiers who were found to be qualified for re-enlistment were to be deemed eligible and that if they re-enlisted they were to be considered as having enlisted immediately after their discharge more than two years earlier. Any such soldier was to receive the "pay, allowances, and other rights and benefits that he would have been entitled to receive according to his rank from said date of discharge as if he had been honorably discharged . . . and had re-enlisted immediately." While some regarded the establishment of the court of inquiry as the "most pointed and signal defeat of Roosevelt's administration," most Negroes looked upon the Brownsville incident as one more evidence of the helplessness of a minority in a hostile land.

The South was not the only land in America that was hostile to the Negro in the early years of the new century. Crowds of white hoodlums frequently attacked Negroes in large Northern cities such as Philadelphia and New York. On several occasions white citizens dragged Negroes off the street cars of Philadelphia, with cries of "Lynch him! Kill him!" As the migration of Negroes to the North increased hostility toward them grew. Some towns tolerated them; others did not. Syracuse, Ohio, forbade any Negroes to settle there, while several towns in Indiana, including Lawrenceburg, Salem, and Ellwood, did not permit any Negro residents within their limits.

Rioting in the North was as vicious and almost as prevalent as in the South. Springfield, Ohio, had two riots within a few years. The one in 1904 conformed perfectly to the pattern of violence that had characterized rioting in other parts of the country. In an altercation a Negro shot and killed a white officer. A mob gathered and broke into the jail where the Negro was being held. The citizens murdered the Negro in the doorway of the jail, hanged him to a telegraph pole, and riddled his body with bullets. They then proceeded to wreak destruction on the Negro section of the town. When they had finished, eight buildings had been burned, many Negroes had been beaten, and others had fled never to return. Two years later, in Greensburg, Indiana, a portion of the act was repeated. A Negro half-wit was convicted for criminally assaulting his employer, a white widow. The mob that gathered did not succeed in taking the Negro from the authorities, but it was not daunted. Many homes of Negroes were damaged; several innocent persons were beaten, and some were driven out of town.

The Northern riot that shook the entire country was the one which occurred in Springfield, Illinois, in August, 1908. The wife of a street car conductor claimed that she had been dragged from her bed and raped by a person whom she identified as a Negro, George Richardson, who had been working in the neighborhood. Richardson was arrested and jailed. Before a special grand jury the woman admitted that she had been severely beaten by a white man whose identity she refused to disclose and that Richardson had no connection with the incident. By this time, however, feeling was running high against Richardson. As a precautionary measure the officials took

Richardson and another Negro, held in connection with the murder of a white man, to a nearby town where they boarded the train for Bloomington. When the mob that was gathering learned that the Negroes had been removed they were furious. They wrecked the restaurant of an operator whose car had been used to transport the Negroes and began to surge through the town.

The town officials saw that the mob was becoming unruly and several unsuccessful efforts were made to disperse it. Finally the Governor called out the militia. The mob, oblivious to the appeals of high state officials to respect the law, raided secondhand stores, secured guns, axes, and other weapons, and began to destroy Negro businesses and to drive Negroes from their homes. They set fire to a building in which a Negro owned a barber shop. The barber was lynched in the yard behind his shop, and the mob, after dragging his body through the streets, was preparing to burn it when the militia from Decatur dispersed the crowd by firing into it. On the following night an 84-year old Negro, who had been married to a white woman for more than 30 years, was lynched within a block of the State House. Before order was restored more than 5,000 militia men were patrolling the streets. In the final count, 2 Negroes had been lynched, 4 white men had been killed, and more than 70 persons had been injured. More than 100 arrests were made and approximately 50 indictments were returned. The alleged leaders of the mob went unpunished.

The news of the riot was almost more than Negroes could bear. It seemed to them a perverse manner in which to celebrate the one hundredth anniversary of the birth of Lincoln. Negroes were actually lynched within half a mile of the only home Lincoln ever owned and within two miles of his final resting place. Their cup was filled, and they hardly had the voice to cry out against this most recent outrage. It was time for drastic action. Somehow, some solution must be found to the problem of color, which DuBois had already called the greatest problem of the twentieth century.

New Solutions for Old Problems

The sordid picture of Negro life in America in the twentieth century had moved a group of young Negroes as early as 1905 to organize for determined and aggressive action in order to secure full citizenship. They reasoned that the day of temporizing was over. A war was on, and they decided to fight to a finish. This group of men, under the leadership of W. E. B. DuBois, met at Niagara Falls, Canada, in June, 1905, and drew up a platform for aggressive action. Among other things they demanded freedom of speech and criticism, manhood suffrage, the abolition of all distinctions based on race, the recognition of the basic principles of human brotherhood, and respect for the working man. Despite the open attack that was made on them for their radicalism, they incorporated themselves as the Niagara Movement and met at Harpers Ferry in the following year.

The resolutions that were drawn up at Harpers Ferry were written by DuBois in what he admitted was a "tumult of emotion." Kelly Miller described this manifesto as "scarcely distinguishable from a wild and frantic shriek." It is palpably the wailings of a despondent but courageous group calling out for consideration on the basis of the common humanity of all men. In part, it said:

> In the past year the work of the Negro hater has flourished in the land. Step by step the defenders of the rights of American citizens have retreated. The work of stealing the black man's ballot has progressed and the fifty and more representatives of stolen votes still sit in the nation's capital. . . . Never before in the modern age has a great and civilized folk threatened to adopt so cowardly a creed in the treatment of its fellow-citizens, born and bred on its soil. Stripped of verbose subterfuge and in its naked nastiness, the new American creed says: fear to let black men even try to rise lest they become the equals of the white. And this in the land that professes to follow Jesus Christ. The blasphemy of such a course is only matched by its cowardice.

The Niagara Movement met in Boston in 1907 and at the session in Faneuil Hall did much to revive the old spirit of abolitionism. Organizations such as the New England Suffrage League and the Equal Rights League of Georgia supported the work of the Niagara Movement. In the following year the meeting was held at Oberlin, Ohio. The organization had now met at Oberlin, a hotbed of Western abolitionism, Boston, the center of Eastern abolitionism, Harpers Ferry, the scene of John Brown's martyrdom, and Niagara Falls, an important terminus on the Underground Railroad. Kelly Miller in commenting on these sites was moved to heckle from the sidelines, "We may expect a future session at Appomattox, so prone is the poetic temperament to avail itself of episodal and dramatic situations." But there were to be no more meetings, for soon the Niagara Movement was to be absorbed by a new and infinitely more resourceful organization. It was significant, however, in being the first organized attempt to raise the Negro protest against the great reaction after the Reconstruction.

The Springfield riots shocked the sensibilities of many whites. Among them was William English Walling, a distinguished writer, who went to the scene and gathered data for an article. In a piece, "Race War in the North" which appeared in the *Independent*, Walling described the Springfield atrocities and declared, "Either the spirit of the abolitionists, of Lincoln and of Lovejoy, must be revived and we must come to treat the Negro on a plane of absolute political and social equality or Vardaman and Tillman will soon have transferred the Race War to the North. . . . Yet who realizes the seriousness of the situation and what large and powerful body of citizens is ready to come to their aid?" Mary White Ovington, a New York social worker already interested in the problems of the Negro, read the article and took the matter up with Walling and Dr. Henry Moskowitz. They decided to call a conference for Lincoln's birthday in 1909 to accept the challenge which Walling had laid down. Oswald Garrison Villard, the grandson of William Lloyd Garrison, wrote the call, in which he said, "We call upon all believers in democracy to join in a National conference for the discussion of present evils, the voicing of protests, and the renewal of the struggle for civil and political liberty." Abolitionism had become reincarnate in the progeny of its greatest exponent.

The young radicals of the Niagara Movement were invited to the conference; most of them accepted. Among those who did not was Monroe Trotter, who was suspicious of the motives of white people. It was a distinguished gathering of educators, professors, publicists, bishops, judges, and social workers. Among those who participated were Jane Addams, William Dean Howells, Livingston Farrand, John Dewey, John Milholland, DuBois, and Villard. Plans were made to establish a permanent organization which came to be known as the National Association for the Advancement of Colored People. A program of action was also agreed upon. The organization pledged itself to work for the abolition of all forced segregation, equal education for Negro and white children, the complete enfranchisement of the Negro, and the enforcement of the Fourteenth and Fifteenth Amendments. A formal organization was perfected in May, 1910, with Moorefield Storey of Boston as president and William E. Walling as chairman of the executive committee. Dr. W. E. B. DuBois, as the director of publicity and research, was the only Negro officer. The presence of Dr. DuBois on the staff branded the organization as radical from the beginning. Many feared that it would be a capricious, irresponsible organization that would draw its main inspiration from the dreamings of the Niagara Movement. It was denounced by most of the white philanthropists, and even some Negroes thought it unwise.

In the first year of its existence the N.A.A.C.P. launched a program to widen the industrial opportunities for Negroes, to seek greater police protection for Negroes in the South, and to carry on a crusade against lynching and lawlessness. Important instrumentalities in carrying out its program were the *Crisis* and the Legal Redress Committee. It was the primary task of DuBois to get the magazine going. In November, 1910, the first issue appeared. One thousand copies were rapidly sold, and the circulation figures increased until they reached 100,000 per month by 1918. In the magazine the campaign against lynching and mob law was waged. Its phenomenal success in circulation was equaled by the effectiveness with which it dealt with the pressing problems of the Negro.

Arthur B. Spingarn, who with his brother Joel had become a member of the bi-racial board of directors, was chairman of the legal committee. White and Negro attorneys worked closely with him, and within fifteen years they had won three important decisions before the United States Supreme Court. In 1915, in the case of *Guinn v. United States*, the Supreme Court after hearing the arguments of Storey declared the grandfather clauses in the Maryland and Oklahoma constitutions to be repugnant to the Fifteenth Amendment and therefore null and void. In 1917, in the case of *Buchanan v. Warley*, the court declared unconstitutional the Louisville ordinance requiring Negroes to live in certain sections of the city. In 1923, in the case of *Moore v. Dempsey*, the Court ordered a new trial in the Arkansas courts for a Negro who had been convicted of murder. The representatives of the Association had argued that the

Arkansas peon had not received a fair trial because, among other things, Negroes were excluded from the jury. The Court accepted this view. Resorting to the courts thus became an effective weapon in the fight for full citizenship.

As the work of the Association became better organized it was extended by the establishment of branches. Shortly after the initial organization the first branch was established in Chicago. Within two years nine others had been formed. Each year down to the outbreak of the first World War the number doubled, and by 1921 there were more than 400 branches scattered all over the United States, gathering information for the Association and carrying out, on the local front, the aims of the parent organization. It was not long before the N.A.A.C.P. extended its activities across national boundaries. DuBois was sent to the International Congress of Races in London, partly to represent the Association at that important gathering and partly to follow Booker T. Washington who had made a tour of Europe in 1910. It had been reported in the United States that Washington was telling English audiences that Negroes in America were making rapid strides toward complete and full citizenship. In his speeches before the Congress DuBois made it clear that Negroes in the United States were suffering under grave legal and civil disabilities, and that only by a fierce struggle would they overcome the many obstacles that beset them. New friends were won for the Association among the delegates from many distant lands. These contacts were to strengthen the program of the Association at home during and after the war, the clouds of which were already gathering by the end of the Congress.

Although the N.A.A.C.P. included in its program a plan for widening the industrial opportunities of Negroes, it did not find time to do much in this area. More and more it concentrated on its crusade to destroy lynching, to secure the franchise for Negroes, and to put an end to all forms of segregation and discrimination. The need for organized effort in the economic sphere was no less pressing, however, and an organization emerged which devoted its attention to this matter. At the time that the Niagara Movement was getting under way in 1905, two organizations were established in New York City which became the nucleus for a national agency. They were the Committee for Improving Industrial Conditions of Negroes in New York and the National League for the Protection of Colored Women. Among the distinguished white persons supporting the latter organization were Mrs. W. H. Baldwin, W. J. Schiefflin, and A. S. Frissell. Meanwhile, George Edmund Haynes, a young Negro graduate student at Columbia University, was making an extensive study of social and economic conditions among the Negroes of New York City. He made a report of his findings to a joint meeting of the two organizations. Interest was so great in his findings, later published as *The Negro at Work in New York City*, that a committee was formed to act as a coordinating agency in the effort to round out a larger program of community life for the Negroes of New York.

Plans were laid before the Committee for improving social and economic conditions among Negroes. Haynes, who maintained a keen interest in the project, went to Fisk University to develop a department of sociology and to establish a training center for social workers. The experience and data he secured were placed at the disposal of the committee, and as the program evolved, a formal organization was perfected. In 1911 the three organizations merged to form the National League on Urban Conditions among Negroes (commonly known as the National Urban League), with Haynes and Eugene Kinckle Jones as executive officers. Professor E. R. A. Seligman of Columbia was the first chairman of the League; it received support from Julius Rosenwald, Mrs. Baldwin, and others. Among the sponsors were Booker T. Washington, Kelly Miller, Roger N. Baldwin, Robert R. Moton, and L. Hollingsworth Wood.

The League undertook to open new opportunities for Negroes in industry and to assist newly arrived Negroes in their problems of adjustment in the urban centers. Branches were opened in many of the large centers with programs for meeting the migrants, directing them to jobs and lodgings, and offering information on how to live in the city. It did an effective job in bringing the employer and employee together and easing the difficulties of mutual adjustment. The League also developed a program for the training of young men and young women for social work. It established fellowships to support students while studying at the School of Philanthropy in New York, and "part fellowships" to make possible in-service training at the national office in preparation for carrying on the work in the field. Its program of training made possible the education of many of America's most distinguished Negro social work leaders in the next generation.

Among the other organizations that assisted in the adjustment of the Negro to city life were the Young Men's Christian Association and the Young Women's Christian Association. The first Negro Y.M.C.A. had been organized as early as 1853 in Washington, but not until after the Civil War was it connected with the white movement. In 1888 William A. Hunton was placed on the national staff as its first salaried Negro officer, and in 1898 Jesse E. Moorland joined him to give special attention to the problems of Negroes in urban areas. Early in the new century several city association branches were organized. Buildings that could be used as headquarters and recreational centers were constructed. In 1907 George Foster Peabody gave a building for colored men and boys in his native city of Columbus, Georgia. In 1910 Julius Rosenwald, in his initial contribution to the Y.M.C.A. movement among Negroes, gave $25,000 toward the erection of the Wabash Avenue building in Chicago. In the succeeding years his gifts for thirteen buildings amounted to $325,000. In the absence of an effective public program of wholesome recreation and guidance the Y.M.C.A. served a useful purpose in the communities where it existed.

By 1906 there were small Y.W.C.A.'s among Negroes in Washington, Philadelphia, New York, and Baltimore. Gradually, with an awakened social consciousness, city and student work developed. Not until the outbreak of World War I did a strong movement develop for the work among Negro women. Several substantial buildings were erected in strategic centers, and with the cooperation of philanthropists like Rosenwald and Rockefeller, the Y.W.C.A. acquired physical plants in which it could carry out a program of social improvement and education among young Negro women that did much to assist them with their problems in urban communities.

There were scattered efforts to solve local problems, such as the establishment of the Flanner Settlement House in Indianapolis and the neighborhood associations of New York. Efforts were made, also, to improve housing, such as the Octavia Hill Association of Philadelphia and the Model Homes Company of Cincinnati. They were, indeed, new solutions for old problems. But the problem of the Negro in the United States at the opening of the twentieth century was so broad in scope and so deep in implication that only a large-scale, comprehensive attack on it could hope to make more than a dent at solving it. The programs of the National Association for the Advancement of Colored People and the National Urban League were so conceived, but there was no guarantee that, however broadly conceived, these agencies had the formula. In the difficult task of social reform and regeneration, science and reason together could scarcely keep the door of hope open, if passion and prejudice were pressing with all their might to close it.

XXIV •

In Pursuit of Democracy

World War I

● *The discerning observer at the Races Congress in London in* 1911 could see the unmistakable signs of the war clouds gathering in Europe. Despite the multiplication of peace agencies in the Old World as well as the New, the armed competition between the two rival coalitions in Europe for markets, cheap materials, and cheap labor was well under way several years before the actual outbreak of the war. What few observers could not see, however, was that civilized countries would be willing to pay a price as dear as a world conflagration for a "place in the sun." Germany and her satellites were more determined than ever to wield a controlling influence in Europe, Africa, and Asia, while Russia, France, and Great Britain were equally determined to see to it that such ambitions were effectively curbed. Confusion and antagonism were everywhere, as the game of intrigue became more complicated and as all semblances of international law broke down.

When war came in 1914 the American people were wholly unprepared even to stand on the sidelines and watch the world plunge itself into the madness and insanity of war. Americans had been peculiarly preoccupied with their own domestic problems, and Woodrow Wilson's promise of a "New Freedom" had focused attention on the economic and social maladjustments that were the legacies of the great industrial upheaval of the previous generation. Negroes certainly were not concerned with

Europe's problems. They had more than enough to claim their attention. Having been skeptical of the Democratic party since the days of Reconstruction, they kept their eyes fastened on Washington to see what the first Southern-born President since the Civil War would do.

In 1912 the Negroes of the United States were sorely distressed by the political picture. They had become suspicious of Theodore Roosevelt because of his handling of the Brownsville incident (see Chapter XXIII) and did not have any confidence in President Taft. Many of them were willing, however, to follow Roosevelt in the formation of a new party if they could receive assurances that the new party would stand unequivocally for full citizenship for the Negro. The officials of the N.A.A.C.P. went so far as to draft a statement to be placed in the Progressive Republican platform and sent it to Chicago by Joel Spingarn. The statement called for the repeal of unfair discriminatory laws and the complete enfranchisement of the Negro. When Roosevelt permitted the Southern white delegates to have their way in excluding the statement from the platform and in barring some of the Negro delegates from the convention, Negroes realized that the Bull Moose movement offered very little for them. As skeptical of the Democratic party as they were, some of them turned to it. They were considerably heartened by Wilson's assertion that he wished to see "justice done to the colored people in every matter; and not mere grudging justice, but justice executed with liberality and cordial good feeling." Many Negroes were won over to the Wilson camp by the candidate's clear-cut expressions of good will. One of them was: "I want to assure them that should I become President of the United States they may count upon me for absolute fair dealing, for everything by which I could assist in advancing the interests of their race in the United States." The Negro support of Wilson was by no means decisive, but it was far greater than many Republicans would have believed possible.

In the early years of the Wilson administration, therefore, Negroes were watching Washington, rather than Paris and Berlin. What they saw dismayed them greatly. They had little immediate interest in the tariff and banking reforms, and since they were excluded from so many labor unions they benefited little from the labor exemption provisions of the Clayton Antitrust Act. Washington had not forgotten them, however. The first Congress of Wilson's administration received the greatest

454 · FROM SLAVERY TO FREEDOM

flood of bills proposing discriminatory legislation against
Negroes that had ever been introduced into an American Congress. At least twenty bills advocated the segregation of the
races on public carriers in the District of Columbia, the exclusion of Negroes from commissions in the Army and Navy,
separate accommodations for Negro and white federal employees, and the exclusion of all immigrants of Negro descent. There
were similar proposals in the next Congress. Although most of
the legislation failed to pass, Wilson, by executive order, segregated most of the Negro federal employees so far as eating and
rest-room facilities were concerned.

When President Wilson issued his proclamation of neutrality
in 1914 the Negroes of the United States, like most Americans,
thought little of the possibility of America's entry into the war.
They continued to concern themselves with their own peculiar
problems. Some of them went to the White House with Monroe
Trotter to protest the segregation of Negro federal employees,
but were dismissed because Wilson regarded Trotter's language
"insulting." Others began the fight against residential segregation ordinances that were springing up all over the country.
When the President ordered the occupation of Haiti by the
Marines in 1915, the Negroes of the United States loudly protested the violation of that country's sovereignty and territorial
integrity; and the killing of several hundred Haitians in order to
restore peace and order was particularly repulsive. In the same
year the most notable motion picture that had yet been produced, "The Birth of a Nation," was released. Based on the
violently anti-Negro writings of Thomas Dixon, it told a most
sordid and obviously distorted story of Negro emancipation,
enfranchisement, and debauchery of innocent womanhood.
Lynchings and other forms of violence increased, to add to the
concern of Negroes. In 1916 Jesse Washington was publicly
burned in Waco, Texas, before a cheering mob of thousands of
men, women, and children. In South Carolina a well-to-do
Negro farmer, Anthony Crawford, was mobbed and killed for
"impudence" in refusing to agree to a price for his cotton seed.
In Mexico 22 Negroes of the Tenth Cavalry were killed while on
a mission pursuing a deserter. As the fires of war slowly enveloped Europe, Negroes in the United States had no time to
extend even an eye across the Atlantic to follow events there.

In the midst of this great distress, late in 1915, Booker T.
Washington died. Now there was no leader among Negroes

whom the majority of the citizens of the United States respected. At the same time, though, there was no one left with the prestige of Washington who would counsel patience and moderation. This was the time, some of the more aggressive leaders believed, to consolidate the group and achieve a unity in thought and action which had been hitherto impossible. To this end a conference was called at Joel Spingarn's home in 1916 to discuss the plight of the Negro. This Amenia Conference brought together perhaps the most distinguished Negroes that had assembled in recent years. It drew up no impassioned manifesto, and its resolutions showed no bitterness. But all of those attending agreed to work quietly and earnestly for the enfranchisement of the Negro, the abolition of lynching, and the enforcement of the laws protecting civil liberties. It was a happy prelude to America's entry into the war. With a calm but firm unanimity of opinion among the Negro leaders of the United States, the black citizens of the Western republic could pursue more intelligently and relentlessly the democracy which the allies were seeking to extend to all the world.

The Enlistment of Negroes

Of the 750,000 men in the Regular Army and the National Guard at the beginning of the war, approximately 20,000 were Negroes. There were 10,000 in the Negro units of the Regular Army, the Ninth and Tenth Cavalries and the Twenty-fourth and Twenty-fifth Infantries. Another 10,000 were in various units of the National Guard: the Eighth Illinois, the Fifteenth New York, the separate battalions of the District of Columbia and of Ohio, and the separate companies of Maryland, Connecticut, Massachusetts, and Tennessee. As early as March 25, 1917, two weeks before the formal declaration of war, Negroes of the District of Columbia National Guard had been called out to protect the national capital. Between July and September, other Negro units were called into active service.

Negroes were among those who thronged the recruiting stations in April, 1917, seeking to volunteer their services; but for the most part they were not received. The passage of the Selective Service Act on May 18, however, provided for the enlistment of all able-bodied Americans between the ages of 21 and 31. On July 5, registration day, more than 700,000 Negroes registered. Before the end of the Selective Service enlistments 2,290,525 Negroes had registered, 367,000 of whom were called into the service. Approximately 31 per cent of the Negroes who registered were accepted, while 26 per cent of the whites who registered were accepted. This was due not to the superior physical and mental qualifications of Negroes, but to the inclination of some draft boards to discriminate against Negroes in the matter of exemptions. One board in Georgia, for example, was discharged because of its flagrant discrimination against Negroes in exemptions. There were numerous similar complaints against other boards. There were no outstanding examples of draft-dodging among Negroes, and even those Negroes who were opposed to the war on the grounds that it was an imperialistic conflict answered the calls of their draft boards.

Negroes were especially eager to participate in the struggle not only as enlisted men but as officers. They were greatly disheartened by the retirement of the highest ranking Negro officer, Colonel Charles Young, because of high blood pressure. To prove his physical fitness, Col. Young rode horseback from Ohio to the nation's capital, but the retirement board remained unconvinced. In the effort to secure provisions for the commissioning of Negro officers Negroes met stern resistance in many high places in Washington. The Congress was creating training camps for white officers, but was making no provisions for the training of Negro officers. A committee of representative citizens, headed by Joel Spingarn, went to Washington and conferred with the military authorities, but it was a fruitless venture. Almost immediately college students at Howard, Fisk, Atlanta, Tuskegee, and other Negro institutions began a program of agitation for the training of Negro officers. When Spingarn took the matter up with General Leonard Wood, the latter said that if 200 Negroes of college grade could be secured he would see to it that a training camp was established for them. Early in May, 1917, a Central Committee of Negro College Men was set up at Howard University, and within ten days it had collected the names of 1,500 Negro college men who wanted to become officers in the United States Army. The Committee interviewed numerous members of Congress and presented them with a statement justifying the establishment of an officers' reserve training camp for Negroes. More than 300 Senators and Representatives approved the proposal and the movement to establish the camp began in earnest. Mass meetings were held, the Negro press vigorously supported the training of Negroes as officers, and students raised funds to carry on the fight.

Some Negroes denounced the idea of a separate camp, contending that such an establishment would defeat the struggle for full citizenship. The N.A.A.C.P., however, supported the proposal. When the government finally authorized the camp, Spingarn, a leader in the association as well as in the fight for the camp, said: "The army officials want the camp to fail. The last thing they want is to help colored men to become commissioned officers. The camp is intended to fight segregation, not to encourage it. Colored men in a camp by themselves would all get a fair chance for promotion. Opposition on the part of Negroes is helping the South, which does not want the Negroes to have any kind of military training." On October 15, 1917, at Fort Des Moines, Iowa, 639 Negroes were commissioned—106 captains, 329 first lieutenants, and 204 second lieutenants. Later, at non-segregated camps and in the field, other Negroes received commissions in the army. At colleges and high schools throughout the country, Negroes prepared to become officer candidates and to serve the army in a variety of ways in the Students' Army Training Corps and the Reserve Officers' Training Corps.

Because of the mounting race friction which attended the migration of Negroes to the North, the continued lynching of Negro men and women, and the German propaganda which was circulated in the United States, it was deemed wise to bring into the government a Negro who could advise on matters affecting his race and who enjoyed the confidence of his people. Consequently, the Secretary of War announced on October 5, 1917, the appointment of Emmett J. Scott, for eighteen years the secretary to Booker T. Washington, as the Special Assistant to the Secretary of War who would serve as "confidential advisor in matters affecting the interests of the ten million Negroes of the United States and the part they are to play in connection with the present war." Newton D. Baker was widely commended by whites and Negroes for making the appointment. *The Mobile News Item* said, "The appointment is a wise move and a wise selection. While the government is coordinating all the interests of the country in the movement to win the war with Germany, it should not overlook the colored people." Kelly Miller of Howard University said, "I regard the appointment of Mr. Scott . . . as the most significant appointment that has yet come to the colored race."

Scott's functions were primarily to urge the equal and impartial application of Selective Service regulations and to formulate plans to promote healthy morale among Negro soldiers and civilians. He was called upon to express an opinion regarding almost every phase of Negro life and was required to answer thousands of inquiries from Negroes on every conceivable subject. He investigated scores of cases in which unfair treatment was charged, and he looked after many cases relating to voluntary and compulsory allotments, war risk insurance, and government allowances and compensation. He worked with the Committee on Public Information in releasing news concerning Negro soldiers as well as various activities on the home front.

While Negroes were barred altogether from the Marines and permitted to serve in the Navy only in the most menial capacities, they served in almost every branch of the army except the pilot section of the aviation corps. After a long struggle they were permitted to join units of coast and field artillery. They were in the cavalry, infantry, engineer corps, signal corps, medical corps, hospital and ambulance corps, veterinary corps, sanitary and ammunition trains, stevedore regiments, labor battalions, and depot brigades. Negroes served also as regimental adjutants, judge advocates, chaplains, intelligence officers, chemists, clerks, surveyors, draftsmen, auto repairers, motor truck operators, and mechanics.

The problem of training the Negro soldiers while in the United States was one that plagued the War Department from the beginning of the struggle. While the army was committed to the activation of an all-Negro division, the Ninety-second, no arrangements were made to train the men at the same camp. Thus the men of the all-Negro division were trained at seven widely separated camps, all the way from Camp Grant in Rockford, Illinois, to Camp Upton in Yaphank, New York. It was the only instance in which a division was never actually brought together until it reached the fighting front. Another Negro division, the Ninety-third, was never brought up to its full strength; and after training in different places the units that were organized were sent overseas at different times to join various fighting units of the French army. Southerners objected strenuously to the army's sending Northern Negroes into the South for training. The objections became so persistent that it was necessary for officials at Washington to call a conference in August, 1917, to discuss the matter. After a series of discussions it was agreed that "while the South might object to having colored men from Northern states sent into the various camps and cantonments of the South, it could not well refuse an acceptance of the principles of having such colored selectmen as might be called in such states trained in the cantonments of the states in which they lived." This arrangement worked such a hardship upon the administration of the army's program that long before the war was over Negroes were being sent to the camp, North or South, which best served the interests of the prosecution of the war.

There was much discrimination in the army and in the civilian agencies that served the army; and it required a great deal of tact and prompt action to prevent more serious outbreaks than there were. The Federal Council of Churches created a Committee on the Welfare of Negro Troops of which Bishop W. P. Thirkield, Robert R. Moton, James H. Dillard, and John R. Hawkins were prominent members. The two field secretaries of the Committee were Charles H. Williams of Hampton and G. Lake Imes of Tuskegee. These secretaries investigated conditions at home and abroad and found many outstanding examples of discrimination and segregation among the service agencies. At Camp Greene, near Charlotte, North Carolina, they found that there were five Y.M.C.A. buildings, but none for the 10,000 Negroes stationed there. A sign over one of the buildings read "This building is for white men only," and the secretary placed outside the building a table which Negro soldiers could use in writing letters. At Camp Lee, near Petersburg, Virginia, white soldiers patrolled the grounds around a prayer meeting to see to it that no Negroes attempted to enter.

Complaints flooded the War Department that Negroes were continuously insulted by white officers. They referred to Negroes as "coons," "niggers," and "darkies," and frequently forced them to work under unhealthy and laborious conditions. Many Negro soldiers contended that white officers made it extremely difficult for them to advance and that they indiscriminately assigned them to labor battalions even when they were qualified for other posts requiring higher skills and intelligence. The friction between Negro soldiers and the Military Police grew in intensity as the war progressed, and although the War Department issued orders calling for fair and impartial treatment of Negro soldiers, there was little discernible improvement. Clashes between white and Negro soldiers continued down to the end of the war.

The hostility which white civilians displayed toward Negro soldiers was especially distressing to Negroes who tried to remain enthusiastic about serving their country. In many places in the North they were denied service in restaurants and admission to theaters. When Negroes insisted on attending the theater at Fort Riley, Kansas, General C. C. Ballou, the commander of the Ninety-second Division, issued an order commanding his men not to go where their presence was resented. He reminded them that "White men had made the Division, and they can break it just as easily if it becomes a trouble maker." Immediately a howl of resentment was raised in the Negro press, and Negroes were not consoled by the fact that General Ballou was pressing legal charges against the theater operators that discriminated against his men.

Friction in the South caused the War Department its greatest concern. In September, 1917, for example, the men of the Twenty-fourth Infantry became involved in a riot with the white civilians of Houston, Texas. After much goading and insults by the citizens, the Negro soldiers were disarmed when it was feared that they would use their weapons in defending themselves. Refusing to be outdone, the soldiers seized arms and killed 17 whites. With only a slight pretense of a trial 13 Negro soldiers were hanged for murder and mutiny, 41 were imprisoned for life, and 40 others were held pending further investigation. Nothing since the Brownsville incident had done so much to wound the pride of American Negroes or to shake their faith in their government. Emmett J. Scott's assertion that the incident "did not dampen the ardor of the colored men who went to the front for the Stars and Stripes" seems hardly accurate. Many men of the Twenty-fourth swore vengeance on the officials whom they accused of unjust treatment of their fellows. A Negro newspaper of Baltimore exclaimed, "The Negroes of the entire country will regard the thirteen Negro soldiers of the Twenty-fourth Infantry executed as martyrs," while the New York Age declared, "Strict justice has been done, but full justice has not been done. . . . And so sure as there is a God in heaven, at some time and in some way full justice will be done."

At Spartanburg, South Carolina, where the Fifteenth New York Infantry was in training, white citizens felt that something was needed to let the jaunty New York Negroes know their place. In October, 1917, when Noble Sissle, the talented drum major of the infantry band, went into a hotel to purchase a newspaper the proprietor cursed him and asked him why he did not remove his hat. Before Sissle could answer, the white man had knocked his hat from his head. As the young soldier stooped to pick up his hat he was struck several times and kicked out of the place. Upon discovering what had happened the Negro militiamen, joined by their incensed white fellows from New York, started to "rush the hotel." But Lieutenant James R. Europe, the bandmaster who happened to be passing, called the men to attention and ordered them to disperse. The following evening the soldiers planned to "shoot up" the town of Spartanburg, but the commanding officer, Colonel William Hayward, overtook them as they were leaving and ordered them back to camp.

Emmett J. Scott rushed to the scene to investigate the incident and to plead with the men to do nothing to bring dishonor on the regiment or on the race. He reminded them of the Houston episode and said that no one wanted that to happen again. The War Department had three possible courses: It could keep the regiment at Camp Wadsworth and face a violent eruption; it could remove the regiment to another camp, thereby conveying the impression that whenever any community exerted sufficient pressure it could force the War Department to remove undesirable soldiers from its midst; or it could order the regiment overseas. The last alternative was decided upon. As the Fifteenth New York Regiment, now the 369th of the United States Army, made its way to Europe to become the first contingent of Negro combat troops to reach the theater of war, it could well reason that there could be a more successful pursuit of democracy in Europe than at home. Many could not have resisted the temptation to conclude that the penalty for insisting upon full equality in the United States was a sentence to face, for a full season, the onslaught of the German armies.

Service Overseas

The first Negroes to arrive in Europe after the United States entered the war, and indeed among the first Americans to reach the war zone, were the laborers and stevedores that were needed to assist in the tremendous task of providing the allies with materials of war. The first Negro stevedore battalion arrived in France in June, 1917. From that date to the end of the war they came in larger numbers. They were classified as stevedore regiments, engineer service battalions, labor battalions, butchery companies, and pioneer infantry battalions. Before the end of the war there were more than 50,000 in 115 different outfits, more than one-third of the entire American force. At Brest, St. Nazaire, Bordeaux, Le Havre, and Marseilles, Negro stevedores worked in mud and rain, sometimes in 24-hour shifts, unloading supplies from the United States. At one port a crew of Negro stevedores amazed the French by unloading 1,200 tons of flour in nine and one-half hours, after it had been estimated that such an undertaking would require several days. In September, 1918, at the American base ports in France, 767,648 tons were handled largely by Negroes, an average of more than 25,000 tons per day. An American war correspondent was moved to remark, "One who sees the Negro stevedores work notes with what rapidity and cheerfulness they work and what a very important cog they are in the war machinery."

The Negro combat troops that were originally intended for the Ninety-third Division were among the first to be sent overseas; they were placed in various divisions of the French army. After many hardships at sea, including breakdown, fire, and collision, the 369th United States Infantry arrived in France early in 1918, and some of the men went immediately to a French divisional training school. There they learned to throw grenades, use bayonets, and handle the French weapons. In April, 1918, almost exactly one year after the formal entry of the United States into the war, they moved up to the fighting front. By May they were in the thick of the fight, in Champagne, holding for a time a complete sector constituting twenty per cent of all the territory held by American troops at the time. After some relief they were placed in the path of the expected German offensive at Minaucourt, where they bore the brunt of the German attacks in the middle of July. From that time until the end of hostilities the men of the 369th were almost continuously in action against the Germans. The feats it could boast at the end of the war were many. It was the first unit of the Allied armies to reach the Rhine. The regiment never lost a man through capture, a trench, or a foot of ground. It saw the first and longest service of any American regiment as part of a foreign army, having been in the trenches for 191 days. It won the unique distinction of being called the "Hell Fighters" by the Germans. The entire regiment won•the Croix de Guerre for its action at Maison-en-Champagne, and 171 individual officers and enlisted men were cited for the Croix de Guerre and the Legion of Honor for exceptional gallantry in action.

The Eighth Illinois Infantry, renamed the 370th United States Infantry, reached France in June, 1918. It was equipped with French arms and sent to the front. After service in the St. Mihiel sector, it was withdrawn and sent to the Argonne Forest where it remained for the better part of July and August. In September, under the Fifty-ninth Division of the French army, it took over a full regimental sector in the area of Mont des Tombes and Les Tueries. From that time until the end of the war, the 370th, in concert with several units of the French army, pursued the enemy out of France into Belgium. Twenty-one men received the Distinguished Service Cross, one received the Distinguished Service Medal, while 68 received various grades of the Croix de Guerre. They were the first American troops to enter the French fortress of Laon when it was wrested from the Germans after four years of war. It fought the last battle of the war, capturing a German wagon train of 50 wagons and crews a half-hour after the Armistice went into effect.

The 371st Infantry Regiment, which had been organized in August, 1917, at Camp Jackson, South Carolina, arrived in France late in April, 1918. It was then reorganized on the French plan and attached to the 157th French Division, the famous "Red Hand," under General Goybet. It remained in the front lines for more than three months, holding first the Avocourt and later the Verrières subsectors, northwest of Verdun. In the great September offensive it took several important places near Monthois and captured a number of prisoners, many machine guns and other weapons, a munition depot, several railroad cars, and many other supplies. For its action its regimental colors were decorated by the French government. Three officers won the French Legion of Honor, while 34 officers and 89 enlisted men won the Croix de Guerre. Fourteen officers and 12 enlisted men won the Distinguished Service Cross.

The 372nd United States Infantry was something of a catch-all outfit, composed of Negro National Guardsmen from the District of Columbia, Ohio, Massachusetts, and Maryland. There were also about 250 men who had entered the army through the Selective Service. After a period of training in the United States the regiment reached France in April, 1918, and was, along with the 371st, brigaded with the French "Red Hand" Division. Late in May it took over the job of holding the Argonne west sector and was in the front line trenches on May 31. During the summer it was subjected to heavy shelling in the Verdun sector, and in September it went "over the top" in pursuit of the retreating enemy. It remained in the thick of the fight until the surrender of the German armies in November. For its gallantry in the final campaign, Vice Admiral Moreau decorated the colors of the regiment with the Croix de Guerre and palm just before the men sailed for America. Many individual honors were also won, especially by the men of the First Battalion of the District of Columbia National Guard.

Because of the rather irregular procedure of the units having been trained in separate camps, the Ninety-second Division was late in becoming welded into an efficient fighting unit. There were eight weeks of intensive training after its arrival in France in June, 1918. By August 7, it was ready to move up to the front by stages and take over its first sector. Late in the month it took over the St. Die sector, relieving several regiments of the American and French forces. At the time, the enemy was on the offensive and almost immediately the only all-Negro division received its baptism of war in the form of shrapnel and gas. The division was eager to attack the enemy, and early in September the opportunity came. The encounter resulted in the capture of several Germans by the Negro troops and the capture of two Negroes by the Germans.

When it became clear to the Germans that the division consisted almost entirely of Negroes they launched their propaganda campaign to accomplish with words what they had not been able to accomplish with arms. The Germans had sought to demoralize other Negro troops, but apparently it had reserved its most powerful propaganda offensive for the Ninety-second Division. On September 12 they scattered over the lines a circular which sought to persuade the Negroes to lay down their arms. They told the Negro soldiers that they should not be deluded into thinking that they were fighting for humanity and democracy. "What is Democracy? Personal freedom, all citizens enjoying the same rights socially and before the law. Do you enjoy the same rights as the white people do in America, the land of Freedom and Democracy, or are you rather not treated over there as second-class citizens? Can you go into a restaurant where white people dine? Can you get a seat in the theater where white people sit? . . . Is lynching and the most horrible crimes connected therewith a lawful proceeding in a democratic country?" The circular asserted that Germans liked Negroes and treated them as gentlemen in Germany. "Why, then, fight the Germans only for the benefit of the Wall Street robbers and to protect the millions they have loaned to the British, French, and Italians?" The Negroes were invited to come over to the German lines where they would find friends who would help them in the cause of liberty and democracy. Apparently the Negroes of the Ninety-second were unimpressed by the solicitations of the Germans. None deserted, and all seemed to have fought more energetically against the enemy.

In September and October the Ninety-second did its share of the fighting by holding two sectors during the heavy fighting of that period. There were numerous casualties from gas and enemy artillery fire. As the fighting became more intense, the men were more determined than ever to see the struggle through to the end. The official reports state that it became difficult in some regiments to send out small patrols, for every officer and man desired to participate. Company commanders solved disputes over priority among the volunteers for night patrols and raiding parties by promising places days in advance. The awards and citations which the men of the Ninety-second received were numerous. The entire first battalion of the 367th Infantry was cited for bravery in its participation in the drive toward Metz and was awarded the Croix de Guerre, while the colors of the regiment were decorated by order of the French high command. In the division 43 enlisted men and 14 Negro officers were cited for bravery in action and awarded the Distinguished Service Cross. Both the French and American governments cited numerous individual soldiers of the division for their heroism and awarded them appropriate decorations.

The feats of gallantry of Negroes in the service were similar to those performed by other American soldiers. Two examples will suffice. On November 10, 1918, a shell struck the house in which the switchboard was being operated at Point-à-Mousson. Sergeant Rufus B. Atwood rendered valuable assistance in reconstructing the switchboard and connecting new lines under heavy shell fire. The official order reported,

When the ammunition dump began to explode in the same neighborhood, he remained on the job, tapping new connections. After repairs were made from the first explosion, there were two to follow which completely wrecked the switchboard room and tore out all the lines which were newly fixed. Sergeant Atwood was left alone, and he established a new switchboard and the same connections they had at first. The coolness with which he went about his work and the initiative he took in handling the situation justifies his being mentioned in orders.

One of the most sensational feats in the war was that performed by Privates Henry Johnson of Albany, New York, and Needham Roberts, of Trenton, New Jersey, both members of the 369th Infantry. While on guard at a small outpost in May, 1918, a strong raiding party of Germans numbering almost twenty made a surprise attack and fired on the two Negroes, wounding both. When the Germans were within fighting distance, Johnson opened fire, and Roberts, lying on the ground, threw grenades. The Germans continued to advance, and as they were about to be captured Johnson drew his bolo knife from his belt and attacked the Germans in a hand-to-hand encounter. He succeeded in freeing Roberts from the Germans who were dragging him away and slashed several so mercilessly that they died of the wounds. Colonel Hayward wrote to Johnson's wife, "The Germans, doubtless thinking it was a host instead of two brave Colored boys fighting like tigers at bay, picked up their dead and wounded and slunk away, leaving many weapons and a part of their shot-riddled clothing, and leaving a trail of blood, which we followed at dawn near to their lines." The killing of at least four of the enemy and the wounding of perhaps twice as many more have caused this encounter to become known—and properly so—as "The Battle of Henry Johnson." Both men received the Croix de Guerre for their gallantry.

The casualties of Negro soldiers seem to indicate the general disregard for personal safety which characterized the American army and which contributed substantially to the victory of November 11, 1918. In the Ninety-second Division, for example, 208 enlisted men were killed in action, while 40 others died of wounds received in battle. There were 551 who were wounded in action, and 672 who were gassed. In some of the Negro regiments attached to the French army the proportion of casualties was even higher. In the 371st Regiment, 113 men were killed in action, 25 died of wounds, and 859 were wounded.

That the price which the Negroes paid for victory was highly regarded by the Allies is clearly seen in the praise accorded them by ranking military officials. General Goybet, the commanding officer of the 157th French Division said, "Never will the 157th Division forget the indomitable dash, the heroic rush of the American regiments (Negro) up the observatory ridge and into the plains of Monthois. . . . These crack regiments overcame every obstacle with a most complete contempt for danger. Through their steady devotion, the 'Red Hand Division' for nine whole days of severe struggle was constantly leading the way for the victorious advance of the Fourth Army." In January, 1919, General Pershing, the commander of the American Expeditionary Forces, said, "I want you officers and soldiers of the 92nd Division to know that the 92nd Division stands second to none in the record you have made since your arrival in France. I am proud of the part you have played in the great conflict which ended on the 11th of November. Yet you have only done what the American people expected you to do and you have measured up to every expectation of the Commander in Chief."

Some effort was made to maintain a high morale among the Negroes during their tour of duty in France. Most of the combat units had their own bands. One of the best known was the 369th Regiment Band under the direction of James R. Europe, assisted by Noble Sissle. Another was the 350th Field Artillery Band under J. T. Bynum. It was said that these musical organizations "filled France with jazz" and won for Negroes the admiration of their hosts. There were no Negro theatrical entertainers overseas. A unit, headed by the Reverend H. H. Proctor, speaker, J. E. Blanton, song leader, and Helen Hagan, pianist, traveled through France and staged programs for the benefit of the soldiers. White entertainment groups almost always bypassed Negro soldiers. In July, 1918, Elsie Janis, the well-known actress, visited the Ninety-second Division, but she entertained only a small group since her coming had not been announced.

Welfare work was carried on largely by the Y.M.C.A. and the Y.W.C.A., although the Knights of Columbus and the Federal Council of Churches devoted some attention to the soldiers. Of the 7,850 "Y" workers who went overseas, 87 were Negroes, 19 of whom were women. Only three of the women, however, were in France during the actual fighting. At the base ports, it was the task of the "Y" huts to provide classes for illiterates, maintain libraries, operate canteens, provide letter-writing facilities, and perform innumerable other services for the comfort of the men. Among the Negroes engaged in this work were Matthew Bullock, J. C. Croom, John Hope, W. J. Faulkner, Max Yergan, Mrs. Addie Hunton, and Miss Kathryn Johnson. Of the 60 Negro chaplains in the United States army, approximately 20 ministered to the spiritual needs of Negro soldiers overseas. As religious speakers, song leaders, and teachers, they contributed to the morale and the morality of the Negro soldier. Although the Negro nurses in the United States offered their services in large numbers, the government did not see fit to accept and send them overseas until the fighting had ended. During periods of rest and recuperation as well as after hostilities were over, Negroes attended several of the Universities of France, including Paris, Bordeaux, Toulouse, and Marseilles.

An important aspect of the welfare of Negro soldiers was the manner in which they were treated by the French. For the most part they moved about freely in France and associated pleasantly with French men and women, much to the chagrin of many white American soldiers. Some whites took it upon themselves to warn the French against the Negroes. American whites told the French that Negroes could not be treated with common civility, that they were rapists, and that Americans were compelled to lynch and burn Negroes in order to keep them in their place. The concern of white Americans became so important that it received official cognizance in an order issued by General James Erwin that Negroes were not to associate with French women. In August, 1918, a document was circulated among the French, *Secret Information Concerning Black Troops*. It was necessary, the document asserted, to maintain complete separation of Negroes and whites, lest Negroes assault and rape white women. It would be unfortunate if French officers associated socially with Negro officers or have any contact with them outside the requirements of military service. Neither the civilians nor the soldiers of France seemed to take seriously the counsel that was offered to them by white Americans, for they continued to welcome Negroes into their homes and sought to make their black defenders as comfortable as possible.

Toward the end of the war reports came to America that Negro soldiers were attacking and criminally assaulting French women in large numbers. The fear was expressed openly that Negroes in France had developed habits and practices that would be detrimental to inter-racial stability upon their return to the United States. The matter became of such concern that in December, 1918, Robert R. Moton, Booker T. Washington's successor at Tuskegee, was asked to go to France to investigate the rumors and to examine the conditions affecting Negro soldiers. The Secretary of War and the President of the United States placed every facility at Dr. Moton's disposal and made it possible for him to travel freely among the Negro troops. The commanding general of the Ninety-second Division asserted that the crime of rape was very prevalent among his men and that there had been at least 26 cases within recent months. Upon examination of the records which the general furnished, Moton found that in the division of more than 12,000 men only 7 cases involved the crime. Only 2 men had been found guilty, and 1 of the 2 convictions had been turned down at general headquarters. In other places it became clear that charges against Negroes were few and that convictions were fewer still. Moton also found that, contrary to persistent rumors, the Ninety-second Division had not been a failure, and that only a very small detachment of a single battalion of one regiment had failed. General Pershing assured him that it was probable that any officers under similar adverse circumstances would have failed.

Dr. Moton made many speeches to groups of Negro soldiers. In his autobiography he reports that he told them:

> You have been tremendously tested. . . . Your record has sent a thrill of joy and satisfaction to the hearts of millions of black and white Americans, rich and poor, high and low. . . . You will go back to America heroes, as you really are. You will go back as you have carried yourselves over here—in a straightforward, manly, and modest way. If I were you, I would find a job as soon as possible and get to work. . . . I hope no one will do anything in peace to spoil the magnificent record you have made in war.[1]

Negro soldiers who heard Dr. Moton reported that he told them not to expect in the United States the kind of freedom they had enjoyed in France and that they must remain content with the same position they had always occupied in the United States. Negro soldiers and civilians were outraged and spoke of Dr. Moton in the harshest manner. Regardless of what he said it

[1] *Finding a Way Out,* by R. R. Moton (Doubleday and Co., 1920), p. 263.

became clear that he did little to allay the fears of Negroes and to prepare them for their return to the United States.

Many Negroes both in the United States and in other parts of the world desired to bring the plight of darker peoples before the Peace Conference that met at Versailles at the end of the war. The only consideration that the darker peoples received was the disposition that was made of the African colonies of the defeated countries. The Mandates system gave England, France, Belgium, and the Union of South Africa the administration of the former German colonies under the supervision of the League of Nations. Some Americans opposed the treaty because they feared that membership of darker countries would make the permanent peace organization a "colored league of nations." Others feared that some agencies of the League might attempt to exercise some influence in the domestic affairs of the United States.

Hoping to place the cause of darker peoples before the world in a dramatic way, W. E. B. DuBois called a Pan-African Congress to meet in Paris simultaneously with the Peace Conference. Dr. DuBois had been asked by the N.A.A.C.P. to go to France in December, 1918, to investigate the treatment of Negro soldiers and to collect information concerning their participation in the war. Through Blaise Diagne, a Senegalese member of the Chamber of Deputies and highly respected in French circles, DuBois secured Clemenceau's permission to hold the Congress in the Grand Hotel in Paris in February, 1919. There were 57 delegates, including 16 American Negroes, 20 West Indians, and 12 Africans. Although the results of the meeting were small, it called the attention of the world to the fact that Negroes in various parts of the world had a material interest in the deliberations at Paris and that they were seeking for themselves the democratic treatment for which they had fought. It served, also, to stimulate interest in the several subsequent congresses that were held in the next few years.

On the Home Front

The Negroes who remained at home during the struggle were no less enthusiastic in their support of the war than those who faced the Germans on the Western Front. It has been estimated, for example, that in the five loan campaigns Negroes purchased more than $250,000,000 worth of bonds and stamps. Mrs. Mary

B. Talbert, president of the National Association of Colored Women, reported that Negro women alone purchased more than $5,000,000 worth of bonds in the Third Liberty Loan. When a Negro cook in Memphis was approached by her employer regarding the purchase of a one hundred dollar bond, she replied that she didn't want such a small bond. "I want a thousand dollar bond, and I'll pay cash for it." A Negro farmer in Georgia, with two sons in the army, bought a $1,000 bond, thereby putting fresh spirit into the local campaign. Negro insurance companies purchased large quantities of bonds in each drive. The North Carolina Mutual Life Insurance Company, for example, purchased $300,000 worth of bonds in less than two years. Similar support was also given to the fund-raising campaigns of the "Y" organizations and the American Red Cross.

The United States found itself especially dependent on Negroes in the program to produce and conserve food, because of the large number of Negro farmers and cooks. Some work was done among Negroes through the educational department of the Food Administration, under the direction of A. U. Craig of the Dunbar High School in Washington. Herbert Hoover, the Director of the Foods Administration, sought to enlarge the work among Negroes, and to that end he appointed Ernest Atwell of Tuskegee as field worker for Alabama and later for the Southern states. In September, 1918, Atwell came to Washington, where he served as director of the activities of Negroes from the headquarters of the Food Administration. Through Atwell the Director circulated an open letter to the Negroes of the United States, asking for their cooperation to help in general food conservation. In part the letter stated, "The Food Administration realizes that the Negro people of this nation can be of the utmost help in food conservation and food production. Every Negro man, woman, and child can render a definite service by responding to the appeal and instructions of the Food Administration and its representatives. The Negroes have shown themselves loyal and responsive in every national crisis. . . . I am confident that they will respond to the suggestions of the Food Administration and thus prove again their patriotism for the winning of this war." Negro directors were appointed in eighteen states, and organizations were perfected to carry forward the program of food conservation.

One of the most important social and economic phenomena

on the home front was the migration of hundreds of Negroes out of the South during the war. The fundamental cause of the exodus was economic, though there were certainly some important social considerations. The severe labor depression in the South in 1914 and 1915 sent wages down to 75 cents per day and less. The damage of the boll weevil to cotton crops in 1915 and 1916 discouraged many who were dependent on cotton for their subsistence. Floods in the summer of 1915 left thousands of Negroes destitute and homeless and ready to accept almost anything in preference to the uncertainty of life in the South. Meanwhile, the wheels of Northern industry were turning more rapidly than ever, and the demand for laborers was increasing. The sharp decline in foreign immigration from more than one million in 1914 to slightly more than three hundred thousand in the following year created a labor shortage that sent agents scurrying to the South to entice Negroes as well as whites to move North to secure employment in industry. Injustice in the Southern courts, the lack of privileges, disfranchisement, segregation, and lynching served as important stimuli for Negroes to move out of the South. The North came to be regarded as the "land of promise," and the Negro press did much to persuade Southern Negroes to abandon the existence which held nothing better for them than second-class citizenship. The *Chicago Defender* exclaimed, "To die from the bite of frost is far more glorious than at the hands of a mob." In 1917 the *Christian Recorder* wrote, "If a million Negroes move north and west in the next twelve-month, it will be one of the greatest things for the Negro since the Emancipation Proclamation."

In 1916 the movement spread like wild. fire among Negroes. By the summer of that year the migration had reached flood tide in the states of the deep South. The Pennsylvania Railroad brought 12,000 to work in its yards and on its tracks; all but 2,000 came from Florida and Georgia. Even Negro professional men moved North to continue to serve their clientele. The South was alarmed. Officials of Jacksonville, Florida, passed an ordinance requiring migration agents to pay a license fee of $1,000. White citizens of many Southern towns threatened Negroes, while the white press urged Negroes to remain in the South. Homes were without servants, farms were without laborers, churches were empty, and houses were deserted. It was estimated that by the end of 1918 more than one million Negroes had left the South. This estimate seems too generous, for the

Bureau of the Census reported that the states of the North and West showed a net gain of 330,000 Negroes for the decade ending in 1920.

Although numerous unfortunate incidents resulted from the wholesale movement of Negroes into the North and West, the migration, coming when it did, gave Negroes an opportunity for industrial employment which they had never enjoyed before, and relieved the labor shortage during the crucial years of the war. The Department of Labor, taking cognizance of the importance of Negro labor early in the war, created a Division of Negro Economics under the direction of George Edmund Haynes. This division was to advise the Secretary of Labor and the heads of bureaus on plans and policies for improving conditions of Negro workers and for securing their full cooperation with white workers and employers for maximum production. Several state and local advisory committees were set up to carry on the work of cooperation and to reduce friction between white and Negro workers. State conferences were held in twelve states, with the cooperation of the governors, employment agencies, employers, and workers. When the year's report of the Negro Worker's Advisory Committee of North Carolina was released, Governor Bickett said, "If every man, white and black, in the United States could read and digest this report, it would go a great way toward solving all our race questions."

The National Urban League was also active in helping with the adjustment of the Negroes who had recently moved to the industrial centers of the North. In 1916 it held a National Conference on Migration in New York, and issued recommendations and advice to employers and migrants. It established branches in cities like Chicago, Detroit, Cleveland, St. Louis, Philadelphia, and Pittsburgh, and assisted in the adjustment and distribution of Negro labor. The League also sought to solve some of the delicate problems arising out of Negro migration, such as housing, recreation facilities, and the relation of Negroes to organized labor.

Negroes were suspicious of organized labor because of their systematic exclusion of black workers in the past. They therefore organized several labor groups of their own, such as the Associated Colored Employees of America. In 1917 the American Federation of Labor expressed the view that the workers of all races should unite and present a common front to industry. It was hoped that Negroes could be brought into the labor movement in order to prevent them from breaking strikes. In 1918 the Council of the American Federation of Labor invited several prominent Negroes to discuss the matter. Among those invited were Robert R. Moton of Tuskegee, Emmett J. Scott of the War Department, Eugene Kinckle Jones of the National Urban League, and Fred Moore of the *New York Age*. Little came of the deliberations except an expression of the willingness of both sides to cooperate further. During the war few unions of organized labor accepted Negroes into full membership.

Negroes found employment in most of the industries of the North during the war. They were engaged in the manufacture of ammunition and of iron and steel products. They were in the meat packing industries, and worked in large numbers in automobile and truck production and in the manufacture of electrical products. There were 26,648 Negroes in 46 of the 55 occupations incident to shipbuilding under the United States Shipping Board. A Negro, Charles Knight, at the plant of the Bethlehem Steel Corporation at Sparrow's Point, Maryland, broke the world's record for driving rivets in building steel ships. A Negro pile-driving crew building shipways at Hog Island, near Philadelphia, broke the world's record for driving piles. More than 75,000 Negroes worked in the coal mines of Alabama, Illinois, Pennsylvania, Ohio, and West Virginia. Approximately 150,000 Negroes assisted in the operation of the railroads, while another 150,000 served to keep up other vital means of communication. In 152 typical industrial plants there were 21,547 Negro women performing 75 specific tasks.

High government officials very properly concerned themselves with the problems of Negro morale during the war, for there were many indications that while there was a vigorous pursuit of democracy in Europe there was a wide-spread destruction of it at home. At least 38 Negroes lost their lives at the hands of lynching parties in 1917, while in the following year the number had risen to 58. Race clashes in the North and South did not diminish. In Tennessee more than 3,000 spectators responded to the invitation of a newspaper to come out and witness the burning of a "live Negro." In East St. Louis, Illinois, at least 40 Negroes lost their lives in a riot that grew out of the employment of Negroes in a factory holding government contracts. Negroes were stabbed, clubbed, and hanged; and one two-year-old Negro child was shot and thrown in the doorway of a burning building. The Germans made the most of these unfortunate incidents in their effort to spread anti-war sentiment among Negroes. They kept a careful record of lynchings and the attacks of whites on Negroes and urged Negroes to desert the struggle out of which they were gaining nothing. While the propaganda had no noticeable effect on the morale of Negroes, the President of the United States saw fit to issue a strong public statement against lynching and mob violence.

The Negro press, for the most part, supported the war enthusiastically. In June, 1918, Emmett J. Scott held a conference of 31 leading Negro newspaper men, who, while pledging their support of the war, drew up a bill of particulars in which they denounced mob violence, called for the use of Negro Red Cross nurses, requested the return of Colonel Charles Young to active service, and asked for the appointment of a Negro war correspondent. Most of their requests were granted, though somewhat belatedly. Ralph Tyler of Columbus, Ohio, was designated by the Committee on Public Information as a war correspondent

SILENT PROTEST PARADE ON FIFTH AVENUE IN NEW YORK. *Staged by the N.A.A.C.P. on July 28, 1917, in protest to the East St. Louis riots and other violence to Negroes. Other banners carried in the parade read, "Mother, do lynchers go to heaven?"; "Mr. President, why not make America safe for Democracy?"; and "Pray for the Lady Macbeths of East St. Louis." Underwood & Underwood.*

and went to Europe to send back dispatches about the exploits of Negro soldiers. Negro newspapers carried his stories which were generally glowing accounts of the gallantry and heroism of the Negro outfits. The *Messenger,* a newspaper published in New York by A. Philip Randolph and Chandler Owen, was one of the few Negro journals that refused to go along in an all-out support of the war. For an article, "Pro-Germanism among Negroes" the editors were sentenced to jail for two and one-half years and their second-class mailing privileges were denied them. The war effort received unexpected support, however, from the *Crisis* whose editor, W. E. B. DuBois, wrote an editorial in July, 1918, entitled, "Close Ranks." In part he said, "Let us not hesitate. Let us, while this war lasts, forget our special grievances and close our ranks shoulder to shoulder with our white citizens and the allied nations that are fighting for democracy."

The talk of democracy during the war had raised vague hopes even among the most militant Negroes. Both at home and abroad they had supported the war that was to make the world safe for democracy. Perhaps it was too much to hope that there could be the full realization of democracy within the foreseeable future. It was not too much, most Negroes reasoned, to hope that the war's end would usher in a new period of opportunity both in the area of economic life and in the sphere of civil rights. Doubtless they realized that the pursuit of democracy was a continuing process that must be carried on long after the last gun was fired. They hardly realized, however, that many of the forces which operated to prevent the establishment of an enduring peace for the entire world, as well as the peculiar local forces which had flourished in the very warp and woof of American civilization, would serve to make democracy seem for them as elusive and as ephemeral as the lengthening shadows of eventide.

XXV •

Democracy Escapes

The Reaction

● *Although some Negro soldiers who served in France were* hesitant about making the return trip to the United States lest they lose what democracy and freedom they had found in faraway places, the great majority seemed anxious to rejoin their loved ones in their native land. Some doubtless believed that conditions would be better than before the war, while others were indifferent to the future, thinking only of the pleasures of being home again. They were not required to wait very long before finding out what changes, if any, had taken place in the United States, for shortly after the Armistice was signed the American military authorities began to make preparations for the return and demobilization of American troops. Some Negro troops were detained to assist in the tasks of cleaning up the camp sites and clearing away the debris left from the battles, but the greater part of them were en route to the United States within four months after the end of the war. By April, 1919, many Negro troops were already in the United States, and some of them were being demobilized.

Since most of the Negro troops disembarked in the New York area, their first reception in the United States was enthusiastic. New York City seemed never to tire of the apparently endless parades of troops, both black and white, that proceeded almost immediately from their ships to make the triumphal march up Fifth Avenue. When New York's own Negro regiment, the

369th, returned on February 17, 1919, approximately one million persons witnessed their parade from lower New York up through Fifth Avenue to Harlem. A similar reception was given various units of the Ninety-second Division, the last of whose troops landed at Hoboken on March 12, 1919. Other cities, however, vied with New York in welcoming their Negro troops. Buffalo turned out en masse to receive its darker brothers, while huge crowds filled the streets of St. Louis to cheer the Negroes who had fought in Europe. When the 370th, the "Old Eighth Illinois," reached Chicago, much of the business of the city was suspended to welcome the veterans. The soldiers paraded through the Loop as well as through the thickly populated Negro South Side, and in many places the crowds were so dense that the troops could not march in regular formation. If the parades were not so large and the enthusiasm not so great in the South, it could easily be attributed to the fact that no Negro units came from single communities, as well as to the fact that Southern whites did not enjoy seeing Negroes armed with powerful weapons. Few stopped to give much consideration to such a matter, however. It was a time of jubilation, and Negroes were determined to enjoy it while it lasted.

The period of jubilation was short-lived, however, for the business of settling down to post-war living became more urgent with every passing day. Indeed, all America was anxious to put the war behind it and return to a peace-time existence. Industry was desirous of beginning its program of filling the huge backlog of orders for goods that were not produced during the war. Labor was ready to press for demands that it could not afford to make during the war, and to perfect its organization to the point where its effectiveness could not be nullified by strike-breakers. Politicians could hardly wait to get the peace treaties out of the way in order to wage a campaign in 1920 that they hoped would be free of the issues of the war. Militant Negro leaders were anxious, too. They did not want to return to a pre-war normalcy, but to move forward to a new basis for democratic living in the United States. In May, 1919, the editor of the *Crisis* undertook to speak for returning Negro soldiers when he said:

We return from the slavery of uniform which the world's madness demanded us to don to the freedom of civil garb. We stand again to look America squarely in the face and call a spade a spade. We sing: This country of ours, despite all its better souls have done and dreamed, is yet a shameful land.

It *lynches*. . . . It *disfranchises* its own citizens. . . . It encourages *ignorances*. . . . It steals from us. . . . It insults us. . . . We *return*. We *return from fighting*. We *return fighting*.

Make way for Democracy! We saved it in France, and by the Great Jehovah, we will save it in the U.S.A., or know the reason why.

The editor had not spoken too early, for if he and other Negroes were determined to secure a larger share of democracy for themselves, there were many white citizens who were as determined to see that there should be no wholesale distribution of the blessings of liberty. Whites had steeled themselves against the day when Negro soldiers would return and make demands for first-class citizenship, and they were ready to put the machinery they had perfected into operation. The Ku Klux Klan had been revived in the Southern states as early as 1915. Its growth was slow until the end of the war, at which time it came forth with a broad program for "uniting native-born white Christians for concerted action in the preservation of American institutions and the supremacy of the white race." Within a year it grew from an impotent organization of a few thousand members to a militant union of more than 100,000 white-hooded knights. It declared itself against Negroes, Japanese and other orientals, Roman Catholics, Jews, and all foreign-born persons. It capitalized on the isolationist reaction that followed the war and spread into areas where previously there had been few manifestations of race hatred. It assumed the responsibility for punishing persons whom it considered dangerous to the growth of its ideas and spearheaded the drive for violence and intimidation toward Negroes. Within ten months, shortly after the close of the war, the Klan made more than 200 public appearances in 27 states. Cells of the organization flourished in several New England states, as well as in New York, Indiana, Illinois, Michigan, and other Northern and Midwestern states. Its assumption of a semi-official role, in taking the law into its own hands and in luring public servants into its membership, stimulated the lawlessness and violence that characterized the post-war period in the United States.

At a public meeting one Klansman exclaimed, "We would not rob the colored population of their rights, but we demand that they respect the rights of the white race in whose country they are permitted to reside." Actually, there were few rights of Negroes that the Klan felt obliged to respect, and it acted in a manner confirming its contention that the United States was a "white man's country." In Texas the Klan became the instrument of a new Negro enslavement, forcing Negroes to work and pick cotton at wages they would not have accepted if the decision had been left to them. Throughout the South and Southwest Negroes lived in constant fear of the hooded bands of night riders who burned crosses to terrify the non-Gentile element of the population. In the West the Klan was also active, especially against the Japanese population. Wherever it established itself it was blamed, correctly or incorrectly, for the atrocities committed in the vicinity. There were floggings, branding with acid, tarring and feathering, hangings, and burnings. The victims were largely, though not entirely, Negroes. It was a new day, indeed—a new day of violence and terror.

White citizens, in and out of the Klan, poured out a wrath upon the Negro population shortly after the war that could hardly be viewed as fit punishment even for a treasonable group of persons. More than 70 Negroes were lynched during the first year of the post-war period. Ten Negro soldiers, several still in their uniforms, were lynched. Mississippi and Georgia mobs murdered three returned soldiers each; in Arkansas two were lynched; while Florida and Alabama each took the life of a Negro soldier by mob violence. Fourteen Negroes were burned publicly, eleven of whom were burned alive. In utter despair a Negro editor of Charleston, South Carolina, cried out, "There is scarcely a day that passes that newspapers don't tell about a Negro soldier lynched in his uniform. Why do they lynch Negroes, anyhow? With a white judge, a white jury, white public sentiment, white officers of the law, it is just as impossible for a Negro accused of crime, or even suspected of crime, to escape the white man's vengeance or his justice as it would be for a fawn to escape that wanders accidentally into a den of hungry lions. So why not give him the semblance of a trial."

It was the summer of 1919, called by James Weldon Johnson "The Red Summer," that ushered in the greatest period of interracial strife the nation had ever witnessed. From June to the end of the year approximately 25 race riots were held in American urban centers. Some were large; others were small; all were indicative of a thoroughly malodorous situation in race relations. Even after the war the migration of Negroes to urban centers continued and, in some areas, increased. Jobs were not so plentiful as they had been during the war years, and competition strained the relations of whites and Negroes. Meanwhile, the high rents in the segregated residential areas continued. Unrest and disappointment seized a considerable portion of the Negro population, and when it became clear that many whites were seeking to deprive them of some of the gains they had made during the war, Negroes bristled into action and showed a willingness to defend themselves that they had not shown before. The riots were not confined to any section of the country. They were Northern and Southern, Eastern and Western— wherever whites and Negroes undertook the task of living together. Egged on by native fascist organizations like the Ku Klux Klan, the lawless element of the population undertook to terrorize the Negroes into submission.

In July, 1919, Longview, Texas, witnessed the nightmare of a race riot. Several white men were shot when they went into the Negro section of the town in search of a Negro school teacher who was accused of sending a release to the *Chicago Defender* concerning the lynching of a Negro during the previous month. Whites of the town were alarmed over this show of strength among the Negroes, and they poured into the Negro section determined to teach the Negroes a lesson. Many homes were burned, a Negro school principal was flogged on the streets, and several leading Negro citizens were run out of town. It was several days before the town returned to normalcy. In the following week a riot of more violent proportions broke out in the nation's capital. Newspaper reports of Negroes assaulting white women whipped the irresponsible elements of the population into a frenzy, although it early became clear that the reports had no basis in fact. Mobs, consisting primarily of white sailors, soldiers, and marines, ran amuck through the streets of Washington for three days, killing several Negroes and injuring scores of others. On the third day the Negroes retaliated when hoodlums sought to invade and burn the Negro section of the city. The casualty list mounted, but before order was restored the number of whites killed and wounded had increased considerably due to the belated but stern action which the Negroes took.

The most serious racial outbreak occurred in Chicago late in July of the "Red Summer." Chicago had become to the Southern Negro "the top of the world," and thousands had migrated there during and after the war in search of employment and freedom. Within less than a decade the Negro population of the city had more than doubled, and the census of 1920 showed approximately 109,000 Negroes living there. There was, of course, some friction in industry, but because of the abundance of jobs it had remained at a minimum. The most serious friction came in housing and recreation. Negroes were spreading into white neighborhoods, whereupon the whites sought to prevent it by bombing the homes of Negroes. Groups of young men took it upon themselves to frighten the Negroes into submission and to prevent their continued movement into white sections of the city. In June two Negroes were murdered, an act that ushered in a month of terror.

The riot that began on July 27 had its immediate origin in an altercation at a Lake Michigan beach. A young Negro swimming offshore had drifted into water that was customarily used by whites. White swimmers commanded him to return to his part of the beach, and some threw stones at him. When the young Negro went down and drowned, the Negroes declared that he had been murdered. Although his recovered body showed no marks of having been stoned, it was too late to save the city from a riot that was already in progress. Distorted rumors circulated among Negroes and whites concerning the incident and the subsequent events at the beach. Mobs sprang up in various parts of the city, and during the entire night there was sporadic fighting. In the next afternoon white bystanders meddled with Negroes as they went home from work. Some were pulled off street cars and whipped. Many persons of both races were injured in these clashes, and at least five were killed. On the Negro South Side a group of young Negroes stabbed an old Italian peddler to death, and a white laundry operator was also stabbed to death. During that day and the next the riot spread, with mobs of both races doing what they could to terrorize the opposite group. For thirteen days Chicago was without law and order, despite the fact that the militia was called out on the fourth day of the riot. When the authorities counted the casualties the tally sheet gave the appearance of the results of a miniature war. Thirty-eight persons had been killed, including 15 whites and 23 Negroes; of the 537 persons injured, 178 were whites and 342 were Negroes. There is no record of the racial identity of the remaining 17. More than 1,000 families, mostly Negroes, were homeless due to the burnings and general destruction of property. It was the nation's worst race war and shocked even the most indifferent persons into a realization that interracial conflicts in the United States had reached a serious stage.

During the next two months riots occurred, among other places, in Knoxville, Tennessee, Omaha, Nebraska, and Elaine, Arkansas. The Knoxville riot was started when a white woman stumbled and killed herself while running from a Negro who was later accused of attempting to assault her. When the Negro was arrested, a mob was formed and an attempt was made to take him from the jail. During the general riot which followed scores of people were injured, some fatally, and more than $50,000 worth of property was destroyed. The troops that were called out went into the Negro section and "shot it up" when a false rumor was circulated that some Negroes had killed two white men. Negroes were stopped on the streets and searched. One man going three blocks was searched seven times. A Negro newspaper declared, "The indignities which colored women suffered at the hands of these soldiers would make the devil blush for shame."

In Omaha a mob almost completely destroyed the county courthouse by fire in order to secure a Negro who was in jail on the charge of attacking a white girl. The group succeeded in seizing the Negro, whereupon he was dragged through the streets, was shot more than a thousand times, and was mutilated beyond recognition. He was finally hanged downtown at one of the busiest intersections. Meanwhile, much damage was done to property, and several Negroes were severely beaten. Negroes in Elaine, Arkansas, met to make plans to force their landlords to make a fair settlement with them. The meeting was broken up by a deputy sheriff and a posse, and in the melee the deputy was killed. A reign of terror began in which scores of Negroes were shot and several killed. In the trials which lasted less than an hour, 12 Negro farmers were sentenced to death and 67 others were given long prison terms. The decisions were later nullified by the Supreme Court which found that the Negroes had not been given a fair trial. (See Chapter XXIII.)

Although rioting continued for the next few years, few outbreaks equaled in proportion those of 1919. Two years later, in June, 1921, the Negroes and whites of Tulsa, Oklahoma, engaged in fighting which some residents prefer to call a "race war," in which 9 whites and 21 Negroes were known to have been killed and several hundred injured. When news reached Negroes of the accusation of an assault of a young white woman by a Negro, Negroes took arms to the jail to protect the accused person, who, it was rumored, would be lynched. Altercations between whites and Negroes at the jail spread to other parts of the city, and general rioting, looting, and houseburning began. Four companies of the National Guard were called out, but by the time order was restored more than one million dollars worth of property had been destroyed or damaged. This progressive young city of the Southwest was thus added to the list of communities in which there was no interracial peace. Detroit, in 1925, joined the ranks by seeking to prevent a Negro physician, Dr. O. H. Sweet, from living in a home he had purchased in a white neighborhood. When a mob gathered around his home and threw stones, a white man was killed by gunfire coming from the house. Dr. Sweet, his brother, and his friends in the house were brought to trial. The National Association for the Advancement of Colored People came to their defense, employing Clarence Darrow and Arthur Garfield Hays as the defense attorneys. All were finally acquitted, but irreparable damage had been done not only to the Sweet family but also to race relations in Detroit.

In the post-war racial strife the Negro's willingness to fight and to die in his own defense injected a new factor into America's most perplexing social problem. It was no longer a case of one race intimidating another into submission. Now it was war in the full sense of the word, and Negroes were as determined to win it as they had been in Europe. The increasing urbanization of Negroes, with its accompanying stimulation of self-respect and racial cohesiveness, had much to do with the resistance that Negroes offered to their would-be oppressors. They had, moreover, imbibed freely of the democratic doctrine that had been expounded so generally during the war. Even if they could not win in the one-sided struggle they were carrying on, they sought to make a good showing. One of the outstanding poets of the period, Claude McKay, expressed the feelings of a great many Negroes when he wrote:

> If we must die, let it not be like hogs
> Hunted and penned in an inglorious spot,
> While round us bark the mad and hungry dogs,
> Making their mock at our accursed lot.
> If we must die, O let us nobly die,
> So that our precious blood may not be shed
> In vain; then even the monsters we defy

Shall be constrained to honor us though dead!
O kinsmen! we must meet the common foe!
Though far outnumbered let us show us brave,
And for their thousand blows deal one deathblow!
What though before us lies the open grave?
Like men we'll face the murderous, cowardly pack,
Pressed to the wall, dying but fighting back!

Many whites freely intimated that it was foreign influences, especially the association on the basis of equality with the French during the war and the propaganda of Bolshevists after the war, that caused Negroes to fight back. Negroes, however, ridiculed this view and contended that they were fighting only for what they thought was right. In October, 1919, the *Pittsburgh Courier* declared, "As long as the Negro submits to lynchings, burnings, and oppressions—and says nothing he is a loyal American citizen. But when he decides that lynchings and burnings shall cease even at the cost of some bloodshed in America, then he is a Bolshevist." The militant *Crusader* regarded such accusations as a compliment. In a scathing denunciation of mob violence and rioting in America its editor asserted, "If to fight for one's rights is to be Bolshevists, then we are Bolshevists and let them make the most of it!"

Negroes loudly protested against practices which they termed injustices and oppressions. They freely admitted that democracy had escaped, despite the fact that they had pursued it with an earnestness and vigor of which few other races could boast. Disillusionment and despair settled over them, and they could express little but dejection in their utterances, which were largely directed rather indiscriminately toward the white population. After describing the burning alive of a young Negro boy in Vicksburg, Mississippi, the *Challenge Magazine* of Chicago exclaimed, "The 'German Hun' is beaten but the world is made no safer for Democracy. Humanity has been defended but lifted no higher. Democracy never will be safe in America until these occurrences are made impossible either by the execution of the law or with double barrel shot guns. . . . I hate every Hun, and the worst I know are the ones that thrive under the free institutions of America." It would take more than utterances to gain a respected place for Negroes in American life. Indeed, it became clearer that it would take more than the feverish fighting back that Negroes courageously performed in times of crisis. Intelligent planning and action were needed; but the difficulty lay in

taking such steps in a climate so completely charged with emotion and tension. Small wonder that the programs for the salvation of the Negro that evolved during the period were of such
varied approaches and such diverse goals.

The Voice of Protest Rises

In the years that immediately followed the first World War no
meeting of a national Negro organization neglected to register
its protest against the failure of the United States to grant
first-class citizenship to the Negro. In July, 1919, the National
Association for the Advancement of Colored People meeting in
Cleveland adopted resolutions which expressed its great concern
over the status of the Negro. In September of the same year the
National Equal Rights League, at its meeting in Washington,
followed the lead of the N.A.A.C.P. In the following month the
National Race Congress also met in Washington and passed
resolutions of protest. At about the same time the National
Baptist Convention declared itself in favor of a more complete
integration of the Negro in American life. It was the
N.A.A.C.P., however, that took the leadership in setting up a
program of assault against bigotry and injustice in America. In
May, 1919, it had held a national conference on lynching at
which the chief speaker was Charles Evans Hughes. The organization decided to carry on a relentless crusade against lynching
and to raise a huge fund to publicize its program and to defend
persecuted Negroes. Largely through the efforts of Mrs. Mary
Talbert and others, the Association had raised more than
$45,000 by 1924.

Late in 1919 the Association took the first steps toward
securing the passage of a federal law against lynching. After
carefully working to secure the support of Senators and Representatives, James Weldon Johnson, the Secretary of the Association, succeeded in 1921 in getting Representative L. C. Dyer of
Missouri to introduce in the House a bill "to assure to persons
within the jurisdiction of every state the equal protection of the
laws, and to punish the crime of lynching." Immediately the
Representatives from the Southern states began organizing to
defeat the proposed bill. They spoke on the floor of the Congress
in favor of mob rule and defied the federal government to

interfere with the police power of the states. It was not possible for them to prevent a vote in the House of Representatives, and the bill passed, 230–119. The task in the Senate was infinitely more difficult, and the Association doubled its efforts to achieve the herculean task of securing its passage in the upper house. A memorial signed by 24 governors, 39 mayors, 29 college presidents and professors, and a large number of editors, jurists, and lawyers was sent to the Senate urging its passage. The Association published full-page advertisements in such newspapers as the *New York Times* and the *Atlanta Constitution* calling attention to the necessity for such a bill. When the bill reached the floor of the Senate the Southern Senators, led by Underwood of Alabama and Harrison of Mississippi, succeeded in organizing a filibuster that ultimately prevented a vote on the measure. The Republicans, showing a decided lack of interest, voted to abandon it. Numerous similar bills have been introduced since that time, including the Costigan-Wagner bill of 1935 and the Wagner-Gavagan bill of 1940, but all of them have met a similar fate.

The N.A.A.C.P. undertook to make a thorough investigation of crimes committed against Negroes and to inform the public concerning them. In 1919 it published *Thirty Years of Lynching in the United States, 1889–1918,* which was a revelation with regard to the causes of lynchings and the circumstances under which the crimes occurred. A young investigator, Walter White, was hired to go to the scenes of crimes and to secure as much data as possible concerning the tragedies. These reports were published by the Association and distributed widely. In 1929 White brought out a work entitled *Rope and Faggot, A Biography of Judge Lynch* which was based on his findings over a period of ten years. The Association held meetings to protest against lynching. In 1921, for example, more than 200 such meetings were held in various parts of the United States. The columns of its official organ, the *Crisis,* were filled with factual reports regarding crimes against Negroes, as well as appeals for support of the program of the organization.

The Association undertook to secure in the courts the rights which Negroes could not otherwise obtain. Encouraged by its success in the cases involving the grandfather clauses, residential segregation, and the Arkansas peons, it sought to break down the practice of the Southern states of excluding Negroes

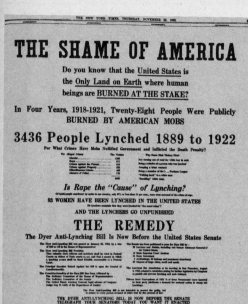

THIS FULL-PAGE ADVERTISEMENT appeared on November 23, 1922, in the New York Times, Atlanta Constitution, and several other leading newspapers. It was part of the N.A.A.C.P.'s campaign to secure passage of the Dyer Anti-Lynching Bill.

from Democratic primaries. It succeeded, in the case of *Nixon v. Herndon*, in having the Supreme Court of the United States declare null and void a Texas statute which excluded Negroes from the Democratic primaries in the state. When the Texas legislature enacted a law giving the executive committee of the party the authority to fix the qualifications for party membership, the Association, in *Nixon v. Condon*, succeeded in having the law nullified by arguing that the statute had set up a party committee and made it a state agency with certain powers and duties. It suffered a setback, however, in 1935 when, in *Grovey v. Townsend*, the Court refused to interfere with the exclusion of Negroes from the Democratic primaries when such an exclusion had been effected by a resolution of the state convention of the party. It recovered its lost ground in 1944, in *Smith v. Allwright*, when the Supreme Court decided that the exclusion of Negroes from the Democratic primary was a clear violation of the Fifteenth Amendment. Thus the Association, as well as many Negroes, came to regard the Court as the most reliable safeguard of the rights of all citizens.

Another interracial organization that interested itself in the plight of the Negro was the Commission on Interracial Cooperation. Organized in 1919, it set out "to quench, if possible, the fires of racial antagonism which were flaming at that time with such deadly menace in all sections of the country." The Commission confined its activities primarily to the South and, through Will W. Alexander and other prominent Southerners, set up a program of education in race relations on the state and community level. Several ten-day schools for whites and for Negroes were held to train leaders in the art of promoting interracial work. Local interracial committees were organized, and upon the creation of sufficient interest state committees were set up. For several years every Southern state had a state committee. While the Commission did not attack segregation, it spoke out against discrimination. Through its monthly publication, *The Southern Frontier*, and through other mediums it pressed for equal participation in government welfare programs, equal justice under the law, the abolition of lynching, and the ballot for all citizens. From its offices in Atlanta it carried on a program of research and education on Southern problems, devoting considerable attention to agriculture, health, and education. The Commission brought into the movement for the improvement of race relations many Southern leaders and public officials that otherwise would not have been identified with any program for the benefit of Negroes in the South.

Despite their vigorous efforts, the National Association for the Advancement of Colored People and the Commission on Interracial Cooperation failed to reach more than a small minority of Negroes and whites; and although they succeeded in achieving ends that were beneficial to all Negroes, they failed to capture the imagination and secure the following of the masses. Negroes on the lower social and economic level were inclined to regard such organizations as the agencies of upper class Negroes and liberal whites who failed to join hands with them in their efforts to rise. It was this feeling, regardless of its justification, that made possible the rise of Marcus Garvey and his Universal Negro Improvement Association. Garvey had begun this organization in his native Jamaica in 1914. Two years later he came to the United States to organize a New York chapter of the U.N.I.A. At the end of the war the Association grew rapidly, and according to the leader there were more than thirty branches by the middle of 1919.

The basis for Garvey's wide popularity was his appeal to race pride at a time when Negroes generally had so little of which to be proud. The strain and stress of living in hostile urban communities created a state of mind upon which Garvey capitalized. Garvey called upon Negroes, especially the ones of the darker hue, to follow him. He exalted everything black. He insisted that black stood for strength and beauty, not inferiority. He asserted that Africans had a noble past, and he declared that Negroes should be proud of their ancestry. In his newspaper, *The Negro World*, he told Negroes that racial prejudice was so much a part of the civilization of the white man that it was futile to appeal to his sense of justice and his high-sounding democratic principles. With an eye on the growing sentiment in favor of the self-determination of dependent peoples, Garvey said that the only hope for American Negroes was to flee America and return to Africa and build up a country of their own. On one occasion Garvey cried out: "Wake up Ethiopia! Wake up Africa! Let us work toward the one glorious end of a free, redeemed and mighty nation. Let Africa be a bright star among the constellations of nations."

As a man of action Garvey began to put his program into operation. He appealed to the League of Nations for permission to settle a colony in Africa and opened negotiations with Liberia. Failing to secure entry into Africa by peaceful means, he organized the Universal African Legion to drive the white usurpers out. Other auxiliary organizations consisted of the Universal Black Cross Nurses, the Universal African Motor Corps, the Black Eagle Flying Corps, and the Black Star Steamship Line. In 1921 Garvey announced the formal organization of the Empire of Africa and appointed himself Provisional President. He ruled with the assistance of one Potentate and one Supreme Deputy Potentate. Among the nobility he created were the Knights of the Nile, the Knights of the Distinguished Service Order of Ethiopia, and the Dukes of the Niger and of Uganda. In New York and other large cities members of the Universal Negro Improvement Association, now citizens of a new empire, paraded in elaborate uniforms and held conferences and conventions.

The effect of the Garvey doctrines on the unlettered and inexperienced Negro urban element, recently removed from the farm, was magnetic. He was hailed by thousands as the true leader of the Negro race. Although Garvey's claim that he had four million followers in 1920 and six million three years later is doubtless exaggerated, even his severest critics admitted that there were perhaps a half million members of the U.N.I.A. Most of the other Negro leaders denounced him bitterly as an insincere, selfish impostor; but he countered that they were opportunists, liars, thieves, and traitors. Dr. DuBois was especially critical of Garvey and called the U.N.I.A. "bombastic and impracticable." Dr. DuBois later admitted that Garvey's schemes made difficult the effective development of the Pan-African Congresses. When the third Congress met in 1923 signs of decline were clearly discernible, and the fourth one in 1927 was nothing more than an "empty gesture to keep the idea alive." Garvey was especially contemptuous of Dr. DuBois and other leaders of the N.A.A.C.P. On one occasion he wrote, "The N.A.A.C.P. wants us all to become white by amalgamation, but they are not honest enough to come out with the truth. To be a Negro is no disgrace, but an honor, and we of the U.N.I.A. do not want to become white. . . . We are proud and honorable. We love our race and respect and adore our mothers."

Garvey's conduct of his steamship line finally put an end to his meteoric rise. According to his wife he had collected ten million dollars between 1919 and 1921. More than one million had been spent in purchasing and equipping ships for the Black Star Line. In 1923 Garvey went on trial before a federal judge on a charge of using the mails to defraud in raising money for his steamship line. He was found guilty, and two years later entered the Atlanta penitentiary to serve a five year term. Perhaps Arthur Brisbane's assertion that to hold him was equivalent to "jailing a rainbow" was an overstatement, but he continued to conduct the movement from his cell in Atlanta. In one letter to his followers he said:

> My months of forcible removal from among you, being imprisoned as a punishment for advocating the cause of our real emancipation, have not left me hopeless or despondent; but to the contrary, I see a great ray of light and the bursting of a mighty political cloud which will bring you complete freedom. . . .

We have gradually won our way back into the confidence of

the God of Africa, and He shall speak with a voice of thunder, that shall shake the pillars of a corrupt and unjust world, and once more restore Ethiopia to her ancient glory. . . .

Hold fast to the Faith. Desert not the ranks, but as brave soldiers march on to victory. I am happy, and shall remain so, as long as you keep the flag flying.

Garvey remained in prison until President Coolidge pardoned him and ordered his deportation as an undesirable alien in 1927. Although he made efforts to revive his movement in Jamaica and later in London, where he died in 1940, "Negro Zionism" was doomed to failure. Regardless of how dissatisfied Negroes were with conditions in the United States they were unwilling in the twenties, as their forebears had been a century earlier, to undertake the uncertain task of redeeming Africa. The widespread interest in Garvey's program was more a protest against the anti-Negro reaction of the post-war period than an approbation of the fantastic schemes of the Negro leader. Its significance lies in the fact that it was the first and only real mass movement among Negroes in the history of the United States and that it indicates the extent to which Negroes entertained doubts concerning the hope for first-class citizenship in the only fatherland of which they knew.

While most Negroes were content to remain in the United States and strive to improve conditions through the regular channels open to all citizens or through special agencies like the N.A.A.C.P., others looked toward a rapid transformation of life into a veritable heaven. Among these were the followers of George Baker, more commonly called "Father Divine." Beginning in 1919 with a small group in Sayville, Long Island, New York, this remarkable character built up a following within the next two decades that amused some observers and perplexed others. Although his followers deserted their churches and began to call him "God," it was as much a social movement as a religious development. By 1930 he was holding open house and feeding thousands in buildings that came to be known as "heavens." When people wondered where he secured the money for the elaborate feasts, he merely answered in an almost unintelligible series of words, "I have harnessed your consciousness as Franklin did electricity and it is for you to use your emotions as Edison handled the electricity uncovered by Franklin." The following grew enormously in the second ten years of its existence, and "heavens" or Peace Missions were founded in many

Eastern cities as well as in some Midwestern communities. It became interracial as early as 1926, and within a few years had attracted a considerable number of white followers, some of whom were wealthy. That such a movement flourished during the period is a testimonial of the extent of the social ills from which the body politic suffered, and was one more indication of the tremendous frustration that characterized the lot of many a Negro, and some whites as well.

Depression

In the decade following the first World War the number of potential Negro wage earners expanded considerably. As the migration to the industrial centers continued, some found employment in the factories and in personal service, while others joined the ranks of the unemployed. They were found in increasing numbers in the automotive and allied industries, in glass factories, paper and bag companies, and in the tobacco factories. They made gains, also, in the clothing and food industries, while thousands were able to earn a living in transportation and communication. The textile industry of the South grew tremendously, but only a small number of Negroes found employment. Almost everywhere white labor tended to exclude Negro workers from the unions. A large number of the affiliated unions of the American Federation of Labor barred or segregated Negroes, while the various railway brotherhoods excluded them altogether. On one large railroad of the South before World War I slightly more than 80 per cent of the firemen were Negroes. Within ten years after the end of the war only 10 per cent of the firemen of that line were Negroes. In 1927 the Atlanta joint terminals entered into an agreement that white firemen were to be given preference over Negro firemen. In some instances white workers violently attempted to drive Negroes out of the transportation field, as in 1932, when the white employees of the Illinois Central Railroad engaged in a fight with Negro workers which resulted in the death of ten Negro trainmen.

Despite the continued employment of Negroes in some industrial centers, hostility to them at the end of the war was sufficient to cause a group to organize, in 1920, the Friends of Negro Freedom. This organization, composed primarily of New York radicals, hoped to unionize Negro migrants, protect Negro tenants, advance Negro cooperation, and organize forums through which to educate the masses. Through the branches which it intended to set up throughout the country the Friends of Negro Freedom hoped to fight racial discrimination in employment by use of the boycott. While only a few locals were established and their work largely ineffective, the Friends existed as a paper organization for approximately three years. A similar organization, the National Association for the Promotion of Labor Unionism among Negroes, was organized about the same time under the direction of Chandler Owen and A. Philip Randolph, publishers of the *Messenger*. An advisory board was composed of white labor radicals and intellectuals, including Morris Hillquit, Joseph D. Cannon, and Charles W. Ervin. After its futile effort to organize Negro laundry workers, the organization ceased to function. The American Negro Labor Congress, meeting for the first time in Chicago in October, 1925, sought to unify the efforts of all organizations of Negro workers and farmers, as well as similar interracial organizations. It desired to abolish discrimination against, and exploitation of, Negroes and workers generally, and looked toward bringing Negroes into trade unions and the general labor movement with the white workers. The Congress hoped to form local councils through which it would work to secure the total integration of the black worker. The local councils were never formed and the objectives of the organization never realized. Like its predecessors, it succumbed under the weight of disunity among Negroes and indifference and hostility among whites.

The most significant step toward the unionization of Negroes was the organization of the Brotherhood of Sleeping Car Porters and Maids by A. Philip Randolph in 1925. When an effort was made to secure from the Pullman Company better conditions of work and higher wages, the employer would have nothing to do with the Brotherhood. It attacked the Brotherhood as a dangerous radical organization, and Randolph was condemned as a professional agitator. Considerable opposition to the Brotherhood arose from both white and Negro groups, but its endorsement by the American Federation of Labor, the N.A.A.C.P., and the National Urban League bolstered its fight considerably. Partial recognition came in 1926 and 1929 in wage agreements; full recognition of the Brotherhood as the bargaining agency for the porters and maids employed by the Pullman Company came only in 1937, when more than 8,000 employees benefited by a wage increase of $1,152,000.

Although the number of Negro business enterprises increased after World War I, the proportion of Negroes among all retail dealers tended to decrease. In the Negro community, however, Negroes who were engaged in business remained important because of their social and political influence, as well as for the economic strength which they wielded. Negro undertakers, beauticians, insurance companies, and mercantile houses constituted the more important enterprises, but a variety of small business institutions performed personal services that increased the number of Negroes in the white-collar group. The success of these businesses depended peculiarly upon the income of the skilled and unskilled Negro laborer who worked, primarily, for whites and who traded with Negroes. When adverse circumstances in the general economic order caused a curtailment of employment or a reduction of wages, Negro businesses were affected immediately. The Negro community in this period was, therefore, hardly more independent of general trends than Negroes had been a century earlier.

The flight of thousands of Negroes from Southern farms during and after the war did not seem to improve the conditions of those that remained. To the general poverty and land exploitation that prevailed were added the ravages of the boll weevil. In many areas the destruction was so extensive that farms were temporarily or permanently abandoned, and Negro and white farm laborers were thrown out of work. The suffering of tenants can hardly be estimated. Early in the twenties the depression had already begun for them. Meanwhile, the number of Negro farm owners was gradually declining. Not only were many of the more enterprising farmers deserting the rural areas, but the depressed conditions caused others to lose their holdings. Soil erosion, the boll weevil, and the southwestern shift in cotton cultivation played havoc on Negro and white farmers alike. The growing importance of foreign tobacco, cotton, and sugar cane on the international market created conditions of competition beyond the control of American farmers, and the tariff legislation of the Republicans did little to relieve conditions. It was an unfavorable sign of the times that the agrarian population of the United States, which included the majority of Negro citizens, was without the necessary purchasing power to enjoy the opulence of the twenties.

As the stock market soared to unprecedented heights, as urban land values increased continuously, and as people spoke confidently of a new era of abundance and prosperity, little attention was given to the fact that the prosperity was unevenly distributed. Only those who were immediately concerned, together with a few "gloomy experts," complained that persons working in agriculture, shipbuilding, coal mining, and the textile and shoe industries were not enjoying the prosperity of the "New Economic Era." In the first signs of recession in the middle of the twenties, thousands of Negroes lost their jobs, but they were counted as casualties of a technological age in which several million persons were expected to be unemployed. When the crash came in October of 1929 many Negroes were already suffering from economic depression. As businesses closed, banks failed, and mines shut down, a larger number of black workers became unemployed. In cities they lost their jobs rapidly, while in the rural areas they were driven to starvation wages. In household jobs and personal service occupations, where so many Negroes were to be found, there was immediate curtailment. Because of the Negro's small or nonexistent reserve of capital, it was not long before there were dire want and untold suffering.

Within a few years after the beginning of the Great Depression millions of American citizens were regarded as incapable of self-support in any occupation. By 1934, for example, 17 per cent of the whites and 38 per cent of the Negroes were placed in this category. Everywhere the relief rolls soared. In October, 1933, between 25 per cent and 40 per cent of the Negroes of several large urban centers were on relief, a figure three or four times the number of whites on relief at the time. Approximately one-fourth of the one and one-half million Negro domestic workers were on relief in 1935. In some Southern cities the size of Negro relief rolls was appalling. In Atlanta, in 1935, 65 per cent of the Negro employables were in need of public assistance, while in Norfolk no less than 80 per cent of the group was on relief. Small wonder that there was utter distress and pessimism among Negroes generally. Added to the denials of freedom and democracy was the specter of starvation.

Even in starvation there was discrimination, for in few places was relief administered on a basis of equality. Some religious and charitable organizations, in the North as well as the South, excluded Negroes from the soup kitchens which they operated to relieve the suffering. In many of the communities where relief work was offered, Negroes were discriminated against, while in the early programs of public assistance there was, in some places, as much as a six dollar differential in the monthly aid given to white and Negro families. This was final proof for the Negroes that democracy had escaped. More and more, they began to feel that if it were to be retrieved at all it could come only through the exertion of a potent political influence. It was an awakened consciousness, brought on by suffering and discrimination, that drove Negroes to this conclusion. The articulation of this consciousness had begun in the early twenties, when the New Negro Movement, which found eloquent expression in what is commonly known as the "Harlem Renaissance," got under way.

XXVI •

A Harlem Renaissance

Socio-Economic Problems and Negro Literature

● *During the post-war period a distinctly new literary move-*ment emerged in the United States. In the early part of the century there had been the shocking revelations of the muckrakers and the tendency toward greater realism in the works of Howells and others. The war had, however, produced such an intense air of patriotism that more energy was expended on praising the American way of life than on criticizing it. It looked as though there would be no further criticism of American life, as everyone appeared content to return to normalcy, to forget whatever was wrong with America, and to concentrate on enjoying the blessings of the existing system. There was, moreover, the spread of Bolshevism, which alarmed Americans so that they became intolerant of cynics who insisted on finding faults with things as they were. There were, nevertheless, a small number of American writers who emerged from the calm surrounding America's enjoyment of peace and prosperity to call attention to the faults and inadequacies of capitalistic democracy in America. In 1920 Sinclair Lewis in *Main Street* emphasized the superficiality and false values of American urban life. Two years later he followed up the theme in a shocking indictment of the American business man in *Babbitt*. In 1925 Theodore Dreiser showed the deleterious effects of the false values of the commercial civilization in *An American Tragedy*.

American writers interested themselves in numerous social

and economic problems. Labor problems received considerable attention, as did housing, crime, social planning, and disarmament. Novelists, dramatists, publicists, and other writers also turned to the problem of the Negro. Perhaps no other subject lent itself to such a variety of treatments, and the writers made the most of it. In 1919 Robert Kerlin collected the points of view of Negro newspapers in his *Voice of the Negro*. Shortly thereafter Moorfield Storey pricked the conscience of America with regard to the Negro in his *Problems of Today;* and in 1924 Frank Tannenbaum described the plight of the Southern Negro in *Darker Phases of the South*. Among the dramatists who experimented with Negro materials, Eugene O'Neill was outstanding with *The Emperor Jones* in 1920 and *All God's Chillun Got Wings* in 1924. In 1926 Paul Green's *In Abraham's Bosom,* produced with a predominantly Negro cast, won for him the Pulitzer Prize. Carl Van Vechten, Victor F. Calverton, H. L. Mencken, Joel Spingarn, and others were lending their pens to the encouragement of Negroes and the use of Negro materials. With such a profusion of writing about the Negro, America became conscious of the Negro problem and was willing to listen to what the Negro had to say about it.

There can be no doubt that the emergence of the Negro writer in the post-war period stemmed, in part, from the fact that he was inclined to exploit the opportunity that presented itself to write about himself. It was more than that, however. The movement that has been variously called the "Harlem Renaissance," the "Black Renaissance," and the "New Negro Movement" was essentially a part of the growing interest of American literary circles in the immediate and pressing social and economic problems. This growing interest coincided with two developments in Negro life that fostered the growth of the New Negro Movement. The migration that began during the war had thrown the destiny of the Negro into his own hands more than ever before. He developed a responsibility and a self-confidence that he had not previously known. During the war he learned from no less a person than his President the promise of freedom, and on the battlefield he served his country. He began to see the discrepancies between the promise of freedom and his experiences in America. The Negro became defiant, bitter, and impatient. It was not the timorous, docile Negro of the past who said, "The next time white folks pick on colored folks, something's going to drop—dead white folks." In the riots and clashes that followed the war Negroes fought back with a surprising audacity. By this time, moreover, the Negro had achieved a degree and kind of articulation that made it possible for him to transform his feelings into a variety of literary forms. Despite his intense feelings of hate and hurt, he possessed sufficient restraint and objectivity to use his materials artistically, but no less effectively. He was sufficiently in touch with the main currents of American literary development to adapt the accepted forms to his own materials, and therefore gain a wider acceptance. These two factors, the keener realization of injustice and the improvement of the capacity for expression, produced a crop of Negro writers who constituted the "Harlem Renaissance."

The literature of the Harlem Renaissance was, for the most part, the work of a race-conscious group. Through poetry, prose, and song, the writers cried out against social and economic wrongs. They protested against segregation and lynching. They demanded higher wages, shorter hours, and better conditions of work. They stood for full social equality and first-class citizenship. Their new vision of social and economic freedom did not force them to embrace the several foreign ideologies that sought to sink their roots in some American groups during the period.

The writers of the Harlem Renaissance, bitter and cynical as some of them were, gave little attention to the propaganda of the socialists and communists. The editor of the *Messenger* ventured the opinion that the New Negro was the "product of the same world-wide forces that have brought into being the great liberal and radical movements that are now seizing the reins of political, social, and economic power in all the civilized countries of the world." Such forces may have produced the New Negro, but the more articulate of the group did not resort to advocating the type of political action that would have subverted American constitutional government. Indeed, the writers of the Harlem Renaissance were not revolting so much against the system as they were protesting against the inefficient operation of the system. In this approach they proved to be as characteristically American as any writers of the period. Like his contemporaries, the Negro writer was merely becoming more aware of America's pressing social problems; and like the others, he was willing to use his art, not only to contribute to the great body of American culture but to improve the culture and civilization of which he was a part.

It seems possible, moreover, for the historian to assign to the Negro writer a role that he did not assume. There were doubtless many who were not immediately concerned with the injustices heaped on the Negro. Some contrived their poems, novels, and songs merely for the sake of art, while others took up their pens to escape the sordid aspects of their existence. If there is an element of race in their writings, it is because the writings flow out of their individual and group experiences. This is not to say that such writings were not effective as protest literature, but rather that not all the authors were conscious crusaders for a better world. As a matter of fact, it was this detachment, this objectivity, that made it possible for many of the writers of the Harlem Renaissance to achieve a nobility of expression and a poignancy of feeling in their writings that placed them among the great masters of recent American literature.

The "New York Wits"

The city of New York had long been the center of intellectual and cultural life of Negro America. It was only natural that the Negro Renaissance should have developed there. The riot of 1900 had stirred the Negro population to a great degree of self-assertion which culminated in the organization of the Citizens Protective League. Under the editorship of T. Thomas Fortune the militant *New York Age* fought for equality of opportunity for Negroes and equal protection of the law. Within a few years James Weldon Johnson had moved from Florida to New York, and shortly after the organization of the National Association for the Advancement of Colored People, W. E. B. DuBois left Atlanta and took up residence there. He continued his creative writings, bringing out two novels, *The Quest of the Silver Fleece* (1900) and *The Dark Princess* (1928), and two volumes of poems and essays, *Dark Water* (1920) and *The Gift of Black Folk* (1924). Militant Negroes from the West Indies migrated to the great city in large numbers and were ready to join in any movement for the improvement of conditions among Negroes. During World War I, with the migration of large numbers of Negroes from Southern states and with greater opportunities for work, the Negro community of Harlem became a prosperous and important part of the metropolitan district.

It was in New York that Negroes made their most eloquent demands for equality during and after World War I. To be sure, there were no serious race clashes, such as those in East St. Louis and Chicago, but there were the impressive silent protest parade in 1917, the vigorous denunciations of injustice in the columns of the *Crisis,* and the radical utterances of the *Messenger.* There was, moreover, a considerable amount of flirtation on the part of Negroes with communists and socialists, though it was short-lived. New York was already the center of American literary and artistic activity. Talented authors, playwrights, painters, and sculptors came to the big city to sell their wares and to increase their output. Publishers and other purveyors of letters and the arts remained sensitive to any production that had the promise of benefiting all parties concerned. It was only natural, therefore, that any substantial growth of Negro literature would take place in a climate so congenial to its development.

A few Negroes, such as DuBois, had written artistic works of protest for many years. "The Litany of Atlanta," which DuBois composed on the occasion of the Atlanta Riot in 1906, was in the spirit of the "New Negro"; but there were too few such works at that time to describe their appearance as part of a movement. As a prelude to the emergence of an abundant crop of Negro writers, James Weldon Johnson published his *Fifty Years and Other Poems* in 1917. The title poem, written on the anniversary of the signing of the Emancipation Proclamation, made it clear that Negroes were determined to remain here in America and to enjoy the full fruits of their labors. Johnson thus became something of an advance herald of the Harlem Renaissance and remained an integral part of it. In 1922 he published *The Book of American Negro Poetry,* which contained the works of the outstanding contemporary Negro poets. His preface to the work, a survey of Negro poetry from Horton to McKay, did much to emphasize the value of such efforts to the cultural life of America. He participated further in the movement by editing, in collaboration with J. Rosamond Johnson, two books of American Negro spirituals in 1925 and 1926. In 1927 there appeared his *God's Trombones,* Negro sermons in verse, and in 1930 his *Saint Peter Relates an Incident of the Resurrection Day,* a burning indictment of the current discrimination against Negro Gold Star mothers. In 1927 his *Autobiography of an Ex-Coloured Man,* originally published in 1912, was reissued as a part of the Renaissance. In two works, *Black Manhattan* (1930) and *Along This Way,* an autobiography (1933), he chronicled the Harlem Renaissance, the first phase of which had come to a close. As a precursor, participant, and historian of the Renaissance, James Weldon Johnson had as much to do with the rise of the new literary movement as any one person.

Claude McKay is regarded by most critics, including James Weldon Johnson, as having been the first significant writer of the Harlem Renaissance. When this West Indian Negro came from his native Jamaica in 1912 at 21 years of age, he had already won distinction as a poet. In 1911 his *Songs of Jamaica* was published, for which he was awarded the medal of the Institute of Arts and Sciences. After attending Tuskegee Institute and the University of Kansas, McKay went to New York and witnessed the evolution of Harlem into an integral part of the great metropolis. He published poems in several magazines, including *The Seven Arts, The Liberator,* and *The Messenger,* but it was the appearance of his volume, *Harlem Shadows,* in 1922 that placed him in the front ranks of post-war America. In "The Lynching," "If We Must Die," and "To the White Fiends" there is expressed in eloquent verse a proud defiance and bitter contempt that became one of the salient characteristics of the Harlem Renaissance. As though he had expended all of his poetic talents, McKay turned most of his attention to prose after the appearance of *Harlem Shadows.* In 1928 he brought out his novel of Negro life in New York, *Home to Harlem.* In the following year there appeared another novel, *Banjo,* the scene of which was laid in Marseilles. Later he was to publish his autobiography, *A Long Way From Home,* and a panorama of Negro life in New York, *Harlem: Negro Metropolis.* Even after McKay turned his attention to other matters the movement that he stimulated grew to enormous proportions.

Jean Toomer was one of the most talented of the Negro writers. He had studied in France, where he developed the art of introspective contemplation. He moved freely among many circles both in Europe and in America and drank deep of a variety of experiences. In 1923 he published *Cane,* which ranked with McKay's *Harlem Shadows* in its significance for the literary movement. This only contribution of Toomer to the Renaissance was a series of realistic stories on Negro life, together with a number of extraordinarily moving lyrics of great beauty.

Both the poetry and prose of *Cane* reflected the capacity for self-revelation which Toomer had developed in France. His writings were unrestrained, yet objective, passionate, but proud. They are full of love and pride of race, and they revealed the inner yearnings as well as the joys and hurts of the New Negro. Shortly after the appearance of *Cane*, Toomer retired from active participation in the literary awakening and disappeared into the larger community of American life.

A new high was reached in the Harlem Renaissance with the appearance of Countee Cullen's first volume of poems, *Color*, in 1925. Though only 22 years old, this New York-born son of a Methodist minister gave numerous evidences of being a true lyric poet. He doubtless felt as keenly about the problem of the Negro as McKay or his other contemporaries, but his protests were couched in some of the most delicate, gentle lyrics that the post-war period witnessed. There was a finesse about his lines that distinguished him from the others, and at times his protests were so subtle as almost to escape detection. He was at his best when writing verse dealing with aspects of the race problem, but the beauty and effectiveness of his lines did not depend on the use of the experience of the race. The lyric quality, rich imagination, and intellectual content of his works make him one of the major poets of twentieth century America. In 1927 he brought out two books, *The Ballad of the Brown Girl* and *Copper Sun*, as well as an anthology, *Caroling Dusk*. Two years later his *Black Christ* appeared, while in 1932 he published *One Way to Heaven*.

During the Renaissance, New York attracted from Missouri via Mexico, Africa, and Europe its most cosmopolitan as well as its most prolific writer, Langston Hughes. Few writers in America have had such rich and varied experiences, and few are so indiscriminate in selecting materials for their writings. While Hughes is a true rebel poet, writing in the best traditions of the New Negro, he did not cry or moan. Frequently he laughed, revealing a freedom from the restrictions of race that equaled his freedom from the restrictions of form. He could pen deeply moving verses full of pride of race, such as "The Negro Speaks of Rivers," or he could write of the most lowly walks of life with a freedom and nobility of expression that raised them many levels higher, such as "Brass Spittoons." In 1926 his *Weary Blues* appeared, followed in the next year by *Fine Clothes to the Jew*. He demonstrated his versatility by bringing out a novel,

Not Without Laughter, in 1930 and a volume of short stories, *The Ways of White Folks*, in 1934. At a later time he experimented with pieces for the theater, and in 1940 his autobiography, *The Big Sea*, appeared. Numerous smaller works of his were published, and as he moved about the country ever broadening the scope of his art and continuously experimenting with new forms of expression, there appeared to be some justification for regarding him as "Shakespeare in Harlem."

The period produced numerous other poets of varying degrees of merit, who published their works either in slender volumes or in the columns of *Opportunity, Crisis*, or other New York periodicals. They were overshadowed, however, by the writers of fiction, some of whom ranked with the major poets. One of those who employed the medium of fiction quite successfully was Jessie Redmond Fauset. She brought to her work an ample education at Cornell University and the University of Pennsylvania, and used her spare moments to translate the works of some of the Negro poets of the French West Indies and to write verse of her own. It was her novel, *There Is Confusion* (1924), that won for her a place among the more select in the new literary movement. In employing characters from well-to-do Negro families, Miss Fauset created a new setting in the treatment of the Negro in literary works. While the problem of race was present in this and subsequent works, it did not obscure the problems which confront any person of similar economic and social position. Because so many of her characters appeared to be normal American citizens, some critics have viewed her creations as unimaginative and dull. It would seem, however, that her characters merely emphasize the growing Americanization of the Negro and the fact that in a given situation Negroes react like other people do. In 1929 Miss Fauset's second novel, *Plum Bun*, appeared, and was followed in 1931 by *The Chinaberry Tree* and in 1933 by *Comedy: American Style*. While there is a pride of race running through most of her works, it cannot be denied that she did much to carry Negro fiction above the complex problem of race and place it in the company of general American literature.

In 1924 Walter White published *Fire in the Flint*, a swiftly moving, tragic story of Negro life in the South. Two years later, in *Flight*, he sought to picture the emotional struggles of a young woman light enough to "pass." In 1929 White deserted the field of fiction and wrote *Rope and Faggot: A Biography of*

Judge Lynch, an authoritative and searching analysis of lynching, based on his own investigations. In *Quicksand* (1928) and *Passing* (1929), Nella Larsen sought to explore the innumerable social problems of young Negro women in their efforts to struggle upward both in America and in Europe. Among the other works of fiction during the period were Wallace Thurman's *The Blacker the Berry* (1929) and *Infants of the Spring* (1932), Eric Walrond's *Tropic Death* (1926), Rudolph Fisher's *The Walls of Jericho* (1928) and *The Conjure Woman Dies* (1932), and George S. Schuyler's *Black No More* (1931).

A considerable amount of non-fiction prose may be regarded as an integral part of the new literary movement. The *Crisis* and *Opportunity* kept their columns open to young Negro authors and offered prizes to stimulate writing. Other periodicals in the New York area also encouraged writers by publishing their works, such as *Survey Graphic, Current History, The Modern Quarterly, The Nation, The New Masses,* and *The American Mercury*. In addition to the writings of DuBois, James W. Johnson, and Schuyler, essays were published by Abram L. Harris, E. Franklin Frazier, Arthur A. Schomburg, Benjamin Brawley, J. A. Rogers, and Alain Locke. In 1925 the Renaissance received its most significant recognition with the appearance of a special Harlem number of *Survey Graphic*, edited by Alain Locke. Later in the same year the articles which appeared in the issue were collected and enlarged in a volume, *The New Negro*. Indeed, the literary aspect of the Renaissance had come of age.

There were other mediums through which the Negro expressed himself during the Renaissance, not the least of which was the stage. After 1910 Negroes disappeared almost altogether from the stages of downtown theaters in New York. In the ensuing years there grew up in Harlem a real Negro theater in which Negro actors performed before predominantly Negro audiences. It was no longer necessary for Negroes to essay only those roles that were acceptable to white audiences. The Lafayette Players presented almost every type of play, including such stalwarts as *Madame X, The Servant in the House, On Trial,* and *Within the Law*. Similar works were produced at the Lincoln Theater. A large group of able and popular players emerged, including Anita Bush, Abbie Mitchell, Ida Anderson, Laura Bowman, Cleo Desmond, Edna Thomas, Charles Gilpin, Frank Wilson, Clarence Muse, and Jack Carter. In 1917 a group of Negro players presented under the sponsorship of Mrs. Emily Hapgood three one-act plays by Ridgely Torrence at the Garden Theater in Madison Square Garden. The presentation of the plays, *The Rider of Dreams*, *Granny Maumee*, and *Simon the Cyrenian* marked the first time that Negro actors in the dramatic theater had commanded the serious attention of the critics and the general press. Because war came to the United States on the day following the opening of the plays, the Negro in the theater was forced to wait until a later period before he could claim a substantial place in American public entertainment of this nature.

In 1919 there was a revival of interest in the Negro in the theater with the appearance of Charles Gilpin as the Reverend William Custis in John Drinkwater's *Abraham Lincoln.* In the following year Gilpin won acclaim for himself and for Eugene O'Neill in the creation of the title role of *The Emperor Jones.* For his outstanding performance he received an award of the Drama League of New York as well as the Spingarn Medal. Some critics predicted for him a career similar to that of Ira Aldridge, who had captivated European audiences with his Shakespearean roles in the previous century. In 1924 Paul Robeson played the leading role in O'Neill's *All God's Chillun Got Wings.* It was the first time in American history that a Negro had taken a principal role opposite a white woman, and the anticipated riot did not materialize. In 1926 Paul Green of the University of North Carolina brought to New York his *In Abraham's Bosom*, in which Jules Bledsoe played the leading role. Bledsoe was ably assisted by Rose McClendon, Abbie Mitchell, and Frank Wilson. The play was a distinct success and demonstrated both the adaptability of Negro life to the theater and the ability of Negroes in the theater. In the following year *Porgy*, a folk-play of Negro life in Charleston by Dorothy and DuBose Heyward, was produced by the Theater Guild. Once more Rose McClendon, Frank Wilson, and the other Negroes in the cast captivated New York audiences by the seriousness with which they plied their art. These plays about Negro life by white authors reached a high-water mark with the production in 1930 of Marc Connelly's *The Green Pastures*, a fable of the Negro's conception of the Old Testament with Richard B. Harrison as "The Lord." With its long run in New York and on the road, the play convinced America that there was a place for the Negro on the legitimate stage.

The Negro playwright made a bid for recognition during the Renaissance, though the success which he enjoyed was somewhat limited. In October, 1925, *Appearances* was produced at the Frolic Theater in New York. The author, Garland Anderson, was a former bellboy and switchboard operator in San Francisco. Anderson eschewed the problem of race and devoted his attention to depicting the doctrines of Christian Science. Although the critics were fairly kind to the production, its general appeal was not sufficient, and it did not last more than a few weeks. In 1927 The Krigwa Players of Harlem gave *The Fool's Errand*, by Eulalie Spence, in the Little Theater Tournament. Although the play did not win the trophy, it was awarded one of the Samuel French prizes for the best unpublished manuscript play in the contest. In later years, Langston Hughes's *Mulatto* and Richard Wright's *Native Son* have had fairly successful runs on Broadway, but the Negro playwright can still, perhaps, look forward to a brighter future than to a successful past.

The Renaissance produced more than writers of serious poetry and prose. It was only natural for New York to expect that in the field of lighter entertainment Negro performances would reach a new high. Ever since Bert Williams and George Walker reached New York in 1896 and introduced their highly successful vaudeville team, Negroes had furnished a considerable portion of New York's entertainment. Aside from making the cake-walk fashionable they appeared in numerous revues and became world-famous for their rollicking, care-free wisecracking. There were also Bob Cole and J. Rosamond Johnson, whose *Shoofly Regiment* and *Red Moon* were successes in the musical comedy field before World War I. By 1920, when Bert Williams was making his final appearances before theatrical audiences, New York was as ready for new Negro musical shows as it was for new Negro poetry.

In the summer of 1921 there opened in New York a Negro musical revue, *Shuffle Along*, that was the most brilliant that New York had ever witnessed. Its popular songs, including "I'm Just Wild about Harry," "Love Will Find a Way," and "Shuffle Along," were worthy of the talented singers and beautiful chorus that sang and danced the tunes. The settings and costumes were in the best traditions of the musical extravaganza. It was written and produced by Negroes—F. E. Miller, Aubrey Lyle, Eubie Blake, and Noble Sissle. It was indeed record-breaking and epoch-making. Its New York run lasted more than a year, and it was on the road for more than two years. It was the highest type of musical comedy entertainment that Negroes had yet produced, and easily the most popular show in New York in 1921 and 1922. There was another fairly popular Negro show, *Put and Take*, by Irving Miller, but because of the extraordinary success of *Shuffle Along* it did not receive the recognition that it deserved.

During the remainder of the twenties, New York witnessed a succession of top-flight Negro musical revues. In 1923 there was Irving Miller's *'Liza*. In the same year there were *Runnin' Wild*, by Miller and Lyle, as well as *Chocolate Dandies* by Blake and Sissle, a show which introduced Josephine Baker to theatergoers. In 1924 *Dixie to Broadway*, starring Florence Mills, opened. Since the Negro revues had previously starred two black-face comedians, the domination of the show by Miss Mills was a break with long established traditions. The production of *Blackbirds* in 1926 was a signal triumph for the talented Florence Mills, who captivated audiences in America and in Europe with her pantomiming, singing, and dancing. Her untimely death in 1927 removed the brightest star on the musical comedy horizon. Ethel Waters in *Africana* and other shows, Adelaide Hall and Ada Ward in *Blackbirds of 1928*, and Bill Robinson in a succession of hits, sought to maintain the high standards set by Florence Mills and others in earlier productions.

There was serious music, too, during the Renaissance. Harry T. Burleigh, R. Nathaniel Dett, Carl Diton, and J. Rosamond Johnson were writing and editing Negro spirituals as well as other musical scores. Paul Robeson, Lawrence Brown, and Taylor Gordon were giving programs made up exclusively of Negro songs, while Jules Bledsoe, Abbie Mitchell, and others included Negro spirituals in their repertoire. Roland Hayes was acclaimed both in Europe and in America for his rare gifts in interpreting songs as well as Negro spirituals. The spirit of the New Negro was as alive in the serious music of the period as in the other mediums.

No Negro artists measured up to the stature of Henry Ossawa Tanner, who was one of the world's outstanding painters at the turn of the century. His works had won medals at the Paris Exposition of 1900, the Pan-American Exposition of 1901, and the St. Louis Exposition of 1904. Today, many of his paintings hang in the better art galleries of Europe and America. In the period after World War I Aaron Douglas began to receive

recognition for his black and white drawings and his illustrations. His growing reputation brought him significant commissions to do extensive work, one of which was the murals of the
Fisk University Library in 1929. Laura Wheeler Waring
painted scenes from the life of upper-class Negroes, examples of
which were "The Co-ed" and "The Musician," while Edward A.
Harleston contented himself with subjects from what may be
called the Negro proletariat, examples of which are his "Old
Servant" and "Negro Soldier." Among the white painters who
gave attention to Negro subjects were Miguel Covarrubias,
whose caricatures of prominent Negroes are well known, and
Winold Reiss, who provided the illustrations for Alain Locke's
The New Negro in 1925. In the field of sculpture Meta Warrick
Fuller, who had won considerable recognition before World
War I, continued to do significant work in the decade following
the war.

It was only natural that these leaders of the Negro Renaissance in New York would tend to move in the same social
circles. There was a community of spirit and point of view that
found its expression not only in the cooperative ventures of a
professional nature, but also in the intimate social relationship
that developed. Perhaps these "New York Wits" felt that form
and substance could be given to their efforts through the inter-
change of ideas in moments of informality. Perhaps, too, they
were merely reflecting the inclination of Americans of the twenties to enjoy to the fullest the days that were at hand. At any
rate there were many "literary parties" in Harlem or downtown
at which most of them could be found. In Harlem the regular
hostess was A'Lelia Walker, the heiress of Madam C. J. Walker,
although Jessie Fauset, the James Weldon Johnsons, Wallace
Thurman, and others entertained the literary set with regularity. Downtown the most regular host was Carl Van Vechten. It
was not at all unusual to discover Clarence Darrow, a distinguished publisher, or a British lord moving freely among the
guests. The fellowship of intellectual colleagues was a cohesive
force in the efforts of the group, while the interracial aspect of
the gatherings doubtless had the effect of giving them a sense of
belonging to the larger community. If the gatherings of the New
York wits were large and, at times, unwieldy, it must be remembered that the problems as well as the tastes of all Americans
had increased greatly over those of the calm and detached
"wits" of a neighboring state in the eighteenth century.

The Circle Widens

While New York was the center of the Negro Renaissance, it could not claim a complete monopoly on Negro literary activity in the decade following World War I. In Boston William Stanley Braithwaite, who had won recognition early in the century with his *Lyrics of Life* (1904) and *The House of Falling Leaves* (1908), continued to issue his yearly anthologies of magazine verse and to write verse of his own. Although none of his poetry reflects the factor of race, he interested himself in the new movement and did what he could to encourage the younger poets. In Washington, Georgia Douglas Johnson emerged as the first outstanding Negro woman poet since Frances Harper. In 1918 her *The Heart of a Woman* was published, followed in 1922 by *Bronze. An Autumn Love Cycle* was published in 1928. Mrs. Johnson's poems are unsophisticated and emotional. Some may be classified as protest pieces. All of them are characterized by a sincerity that gives them their greatest appeal. In the same city Angelina W. Grimké, while teaching at the Dunbar High School, wrote a number of poems that have never been collected. Among them were "A Winter Twilight" and "When the Green Lies over the Earth."

Two young Washington poets emerged toward the end of the literary movement and won immediate recognition as writers of talent. Waring Cuney won the *Opportunity* poetry contest of 1926 with his "No Images" and followed this up with the composition of several poems of protest that have been recorded by Josh White in an album entitled *Southern Exposure*. Although his first volume of poems, *Southern Road*, was. not issued until 1932, Sterling Brown had been writing verse for several years. His "Long Gone," "Slim in Hell," and "Break of Day" reveal a remarkable capacity for using Negro materials. In Washington, also, while professor of philosophy at Howard University, Alain Locke was active in the new literary movement. He did much to steer its course and to interpret it to the world at large. In many respects he may be regarded as the liaison officer of the Negro Renaissance.

The circle widened to include Negroes who were removed from New York and the forces that produced a profusion of writers in that city. In Lynchburg, Virginia, Anne Spencer lived and worked but found time to write verse which reflected both maturity and detachment from race. Her "Before the Feast of

Shushan," "At the Carnival," and "Dunbar" won for her a secure place in the new movement. Out in Louisville, Kentucky, Joseph Seamon Cotter, Jr., had already begun to follow in the footsteps of his poet-father by publishing in 1918 a slender volume of verse, *The Band of Gideon*. His death in his twenty-fourth year cut off what promised to be a rich and influential life. Frank Horne, a New Yorker who worked in Chicago and Fort Valley, Georgia, won the *Crisis* contest of 1925 with his "Letters Found Near a Suicide." Other well-known poems of his are "Nigger: A Chant for Children," and "On Seeing Two Brown Boys in a Catholic Church." In California, Arna Bontemps, who later was to join the New York group, began writing verse; and in 1926 he won *Opportunity's* Alexander Pushkin Award for Poetry with "Golgotha Is a Mountain." In the following year he received the same award for his "Nocturne at Bethesda."

Gradually the scope of the Harlem Renaissance came to be the whole of the United States. Negroes everywhere became more articulate. There were poetry circles in Houston and Detroit, little theaters in Chicago and Los Angeles, and interested students of painting in Cleveland and Nashville. Long before the beginning of the Depression the groups in Harlem could claim no monopoly on the awakening, but they could claim some credit for the widespread interest in the new efforts at self-expression in various parts of the country. DuBois lectured in almost every community where there was a substantial number of Negroes, and frequently he spoke on subjects somewhat removed from the crusading activities of the N.A.A.C.P. Negro book dealers and publishers effectively distributed the works of the "New York Wits." Richard B. Harrison gave dramatic readings in the South and Midwest long before he became famous in *The Green Pastures*. It was no more possible for the Harlem Renaissance to remain confined to upper Manhattan than it was for other elements in American social and cultural life to remain isolated in one area of the United States. The literary and cultural aspects of the New Negro Movement had indeed become national before the end of the twenties.

Many students of the period regard the Renaissance as having ended with the production of *The Green Pastures* in 1930. To be sure, there was less activity among the "Wits" at that time, and their works were not so sensational. The group that had been concentrated in New York scattered to all parts of the world. Claude McKay spent much of his time in France; Langston Hughes resumed his world-wide travels; and James Weldon Johnson accepted a professorship in creative literature at Fisk University. The Depression settled over the country, and it was, naturally, more difficult for persons in the arts and letters to ply their trades. Many of the writers, singers, and artists found it impossible to stay off relief; and thanks to the broad scope of the federal relief projects they could continue to write and to sing and receive a check from the government for their efforts.

Out of the Federal Writers' Project, of which Sterling Brown was the Negro adviser, came many evidences that the Renaissance had not ended. At best, there was merely a lull. Even the older writers continued their efforts. Langston Hughes continued to write, as did Jessie Fauset, Countee Cullen, Claude McKay, and others. There were, moreover, several persons who, having begun toward the so-called end of the Renaissance, seemed to flourish in the darkest days of the Depression. One of them, Zora Neal Hurston, effectively bridged the gap between what may be described as the first and second stages of the Renaissance. This young anthropologist, a student of Franz Boas at Columbia, began to write short stories in the late twenties and collected a mass of folk lore in the United States and the Caribbean area on which many of her later works were to be based. In rapid succession she wrote novels, collected short stories, issued scholarly pieces on folk lore, and wrote authoritatively on Haiti and Jamaica. Between 1931 and 1943 she published *Moses, Man of the Mountain; Jonah's Gourd Vine; Mules and Men; Their Eyes Were Watching God; Tell My Horse;* and *Dust Tracks on a Road.* Certainly with such works as Miss Hurston produced one could hardly say that the Renaissance was over.

In the second period of the Renaissance, which may be regarded as still in progress, many white writers demonstrated the same interest in Negro materials and writers that had been shown in the earlier period. Paul Green and a number of his colleagues at the University of North Carolina continued to employ Negro materials and themes in their works. Carl Van Vechten maintained the lively interest that he showed from the beginning, and the group was widened to include such sponsors as Fannie Hurst, Stephen Vincent Benét, and H. A. Overstreet. New white writers such as Lillian Smith, Hodding Carter, Frances Gaither, Henrietta Buckmaster, and Howard Fast won recognition for their works with Negro themes, and some of them consciously sought to argue the case for the American Negro through their prose or poetry. If depressions and war years serve to inhibit certain cultural and social activities, it cannot be said that they either dampened the interest in the Negro or stifled creative expression on the part of the Negro. The thirties and forties were years of rich harvest for Negroes in almost all fields of creative activity.

Among the poets of the second period was Melvin B. Tolson, then a professor of English at Wiley College. He published poems in newspapers and magazines during the thirties and won numerous prizes and awards. Although his volume of poems was not issued until 1944, under the title of *Rendezvous with America*, one of the principal poems, "Dark Symphony" had been published previously in the *Atlantic Monthly*. While at the University of Michigan, Robert Hayden won the Jule and Avery Hopwood Prize for his poems, and in 1940 his first volume, *Heart-Shape in the Dust*, was published. In 1966 his poetry won first prize at the World Festival of Negro Art at Dakar, Senegal. Owen Dodson, one of the youngest of the well-known poets and playwrights, became seriously interested in writing while a student at Bates College. After writing traditional and experimental verse for several years, he collected his works in a volume, *Powerful Long Ladder*, in 1946. Two young women who have won recognition in the field of poetry during recent years are Margaret Walker and Gwendolyn Brooks. While on the Chicago Federal Writers' Project, Miss Walker wrote "For My People," which later won the first prize in the Yale University competition for younger poets. Stephen Vincent Benét praised Miss Walker's work generously when it was published in 1942. Her novel *Jubilee*, winner of the Houghton Mifflin Literary Fellowship, was published in 1966. Miss Brooks's volume, *Street in Bronzeville*, appeared in 1945. Five years later her *Annie Allen* won the Pulitzer prize.

There was a profusion of prose writers who appeared on the scene during and after the Depression. Among them, Arna Bontemps, who said that he had watched the early stages of the Renaissance from a grandstand seat, now became one of the most productive. In 1931 his *God Sends Sunday* appeared. Then came two historical novels, *Black Thunder* (1936) and *Drums at Dusk* (1939). Bontemps also became one of the most successful writers of children's books. More recently he has turned to non-fiction materials. With Jack Conroy he wrote *They Seek a City* (1945), an engrossing story of the urbanization of the Negro. The revised edition appeared in 1966 under the title, *Any Place But Here*. His *They Have Tomorrow* (1945) is a series of biographical sketches of promising young Negroes. Two Southern writers brought out novels of Negro life in the deep South: George W. Henderson wrote *Ollie Miss* in 1935, and in 1946 his second novel, *Jule*, appeared. George W. Lee shed considerable light on Negro life in Memphis with his *Beale Street* (1934). Two years later his *River George* appeared. Meanwhile, a promising young writer, Waters Turpin, was using materials of the upper South for his novels. As a native of the Eastern Shore of Maryland, Turpin dealt with a familiar area, and his works, *These Low Grounds* (1937) and *O Canaan* (1939), have an authoritativeness about them that is lacking in many similar works.

William Attaway pointed to new areas and materials for the Negro writer in his novels of the second period. In *Let Me Breathe Thunder* (1939) Attaway showed that a Negro writer could deal successfully with a work made up primarily of white characters. In *Blood on the Forge* (1941) he indicated the wealth of materials that was to be found in industrial communities where there was a problem of racial competition in the struggle for existence. The theme was exploited to a greater degree by Chester Himes in his novel of race friction in a wartime industrial community, *If He Hollers, Let Him Go* (1945). Himes, who had attracted attention with his short stories in *Opportunity*, *Esquire*, and *Coronet*, demonstrated vividly the impact of the war upon Negro migrants to industrial communities and the bitterness which stems from frustration and despair. Ann Petry, winner of the Houghton Mifflin Literary Fellowship, depicted the problems of a young Negro woman attempting to live a respectable life in the undesirable section of a large urban center. *The Street*, published in 1946, had wide circulation and considerable praise.

In the 1940's the best known of the younger Negro writers was Richard Wright. It became clear that he was the master of the short story when his *Uncle Tom's Children* appeared in 1938. *Native Son*, which came out in 1940, immediately placed Wright in the front ranks of contemporary American writers. The stark, tragic realism with which he described the frustrations of a young Negro living in the blighted slums of a great

American city may be compared favorably with the best similar works in American literary history. The work was widely circulated by the Book-of-the-Month Club as one of its selections and also through the general bookstores. In 1941 Wright brought out his *Twelve Million Black Voices*, a folk history of the American Negro. In 1945 *Black Boy*, a record of Wright's childhood and youth in Mississippi, was a Book-of-the-Month Club selection. Although there was disagreement over the accuracy of the work as autobiography, there was no dissent about its power as a story of life among poor, underprivileged, Southern Negroes. *The Outsider*, which appeared in 1953, did not receive the favorable critical acclaim that Wright's earlier works enjoyed, but by that time he was firmly established as one of the major writers of modern America.

Ralph Ellison has been compared by some critics with Richard Wright for his talents as a writer and for his insight into important social problems. *The Invisible Man* received the National Book Award in 1952, and in 1955 Ellison received the Prix de Rome and went to the American Academy in Rome to complete his work on a second novel. His volume of essays, *Shadow and Act*, was published in 1964. The most widely read writer was Frank Yerby. In 1944 he won the O. Henry Memorial Award with his short story, "Health Card." In 1946 *The Foxes of Harrow* remained on the best-seller list for many months and was reported to have approached the million-copy mark. In succeeding years he published numerous novels; all of them reached the best-seller list and some were filmed in Hollywood.

In the post-war years several young Negro writers won wide critical acclaim. John Oliver Killens showed great talent in his novel of Southern life, *Youngblood* (1954) and in the film scripts he wrote for Harry Belafonte. His *And Then They Heard the Thunder* was regarded by many as the most important novel about the Negro during World War II, while *Blackman's Burden* (1965) contains lively essays on the question of race. James Baldwin, who early showed much promise as an essayist and novelist, followed Richard Wright into a Paris exile. Unlike Wright, he returned. The promise one saw in *Go Tell It On the Mountain* (1953) and *Notes of A Native Son* (1955) was fulfilled in *Nobody Knows My Name* (1960) and *Another Country* (1962) in the sixties. Baldwin's *The Fire Next Time* (1963) is one of the most important pieces of writing to come out of the Negro Revolution. LeRoi Jones, an angrier and more solemn writer, has used his ample talents in a volume of poetry, *Preface to A Twenty Volume Suicide Note* (1961), a non-fiction work, *Blues: Negro Music in White America* (1963) and his highly controversial and thoroughly engaging *System of Dante's Hell* (1965).

In dramatic arts Negro writers contented themselves, for the most part, with writing one-act plays for the little theater. Most of the writing was done by teachers of dramatic art in Negro colleges. Randolph Edmonds of Florida Agricultural and Mechanical University published several volumes of plays about Negro life, including *Six Plays for a Negro Theater* (1934), and *Land of Cotton and Other Plays* (1942). At Howard University James W. Butcher, Jr., wrote "The Seer" and several other plays. Owen Dodson, also of Howard University, wrote "The Divine Comedy" and "The Garden of Time" while a student at Yale University, and they were produced at Yale and several other Eastern institutions. Thomas D. Pawley, Jr., of Lincoln University in Missouri published several plays in 1938, including *Jedgement Day, Smokey,* and *Son of Liberty.*

While many Negro colleges stimulated an interest in the dramatic arts through the work of the little theaters on the campuses, there was little opportunity for young Negroes to pursue acting as a career because of the limitations placed upon the Negro by the demands of the theater-going public. Negroes in roles other than as servants were likely to hamper the success of a play, especially on cross-country runs, and few authors were willing to run the risk. Some substantial progress was made with Paul Robeson as *Othello,* which he had previously played in London, Hilda Simms in *Anna Lucasta,* Gordon Heath in *Deep Are the Roots,* and Canada Lee in *On Whitman Avenue.* The last two plays dealt with two of America's most pressing social problems: the return of Negro soldiers to Southern communities and the housing of Negroes in Northern cities. With these advances the Negro could look forward to a more secure place in the American theater. The Negro in the field of drama made a significant step forward with the production in 1959 of Lorraine Hansberry's *A Raisin in the Sun.* A moving story about the housing problems of a Negro family, it won the New York Critics Circle Award. Miss Hansberry's second play, *The Sign in Sidney Brustein's Window,* was produced shortly before her death in 1964. Although his novels and essays won for him his greatest acclaim, James Baldwin enjoyed moderate success with his plays, the outstanding of which was *Blues for Mister Charlie*, produced in 1964. Other Negro writers who produced works for the stage included LeRoi Jones, Langston Hughes, and Owen Dodson.

In motion pictures the problem of handling Negro actors was more serious because of the tremendous influence of Southern box-offices on motion picture production. In 1929 the first major all-Negro picture, *Hallelujah*, was produced by King Vidor. Although it was well received, it did not open the doors for the general participation of Negroes as actors in Hollywood. In 1934 Fannie Hurst's *Imitation of Life*, with Louise Beavers and Fredi Washington as well as several outstanding white actors and actresses, emphasized the difficulties confronting Negroes of light complexion. This, however, was not the typical role of the Negro in Hollywood. Negroes such as Etta Moten, Bill Robinson, Hazel Scott, and Lena Horne succeeded in securing contracts from major producers which made it possible for them to play respectable roles as entertainers. Until World War II the greater portion of Negroes who secured parts in movie productions were servants, laborers, or criminals. As a servant in *Gone With the Wind*, Hattie McDaniel won the Academy Award for the best supporting role of 1939. Unlike the legitimate stage there was little inclination in Hollywood to undertake the integration of Negroes into productions on the basis of equality. Except in the area of purveying news, the Negro film companies experienced little success in the field of motion picture production.

In more recent years talented and versatile Negroes had careers that took them from the New York stage to Hollywood films and points in between. Ossie Davis and his wife, Ruby Dee, starred in the Broadway hit, *Purlie Victorious*, written by Davis, and in the film version, *Gone Are the Days*. Sammy Davis, Jr. played numerous roles in motion pictures, became a television star, and had a long, successful run on Broadway in the title role of *Golden Boy*. Comedians such as Dick Gregory and Godfrey Cambridge introduced biting satire on the racial theme in their night club and television performances. Harry Belafonte attracted huge audiences with his unique singing of folk music and his dramatic roles in motion pictures. In the latter medium, however, the outstanding star was Sidney Poitier who won the coveted Academy Award as the best actor in 1963 for his performance in *Lilies of the Field.* In 1966 Bill Cosby received the "Emmy Award" for his acting role in the television series, "I Spy."

Though the second period saw little in the way of a revival of the large, all-Negro musical revues similar to the smash hits of the early twenties, Negroes continued to play an important part in the light entertainment field. Count Basie, Louis Jordan, Louis Armstrong, Cab Calloway, and others were in great demand for their uninhibited renditions of jazz music, and Jimmie Lunceford, Noble Sissle, Duke Ellington, and others were equally successful in the field of "sophisticated swing." The major night clubs of New York, Chicago, and other cities frequently employed Negro orchestras, singers, and dancers. Billy Rose gave many Negroes an opportunity in his New York World's Fair production of a popular version of Gilbert and Sullivan's *Mikado.* Later, both Murial Rahn and Muriel Smith rose to fame in the title role of Rose's *Carmen Jones.* Still later singers like Lena Horne, Diahann Carroll, and Nat "King" Cole became popular on the stage and in recordings.

In serious music William Grant Still was the outstanding composer of the recent period. His symphonies, *Africa, Afro-American Symphony*, and *Symphony in G Minor: Song of a New Race* were performed by many of the major orchestras of America. He was commissioned to write many serious pieces, including the work he did for the New York World's Fair in 1939, and was named by Howard Hanson as one of the four leading composers of America. Meanwhile, R. Nathaniel Dett continued to compose works for the piano and voice ensembles until his death in 1943. William L. Dawson of Tuskegee Institute, John W. Work of Fisk University, and Warner Lawson of Howard University composed and arranged numerous works, primarily for choruses and choirs. Among the conductors who achieved international reputations were Dean Dixon, the conductor of the American Youth Symphony Orchestra, and Rudolph Dunbar, who was the guest conductor of several major orchestras both in Europe and the United States.

In recent years there has been a steady increase of widely acclaimed Negro singers. Paul Robeson and Roland Hayes continued to draw large audiences and generous critical praise during the second period. They shared the spotlight with Edward Matthews, Aubrey Pankey, Kenneth Spencer, and William Warfield. In 1935 Marian Anderson, acclaimed in Europe by

Sibelius and Toscanini as one of the great singers of the world, returned in a veritable blaze of glory and twenty years later was still regarded by many as the greatest living contralto. Dorothy Maynor and Carol Brice won the praise of Serge Koussevitsky as well as thousands of music lovers. Ann Brown and Todd Duncan added to their laurels in their interpretations of the title roles of George Gershwin's folk opera, *Porgy and Bess*. Even before major opera companies of the United States were using Negroes in their casts, Camilla Williams sang the title role of *Madame Butterfly* with a group of New York artists in 1946. At the same time Ellabelle Davis was invited to sing *Aïda* with the Mexican Grand Opera Company.

Only here and there did the color line appear on the American concert stage. There were some incidents, such as the refusal of the Daughters of the American Revolution to permit Marian Anderson to use Constitution Hall in Washington in 1939; but a smashing victory over segregation was rendered when she was invited by Harold L. Ickes, Secretary of the Interior, to sing from the steps of the Lincoln Memorial on Easter Sunday, 1939. The victory of the Negro singers in later years was symbolized not only by the opening of Constitution Hall to many of them but also by their acceptance in the major opera companies of the United States. By 1956 the Metropolitan Opera Association of New York had signed contracts with several Negro singers, including Marian Anderson, Robert McFerrin, and Mattiwilda Dobbs, who had already sung with several major opera companies in Europe. Meanwhile, singers like Leontyne Price and Lawrence Winters were singing opera on television and with the New York City Opera company.

This was merely the beginning of the operatic triumphs of Negro singers. In the nineteen sixties Gloria Davey, Thurman Bailey, and Grace Bumbry became regular members of European companies. At the Metropolitan in New York, the number of Negroes on the roster climbed steadily. In 1961 Leontyne Price sang the title role on opening night and received this signal honor again in 1966, when the new home of the Metropolitan Opera Association was opened. Meanwhile, George Shirley became one of the most durable and admired tenors with the New York company.

Several outstanding Negro painters were also receiving recognition at this time. Hale Woodruff of Atlanta University and New York University won numerous prizes for his works; his

MARIAN ANDERSON AT THE LINCOLN MEMORIAL. When the Daughters of the American Revolution refused to permit Marian Anderson to sing in Constitution Hall, the Secretary of the Interior invited her to give a recital on the steps of the Lincoln Memorial. More than 75,000 people gathered on Easter Sunday 1939, to hear her. Courtesy Hurok Attractions.

LEONTYNE PRICE SANG THE LEADING ROLE in Samuel Barber's "Antony and Cleopatra" when the new Metropolitan Opera House at Lincoln Center opened on September 16, 1966. Shown backstage at the close of the performance are Rosalind Elias as Charmian, Justino Diaz as Antony, Franco Zeffirelli, director, Rudolf Bing, manager, Miss Price, Mr. Barber, and Thomas Schippers, conductor. Courtesy of Metropolitan Opera Company.

murals in the Talladega College Library portraying the Armistad incident were regarded as artistic history at its best. Charles Alston of New York proved to be one of the most versatile of the Negro artists. His portraits, caricatures, and pieces of sculpture were to be found in several major American museums. Lois Mailou Jones and James Porter of Howard University won recognition for their works in oils. Ernest Crichlow, Romare Bearden, and E. Simms Campbell of New York were among the leading illustrators and caricaturists in America by midcentury. In sculpture three women and two men were among the leaders in the field. Elizabeth Prophet's work in wood and stone was well known. Her "Congolaise" and "Head of a Negro" were widely reproduced as examples of the successful use of Negro subjects in this difficult medium. Augusta Savage's "Head of Dr. DuBois" was one of the best known pieces of Negro sculpture in America, her "Lift Every Voice and Sing" was praised by many at the New York World's Fair of 1939 as a noble expression of the Negro in music. Selma Burke achieved wide recognition for her work on the head of Franklin D. Roosevelt for the Recorder of Deeds Building in Washington. Sargeant Johnson enjoyed success as a decorative sculptor, while Richmond Barthé became the foremost Negro sculptor of the postwar years. His series of busts of famous actors and actresses, including John Gielgud, Phillips Holmes, and Katherine Cornell displays his talents in his field. "Shoe Shine Boy" and "The Boxer" were praised by critics in the field. His pre-eminence was acknowledged in 1946 when he was commissioned to do the bust of Booker T. Washington for the Hall of Fame at New York University.

It takes little perspective to realize that the Renaissance that began shortly after the close of World War I is still in progress. The interruptions of the Depression and World War II were slight, and, in some respects, these two disturbances served as stimuli for the greater articulation of the American Negro. It does not seem too much to assert that the peak of the second stage of the Renaissance has not been reached. With greater opportunities for education, with rich experiences, and with the fearlessness that comes from greater security and a greater sense of belonging, there is every reason to believe that future historians will regard the first fifty years of the Renaissance as merely the beginning of a long period of self-expression and self-revelation of the Negro in American life.

XXVII •

The New Deal

Political Regeneration

● *Although there was little opportunity for him to participate in* the affairs of government, the Negro remained an issue in American politics from the Civil War down to the end of World War I. What patronage he enjoyed under the Republican Presidents during the late nineteenth and early twentieth centuries had diminished perceptibly under Wilson, and an almost impenetrable pall of gloom settled over the Negro's political prospects before the end of the first administration of the exponent of the New Freedom. The period of the war brought new economic opportunities to the Negroes of the United States; too, there came in its wake a new hope for the greater exercise of political power. This hope stemmed from practical situations much more than it did from the ideological expressions of the war-time leaders. The migration of large numbers to Northern urban centers and the ambitious and restless nature of many of the newcomers combined to produce a new power which some of them were quick to realize. In consequence of the concentration of Negroes in the Northern cities there developed a political resurgence on the part of Negroes that placed them once more in the thick of American politics and gave them the kind of strength that they had not exercised since the period of the Reconstruction.

It was only natural that the resurgence would manifest itself first in the centers where the Negro population had grown most rapidly. In Chicago political leaders realized that the Negro vote had become potent when, in 1915, Oscar DePriest was elected alderman from the densely populated South Side. In New York Negroes had gained enough strength by 1917 to send Edward A. Johnson to the state assembly. In each succeeding year they became more aware of their political potentialities and took advantage of their opportunities. The breaking away from tradition which had characterized the literary movement in the twenties was likewise found in politics. There seemed to be an interest not so much in patronage as in an over-all program for the improvement of the condition of Negroes. While many Negroes had early been satisfied with President Taft's appointment of William H. Lewis of Boston as Assistant Attorney General of the United States and with President Wilson's appointment of Robert H. Terrell of Washington as judge of the municipal court of the District of Columbia, few regarded such appointments as more than political crumbs by 1920. In 1924 when the Democratic candidate for President, John W. Davis, promised that if elected he would make no distinctions on the basis of race or creed, and when the Progressive candidate, Robert LaFollette, made a similar statement, Negroes deserted the Republican party in considerable numbers.

The real disaffection of Negroes in the party of Lincoln began in 1928 when Republicans attempted to resurrect a strong party in the South with white leadership. Prominent Negro Republican leaders, such as Benjamin Davis of Georgia, Perry Howard of Mississippi, and William McDonald of Texas, lost influence in their states as the Republican high command began to recognize white leaders in those states and to seat white delegates at the National Convention instead of the Negro delegates who presented themselves. Leaders like Robert Church of Memphis were so incensed over the lily-white Republican movement in the South that they refused to serve on the national advisory committee. The Baltimore *Afro-American*, Norfolk *Journal and Guide*, and Boston *Guardian*, all Negro newspapers, supported Alfred E. Smith rather than Herbert Hoover.

The Hoover upset—he carried Florida, Kentucky, North Carolina, Tennessee, Texas, Virginia, and West Virginia—demonstrated the Republicans' possibility of amassing strength among white Southerners, especially when the Democratic candidate was a Roman Catholic and an advocate of the repeal of prohibition. It also showed the extent which the Republican party was willing to alienate the Negro vote in an effort to build up a following that could crack the Southern Democratic stronghold. By 1928 Negroes had learned to vote in considerable numbers for candidates who were not Republicans. At a time when more and more independent thought was motivating the actions of Negroes the Republicans could ill afford to jeopardize their leadership of a group that was becoming a political power to be reckoned with in some sections of the country. After the election, to add insult to injury, the new President is reported to have said that he was very much interested in building up a Republican party in the South "such as could commend itself to the citizens of those states."

The election of Oscar DePriest to the national House of Representatives in 1928 compensated for the disappointment of the Negroes who opposed Herbert Hoover, and it also gave all Negroes new hope concerning their political possibilities in American life. DePriest had moved to Chicago from his Alabama home in 1899, and almost immediately he developed an interest in politics and worked up from a ward committeeman to become the first Negro alderman. As early as 1923 he was mentioned as a possible candidate for Congress, and with the cooperation of William H. Thompson his influence steadily increased. With the death of Martin B. Madden, who had been renominated by the Republicans in 1928, DePriest's big opportunity came. He announced his candidacy, and with the help of powerful Republican interests he was able to overcome the opposition of his enemies and to win the seat from the First Illinois Congressional District by a plurality of 3,800. George White's prediction of 1901 that Negroes would return to Congress had come true. The Negro had returned to the halls of Congress, and for the first time in the nation's history a Northern Negro sat in the nation's lawmaking body. By 1956 there were three such persons in the House of Representatives. (See Chapter XXX.)

DePriest's position was peculiar. He represented not only his own district, but all the Negroes of the United States. During his three terms in office he was in great demand as a speaker and was pointed to by Negroes everywhere as the realization of their fondest dreams. One Negro newspaper said that his presence in Washington gave the Negro "new hope, new courage, and new inspiration." The white South was alarmed that a Negro had achieved so high a distinction in American political life. When Mrs. DePriest attended a tea at the White House for the wives and families of Congressmen, Southerners were outraged, and several Southern legislatures passed resolutions "condemning certain social policies of the administration in entertaining Negroes in the White House on a parity with white ladies." In Birmingham, where DePriest was scheduled to speak, the Ku Klux Klan burned him in effigy. Through all the insults that were heaped upon him DePriest maintained an imperturbable calm and continued to try to secure greater recognition for the Negro in the national government. Many of his energies were doubtless dissipated by the peculiar demands of his role, but his presence in Washington symbolized the regeneration of the Negro in politics and prepared the way for his successors both in Congress and in other high places.

More and more Negroes were using their votes to register their protests. They studied the voting records of members of Congress and watched the utterances and policies of the Presidents in order to ferret out those whom they considered their enemies. As early as 1923 they began to fight those Senators who were responsible for the death of the Dyer anti-lynching bill. In 1930 they vigorously opposed the confirmation of John J. Parker to the United States Supreme Court because he was reported to have said that the "participation of the Negro in politics is a source of evil and danger to both races." When his name was finally rejected by the Senate, Negroes began to turn their guns on those Senators who had voted for his confirmation. Thus, they helped to defeat Henry J. Allen of Kansas and Roscoe McCulloch of Ohio. Despite the fact that Negroes had helped elect Samuel Shortridge of California to the Senate in 1926, they turned against him in 1932 and helped to bring about his defeat. Many Negroes who had supported President Hoover now began to regard him as their enemy. They did not like the manner in which he supported the lily-white Republican movement in the South, and they openly censured him for his appointment of Judge Parker to the Supreme Court. They noticed, also, a decline in the patronage that was given to Negro Republicans. Like many other Americans, moreover, some Negroes placed the responsibility for the Depression on the shoulders of the President and roundly condemned the relief policy which he fostered. Some Negro leaders grumbled that it would take a long time for the funds of the Reconstruction Finance Corporation to trickle down through the giant but defunct industrial firms to the Negroes who were at the bottom. They were ready, therefore, to try something else at the end of Hoover's first term in office.

It was not easy for the Negroes to desert the Republican party in 1932, and many of them remained true to the tradition and voted for the party of Lincoln. They continued to have the feeling that the "best people" voted Republican; it meant a great deal to many Negroes to be identified with that group. Few Negroes outside New York were acquainted with Roosevelt, and he had aroused little enthusiasm as a public figure. They were fearful, moreover, that a Democratic victory would lead to the ascendancy of Southern politicians in Washington, with the consequent degradation of the Negro, as had happened during Wilson's administration. Finally, rumors of Roosevelt's ill health terrified some Negroes as they thought of the possibility of the succession of John Nance Garner of Texas to the Presidency. Only in New York City had Negro Democratic organizations been able to draw large numbers into their folds. Theirs was a difficult task, and Negroes showed great reluctance to break with the past and vote Democratic. In Chicago, for example, only 23 per cent of the Negro vote was for Democrats in the election of 1932. Among those who deserted the Republican party few were willing to "throw their votes away" by voting the Communist ticket, although a Negro, James W. Ford, was the vice-presidential candidate in 1932, 1936, and 1940.

President Roosevelt was not long in office before he gained a large following among Negroes. The dramatic manner in which he tackled the problems before him captured the imagination of Negroes as it did most Americans; and his fireside chats gave many a feeling of belonging that they had never experienced before. Negroes early regarded the relief and recovery programs which he advocated as especially beneficial to them, although there were later to be many Negro critics of the administration of relief under the New Deal. The President frequently received Negro visitors, and it was widely known that Robert L. Vann of Pittsburgh, Julian Rainey of Boston, William T. Thompkins of Kansas City, and F. B. Ransom of Indianapolis were high in the Democratic councils. Roosevelt visited Negro institutions and sent messages to Negro organizations, thus adding to his popularity with Negro groups. His physical handicap was an inspiration to them. He had overcome his; perhaps, some day, they could overcome theirs. Mrs. Roosevelt was especially friendly to Negroes. She was known to be on intimate terms with Mrs. Mary McLeod Bethune, and she invited the National Council of Negro Women, of which Mrs. Bethune was president, to have tea at the White House. She visited Negro schools and federal projects and spoke to numerous groups. When she was photographed while being escorted by two R.O.T.C. cadets of Howard University, Negroes circulated the picture widely as an example of the broad equalitarianism of the occupants of the White House, while Southern whites circulated it to show the depth to which the occupants in the White House had descended in their dealings with Negroes. These manifestations of interest caused thousands of Negroes to change their party allegiance in the years following Roosevelt's election in 1932.

The extent of the shift of the Negro's allegiance was demonstrated in 1934 when Arthur W. Mitchell, who only four years earlier had been registered as a Republican, was elected to the Congress on the Democratic ticket to replace Oscar DePriest. Mitchell was the first Negro Democrat ever to sit in the Congress, and it was a source of considerable embarrassment to his

THE PRESIDENTS EXCHANGE VISITS. When President Roosevelt went to Africa in 1943 he took the opportunity to inspect American troops stationed in Liberia and to cement the friendship between that country and the United States. In May 1943, President Edwin Barclay and President-Elect William V. Tubman returned the visit and consulted with State Department officials. The close relationship that developed during the war was described by some writers as the "Washington-Monrovia Axis." Photo by Army Air Forces from Wide World Photos.

Southern colleagues to have him as a member of their majority. All over the country Negroes were not only changing from the party of Lincoln to the party of Roosevelt, but were becoming more active in politics. Negro newspapers showed a spirited interest in the campaign of 1936, and while the majority of them supported Roosevelt, Landon and the Republicans were not without their Negro enthusiasts. The Republicans made a desperate bid for Negro support and received it in some quarters. By 1940 some opposition to Roosevelt had developed, and there was a substantial decline in the Negro support which he received. Negroes accused the administration of discriminating in some of the relief agencies and of excluding Negroes from preliminary defense preparations that were being made. Some Negroes, moreover, discovered a ring of sincerity in Wendell Willkie's promises and were inclined to desert what they were pleased to call "The Dirty Deal."

In the years that followed the Negro vote came to be more evenly divided, with the groups in the great urban centers of the North still showing an inclination toward the politics of the New Deal, but wielding sufficient influence in pivotal states such as Illinois, Ohio, Pennsylvania, and New York to cause much anxiety in both Republican and Democratic circles. Labor matters, foreign policies, and innumerable other issues influenced the urban Negro voters just as they did the white voters. The Negro, feeling his strength and importance as a voter, felt that he could now demand a high price for his support. In addition to demanding that the candidates reflect his views on public questions that interested all Americans, he could also demand that the candidate's views on questions touching on race be acceptable. It was a large order, but in many communities the candidates had bitter regrets when they ignored these demands. By 1946, with President Roosevelt out of the picture, Negroes felt that they could defect without appearing to be disloyal. They had already become wary of the domination of the Congress by Southern leaders who had blocked anti-lynching and fair employment legislation. Like many another American in 1946, moreover, the Negro voter had come to feel that change in itself was healthy; and he joined his fellows in bringing about that change.

The strength of Negroes during the period of political regeneration was manifested not only in the consideration which both major parties gave to them in national elections, but also in their successes in state and local elections. An increasing number of Negroes secured seats in state legislatures in the thirties and forties. After 1932 Negro legislators in California, Illinois, Indiana, Kansas, Kentucky, New Jersey, New York, Ohio, Pennsylvania, and West Virginia became commonplace; and both the Republican and Democratic parties were represented. The reapportionment of seats in state legislatures, ordered by the United States Supreme Court in 1962, increased the opportunities for Negroes to win elections. The greater concentration of Negroes in urban centers and their increased political consciousness were additional factors. In 1946 some thirty Negroes secured seats in the legislatures of ten states. Twenty years later one hundred and four Negroes—four Republicans and one hundred Democrats—sat in the legislatures of twenty-four states, including ten Negroes in the two houses of the Georgia legislature.

After 1930, when two Negroes were elected to municipal judgeships in New York City, other municipalities elected or appointed Negroes to judicial positions. In 1947 there were Negro judges in Cleveland, Chicago, Los Angeles, Washington, and several other cities, while the number had increased to seven in New York City. In 1966 the number of Negro judges in New York had more than doubled while the number had significantly increased in the other cities mentioned above. And more than a dozen new cities boasted Negro judges. In many American cities Negroes helped to manage the affairs of government as members of boards of education and city councils, as members of the prosecuting attorneys' staffs and policemen, and as tax commissioners and corporation counsels. The fruits of political activity were enjoyed in a very real way by the faithful servants of parties, and there was an increasing recognition of the contributions that qualified Negroes could make to the improvement of the life of the whole community. There were few who would doubt that a political regeneration had taken place among Negroes that made it possible for them to demand a great deal of consideration from both major parties.

Roosevelt's Black Cabinet

One of the most important factors in the achievement of political respectability on the part of the Negroes of the United States was the New Deal policy of securing the assistance of Negro specialists and advisers in various governmental departments. Seeking the advice of Negroes was not a Roosevelt innovation. Many a President had sought to feel the pulse of the Negro population through one or more Negroes in whom he had confidence. Booker T. Washington was merely an outstanding example of a long-established practice. In most instances, of course, the Negro advisers were faithful members of the President's party who gave counsel in the matter of patronage. Roosevelt's group of Negro advisers differed from the others in at least four important respects. In the first place, the number of "Black Cabineteers" was fairly large, in contrast to the small number on whom previous Presidents had relied for advice. It is not possible to set an arbitrary number because it was changing constantly and because one cannot always be sure as to whether certain appointees were members of a select circle that may be regarded as a "cabinet." In the second place, they were placed in positions of sufficient importance that both the government and the Negro population generally regarded the appointment as significant. They were not persons whose relationship with the government was nebulous and unofficial. They were oath-bound servants of the people of the United States.

Members of Roosevelt's "Black Cabinet" were not politicians, for the most part. To be sure, there were Negro political advisers to the President; but few of them were in high positions of trust in the government. It was later said that they were mere salesmen for the New Deal, but of many of them it could not be said that they were brought in because of faithful political service during campaigns; and finally, they were highly intelligent and highly trained persons who were called in to perform a specific function. To that extent their appointments were in line with the tendency of the New Deal administration to commandeer the services of the best trained persons in the country to assist in developing a program of relief, recovery, and reform. They were called by some, therefore, the "Black Brain Trust," for among them were doctors of juridical science, doctors of philosophy, and college presidents. Some Negroes complained that it was most unfortunate that they were confined to problems affecting the Negro, and one severe critic said that they could be described as "Porkbarrelensis Africanus" because of that fact. Few could deny, however, that they were well qualified to perform many functions; and indeed, on occasion, many of them worked in areas that only indirectly touched on the Negro.

It was Harold L. Ickes, a former president of the Chicago branch of the N.A.A.C.P., who, as Secretary of the Interior, began to hire racial advisers in the early days of the New Deal. The first was Clark Foreman, a white Liberal of Atlanta. He used Negroes as his own advisers, on the legal staff of the Department, and in other agencies such as the National Parks Service. Later, some of them transferred to other departments, thereby enlarging the area in which Negroes were exercising some influence in the national government. Mrs. Roosevelt is credited with the responsibility of enlarging the size of the "Black Cabinet," while Dr. Will W. Alexander, who was for a time the head of the Farm Security Administration, was also instrumental in having Negroes appointed to positions that were regarded as having "cabinet" rank.

Among the Negroes who occupied high places in New Deal counsels was Robert L. Vann, the editor of the *Pittsburgh Courier*, who served as Special Assistant to the Attorney General. William H. Hastie, the Dean of the Howard University Law School, entered government service as Assistant Solicitor in the Department of the Interior. He went on to serve as the Judge of the Virgin Islands and later as Civilian Aide to the Secretary of War. In 1946 he was appointed as Governor of the Virgin Islands. Robert C. Weaver was the first Negro to be the racial adviser in the Department of the Interior. Subsequently he served in several agencies, including Federal Housing Authority, Office of Emergency Management, and War Manpower Commission. In 1966 he became the first Negro member of the President's Cabinet when the Housing and Home Finance Agency, which he headed, became a Department in the Executive branch of the federal government. Eugene Kinckle Jones, Executive Secretary of the National Urban League, went to Washington in the early days of the New Deal and for a period was Adviser on Negro Affairs in the Department of Commerce. Lawrence A. Oxley, veteran social worker, was chief of the Division of Negro Labor in the Department of Labor. Mrs. Mary McLeod Bethune, founder-president of Bethune-Cookman College, was active for several years as the Director of the Division of Negro Affairs of the National Youth Administration. Edgar Brown, president of the United Government Employees, was Adviser on Negro Affairs in the Civilian Conservation Corps. Frank S. Horne, poet and teacher, has served in several capacities, primarily with the federal housing programs. William J. Trent was racial adviser in the Department of the Interior before going to the Federal Works Agency as the racial relations officer.

The list of Negroes in such positions with the federal government could be expanded almost indefinitely. Some of them remained only a few months, while others found the government service so much to their liking that they stayed on during the Truman administration. With the onset of the war emergency the number was substantially increased. Mrs. Crystal Bird Fauset, a former member of the Pennsylvania legislature, went to Washington as the racial relations adviser in the Office of Civilian Defense. Ted Poston, veteran New York newspaper man, served as racial adviser in the Office of War Information. Colonel Campbell Johnson became an executive assistant to General Lewis B. Hershey, the head of the National Selective Service. Others served with the War Production Board, War Manpower Commission, Office of Price Administration, and Social Security Board. Numerous consultants served only temporarily: Abram L. Harris with the National Recovery Administration, William H. Dean with the National Resources Planning Board, Ralph Bunche with the Library of Congress and later more permanently with the Department of State, Rayford W. Logan with the Coordinator of Inter-American Affairs, and Ira DeA. Reid with the Social Security Board's Bureau of Employment.

The task of "top" Negroes in the federal government was a difficult and delicate one: to press for the economic and political equality of the Negroes in the United States. This task was all the more peculiar because they were seeking to bring about an integration that was antithetical to their own roles. Almost all of them were unalterably opposed to any suggestion of racial separatism. When the suggestion was made that there should perhaps be a Negro bureau to deal with all matters affecting the Negro, several of the "Black Cabineteers" combined their energies to oppose it on the grounds that it would tend to make the Negro a ward of the government, thus extending and perpetuating segregation. These leaders also sought to increase the opportunities for the employment of Negroes in the government and in industry. They attempted to secure employment for Negroes on the basis of ability and training rather than color. They worked closely with the Negro press and with other agencies of influence, through influential members of Congress, and through powerful white citizens in public and private stations. The aggressive temper of the Negro population, the war emergency, and the inclination of many New Dealers to grant to Negroes equal opportunities served to make possible the achievement of a measure of success on the part of these Negro government officials.

If these officials smarted under the roles assigned to them as advisers on Negro affairs, they could look with satisfaction at the increasing number of Negroes who were serving their government in innumerable capacities. Thanks to new Civil Service regulations it was no longer necessary to indicate one's race on applications or to attach a photograph to the forms, but after personal interviews, hiring officials sometimes avoided hiring Negroes by availing themselves of the Civil Service Commission's "rule of three." Even so, Negro employees on the federal payroll increased from about 50,000 in 1933 to approximately 200,000 before the end of 1946. It is only fair to add that the majority of the newly employed Negroes were in the low, unskilled, and semi-skilled brackets, but there was a fairly generous sprinkling of economists, statisticians, chemists, physicists, and other specialists. In some portions of the government the segregation of whites and Negroes was abolished, while most of the government cafeterias were opened to Negroes. While the "Black Cabineteers" were not responsible for all of the improvements of the conditions of Negro federal employees, they could view with pride all of the changes and could claim as their handiwork a considerable number of them.

Government Agencies and Negro Relief

It was only natural that as the Roosevelt administration established innumerable agencies to aid in the recovery from the severe depression Negroes would benefit from the amelioration of the suffering of the total population. Because of the long custom of discriminating against Negroes, however, it was equally natural that in these agencies there would be variations between Negro and white relief grants, numbers of workers, salaries, and the like. The National Industrial Recovery Act, which sought to stimulate industry, established "codes of fair competition" which provided for a minimum wage scale of twelve to fifteen dollars per week, a forty-hour week, and the abolition of child labor under the age of sixteen. Few Negroes represented their group at code hearings, and cost of living differentials were set up which discriminated against the groups in which most Negro workers were to be found. In the steel, laundry, tobacco, and other codes Negroes frequently received lower minimum wages than whites. The compliance boards that were to enforce the codes were frequently made up of employers who were themselves violating the codes. Negroes seldom complained, for fear of losing their jobs. When wages were raised, in compliance with the codes, employers frequently dismissed Negro workers and paid higher wages to whites. Few Negroes lamented the fact that the Supreme Court in 1935 declared the NIRA unconstitutional.

A larger number of Negroes was affected by the various New Deal measures to provide for relief to farmers and agricultural workers. In the crop reduction program of the Agricultural Adjustment Administration farmers were given cash benefits for plowing under their cotton, wheat, and tobacco crops and for slaughtering their hogs. While the farmers' cash benefits rose to billions of dollars under the AAA, many of the grants intended for Negro farmers were dissipated and misappropriated. Many landlords took advantage of the illiterate sharecroppers and tenants and kept the checks intended for them. It was this dishonesty, which hurt both white and Negro farm workers, that led to the organization of the unfortunate victims into such groups as the Southern Tenant Farmers Union. The planters vigorously opposed the unions and appealed to race prejudice in an effort to break up the cooperation of Negro and white farmers. Even after administrative rules were changed to provide for payments to be made direct to the tenants, many Negroes suffered; for then white landlords would merely remove them from the land and receive the benefits themselves. Aside from the benefits which some Negro farmers received in the form of cash payment, they obtained valuable experience in voting in the AAA referenda on such important questions as establishing marketing quotas. They demonstrated conclusively that Negroes and whites could vote together on important economic questions, even though Negroes were being effectively disfranchised in the regular elections of most Southern states.

In the Tennessee Valley Authority, Rural Electrification Administration, Federal Land Bank, and local production credit associations, Negroes received benefits, though infrequently in proportion to their numbers or their needs. They were substantially aided by the program of the Farm Security Administration which, in 1937, took over the work of the Resettlement Administration. Unfortunately, the FSA had an appropriation only one-fifth of the amount appropriated for the AAA, but it undertook to establish communities of small farmers who rented land from the FSA and to make loans to persons who desired to purchase their own farms. An extensive educational program was carried on in which, among other things, new methods of production and marketing were introduced. Under the program Negroes received a large share of the benefits, and thousands, for the first time in their lives, were able to purchase land. The FSA, to a considerable extent because of the leadership of Will W. Alexander, insisted that there be no discrimination between white and Negro farmers. Because of its racial policies and because of its program of settling farmers in communities it was almost always under fire. The attacks grew to the point that its enemies were successful in 1942 in cutting its appropriations so drastically that the greater part of its program had to be curtailed.

The National Youth Administration and the Civilian Conservation Corps undertook to provide relief for the youth of America. Under Aubrey Williams, a white Mississippian, the NYA set up a liberal program for the benefit of Negro youth. Not only was Mrs. Bethune invited to Washington to head the Division of Negro affairs, but state and local supervisors were appointed in the districts in which large numbers of Negroes lived. In the out-of-school programs, 13 per cent of the enrollees were Negroes; and they were learning a variety of trades that were to be beneficial in the war emergency. In the student-work program, more than 64,000, or 10 per cent, were Negroes. Young Negroes, all the way from grade schools to graduate schools, found it possible to continue their education by means of the benefits under NYA. The CCC maintained a policy of strict segregation, but during its lifetime from 1933 to 1942, approximately 200,000 Negro boys worked in camps established by the agency. In addition to the work of conservation, reforestation, and the prevention of soil erosion, the agency set up an educational program under the supervision of Negro advisers. A measurable amount of illiteracy was eliminated and juvenile delinquency was doubtless curtailed. Although many critics raised serious doubts as to the wisdom of the program, it can hardly be argued that the CCC did not relieve the suffering of many young men during the height of the Depression.

The New Deal housing program aided Negroes not only in their efforts to keep their homes and to acquire better living accommodations, but also in the matter of providing employment on projects under construction. Some Negroes secured loans from the Home Owners Loan Corporation in order to make payments on their homes during the Depression. A limited number were able to borrow money to build homes on loans that were guaranteed by the Federal Housing Authority. In many communities, however, some banks were not inclined to lend money to Negroes because such an investment was regarded as a poor risk and because of the uncertain future value of houses occupied by Negroes. The most widely beneficial federal housing program for Negroes was the encouragement which local housing authorities received to construct low-cost housing projects with subsidies from the United States Housing Authority, later the Federal Public Housing Authority. In some Northern communities the projects were occupied jointly by Negroes and whites, while in each Southern community where the program was undertaken, a project was constructed for Negroes as well as for whites. Approximately one-third of the units constructed were occupied by Negro families. These modern units, with electric or gas appliances and facilities for recreation, gave thousands of Negro families an opportunity to live in a kind of environment that previously was wholly unknown to them.

Under the Public Works Administration and similar agencies, a considerable number of Negro hospitals and other public buildings were constructed. Through an arrangement with local and state governments, these federal agencies subsidized the construction of buildings at Negro colleges, playgrounds, community centers, and the like. Despite the provisions of the contracts which called for the employment of a proportionate number of Negro workers in the construction of these buildings, there was frequent disregard for the stipulations. In some cities, where as many as a score of buildings were constructed with public funds, no Negroes were employed. In some others, however, there was some employment of Negro workers. In very few instances did Negroes secure the amount of employment to which they were entitled under the provisions of the contracts.

During the darkest days of the Depression, it was not possible, either for the government or private business, to employ a sufficient number of persons to relieve satisfactorily the plight of the unemployed portion of the population. The Federal Emergency Relief Administration and, later, the Works Progress Administration (renamed the Work Projects Administration) provided both for relief in kind—food, clothing, and commodity surpluses—and in employment. There was a greater inclination toward fairness to Negroes in providing material relief than in providing employment. Under the WPA there was such a variation in policy from place to place as to make impossible any general statement with regard to the treatment of Negroes. In some communities Negroes secured employment on professional and clerical levels. Thus, Negro actors, writers, and artists in cities like New York and Chicago carried on their activities under the WPA. In some other localities, however, it was almost impossible even for unskilled Negroes to secure any benefits from the relief agencies. The wage differentials in some communities were great, and the administrators made no apologies for them. Even so, more than a million Negroes owed their living to the WPA in 1939, and this and similar agencies of relief had become so important that they were surpassed only by agriculture and domestic service as sources of income for the Negro population.

When the Social Security Board was established in 1935, provisions were made for old age assistance and unemployment benefits in a large number of occupational categories. Since agricultural and domestic workers were excluded, however, a tremendous proportion of the Negro population failed to qualify for the benefits provided by the act. Even in the program of old age assistance, there was a tendency to grant lower sums, especially in the South, to aged Negroes than to aged whites.

Although there was outright discrimination against Negroes in the local administration of most of the New Deal measures in the South, some substantial progress was made toward breaking down the pattern of discrimination as it had existed. Many Southern leaders found the New Deal distasteful because it concentrated too much power in Washington, it relieved the suffering of many whites and Negroes on whose poverty many Southern politicians had climbed to power, and it undertook to force equality in the administration of its benefits. They could ill afford to break with the Roosevelt administration, however, because it gave them national power through their control of Congressional committees and their voice in party politics. They had to pay lip service, for the most part, to the liberal measures of the New Deal and to compromise on many issues. The entrance of highly trained Negroes into the government in Washington and federal agencies in the South gave Southerners a new experience in their relationships with Negroes. The consequences of this new experience could not be measured until years after the New Deal had passed out of existence.

Unemployed, poverty-stricken Negroes could not always wait for the New Deal to provide them with the necessaries of life. At times they found it desirable to use what force they could command to secure employment and relief. In 1929 Albon Holsey of the National Negro Business League organized the Colored Merchants Association which undertook to establish stores in New York and to purchase their merchandise cooperatively. Negroes were urged to buy from these merchants because their patronage would provide jobs for Negroes. The stores survived less than two years of the severe Depression, however. Shortly thereafter the "Jobs-for-Negroes" movement began in earnest in St. Louis, where the Urban League led a boycott against a white-owned chain store whose trade was almost exclusively Negro but employed no Negroes. The movement spread to Pittsburgh, Chicago, Cleveland, and other Midwestern cities; and many Negroes found employment because of the pressure brought on white employers in Negro sections. The most intensive campaign was carried on in New York City where Negroes organized the Citizens' League for Fair Play in 1933. Under the leadership of the Reverend John H. Johnson the Committee attempted to persuade white merchants to use Negro clerks. When their first efforts failed they resorted to picketing the stores and appealing to Negroes with the motto, "Don't Buy Where You Can't Work." On street corners Negroes harangued their listeners concerning the injustice of whites refusing to hire Negro workers. Intense feeling developed, and the movement almost got out of hand when imposters, such as Eugene Brown, alias Sufi Abdul Hamid, took advantage of the situation to advance their own interests. The campaign resulted in hundreds of Negroes obtaining employment in stores in Harlem and with public utilities, such as the telephone, electric, and bus companies.

In 1935 the intense feeling against the white merchants and

landlords in Harlem led to a riot of considerable proportions. A Negro lad was caught stealing a small knife from the counter of one of the stores in 125th Street. He succeeded in escaping, but there were rumors that he had been beaten to death. Negro crowds gathered and loudly accused the police of brutality and the white merchants of discrimination in employment. They began to smash store windows and to raid the shelves. During most of the night of March 19 the rioting went on. Three Negroes were killed, 200 stores were smashed, and more than two million dollars worth of damage was done. The city was both outraged and ashamed. Mayor LaGuardia appointed an interracial Committee on Conditions in Harlem. A staff of investigators, headed by E. Franklin Frazier, studied the causes of the riot and concluded that the lawlessness was provoked by "resentments against racial discrimination and poverty in the midst of plenty." There was insufficient relief of a private and public nature to stem the tide of social unrest that prevailed in Harlem and other Negro communities in America. Picketing and other measures of pressure continued to be employed. Negroes were encouraged greatly by the decision of the Supreme Court in 1937 which declared that the picketing of firms which refused to employ Negroes was a legal technique of securing relief.

Negro Labor and the Unions

The Great Depression worked a real hardship on the labor movement in the United States; and Negro workers, who, even during the days of prosperity, found the going very difficult, now met almost insurmountable barriers against their employment. Section 7a of the National Industrial Recovery Act provided that employees should have the right to organize and bargain collectively through representatives of their own choosing without "interference, restraint, or coercion of employers of labor." The National Labor Board was set up to enforce those provisions of the statute. While the average employee found it especially difficult to press for higher wages and keep his job, Negro workers found it almost impossible. Indeed, the discriminatory policies of the major labor unions were still in effect, and, therefore, the majority of the Negro workers were outside whatever protection section 7a offered. In 1935 the Wagner Act gave permanency and strength to the National Labor Relations Board that had replaced the NLB during the previous year. It established clear-cut rules for collective bargaining and set up 22 regional boards to conduct elections in industry to determine what group of employees was entitled to bargain with the employer. It was also given wide powers in handling labor disputes and in settling strikes. It was, indeed, labor's "bill of rights"; and if the Negro worker could succeed in breaking the barriers which excluded him from the unions he could enter a new period of security and prosperity in the enjoyment of these rights.

In 1938 the Congress passed the Fair Labor Standards Act, better known as the Wages and Hours Bill. It was another step in the direction of the emancipation of the worker in that it established a minimum wage of 25 cents per hour which was to be increased to 40 cents by 1945 and a maximum week of 40 hours, any excess of which was to be paid on the basis of time and one-half. While perhaps better than a million Negroes were affected by the Act, several millions were not; since it excluded agricultural and domestic workers, just as the Social Security Act did. Here again, the Act meant little if Negroes were unable to secure employment in those industries covered by it.

In an effort to keep whites employed during the Depression labor unions maintained their exclusion policies on a stricter basis than ever. The bulk of Negroes that found employment fell into the unskilled and semi-skilled categories where there was little or no union organization. They were thus without the protection which the NLRB granted to workers. There were few unions like the United Mine Workers which brought together in one union all the workers in a given industry and which, since its organization in 1890, had encouraged the organization and participation of Negro workers. By 1934 even a considerable number of white workers had come to the conclusion that the labor movement in the United States could have great success only by organizing the mass production industries which employed hundreds of thousands, indeed millions, of men. William Green, the president of the American Federation of Labor, had said that he would organize 25,000,000 workers, but he had failed miserably. Meanwhile, the industrial bloc in the American Federation of Labor was demanding that mass production industries be organized, and on an industry-wide basis rather than on the basis of crafts.

In 1935 the industrial bloc, led by John L. Lewis of the United Mine Workers, become more insistent, and when the American Federation of Labor remained adamant, Lewis called a meeting for November 9, 1935, out of which grew the Committee for Industrial Organization. Even after the organization of the C.I.O., Lewis attempted to force the American Federation of Labor to foster the organization of the mass production industries on a craft basis, but the older organization spurned all offers by Lewis, even to the $500,000 which he offered to finance such a campaign. The break with the American Federation of Labor became clean; and the C.I.O. began to make plans to conduct such a campaign itself. With the resources of its own member unions, among which were the United Mine Workers, the Amalgamated Clothing Workers, and the International Ladies' Garment Workers, the C.I.O. undertook to organize the mass production industries. From the beginning the C.I.O. made it clear that it sought to organize workers regardless of race, and in its early campaigns it made a special appeal to Negroes. When the Steel Workers Organizing Committee set out in 1936 to organize the workers in the steel industry, the United Mine Workers transferred many of its Negro organizers to the S.W.O.C. In some places Negroes joined enthusiastically, but in others they were skeptical, having learned through bitter experience to distrust all labor unions. The National Urban League and other Negro organizations urged Negro steel workers to join the C.I.O. affiliate. Finally, the vast majority of Negro workers joined the S.W.O.C., and when the great steel companies capitulated in 1937 and agreed to bargain with the organization under the NLRB, thousands of Negro workers benefited from the pay raises for which the contract called.

In the meat-packing industry, where many Negroes were already employed, 5,000 enrolled in the Chicago locals of the Amalgamated Meat Cutters and Butcher Workmen after the adoption of the blanket code under the NRA. There was similar affiliation in Kansas City and St. Louis. When the union showed signs of weakness, especially after the demise of the NRA, many Negroes dropped out. In 1936 the C.I.O., with its United Packing House Workers' Industrial Union, sought to organize the industry, but its efforts gave new life to the older union. Although there was some considerable success on the part of the C.I.O. union, to which many Negroes belonged, the competition was keen, and both unions still maintained organizations in the meat-packing industry.

In the clothing industry the Ladies' Garment Workers Union and the Amalgamated Clothing Workers long had a liberal policy toward the organization of Negro workers. Although relatively few Negroes were employed in the clothing industry, by far the great majority of them belonged to these two unions, with the ILGWU having the larger number. When the C.I.O was organized the program of equality among the workers was extended, and they became exemplary unions in equality of treatment of their members. In the textile industry, on the other hand, Negroes had little opportunity to work either in Northern or Southern mills. The C.I.O. affiliate, the Textile Workers Union, undertook to organize the workers; but it made little headway, except in the North. In the unions of Virginia and North Carolina, there were separate white and Negro locals, perhaps the only C.I.O. unions where such an arrangement existed. In making this compromise with its policy the C.I.O. attempted to face realistically the extremely difficult task of organizing an industry whose white workers historically have viewed these jobs as belonging to them. Negro machine operators in Southern textile mills were almost as unthinkable as Negroes dining in white restaurants in the South.

In 1940 Negroes constituted more than 30 per cent of all the longshoremen in the United States. Because of the hazards involved in the work and because of its irregularity, whites viewed work on the docks as undesirable. Since its beginning in 1892, the International Longshoremen's Association, an affiliate of the American Federation of Labor which dominated the Atlantic and Gulf ports, opposed racial discrimination. Several of its vice-presidents were Negroes; but in some ports there were separate Negro and white locals. In 1937 the International Longshoremen's and Warehousemen's Union was organized on the West Coast and affiliated with the C.I.O. In the beginning it did not seem to welcome Negro workers, but after the strike of 1934 Harry Bridges, the leader, made it clear that Negro labor would receive equality of treatment in the I.L.&W.U. Special anti-discrimination committees were organized to see that no worker was discharged or intimidated on account of race or color. An effort was made to see to it that all loading and unloading gangs were interracial. Various efforts were made on the part of the I.L.&W.U. to organize the workers of the Atlantic and Gulf ports, but because of the fairly satisfactory policy of the ILA, little headway was made. Some observers believed that the vigorous non-discrimination policy of the West Coast union had a salutary effect on the policy of the ILA.

It was during World War I that Negroes forced open the doors of the automobile industry. Even so, there were only 20,720 Negro automobile workers as late as 1940, constituting 3.8 per cent of the total number. After that time, however, both the number and proportion of Negroes in the industry increased substantially. Except in Ford's River Rouge factory, the great majority of Negroes in the automobile industry were employed in unskilled jobs. The unionization of automobile workers was largely the work of the C.I.O., and since Negroes were not in special crafts in the industry, they were fortunate that a union adhering to the industrial principle organized the workers. The United Automobile Workers of the C.I.O. succeeded in forcing all the major automobile manufacturers to recognize it as the legal collective bargaining agent for the workers, with the Ford plant finally capitulating after a bitter fight in 1941. Negroes, who feared that the encroachments of the U.A.W.–C.I.O. would hurt their status in the Ford plants, supported the union enthusiastically when they found that their conditions were actually improved under the new contract. Although some white members opposed the union's fight for more equitable opportunities for Negroes in the automobile industry, the union continued its fight. The new opportunities which the war provided for the employment of Negroes in the automobile industry created innumerable social as well as economic problems, especially in the Detroit area, which the shedding of blood did not altogether solve.

Substantial progress was made in the organization of Negroes in other industries. In the tobacco industry, the building trades, and the aircraft industry, for example, Negroes were included in the organization. The C.I.O. was, for the most part, consistently opposed to discrimination on the basis of race; and while it did not always have great success in its efforts to organize, as with the tobacco workers, for example, its use of Negro organizers and its election of Negro officers had wide appeal among Negroes. The stand of the C.I.O. Committee to Abolish Racial Discrimination and the liberal program of the Political Action Committee gave new hope to many Negroes. They were no longer suspicious of labor organizations and were inclined to join in the program of strikes with as much enthusiasm as other workers. A feeling of security and belonging arose among Negro workers that was one of the most significant developments in the direction of their more complete integration into American life.

XXVIII •

Social and Cultural Strivings

Trends in Education

● *In the twentieth century Negroes manifested the same intense* interest in education that characterized their attitude in the period immediately following emancipation. More and more the public assumed the responsibility that earlier had been borne by philanthropy and self-help; but the triumph of white supremacy implied that Negroes would not share in educational opportunities on any basis that even remotely approached equality. The enrollment of Negroes increased steadily. In 1880 there were 714,884 Negroes in school in Alabama, Arkansas, Florida, Georgia, Louisiana, Mississippi, North and South Carolina, Tennessee, and Texas. By 1910 the number had increased to 1,426,102; while in 1930 there were 1,893,068 in school. In the same states the enrollment of white children increased even more rapidly, with the consequent diversion of educational funds to schools for whites, thereby depriving Negroes of adequate facilities and well-trained teachers. For the last two generations the bulk of the Negro children have attended impoverished, small, short-term schools with pronounced inadequacies in every phase of the educational program.

The movement of large numbers of Negroes from the rural areas to urban centers has resulted in some substantial improvement of educational opportunities. In urban areas there is much more taxable wealth, the income from which is sometimes made available for educational purposes. The concentration of the population in urban centers, moreover, has had the effect of reducing the per capita cost of education even when many inadequacies remain. Finally, in cities there is a greater opportunity to impose various forms of taxes, thereby increasing the opportunities for the diversion of some of the income to schools for Negroes. This is not to say that Negroes have received an equitable share of the school funds in any of the Southern states. By 1900 every state in the South had enacted laws that provided for separate schools, and through the years the courts have made it clear that even though the laws did not specify that the schools for both races should be equal, they, nevertheless, must be equal. The compliance with the provision of equality in educational facilities has nowhere been more than slight; and in most instances there has been a studied disregard for the principle of equality. The inability of the South to support a dual system of education has been reflected largely in its neglect of schools for Negroes.

Nothing has been more persistent in the twentieth century than the tendency to continue the disparity between the money spent for the education of white children and that spent for the education of Negro children. In fact, in many instances the differential has increased. In 1900 for every $2 spent for the education of Negroes in the South, $3 was spent on whites; but in 1930 $7 was spent for whites to every $2 spent for Negroes. As recently as 1935–36, the current expenditures per white pupil in ten Southern states averaged $37.87, while such expenditures per Negro pupil averaged $13.09, slightly more than one-sixth as much as for all schools of the United States. In the new services, such as transportation, visual aids, laboratory equipment, modern buildings, and the like, the differentials are even greater. In North Carolina, for example, where greater attention has consistently been given to the education of Negroes than in most Southern states, more money was spent in 1929–30 for school trucks for white children than was spent for new schools for Negro children.

The work of the Julius Rosenwald Fund in assisting in the construction of school buildings for Negroes in the South has helped greatly in providing better facilities. Between 1913 and 1932 the Fund aided in the construction of more than 5,000 Negro school buildings in 15 Southern states. Approximately 64 per cent of the expenditure of $28,000,000 came from the tax funds; 15 per cent was contributed by the Rosenwald Fund;

interested white persons contributed 4 per cent; while 17 per cent was made up of a "flood of small contributions of Negroes themselves—striking evidence of the desire of members of this race for schooling for their children." When the program was completed more than 30 per cent of all the Negroes in school in the South were housed in buildings that had been constructed under the Rosenwald aid program. By 1935, however, the value of Negro school sites, buildings, and equipment per pupil enrolled was less than one-fifth as great as the per pupil value of property in white schools.

Only in teachers' salaries was there a noticeable decline in the differentials between Negro and white education by 1945. In most instances where equalization was achieved it came only after a court battle which was vigorously contested by school authorities. Several counties of Virginia, Maryland, and South Carolina equalized the salaries of white and Negro teachers after court action was either instituted or threatened. In 1940 Judge John J. Parker of the United States Circuit Court of Appeals ruled in a case arising in Norfolk, Virginia, that a double salary standard based on race was an unconstitutional discrimination. Although this had the effect of forcing equalization in the county in which the case arose, there was no wholesale equalization in the South as a result of the Parker decision. In 1944 North Carolina completed its program of gradually reducing the differential and proudly announced that it had brought about equalization without court action. Even with the help of teachers' associations and the N.A.A.C.P. the program of equalization moved slowly; in some communities where it was formally achieved, devices such as city supplements had the effect of creating the disparity once more.

While the Great Depression hurt education all over the country, it worked a special hardship on Southern Negro schools. Construction of new school buildings stopped almost entirely, the teaching staff was curtailed to the point that effective teaching was practically impossible, and miserably low salaries were further reduced. Southern states curtailed expenditures for Negro schools in the same or greater proportion that they were curtailed in white schools. While no Southern communtiy could afford to cut its educational expenditures without seriously impairing the effectiveness of its program, the slightest cut in Negro education often had the effect of taking away the barest essentials in the educational program, including the teacher.

As the Negro population moved North in the twentieth century, especially during and after World War I, Negro children were forced, or at least urged, to attend schools predominantly Negro. This was not too difficult, since in most communities Negroes lived in restricted areas. Few states followed the lead of New York, which, in 1900, prohibited separate schools. Most of the Northern states were inclined to provide separate schools for Negroes, especially where white patrons brought pressure to bear upon school officials. The practices varied greatly from place to place. In several Northern states there were separate schools as well as institutions where all races could attend, such as New Jersey, Ohio, Illinois, and Indiana. In two states, Kansas and Arizona, only on the elementary level was separate education mandatory; but in both cases several communities had separate schools on the secondary level. In large cities, such as Gary and Indianapolis, Indiana, where separate high schools were established, the schools constructed for the use of Negroes were modern and adequate in almost every detail. Some have suggested that meticulous care was taken in the construction of Negro schools in such communities in order that Negroes would not feel that they were being deprived of equal education in attending exclusively Negro institutions. The tendency toward segregation increased as white students engaged in strikes and violence in the effort to prevent Negro students from attending schools open to all, and as white parents kept children away from school in the effort to force the authorities to set aside separate facilities for Negro pupils. In the 1950's, however, there were some evidences of a slow and painful movement toward the democratization of education.

It is not possible to measure the effects that separate and unequal education have had on both white and Negro populations in the areas where it has been maintained. There can be no doubt that separate schools have been one of the strongest supports of the concept of white supremacy in the South, by emphasizing the greater importance of the white population which enjoys superior training to that which the Negroes have. Separate schools have, moreover, contributed to the perpetuation of a leadership that is devoted not only to the idea of separate education but also to the maintenance of economic and political inequalities between the white and Negro populations of the South. Even under such handicaps, there has been a notable decline in illiteracy among Negroes. In 1870 at least

81 per cent of all Negroes above ten years old were illiterate. Sixty years later only 16 per cent of the Negroes of the United States were illiterate. In 1946 Ambrose Caliver of the United States Office of Education undertook to establish a program which would wipe out the last remnants of illiteracy among the Negro population. The decline of illiteracy is a clear indication that Negroes are gradually coming into possession of the "fundamentals of civilized intercourse" and that, in due time, they will not suffer the personal handicaps that have so often made them the dupes of those who have sought to control them.

Institutions for the higher education of Negroes increased from one in 1854 to more than 100 in 1955. They are of three general types: church colleges, privately endowed colleges, and public colleges. While the period of their most rapid growth was the thirty years following the Civil War, the twentieth century has witnessed a considerable increase. During the last fifty years the most notable growth has been in colleges supported by the public. States and cities established colleges for the education of Negroes and also took over church-supported institutions and supported them out of public funds. An example of the latter procedure was the assumption by North Carolina in 1923 of the support of the National Religious Training School of Durham that had been founded in 1910 by Dr. James E. Shepard. The name of the institution was changed to the North Carolina College for Negroes (again changed to the North Carolina College at Durham in 1947) and became the only state-supported liberal arts college for Negroes in the country.

While some of the larger philanthropic agencies continued to support Negro institutions of higher learning in the twentieth century, the contributions of wealthy industrial magnates of the North declined noticeably. Consequently many smaller private institutions found it necessary to curtail their programs or to close down altogether. Only a few were able to secure aid from the states. Others did not seek such support. Institutions such as Virginia Union University and Shaw University discontinued the training of lawyers and physicians. Walden University and Roger Williams University were among those that went out of existence. In 1916 the situation among the Negro institutions of higher learning was described as deplorable. In a survey made by the United States Office of Education under the direction of Thomas Jesse Jones it was disclosed that only 33 of the 653 existing private and state schools were teaching any subjects of college grade; and only three, Howard, Fisk, and Meharry Medical College, "had a student body, teaching force, equipment and income sufficient to warrant the characterization of 'college.'" Jones's recommendation that some institutions should be closed and his influence in directing Northern philanthropy to those schools which he favored brought a shower of criticism from many Negro leaders. They accused Jones of favoring institutions that were controlled by white educators and industrialists, and of undertaking to determine what kind of education was best for Negroes. Although some of the criticisms against Jones were doubtless valid, the survey did bring about a more scientific approach to the problem of higher education for Negroes and stimulated both states and churches to make many needed improvements in their schools.

The enrollment of Negroes in institutions of higher learning increased steadily in the years following World War I. By 1933 more than 38,000 Negroes were receiving collegiate instruction, 97 per cent of whom were in colleges in the Southern states. Despite the Depression which forced the curtailment of expenditures, the physical plants of Negro colleges were improved and teachers continued to increase their training. The problems of Negro colleges had not been solved, however, and several gave evidence of long-term planning by consolidating their resources. In 1929 Morehouse College, Spelman, and Atlanta University combined to form the Atlanta University System under John Hope. A few years later two institutions in New Orleans, Straight College and New Orleans University, gave up their separate identity and became Dillard University, receiving considerable support from the Rosenwald Fund and the General Education Board. The operating expenses had become such a problem to private institutions by 1943 that 33 of them pooled their solicitation resources and organized the United Negro College Fund. White philanthropists, such as John D. Rockefeller, Jr., Winthrop W. Aldrich, Walter Hoving, and Thomas A. Morgan, have assisted in the annual campaigns which have averaged approximately one million dollars.

In the last thirty years many Negro colleges and secondary schools have achieved standards sufficiently high to receive class "A" accreditation from several rating agencies. The fact that private institutions led in accreditation emphasizes the disparity that existed between white and Negro public institutions. In very recent years, however, a larger number of public institutions have measured up to the requirements set up by the rating agencies. By 1944, for example, 22 of the 231 high schools for Negroes in North Carolina had been accredited by the Southern Association of Colleges and Secondary Schools. Today, only a few of the major state-supported Negro colleges have failed to receive class "A" ratings.

Three significant and unusual trends of Negroes in higher education have become noticeable in recent years. In the first place, more Negroes than ever before are enrolling in the large Northern colleges and universities. Before World War I it was most unusual to see more than a dozen Negroes at a Northern institution. In recent years, however, as many as several hundred have been in attendance at the University of Michigan, the Ohio State University, Columbia University, and New York University, with a generous sprinkling of Negroes at many other such institutions. Meanwhile, the Negro enrollment at Southern white colleges has steadily increased. By 1967 few Southern colleges had no Negro students. In the second place, the number of Negro administrators of Negro colleges has increased markedly. Thirty years ago Knoxville College, St. Augustine's College, Shaw University, Virginia Union University, and Fisk University were administered by white presidents. By 1956, Negro presidents administered all these institutions, and very few of the leading colleges for Negroes were in the hands of white presidents. Finally, there has been a growing tendency on the part of white colleges to employ Negroes on their instructional staffs. At the turn of the century W. E. B. DuBois was on the faculty of the University of Pennsylvania. Later, Harvard University Medical School employed William A. Hinton in a non-teaching capacity. In recent years the number has increased considerably. In 1956 more than 40 Northern colleges and universities had Negro teachers. Among them were the University of Chicago, Rhode Island State College, Roosevelt University, the University of Louisville, Antioch College, New York University, Princeton University, the New School for Social Research, and the municipal colleges of New York City. By 1966 many other colleges and universities, including some in the Southern states, were employing Negroes on their faculties.

The problem of graduate and professional training of Negroes increased as a larger number of Negroes sought such training. Early in the century graduate training was available at only a few privately supported Negro institutions. After World

War I Howard University, Fisk University, and Atlanta University increased their emphasis on graduate education; but it was not possible for these institutions to serve Negroes in all the areas of training in demand. The feeling increased, moreover, that the public should provide graduate and professional training for Negroes as well as for whites. Several states took cognizance of this point of view and appropriated money for out-of-state graduate training of Negroes. By 1935 several states had made such appropriations, and in succeeding years other Southern states sought to solve the problem in that manner. The temper of Negroes was clearly shown by their willingness to resort to court action to force states to discharge their obligations to Negro citizens. As early as 1933 Thomas Hocutt of North Carolina sought to force admission to the school of pharmacy of the University of North Carolina by bringing court action against the officials of the University. The applicant lost his suit on a technicality when he failed to establish his eligibility for admission. In 1935 Donald Murray was successful in his effort to be admitted to the law school of the University of Maryland. The Maryland Court of Appeals made it clear that it regarded out-of-state tuition scholarships as unequal and, therefore, a violation of the law.

The most significant step toward providing graduate and professional training for Negroes grew out of the decision of the United States Supreme Court in the case of *Missouri* ex rel. *Gaines v. Canada, Registrar of the University, et al.* In 1936 Lloyd Gaines applied for admission to the law school of the University of Missouri. When refused he carried his case to the courts, and when the state courts denied him relief he appealed to the federal courts. In the decision of the Supreme Court in 1938 Chief Justice Hughes said that it was the duty of the state to provide education for all its citizens and that the provision must be made *within the state*. To provide legal education for white residents within the state and to fail to do so for Negroes "is a denial of the equality of legal right to the enjoyment of the privilege which the State has set up, and the provision for the payment of tuition fees in another State does not remove the discrimination."

The decision caused immediate consternation in the states having separate systems of education. The reaction to the decision varied in different states. Some states gave more attention to the matter of appropriating out-of-state tuition, while others sought to establish opportunities for graduate and professional training at colleges already in operation. Missouri established a law school; Virginia increased its provisions for out-of-state aid; North Carolina, having made some moves in the direction of providing graduate training, accelerated its program. States of the lower South reluctantly appropriated funds to educate Negroes out of the state. South Carolina established a "chair of law" at the State Agricultural and Mechanical Institute at Orangeburg. Only Maryland and West Virginia moved in the direction of making it possible for Negroes to attend institutions that had heretofore been used exclusively by white residents.

In succeeding years the fight for graduate education within the Southern states continued. Texas was attempting to comply with a recent decision of its state court that a Negro who applied for admission to the University of Texas Law School must either be admitted or a law school established for him that was substantially equal. The problem had plagued the Conference of Southern Governors, as well as the Conference of Deans of Southern Graduate schools. In 1945 the latter organization made a thorough study of the needs of Negroes for graduate instruction and found that Negroes were, on the whole, strong in their demands for equal educational opportunities within the states where they resided. The idea of regional graduate and professional schools for Negroes was receiving much more support from whites than from Negroes by 1946.

In that year the struggle assumed critical proportions when Ada Sipuel sought admission to the law school of the University of Oklahoma. Two years later, when the United States Supreme Court ordered the state to provide facilities for her to secure a legal education, the university regents arranged for the establishment of a separate law school for Negroes. She declined to attend this institution that had been set up within two weeks, began the litigation all over again, and finally gained admission to the university law school in 1949. Meanwhile, another Oklahoma Negro, G. W. McLaurin, demanded and gained admission to the graduate school of the state university. When university officials segregated him in the classroom, library, and cafeteria, McLaurin sued again; on June 5, 1950, the Supreme Court ordered an end to these segregation practices. On the same day the Court ordered the law school of the University of Texas to open its doors to a Negro applicant despite the fact that the state maintained a separate law school for Negroes. It was not possible, Chief Justice Vinson declared, for the Negro law school to provide the student with an education equal to that of the university law school, which had a strong faculty, experienced administrators, influential alumni, standing in the community, tradition, and prestige.

To white Southerners this was a frightening departure from the "separate but equal" doctrine that had been laid down in *Plessy v. Ferguson* in 1896. For most Southern states, it also was convincing proof that the Court would, in time, open all public institutions of higher education to Negroes. Arkansas had already voluntarily admitted its first Negro in 1947. In 1951 the University of Louisville absorbed the Negro municipal college and employed one Negro professor. Within a few years, either voluntarily or by court order, several Southern state universities had admitted Negroes. In 1956 only South Carolina, Georgia, Florida, and Mississippi had admitted no Negro students to their state universities.

Both the friends and foes of segregation in education conceded that the bitter fight would be waged on the level of the elementary and secondary schools, and the fight was not long in coming. The segregationists hoped that they would be able to prevent or forestall indefinitely the admission of Negroes to white elementary and secondary schools by moving toward the equalization of Negro schools. Thus, as the Supreme Court moved away from the doctrine of "separate but equal" in a succession of cases, the Southern states spent funds, almost desperately, on Negro schools. By 1956 some of the most modern schools to be found anywhere in the United States had been constructed for Negro children in Southern communities. Southern leaders pledged themselves to equalize white and Negro schools as rapidly as possible.

The determination of the South to provide better public schools for Negroes brought its resources to one of its major problems in a tardy and inadequate fashion. Not only were the Negro schools so inadequate that it would take years to achieve even a semblance of equality, but by 1951 the N.A.A.C.P. had decided to attack the very principle of segregation as unconstitutional and a clear contravention of the "basic ethical concepts of our Judaeo-Christian tradition." To test the validity of segregated schools the N.A.A.C.P., in 1952, carried to the Supreme Court five cases arising in South Carolina, Virginia, Kansas, Delaware, and the District of Columbia. Many organizations entered briefs in behalf of the Negroes' position, and the Attorney General of the United States asked that the "separate but equal" doctrine be stricken down. "Racial discrimination," he declared, "furnishes grist for the Communist propaganda mills, and it raises doubt even among friendly nations as to the intensity of our devotion to the democratic faith."

Perhap no public question in the United States in the twentieth century aroused more interest at home and abroad than the debate about the constitutionality of segregated public schools. It was presented on the platform and in the press as well as before the Supreme Court of the United States. The decision of the Court on May 17, 1954, was unequivocal in outlawing segregated public schools. Speaking for a unanimous court Chief Justice Earl Warren said:

> Separate educational facilities are inherently unequal. Therefore, we hold that the plaintiffs and others similarly situated for whom the actions have been brought are, by reason of the segregation complained of, deprived of the equal protection of the laws guaranteed by the Fourteenth Amendment. . . .

The Chief Justice then conceded that the formulation of the decrees presented problems of "considerable complexity" because of the great variety of local conditions and because of the wide applicability of the decision. He, therefore, invited the parties to the suits, the Attorney General of the United States, and the attorneys general of the states requiring or permitting segregation in public education to offer suggestions during the next term of court regarding the manner in which relief should be granted.

Reaction to the decision was mixed. There was the anticipated defiance in such states as South Carolina, Georgia, and Mississippi, whose governors had threatened to abolish public schools rather than permit white and Negro children to attend the same schools. Fiery crosses were burned in some Texas and Florida towns, and scattered groups of whites organized to resist the decision. But the *Knoxville Journal* spoke for many Southerners when it said, "No citizen, fitted by character and intelligence to sit as a justice of the Supreme Court, and sworn to uphold the Constitution of the United States, could have decided this question other than the way it was decided." A group of leading Negro educators praised the decision in a statement entitled "It Was The Right and Moral Thing To Do," and several groups of white church women in the South declared that they accepted the decision "with humility."

Meanwhile, most of the communities with segregated schools waited for the final decree before taking any specific steps. Exceptions were Topeka, Kansas, Baltimore, Maryland, Washington, D.C., and some towns in West Virginia and Delaware. These communities were following the lead that some border cities had taken before the decision, among which were Cairo, Illinois, and Evansville, Indiana.

A year later, May 31, 1955, the Supreme Court remanded the cases to the courts of origin, "because of their proximity to local conditions." The Court made it clear, however, that although the lower courts should be guided by equitable principles including practical flexibility, adjustment, and reconciliation of public and private needs, the vitality of the constitutional principles set forth in its 1954 decision could not "be allowed to yield simply because of disagreement with them." It then instructed the courts to require the defendants to make "a prompt and reasonable start toward full compliance" with the ruling of May 17, 1954.

Indefinite delay now seemed impossible, and adverse Southern reaction to the Court's decision was pronounced. An editorial in a Richmond newspaper referred to the Supreme Court justices as "that inept fraternity of politicians and professors" and declared that the Court "repudiated the Constitution, spit upon the Tenth Amendment, and rewrote the fundamental law of this land to suit their own gauzy concepts of sociology." The legislature of one state, by unanimous vote, passed a resolution declaring it impossible to educate the children of both races in the same school. Several states enacted stand-by legislation to turn the public schools over to private organizations if Negroes succeeded in gaining admission to white public schools. But the President of the Southern Regional Council called the decree "wise, moderate, and workable," while a South Carolina newspaper, in an editorial entitled, "We Can't Win," said "Segregation is going—it's all but gone. South Carolina and the rest of the South can't reverse the trend." Even if the South could not win, it was not ready to admit defeat. (See Chapter XXX.)

Among the other mediums of education in which Negroes manifested an interest in the twentieth century was the public library. In the South, the public library lagged behind the rest of the nation. Between 1900 and 1910, a number of public libraries in the South began to extend their services to Negroes, either through restricted privileges at the main library or the establishment of Negro branches. In 1903 the Cossitt Library of Memphis agreed to furnish a librarian and the books if Lemoyne College would furnish a room for Negro readers. In the same year the Charlotte, North Carolina, Carnegie Public Library fostered the establishment of a separate library for Negroes with its own board of management. The extension of public service to Negroes in the South was indeed slow. As late as 1935, for example, only 83 of the 565 public libraries in 13 Southern states were reported to be giving Negroes service. The Hampton Library School furnished the major portion of the trained Negro librarians during its years of existence between 1925 and 1939. Later, schools of library service were established at Atlanta University and the North Carolina College. Negroes of the South continue to be without adequate library facilities or trained librarians.

Surprisingly enough, out of the confused pattern of education for Negroes in the United States there emerged a body of highly trained men and women who may be regarded as scholars by any criterion. While almost all of them received their graduate and professional training in Northern and European universities, many of them were products of separate schools on the lower levels. While W. E. B. DuBois may be regarded as the pioneer Negro scholar in the period following the Civil War, there were numerous others with whom he had to share honors. Others who wrote widely in the field of sociology and came to be regarded as authorities in their fields were George E. Haynes, Charles S. Johnson, E. Franklin Frazier, and Oliver Cox. Scholars in the field of economics included Abram L. Harris, W. H. Dean, Robert C. Weaver, B. R. Brazeal, Charles L. Franklin. Carter G. Woodson, Charles H. Wesley, Rayford Logan, A. A. Taylor, Lawrence D. Reddick, Benjamin Quarles, W. Sherman Savage, Lorenzo Greene, Ralph Bunche, and Kenneth Clark were among the most distinguished in the other social sciences. In the humanities some leading figures were Alain Locke, J. Saunders Redding, Sterling Brown, Arthur Davis, Charles E. Burch, and Ulysses Lee. A growing number of scholars in the various scientific fields included George W. Carver, Elmer S. Imes, Ernest E. Just, Charles H. Turner, Julian Lewis, James A. Parsons, William A. Hinton, Percy Julian, and Charles Drew.

Negro scholars became increasingly articulate and contributed articles to learned journals and published numerous books. While their works were accepted in many of the white journals, they saw fit, in several fields, to establish journals of their own. In 1916 the Association for the Study of Negro Life and History began publishing the *Journal of Negro History*, which, under the editorship of Carter G. Woodson, remained one of the major historical journals for more than 30 years. In 1931 the Bureau of Educational Research of Howard University began publishing the *Journal of Negro Education*, edited by Charles H. Thompson. Its Yearbook issue became one of the most important sources of information on the historical, sociological, and educational aspects of Negro life. In 1940 W. E. B. DuBois started at Atlanta University a magazine entitled *Phylon, A Journal of Race and Culture*, which served as a broad medium of articulation for Negro scholars. White scholars contributed generously to all these publications. Some colleges sponsored periodicals for Negro scholars, such as Johnson C. Smith University's *Quarterly Review of Higher Education Among Negroes* and Wilberforce University's *Negro College Quarterly*. Others issued works of Negro scholars in their bulletins or other publications. By the middle of the twentieth century, there were many signs of maturity among Negro scholars.

The Negro's World

The forces that have operated on the Negro population during the last three centuries have been of such nature as to create a distinctly separate Negro world within the American community. It was the system of slavery with its basic assumption of an inherent difference between the white and Negro population that gave rise to the careful separation of the races. During the period of freedom, moreover, that assumption has survived the most searching scientific findings; and it has given strength and persistence to the separate Negro world. Not even the social upheaval brought about by the migration of large numbers of Negroes from rural to urban industrial centers did much to disturb the existence that Negroes led apart from the rest of the community. Indeed, the policy of forcing them into ghettoes in the larger cities had the effect of creating new forces for the perpetuation of the Negro's world. In a nation dedicated to the idea of the essential equality of mankind and in which there is a general commitment to the policy of the integration of races and cultures, the existence of a separate Negro community constitutes one of the remarkable social anomalies of the twentieth century. It is needless to add that this situation has created innumerable problems of a political, social, and economic nature that have confounded both Negroes and whites who have sought solutions to them.

Because of the laws and mores of the American community, the Negro family remained intact despite the disorganizing forces that operated to contribute to its instability. With the migration of large numbers of Negroes to American cities during and after World War I it became difficult even for Negro families with traditions of stability to remain immune to the unfavorable conditions that tended to destroy normal and healthy human relationships. Poor housing, unemployment, inadequate recreational facilities, and similar conditions contributed to delinquency among children and crime and separation among parents. The occupational differentiation which followed in the wake of industrialization and urbanization in the twentieth century drew class lines more distinctly among Negroes. While few could be regarded as upper class, a substantial middle class emerged, composed of people in the professions. The great mass of Negro industrial workers formed the broad base on which the Negro social structure was built. The contact that these various segments of the Negro population had with white Americans served to bring about a considerable amount of similarity between the social structure, interests, and tastes of the two groups. Seldom, however, did the contact reach the point where racial identity and interests disappeared. The Negro's world continued to exist apart from the larger community.

As far as new religious institutions in the post-war years were concerned, none attracted more outside attention or more dramatically pointed up the theme of Negro alienation than the Nation of Islam, commonly called the Black Muslims. The religious group undertook, modestly enough, to offer encouragement and some security to the unemployed, disinherited Negroes who had sought in vain for some sign of faith in them on the part of the larger community. Accepting the general tenets of the religion of Islam, the Black Muslims, under the leadership of Elijah Poole, who renamed himself Elijah Muhammad, renounced their faith in the ultimate solution of the race problem in the United States, rejected all names that might imply a connection with white America, and sought complete separation from the white community. The ablest and most eloquent spokesman was Malcolm X, who was read out of the Black Muslims when he described the assassination of President Kennedy as "chickens coming home to roost" and who was himself assassinated early in 1964 at a New York mass meeting of his newly formed group that competed with the Black Muslims. The Nation of Islam, bitter in its denunciation of American racism, was a voice of disgust and despair. It was as much a political and social movement as it was a religious organization.

Perhaps the most powerful institution in the Negro's world is the church. Barred as he was from many areas of social and political life, the Negro turned more and more to the church for self-expression, recognition, and leadership. Nothing in his world was so completely his own as his church. Early in the century church membership grew as it had in the post-Reconstruction period. Negroes migrated to the cities, old denominations increased in membership, and new denominations sprang up. It was an exhilarating experience for Negroes to participate in the ownership and control of their own institutions. It stimulated their pride and preserved the self-respect of many who had been humiliated in their efforts to adjust themselves in American life. The lack of opportunities of Negroes to participate fully in the affairs of other institutions caused many to concentrate their energies and attention on the church. The consequent scramble for leadership and control led to schisms, withdrawals, and reorganization. In 1917 the National Baptist Convention split into two organizations, with the older organization keeping almost twice as many members as the new group. In 1944 the National Baptist Convention, Incorporated, had more than four million members, while the National Baptist Convention of America had more than two million members.

Among the new Negro denominations that came into existence in the early twentieth century were the Triumph of the Church and Kingdom of God in Christ (1902), the Free Christian Zion Church of Christ (1905), and the Apostolic Overcoming Holy Church of God (1916). After World War I other Negro denominations emerged including the African Orthodox Church (1921), the National Baptist Evangelical Life and Soul-Saving Assembly of the U.S.A. (1921), the House of Lord (1925), and the Kodesh Church of Immanuel (1929).

Meanwhile, older denominations continued to grow, giving little evidence of being hurt by the schisms that gave birth to the new groups. By mid-century thirty-four all-Negro denominations claimed a membership of more than five million Negroes, more than 35,000 churches, and property valued at nearly $200,-000,000. The Roman Catholic Church made substantial gains among Negroes in some parts of the country, while the Protestant Episcopal Church and other Negro-white denominations seemed to hold their own.

As the Negro community came more and more to take on the attributes of an entirely separate world the Negro press performed an increasingly important function. Whereas Douglass's *North Star* fought the institution of slavery and Fortune's *New York Age* fought the relegation of Negroes to second-class citizenry, Negro newspapers of the twentieth century took up the cudgel in behalf of the underprivileged fellows. They became the medium through which the yearnings of the race were expressed, the platform from which the Negro leaders could speak, the coordinator of mass action which Negroes felt compelled to take, and the instrument by which many Negroes were educated with respect to public affairs. During the first World War the Negro newspaper came into its own. It encouraged Negroes to move to industrial centers in search of work; it urged support of the war; but it also led in the fight for the complete integration of Negroes into American life. Older newspapers, such as the Baltimore *Afro-American* and the *Chicago Defender*, enjoyed a growth such as they had never before experienced; while newer sheets, like the *Pittsburgh Courier* and the *Norfolk Journal and Guide*, made rapid strides both in circulation and influence. Editors, notably John Murphy of the *Afro*, Robert S. Abbott of the *Defender*, Robert L. Vann of the *Courier*, and P. B. Young of the *Journal and Guide*, seemed to have the capacity to combine an effective editorial policy with shrewd business sense to make their newspapers important business institutions in the Negro's world. By 1920 several of them had reached a weekly circulation of more than 100,000, while twenty years later several reported circulations above 200,000.

In the decades following World War I the number of Negro newspapers increased steadily. Every Negro community apparently felt the need for its own newspaper to perform the services that few white newspapers could or would undertake to perform. Here and there a white paper devoted a part of a page to Negro news, while most of them reported a generous share of news of crimes committed by Negroes. None of the Southern white papers, however, had an editorial policy or an interpretation of the news that satisfied the Negro ghetto. Therefore, most communities where there was an appreciable Negro population saw fit to support Negro newspapers: Houston had its *Informer;* Los Angeles, its *Eagle* and *Sentinel;* Kansas City, its *Call;* and Oklahoma City, its *Black Dispatch.* The larger papers began to publish several editions to serve various areas of the country, while some, such as the *Afro-American* and the *Houston Informer,* established chains of newspapers. Several newsgathering agencies were established, the most important of which was Claude Barnett's *Associated Negro Press.* The editors organized the Negro Newspaper Publisher's Association, and together they sought to establish uniform policies and views with regard to the important issues affecting Negroes.

By 1966 there were more than 350 Negro newspapers, magazines, and bulletins that were issued on a regular weekly, monthly, or quarterly basis. Only two newspapers, *The Atlanta World* and the *Chicago Defender,* were published daily. In recent years the most significant growth was in the field of the monthly or quarterly magazine where a number of publications vied for control of the field. Among them were *The Negro Digest, Ebony, Jet, Color,* and *Headlines.* Each Negro fraternity and sorority had an official journal, while numerous large business institutions issued weekly or monthly periodicals for their employees and patrons. The Negro world thus produced a journalistic business that represented an investment of more than $10,000,000 and provided employment for 8,000 persons.

While it cannot be said that the rise of Negroes in the professions was altogether an achievement of the post-Civil War period, it was the growth of the free, separate Negro community that provided the greatest stimulation for such a development. The Negro world needed not only teachers and clergy, but also physicians, dentists, pharmacists, nurses, attorneys, social workers, recreation leaders, morticians, and others to perform a variety of personal services. The great growth in the Negro professional class followed World War I, and the numbers in each group have continued to increase down to the present day. As the standards for qualification were raised by the state or municipal licensing boards, Negro professionals increased their training at white or Negro educational institutions. Today, they are the most highly trained group in the Negro community. The members of practically every group have come together to organize associations for their protection and mutual assistance. In so doing, they conformed to the American practice whereby persons of similar interests translate this fact into the erection of a formal organization. Through these associations Negro professionals were able to wield influence not only in the Negro world but in the larger community as well.

Negroes experienced great difficulty in developing satisfactory programs for wholesome recreation. The Y.M.C.A. and the Y.W.C.A. were able to flourish only in cities of considerable size, and community centers which received public support were likely to be as inadequately equipped and staffed as the separate school. The fraternities and sororities, which seldom had physical facilities to provide for recreation, still provided a nucleus from which both civic and recreational activities emanated. The membership of these organizations, however, was confined to college-trained men and women. The fraternal organizations, such as the Masons and Odd Fellows, increased both in membership and in numbers in the twentieth century and many of them established club-houses and centers where members and friends could enjoy the fellowship that comes from association. The most important of the newer fraternal organizations of a semi-social nature was the Improved Benevolent and Protective Order of Elks of the World.

The Boy Scout and the Girl Scout movement did not seek to incorporate the Negro youth into its organization until the late twenties. After that time Negro membership grew rapidly. Still, the majority of Negro boys and girls were without any organized out-of-school recreational activity and only a small number of Negro associations, fraternities, and clubs had programs which embraced the younger people. Motion pictures in the Negro community, frequently operated by white businessmen, became one of the most important sources of recreation for Negroes, both young and old. By mid-century, many cities were employing Negro recreational leaders who undertook to set up programs for young people which were designed to reduce the social maladjustments of the Negro population.

The growth and persistence of the Negro world did not result in the resignation of the Negro to life in this relatively small orbit. There were numerous manifestations of the effort to rise above the proscriptions that were thrown around the Negro community. These manifestations were reminiscent of the efforts that many Negro slaves made to escape their bondage and were also similar to them. Negro editors, for the most part, fought against the existence of a Negro world, as did numerous other groups and individuals. The National Negro Congress, which was organized in 1936, represented one of the most vigorous of the recent efforts of Negroes to present a solid front against the confinements to which their color apparently condemned them. It consisted of more than 500 Negro organizations and represented a large cross-section of Negro life. Its protests against various forms of discrimination and segregation were vehement, but after its meeting in 1940 it disintegrated rapidly, and many members withdrew because they believed that it was becoming a Communist front.

The Southern Negro Youth Congress which was formed in 1937 was composed of various types of youth organizations. Local councils were established and efforts were made to help young Negroes out of their many difficulties. Its program had only limited success, however. Numerous local protests and fights against restrictive covenants, separate schools, segregation in public carriers, and other policies which Negroes considered un-American showed clearly that they were consistently determined to eradicate all practices which implied their racial inferiority. Evidence of the relentless drive against segregation, for example, was their successful attack, in 1946, against a Virginia bus company which segregated interstate Negro passengers. The Supreme Court held that such segregation was unconstitutional, since it placed an undue burden on interstate commerce.

The protests of Negroes against their status did not imply that they took no pride in their race and in its possibilities. The pride of Negroes grew almost as rapidly as institutions in the Negro community. In inaugurating "Negro Health Week" Booker T. Washington hoped to inspire Negroes to guard their health and to develop habits of cleanliness which would help them become a stronger and more effective racial group. Carter G. Woodson conceived "Negro History Week" as a period in which the contributions of the Negro to the development of civilization would be sufficiently emphasized to impress Negroes as well as whites. In 1914 the N.A.A.C.P. instituted an annual award—the Spingarn Medal—to the Negro who "shall have reached the highest achievement in his field of activity." Beginning in 1926, the William E. Harmon Foundation undertook to select for awards those Negroes who had contributed most notably to the fields in which they were working. Both the Spingarn and Harmon medalists have come from a variety of fields, but the racial nature of the achievement has always been emphasized; this has doubtless stimulated the pride in race of many Negroes.

Negroes paid considerable respect to their leaders and heroes, even when dissension against them arose. They pointed with pride to the fact that Matt Henson was with Admiral Peary when he reached the North Pole in 1909; that in the twentieth century they boasted of seven heavyweight champions including, Jack Johnson and Joe Louis, and a host of other greats in the athletic world; and that in few walks of life did Negroes fail to achieve. It was the kind of pride that naturally and pardonably stemmed from a racial group as peculiarly situated as the Negro was. His world was a small one; the opportunities were relatively few; and what achievements there were, of course, loomed up all the greater.

Americanization

In the three centuries that the Negro had been a part of the evolving American civilization two important processes vitally affecting him were in operation. He was compelled to live in a world apart from the dominant group in the community and, therefore, developed institutions of his own in order to preserve his identity and individuality. At the same time, however, he participated in the affairs of the larger community to the extent that the experience helped to shape his own institutions and also promoted his integration, to a limited degree, into the pattern of life of the community. It seems unnecessary to add, of course, that his presence in America vitally affected the course of its development, for the most cursory glance at what has already been said will reveal that fact. These two processes that went on simultaneously imposed on the Negro a most difficult task, that of trying to live in two worlds at the same time. Meanwhile, there was a considerable attempt to move from one world into the other. These efforts were motivated by the desire to make the problem of existence easier by reducing the many duplications of effort involved in living in two worlds and to move closer to realization of the American concept of equalitarianism which the Negro took as seriously as any group in American life.

In the period following the Civil War America was first compelled to consider the problem of the extent to which Negroes would be permitted to move into the main stream of American life. There was no general agreement on the way in which the problem should be solved, and the heritage of the slave period served to resist any suggestion of integration. It was not a problem that Negroes could solve, for it involved acceptance. Negroes persistently sought opportunities to enter more fully into the affairs of American life, but the overtures were more frequently spurned than not. They were forced back into their own world, and as they erected more institutions and ways of life of their own the prospect of Americanization became more remote.

The effect of this whole experience upon Negroes cannot be measured accurately. Many students of race relations and inter-group relations had much to say about the matter. Opponents of the integration of the Negro concentrated their attention on the Negro community; when they found crime, delinquency, disease, and illiteracy, they insisted that these shortcomings were proof positive of the inability of the Negro to become an equal participant in the affairs of a civilized community. Friends of the idea of integration held that such shortcomings were manifestations of frustration and were, in themselves, suggestive of the abnormality, as well as the difficulty, of living in a world that had the stigma of inferiority and instability placed upon it. Unfortunately, there were many studies, especially those of the early twentieth century, that had little value because the conclusions were colored by the subjectivity and motives of the students.

Recently, a greater interest in the Negro's Americanization than ever before has been manifested. The years since emancipation are sufficient to warrant some acceptable evaluations of the manner in which Negroes have adjusted themselves, and of the extent to which they have become accepted as participants in activities in the whole of American life. Moreover, during this period new psychological and sociological techniques of studying the problems of race and community have been developed and applied. There has been, also, some interest in investigating the influence of the American democratic tradition on groups of diverse racial origins. The nation's serious economic problems in recent years have had to be considered in terms of the whole community; this has meant, of course, that the Negro's relation to the larger group has been frequently looked into. Finally, the Negro Revolution of the sixties has required a full scale re-examination of the Negro's place in American life, and this has in turn, greatly affected the evaluation of the process by which the Negro moves toward complete acceptance.

Many studies of the Negro's place in American social and economic life came out of the research of federal departments such as the Office of Education, the Department of the Interior, and the Department of Commerce. Educational institutions such as the Institute for Research in Social Science of the University of North Carolina and the Department of the Social Sciences of Fisk University undertook to present graphic and scientific pictures of the status of the Negro in American society. The works of Howard Odum, Charles S. Johnson, Rupert Vance, Gordon Blackwell, Guy B. Johnson, and others provided hitherto unavailable information concerning the Negro and his relation to the worlds in which he lived. In a series of significant volumes the American Council on Education published the findings of the American Youth Commission, which had studied the effect of the proscriptive influences of American society on personality development of Negro youth. Studies of these investigators—among whom were Allison Davis, E. Franklin Frazier, Charles S. Johnson, John Dollard, W. Lloyd Warner, J. H. Atwood, Donald W. Wyatt, Ira DeA. Reid, and Robert L. Sutherland—led one to conclude that the vast majority of Negro youth do not get an opportunity to share in the American dream of equal opportunities. They pointed out that the environment in which Negro youth is compelled to live often forces him to react in a manner that seems, to many, shiftless, irresponsible, and aggressive. The real opportunities for young Negroes to become Americanized are so few as to challenge any serious students who would be interested in seeing even an approximation of the American dream.

The most ambitious study of the place of the Negro in American life was undertaken by Gunnar Myrdal of the University of Stockholm and a large staff of sociologists, historians, economists, political scientists, psychologists, anthropologists, and other specialists under the Carnegie Corporation of New York. Several major works were published: *Myth of the Negro Past*, by Melville J. Herskovits; *Patterns of Negro Segregation*, by

Charles S. Johnson; *The Negro's Share*, by Richard Sterner and others; *Characteristics of the American Negro*, by Otto Klineberg; and *An American Dilemma*, by Gunnar Myrdal. In addition, more than a score of exhaustive studies of various aspects of the Negro were made, but were not published. An inescapable conclusion running through all the studies is that the treatment of the Negro is America's greatest scandal, and the almost universal rejection of the Negro is America's outstanding denial of its own profession of faith in the equality of mankind.

While most of the recent significant studies of the Negro contained recommendations for the improvement of his status in American life, they were primarily concerned with revealing facts and did not concentrate on programs of action. This phase was not neglected, however. Negro organizations, in recent years, continued to fight for a larger share of every aspect of American life for Negroes. To these may be added a growing number of white and interracial organizations which evolved programs for the greater integration of the Negro in American life. In 1944 a group of white and Negro Southerners met and organized the Southern Regional Council, which was, in fact, a revitalized and expanded Commission of Interracial Cooperation. The new organization was the result of a series of meetings that began with a conference of Southern Negro leaders at Durham, North Carolina, in October, 1942, followed by a similar conference of white leaders at Atlanta in April, 1943. Out of these conferences grew a collaboration committee which drew up the plan of organization of the Southern Regional Council. It declared itself to be "A Council to attain, through research and action, the ideals and practices of equal opportunity for all peoples in the South." A preliminary statement in August, 1943, contained the assertion that "the Negro in the United States and in every region is entitled to and should have every guarantee of equal opportunity that every other citizen of the United States has within the framework of the American democratic system of government." The Council participated actively in an attempt to secure political and economic equality for the Negroes of the South; if the Council undertook no drastic measures, it failed to do so because it acquiesced to the views of its first Executive Director, Guy B. Johnson, who asserted that the foothills must be captured before the mountain can be taken.

An organization which sought to secure a larger following of the masses, and whose program was more insistent about immediate concessions to the Negro, was the Southern Conference for Human Welfare. Organized in 1938, the Southern Conference tried to promulgate a program of aggressive action to raise the general level of underprivileged groups in the South. Through its state committees and local chapters it endeavored to create a wide interest in political affairs and, in some instances, went so far as to throw its support behind some candidates for public office and to oppose others. Its stand against lynching, discrimination, the poll tax, and similar matters was unequivocal, and it usually allied itself with liberal labor forces. It was frequently accused of left-wing leanings. Each year it made the Thomas Jefferson Award to the Southerner whom it considered to have made the most significant contribution to the improvement of the South. Among the recipients were Mrs. Mary McLeod Bethune, Frank P. Graham, and Ellis Arnall.

Persons in the Midwest found it necessary, in 1944, to concentrate on the matter of race relations and to seek more satisfactory adjustments for minority groups in community life. Accordingly, they established the American Council on Race Relations, with headquarters in Chicago. As a consultant organization the American Council was instrumental in advising in the adjustment of minority group problems, especially in industrial communities, and in establishing programs for inter-group education where they were deemed necessary. With ample funds and a staff of highly trained white and Negro specialists, the American Council moved from the experimental stage to a position where it was recognized as an important force in furthering the Americanization of all groups in the areas where it served. The activities of other organizations, such as the Fellowship of Southern Churchmen and the American Missionary Association, were significant both in their action programs and in their publications.

In recent years there has been a growing recognition of the fact that any successful program of Americanization must be community-wide and must undertake to develop tolerance in the schools. In 1933 several public school teachers in the vicinity of New York City, aware of the need for an educational program in human relations, united to this end; after several years of experimentation, their group evolved into the Bureau for Intercultural Education. The Bureau fostered a broad plan of intergroup education through the schools and community organizations. Although it hoped to educate the community to tolerate all ethnic and religious groups, it gave special attention to the problem of the Negro. Through radio programs, plays, magazine and newspaper articles, visual aids, and other mediums of communication, the problems of race and culture in American education were discussed, and suggestions were made for increased tolerance through better understanding. A series of significant volumes was published, including *Intercultural Education in American Schools* by W. E. Vickery and S. G. Cole, *Probing Our Prejudices* by Hortense Powdermaker, *Minority Problems in the Public Schools* by Theodore Brameld, and *Educating the Culturally Disadvantaged Child* by Lester Crow, Walter Murray, and Hugh Smythe.

In the fifties and sixties the efforts in this general field were greatly expanded. Outstanding psychologists, such as Kenneth Clark, showed how prejudice among children merely reflected the attitudes of their parents. School officials began to introduce courses designed to explain racial and cultural differences and, at the same time, to stimulate greater achievement by Negro children. From "Operation Headstart," adopted by several cities with the encouragement of the United States Office of Education, to enrich the training of pre-school children, to the Higher Horizon program of New York City and the program of compensatory education in San Francisco, educators demonstrated a greater understanding of the problem of minorities. To offset the unfavorable image or, indeed, the neglect of Negroes in many texts, some school officials even prepared supplements covering the history of the Negro, while others began to adopt textbooks that gave a more adequate treatment of the Negro in the history of the United States.

While it was not possible to measure the results of the numerous efforts to foster a greater Americanization of the Negro and other minority groups, there was rather general agreement that some of them at least helped to check the increase of racial antipathy. If the agencies, councils, and bureaus did not succeed in accomplishing their aims in trying to get America's melting pot to boil to the point of blending the races and cultures that comprise America, they did dramatize the importance of the problem. They called attention to the fact that the great test of America's democratic tradition is the acceptance of the Negro with other minority groups into the mainstream of American life. They provided, moreover, innumerable suggestions for approaches to the solution of these problems. With more scientific data than had ever been previously available, with a variety of blueprints for tackling the problem, and with a persistent reaffirmation of the equalitarianism inherent in American life, the people of the United States were given the greatest opportunity in their history to bring about the complete Americanization of their Negro citizens.

XXIX •

Fighting for the Four Freedoms

Arsenal of Democracy

● *The international anarchy that characterized the period be-*fore the outbreak of World War I reasserted itself shortly after the "War to End Wars" was over. To be sure, there were gestures in the direction of a lasting peace. The machinery of the League of Nations sought feebly to check aggression and to settle international disputes amicably; but the powerful nations too frequently used the organization as a cloak behind which they imposed their will on weaker members. The Washington Conference of 1921 looked toward the naval disarmament of great powers; but the anxiety of all participants to secure an advantage over each other insured the failure of any comprehensive plan to discourage an armament race. The Briand-Kellogg Peace Pact of 1928 in which more than 60 nations renounced war as an instrument of national policy appealed to the consciences of men; but without effective means of enforcement it was impotent as long as nations could hide their aggressiveness behind the pretext of self-defense. The seizure of Manchuria by Japan in 1931, and the failure of various international organizations to do anything about it, demonstrated the ineffectiveness of such agencies in the face of determined cupidity. As early as 1922, Mussolini had come to power in Italy; and by 1935 he was seeking to resurrect the Roman Empire by overrunning Ethiopia. These developments gave encouragement and comfort to Adolph Hitler, who was waiting for a chance to use his newly won authority in Germany to extend his control to neighboring nations.

Negroes watched events in other parts of the world with growing concern. They cheered China in her efforts to stem the tide of Japanese aggression, but when Italy invaded Ethiopia, they protested with all the means at their command. Almost overnight even the most provincial among the American Negroes became international-minded. Ethiopia was a Negro nation, and its destruction would symbolize the final victory of the white man over the Negro. In many communities funds were raised for the defense of the African kingdom, while in larger cities elaborate organizations were set up. In New York the International Council of Friends of Ethiopia was organized, with Willis N. Huggins as executive secretary. In 1935 Dr. Huggins pleaded for Ethiopia before the League of Nations, contending that an Italian victory there would imperil the peace of the world and bring into deeper disgrace the principles of Christianity. Other organizations were the United Aid to Ethiopia and the Ethiopian World Federation, both of which raised funds for the embattled brother in Africa. The *Pittsburgh Courier* sent its historian news-analyst, J. A. Rogers, to the front to cover the war, and upon his return he issued a booklet, *The Real Facts About Ethiopia,* and lectured to many Negro and white groups.

Negroes were among the earliest and most energetic Americans to condemn the fascism that was rising in Europe. They early learned to hate Nazism and its Aryan doctrines. Some had read Hitler's *Mein Kampf* and had resented its unfavorable comments concerning Negroes. It had been rumored, moreover, that in 1936 Hitler had refused to treat the Negro Olympic participants with civility at Berlin. When Max Schmeling knocked out the athletic idol of the Negro race, Joe Louis, in 1936, Negroes had little to say for Hitlerism. Not until Louis gained complete revenge in 1938 could the average Negro speak of Nazis without a feeling of personal antagonism. By that time, however, public opinion in America was generally censuring Hitler's tactics in overthrowing Austria and dismembering Czechoslovakia; and Negroes joined in the loud condemnation.

When Europe was plunged into war as a result of Hitler's invasion of Poland early in September, 1939, the position of the United States as a neutral nation pursuing a policy of isolationism became more and more untenable. Within two months after

THE EMPEROR RECEIVES AN HONORARY DEGREE. More than 15,000 people witnessed the ceremony at Howard University in 1954 when Emperor Haile Selassie of Ethiopia received the honorary degree of Doctor of Laws. Here, the Emperor responds in a brief address. Scurlock Studio.

the beginning of the war the Congress, at the stern insistence of the President, passed an act permitting arms to be purchased on a cash-and-carry basis. When Germany unleashed its furious attack in the West in the spring of 1940, conquering Denmark, Norway, the Netherlands, Luxembourg, and Belgium, the people of the United States became alarmed. The fall of France in June, 1940, added to the panic. It looked as though Britain would fall before the Nazi *Blitzkrieg.* As Americans asked themselves what disposition Germany would make of the New World colonies of the conquered nations, they realized that the war had come frightfully close to them. It was time to prepare, and the following year witnessed a feverish race to construct a two-ocean navy, to build up an efficient air arm, and to train a soldiery that would be ready for any emergency.

The low state of America's army by 1940 stemmed not so much from the fact that the people of this nation were pursuing a policy of disarmament in the search for peace as it did from the almost natural disinclination to support a large standing army in time of peace. As the number of officers and soldiers steadily decreased after World War I, the number of Negro soldiers in the army of the United States diminished to one of relative inconsequence. By 1940 there were less than 5,000 Negroes in an army composed of 230,000 enlisted men and officers. Only four Negro units, the 24th and 25th Infantries and the 9th and 10th Cavalries were up to their full strength. As early as 1939, however, several other Negro units were activated, including three quartermaster regiments, two antiaircraft battalions, one field artillery unit, a chemical warfare company, and several corps of engineers. At the beginning of the emergency there were less than a dozen Negro officers in the regular army. The difficulties involved in maintaining an active status in the Reserve Officers Corps had caused many Negroes who were eligible for commissions to allow their eligibility to lapse. There were, therefore, neither Negro enlisted men nor officers in any considerable numbers that were ready to participate in the first stages of building up a large fighting force.

As the United States began to put itself on a war footing, Negroes raised the question as to what consideration would be given them, both in the building up of a large fighting force and in the manufacture of the materials of modern warfare. When the Selective Service Act was passed in 1940 it was amended by a clause forbidding discrimination in the drafting and training of men. For a period of time, however, some draft boards accepted only white men for training, on the grounds that there was a lack of housing facilities for Negroes in the camps. At the first signs of discrimination Negroes began to protest loudly. In September, 1940, a group of outstanding Negro leaders, including A. Philip Randolph, Walter White, and T. Arnold Hill, submitted a seven-point program to President Roosevelt outlining minimum essentials in giving Negroes just consideration in the defense program. They urged that all available reserve officers be used to train recruits; that Negro recruits be given the same training as whites; that existing units in the army accept officers and men on the basis of ability and not race; that specialized personnel, such as physicians, dentists, and nurses be integrated; that responsible Negroes be appointed to draft boards; that discrimination be abolished in the Navy and Air

Forces; and that competent Negroes be appointed as civilian assistants to the Secretaries of War and Navy.

The policy of the War Department with regard to Negroes became clearer in the fall of 1940 when a statement was issued that Negroes would be received into the army on the general basis of the proportion of the Negro population of the country. Negroes, however, were to be organized into separate units; and existing Negro units which were officered by whites would receive no Negro officers other than medical officers and chaplains. Negroes were furious and made known their indignation in the press. They admitted that Hitlerism was to be despised, but they insisted that discrimination against the Negro in the United States was to be fought with desperate vigor. Significant appointments and promotions of Negroes did little to quiet the voice of protest. On October 25, 1940, Colonel B. O. Davis became the first Negro to be promoted to the rank of Brigadier General; but election day was too close to convince all Negroes that the promotion was made without political considerations. William H. Hastie was appointed the Civilian Aide to the Secretary of War, and Colonel Campbell Johnson became an Executive Assistant to the Director of Selective Service. Senior R.O.T.C. units were added at West Virginia State College, Hampton Institute, A. and T. College, Prairie View College, and Tuskegee Institute. Although these steps pleased Negroes, they were insufficient to convince them that Washington had made a significant change of policy with regard to the Negro. Too many clear signs indicated that the United States had committed herself to a white army and a black army that somehow must be used together to carry on the fight against the powerful threat of fascism and racism in the world.

As industrial plants began to convert for the purpose of producing weapons of war, Negroes found great difficulty in securing employment. Approximately five million whites were still unemployed—a significant contrast with the situation immediately before World War I—and employers were generally inclined to absorb them first. Since the vast majority of Negroes were unskilled, the explanation for failure to employ them was usually that skilled workers were needed. The first benefits which Negroes derived from the boom in defense industries were in securing jobs that had been deserted by whites who were attracted by higher wages to plants making weapons of war. The federal government made several gestures to discourage discrimination. The United States Office of Education declared that in the expenditure of funds in the defense training program there should be no discrimination on account of race, creed, or color. In August, 1940, the National Defense Advisory Committee issued a statement against the refusal to hire Negroes in defense plants. In September, the President in a message to the Congress spoke out against discrimination. The Office of Production Management established a Negro Employment and Training Branch in its Labor Division in the effort to facilitate the hiring of Negroes in defense industry. None of these actions brought satisfactory results, and Negroes made it clear that they wished more than gestures from their government.

As Negroes saw wages skyrocket in plants holding large defense contracts and as they saw few signs that the rigid anti-Negro policy in industry was undergoing any change, they developed a program for drastic action. In January, 1941, A. Philip Randolph, the president of the Brotherhood of Sleeping Car Porters, advanced the idea of fifty to one hundred thousand Negroes marching on Washington and demanding that their government do something to insure the employment of Negroes in defense industries. Almost immediately, Negroes showed enthusiasm for the idea, and as the plans were laid for carrying out the march, high government officials became alarmed. Frequently, around Washington, the question was asked, "What will they think in Berlin?" Negroes became accustomed to replying, "Oh, perhaps no more than they already think of America's racial policy." By June, Negroes all over the United States—certainly, many thousands, if not a hundred thousand—were making preparations to entrain for Washington to be ready to march to the Capitol on July 1. Seeking redress for grievances was an old American custom, and in this form it was reminiscent of the march on Washington of Coxey's army of unemployed men in 1894 and of the Bonus Expeditionary Force in 1932.

During the last three weeks of June, 1941, many things were done to prevent the march on Washington. Mayor Fiorello LaGuardia of New York, Mrs. Eleanor Roosevelt, Aubrey Williams of the National Youth Administration, Walter White of the N.A.A.C.P., and Randolph discussed the matter in New York. Several, including Mrs. Roosevelt and Mayor LaGuardia, asserted that the march would do no good and would, perhaps, cause reprisals against the Negro. Randolph, however, would entertain no thought of calling off the march. The President sent for Randolph and conferred at length with him, along with Secretary of War Stimson, Secretary of the Navy Knox, and other officials. None of their pleas could dissuade Randolph. As the time for the march drew closer, government officials became more desperate. After several conferences, the President said that if Randolph would call off the march, he would issue an order "with teeth in it," prohibiting discrimination in employment in defense industries and in the government. On June 25, 1941, the President issued his famous Executive Order 8802, in which he said that, "there shall be no discrimination in the employment of workers in defense industries or Government because of race, creed, color, or national origin. . . . And it is the duty of employers and of labor organizations . . . to provide for the full and equitable participation of all workers in defense industries, without discrimination because of race, creed, color or national origin. . . ."

In pursuance of the Executive Order a clause prohibiting discrimination was placed in all defense contracts, and a Committee on Fair Employment Practices was set up to receive and investigate complaints of discrimination in violation of the order. The Committee, which was composed of representatives of the public, of management, and of labor, held hearings in important industrial centers, such as Los Angeles, Chicago, and New York. Many evidences of discrimination were, of course, uncovered. Although the Committee had no power to institute punishment and although it was disinclined to recommend the cancellation of war contracts because of the emergency, its existence had a salutary effect on the employment status of Negroes. Employers and trade unions did not like to appear at hearings as defendants, and, occasionally, they were willing to change their policies to avoid being called up. The unfavorable publicity involved in an appearance before the Committee, moreover, caused some employers to revise their employment policy. Finally, the embarrassment which some employers suffered as a result of their proved misrepresentation of employment practices moved them to change their practices in an effort to restore their good name.

The reaction to the Executive Order and the Committee was varied. Negroes hailed the Order as the most significant document affecting them since the issuance of the Emancipation Proclamation. They were, of course, disappointed when widespread discrimination continued in defiance of the Committee. White employers and Southern whites generally were opposed to it. Mark Ethridge, a Louisville newspaper man and an original member of the Committee, said that the Order was not a social document and it had no concern with racial segregation. He added, significantly, "All the armies of the world, both of the United Nations and the Axis, could not force upon the South the abandonment of racial segregation." A white Alabama lawyer was so furious that he organized a League to Maintain White Supremacy, while the governor of that state declared that he would refuse to sign a contract that would force him to abandon a policy which he regarded as essential to racial peace.

Thus did the United States struggle in the early days of the European War when it was called upon by the enemies of the Axis powers to be the arsenal of democracy. It was expected to provide an increasing amount of the goods of war through sale, lend-lease, gift, relief, and the like. It experienced a major difficulty in seeking to serve as the arsenal of democracy and, at the same time, hold fast to its pattern of a free economy in which labor has the right to strike and management has the right to hire only those persons whom it deems to be desirable for its purposes. If it could overcome this difficulty, it would doubtless weaken its position in seeking to overcome another, namely, that of reinforcing the democratic ideology among the faltering nations of Western Europe. The task of giving spiritual as well as material succor to nations under the Axis heel and maintaining simultaneously discriminatory policies based on race, creed, and national origin required remarkable ambidexterity. The inability of the United States to enunciate a strong ideology of democracy that stemmed from honest practices doubtless had the effect of weakening its position as the arsenal of democracy.

Negroes in the Service

Under the Selective Service Act of 1940 more than three million Negro men registered for service in the armed forces of their country. Largely because of educational deficiencies and social diseases, however, the rate of rejections of Negroes was 18.2 per cent as compared with 8.5 per cent for whites. In the first year of the operation of the Act only 2,069 Negroes were drafted into the armed services. In the following year, more than 100,000 entered the service, while in 1942 approximately 370,000 Negroes joined the armed forces of the United States. In September, 1944, when the Army was at its peak, there were 701,678 Negroes in that branch of the service alone. Approximately 165,000 served in the Navy, 5,000 in the Coast Guard, and 17,000 in the Marine Corps. A rough estimate of the total number of Negroes in the armed services during World War II places the figure in the neighborhood of one million men and women, which approximates the ratio that Negroes bear to the general population.

The participation of Negroes in the administration of the Selective Service doubtless reduced discrimination in accepting men into the armed forces. In various parts of the United States Negroes served in almost every capacity under Selective Service. On the national level, in addition to the Executive Assistant to the Director, a Negro served on the President's Advisory Committee on Selective Service. On the lower levels Negroes served as local board members, as members of the registrants' advisory board, as examining physicians, as appeal board members, and in other capacities. The impression was rather general among Negroes that the Selective Service in World War II was administered more impartially than in World War I. There were not nearly so many complaints of discrimination on the part of draft boards.

Although discrimination did occur within the armed forces, Negroes had a greater opportunity to serve their country than in any previous war. They were in the infantry, coast and field artillery, cavalry, tank battalions, transportation units, signal corps, engineer corps, medical corps, and many other branches in most of which they had previously served. When the Womens' Auxiliary Corps was organized, Negroes were received; and before the end of the war more than 4,000 Negro women had enlisted. Late in 1940 the War Department announced that Negroes would be trained as aviation pilots at Tuskegee, Alabama. While some Negroes violently objected to the segregation of Negroes in the Air Force, others viewed the announcement as a step forward, since no provisions had hitherto been made. As pilots began their training at Tuskegee, ground crews were prepared at Chanute Field, Illinois. Late in 1941 the 99th

NEGRO COAST GUARDSMEN.
On the U. S. S. Big Horn, north-
west of the Azores these men
engage in target practice. U. S.
Coast Guard photo no. 26-G-4284,
National Archives.

THE S. S. HARRIET TUBMAN. This vessel was named for the "Moses of
her people" who was active in the Underground Railroad and served as a
Union spy during the Civil War. Completed in 1943 at the New England Ship-
building Corporation, it was one of fourteen Liberty ships named for outstand-
ing Negroes. U. S. Maritime Administration.

NEGRO WOMEN SERVE. Lt. Stella G. Garvin of the Women's Army Corps interviews a job applicant at the rapidly expanding Jersey City Quartermaster Repair Sub-Depot. U. S. Signal Corps Photo.

NEGRO PILOTS. Taking time out between missions in Italy in 1944, these five pilots of the all-Negro Mustang Group of the 15th Air Force were among the first Negroes to be admitted to the pilot training program in the Air Force. Office of War Information photo no. 208-NP-6XXX-1, National Archives.

Pursuit Squadron was ready for organization into a fighting unit, and other groups of Negro fighter pilots were undergoing training. Approximately 600 Negro pilots had received their wings before the end of the war.

In June, 1940, there were only 4,000 Negroes in the Navy, a majority of whom served as messmen. Negroes had no opportunity either to learn the many trades provided in the naval training program or to become combat seamen. After the beginning of the war Negroes protested the discrimination in the Navy, and for several months officials of that branch of the service made it clear that they had no intention of revising their policy regarding Negroes. In April, 1942, however, the Secretary of the Navy announced that the Navy would accept the enlistment of Negroes for general service and as noncommissioned officers. A separate unit, Camp Robert Smalls, was established for Negroes at the Great Lakes Naval Training Station. Promising recruits were sent from there to Hampton for further training. Others were sent to sea or to naval ammunition depots. Later, Negro women were permitted to enlist in the WAVES. At the same time it was announced that Negroes would be received into the Marine Corps, thereby smashing a tradition of excluding Negroes that was as old as the Corps itself. Negro "Leathernecks" began their training late in the summer of 1942 at the Marine base at Camp Lejeune, North Carolina. Within a short period of time the 51st Composite Defense Battalion was in the process of organization.

The question of the Negro officer was a delicate one, because of the experience of Negroes as well as military officials during the previous war. Negroes were determined to secure equal and integrated training as officers, and the fight to accomplish this was high on the agenda of the Negro leaders. There was no long struggle, however. In October, 1940, the War Department stated, "When officer candidate schools are established opportunity will be given for Negroes to qualify for reserve commissions." It was decided, moreover, that Negro and white soldiers should be admitted to the same officer candidate schools and classes, after qualifying under a single standard. In the following summer classes began in officer candidate schools. The problem that developed was that of getting commanding officers at the various camps to recommend Negroes for the advanced training. In the first six months, less than 30 Negroes were admitted to the schools. Only after the Secretary issued a stern order that Negroes be sent to the candidate schools on the basis of no discrimination did Negroes get into the schools in any considerable numbers. By the middle of 1942 Negroes were graduating at the rate of approximately 200 per month. They received commissions in the Armored Forces, Air Corps Administration, Cavalry, Coast Artillery, Infantry, Chemical Warfare, Quartermaster Service, from the Adjutant General's School, and other branches. In each instance they studied and graduated with their white fellows. Only in the Air Corps were commissions given at a segregated school. Even the Navy commissioned Negroes as officers in 1944. Before the end of the War more than 50 Negroes were ensigns, lieutenants, medical and dental officers, nurses, WAVES officers, and chaplains. In the Marines and Coast Guard there was also a small number of Negro officers.

Approximately a half-million Negroes saw service overseas during World War II. On September 30, 1944, there were 411,368 in foreign theaters, while on February 28, 1945, the number had reached 497,566. In the European theater almost half of the Transportation Corps was composed of Negroes. They served in Port Battalions, Truck Companies, and in other similar units. Port Battalions composed of Negroes came ashore shortly after the invasion and unloaded supplies for the use of the assault troops. During the summer of 1944 and the remainder of the war Negro Amphibian Truck Companies made a significant contribution to the successful drive across France. After D-Day more than 50,000 Negro engineers erected camps, tents and buildings, cleared debris, rebuilt cities, and performed other important services. They constituted approximately one-fifth of the American engineers in the European theater. Approximately 11 per cent of the ordnance men in Europe were Negroes. The Chief of Ordnance reported that not only did these Negroes "pass the ammunition" but on numerous occasions they fought the Germans, participating in patrols and taking prisoners.

Twenty-two Negro combat units participated in the ground operations in the European theater. There were 9 field artillery battalions, 1 antiaircraft battalion, 2 tank battalions, 2 tank destroyer battalions, and 8 engineer combat battalions. The 761st Tank Battalion was one of the outstanding fighting units in the European theater. It fought in the Battle of the Bulge and saw service in six European countries. Four major generals and the Undersecretary of War commended it for its gallant service. The 614th Tank Destroyer Battalion served in several important actions, and one of its officers, Captain Charles L. Thomas, received the Distinguished Service Cross for heroism in the action before Climbach, France. Negro units of field artillery were in France within ten days after the invasion. The 333rd fought through Brittany and Northern France and against vicious German attacks in the fall of 1944. Several other units provided artillery backing for other divisions.

In January, 1945, it was announced that Negro troops would be integrated with white troops in a unit to fight on German soil. The integration was of platoons rather than of individual men. Volunteers called for soon doubled the quota of 2,500 men. After a short period of training they were in action on the east side of the Rhine, with various divisions of the First Army. Negroes everywhere were elated at the news of the experiment and were delighted to learn that the mixed units were a success. On April 30, 1945, the War Department said that the volunteer Negro infantrymen had "established themselves as fighting men no less courageous or aggressive than their white comrades." Their performance was short, for the war was soon over, but not before they won the plaudits of many high ranking officers. One said to them, "I have never seen any soldiers who have performed better in combat than you." When the units were broken up at the end of the European conflict, Negroes protested, but the War Department seemed done with experimenting.

In the Mediterranean theater the principal Negro combat unit was, of course, the 92nd Division, which had been reactivated at Fort McClellan, Alabama, in 1942. In 1943 it was moved to Ft. Huachuca, Arizona, where it went into intensive training. In June, 1944, it was sent to Africa and later to Italy, where it served with the Fifth Army. It was composed of four regiments of infantry and four battalions of field artillery, as well as other service units. Its first major offensive action was in crossing the Arno River in September, 1944. Its drive was successful until December, when it was driven out of several towns that it had taken. Within a few days, however, all of the lost ground had been retaken. In the following February the 92nd suffered serious reverses, for which it was severely criticized. After a visit to the Division, William Hastie's successor as Civilian Aide to the Secretary of War, Truman K. Gibson, Jr., was reported to have said that the 92nd had not made a good showing. Immediately many critics of Negro combat troops took up the report and, by quoting it out of context, used it to bolster their arguments that Negroes could not fight. Negroes severely criticized Gibson for his statements. Later it became clear that Gibson had been misquoted in the first place. He only said that whatever poor showing there was of the 92nd was doubtless due to the low educational equipment of a large part of the rank and file of the Division. He pointed out that 17 per cent belonged in Class Five, the lowest literacy class admitted to the Army. The more than 12,000 decorations and citations which the Division received seem to indicate that its performance was a creditable one under unusually unfavorable circumstances.

The two major Negro combat air units overseas were the 99th Pursuit Squadron and the 332nd Fighter Group. The 99th went overseas in April, 1943, and in February of the following year the 332nd went to the Mediterranean theater. Both groups participated in various types of fighting over Europe. They escorted bombers and went on strafing and other missions. The 332nd was instrumental in sinking an enemy destroyer off the Istrian Peninsula and protected the 15th Air Force bombers in their important attacks on the oil fields of Rumania. Under the command of Colonel Benjamin O. Davis, Jr., the fighter group won the admiration of Negroes everywhere and the generous praise of high officials in the Air Force. More than 80 pilots won the Distinguished Flying Cross, having destroyed 111 planes in the air and 150 on the ground. The 477th Bombardment Group which was activated late in the war did not see action.

From the time that engineers landed in New Guinea to prepare landing strips, Negroes took an increasingly active part in the war in the Pacific and the Orient. Approximately 10,000 Negro troops worked on the construction of the Ledo Road; and it was necessary for many of them to fight the enemy as well as build the road. There were also the usual service troops, including engineers, port companies, quartermasters, amphibians, and chemical warfare units. Among the combat units that saw service against the Japanese was the 24th Infantry which helped take the New Georgia Islands in May, 1942. There were several other outfits, including two battalions of coast artillery and one antiaircraft barrage balloon battalion. The main Negro combat unit was the 93rd Division, which saw its first action at Bougainville in the Solomons. From there it proceeded against the Japanese in the Treasury Islands, the Dutch East Indian Island of Morotai, and the Philippines. While the 93rd Division did not perform the kind of sensational deeds that captured the imagination of citizens on the home front, it can be said that their fighting was steady and consistent under adverse tropical conditions and that they were never severely criticized for failures in any way.

The opportunities which Negroes had to serve in the Navy were in distinct contrast to those which they had in World War I. Thousands of Negroes received training to perform numerous technical tasks and were given ratings accordingly. On March 20, 1944, the destroyer escort, *Mason,* was commissioned, and Negroes of various grades were assigned to duty on it. Later, Negroes manned a patrol chaser and hunted enemy submarines in the Atlantic. By the fall of 1944 the Navy was able to announce that 500 Negro seamen were on duty on 25 large auxiliary vessels operating primarily in the Pacific. Among the Negroes with ratings were storekeepers, yeomen, radiomen, ship-fitters, carpenter's mates, gunner's mates, quartermasters, and coxswains. Meanwhile, approximately 12,500 Negro Seabees served in the Pacific, constructing advanced naval bases and doing other jobs. The work they performed, frequently under severe enemy attack, was praised by high Navy officials. Negro Marines were stationed at several strategic Pacific outposts to defend areas taken from the enemy. Their conduct caused the commander of the Corps to say, "Negro Marines are no longer on trial. They are Marines, period." The more than 900 Negroes in the Coast Guard did rescue work in the Atlantic, Pacific, and in Alaskan waters. They were among the first to go ashore at Okinawa early in 1945, and, upon occasion, performed invaluable services on shore duty both at home and abroad.

Approximately 24,000 Negroes served in the Merchant Marine, and some of them had enlisted before the Navy had relaxed its restrictions on the enlistment of Negroes. There seemed to be a minimum of segregation and discrimination; and Negroes were given numerous opportunities to serve in responsible capacities. They worked as able and ordinary seamen, engineers, radio operators, and the like. Four Negro captains commanded Liberty ships, the crews of which were made up of various races. Eighteen ships were named for Negroes—fourteen for noted Negro Americans and four for Negro merchant seamen who lost their lives while in active service with the

Merchant Marine. During the course of the war two Liberty ships named for Negroes were sunk, S.S. *Frederick Douglass* and S.S. *Robert L. Vann.* The Negro press and Negro leaders did not fail to use the Merchant Marine as an outstanding example of an enterprise in which Negroes and whites could work together successfully.

The problem of maintaining a high morale among Negroes in the service was one of the most difficult which the government faced. To be sure, the War and Navy Departments made some concessions; but the Negro press and Negro leaders were always demanding more. Negro soldiers, taking their cue from the more articulate Negroes, demanded equality of treatment whenever it was possible to do so without breaking military discipline. Even among the considerable number of Negro soldiers and sailors with a small amount of formal training, there was much dissatisfaction with the discriminatory policies of the Army and Navy and disgust with the way in which they were treated by many white civilians. In Durham, North Carolina, a white bus driver was found not guilty of murder after he left his bus in July, 1944, and killed a Negro soldier after an argument. In several communities in the South Negro soldiers were refused food in places where German prisoners of war were eating and enjoying American hospitality. In a Kentucky railroad station three Negro WACS were beaten by civilian policemen when the women did not move promptly enough from the white waiting room when asked to do so. In South Carolina a white policeman gouged out a Negro soldier's eyes in an altercation.

On military posts the situation was scarcely any better. Several commanding officers forbade the reading of Negro newspapers, and there were instances in which Negro newspapers were taken from newsboys or soldiers and burned by the scores. At many camps transportation for Negro soldiers was most unsatisfactory. They were frequently forced to wait until buses had been loaded with white soldiers before they were permitted to board them. At post exchanges they were segregated and given inferior merchandise. The theaters and other entertainment facilities were frequently set apart, and the accommodations for Negroes were below the standard of those provided for white soldiers. The War Department took cognizance of the discrimination against Negro soldiers in its order of July 8, 1944, which forbade racial segregation in recreational and transportation facilities at all Army stations. A veritable storm of protest arose in the South as the order was made known. The Montgomery *Advertiser* said, "Army orders, even armies, even bayonets, cannot force impossible and unnatural social race relations upon us." The order was regarded as a "directive" by some commanding officers, and it was not strictly enforced; others sought to wipe out the discrimination as the order required. Many Negro soldiers, seeking equal treatment in pursuance of the order, were rebuffed and denied service in post exchanges and theaters.

The attempts of Negroes to resist segregation and discrimination led, of course, to innumerable clashes both on and off the military posts. Few camps could boast at the end of the war that there had been no clashes that had arisen from disputes over the treatment of Negroes. There were serious riots at Fort Bragg, Camp Robinson, Camp Davis, Camp Lee, and Fort Dix. At Freeman Field, Indiana, more than 100 Negro officers were arrested for attempting to enter an officers' club maintained for whites. They were later exonerated, but irreparable damage had been done to the morale of the 477th Bombardment group. At Mabry Field, Florida, and at Port Chicago, California, Negro servicemen were charged with mutiny when they refused to perform work which they felt was assigned to them because of their color. There were more experiences which depressed the morale of Negro soldiers than those that raised their morale. The emotional conflicts and frustrations they went through as they sought to reconcile the doctrine of the Four Freedoms with their own plight discouraged many of them. Neither the anti-discrimination orders of the War Department nor the concessions made in the commissioning of Negro officers in the Navy could compensate for the hurt which Negroes felt when rebuffed while wearing the uniform of their country. At the end of the war realists would admit that the morale of Negro soldiers could be substantially raised only by granting to them the Four Freedoms for which they were fighting.

There were, of course, many critics of the Negro soldier who insisted that he was incapable of participating efficiently in modern warfare. To be sure, it was strange indeed that no Negroes had been awarded the Congressional Medal of Honor since the Spanish-American War, but Negroes could well argue that there had been a change in the policy of those responsible for the awards rather than any change in the heroism and gallantry of the Negro soldier. In the Civil War sixteen soldiers and five sailors won the coveted Medal, while in the Spanish-American War seven Negro servicemen had received it. Fifteen Negroes on other occasions had served their country in such a manner as to merit it. In World War I not even Henry Johnson was awarded the Medal of Honor, and Negroes began to ask if the nation was reserving its highest award for white soldiers. Negro soldiers concluded that they would have to content themselves with less significant recognitions, and of these there were plenty. The Secretary of War, the Chief of Staff, and the high military officials in the various theaters of war praised the heroism and service of the Negro soldier. Through their own newspapers Negroes followed the exploits of their soldiers, and they were satisfied with their performance.

Many units received the Presidential Citation for their gallantry. Individual men received recognitions that ranged from good conduct medals to Distinguished Service Crosses. Five Negroes received the Distinguished Service Cross: Captain Charles L. Thomas, Lt. Vernon J. Baker, S/Sgt. Edward A. Carter, Jr., Pfc. Jack Thomas, and Pvt. George Watson. For the late Pvt. Watson the citation read, "Extraordinary heroism—on March 8, 1943, when he lost his life in Portlock Harbor, New Guinea, after assisting several men to safety on a raft from their sinking boat, which had been attacked by Japanese bombers. Overcome by exhaustion, he was pulled under and drowned by the suction of the craft." Steward's Mate 2/c Eli Benjamin, Mess Attendant Leonard Harmon, Messman Dorie Miller, and Cook William Pinckney received the Navy Cross for their outstanding heroism. In the now famous incident at Pearl Harbor, Dorie Miller, "Without previous experience . . . manned a machine gun in the face of serious fire during the Japanese attack on Pearl Harbor, December 7, 1941, on the Battleship *Arizona*, shooting down four enemy planes." Eighty-two Negro pilots received the Distinguished Flying Cross for their services in the Air Force. Other Negroes received the Croix de Guerre, the Partisan Medal for Heroism from Yugoslavia, and one received the Order of the Soviet Union. With some justification the Negro service man and woman could feel that they had made their contributions to the preservation of, at least, the ideal of the Four Freedoms.

592 · FROM SLAVERY TO FREEDOM

The Home Fires

The global nature of the war and its demands on the resources of the belligerents implied, from the beginning, that its success-ful prosecution involved the utilization of every factor that could possibly contribute strength. For the United States the waging of total warfare presented innumerable difficult prob-lems. It could not be achieved without erecting some controls that served to reduce the freedom of the individual, a move which was strenuously resisted by a considerable portion of the population. Nor could total warfare be achieved without the country's making substantial concessions to its minority groups so that they could make their contribution to the defeat of the Axis powers. This, also, found considerable opposition among groups that were determined to carry on the fight abroad with-out upsetting the existing pattern of race relations at home. Many admitted, however, that for the sake of consistency with the ideology of the United Nations, as well as for the purpose of increasing efficiency, the United States would have to deal more justly with all its people during the course of the war. On numerous occasions Negroes at various levels of social and economic life pointed to the tremendous wastage of human effort in their struggle for the right to work and fight for victory. It was, indeed, embarrassing to Americans, and more than once they asked themselves, "What will Berlin say?"

Thanks to the training programs of the NYA and the WPA, thousands of Negroes were ready for employment in industry when the defense program began. The number was increased substantially by the training programs of the United States Office of Education, the Vocational Training for War Production Workers, and the Engineering, Science, and Man-agement War Training Program. By December, 1942, more than 58,000 Negroes were enrolled in pre-employment courses. In the summer of 1943 sixty-five Negro colleges were participat-ing in the ESMWT program, and more than 50,000 students were enrolled. In such a way Negroes prepared for work in aircraft industries, ship-building, welding, automotive mechan-ics, electricity and radio, and in numerous other defense activi-ties. The non-discriminatory provisions of the federal training programs insured the preparation of Negroes for defense work, but the problem of securing employment for them was one which plagued both Negroes and the federal government all during the war.

Before the establishment of the FEPC the Negro Employment and Training Branch in the Labor Division of the Office of Production Management had a limited amount of success in negotiating with employers and persuading them to use Negroes on war construction projects and in defense plants. Within a year after the creation of the FEPC it was evident that it had experienced some success both directly and indirectly in increasing the number of Negroes in government service and in war industries. After its transfer to the War Manpower Commission its techniques were improved and the results were more gratifying. Considerable antagonism to the FEPC developed, however, because of its practice of citing industries for the violation of the President's Executive Order, even after those industries had initiated programs for the integration of minorities. The FEPC was also instrumental in exercising pressure on the United States Employment Service to give preference, in job referrals, to those employers who did not discriminate against minority groups. These various forms of government pressure resulted in much greater utilization of the total manpower of the country.

Despite serious criticisms leveled against the FEPC and other agencies of the government which tried to eliminate discriminatory policies, their activities showed clearly that the federal government could do much to modify racial employment practices. By the end of the war few major industries were without at least some Negroes in their plants. At the beginning of the emergency almost no Negroes were employed in aircraft industries; but at the end of the war thousands worked in them. The shipyards increased their Negro workers, both in quantity and quality. More than 100,000 found employment in the iron and steel industries. Although the problem of upgrading remained, on the whole, unsolved during the war, there were indications that industries were becoming more liberal in this important matter. Perhaps the increased participation of Negroes in labor organizations had something to do with this, as well as with other trends for improving the status of Negro workers. During and after the war Negroes played an increasingly important part in the conventions of organizations like the United Automobile Workers, the United Steel Workers, the National Maritime

WOMEN PARACHUTE MAKERS. In our Eastern Navy Yard in 1942 Negro and white women worked together making parachutes for the armed forces. Photo by Office of War Information.

WORKER IN NORFOLK NAVY YARD. This worker is in the plate-bender's shop, where steel plates are bent to fit the sidings of warcraft under construction. This operation requires a high degree of skill. OEM defense photo by Palmer.

Union, and the United Rubber Workers, and in the national councils of the C.I.O. A larger number of American citizens have become convinced, that the public, through its government, should guarantee employment to its citizens on a basis of non-discrimination. As a result there has been considerable discussion of a permanent FEPC in the federal government, and the National Committee for a Permanent FEPC has done much to rally public sentiment behind such a proposition. In the campaign of 1944 both major parties committed themselves to the proposal, but no headway was made in securing the necessary legislation. Meanwhile, several states, such as New York and Massachusetts, set up such agencies, and others were giving the matter serious consideration. (See Chapter XXX.)

As a matter of course, Negroes gave generous support to the war effort on the home front. They purchased bonds enthusiastically, and many corporations reported that Negro employees signed up for the payroll savings plan, whereby regular amounts were deducted from wages for the purchase of bonds. In every bond campaign Negroes held rallies in schools, churches, and community centers to sell war bonds. With the help of Negroes on the staff of the Treasury Department, especially William Pickens and Mrs. Nell Hunter, the campaigns among Negroes were almost always successful.

When the Office of Civilian Defense was established, Negroes became active in the preparations to defend the country against possible enemy attack. On the national level Mrs. Crystal Bird Fauset served as race relations adviser, while on the local levels Negroes served as block managers, messengers, auxiliary firemen and policemen, and in numerous other capacities. In air raid drills they were especially cooperative. Since Negroes lived in ghettoes in most American communities, violations by Negroes could be easily detected; and they were determined that there would be none. In Southern communities Negroes facetiously speculated on what accommodations would be made for them in shelters in case of an air raid; but fortunately the South was never called upon to provide such facilities. It was, perhaps, the fear of what would happen in such a case that prompted a Southern Senator to charge that Senegalese soldiers were criminally assaulting large numbers of German women in the subway shelters of Stuttgart, although the German city had no subways at all.

In the program to conserve foods and other essential commodities and to control prices, Negroes played their part. When the Office of Price Administration was established, Negroes were employed as attorneys, price analysts, economists, and in other specialized fields. They were in regional and state offices as information specialists and in the local offices of some communities as clerks as well as members of the ration boards. There seemed to be more general satisfaction among Negroes with the way in which the OPA was administered than with any other war-time agency, perhaps, because of the rather general policy of the agency to employ persons for jobs regardless of race. It was not difficult, moreover, for Negroes to cooperate with programs of conservation because of their traditionally impoverished condition. When a representative from the War Foods Administration was lecturing to a Negro audience concerning the ways of saving fats, a housewife asserted that many Negroes, through the years, had been forced to use fats over and over again and were, therefore, already quite familiar with the techniques of saving them.

In the agencies for the building of morale, Negroes participated in larger numbers than during World War I. They served the Red Cross as Gray Ladies, Nurses Aides, and as drivers in the Motor Corps. In the fighting areas they worked in camps, clubs, and hospitals. During the war approximately 200 professional workers served as club directors and in other capacities in four theaters of war. There were, to be sure, segregation and discrimination; but even the workers themselves, as well as the soldiers, protested against such practices. The United Service Organizations, organized in February, 1941, undertook to channel the activities of the Y.M.C.A., Y.W.C.A., National Catholic Community Service, Salvation Army, Jewish Welfare Board, and Travelers Aid Society, into one great effort for sustaining the morale of the fighting men and women. During the course of the war more than 300 USO clubs were staffed by Negro personnel, while approximately a dozen were staffed by Negroes and whites. There were, moreover, approximately 30 Travelers Aid Case Service Units with interracial staffs and 25 Travelers Aid Lounges staffed by Negroes. In the Southern states these services were dispensed on a segregated basis, but in most Northern communities both Negro and white servicemen enjoyed the same facilities. Several Negro USO shows were organized and sent overseas to entertain those in the war zones.

In contrast to their state of mind at the outbreak of World

War I, Negroes had no illusions about the benefits they would derive from World War II. Had there been any doubts in their minds, they would have been dispelled during the period of the emergency before the beginning of hostilities, when Negroes had such great difficulties in securing opportunities to work in defense industries. At the outbreak of the war Negro civilians made it clear that they were suspicious of the white man's good intentions, and one went so far as to say, "This is very likely to be the last war that the white man will be able to lead humanity to wage for plausible platitudes." Upon occasion of mistreatment Negro soldiers were heard to grumble that they would prefer to die for some rights in the United States than to die overseas to secure those rights for peoples in foreign lands.

Experiences on the home front during the war drove the morale of Negroes to a new low. The migration of large numbers of Negroes to the North and the West in search of employment raised anew the difficult question of how Negroes and whites could live together peacefully in communities where the patterns of race relations were not defined. Within the five-year period between 1940 and 1945 the Negro population of Los Angeles County, for example, increased from 75,000 to 150,000. Added to that community's problems of Mexicans and Japanese were the newly arrived Negroes, and interracial clashes seemed inevitable. In the industrial communities of San Francisco, Portland, and Seattle there was a similar growth, with correspondingly increased problems in the field of race relations. Among the Midwestern cities that witnessed an influx of Negroes and whites, Detroit showed the greatest strains in the problem of achieving adjustment. Approximately 50,000 Negroes had come into the city, along with 450,000 other persons in the three years preceding 1943. The lack of housing, the presence of race-baiters and demagogues, the problem of organizing newly arrived workers, and the impotence of the government created an ideal atmosphere in which a riot could flourish.

On June 20, 1943, the most serious race riot of the war period broke out in Detroit. The months of tension were climaxed on that day when a fist fight occurred between a Negro and a white man. The altercation rapidly spread to involve several hundred persons of both races. Wild rumors, as usual, swept through the town. Within a few hours Negroes and whites were fighting through most of Detroit. When the governor hesitated to declare martial law and call out troops, whites began to roam the streets burning Negro cars and beating Negroes in large numbers. Nothing effective was done to bring order out of the chaos until President Roosevelt proclaimed a state of emergency and sent 6,000 soldiers to patrol the city. At the end of more than 30 hours of rioting 25 Negroes and 9 white persons had been killed, and property valued at several hundred thousand dollars had been destroyed.

Other Northern cities feared that they would have the same experience as Detroit, and numerous efforts were made to stem the tide toward interracial clashes. New York City and Los Angeles did not escape completely, but many communities were able to avert riots by making intelligent and careful approaches to the solution of the problems that created riots. Negroes, however, continued to protest for better treatment and for a larger share of the benefits that came from the huge expenditures in the war effort. They were willing to do their part and to make necessary sacrifices to insure victory, but they never failed to remind the people of the United States that they resented all forms of mistreatment. Negroes even criticized Joe Louis when he fought Buddie Baer in January, 1942, and gave his entire purse for Navy relief at a time when the Navy was not permitting Negroes to enter the service in other than menial capacities. The *Pittsburgh Courier* waged a vigorous "Double-V" campaign, victory at home as well as abroad. Everywhere Negroes registered their protest against the practice of the Red Cross of separating Negro and white blood in the banks that had been established for the relief of wounded service men. They were quick to point out that there would, perhaps, have been no blood banks without the work of a Negro, Dr. Charles Drew. They also censured the USO when that organization banned the circulation of Ruth Benedict's *Races of Mankind* through its clubs.

The government took official cognizance of the importance of Negro morale by appointing Ted Poston, a veteran Negro newspaperman, as racial adviser in the Office of War Information. Through Poston's office the news of how the Negro was faring in the armed services and on the home front was sent to newspapers that were read by Negroes. The OWI also employed Negro artists, photographers, and others to assist in telling the story of what the Negro was doing to help win the war. Early in 1943 the OWI distributed two million copies of a large pamphlet entitled,

"Negroes and the War," which contained numerous pictures of Negro servicemen, war workers, scholars, scientists, and artists. It was, of course, calculated to raise the morale of the Negroes, but there are serious doubts if it succeeded. Lester Granger of the National Urban League asserted that the publication was a "monumental mistake and a disservice to the government and the Negro. I say this . . . because it is like kicking a man who is down and congratulating him because he is not yet dead. . . ." Other Negroes resented what they described as "its implication of possible group disloyalty and its half-truths."

The War Department sought to raise the morale of Negroes not only by maintaining a Negro officer in its press section, but also by accrediting Negro newspapermen as war correspondents. During the war about twenty Negroes covered various theaters of war for the press, but far from raising the morale of Negroes, some of the reports had the opposite effect. The reports of correspondents like Ollie Stewart of the *Afro-American* and Lem Graves of the *Journal and Guide* made it clear that all was not well with Negro service men and women overseas, while the book of Walter White, *A Rising Wind,* which was based on his visits to the war fronts, contained revelations which depressed Negroes at home even more. Both the War and Navy Departments made possible the visits of leading Negroes to the war fronts in order to raise the morale of the servicemen and to inform civilians at home of the activities of the men on the front. Among those who went to the theaters of operation were Bishop J. A. Gregg, of the A M E Church, Lester Granger of the National Urban League, and Matthew Bullock of the Massachusetts Parole Board.

The experience of living in two worlds had prepared Negroes to wage two fights simultaneously. They felt compelled to carry on the fight for better treatment at home so as to give real meaning to the ideal of the Four Freedoms. While it cannot be denied that the double preoccupation must have caused both efforts to suffer, there is merit in the argument that both efforts were necessary. Mrs. Roosevelt had said early in the war, "The nation cannot expect colored people to feel that the United States is worth defending if the Negro continues to be treated as he is now." Negroes were determined to do all within their power to improve their own status. For them the task of keeping the home fires burning involved the elimination of discrimination and maltreatment. For them that task was as important as that of protecting the Four Freedoms abroad. If their morale continued to sink, it was because the people of the United States failed to agree with one Negro psychologist who observed that the morale of the Negro will not be appreciably raised "as long as concessions are made within a rigid framework of segregation." At the end of the war most Negroes realized that the struggle to save America's own ideals from destruction had just begun. If America was to assume a more important role in world affairs, many Negroes became determined to see to it that race hatred was not one of the items on America's export list. Perhaps, moreover, in the broader sphere and through contact with the hundreds of millions of darker peoples the world over, America could face her own problem and solve it more effectively. At the end of the war, discerning Negroes, therefore, began to look to world organizations to help in the solution of their problems at home. It was a desperate, almost forlorn, hope, but in the face of growing reaction at home, it was one worth pursuing.

The United Nations and Human Welfare

The interest of the Negro in world affairs lagged very little after Italy invaded Ethiopia in 1935. In the following year American Negroes manifested considerable interest in the Spanish Civil War, and some went to Spain to fight with the Loyalist forces. The Negro press loudly condemned Franco and even warned that if he went unchallenged, his regime would constitute a threat to peace and freedom throughout the world. World War II greatly stimulated Negroes' interest in world affairs, as it did for most Americans. A noticeable interest in colonial problems was displayed by the Negro press, as several newspapers engaged Japanese, Hindu, and Chinese columnists. Long before the end of the war Negroes sought to influence the course of post-war adjustment by calling attention to the importance of establishing a peace based on justice without regard to race. In 1943, Merze Tate, for example, grimly warned that, "the peace that follows World War II may prove only an interlude—a breathing spell before the race and class war—unless Great Britain and the United States act to implement their professed aims. In the coming global order there must be freedom for all or freedom for none." In 1945 Alphonse Heningburg asserted that Negroes, like others, wanted a just and durable peace, security in their work, and an opportunity for creative living. Most Negroes seemed to feel that this was not asking too much. More and more they looked toward San Francisco to see if their desires had any possibility of realization.

When the conference for the establishment of the United Nations Organization opened in San Francisco late in April, 1945, Americans were deeply mourning the recent death of President Franklin D. Roosevelt. Negroes were especially dejected. Some had deserted him in the election of 1944, but the great majority still regarded him as their best President since Lincoln. Many heaped extravagant praise on him. Some Negro writers "revealed" that Roosevelt had wanted to do much more for Negroes than he was able to do; that he was instrumental in securing commissions for Negroes in the Navy; and that he deplored conditions among colonials the world over. Now that he was gone, they seemed to feel that their problems could not be solved without help from the outside. More and more they thought in terms of bringing world opinion to bear on their plight, in the hope that a healthier atmosphere, in which they could raise their status, would be generated. The meeting at San Francisco, coming so close to the death of the President, was, to many Negroes, "the last best hope of earth." Such a point of view could be born only of the most abject disillusionment and the most desperate plight.

They did not exaggerate the importance of the San Francisco conference. The peoples of all the continents of the world looked to the meeting for formulas to eliminate war and its causes and to guarantee a measure of freedom and security. They interpreted the importance of the meeting in terms of their own difficulties. Big powers wanted machinery that would make German and Japanese aggression impossible. Colonial peoples wanted guarantees against the encroachments upon their rights by the imperial powers. Minority groups wanted guarantees that they, too, would have the opportunity to enjoy the Four Freedoms for which they had fought. American Negroes, one of the world's most important minority groups, wanted relief from the discrimination, segregation, and oppression that the world's "arsenal of democracy" had imposed upon them.

Among American observers who were accredited by the State Department to attend the organizational meeting at San Francisco were several Negroes, including Mrs. Mary McLeod Be-

thune of the National Council of Negro Women, Dr. Mordecai
W. Johnson of Howard University, and Dr. W. E. B. DuBois
and Walter White of the N.A.A.C.P. Dr. Ralph Bunche, Acting
Chief of the Division of Dependent Territories of the Department of State, went as a member of the official staff. Most of the
Negro newspapers with national circulations sent reporters to
cover the conference. Negroes from all over the United States
went to San Francisco in considerable numbers for no reason
except to see if the nations of the world were capable of establishing an organization that could give relief to the many
peoples that were seeking it. Most of the Negroes who went to
San Francisco, as well as many of those who remained at home,
maintained a lively interest in the official delegates from the
darker countries, especially those from India, Liberia, Ethiopia,
and Haiti. There was the feeling that when these delegates
spoke, they voiced the yearnings of underprivileged peoples
everywhere. Conversely, the delegates from certain imperial
powers, especially those from Holland, Belgium, and South
Africa, were viewed with utter disgust by American Negroes,
who made their feelings known in their speeches and in their
writings.

Negroes were not the only Americans who had considerable
difficulty in following the deliberations at San Francisco. Few
people in the United States understood the intricacies of international politics, and too frequently reporters and observers
regarded the meeting as any other large gathering of peoples of
different tongues and cultures. Many had little background to
understand the numerous problems involved in establishing an
organization that transcended national boundaries and, at the
same time, sought to reconcile the desires of scores of different
peoples. Negroes kept their eyes on developments that suggested
that consideration was being given to underprivileged peoples.
"Small Nations Demand Race Plank" and "British Evasive on
Colonial Question" were typical headlines in the Negro newspapers during the conference. When it became known that the
colored people of South Africa protested the treatment they
received at the hands of their government, the Negro press of
the United States emphasized the fact and pointed out that Jan
Smuts had devoted his whole life to entrench a "Nazi-like domination" over his subjects. When General Smuts pleaded for an
article on human rights in the United Nations Charter, Negroes
remembered that he had once said that every white man in

South Africa except those that are "mad, quite mad" believes in the suppression of the Negro.

No previous international document had given such great attention to the rights of human beings as the United Nations Charter. Small nations, minority groups, and colonials were pleased with the preamble of the charter which, instead of speaking of "high contracting parties" began simply, "We, the peoples of the United Nations." They begrudgingly gave General Smuts credit for wording it and wondered exactly what he meant by it. The preamble further reaffirmed "faith in fundamental human rights, in the dignity and worth of the human person, in the equal right of men and women and of nations large and small." Negroes were especially pleased with the chapter which asserted that the United Nations would promote "Universal respect for, and observance of, human rights and fundamental freedoms for all without distinction to race, sex, language, or religion." They reasoned that if there was any conscientious effort on the part of the international organization to live up to this provision, Negroes in the United States would benefit considerably.

Of the agencies provided for by the Charter, Negroes took the liveliest interest in the Economic and Social Council and the Trusteeship Council. Under the Economic and Social Council there was established the Educational, Scientific and Cultural Organization whose responsibility was to develop a world-wide program in fundamental education. It was to be concerned with those tensions that are conducive to misunderstanding and distrust. If it could provide constructive programs of action to identify, counteract, and overcome the forces that disrupt human relations, it would be able to make a significant contribution to the maintenance of peace and the elevation of the rights of human beings everywhere. At the first meeting of UNESCO in Paris, late in 1946, a Negro, Charles S. Johnson, was in attendance as a member of the United States National Commission. There seemed to be much hope that this agency would do a great deal to promote the program that was originally conceived for it. Negroes in America hoped, too, that UNESCO would develop a program of fundamental education for Americans as well as for Europeans. Later, the creation of a Commission on Human Rights and the appointment of Mrs. Eleanor Roosevelt to that body encouraged Negroes even more. The Trusteeship Council was provided in order to safeguard

the interests and welfare of non-self-governing peoples in territories held either under League of Nations mandates or detached from enemy countries after World War II. The Mandates Commission had failed to safeguard satisfactorily the
welfare of dependent territories, and the mandatories too frequently administered the territories in their own interests. Membership in the Trusteeship Council was to be divided equally
between countries administering trust territories and countries
that had no such responsibility. Even before the formal establishment of the Council, Negroes complained that it was
unsatisfactory. George Padmore, writing in London, asserted
that it was nothing more than a continuation of the Mandates
System, "modified and refurbished to accommodate the conflicting ideologies of the great powers." He admitted, however,
that the provision that the Council could receive petitions from
people in trust territories was a "small advance." Negroes were
heartened, however, when Ralph Bunche of the State Department's Division of Dependent Territories joined the United
Nations to work with the Trusteeship Council. They hoped that
this Negro specialist would, somehow, be able to advance substantially the welfare and interests of those peoples who would
be unable to promote their own interests. In 1947 observers still
wondered if the Trusteeship Council would be any real improvement over the system that was established by the League of
Nations.

Viewing the Charter as a whole, minority groups could see it
as an important step in the process by which the problems of
domestic minorities are attaining world significance and a world
hearing. Negroes admitted that it would be naïve to imagine
that the United Nations would be able to end immediately the
discrimination against them in the United States, but it seemed
not too much to hope that they would benefit by the general
tendency to give greater consideration to underprivileged peoples the world over. At the meeting of the United Nations
General Assembly in the autumn of 1946, that body recognized
India's charges of racial discrimination practiced against East
Indian nationals and their descendants in South Africa. The
two-thirds majority by which the resolution was passed requiring South Africa to report to the next meeting on the steps that
had been taken to rectify the situation was a signal victory for
domestic minorities. The delight which Negroes in the United
States took in the defeat of General Smuts was dampened,

somewhat, by the fact that the United States, along with Great Britain, voted against the resolution. The Assembly also approved a resolution asking that the extermination of minorities and racial and ethnic groups, such as the Nazis practiced, be declared an international crime. This seemed to be further recognition of the rights of minorities. The editor of the *Crisis* could correctly observe that the UN discussions on race were "far ahead of Versailles when President Wilson and the British would not even permit race to be discussed formally even in a committee meeting."

Encouraged by the rather liberal Charter of the United Nations and the early actions of its agencies, the National Negro Congress, late in 1946, filed a petition with the Economic and Social Council. On behalf of the colored people of America, the Congress sought the aid of the United Nations in the struggle to eliminate political, economic, and social discrimination imposed on them in the United States. Opponents of such petitions argued that the treatment of Negroes in the United States is purely a domestic matter. They reminded Negroes that the Charter of the United Nations prevents it from intervening in local and domestic problems. Negroes countered with the argument that one of the main purposes of the UN is to achieve international cooperation in solving problems of an economic, social, cultural, or humanitarian character. Writing on the subject, Charles H. Houston admitted that the UN does not have jurisdiction to investigate every lynching in Georgia or the denial of the ballot in Mississippi, but "where the discrimination and denial of human rights reach a national level or where the national government either cannot or will not afford protection and redress for local aggression against colored peoples, the national policy of the United States itself becomes involved." He further pointed out that at the national policy level the UN can take jurisdiction. "A national policy of the United States which permits disfranchisement in the South is just as much an international issue as elections in Poland or the denial of democratic rights in Franco Spain," Houston concluded.

Houston's point was illustrated graphically by a series of events which occurred in the United States in the early months of 1947. In February the State Department inaugurated a series of broadcasts to communist Russia to keep the people of that country informed of events in democratic America. One of the events that the Voice of America felt compelled to report on its first broadcast was the brutal lynching of a young South Carolina Negro who was being held in connection with the murder of a taxicab driver. In May an all-white jury exonerated 28 men who had confessed that they participated in the lynching. Repercussions of the verdict could be heard in London, Paris, and Moscow. Negroes began to wonder if the outcome of the trial was a signal for a reign of terror. Within a few days a group of white North Carolinians attempted to lynch a Negro accused of attempted assault; only his agility in getting away prevented a repetition of the South Carolina atrocity. Again, foreign capitals manifested great interest in the form of "justice" peculiar to America. Again, Negroes wondered if America was prepared to lead the world toward a saner approach to human relations.

Some Negroes had the opportunity to serve the cause for peace and freedom by working in the United Nations. Ralph Bunche was not only the Director of the Trusteeship Council, but he also won the Nobel Peace Prize in 1950 for his work as United Nations mediator in the Palestine dispute and later became Deputy Secretary General. For several years William H. Dean was an economist with the Trusteeship Council, and E. Franklin Frazier was for two years chairman of the Department of Applied Social Sciences in UNESCO. Meanwhile, Negroes served regularly on the United States National Commission for UNESCO. The United States delegation to the General Assembly of the United Nations usually included a Negro as alternate, among them Mrs. Edith Sampson, Channing Tobias, Archibald Cary, and Robert Brokenburr. In 1955 Charles H. Mahoney of Detroit became the first Negro to have the status of a delegate from the United States to the General Assembly of the United Nations.

The presence at the United Nations headquarters in New York of delegations of distinguished Africans aroused a new interest in the international organization on the part of Negro Americans. It was heartening to see almost thirty new African states take their places in the family of nations, and particularly thrilling in 1963–1964 to see Alex Quaison-Sackey of Ghana preside over the General Assembly. Negro Americans regarded these events as concrete evidence that black peoples could reach the summit in world affairs; and they hoped that white Americans would take notice. They believed, moreover, that as Africans proceeded to enjoy civil rights in the United States, except among the crudest, most bigoted Americans, they too would be the beneficiaries. Even more important for Negro Americans was the new stance of the United States government that sought to improve its racial policies in order to win support from the African states in the continuing rivalry with the communist bloc.

XXX •

The Post-War Years

Progress

● *Among the numerous adjustments the American people had* to make at the end of World War II was adaptation to a new position of the Negro in the United States. This new status arose not merely because a substantial portion of the gains made during the war were retained but also because of an intensification of the drive, in several quarters, to achieve complete equality for the Negro. The war had created a climate in which substantial gains could be made, but the very nature of the emergency imposed certain restraints that could no longer be justified after 1945. Negro organizations, notably the N.A.A.C.P., began to press more vigorously for full equality; they were effectively assisted by numerous groups in various parts of the country, including political organizations and civic, labor, and religious groups. The courts, chiefly but not exclusively the federal ones, showed a disposition to take cognizance of racial questions and rather frequently ruled in favor of the advancement of the status of the Negro. The executive branch of the federal government itself, moreover, sensitive both to domestic and foreign pressures, exerted considerable influence in eradicating the gap between creed and practice in American democracy. The interaction of these forces created a better place for Negro Americans as the nation moved into the second half of the twentieth century.

In several significant ways President Harry S. Truman contributed to the creation of a climate in which the status of the Negro could be improved after the close of the war. In 1946 he appointed a committee of distinguished Negro and white Americans to inquire into the condition of civil rights and to make recommendations for their improvement. The report, *To Secure These Rights*, strongly denounced the denial of civil rights to some Americans, and it called for a positive program to strengthen civil rights including "the elimination of segregation, based on race, color, creed, or national origin, from American life." In the same year the President appointed another interracial committee to look into the problem of higher education. In their report this committee recommended not only the elimination of inequalities in educational opportunities but the abandonment of all forms of discrimination in higher education.

The President's efforts in the armed services did more than lend moral support to the cause for equality. The integration that had been inaugurated in the closing years of World War II was greatly accelerated in the post-war years. In 1948 the President appointed a committee to study the problem, and its report, *Freedom to Serve*, was a blueprint of the steps by which integration was to be achieved. Acting on the recommendations of the committee, the Army adopted a new policy in 1949 opening all jobs to qualified personnel without regard to race or color and abolishing the racial quota. The Navy and Air Force adopted similar policies; with very few incidents to mar the transition, the armed services of the United States moved toward complete integration, and this progress was significant.

In Korea, in 1950, a battlefield test of integration was in the making. When the North Korean forces began pressing the United Nations forces, especially the Ninth United States Infantry Regiment, the commanding officer began to use men from his all-Negro Third Battalion. They were immediately acceptable to the whites "because at a time like that, misery loves company." After General Matthew Ridgway assumed command of all forces in the Far East he asked permission from the Defense Department to integrate all Negroes throughout his command. Between May and August, 1951, the extent of integration in Korea jumped from 9 per cent to 30 per cent of troops in the field. A special Army report declared that the integration of Negroes had resulted in an overall gain for the Army. At long last, the sixteen million Negroes of the United States had become a vital and integral part of the manpower pool of the nation.

In public statements President Truman also lent the prestige of his office to the improvement of the status of the Negro. In 1948 he issued an executive order requiring fair employment in the federal service and declared that "the principles on which our Government is based require a policy of fair employment throughout the Federal establishment without discrimination because of race, color, religion, or national origin. . . ." Despite the fact that enough Southerners were outraged with certain portions of Truman's Fair Deal policy to form the Dixiecrat Party and oppose his election in 1948, the President remained firm on these matters. Four years later, after announcing his retirement from office, he said at the Howard University commencement that there should be a civil rights program backed "by the full force and power of the Federal Government" to end discrimination against minorities. He declared that the more the nation practiced the belief in equality "the stronger, more vigorous, and happier" it would become.

The armed services were not alone in reflecting the assault on discrimination and segregation. In public housing the trend was away from segregation and toward integration. In 1950, for example, there were 177 local housing projects open to families of all races and creeds; in addition, nine states and eight cities had forbidden discrimination or segregation in public housing. In 1955 the Administrator of the Federal Housing and Home Finance Agency called on the nation's lending agencies to lend money for the purchase and construction of homes by minority groups. Meanwhile, as the full implications of the 1948 decision of the Supreme Court outlawing the enforcement of restrictive covenants were felt, the opportunities of Negroes to secure satisfactory housing increased in many communities.

There were difficulties in the area of housing, however, and some Negroes met stern resistance, hostility, and even violence as they sought to move into neighborhoods where they were not wanted. In 1951 a Negro couple was all but driven from a home they had purchased in Cicero, Illinois. The angry mob broke windows, mutilated the exterior, and shouted vile epithets at the couple. In Birmingham, Chicago, and Detroit, homes of Negroes were attacked by whites who resented their presence. In New York City, the policy of excluding Negroes from the Stuyvesant Town housing project aroused a controversy that stimulated the drive for legislation against discrimination in housing.

The northward migration of Negroes that began during the war continued for the next decade, thus complicating not only the problem of housing but that of employment as well. While the pattern of employment of Negroes in the South did not change substantially, despite the growth of industry there, many of the gains that had been made in the North during the war were retained, and new opportunities appeared. In 1947 the President's Committee on Civil Rights recommended the enactment of fair employment legislation at both the federal and state levels. Since no federal legislation was forthcoming, President Truman and President Eisenhower established committees to see that there was no discrimination in industries that were filling government contracts. Meanwhile, some states had already begun to set up fair employment committees, and by 1956 sixteen states and thirty-six cities had committees working toward the elimination of discrimination in employment.

Notable among the increased employment opportunities for Negroes were those in the aircraft, electronics, automotive, and chemical industries. There were signs of change, moreover, in retailing establishments when firms began to employ Negroes as clerks, bookkeepers, and buyers. Upgrading of Negro workers and recognition of seniority rights made it possible for some Negroes to move into positions of responsibility hitherto closed to them.

An important factor in the increased opportunities of the Negro worker was the role of the unions, especially the C.I.O. When the much-heralded drive of the C.I.O. to unionize Southern workers failed, Negroes in that region were left without a vigorous protagonist. Elsewhere, however, there was a general tendency for unions to increase their Negro membership and to elevate Negroes to positions of leadership. When the American Federation of Labor merged with the C.I.O. in 1955, two Negroes, A. Philip Randolph and Willard Townsend, were elected vice presidents of the new organization. As the Negro worker came to be accepted as a union member and a participant in the formulation of union policy, there was a real possibility that the second half of the twentieth century would witness the elimination of much of the racial discrimination in employment.

One of the most important influences in improving the position of the Negro in American life at mid-century was the role of religious institutions and organizations. Groups like the

American Friends Service Committee and the American Missionary Association gave specific attention to the problem of race tensions in communities, set up programs to improve intergroup relations, and published reports and studies involving race. The social action divisions of the major denominations became involved in racial matters, while the National Council of Churches employed staff members who gave full time to social problems of this nature. The Anti-Defamation League of B'nai B'rith and numerous Roman Catholic priests and bishops issued statements and adopted policies which supported the elimination of segregation and discrimination from American life. Here and there churches began to integrate. The Church of All People in San Francisco had Negro and white ministers, while the white and Negro Baptists in a small Arkansas community merged their churches, to the amazement of most observers.

Nowhere was the improvement of the status of the Negro more dramatic than in the nation's capital. As early as 1947 the larger hotels in Washington began to accept Negro guests, and by 1956 most of them were doing so. The motion picture houses and theaters followed suit. The desegregation of the facilities of the Department of the Interior and the City Recreation Board made it possible for Negroes to use all the public parks, playgrounds, and swimming pools within the District of Columbia. In 1953 all restaurants in Washington were opened when the Supreme Court upheld the validity of an 1872 statute requiring such establishments to serve "all well-behaved" persons. One of the school desegregation cases arose in the District of Columbia, and when the decision was handed down, President Eisenhower expressed the hope that the nation's capital would be a model for the rest of the country. Plans to desegregate went forward immediately, and although the process has not been completed, it is well under way.

By mid-century the courts and the Interstate Commerce Commission were protecting the rights of Negroes to travel about the country without the restrictions imposed by state segregation laws. In 1950 the Supreme Court ruled that the segregation of Negroes on dining cars of interstate railways was an undue burden on interstate commerce. Although an increasing number of Negroes were traveling on commercial airlines that had never been segregated, those who continued to travel by rail experienced little or no difficulty in securing first-class accommodations and in traveling across state lines without being segregated. In 1955 the Interstate Commerce Commission decreed that all racial segregation on interstate trains and buses must end by January 10, 1956. The decree applied also to waiting rooms in railway and bus terminals. As the Southern states reluctantly began to comply with the decree, some of them held to the principle of segregation by setting up separate waiting rooms for intrastate Negro passengers.

The steady migration of Negroes to the North and West and their concentration in important industrial communities gave them a new powerful voice in political affairs. In cities like Chicago, Detroit, and Cleveland they frequently held the balance of power in close elections, and in certain pivotal states the votes of Negroes came to be regarded as crucial in national elections. Meanwhile, an increasing number of Negroes in the South were registering and voting. In 1947 Federal District Judge J. Waties Waring declared that Negroes could not be excluded from the Democratic primary in South Carolina. In the following year 35,000 Negroes voted in the Democratic primary in that state. By 1948 the number of registered Negro voters in Georgia had already exceeded 150,000, and this number was even higher by the time of the next Presidential election. In 1952 it was estimated that 63 per cent of the eligible Negro electorate in Durham, North Carolina, voted regularly.

While the efforts of Southern Negro leaders to raise the number of Negro voters to two million in the election of 1952 perhaps fell short of the mark, the influence of the Negro voters could clearly be seen in some areas. It was held by some that the Negro vote was an important factor in holding Louisiana and South Carolina in the Democratic column. A survey of the vote in predominantly Negro districts revealed a majority for the Democratic Presidential candidate, Adlai Stevenson, ranging from 56 per cent in two Jersey City wards to 99 per cent in one ward in Darlington, South Carolina. In 1952, as twenty years earlier, Negro voters did not follow the national trend. While some Negro newspapers attributed the widespread opposition of Negroes to Eisenhower's candidacy to his stand on Army segregation as late as 1948, others said that Negroes were more concerned with retaining the gains made under the New Deal and Fair Deal programs of Roosevelt and Truman.

At state and local levels the rising influence of the Negro electorate was clearly perceptible. In 1954 Illinois sent Negro Democrat William Dawson to the House of Representatives of the United States Congress for his seventh consecutive term, while Adam C. Powell was returned from New York for his sixth term. When Charles C. Diggs, Jr., of Detroit was elected to the House on the Democratic side in the same year, it marked the first time in the twentieth century that as many as three Negroes were in the Congress. Detroit would send a second Negro to Congress in 1964, by which time six Negroes were in the Lower House. By 1956 there were some forty Negroes in state legislatures, all in the North and West. The number of Negroes elected to city councils, judgeships, boards of education increased each year. Significant among such victories were the election of Rufus E. Clement, the President of Atlanta University, to the Atlanta School Board in 1953, and, in the same year, the election of Hulan Jack to the presidency of the borough of Manhattan of New York City.

Appointments of Negroes to high posts in the national government were indicative of a new position of influence and respect. In 1949 William H. Hastie, with many years of distinguished public service behind him, became a judge of the Third United States Circuit Court of Appeals. Thurgood Marshall went to the Circuit Court in 1961 but resigned in 1965 to become Solicitor General of the United States. In 1953 J. Ernest Wilkins became Assistant Secretary of Labor, while E. Frederick Morrow became an administrative assistant in the executive offices of the President and Scovel Richardson was appointed chairman of the United States Parole Board. In the offices of several Senators and members of the House of Representatives there were Negro secretaries and assistants, and others served as Register of the Treasury, Governor of the Virgin Islands, Assistant to the Director of Selective Service, and Assistant to the Secretary of Health, Education, and Welfare.

Reaction

The improvement of the status of Negroes was neither uniform nor without vigorous opposition in some quarters. On the job, white workers frequently threatened to quit if Negroes were employed or upgraded. While the threats were not always successful, they served to retard the advancement of Negroes, as in the case of the proposed integration of the fire department of Washington, D.C. There was, likewise, resistance to any change

END OF THE WHITE PRI-
MARY IN SOUTH CAROLINA.
A Negro registers as a South
Carolina Democrat after Judge
J. Waties Waring issued an order
directing the Democratic party
to grant Negroes full participa-
tion in party affairs. Wide World
Photos.

in the voting habits of Negroes. When Judge Waring ordered that the South Carolina Democratic primary be opened to Negroes in 1947, there was the most bitter denunciation of the decision; the Waring family was ostracized by whites in Charleston, and hoodlums threatened them with bodily harm. In 1956, when a Louisiana registrar disqualified whites as well as Negroes who did not satisfactorily demonstrate their understanding of the Constitution, she was summarily dismissed— obviously because she failed to discriminate against Negroes who sought to qualify as voters.

Negroes who sought to improve their own status were frequently singled out for attack. In 1956 the Negroes of Montgomery, Alabama, boycotted the city bus lines to avoid the alleged abuse of Negro passengers by white drivers, to obtain a more satisfactory seating regulation, and to secure the employment of Negro drivers on buses serving predominantly Negro sections. Almost immediately about ninety Negroes were indicted under a 1921 anti-union law forbidding conspiracy to obstruct the operation of a business. The leader, the Reverend Martin Luther King, was the first to be tried. He was found guilty. Immediately he served notice of appeal, while the bus company frantically sought to settle the problem lest it go into bankruptcy. But the effective weapon of the boycott gained in popularity as the Negroes of Tallahassee, Florida, in June, 1956, cut the local bus company's business by almost 75 per cent by following the Montgomery plan.

There was, moreover, an intensification of resistance that corresponded roughly to the improvement in the status of Negroes. As Negroes pressed to desegregate schools, whites organized for a last-ditch stand. Among the new anti-Negro groups was the National Association for the Advancement of White People, with national headquarters in Washington, D.C. The organization became discredited in 1954, however, as a result of the numerous legal entanglements in which its executive director became involved. More widespread and more effective were the White Citizens' Councils, which a leading white Mississippi editor called the "Uptown Ku Klux Klans." Frankly admitting their determination to resist the enforcement of the school desegregation decision, the councils called on their members to use economic reprisals against Negroes who were active in the fight to desegregate the schools and against whites who favored compliance with the law. In some communities, in retaliation, Negroes began to boycott businesses operated by members of the councils. Thus, by 1956, something akin to economic warfare was being waged in the South, with many business firms caught in the middle for being regarded either as "soft" on the N.A.A.C.P. or as favorable to the program of the councils.

In other ways Southern leaders fought the school desegregation decisions. They considered numerous plans to avoid compliance, including turning over the public schools to private organizations, punishing as criminals any persons who attended or taught mixed classes, and encouraging "voluntary segregation." In the area of political theory they resurrected the doctrine of interposition set forth by South Carolina's Chancellor William Harper in 1832. Early in 1956 the governors of South Carolina, Georgia, Mississippi, and Virginia called on the Southern states to declare that the federal government has no power to prohibit segregation and to "protest in appropriate language, against the encroachment of the central government upon the sovereignty of the several states and their people." Among the states that passed resolutions of interposition were Georgia, Mississippi, and Virginia, while several others considered such action.

Southern members of Congress also came forth with a vigorous denunciation of the desegregation decision. In March,

1956, more than ninety Southerners, led by Senator Walter George, presented in Congress their "Declaration of Constitutional Principles," commonly known as the "Southern Manifesto." The document condemned the decision as a usurpation of the powers of the states and encouraged the use of "every lawful means" to resist its implementation. Of the three North Carolina members of Congress who refused to sign the manifesto, two were defeated in the Democratic primary in the following May.

Since the N.A.A.C.P. had led in the fight for desegregation, it was natural that it should become the special object of attack in the resistance to change. It was widely attacked in the South as subversive, and in 1956 several states, by means of legal devices, virtually stopped its operations. In Louisiana an injunction was granted which restrained the N.A.A.C.P. from holding meetings until it had filed with the secretary of state a complete

INADEQUACY OF NEGRO SCHOOLS. In Greene County, Georgia, in 1941, the teacher's resourcefulness in teaching reading, writing, and arithmetic was sorely tried. Courtesy Library of Congress.

list of its membership. In Alabama a local judge granted an injunction against any further activities by the N.A.A.C.P. In South Carolina the General Assembly called for its classification as a subversive organization. Meanwhile, a member of Congress from Arkansas entered into the *Congressional Record* some forty pages of "evidence" in his attempt to show that the officers and leading members of the N.A.A.C.P. were un-American.

Southern resistance to any change in the status of Negroes often degenerated into violence; the "machinery" for maintaining law and order apparently was unable or unwilling to operate. While the bombing of Negro homes was not confined to the South, there were other forms of violence that were to be found primarily in the South. Encouraged by many of their leaders to defy and disobey the law and inspired by citizens' councils and similar groups to take matters into their own hands, many white Southerners assumed responsibility for maintaining segregation at all costs. In some parts of the South the amount of violence rose to the proportions of a reign of terror. In Mississippi, for example, several Negro leaders who had urged their people to vote were murdered, one of them on the courthouse lawn in Brookhaven in the summer of 1955. A few months later the president of the N.A.A.C.P. in Belzoni was shot when he ignored an order to remove his name from the voting register, but he recovered. Near Greenwood a fourteen-year-old Negro boy from Chicago was murdered for allegedly whistling at a white storekeeper's wife. In few of these incidents was any white person even accused of having committed a crime, and in none of them was there a conviction.

By early 1956, as Southern whites despaired of retaining segregation, they became increasingly immoderate in their actions. When the state of Alabama was ordered to admit Autherine Lucy, a Negro applicant, to the University of Alabama the students and townspeople of Tuscaloosa resorted to violence to prevent her from remaining at the university. Even with heavy police escort and in the company of the dean of women, her car was pelted with stones, and some persons even jumped on top of the car. When she was suspended because of the rioting, she accused university officials of conspiring to keep her out of the university. As a result she was expelled by the board of regents. A few weeks later, in Birmingham, Nat "King" Cole, a Negro singer, was attacked by a group of whites while he was performing on the stage of the city auditorium before an all-white audience.

Responsible citizens in the North and South began to express concern over mounting race tensions. Some called for moderation, without too carefully defining it. Others called for federal action, but neither the President nor the Congress seemed inclined to enter the picture. All were agreed, however, that the problem of the Negro's status continued to be disturbing at home and embarrassing abroad.

The Road to Revolution

Many factors stimulated the resort to direct, more drastic action to secure the rights of Negro Americans. Few, if any, were more important than the widespread, massive resistance to the extension of these rights. In many Southern communities economic sanctions were invoked against Negroes who were active in civil rights. Dismissals from jobs, denials of loans, and foreclosures of mortgages were some of the tactics used to decimate the ranks of "aggressive Negroes." Violence was a cruder and more direct method. From the time that George Lee, an N.A.A.C.P. leader in Belzoni, Mississippi, was killed by a shotgun blast in early 1955, violence spread; and within the next two years Negroes were murdered with impunity in South Carolina, Alabama, Georgia, and other Southern states. Such incidents were extremely discouraging to those who hoped for an early and peaceful extension of civil rights to all.

Equally discouraging was the official opposition in many Southern states, and complacency and indifference elsewhere. Taking their cue from the call for massive resistance by the Virginia Senator, Harry F. Byrd, all of the eleven states of the old Confederacy enacted interposition, nullification, or protest resolutions against the Supreme Court decision in the school desegregation cases. *Black Monday*, a bitter tirade against the decision, written by a Mississippi circuit court judge, Tom P. Brady, helped to stiffen the opposition by arguing that Negroes were not capable of becoming equal citizens. In 1957 the segregationists cheered the active opposition of Governor Orval Faubus to the desegregation of Central High School in Little Rock, Arkansas. Not until President Eisenhower sent federal troops in response to the governor's defiance of a court order did the Negro children gain admission to the school. The weeks and months of intimidation and harassment of the children on the part of the white students and their parents suggested how bitter and harsh the resistance could be.

Negroes themselves manifested a growing impatience with the intransigence of the opponents of civil rights. Negroes were becoming bolder and more aggressive and began to press for their rights with relentless vigor. Their action in boycotting the Montgomery buses set an example that was followed in other Southern communities. It was in the cities that they most clearly began to manifest their impatience; and Negroes were steadily becoming urban dwellers. Between 1940 and 1960 the Negro population outside the old Confederacy increased two and one-fourth times, from nearly four million to more than nine million, representing 48 per cent of the total Negro population. Most of the growth outside the South was in the central cities of the twelve largest metropolitan areas: New York, Los Angeles, Chicago, Philadelphia, Detroit, San Francisco-Oakland, Boston, Pittsburgh, St. Louis, Washington, Cleveland, and Baltimore. By 1960 these twelve areas held 31 per cent of all the Negroes in the United States. There were 1,100,000 Negroes in New York City, 813,000 in Chicago, 529,000 in Philadelphia, 500,000 in Detroit and 464,000 in Los Angeles. In Southern cities, such as Atlanta, Birmingham, Houston, and Dallas the Negro population grew steadily. The Northern Negro was already a city dweller; and the Southern Negro was rapidly becoming one.

If Negroes moved to the cities to solve their problems, they soon discovered that their problems persisted, even increased. Poor housing and unemployment were twin evils that spawned new frustrations and difficulties. But new contacts and new associations provided opportunities to discover the strength that they possessed. Some Negroes, in such cities as Chicago, Detroit, Washington, and New York, turned to the racial separatism advocated by the Nation of Islam, commonly known as the Black Muslims. From its modest beginnings in the mid-thirties, the Nation by 1960 had grown under the leadership of Elijah Muhammad into a vocal and vigorous religious sect.

In welcoming all Negroes, including social outcasts and ex-convicts, Elijah Muhammad emphasized the common bond that all Negroes shared against what he called "the white devil" and the hopelessness of any effort at racial integration. Members of the Nation paid strict attention to dress and dietary laws and pressed their case by standing on street corners in most Northern cities and selling such publications as *Muhammad Speaks*. They changed their names that indicated their relationship to the white man to such designations as Brother Leonard IX and Minister Malcolm X. The best known of all Black Muslims was the world heavyweight champion, Muhammad Ali, formerly Cassius Clay. Malcolm X was the most eloquent exponent of the ideas of the Black Muslims until he broke with the the sect in 1964. In the following year he was assassinated in New York during a rally of his newly organized group. By the early sixties, conservative estimates indicated that the Black Muslims numbered nearly 50,000, with a much larger number of sympathizers.

A more likely response to their plight—and one that appealed to a much larger number of urban Negroes—was to seek improvement through political action. To most Negroes city hall, the state capitol, and Washington seemed proper targets for their efforts. They had seen government wield enormous power in new areas during the depression and the war. They began to feel that government would do more for Negroes if they could harness and use their political strength wisely. In the Northern cities more Negroes had begun to vote, while even in the South—after the white primary was outlawed—they became more active politically. Political activity had undoubtedly influenced the enactment of fair employment laws in New York (1945), Michigan, Minnesota, Pennsylvania (1955), and California and Ohio (1959). Fifteen other states would pass such laws by 1962. Political influence could, perhaps, secure more favorable action on behalf of Negroes on the state level and even on the national level.

There were important indications that the national government might soon act to improve the status of Negro Americans. From the time of President Truman's civil rights proposals in 1948 Congress had begun to consider civil rights legislation. Indeed, between 1953 and 1957 the House of Representatives passed civil rights bills several times, but none ever came to a vote in the Senate. In 1957 President Eisenhower presented a four-point proposal for civil rights, a very important feature of which was that the attorney general should be empowered to seek injunctive relief in the federal courts for persons whose constitutional rights had been violated. Although this feature was stricken from the bill that was introduced following the President's suggestion, Congress did pass a civil rights bill after much bitter debate and much pressure from civil rights advocates.

The new law, the first civil rights act since 1875, authorized the federal government to bring civil suits in its own name to obtain injunctive relief, in federal courts, where any person was denied or threatened in his right to vote. It elevated the Civil Rights Section of the Department of Justice to the status of a Division, with an assistant attorney general over it. It also created the United States Commission on Civil Rights, with authority to investigate allegations of denials of the right to vote, to study and collect information concerning legal developments constituting a denial of equal protection of the laws, and to appraise the laws and policies of the federal government with respect to equal protection. One senator called the new law a "sham," while another called it "a limited and modest step." The real significance of the legislation lay not so much in its provisions as in its recognition of federal responsibility and its reflection of a remarkable and historic reversal of the federal policy of hands-off in matters involving civil rights.

Congress was impelled to enact civil rights legislation not merely in response to the President's suggestion or even to the mounting pressure by advocates of civil rights. It was also responding to the rapidly changing international scene, in which the status of the Negro in the United States was playing an increasingly important part. On March 8, 1957—six months before the new civil rights act was passed—Ghana became the first former African colony to join the United Nations. As Professor Talcott Parsons has aptly observed, the emergence into independence of the sub-Saharan nations enormously changed the world-wide significance of the American race problem and provided a considerable stimulus to the movement for racial equality in the United States. As Congress began to debate the proposed civil rights bill in the summer of 1957, the diplomatic representatives from Ghana had taken up residence at the United Nations and in Washington. This important fact could not be ignored by responsible members of Congress. It seemed that black men from the Old World had arrived just in time to help redress the racial balance in the New.

XXXI •

The Negro Revolution

The Beginnings

● *On February 1, 1960, four students from the Negro* Agricultural and Technical College in Greensboro, North Carolina, entered a variety store, made several purchases, and then sat down at the lunch counter and ordered coffee. They were refused service because they were Negroes. They sat at the counter until the store closed. This was the beginning of the sit-in movement which spread rapidly through the South and to numerous places in the North. In the spring and summer young people, white and Negro, participated in similar peaceful forms of protest against segregation and discrimination. They sat in white libraries, waded in white beaches, and slept in the lobbies of white hotels. Many were arrested for trespassing, disorderly conduct, and disobeying police officers. A Southern journalist called the sit-ins the South's new time bomb. When Negro students were criticized for sitting-in they placed full page advertisements in several newspapers, including the Atlanta *Constitution* in which they said, "We do not intend to wait placidly for those rights which are already legally and morally ours to be meted out to us one at a time." Soon, many lunch counters across the South began to serve Negroes; and other facilities were opened.

By the time the four Negro students launched the sit-in movement, the stage was already set for the beginning of the most profound, revolutionary changes in the status of Negro Americans that had occurred since emancipation. The road to revolution had been paved by Supreme Court decisions on voting and school desgregation, by the Montgomery bus boycott and the emergence of Martin Luther King, the passage of the Civil Rights Act of 1957, and the rise of national states in Africa. The revolution would have many facets. The changes in public policy, in the way that Negroes viewed themselves and their place in American life, in the attitudes and thoughts of the larger community toward Negroes, were about as far-reaching as the changes in the status of Negroes themselves. The decision of the young Negro college students to sit in symbolized some of these changes and suggested the nature of others yet to come.

In the months and years that followed an interesting and, at times, exciting interplay of action and response developed between government and civil rights advocates. And it was this interplay that did so much to carry the revolution forward. After the passage of the act of 1957 the federal government increased its activity in the civil rights field; and so did the opponents. The Commission on Civil Rights held hearings on Negro voting in several cities, North and South, and discovered that Negroes were being regularly denied the right to vote by certain Southern white registrars. The Department of Justice then instituted suits in Alabama, Georgia, and Louisiana charging that registrars had failed to register qualified Negro voters solely because of their race. Although the Supreme Court upheld the right of the Department of Justice to bring such suits, that had been bitterly challenged in the South, it became clear that the act needed strengthening to prevent evasive actions by registrars.

In 1960, after much debate and some filibustering in the Senate, Congress passed another civil rights bill. It provided that if a registrar resigned after complaints had been filed, the proceeding could be instituted against the state. The act further required that voting records be preserved for twenty-two months following any primary, special, or general election. The records were to be available to the attorney general in order to determine whether proceedings were warranted. To strike at a malicious practice that had sprung up in recent years, the law singled out for punishment any persons found guilty of defacing churches, synagogues, or other buildings. The Department of Justice then proceeded successfully to enjoin many white citizens of Haywood and Fayette County, Tennessee, from using a variety of methods of economic reprisals against Negroes who had attempted to vote. By 1962 more than thirty cases had been brought by the attorney general to protect Negroes in their efforts to vote in Mississippi, Louisiana, Alabama, Tennessee, and Georgia.

By the summer of 1960 the question of the status of the Negro had become such a burning issue that neither major party, facing the Presidential campaign, could fail to recognize its importance. There were already more than one million registered Negro voters in twelve Southern states. In at least six of the eight most populous states in the country Negroes held the balance of power in closely contested elections. In their platforms in 1960 both major parties took strong stands for racial justice and equality. They hoped not to be guilty of what Theodore White observed in his *The Making of the President 1960* when he said, "To ignore the Negro vote and Negro insistence on civil rights must be either an act of absolute folly—or one of absolute miscalculation."

Senator John F. Kennedy easily outmaneuvered his opponent, Vice-President Richard M. Nixon, in their quest for the Negro vote in 1960. Long before his nomination, Negro members of Kennedy's staff had briefed him well on the problems of Negroes as well as their aspirations. During the campaign Kennedy chided the Republicans for not having done more to advance the cause of the Negro. He criticized President Eisenhower for not having put an end to discrimination in federally supported housing and declared that it could be done "with the stroke of a pen." (President Kennedy did not take that step until November, 1962, two years after his election.)

Even more astute was Kennedy's action regarding the imprisonment of Martin Luther King. On October 19, King and some fifty other Negroes were arrested for sitting in at the Magnolia Room of Rich's Department Store in Atlanta. The others were released, but King was sentenced to four months of hard labor in the Reidsville State Prison, to the dismay and fear of those who knew what Georgia justice might lead to. On the morning of October 26, Kennedy called Mrs. King and expressed his sympathy and concern. His campaign manager and brother, Robert F. Kennedy, telephoned the Georgia judge who had sentenced King and pleaded for his release. On the following day King was released, although it is not clear what effect Robert Kennedy's intervention had on the judge. The news of the action of the Kennedy brothers swept through the Negro community, assisted by the distribution in Negro churches and elsewhere of more than a million pamphlets telling of their deed. The point was not lost on the Negro voters that neither Dwight D. Eisenhower, the President, nor Vice-President Nixon, the candidate, took any action at all.

By 1960 Negroes were so preoccupied with civil rights that they were scarcely influenced by other considerations in their decisions to support parties and candidates. Southern Negroes who could vote overcame their Protestant bias and cast their votes for the Catholic Presidential candidate, who appeared to them to be more prepared to advance the cause of civil rights. Northern Negroes, aware of their critical strength, were determined to use it to compel equality for their less privileged kinsmen. When the votes were counted—in the closest Presidential election of the century—Negroes had reason to believe that they were responsible for the election of John F. Kennedy. In Illinois, which Kennedy carried by 9,000 votes, it was estimated that 250,000 Negroes voted for him. In Michigan, where he won by a margin of 67,000 votes, some 250,000 Negroes supported him. He carried South Carolina by 10,000 votes, including an estimated 40,000 Negro votes. Negroes now hoped that the New Frontier would also be theirs.

The young President had no ambitious plans for new legislation to elevate the Negro in American life. Instead, he looked toward expanded executive action, especially in those areas where federal authority was most complete and undisputed. He hoped, moreover, to use the prestige of his office to exercise the "moral leadership" to which he had referred during the campaign. He encouraged the Department of Justice, headed by his brother Robert, to carry forward its efforts to secure the right to vote through negotiation and litigation. He pressed for increased employment of Negroes in federally connected programs and established the Committee on Equal Employment Opportunity, with Vice-President Lyndon B. Johnson as chairman. The Committee took steps to eliminate discrimination in employment in government and private enterprise. After President Kennedy issued the order to prevent discrimination in new federally supported housing, he appointed a Committee on Equal Opportunity in Housing, headed by former Governor David Lawrence of Pennsylvania.

Kennedy showed little hesitation in appointing Negroes to

important federal positions. As judges he appointed Thurgood Marshall to the Circuit Court in New York, Wade McCree to the District Court for Eastern Michigan, James Parsons to the District Court of Northern Illinois, and Marjorie Lawson, Joseph Waddy, and Spottswood Robinson to the bench in the District of Columbia. Robert Weaver became head of the Housing and Home Finance Agency; and when the Agency was elevated to cabinet rank in 1965 President Johnson appointed Weaver Secretary of the new Department of Housing and Urban Development, the first Negro to hold a cabinet office. The President also appointed George L. P. Weaver to be Assistant Secretary of Labor, Carl Rowan as Deputy Assistant Secretary of State and later Ambassador to Finland, and Clifton R. Wharton and Mercer Cook to be Ambassadors to Norway and Niger respectively. He appointed two Negroes, Merle McCurdy and Cecil F. Poole, as United States Attorneys, several others to Presidential Committees working in the civil rights field and to other boards and commissions, including John B. Duncan to the Board of Commissioners of the District of Columbia.

On the whole, however, the picture of federal employment for Negroes continued to be dark. Between June, 1961, and June, 1962, the federal employment of Negroes increased by only 11,000, while the total number of federal employees increased by more than 62,000. At the very lowest levels, GS–1 through GS–4, less than 2,000 Negroes found employment; almost 5,000 in the categories GS–5 through GS–11 were hired; while the number of Negroes in the upper ranks, GS–12 through GS–18, increased from a mere 1,037 to a slightly higher figure, 1,406. Discrimination in federal employment persisted. Indeed, in some agencies there were scarcely any Negro employees at all. Only in the sub-professional categories, paying less than $5,000 per year did Negroes constitute any substantial proportion, 23 per cent, of the federal service.

The anxieties of Negroes and others in the civil rights field were not satisfied by the actions of the Kennedy administration. Soon, civil rights advocates were applying new pressures to secure equal rights for Negroes. In May, 1961, the Congress of Racial Equality, an interracial direct action group founded in 1942, sent "Freedom Riders" into the South to test segregation laws and practices in interstate transportation. In Anniston and Birmingham, Alabama, the interracial teams were attacked by angry segregationists. Attorney General Robert Kennedy was obviously a bit annoyed by the aggressiveness of these unorthodox fighters for civil rights and expressed a desire for a "cooling off" period. He nevertheless ordered an investigation by the Federal Bureau of Investigation and made it clear that the Freedom Riders would be protected. When the Riders were set upon by a mob in Montgomery, where the police intervened only belatedly, the Attorney General dispatched a force of 600 deputy marshals and other federal officers to the scene, thus narrowly averting further violence.

Other groups, including the new Student Nonviolent Coordinating Committee, the Southern Christian Leadership Conference, and the Nashville Student Movement, became interested and joined in sending more than a thousand volunteers on freedom rides through the South. Federal marshals escorted them to Jackson, but local officials arrested at least three hundred of them, including fifteen priests. Reacting to the pressures of the Freedom Riders and the intervention of the Attorney General, the Interstate Commerce Commission ruled on September 22, 1961, that passengers on interstate carriers would be seated without regard to race and that such carriers could not use segregated terminals.

School desegregation had moved at a snail's pace since the Supreme Court issued its decrees in the school desegregation cases in 1955. In the North *de facto* segregation of the schools was deeply entrenched, thanks to rigid patterns of segregation in housing. In such cities as New Rochelle, New York, Englewood, New Jersey, Chester, Pennsylvania, and Chicago, however, strong protest actions in 1960 and 1961 were a portent of what was to come. In the South, resistance to school desegregation had stiffened to the point that by 1958 the slow pace had come to a virtual standstill. In 1961 a total of 775 of the 2,839 biracial school districts in the seventeen Southern and border states had some desegregation, an increase of only 1.5 per cent in the two preceding years. Most of the increase had been in the border states.

Since Autherine Lucy's expulsion from the University of Alabama in 1956 Negroes had been admitted in small numbers to Southern white colleges and universities, public and private. Although there were some local objections, the Universities of Georgia and South Carolina admitted Negroes without much excitement. The most dramatic and violent effort to bar a Negro from public higher education was the attempt by the state of

Mississippi in 1962, in defiance of a court order, to prevent the enrollment of James Meredith. When it became clear that the state would not maintain order and admit Meredith, despite Governor Ross Barnett's promise to the President, the latter sent deputy marshals and, later, federalized national guardsmen to secure Meredith's admission and maintain order. Before the rioting had subsided, two persons had been killed and many injured. Meredith's enrollment and graduation the following year indicated the futility of attempting to deny higher education to a Negro in the face of a federal government determined to secure it for him. George Wallace, governor of Alabama, would learn that lesson anew in 1963, when he unsuccessfully attempted to block the enrollment of a Negro at the University of Alabama by "standing in the schoolhouse door." Another disadvantage from which Wallace suffered was the fact that by 1963 the Negro Revolution was at full tide.

Marching for Freedom

For several years before 1963 the National Association for the Advancement of Colored People used the motto "Free by '63." Other groups adopted the motto and focused more attention on the drive for equality. Many leaders were especially sensitive to the significance of the Emancipation Centennial in pointing up racial inequality in American life. On September 22, 1962, when Governor Nelson Rockefeller of New York spoke in Washington to open the exhibit of the Preliminary Emancipation Proclamation, "the state's most treasured possession," he said, "The very existence of this document stirs our conscience with the knowledge that Lincoln's vision of a nation truly fulfilling its spiritual heritage is not yet achieved."

During the centennial year itself, the United States Commission on Civil Rights presented to the President a report on the history of civil rights, *Freedom to the Free*, in which it declared that "A gap between our recorded aspirations and actual practices still remains." On Lincoln's birthday, 1963, President and Mrs. Kennedy received more than a thousand Negro and white citizens at the White House and presented to each of them a copy of the report. Speaking at Gettysburg that year, Vice-President Lyndon B. Johnson said, "Until justice is blind, until education is unaware of race, until opportunity is unconcerned

A JOHNSON PUBLICATION

EBONY

SPECIAL ISSUE

SEPTEMBER 1963 50¢

FREDERICK DOUGLASS
Father Of The
Protest Movement

*In
Commemoration
of the
100th Anniversary of*

THE EMANCIPATION PROCLAMATION

THIS SPECIAL ISSUE OF EBONY *to commemorate the centennial of the Emancipation Proclamation sold more than a million copies. Courtesy EBONY Magazine.*

with the color of men's skins, emancipation will be a proclamation but not a fact." President Kennedy took note of the absence of equality when he said, "Surely, in 1963, one hundred years after emancipation, it should not be necessary for any American citizen to demonstrate in the streets for an opportunity to stop at a hotel, or eat at a lunch counter . . . on the same terms as any other American."

Theoretically, the President was right; but Negroes had discovered that demonstrations had accomplished what other measures had not. They had gained valuable experience at Montgomery, Greensboro, Albany, Georgia, and elsewhere. They were determined to use that experience during the centennial year in pressing for equality. Consequently, demonstrations "broke out" in many places during the spring of 1963. The most critical demonstration began in Birmingham on April 3, under the leadership of Dr. Martin Luther King and the Southern Christian Leadership Conference. As they marched the demonstrators demanded fair employment opportunities, desegregation of public facilities, creation of a committee to plan desegregation, and the dropping of charges against King and the other 2,500 persons who were arrested in the course of the demonstrations.

Up to May 3 the demonstration was notable merely because of the large number of participants, including many school-children, and the large number of arrests. On that day the Birmingham police began to use dogs and high pressure water hoses on the marchers, who defended themselves with rocks and bottles. The action of the police caused consternation and dismay in many parts of the country, where sympathy demonstrations were held. During the week of May 18, the Department of Justice noted forty-three major and minor demonstrations, ten of them in Northern cities. More such demonstrations were held the following month when Medgar Evers, the leader of the Mississippi N.A.A.C.P., was shot in the back outside his home in Jackson. The border town of Cambridge, Maryland, was the scene of many weeks of peaceful demonstrations in the spring, but rioting erupted in July, and the national guard was called out. A semblance of peace was restored only when an agreement was reached with Cambridge officials to desegregate schools and public accommodations, to enlarge employment opportunities for Negroes, and to build low-rent housing that would be available to them.

There were about as many demonstrations in the North and West as in the South. The emphasis was on increased job opportunities and an end to *de facto* segregation in housing and education. In New York and Philadelphia demonstrators sought to block tax-supported construction on which Negroes received little or no employment. They also sought to prevent the construction of schools in all-Negro neighborhoods. They staged sit-ins in the offices of Mayor Robert Wagner of New York City and Governor Nelson Rockefeller of New York. In Boston, Chicago, New York, and Englewood, New Jersey, they sat in schools or staged school strikes to protest racial imbalances. In Los Angeles and San Francisco crowds of more than 20,000 held rallies to protest the slaying of Medgar Evers and of William Moore, a Baltimore postal employee who was shot from ambush while making a one-man freedom march to Mississippi.

Neither the President nor Congress could be indifferent to the large-scale demonstrations and the resistance of the white segregationists. In February, before the demonstrations reached their peak, President Kennedy sent a special message to Congress recommending legislation to strengthen voting rights. In June, largely because of events in Birmingham and elsewhere, he submitted a new and broadened civil rights program. A few days earlier he had spoken to the American people by radio and television—on the same day that national guardsmen had been used to secure the admission of two Negroes to the University of Alabama. In part, the President said, "We face . . . a moral crisis as a country and as a people. It cannot be met by repressive police action. It cannot be left to increased demonstrations in the streets. It cannot be quieted by token moves or talk. It is a time to act in the Congress, in your state and local legislative body and, above all, in all of our daily lives."

The bill containing the President's recommendations occupied much of the attention of Congress during the summer of 1963. There was bitter opposition to the public accommodations provision on the ground that it interfered with property rights. Opponents of the bill also declared that the proposal to withhold federal funds from programs where discrimination was practised was vindictive and, perhaps, unconstitutional. Advocates of the measure pointed to the unconscionable delay in granting Negroes equal rights; and they called on Congress to pass the bill as a first step toward the achievement of racial equality. Attorney General Robert F. Kennedy testified before Congressional committees ten times in support of the proposed legislation.

As Congress and the nation debated the proposed civil rights bill, the "March on Washington for Jobs and Freedom" occurred. Those who regarded the March as an idle threat were astounded to discover that even in the planning stages it was receiving broad support from many sectors of American life. All of the major civil rights groups were joined by many religious, labor, and civic groups in planning and executing the gigantic demonstration. The American Jewish Congress, the National Conference of Catholics for Interracial Justice, the National Council of Churches, and the A.F.L.-C.I.O. Industrial Union Department were among the strong supporters of the March. On August 28, 1963, more than 200,000 Negroes and whites from all over the United States staged the largest demonstration in the history of the nation's capital. The orderly procession moved from the Washington Monument to the Lincoln Memorial, where A. Philip Randolph, Martin Luther King, Roy Wilkins, Walter Reuther, and others addressed the throng. Two noted civil rights leaders were absent. James Farmer, in a Louisiana jail for his activities in a demonstration, sent a message. After seventy years of crusading for civil rights, W. E. B. DuBois had joined the Communist Party, renounced his United States citizenship, and moved to Ghana in 1961. In his ninety-sixth year, he died in Accra on the eve of the March.

Congressional opponents of civil rights legislation had insisted that they could not be intimidated by the marchers. Some members of Congress were "out of town" or "previously engaged" when the marchers who were their constituents called on them to enlist their support. Some other members of Congress, however, supported the March and cordially received the demonstrators. President Kennedy, who had refused to criticize the March, received the leaders and pledged his continued support of the drive for equality. As Congress continued to debate the bill and as the threat of a filibuster held out the promise of killing the bill, many civil rights supporters became discouraged and pessimistic.

The September bombing of a Negro church in Birmingham in which four Negro children were killed was as discouraging as the delay in enacting the civil rights bill. The election in November of numerous Southerners who ran for public office on strong pro-segregation platforms was also discouraging. Nothing, however, filled Negroes with such despair as the murder of the young President in Dallas on November 22, 1963. President Kennedy had said that the enactment of the pending civil rights bill was imperative, regardless of how long it took. The year of

THE MARCH ON WASHINGTON FOR JOBS AND FREEDOM. August 28, 1963, more than 200,000 people gathered at the foot of the Lincoln Memorial and heard speeches from leaders in the civil rights movement. Courtesy EBONY Magazine.

'63 was drawing to a close; and Negroes were not yet free. They had not even been guaranteed the right to sit down at a lunch counter and have a cup of coffee. But they had gained a few victories. The Supreme Court, in *Edwards* v. *South Carolina*, had upheld their right to demonstrate and in *Johnson* v. *Virginia* had reversed the contempt conviction of a Negro who refused to obey a judge who ordered him to sit in the section of the courtroom reserved for Negroes. And more people openly supported racial equality than ever before in the history of the country.

THE PRESIDENT AND THE LEADERS. At the end of the March on Washington, August 28, 1963, President Kennedy met with the leaders of the March. From the left: Whitney Young, National Urban League; Dr. Martin Luther King, Southern Christian Leadership Conference; John Lewis, Student Non-Violent Coordinating Committee; Rabbi Joachim Prinz, American Jewish Congress; Dr. Eugene P. Blake, National Council of Churches; A. Philip Randolph, AFL-CIO Vice President; President Kennedy; Walter Reuther, United Auto Workers; Vice President Johnson (Rear), and Roy Wilkins, N.A.A.C.P. Wide World Photos.

The Illusion of Equality

Lyndon B. Johnson, who became the thirty-sixth President of the United States on November 22, 1963, was quick to make known his strong support of the late President's civil rights program. Five days after he took office he told Congress that he desired "the earliest possible passage of the civil rights bill." In the weeks and months that followed, the acrimonious debate in Congress continued, with the usual parliamentary maneuvers and delays. The only bright spot on the horizon as the New Year opened was the ratification in January, 1964, of the Twenty-fourth Amendment to the Constitution, which outlawed the requirement of the poll tax, long a means of disfranchising Negroes in federal elections. In the following month, however, the pressure of the President and of civil rights groups began to take effect; and the House of Representatives passed the civil rights bill by a substantial majority, 290–130. In June the Senate, for the first time, voted cloture to break a civil rights filibuster, thus assuring final passage of the bill. The vote in the Upper House was 73–27, with the Republican leader, Everett M. Dirksen of Illinois, voting for the bill, and the front-running Republican candidate for the Presidency, Barry Goldwater of Arizona, voting against it.

The Civil Rights Act of 1964 was the most far-reaching and comprehensive law in support of racial equality ever enacted by Congress. It gave the attorney general additional power to protect citizens against discrimination and segregation in voting, education, and the use of public facilities. It forbade discrimination in most places of public accommodation and established a federal Community Relations Service to help individuals and communities solve civil rights problems. It established a federal Equal Employment Opportunity Commission and extended the life of the Commission on Civil Rights to January, 1968. One of the most controversial provisions required the elimination of discrimination in federally assisted programs, authorizing termination of programs or withdrawal of federal funds upon failure to comply. Finally, the United States Office of Education was authorized to provide technical and financial aid to assist communities in the desegregation of schools. While some Negroes criticized the Act for not going far enough, others were delighted that a semblance of equality might now be attainable.

While there was a notable decline in discrimination in some fields, the period following the passage of the Civil Rights Act of 1964 was marked by strong resistance to its enforcement and, indeed, considerable violence in some places. There was what some called a "white backlash" created by Negroes who pushed "too hard" for equality. In the North it manifested itself in the actions of whites who discovered their prejudices for the first time or who resented direct action protests to eliminate discrimination in their own communities. It accounts, at least in part, for the strong showing that the segregationist governor of Alabama, George Wallace, made in the presidential primaries in Wisconsin, Indiana, and Maryland. The backlash in the South was merely the normal determination with which some segregationists went about the task of preserving the old order. Some public places transformed themselves into private clubs—as they had done after the passage of the Civil Rights Act of 1875. The proprietor of an Atlanta restaurant specializing in fried chicken vowed that he would go out of business before he would desegregate it; and he finally did. Before the end of the year it was the segregationists' turn to be discouraged, when the United States Supreme Court on December 14 upheld the constitutionality of the public accommodations section of the Civil Rights Act.

Neither congressional legislation nor executive action could stem the violence that was a feature of the "long hot summer" of 1964. In mid-July, the violence that broke out in the Yorkville section of New York City was touched off by the killing of a Negro teenage youth by an off-duty policeman. Protest demonstrations against "police brutality" spread to Harlem, Bedford-Stuyvesant, and other parts of the city, often accompanied by rioting and looting. There were similar disturbances in Rochester, New York, Paterson, Elizabeth, and Jersey City, New Jersey, Philadelphia, and Chicago. It was reported by one observer that roving gangs of "unemployed youths were conspicuously involved in most of the disorders."

Following the decision in the school desegregation cases the Ku Klux Klan had surrendered to the Citizens Councils its position as leading defender of white supremacy. During the debates over the Civil Rights Act of 1964, however, the Klan reclaimed its position of leadership. In Mississippi, Alabama, Louisiana, and Georgia, its members paraded in protest against racial equality. In Georgia, Klansmen picketed a hotel that had desegregated, carrying posters stating, "Don't trade here! Owners of this business surrendered to the race mixers." Much more serious was the violence, attributed to the Klan and similar groups, that broke out in the South during the summer as the SNCC and SCLC stepped up their voter registration drives. In July a Negro educator, returning to his home in Washington from reserve officer training, was killed in Georgia by a shotgun blast from a passing automobile. Two men, identified as Klansmen, were tried for the crime but were acquitted. In July three young civil rights workers, one Negro Mississippian and two white New Yorkers, disappeared after having been arrested in Mississippi on speeding charges. Weeks later their bullet riddled bodies were discovered buried in an earthen dam. During the search for the civil rights workers the bodies of two Negroes were found floating in the Mississippi River. Several whites were arrested in connection with both crimes, but there were no convictions. Between June and October some twenty-four Negro churches in Mississippi were totally or partially destroyed by bombings and fire.

Although both major parties continued to recognize the importance of the Negro vote in national elections, the odds greatly favored the Democrats capturing it in 1964. Negroes were generally pleased with the civil rights record of Lyndon B. Johnson as Vice-President and President. His choice for second place on the ticket, Senator Hubert Humphrey of Minnesota with a strong pro-civil rights record, was additional reassurance that the executive was committed to continued support of the Negro's cause. If the Democrats failed to seat the delegates from the Mississippi Freedom Democratic Party, who argued that the regular Mississippi Democrats were "lily white," they did mollify the Negroes by outlawing segregated delegations at future conventions. On the other hand the Republicans nominated Barry Goldwater for President, who had voted in the Senate against the Civil Rights Act of 1964 and for Vice-President the little-known Representative William E. Miller of New York. Most Negroes regarded Goldwater's persistent references during the campaign to "crime in the streets" as a thinly veiled condemnation of civil rights demonstrations. The overwhelming victory for the Johnson-Humphrey ticket was one to which the vast majority of Negro voters contributed.

Despite existing civil rights legislation, hundreds of thousands of Negroes in the South continued to have difficulty in voting or were barred altogether. During the summer and fall of 1964 the Council of Federated Organizations, composed of the major civil rights groups, the National Council of Churches, and others, experienced great difficulty in their drive to increase voter registration among Negroes. Even after the election, they continued to face bitter opposition. Southern whites, especially in areas where the Negro population was large, seemed more opposed to the voter registration drives than to demonstrations to desegregate public accommodations. In Selma, Dallas County, Alabama, the opposition, led by the county sheriff, was particularly fierce. In February a Negro civil rights worker was killed, and a few weeks later a young white minister from Boston was killed. These acts of violence, together with the sheriff's use of tear gas, whips, and clubs against the demonstrators, attracted world-wide attention.

Still further attention was attracted by the demonstrators' decision to march from Selma to Montgomery. When Alabama public officials sought to prevent the march, the United States District Court judge in Montgomery ordered state officials to permit the march; and President Johnson called the Alabama National Guard into federal service to protect them. On the final day of the march the three hundred demonstrators were joined by some 35,000 supporters from all over the country. Martin Luther King, who a few months earlier had received the Nobel Peace Prize for his civil rights leadership, told the crowd in Montgomery that "no tide of racism can stop us." Nobel Prize winner Ralph Bunche, another speaker, apologized for having to speak from the steps of a state capitol over which waved the flag of the Confederacy. That night, as if to reaffirm the motto, "The Deep South says 'Never,' " snipers shot and killed a white woman from Detroit as she transported passengers from Montgomery back to Selma. In December her assailants, who had been exonerated on a charge of murder, were convicted, under an 1870 federal statute, for violating her civil rights.

As the Selma-Montgomery march got under way the President recognized the clear need for additional legislation to protect the rights of voters. In an address to Congress and the nation he said that the real hero in the struggle for equality was the Negro American. "His actions and protests—his courage to risk safety and even life—have awakened the conscience of the nation. His demonstrations have been designed to call attention to injustice, to provoke change and stir reform. He has called upon us to make good the promise of America. And who among us can say we would have made the same progress were it not for his persistent bravery, and his faith in American democracy. . . . We intend to fight this battle where it should be fought—in the courts, in the Congress, and in the hearts of men. And we shall overcome." Negroes everywhere were gratified that the President of the United States should end his stirring address with the words that were the theme song of the civil rights movement.

A few days later the President sent to Congress his proposals for a right-to-vote law. Congress passed the law with unusual swiftness. It authorized the attorney general to send federal examiners to register Negro voters when he concluded that local registrars were not doing their job. It suspended all literacy tests and other devices in states and counties that used them and where less than 50 per cent of the adults had voted in 1964. States affected were Alabama, Georgia, Louisiana, Mississippi,

IN MONTGOMERY, ALABAMA, IN MARCH 1965, approximately 50,000 people joined those who had marched from Selma and then proceeded to the capitol grounds to air their grievances. Courtesy EBONY Magazine.

South Carolina, Virginia, twenty-six counties in North Carolina, Alaska, and scattered counties in Arizona, Idaho, and Hawaii. There was opposition to the measure; and some Negroes accused Attorney General Nicholas Katzenbach of not sending federal examiners quickly enough. Nevertheless, by the end of the year nearly a quarter of a million new Negro voters had registered, one-third by federal examiners and two-thirds by local officials. Even in that year Negroes won seats in the Georgia legislature and in city councils of several Southern cities.

Even before larger numbers of Negroes began to register to vote under the protection of the new legislation, it became clear that they needed much more than the franchise if they were to enjoy equality. After World War II Negroes moved from the rural areas to the cities at an enormous rate; but the move failed to solve many of their problems. Between 1940 and 1960 the Negro population of New York City increased two and one half times, but fully 85 per cent of the newcomers were crowded into the already overcrowded Negro ghettoes. The situation was similar in other cities. As whites departed from the inner city to more attractive sections of the city or to the suburbs, Negroes found housing, not on their own terms but on those arranged by owners, mortgage companies, and other beneficiaries. All too often they paid premium prices for housing that was already outmoded and becoming dilapidated.

Discrimination in housing was not only private practice but public policy. Between 1935 and 1950 eleven million homes were built. Wherever there was federal assistance, the racial policy was laid down in the manual of the Federal Housing Administration that declared, "If a neighborhood is to retain stability it is necessary that properties shall be continued to be occupied by the same social and racial classes." One housing authority has claimed that this policy did more to entrench housing bias in American neighborhoods than any court could undo by a ruling. Despite the fact that by 1962 some seventeen states and fifty-six cities had passed laws or resolutions against housing discrimination, the bias persisted. Banks, insurance companies, real estate boards, and brokers greatly benefited from segregated housing for which they received a maximum profit from a minimum of expenditure.

Negroes were greatly embittered to discover that they were being exploited by landlords and real estate brokers who took their rents but refused to comply with the minimum housing and health standards established by the city and state. As they paid high rents for rat-infested slums, they discovered that in such neighborhoods their children received inferior education, fewer job opportunities, and few, if any, public facilities. What was even worse, they discovered that cities were unwilling to enforce their own anti-bias housing codes. This led Negroes in New York City in 1963 to launch rent strikes against "slumlords" and in Chicago in 1966 to engage in an all-out war against discrimination in housing. In California, the supporters of equal opportunity in housing suffered a setback in 1964 when the voters adopted, by an overwhelming vote, a cleverly framed constitutional amendment ostensibly guaranteeing a property owner the right to dispose of his property to any person he chose. Backed by the California Real Estate Association and the National Association of Real Estate Boards, the amendment was in fact a bulwark against open occupancy in housing. It was so construed in 1966 by the California Supreme Court that declared the amendment unconstitutional. But Negroes in the American city continued to experience untold difficulty in finding decent housing.

Urban Negroes suffered even more, if possible, from a lack of equal opportunity in employment. President Johnson attempted to set a pattern of fair employment by continuing to appoint Negroes to high government posts. As ambassadors he appointed Mercer Cook to Senegal, Hugh Smythe to Syria, Franklin Williams to Ghana, Elliott Skinner to Upper Volta, and Patricia Harris to Luxembourg. He promoted Wade McCree from the U.S. District Court to the Circuit Court, appointed Circuit Judge Thurgood Marshall to be Solicitor General of the United States, Hobart Taylor to the Board of the Export-Import Bank, and Andrew Brimmer to the Federal Reserve Board. Early in 1965, moreover, he set up the Council on Equal Opportunity, composed of cabinet officers and heads of agencies with major civil rights responsibilities and appointed Vice-President Humphrey as chairman. The council with overall responsibility in the civil rights field was to have a staff and could require reports from agencies and departments. This arrangement was terminated in September, 1965, and the Vice-President was relieved of his civil rights assignments. The attorney general became head of the administration's civil rights program; and the emphasis shifted from economic opportunity to the problems of compliance under the Civil Rights Act of 1964. There remained some of the momentum created during the Kennedy years in seeking to persuade private industry to increase employment opportunities for Negroes. This, however, was not sufficient to change the picture significantly.

During the years of the Negro revolution it was widely assumed that the vigorous thrust for equality had begun to close the economic gap between Negroes and whites. The assumption was entirely erroneous, caused in part by the opening of a few widely publicized opportunities that can best be described as "massive tokenism." The economic differences between Negroes and whites not only failed to decrease but actually increased. Between 1949 and 1964 the relative participation of Negroes in the total economic life of the nation declined significantly. During that period the unemployment rate of Negroes was at least double that of whites. Even in 1963, a prosperous year, the unemployment rate of Negroes was 114 per cent higher than whites. Where Negroes were employed, more than 80 per cent worked at the bottom of the economic ladder, as compared with 40 per cent of the employed whites. And the opportunities for Negroes to move up were greatly restricted not only by general race bias but also by the meager opportunities for apprenticeship training and by discrimination in the labor unions.

In 1962 the Council of Economic Advisors estimated the overall cost of racial discrimination at about $17.3 billion, or 3.2 per cent of the gross national product. This cost resulted primarily from the failure to utilize fully the existing experience and skills of the total population and the failure to develop potential experience and skills fully. The effect of this discrimination on Negro Americans themselves could be seen in their inability to secure adequate housing even when it was available, to provide a wholesome environment in which to rear and educate their children, and to participate more fully in the economic and social life of the country. There was also the shattering sense of frustration and alienation which could not be measured in monetary terms—at least not until it exploded into violence such as that which occurred in Los Angeles in August, 1965.

The immediate cause of the explosion in the Watts area of Los Angeles was the arrest of a young Negro who was charged with reckless driving. When a policeman drew a gun, an angry crowd assembled and began to fight the police. On the following day, after an unsuccessful attempt to quiet the tensions, the rioting was resumed, accompanied by looting and burning. At the height of the holocaust Negroes were heard to exclaim, "Burn, Whitey, Burn" and "Get Whitey." It was indeed an explosion of tension, bitterness, and hatred. By the time that the police, assisted by the California National Guard, restored peace, the toll had reached 34 dead, 1,032 injured, and 3,952 arrested. Property damage was estimated at $40 million.

The underlying cause of the Watts riot was the demoralization of the Negro population of Los Angeles. Despite the fact that 20 per cent of the houses in Watts were dilapidated, one-sixth of Los Angeles' half million Negroes were crowded into the area in conditions four times as congested as those in the rest of the city. Because of discrimination and bias, few Negroes were able to secure housing elsewhere, even when they could afford it. The employment picture was no better. More than 30 per cent of the potential Negro wage earners were unemployed at the time of the riot. Thousands of skilled and unskilled Negroes had no hope of employment. Even in the shops in the Watts area many seeking employment had been turned away by the white owners who preferred white employees, who, like the owners, did not live in Watts. Many Negroes resorted to plying a variety of illegal trades. Others, taking counsel with the Black Muslims whose influence there was growing, concluded that their plight was caused by the injustices of the white man. Thus, they were psychologically prepared to loot and burn. Watts was indicative of the tragedy of the illusion of equality.

At still another level the sense of hopelessness was in evidence. The Student Nonviolent Coordinating Committee had been, for several years, the heaviest contributor of shock troops to the civil rights battle. Its members had braved insults and risked their lives in order to increase voter registration among Southern Negroes. They had lived among Negroes, taught them, and built up their self-esteem. Gradually, disillusionment and pessimism overtook some of the members. They felt that some of the Negro leaders were not pressing hard enough and might be willing to settle for less than full equality. They lost confidence in most public officials and saw a collusion between federal officials and state and local leaders, to the detriment of Negroes. Laws were weak, they felt, and when they were strong, officials would not enforce them. Members of SNCC, therefore, began to express their own sense of futility in working along traditional lines in fighting for equality. In 1966 the new chairman, Stokely Carmichael, insisted that Negroes must think in terms of "Black Power" and use it to combat the "white power" that has held them down. It was not clear how much white support SNCC was rejecting. It was clear, however, that it preferred Negro leadership for Negro goals.

The process of school desegregation also showed how illusory freedom could be. Because of the opposition to the decision in the school desegregation cases and the techniques used to delay desegregation altogether, Negroes soon discovered that desegregation both in the South and the North would be a very slow process. As late as 1964 less than 2 per cent of the Negro students in the eleven states of the former Confederacy were in desegregated schools. In that year, however, the intransigence of the officials of Prince Edward County, Virginia, was broken when the Supreme Court ruled that the county was required to maintain a public school. For the first time since 1959 Negro children were able to attend public school.

Under the Civil Rights Act of 1964 the executive branch of the government gained the means of doing what the Court had been unable to do. Since the Act barred discrimination in federally aided projects and programs, school districts receiving federal funds were required to desegregate or to present acceptable plans for desegregating their schools. The Elementary and Secondary Education Act of 1965, with an appropriation of $1.3 billion, was an added incentive to compliance. By September, 1965, all but 124 of the school districts in the Southern and border states had presented acceptable plans for compliance, including freedom-of-choice plans, which required Negro pupils to take the initiative in seeking admission to all-white schools. In the eleven Southern states of the former Confederacy, however, only 6 per cent of the Negro children were attending desegregated schools in the 1965–1966 school year. Southern States were rapidly learning how to satisfy the federal requirement and receive federal funds and, at the same time, preserve the old order.

The application of the compliance provision of the Civil Rights Act to *de facto* segregation in Northern schools presented difficulties. New aid grants to Boston were delayed in 1965 because of complaints that Negro pupils were treated unfairly. The funds were released during the investigation. In the same year the Office of Education held up more than $30 million in aid to Chicago schools because of complaints that

Negroes were kept out of trade schools and that school district lines were gerrymandered. The school board of Chicago agreed to study the situation, and after strong intervention by the mayor and some Illinois members of Congress, the funds were freed. There were complaints in other cities—San Francisco and New York City, for example—but the funds were not held up. Even with its new powerful weapon the Office of Education had not yet learned to use it in moving effectively toward equalizing educational opportunities.

The Negro American and the World

In the months that followed the close of World War II Negroes more and more viewed their fate as inextricably connected with the fate of darker peoples throughout the world. Regardless of what attitude the UN took toward the domestic problems of the United States, Negro Americans sensed, more than many people of the United States, the implications of the interdependence of the world brought about by the revolutionary developments in transportation and communication and by the use of atomic energy. It was no sudden, newly awakened realization on the part of Negroes. Diplomacy, disarmament, colonial problems, and international relations had for years occupied the attention of a growing number of Negro scholars, including W. E. B. DuBois, Ralph Bunche, Rayford Logan, and Merze Tate. The Negro press, as well as a considerable number of Negro organizations, became interested in the international aspects of the struggle for freedom. They sought to define the roles which they as well as their country should play in the achievement of the great dream of peace and equality.

Negro Americans assumed a strong moral position as they became more articulate in the area of peace and freedom for the world. They praised America's goal of a world community of peaceful nations. They were quick to point out, however, that in order to achieve such a goal, discrimination, race hatred, and segregation must be replaced by equality for all citizens at home. They went so far as to chide the Truman administration for embarrassing the United States in appointing as Secretary of State, James F. Byrnes of South Carolina, where Negroes were excluded from white primaries, at a time when it became necessary to protest against the "undemocratic character" of elec-

DR. RALPH BUNCHE, Under Secretary for Special Political Affairs of the United Nations, who received the Nobel Prize for Peace in 1950, confers with the United Nations Secretary-General, U Thant. Courtesy United Nations.

tions in Bulgaria. Later, many Negroes would question their country's involvement in a war in Vietnam to achieve there what had not been achieved at home. They also reminded their government that the people of India, Indonesia, Burma, and elsewhere, were following in the footsteps of the United States in their struggle for independence. It would be most unfortunate if the country that had early set the example for the right of peoples to be independent should now seek to thwart the effort of others to become self-governing.

When the Fifth Pan-African Congress met at Manchester, England, in October, 1945, it was concerned not so much with problems peculiar to Africa as it was with the matter of taking steps toward implementing the efforts of darker peoples everywhere to secure a greater share of democracy for themselves. Negro Americans who were in attendance hoped that the Congress would inspire a greater measure of cooperation between Africans and their descendants in the United States. Even if the sons of Africa in the United States were not enthusiastic about working within the framework of such an organization, there was little doubt that they were anxious to take up the cudgel in behalf of darker peoples everywhere.

As Negroes wrote and spoke in support of freedom and democracy in Africa and Asia, it became rather difficult to determine whether they had achieved a breadth of understanding of international problems that their white brothers did not possess or whether it was a masterful merging of their own problems with similar ones in other parts of the world. While it can be said that many Negroes did have a broad interest in human welfare everywhere, it seems to be a fair conclusion to state that they never lost sight of their immediate difficulties. The struggle to attain freedom all over the world was essentially a struggle to attain a measure of it at home. As the editor of *Opportunity* said, "what happens to human rights in Manila, Martinique or Lagos will affect in no small measure development in Detroit."

Negro Americans were particularly interested in the movement for self-government in West Africa, and they applauded the leaders of Nigeria and the Gold Coast who were moving nearer their goals. As they became world-minded, thousands of them traveled to Europe, Asia, and Africa. In Africa they examined conditions and, on occasion, assisted in the improvement of them. Expatriate Richard Wright left his Paris home, visited numerous countries in Africa, and wrote a moving account of the continent's progress and problems in *Black Power*. Era Bell Thompson left her post with *Ebony* magazine in Chicago and recorded her impressions in *Africa, Land of My Fathers*. Negro observers, newspaper editors, and one member of Congress attended the Conference on Asian-African problems at Bandung, Indonesia, in the spring of 1955 and reported the proceedings to their constituents in the United States. Meanwhile, Negro physicians, engineers, teachers, and other highly trained personnel went to Ethiopia, Liberia, and other countries to contribute what they could to the growth and development of these countries.

When Africans south of the Sahara began to win their independence, they could hardly have been more delighted than Negro Americans. They were present in large numbers for the ceremonies marking the independence of Ghana, Tanganyika, Kenya, Zanzibar, Sierra Leone, and Uganda. They agonized over the tribulations and the conflicts in Rhodesia. It was clear that they wished to be identified with the peoples of "Mother Africa" who were moving to an important position on the world stage. They were not unaware of the effect that the emerging black nations might have upon their own status. The studied insult of a black finance minister of an African nation by a Maryland coffee shop or the presence of a black man on the United Nations Security Council was enough to elicit support from the highest United States officials for the equal treatment of all peoples, including Negro Americans. Nor could they lose sight of the fact that the entire world was interested in the fight over the admission of a Negro to the University of Mississippi, the bombing of Negro churches by white hoodlums, or the denial of equal employment and housing opportunities to Negroes.

The widening horizons of Negroes, the increasing world interest in the American race problem, and the leadership of the United States in world affairs were factors that commended the greater participation of Negroes in the foreign relations work of the United States government. One of the duties of Assistant Secretaries of Labor J. Ernest Wilkins and George L. P. Weaver was to represent the United States at international labor meetings. In 1965 James M. Nabrit became Deputy Chief of the United States Mission to the United Nations. By 1966 Negroes were serving their government in many parts of the world—as ambassadors in six countries, as cultural officers in many places, with the Agency for International Development and the United States Information Agency in dozens of countries.

Negroes served, moreover, as intellectual and cultural ambassadors of good will for the United States. With the endorsement of the United States and, at times, with government support, the Howard University Players toured Scandinavia and Germany, the cast of *Porgy and Bess* presented that show in the Soviet Union as well as in other parts of the world, and the Jubilee Singers gave concerts in Asia, South America, and Europe. Negro scholars worked, lectured and studied abroad under the Fulbright program and the Agency for International Development. Negro leaders toured the world with "teams" of Americans, and Negro athletes and entertainers performed the world over. The peoples of the world could begin to believe that the Negro was finally taking his place in the life of his country.

The war in Vietnam underscored this belief in the Negro American's increased involvement. At home many Negroes raised questions about the presence of American troops in Southeast Asia. Some joined with other Americans who insisted that the United States could not and should not undertake the task of policing the world. Others insisted that the escalation of the war and the bombing of North Vietnam went beyond the commitment of the United States and, indeed, rendered impossible any

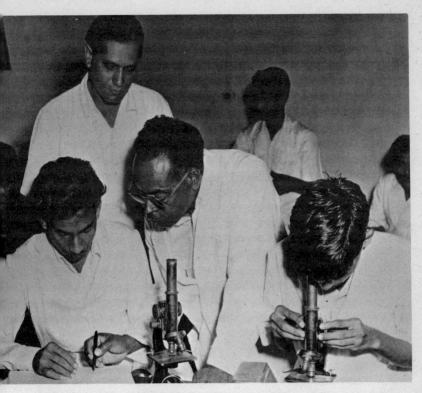

NEGROES SERVE ABROAD. Dr. Roscoe L. McKinney, Howard University anatomy professor, makes suggestions to a tutor in anatomy at the Osmania University Medical College in Hyderabad. Courtesy A.I.D.

PEACE CORPS VOLUNTEER Theresa Hicks serves as a nurse in a hospital in Rio de Janeiro. Peace Corps photo by Paul Conklin.

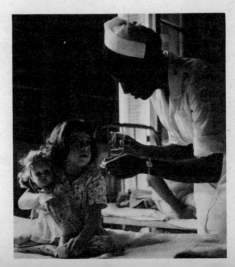

THE WAR IN VIETNAM. The Negroes in these photographs were among the 22,000 Negro Americans in Vietnam in 1966, comprising some 15 per cent of the total United States Armed Forces there. In the first eleven months of 1966, 22.4 per cent of all Army troops killed in action were Negroes. After receiving a fresh supply of ammunition and water flown in by helicopter, the men of the 173rd Airborne Brigade continue on a jungle "Search and Destroy" patrol in Phuoc Tuy province (top). A paratrooper medic with the same brigade gives help to a Vietnamese girl with a foot injury (bottom). Courtesy Department of Defense.

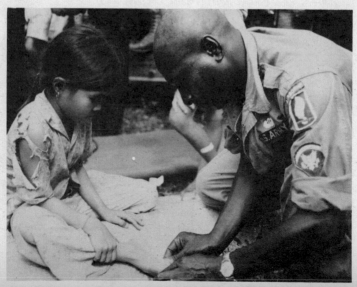

meaningful peace talks. Some opposed the war because it used up resources that could better be utilized in fighting for equal economic and civil rights at home or because it was a war against other darker peoples.

Civil rights groups were divided over the Vietnamese question. The older organizations tended to be less critical of United States policy and to view their role as that of continuing to fight for their stated objectives. The newer ones, such as the Congress of Racial Equality and the Student Nonviolent Coordinating Committee, viewed the war as closely related to the civil rights question. Some of the leaders declared that they would not fight in the war even if drafted. Julian Bond, the director of publicity for S.N.C.C., was denied his seat in the Georgia legislature because he had praised young men who burned their draft cards. He was not seated until the United States Supreme Court decided that he could not be denied his seat because of the opinions he held. More than in any other war in the nation's history Negro Americans were signing peace petitions, participating in peace rallies, and criticizing the administration of the armed services and their country's role in the war.

In contrast to the critical view of the war that many Negroes held was the participation of Negroes in the war itself. In the 1960's proportionately more Negroes (30 per cent) than whites (18 per cent) from the group qualified for military service were drafted. While enlistment rates of Negroes and whites were about equal, first term re-enlistments of Negroes were more than double that of whites. At the end of December 1965, there were more than 20,000 Negroes in Vietnam, including 16,531 in the Army, 500 in the Navy, 3,580 in the Marine Corps, and 908 in the Air Force. In 1967 Negroes constituted 11 per cent of the total United States enlisted personnel in Vietnam, but Negro soldiers comprised 14.5 per cent of all Army units, and in Army combat units the proportion was, according to the Department of Defense, "appreciably higher" than that. During the first eleven months of 1966, Negro soldiers constituted 22.4 per cent of all Army troops killed in action. By the spring of 1967 two Negroes had received the Medal of Honor for gallantry in Vietnam, one of them posthumously.

Looking back on their 350 years of residence in the Western world, Negroes could correctly visualize themselves, from the beginning, as an integral part of the struggle for freedom. At times they were passive symbols for the struggle that was car-

ried on by others. Frequently, however, they were active participants in the valiant warfare to destroy bigotry, repression, and
subjugation. Studying carefully their role in the growth and
development of the United States they could see that they were
more than very important contributors to the economic, political, and social development of their country. They had also
been important factors in the ageless struggle between freedom
and slavery. They had been the nation's constant reminders of
the imperfection of its social order and the immorality of its
human relationships. They had witnessed a nation dedicated to
liberty move toward the brink of destruction in the struggle to
settle the question of freedom. They had seen that same nation
compromise its position in the family of nations because of its
inability to face squarely the problem of freedom for all at
home.

This was a rich experience that Negroes had undergone. As
they moved together with other peoples into another era at the
close of World War II, they gave evidences of greater maturity
as a result of their experiences. They had become an integral
part of Western culture and civilization, and their fate was
inextricably connected with it. The rejections which they had
suffered doubtless wounded them considerably, but such treatment also gave them a perspective and an objectivity that others
had greater difficulty in achieving. They could, therefore, point
out more clearly than some others the weaknesses that seemed
to be inherent in Western civilization. They could counsel their
country, if it cared to listen, concerning its own position in an
atomic world. They could tell it, as the National Urban League
did twenty years ago, "The United States must hold to the
elemental principles of cooperation in a family of diversified
nations, none of which can escape the obligations of world
responsibility. Back of all that is planned or achieved is the fact
that henceforth it is ONE WORLD OR NONE." If America's
role in the atomic age was to lead the world toward peace and
international understanding, the Negro element in the population had a peculiar function to perform in carrying forward the
struggle for freedom at home, for the sake of America's role,
and abroad, for the sake of the survival of the world.

Bibliographical Notes

I shall make no attempt here to list all of the primary and secondary works that I consulted in the writing of this book. Instead, I shall cite a selected number of the more important works, primarily in English and fairly generally available, with a view to guiding the interested reader to further study. For many years the best general bibliographical aid in the study of the Negro was Monroe N. Work's *A Bibliography of the Negro in Africa and America* (New York, 1928). Although out of date, it continues to have value; but it should be supplemented by other aids. Among them are Dorothy B. Porter, *A Selected List of Books By and About the Negro* (Washington, 1936); Erwin K. Welsch, *The Negro in the United States, A Research Guide* (Bloomington, 1965); Erwin A. Salk, *A Layman's Guide to Negro History* (Chicago, 1966); and, for the period since 1954, Elizabeth W. Miller, *The Negro in America, A Bibliography* (Cambridge, 1966). The lists of materials in the major Negro collections should also be consulted. Among them are the Negro collections at Fisk University and Hampton Institute, the Moorland Collection at Howard University, the Slaughter Collection at Atlanta University, the James Weldon Johnson Collection at Yale University, and the Schomburg Collection at the New York Public Library.

It is widely known that a large and curious assortment of general histories of the Negro have appeared in the past century. While some have only historiographical value, others are important sources of information. Among the former are James W. C. Pennington, *Text Book of the Origin and History of the Colored People* (Hartford, 1841); William T. Alexander, *History of the Colored Race in America* (Kansas City, 1887); Harold M. Tarver, *The Negro in the History of the United States from the Beginning of the English Settlements in 1607, to the Present Time* (Austin, 1905); and E. A. Johnson, *School History of the Negro Race* (Raleigh, 1893). Of much greater value is George W. Williams, *History of the Negro Race in America*, two volumes (New York, 1882), which was the first such work to attract the attention of serious students. Two works of a similar nature, but less exhaustive, are Booker T. Washington, *The Story of the Negro: The Rise of the Race from Slavery*, two volumes (New York, 1909) and Willis D. Weatherford, *The Negro from Africa to America* (New York, 1924). A work dealing with the Negro on both American continents and the Caribbean is Sir Harry Johnston, *The Negro in the New World* (London, 1910). Other efforts in the general field include Benjamin Brawley, *A Short History of the American Negro* (New York, 1913);

Merle R. Eppse, *The Negro, Too, in American History* (Chicago, 1939); and Edwin R. Embree, *Brown Americans: The Story of a Tenth of the Nation* (New York, 1945).

The pioneer modern work was written in 1922 by Carter G. Woodson. The tenth edition was prepared by Charles H. Wesley under the title, *The Negro in Our History* (Washington, 1962). For certain aspects of the history of the Negro, W. E. B. DuBois, *Black Folk, Then and Now; An Essay in the History and Sociology of the Negro Race* (New York, 1939), is invaluable. In recent years the number of general histories of the Negro has greatly increased. Among them are Roi Ottley, *Black Odyssey* (New York, 1948); Rayford W. Logan, *The Negro in the United States* (New York, 1957); Lerone Bennett, *Before the Mayflower*, revised edition (Chicago, 1964); J. Saunders Redding, *They Came in Chains* (New York, 1952) and *Lonesome Road* (New York, 1958); W. Z. Foster, *The Negro People in American History* (New York, 1954); Benjamin Quarles, *The Negro in the Making of America* (New York, 1964); Eli Ginzberg and Alfred S. Eichner, *The Troublesome Presence; Democracy and the Negro* (Glencoe, 1964); and August Meier and Elliott Rudwick, *From Plantation to Ghetto: An Interpretive History of American Negroes* (New York, 1966).

A different approach to the history of the Negro is Earl E. Thorpe, *The Mind of the Negro: An Intellectual History of Afro-Americans* (Baton Rouge, 1961). The interest of foreign writers in the subject can be seen in J. W. Schulte Nordholt, *The People that Walk in Darkness* (London, 1960), Frank L. Schoell, *Histoire de la race noire aux États-Unis du XVIIe siècle à nos jours* (Paris, 1959) and Jean Daridan, *de Lincoln à Johnson: noirs et blancs* (Paris, 1965). There is much historical material in Gunnar Myrdal, *An American Dilemma; The Negro Problem and Modern Democracy* (New York, 1944 and 1964); E. Franklin Frazier, *The Negro in the United States*, revised edition (New York, 1957); Margaret J. Butcher, *The Negro in American Culture* (New York, 1956), and John P. Davis, editor, *The American Negro Reference Book* (Englewood Cliffs, N.J., 1966).

Volumes documenting the general history of Negro Americans have not been numerous. The outstanding one is Herbert Aptheker, *A Documentary History of the Negro People in the United States* (New York, 1951). See also Richard Wade, *The Negro in American Life, Selected Readings* (New York, 1965) and Milton Meltzer, *In Their Own Words: A History of the American Negro, 1619–1865* (New York, 1964). There is some documentary material in the multi-volume *American Negro Heritage Library*, now in process. Richard Bardolph, *The Negro Vanguard* (New York, 1959) contains a wealth of material on individual Negroes. Among pictorial representations are the following: Langston Hughes and Milton Meltzer, *A Pictorial History of the Negro in America* (New York, 1956); T. O. Fuller, *Pictorial History of the American Negro* (Memphis, 1933); Russell L. Adams, *Great Negroes, Past and Present* (Chicago, 1963); Year's *Picture History of the American Negro* (New York, 1965), and Lucille A. Chambers, *America's Tenth Man* (New York, 1957).

There have been many books and articles dealing with the treatment of the Negro in American history. Among them are Louis R. Harlan, *The Negro in American History* (Washington, 1965); Earl E. Thorpe,

Negro Historians in the United States (Baton Rouge, 1958); John Hope Franklin, "The New Negro History," *Journal of Negro History*, XLII (April, 1957); and Ernest Kaiser, "Trends in American Negro Historiography," *Journal of Negro Education*, XXXI (Fall, 1962).

More and more the Negro has become the subject of serious study; and numerous monographs have appeared which shed considerable light on his condition. While they are specialized in subject matter, their scope in time or approach is sufficiently broad to be considered among the studies that are generally useful in a work of this nature. The problems of adjustment and integration are extensively discussed in Gunnar Myrdal, *An American Dilemma*; Melville J. Herskovits, *The American Negro: A Study in Racial Crossing* (New York, 1928) and *Acculturation; The Study of Culture Contact* (New York, 1938); Charles S. Johnson, *The Negro in American Civilization* (New York, 1930); John G. Van Deusen, *Black Man in White America* (Washington, 1944); E. Franklin Frazier, *The Negro in the United States;* Maurice R. Davie, *Negroes in American Society* (New York, 1949) and Oscar Handlin, *Race and Nationality in American Life* (Boston, 1948). The outstanding study of the history and sociology of the Negro family is E. Franklin Frazier, *The Negro Family in the United States* (Chicago, 1939). See also Daniel P. Moynihan, *The Negro Family: The Case for National Action* (Washington, 1965). Socio-biological problems are treated in Samuel J. Holmes, *The Negro's Struggle for Survival: A Study in Human Ecology* (Berkeley, 1937) and Julian H. Lewis, *The Biology of the Negro* (Chicago, 1942).

The political and legal aspects of the Negro's history and status have been treated in several books, among which the following are the most satisfactory: William F. Nowlin, *The Negro in American National Politics* (Boston, 1931); Paul Lewinson, *Race, Class and Party: A History of Negro Suffrage and White Politics in the South* (London, 1932); Charles S. Mangum, *The Legal Status of the Negro* (Chapel Hill, 1940); and Fitzhugh Lee Styles, *Negroes and the Law* (Boston, 1937). More recent and more sophisticated are Pauli Murray, *States' Laws on Race and Color* (Cincinnati, 1950); V. O. Key, *Southern Politics in State and Nation* (New York, 1949); and Jack Greenberg, *Race Relations and American Law* (New York, 1959).

In the field of the economic history of the Negro, Charles H. Wesley, *Negro Labor in the United States, 1850–1925* (New York, 1927) is much more comprehensive than the title suggests, while *The Negro Wage Earner* (Washington, 1930) by Lorenzo J. Greene and Carter G. Woodson confines itself primarily to the history of the Negro as a laborer. A penetrating study of the history of the Negro and organized labor is the work by Sterling D. Spero and Abram L. Harris, *The Black Worker; The Negro and the Labor Movement* (New York, 1931), while another phase of economic life is treated in Abram L. Harris, *The Negro As Capitalist; A Study of Banking and Business among American Negroes* (Philadelphia, 1936).

Among the better general studies in the social and intellectual history of the American Negro are the following: For education there are Horace M. Bond, *The Education of the Negro in the American Social Order* (New York, 1934); Dwight O. W. Holmes, *The Evolution of the Negro College* (New York, 1934); and the numerous studies made by the United States Office of Education, primarily under the supervision of Ambrose Caliver. In the area of the fine arts two works by Alain Locke, *Negro Art; Past and Present* (Washington, 1936) and *The Negro and His Music* (Washington, 1936) should be consulted, as well as James Porter, *Modern Negro Art* (New York, 1943) and Maude Cuney Hare, *Negro Musicians and Their Music* (Washington, 1936). The best studies in religion are Carter G. Woodson, *History of the Negro Church* (Washington, 1921); *The Negro's Church* (New York, 1933) by Benjamin E. Mays and Joseph W. Nicholson; E. Franklin Frazier, *The Negro Church in America* (New York, 1963); and Joseph R. Washington, *Black Religion* (Boston, 1964). The literary history of the Negro may be traced in Benjamin Brawley's *The Negro in Literature and Art in the United States* (New York, 1921); Vernon Loggins, *The Negro Author; His Development in America* (New York, 1931); Sterling Brown, *The Negro in American Fiction* (Washington, 1937); Hugh Gloster, *Negro Voices in American Fiction* (Chapel Hill, 1948); and Robert Bone, *The Negro Novel in America* (New Haven, 1958). Satisfactory collections of Negro writings are Victor F. Calverton, *Anthology of American Negro Literature* (New York, 1929); Otelia Cromwell and others, *Readings from Negro Authors* (New York, 1931); *The Negro Caravan* (New York, 1941) by Sterling Brown and others. Herman Dreer, *American Literature by Negro Authors* (New York, 1950); and, for representative recent writing, Herbert Hill, *Soon One Morning; New Writing by American Negroes* (New York, 1963). Edith J. R. Isaacs, *The Negro in the American Theater* (New York, 1947) should not be overlooked. The pioneer study on Negro newspapers was made by Irvine Garland Penn in *The Afro-American Press and Its Editors* (Springfield, 1891). Less encyclopedic but more critical is Frederick G. Detweiler, *The Negro Press in the United States* (Chicago, 1922).

Among the major general works in the field of American history that are of value in studying the history of the Negro American are the following: Henry S. Commager and Richard B. Morris, editors, *The New American Nation Series* (New York, 1954); Allen Johnson, editor, *Chronicles of America*, fifty volumes (New Haven, 1918–21); Arthur M. Schlesinger and Dixon R. Fox, editors, *A History of American Life*, twelve volumes (New York, 1927–45); and Charles and Mary Beard, *The Rise of American Civilization*, two volumes (New York, 1927). Of value also is John R. Commons and others, *History of Labour in the United States*, four volumes (New York, 1918–35). The most satisfactory intellectual history of the United States is Merle Curti, *The Growth of American Thought* (New York, 1943). Sketches of leading Americans, including some Negroes, are in the *Dictionary of American Biography*, twenty volumes (New York, 1928–37). Other aids are the *Encyclopaedia of the Social Sciences*, fifteen volumes (New York, 1930–35) and the *Dictionary of American History*, five volumes (New York, 1940).

I. A Cradle of Civilization

An excellent description of Egyptian geography may be found in M. I. Newbigin, *Mediterranean Lands* (New York, 1924), while a popular, but satisfactory account may be found in Emil Ludwig, *The Nile* (New York, 1937). W. Z. Ripley, *The Races of Europe* (New York, 1899) is still one of the most reliable treatments of that subject, but a more recent acceptable study is *The Racial History of Man* (New York, 1923) by R. B. Dixon. A healthy revision of the view of the Nordic origin of civilization is Frank H. Hankins, *The Racial Basis of Civilization; A Critique of the Nordic Doctrine* (New York, 1926).

Among the standard histories of Egyptian civilization James H. Breasted, *History of Egypt*, second edition revised (New York, 1950) is good. A work of merit of greater length is W. M. F. Petrie, *History of Egypt*, six volumes (London, 1894–1925) as well as *Social Life in Ancient Egypt* (Boston, 1923) by the same author. See also A. H. Gardiner, *Egypt of the Pharaohs* (Oxford, 1961). Negro contributions are given some consideration in Edouard Henri Naville, "The Origin of Egyptian Civilization," *Annual Report of the Smithsonian Institution for 1907* and in Alexander Francis Chamberlain, "The Contribution of the Negro to Human Civilization," *The Journal of Race Development*, II (April, 1911). The cultural development of Egypt during the period of Ethiopian domination is discussed in *A History of Art in Ancient Egypt*, two volumes (London, 1883). A suggestive article along these and similar lines is Leo Hansberry, "Sources for the Study of Ethiopian History," *Howard University Studies in History* (November, 1930).

II. Early Negro States of Africa

Maurice Delafosse has made many important contributions to the history of African civilization. Among those that have been translated from the French is *The Negroes of Africa: History and Culture* (Washington, 1931), which contains a mine of information on the early Negro states. Carter G. Woodson, *African Background Outlined* (Washington, 1936) is excellent for its bibliographical and other study aids, while his *African Heroes and Heroines* contains informal, human interest accounts of many of the leaders in West Africa. Basil Davidson, *The Lost Cities of Africa* (Boston, 1959) is especially valuable. W. E. B. DuBois's *Black Folk, Then and Now* has excellent chapters on the early Negro states. A classical and reliable description of the political and social scene may be found in the writings of a contemporary, Joannes Leo Africanus, *The History and Description of Africa* (London, 1896). A popular but generally reliable account of the early history of the Western Soudan is Flora Louisa Lugard, *A Tropical Dependency* (London, 1905).

III. The African Way of Life

Perhaps the best general accounts of the culture and civilization of West Africa are to be found in Delafosse, *The Negroes of Africa*; DuBois, *Black Folk, Then and Now*; Davidson, *Lost Cities of Africa* and *The African Past* (Boston, 1964); E. W. Bovill, *Golden Trade of the Moors* (New York, 1958); and Woodson, *The African Background Outlined*. The works of Melville J. Herskovits in the field have long been regarded as highly significant. Among them are *Dahomey; An Ancient West African Kingdom*, two volumes (New York,

1938), a modern anthropological study which sheds considerable light on the earlier period, and "The Art of the Congo," *Opportunity*, V (May, 1927). A provocative work by the same author is *Myth of the Negro Past* (New York, 1941), in which he contends that the Negroes of West Africa had developed a complex civilization and that much of it survived in the New World. In this connection one should also read his "On the Provenience of the New World Negroes," *Social Forces*, XII (December, 1933). A scholarly general treatment is Leo Frobenius, "The Origin of African Civilizations," *Annual Report of the Smithsonian Institution for 1898*. See also J. D. Fage, *Introduction to the History of West Africa* (Cambridge, 1959). *An Introduction to African Civilizations* (New York, 1937) by Willis N. Huggins and John G. Jackson is not generally satisfactory, but it contains some suggestions for study that may not be found elsewhere. George W. Ellis, *Negro Culture in West Africa* (New York, 1914) is valuable largely for its discussion of how a Negro group developed its own alphabet and written language. Two brief studies which emphasize the importance of the culture of the Africans are *Old African Civilizations* (Atlanta, 1906) by Franz Boas and *Native African Races and Culture* (Charlottesville, 1927) by James Weldon Johnson.

Special aspects of African culture are treated in the *Harvard African Studies*, No. I (Cambridge, 1917) and No. II (Cambridge, 1918), edited by Oric Bates. These studies are especially satisfactory for their treatment of early African art and of implements. A. O. Stafford's "The Tarik E. Soudan," *Journal of Negro History*, II (April, 1917) is a valuable study of an early African literary work. In addition to several works already mentioned, two special studies of African art will prove helpful. They are Paul Guillaume and Thomas Munro, *Primitive Negro Sculpture* (New York, 1926) and James J. Sweeney, *African Negro Art* (New York, 1925).

IV. The Slave Trade

In the history of the slave trade there is nothing to compare with the monumental four-volume work of Elizabeth Donnan, *Documents Illustrative of the History of the Slave Trade to America* (Washington, 1930–35). The introductions to each volume provide a most satisfactory running account of the traffic, and the notes on the documents themselves illuminate the period considerably. A good general account of the trade is presented in Daniel P. Mannix, *Black Cargoes: A History of the Atlantic Slave Trade, 1518–1865* (New York, 1962). The significance of the trade in the growth of capitalistic enterprise is discussed in Wilson E. Williams, *Africa and the Rise of Capitalism* (Washington, 1938) and Eric Williams, *Capitalism and Slavery* (Chapel Hill, 1944). Two pioneer works which give some attention to the slave trade are W. E. B. DuBois, *Suppression of the African Slave Trade to the United States, 1638–1870* (Cambridge, 1896) and U. B. Phillips, *American Negro Slavery* (New York, 1918). The slave trade as an integral part of the evolving imperial economy is discussed in the standard works of George L. Beer, *The Old Colonial System, 1660–1754*, two volumes (New York, 1933) and L. H. Gipson, *The British Empire before the American Revolution*, volume I (New York, 1939) and volume V (New York, 1942). Specific phases of the trade are discussed in several papers published in the *Journal of Negro History:* Jerome Dowd, "The African Slave Trade," II (January, 1917) ; George F. Zook, "The Company of Royal Adventurers Trading in Africa," IV (April, 1919) ; Luther P. Jackson, "Elizabethan Seamen and the African Slave Trade," IX (January, 1924) ; and Eric Williams, "The Golden Age of the Slave System in Britain," XXV (January, 1940).

The participation of Negroes in the exploration of the New World first received attention at the hands of Richard R. Wright in an article published in *The American Anthropologist* in 1902. It is reprinted under the title, "Negro Companions of the Spanish Explorers," *Phylon,* II (Fourth Quarter, 1941), to which Rayford W. Logan has appended some valuable notes. Other papers on the subject include J. F. Rippy's "The Negro and Spanish Pioneers in the New World," *Journal of Negro History,* VI (April, 1921) ; James B. Browning, "Negro Companions of the Spanish Pioneers in the New World," *Howard University Studies in History* (Washington, 1930) ; and Rayford W. Logan, "Estevanico, Negro Discoverer of the Southwest," *Phylon,* I (Fourth Quarter, 1940).

The horrors of the middle passage are described in several of the above works, notably in the *Documents* edited by Miss Donnan and in the work by Phillips. See also DuBois, *Black Folk, Then and Now;* Weatherford, *The Negro from Africa to America* and Mannix, *Black Cargoes.* H. A. Wyndham, *The Atlantic and Slavery* (London, 1935) deals in a scholarly manner with this and many other aspects of the slave trade.

V. Seasoning in the Islands

One of the most distinguished works in the economic history of the Caribbean is Lowell J. Ragatz, *The Fall of the Planter Class in the British Caribbean* (New York, 1928), in which ample attention is given to the institution of slavery. Frank W. Pitman has also made significant contributions in his "Slavery on the British West India Plantations in the Eighteenth Century," *Journal of Negro History,* XI (October, 1926) and in his larger work, *The Development of the British West Indies, 1700–1763* (New Haven, 1917). The rivalry of the European countries is treated in the definitive work by Arthur P. Newton, *The European Nations in the West Indies, 1493–1688* (London, 1933), while the problem of slavery in specific colonies is treated in W. J. Gardner, *A History of Jamaica* (London, 1909) and C. L. R. James, *The Black Jacobins: Toussaint Louverture and the San Domingo Revolution* (New York, 1938). A satisfactory summary of conditions in most of the islands may be found in Weatherford's *The Negro from Africa to America,* while the imperial problem which slavery in the islands presented is amply treated by Charles M. Andrews in *The Colonial Period of American History,* four volumes (New Haven, 1934–38).

VI. Servitude and Slavery in the Southern Colonies

The view that the first Negroes in Virginia were servants rather than slaves is set forth by John H. Russell in *The Free Negro in*

Virginia, 1619–1865 (Baltimore, 1913). Details concerning the early years of slavery in Virginia are provided in James C. Ballagh, *A History of Slavery in Virginia* (Baltimore, 1902) and P. A. Bruce, *Economic History of Virginia in the Seventeenth Century,* two volumes (New York, 1895), while *The Negro in Virginia* (New York, 1940) by the Writers' Program of the Work Projects Administration furnishes valuable additional information. See also Thad W. Tate, Jr., *The Negro in Eighteenth-Century Williamsburg* (Williamsburg, 1965). Jeffrey R. Brackett, *The Negro in Maryland: A Study of the Institution of Slavery* (Baltimore, 1889) gives the essential information concerning slavery in that colony. The problem for North Carolina has been treated by John Spencer Bassett in *Slavery and Servitude in the Colony of North Carolina* (Baltimore, 1896) but Guion G. Johnson's *Ante-Bellum North Carolina* (Chapel Hill, 1937) deals most satisfactorily with the colonial as well as with the later period. Edward McCrady has handled the problem of slavery in South Carolina in several studies, including *The History of South Carolina under Proprietary Government, 1670–1719* (New York, 1897); but the best study of the Negro in that colony is Frank J. Klingberg, *An Appraisal of the Negro in Colonial South Carolina* (Washington, 1941). Beginnings in Georgia are covered in Ralph B. Flanders, *Plantation Slavery in Georgia* (Chapel Hill, 1933) and Ellis M. Coulter, *A Short History of Georgia* (Chapel Hill, 1933). Marcus W. Jernegan, *Laboring and Dependent Classes in Colonial America, 1607–1783* (Chicago, 1931) illuminates many aspects of the problem.

VII. Experimenting in the Middle Colonies

The social and economic life of the Negro in early New York is treated in Samuel McKee, *Labor in Colonial New York, 1664–1776* (New York, 1935) and Edwin V. Morgan, *Slavery in New York* (Washington, 1891). William R. Riddell's "The Slave in Early New York," *Journal of Negro History,* XIII (January, 1928) is a valuable addition to the literature. Henry S. Cooley, *A Study of Slavery in New Jersey* (Baltimore, 1896), Marian T. Wright, *Education of Negroes in New Jersey* (New York, 1941), and "New Jersey Laws and the Negro," *Journal of Negro History,* XXVIII (April, 1943) by the same author shed considerable light on the Negro in that colony. Standard works on Pennsylvania are Rufus M. Jones, *The Quakers in the American Colonies* (London, 1911), Edward R. Turner, *The Negro in Pennsylvania* (Washington, 1911), and Thomas E. Drake, *Quakers and Slavery in America* (New Haven, 1950).

VIII. Puritan Masters

The most important single volume on the subject is Lorenzo J. Greene, *The Negro in Colonial New England* (New York, 1942). William B. Weeden, *Economic and Social History of New England,* two volumes (Cambridge, 1890) can be read with profit. Valuable studies on states are George H. Moore's anti-Puritan *Notes on Slavery in Massachusetts* (New York, 1866), William Johnston, *Slavery in Rhode Island, 1755–1776* (Providence, 1894), Edward Channing, *The Narragansett Planters* (Baltimore, 1886), and Bernard C. Steiner,

A History of Slavery in Connecticut (Baltimore, 1893). The New England slave trade is given further treatment in Lorenzo J. Greene, "Slave-holding New England and its Awakening," *Journal of Negro History*, XIII (October, 1928) and William B. Weeden, "The Early African Slave Trade in New England," *Proceedings of the American Antiquarian Society*, New Series, V (Worcester, 1889). A sidelight on New England social history is provided in Lorenzo J. Greene, "The New England Negro As Seen in Advertisements for Runaway Slaves," *Journal of Negro History*, XXIX (April, 1944).

IX. Latin America's Bondmen

Among general works on Spanish America, the following give some attention to various aspects of Negro life: Charles E. Chapman, *Colonial Hispanic America: A History* (New York, 1933); Bernard Moses, *South America on the Eve of Emancipation* (New York, 1908); and *Spanish Dependencies in South America*, two volumes (New York, 1914) by the same author. James F. King's studies have been reported in numerous articles, the most significant and suggestive of which are "Evolution of the Free Slave Principle in Spanish Colonial Administration," *Hispanic American Historical Review*, XXIII (February, 1942); "Descriptive Data on Negro Slaves in Spanish Importation Records and Bills of Sale," *Journal of Negro History*, XXVIII (April, 1943); and the highly important "Negro History in Continental Spanish America," *Journal of Negro History*, XXIX (January, 1944). Considerable statistical data as well as provocative interpretations are provided in Frank Tannenbaum, *Slave and Citizen* (New York, 1947). One of the best travel accounts of slavery in Latin America is Alexander von Humboldt, *Personal Narrative of Travels to the Equinoctial Regions of the New Continent*, seven volumes (London, 1814–29). The acculturative process is discussed in Ildefonso Pereda Valdes, "Negroes in Uruguay," *Phylon*, IV (Third Quarter, 1943) and G. Aguirre Beltran, "Races in Seventeenth Century Mexico," *Phylon*, VI (Third Quarter, 1945). The growing interest in the study of the Negro in Latin America is shown by several significant volumes that have recently appeared: *The Negro in the Americas* (Washington, 1940), edited by Charles H. Wesley; *Negro Studies in Latin America*, Bulletin No. 32 of the American Council of Learned Societies, by Richard Pattee; and the entire issue of the *Hispanic American Historical Review*, XXIV (August, 1944). Especially important is Herbert S. Klein, *Slavery in the Americas: A Comparison of Cuba and Virginia* (Chicago, 1966).

The literature on Brazil is abundant. Perhaps the three most important works to appear in English in recent years are Gilberto Freyre, *The Masters and the Slaves: A Study in the Development of Brazilian Civilization* (New York, 1946); Donald Pierson, *Negroes in Brazil, A Study of Race Contact at Bahia* (Chicago, 1942); and Arthur Ramos, *The Negro in Brazil* (Washington, 1939). A searching analysis of the institution of slavery is made by Mary W. Williams in "The Treatment of Negro Slaves in the Brazilian Empire: A Comparison with the U.S.A.," *Journal of Negro History*, XV (July, 1930). Social relationships are treated in Gilberto Freyre, "Social Life in Brazil in the Middle of the Nineteenth Century," *Hispanic American Historical Review*, V (November, 1922). Resistance is discussed in Charles E. Chapman,

"Palmares, The Negro Numantia," *Journal of Negro History*, III (January, 1918).

X. *That All Men May Be Free*

The outstanding work covering this period is Benjamin Quarles, *The Negro in the American Revolution* (Chapel Hill, 1961). The paradoxes of slavery and the revolutionary philosophy are discussed in George Livermore, *An Historical Research Respecting the Opinions of the Founders of the Republic on Negroes as Slaves, as Citizens, and as Soldiers* (Boston, 1862); George H. Moore, *Historical Notes on the Employment of Negroes in the American Army of the Revolution* (New York, 1862); and Walter H. Mazyck, *George Washington and the Negro* (Washington, 1932). Among the studies of Negroes as fighters in the War for Independence, the following are outstanding: Laura E. Wilkes, *Missing Pages in American History* (Washington, 1919); William C. Nell, *The Colored Patriots of the American Revolution* (Boston, 1855); W. B. Hartgrove, "The Negro Soldier in the American Revolution," *Journal of Negro History*, I (April, 1916); and Luther P. Jackson, "Virginia Negro Soldiers and Seamen in the American Revolution," *Journal of Negro History*, XXVII July, 1942). In George W. Williams, *A History of the Negro Troops in the War of the Rebellion* (New York, 1888) and Joseph T. Wilson, *The Black Phalanx* (Hartford, 1888) there are chapters on Negro soldiers in the War for Independence. Numerous addresses have been made on the subject, an example of which is the one by William Lloyd Garrison, *The Loyalty and Devotion of Colored Americans in the Revolution and the War of 1812* (Boston, 1861).

The anti-slavery movement in the Revolutionary period is treated in detail in Mary S. Locke, *Anti-Slavery in America* (Boston, 1901). Important for its interpretation is John Franklin Jameson, *The American Revolution Considered as a Social Movement* (Princeton, 1926). The problem of slavery at the Constitutional Convention is excellently treated in Charles A. Beard, *An Economic Interpretation of the Constitution of the United States* (New York, 1913). One of the best brief accounts of the convention is Max Farrand, *The Framing of the Constitution* (New Haven, 1913), and a recent one is Catherine Drinker Bowen, *Miracle at Philadelphia* (Boston, 1966); but there is no substitute for the monumental *Records of the Federal Convention of 1787*, three volumes (New Haven, 1911), edited by Max Farrand. It contains much discussion on the status of Negroes at the time which has not yet been used in other works.

XI. *The Turn of the Century*

The best source of information concerning the numbers and distribution of the Negro population is the publication of the United States Bureau of the Census, *Negro Population, 1790–1915* (Washington, 1918). Significant changes of an economic and social nature are dealt with in Charles A. Beard, *Economic Origins of Jeffersonian Democracy* (New York, 1915). Perhaps the best description of social conditions at the turn of the century is to be found in Henry Adams, *History of the United States during the Administrations of*

Jefferson and Madison, volume one (New York, 1889). The impact of the Industrial Revolution on slavery is treated adequately in Lewis C. Gray, *History of Agriculture in the Southern United States to 1860* (Washington, 1933) and E. C. Kirkland, *A History of American Economic Life* (New York, 1932). The uprising in the Caribbean is vividly described in James, *The Black Jacobins.* An early but still authoritative account of the movement to close the slave trade is in DuBois, *The Suppression of the African Slave Trade.*

Brief discussions of the works of early Negro writers are given in Benjamin Brawley, *Early Negro American Writers* (Chapel Hill, 1935) and Brown and others, *The Negro Caravan.* The following are satisfactory treatments of individual Negroes: Edward D. Seeber, "Phillis Wheatley," *Journal of Negro History,* XXIV (July, 1939); Henry Baker, "Benjamin Banneker, Negro Mathematician and Astronomer," *Journal of Negro History,* III (April, 1918); P. L. Phillips, "The Negro, Benjamin Banneker: Astronomer and Mathematician," *Records of the Colombia Historical Society,* XX (Washington, 1917); H. N. Sherwood, "Paul Cuffe," *Journal of Negro History,* VIII (April, 1923); and W. H. Morse, "Lemuel Haynes," *Journal of Negro History,* IV (January, 1919). For discussions of education see Carter G. Woodson, *Education of the Negro Prior to 1861* (New York, 1915) and Charles C. Andrews, *History of the New York African Free Schools* (New York, 1830). The best accounts of the beginnings of the church are Woodson, *History of the Negro Church* and Charles H. Wesley, *Richard Allen, Apostle of Freedom* (Washington, 1935). For Negro Masonry see George W. Crawford, *Prince Hall and His Followers* (New York, 1914) and William Upton, *Negro Masonry* (Cambridge, 1902).

XII. The Westward March

Frontier influences are treated in a series of highly significant essays in Frederick J. Turner, *The Frontier in American History* (New York, 1920). Dan E. Clark, *The West in American History* (New York, 1937) and F. L. Paxson, *The History of the American Frontier, 1763–1893* (Boston, 1924) may also be read with profit. The movement of the Negro into frontier areas has been discussed in several essays in the *Journal of Negro History,* among which are the following: W. Sherman Savage, "The Negro in the Westward Movement," XXV (October, 1940); Eugene P. Southall, "Negroes in Florida prior to the Civil War," XIX (January, 1934); Harry E. Davis, "John Malvin, A Western Reserve Pioneer," XXIII (October, 1938); Alrutheus A. Taylor, "The Movement of Negroes from the East to the Gulf States from 1830 to 1850," VIII (October, 1923); and Carter G. Woodson, "Freedom and Slavery in Appalachian America," I (April, 1916). The War of 1812 is treated in Wilkes, *Missing Pages in American History;* Williams, *A History of Negro Troops;* and Wilson, *The Black Phalanx.* William C. Nell, *Services of Colored Americans in the Wars of 1776 and 1812* (Boston, 1851) should also be read.

The growth of the Cotton Kingdom is treated in William E. Dodd, *The Cotton Kingdom* (New Haven, 1919); Gray, *History of Agriculture in the Southern United States;* Frederick J. Turner, *Rise of the New West* (New York, 1906); and Ulrich B. Phillips, *American Negro*

Slavery (New York, 1918). For a critical discussion of the highly questionable conclusions reached by Phillips, see Richard Hofstadter, "U. B. Phillips and the Plantation Legend," *Journal of Negro History*, XXIX (April, 1944). The influence of the doctrine of Manifest Destiny on the emergence of the Cotton Kingdom is handled in Albert K. Weinberg, *Manifest Destiny, A Study of Nationalist Expansionism in American History* (Baltimore, 1935). Most of the works on slavery deal with the domestic slave trade, but the best account is in Frederic Bancroft, *Slave Trading in the Old South* (Baltimore, 1931). An important supplement is W. H. Stephenson, *Isaac Franklin, Slave Trader and Planter of the Old South* (University, La., 1938). See also William T. Laprade, "The Domestic Slave Trade in the District of Columbia," *Journal of Negro History*, XI (January, 1926). For discussions of the persistence of the African trade, see DuBois, *Suppression of the African Slave Trade;* Charles H. Wesley, "Manifests of Slave Shipments along the Waterways, 1808–1864," *Journal of Negro History*, XXVII (April, 1942) ; and Eric Williams, "The British West Indian Slave Trade after Its Abolition in 1807," *Journal of Negro History*, XXVII (April, 1942).

XIII. That Peculiar Institution

Most of the works on slavery in the United States should be read with critical care because of the tendency to emphasize the large plantation at the expense of the smaller unit, on which most of the slaves were to be found. In addition to the works already mentioned, the following may be consulted: Emory Q. Hawk, *Economic History of the South* (New York, 1934), which has discussions on the economic aspects of slavery that are uncritical and, at times, sentimental; William B. Hesseltine, *The South in American History* (New York, 1943), which contains a cursory but critical discussion of the institution; and Ulrich B. Phillips, *Life and Labor in the Old South* (Boston, 1929) which, like his *American Negro Slavery*, tends to apologize for the institution.

Kenneth M. Stampp, *The Peculiar Institution* (New York, 1956) is a more recent, exhaustive study of slavery that takes sharp issue with Phillips on many points. Eugene D. Genovese, *The Political Economy of Slavery* (New York, 1965), discusses slavery as a part of a total way of life in the South. Stanley Elkins, *Slavery: A Problem in American Institutional and Intellectual Life* (Chicago, 1959) is concerned primarily with the effect of slavery on personality. Richard C. Wade, *Slavery in the Cities: The South, 1820–1860* (New York, 1964) successfully shows that slavery in urban areas was different in virtually every way from slavery in rural areas. For a discussion of the problem of determining the profitability of slavery see Alfred H. Conrad and John R. Meyer, *The Economics of Slavery and Other Econometric Studies* (Chicago, 1964). See also Thomas P. Govan, "Was Plantation Slavery Profitable," *Journal of Southern History*, VII (November, 1942) and Harold D. Woodman, "The Profitability of Slavery: A Historical Perennial," *Journal of Southern History*, XXIX (August, 1963). Other problems of management are discussed in John S. Bassett, *The Southern Plantation Overseer as Revealed in His Letters* (Northampton, 1925).

The following are among the more satisfactory discussions of slavery in specific states: Guion Johnson, *Ante-Bellum North Carolina*; Charles S. Sydnor, *Slavery in Mississippi* (New York, 1933) ; Roger W. Shugg, *Origins of Class Struggle in Louisiana* (University, La., 1939) ; Chase C. Mooney, *Slavery in Tennessee* (Bloomington, 1957) ; J. Winston Coleman, *Slavery Times in Kentucky* (Chapel Hill, 1940) ; Harrison A. Trexler, *Slavery in Missouri, 1804–1865* (Baltimore, 1914), and James B. Sellers, *Slavery in Alabama* (University, Ala., 1950). The best travel account, more authoritative than many secondary works, is Frederick L. Olmsted, *The Cotton Kingdom; A Traveller's Observations on Cotton and Slavery in the American Slave States*, two volumes (New York, 1861).

The laws affecting slaves are summarized in John C. Hurd, *Law of Freedom and Bondage in the United States*, two volumes (Boston, 1858), while interpretations of the law may be found in Helen T. Catterall, editor, *Judicial Cases Concerning American Slavery and the Negro*, five volumes (Washington, 1926). The problem of enforcing the black codes is discussed in Howell M. Henry, *The Police Control of the Slave in South Carolina* (Emory, Va., 1914) and Wilbert E. Moore, "Slave Law and the Social Structure," *Journal of Negro History*, XXVI (April, 1941). Numerous slaves have told of their own experiences, often with the assistance of others. *The Narrative of Frederick Douglass* (Boston, 1845) is the best known. Another is *Father Henson's Story of His Own Life* (Boston, 1858). The reminiscences of several slaves are recorded in B. A. Botkin, editor, *Lay My Burden Down: A Folk History of Slavery* (Chicago, 1945).

The best source of information concerning the problems of the slave family is Frazier, *The Negro Family in the United States*. A special aspect of social relationships is considered in E. Ophelia Settle, "Slave Attitudes during the Slave Regime: Household Servants versus Field Hands," *Publications of the American Sociological Society*, XXVIII (1934). The relationships of slaves with others is discussed in several works, including the following: James H. Johnston, *Miscegenation in the Ante-Bellum South* (Chicago, 1939) ; Carter G. Woodson, "Beginnings of the Miscegenation of the Whites and Blacks," *Journal of Negro History*, III (October, 1918) ; Avery O. Craven, "Poor Whites and Negroes in the Antebellum South," *Journal of Negro History*, XV (January, 1930) ; and Kenneth W. Porter, "Relations between Negroes and Indians within the Present Limits of the United States," *Journal of Negro History*, XVII (July, 1932). In addition to Woodson, *History of the Negro Church*, Henry J. Cadbury, "Negro Membership in the Society of Friends," *Journal of Negro History*, XXI (April, 1936) and Luther P. Jackson, "Religious Development of the Negro in Virginia from 1760 to 1860," *Journal of Negro History*, XVI (April, 1931) may be read with profit. For a discussion of the origins of the spirituals and work songs, see Miles M. Fisher, *Negro Slave Songs in the United States* (Ithaca, 1953). An interesting form of slave recreation is handled in Ira DeA. Reid, "The John Canoe Festival," *Phylon*, III (Fourth Quarter, 1942).

The best account of resistance to slavery is Herbert Aptheker, *American Negro Slave Revolts* (New York, 1943). His "Maroons within the Present Limits of the United States," *Journal of Negro*

666 · BIBLIOGRAPHICAL NOTES

History, XXIV (April, 1939) is also valuable. Other studies are Joseph C. Carroll, *Slave Insurrections in the United States, 1800–1860* (Boston, 1938); Raymond and Alice Bauer, "Day to Day Resistance to Slavery," *Journal of Negro History*, XXVII (October, 1942); and Lorenzo J. Greene, "Mutiny on the Slave Ships," *Phylon*, V (Fourth Quarter, 1944). An engrossing account of one slave uprising is in John Lofton, *Insurrection in South Carolina; The Turbulent World of Denmark Vesey* (Yellow Springs, 1964), but see Richard Wade, "The Vesey Plot: A Reconsideration," *Journal of Southern History*, XXX (May, 1964).

XIV. Quasi-Free Negroes

There is no general history of the free Negro. An excellent summary statement concerning the group is found in Carter G. Woodson, *Free Negro Heads of Families in the United States in 1830* (Washington, 1925). The problem in the North is treated in Leon Litwack, *North of Slavery, The Negro in the Free States, 1790–1860* (Chicago, 1961) and Emma L. Thornbrough, *The Negro in Indiana, A Study of a Minority* (Indianapolis, 1957). Several monographs deal with the subject in different states. They are: James M. Wright, *The Free Negro in Maryland, 1634–1860* (New York, 1921); John Russell, *The Free Negro in Virginia, 1619–1865* (Baltimore, 1913); Luther P. Jackson, *Free Negro Labor and Property Holding in Virginia, 1830–1860* (New York, 1942); and John Hope Franklin, *The Free Negro in North Carolina, 1790–1860* (Chapel Hill, 1943). A rare personal testimony is W. R. Hogan and E. A. Davis, editors, *William Johnson's Natchez: The Ante-Bellum Diary of a Free Negro* (Baton Rouge, 1951). Briefer works deal with the free Negro in other localities: E. Horace Fitchett, "The Origin and Growth of the Free Negro Population of Charleston, South Carolina," *Journal of Negro History*, XXVI (October, 1941); Ralph B. Flanders, "The Free Negro in Ante-Bellum Georgia," *North Carolina Historical Review*, IX (July, 1932); W. McDowell Rogers, "Free Negro Legislation in Georgia," *Georgia Historical Quarterly*, XVI (March, 1932); David Y. Thomas, "The Free Negro in Florida before 1865," *South Atlantic Quarterly*, X (October, 1911); J. Merton England, "The Free Negro in Ante-Bellum Tennessee," *Journal of Southern History*, IX (February, 1943); William L. Imes, "The Legal Status of Free Negroes and Slaves in Tennessee," *Journal of Negro History*, IV (July, 1919); Charles S. Sydnor, "The Free Negro in Mississippi before the Civil War," *American Historical Review*, XXXII (July, 1927); Alice D. Nelson, "People of Color in Louisiana," *Journal of Negro History*, I (October, 1916) and II (January, 1917); and Harold Schoen, "The Free Negro in the Republic of Texas," *Southwestern Historical Quarterly*, XL .(April, 1926) and succeeding issues. A special phase of the free Negro's legal status is treated in Roger W. Shugg, "Negro Voting in the Ante-Bellum South," *Journal of Negro History*, XXI (October, 1936). For the fortunes and misfortunes of an individual free Negro see John Hope Franklin, "James Boon, Free Negro Artisan," *Journal of Negro History*, XXX (April, 1945).

The ownership of slaves by free Negroes is discussed in John H.

Russell, "Colored Freemen as Slave Owners in Virginia," *Journal of Negro History*, I (July, 1916) and C. D. Wilson, "Negroes Who Owned Slaves," *Popular Science Monthly*, LXXXI (November, 1912). Statistics are provided in Carter G. Woodson, *Free Negro Owners of Slaves in the United States in 1830* (Washington, 1925).

Some of the peculiar social problems of the free Negro are treated in E. Franklin Frazier, *The Free Negro Family* (Nashville, 1932). Economic matters are handled in Martin R. Delany, *The Condition, Elevation, Emigration, and Destiny of the Colored People of the United States* (Philadelphia, 1852) and Wesley, *Negro Labor in the United States*. Among the works which deal with the problems that Northern free Negroes faced are Edward R. Turner, *The Negro in Pennsylvania* (Washington, 1911) and Carter G. Woodson, "The Negroes of Cincinnati prior to the Civil War," *Journal of Negro History*, I (January, 1916). Early Negro organizations are considered in John W. Cromwell, *The Early Negro Convention Movement* (Washington, 1904) and Bella Gross, "The First National Negro Convention," *Journal of Negro History*, XXXI (October, 1946). For an important phase of cultural history, see Dorothy B. Porter, "The Organized Educational Activities of Negro Literary Societies, 1828–1846," *Journal of Negro Education*, V (October, 1936).

The pioneer work on the major colonization organization is Early L. Fox, *The American Colonization Society, 1817–1840* (Baltimore, 1919). It has been superseded by Philip J. Staudenraus, *The African Colonization Movement, 1816–1865* (New York, 1961) and the essays by Frederic Bancroft in Jacob E. Cooke, *Frederic Bancroft, Historian* (Norman, 1957). H. N. Sherwood's "The Formation of the American Colonization Society," *Journal of Negro History*, II (July, 1917) should also be read. Additional works on various phases of the subject are: Charles A. Earp, "The Role of Education in the Maryland Colonization Movement," *Journal of Negro History*, XXVI (July, 1941); Miles M. Fisher, "Lott Cary, the Colonizing Missionary," *Journal of Negro History*, VII (October, 1922); H. N. Sherwood, "Early Negro Deportation Projects," *Mississippi Valley Historical Review*, II (March, 1916); N. Andrew Cleven, "Some Plans for Colonizing Liberated Negro Slaves in Hispanic America," *Journal of Negro History*, XI (January, 1926); and Louis R. Mehlinger, "The Attitude of the Free Negro toward Colonization," *Journal of Negro History*, I (July, 1916).

XV. Slavery and Intersectional Strife

The beginnings of abolition are discussed in Alice D. Adams, *The Neglected Period of Anti-Slavery in America, 1808–1831* (Boston, 1908). For the relationship between abolitionism and the other reform movements see Alice F. Tyler, *Freedom's Ferment; Phases of American Social History to 1860* (Minneapolis, 1944). One of the best discussions of the abolition movement is Gilbert H. Barnes, *The Antislavery Impulse, 1830–1844* (New York, 1933). Several recent works of excellent quality deal with abolitionism. They are Louis Filler, *The Crusade Against Slavery, 1830–1860* (New York, 1960); Dwight L. Dumond, *Anti-Slavery: The Crusade for Freedom in America* (Ann Arbor, 1961); and Martin L. Duberman, editor, *The Antislavery Van-*

guard (Princeton, 1965). Biographies of abolitionists that should be consulted include Irving Bartlett, *Wendell Phillips, Brahmin Radical* (Boston, 1961) and John L. Thomas, *The Liberator: William Lloyd Garrison* (Boston, 1963). Herbert Aptheker, "Militant Abolitionism," *Journal of Negro History*, XXVI (October, 1941) is excellent. The international aspects of abolitionism are treated in Frank J. Klingberg, *The Anti-Slavery Movement in England* (New Haven, 1926). The growth and dissemination of ideas in the abolition movement may be studied in Lorenzo D. Turner, *Anti-Slavery Sentiment in American Literature* (Washington, 1929) and W. Sherman Savage, *The Controversy over the Distribution of Abolition Literature* (Washington, 1938). Sketches of the lives of the leading abolitionists appear in the *Dictionary of American Biography* or W. J. Simmons, *Men of Mark* (Louisville, 1887).

The exciting story of black abolitionists is excellently told by Herbert Aptheker in *The Negro in the Abolitionist Movement* (New York, 1941) and Charles H. Wesley in "The Negroes of New York in the Emancipation Movement," *Journal of Negro History*, XXIV (January 1939). The outstanding piece of abolitionist writing by a Negro is David Walker, *Appeal in Four Articles* (Boston, 1830), two paperback editions of which appeared in 1965. The narratives mentioned in the text of Chapter XIV furnish valuable information concerning Negroes in the abolition movement as does Carter G. Woodson, *The Mind of the Negro As Reflected in Letters during the Crisis, 1880–1860* (Washington, 1926). There are numerous biographies and sketches of individual Negroes. *The Life and Times of Frederick Douglass* (Hartford, 1881) is one of the classics of American autobiography. The work by Shirley Graham, *There Was Once a Slave* (New York, 1947) is one of the best recent biographies. The definitive biography of Douglass is Benjamin Quarles, *Frederick Douglass* (Washington, 1948). See also Earl Conrad, *Harriet Tubman* (Washington, 1943); Arthur H. Fauset, *Sojourner Truth, God's Faithful Pilgrim* (Chapel Hill, 1938); Dorothy B. Porter, "David M. Ruggles, An Apostle of Human Rights," *Journal of Negro History*, XXVIII (January, 1943); and Monroe N. Work, "The Life of Charles B. Ray," *Journal of Negro History*, IV (October, 1919). The conflict between the leading white and Negro abolitionists is discussed in Benjamin Quarles, "The Breach between Douglass and Garrison," *Journal of Negro History*, XXIII (April, 1938).

The works of Wilbur H. Siebert have made him the outstanding authority on the Underground Railroad. His major work is *The Underground Railroad from Slavery to Freedom* (New York, 1898). Others include "The Underground Railroad in Massachusetts," American Antiquarian Society, *Proceedings*, New Series, XLV (Worcester, 1935) and "Light on the Underground Railroad," *American Historical Review*, I (April, 1896). An invaluable collection of documents and incidents by a participant is William Still, *The Underground Railroad* (Philadelphia, 1872). See also Horatio T. Strother, *The Underground Railroad in Connecticut* (Middletown, 1962). A recent popular account is Henrietta Buckmaster, *Let My People Go* (New York, 1941). Two articles by E. D. Preston in the *Journal of Negro History* shed considerable light on two aspects of the Railroad: "Genesis of the Underground Railroad," XVIII (April, 1933) and "The Underground Railroad in Northwest Ohio," XVII (October, 1932). A critical view of the "Railroad" is given in Larry Gara, *The Liberty Line: The Legend of the Underground Railroad* (Lexington, 1961).

The fate of the anti-slavery movement in the South is discussed in John S. Bassett, *Anti-Slavery Leaders in North Carolina* (Baltimore, 1931); Ruth Scarborough, *The Opposition to Slavery in Georgia Prior to 1860* (Nashville, 1933); and Kenneth M. Stampp, "The Fate of the Southern Antislavery Movement," *Journal of Negro History*, XXVIII (January, 1943). The growth of pro-slavery sentiment in the South is carefully traced and analyzed in William S. Jenkins, *Pro-Slavery Thought in the Old South* (Chapel Hill, 1935). See also William R. Stanton, *The Leopard's Spots: Scientific Attitudes toward Race in America, 1815–1859* (Chicago, 1960) and also William B. Hesseltine, "Some New Aspects of the Proslavery Argument," *Journal of Negro History*, XXI (January, 1936). The disappearance of liberalism is treated in Clement Eaton, *Freedom of Thought in the Old South* (Durham, 1940), while the psychological effect of the pro-slavery thought is discussed in Jesse Carpenter, *The South as a Conscious Minority, 1789–1861* (New York, 1930). The breakdown of intersectional relations is discussed in two works by Dwight L. Dumond, *The Secession Movement* (New York, 1931) and *Antislavery Origins of the Civil War in the United States* (London, 1939). In this connection see also Arthur C. Cole, *The Irrepressible Conflict* (New York, 1938) and John Hope Franklin, *The Militant South 1800–1861* (Cambridge, 1956).

XVI. Civil War

For general works on the Negro in the Civil War see the able study by the pioneer Negro historian, George W. Williams, *A History of the Negro Troops in the War of the Rebellion.* Another study which may also be consulted with profit is Wilson, *The Black Phalanx.* Of less importance, but of some value, is William W. Brown, *The Negro in the American Rebellion* (New York, 1888). Easily the outstanding modern treatment is Benjamin Quarles, *The Negro in the Civil War* (Boston, 1953). See also his *Lincoln and the Negro* (New York, 1962) and William O. Douglas, *Mr. Lincoln and the Negroes: The Long Road to Equality* (New York, 1963). Herbert Aptheker, *The Negro in the Civil War* (New York, 1938) is a brief, but valuable, work. Bell Irvin Wiley, *Southern Negroes, 1861–1865* (New York, 1953) ably deals with numerous aspects of the Union and the Confederate policies. The policy of the Union government is discussed in Fred Shannon, *The Organization and Administration of the Union Army,* two volumes (Glendale, 1928) and "The Federal Government and the Negro Soldier, 1861–65," *Journal of Negro History*, XI (October, 1926) by the same author. The controversy over the use of Negro soldiers is treated in Thomas R. Hay, "The Question of Arming the Slaves," *Mississippi Valley Historical Review*, VI (June, 1919) and N. W. Stephenson, "The Question of Arming the Slaves," *American Historical Review*, XVIII (January, 1913). The effect of the draft laws on Negroes is handled by Emerson D. Fite, *Social and Industrial Conditions in the North During the Civil War* (New York, 1910). The problem of emancipation is covered in

John Hope Franklin, *The Emancipation Proclamation* (New York, 1963). See also two articles that shed light on the evolution of Lincoln's policy regarding Negroes: Harry S. Blakiston, "Lincoln's Emancipation Plan," *Journal of Negro History*, VII (July, 1922) and Charles H. Wesley, "Lincoln's Plan for Colonizing the Emancipated Negro," *Journal of Negro History*, IV (January, 1919). Among the many works on the service of Negro soldiers, Thomas W. Higginson, *Army Life in a Black Regiment* (Boston, 1870) is outstanding. Of great merit in covering this subject is Dudley T. Cornish, *The Sable Arm: Negro Troops in the Union Army, 1861–1865* (New York, 1956). Herbert Aptheker's "Negro Casualties in the Civil War," *Journal of Negro History*, XXXII (January, 1947) is the most recent and best study on the subject. The Negro's own experience is conveyed in James McPherson, *The Negro's Civil War: How American Negroes Felt and Acted during the War for the Union* (New York, 1965).

Works that deal primarily with the condition of Negroes under the Confederacy are: Brainerd Dyer, "The Treatment of Colored Union Troops by the Confederates, 1861–1865," *Journal of Negro History*, XX (July, 1935); H. J. Eckenrode, "Negroes in Richmond in 1864," *The Virginia Magazine of History and Biography*, XLVI (July, 1938); Charles H. Wesley, "The Employment of Negroes as Soldiers in the Confederate Army," *Journal of Negro History*, IV (July, 1919); and Harvey Wish, "Slave Disloyalty under the Confederacy," *Journal of Negro History*, XXIII (October, 1938).

XVII. The Effort to Attain Peace

For many years a great portion of the literature on the Reconstruction, while written in the framework of "scientific" history, contained such strong presuppositions regarding the inherent unfitness of the Negro for citizenship and the justification for Ku Kluxism to restore "order" in the South that its value was limited by its bias. That was especially true of the works written under the supervision of William Archibald Dunning at Columbia University early in the century. Among the outstanding works of this "school" of writing are Walter L. Fleming, *Civil War and Reconstruction in Alabama* (New York, 1905) and Joseph G. DeRoulhac Hamilton, *Reconstruction in North Carolina* (New York, 1914). The problems involved in the writing of Reconstruction history have been ably discussed by several historians: Howard K. Beale, "On Rewriting Reconstruction History," *American Historical Review*, XLV (July, 1940); Francis B. Simkins, "New Viewpoints of Southern Reconstruction," *Journal of Southern History*, V (February, 1939); A. A. Taylor, "Historians of the Reconstruction," *Journal of Negro History*, XXIII (January, 1938); and Bernard Weisberger, "The Dark and Bloody Ground of Reconstruction Historiography," *Journal of Southern History*, XXV (November, 1959). See also, W. E. B. DuBois, "Reconstruction and Its Benefits," *American Historical Review*, XV (July, 1910). A broader approach to the problems of Reconstruction was made by Francis B. Simkins and R. H. Woody in *South Carolina during Reconstruction* (Chapel Hill, 1932), while an attempt to redress the balance was made by W. E. B. DuBois in *Black Reconstruction* (New York, 1935) which, unfortunately, contains a distended application of the Marxist doctrine to the problems of Reconstruction. See also James Allen, *Reconstruction: The Battle for Democracy* (New York, 1937).

Several Negroes who lived through the period have attempted to tell their story. Among them are John R. Lynch, *The Facts of Reconstruction* (New York, 1913); John Wallace, *Carpetbag Rule in Florida* (Jacksonville, 1888); and Ray Billington, *The Journal of Charlotte Forten* (New York, 1953). The works of Alrutheus A. Taylor should be consulted. They are *The Negro in the Reconstruction of Virginia* (Washington, 1926); *The Negro in South Carolina during Reconstruction* (Washington, 1924); and *The Negro in Tennessee, 1865–1880* (Washington, 1938). In recent years studies of Reconstruction in the several states have illuminated the general picture. One of the most significant was Vernon L. Wharton, *The Negro in Mississippi, 1865–1890* (Chapel Hill, 1947). Others were Joel Williamson, *After Slavery, The Negro in South Carolina During Reconstruction* (Chapel Hill, 1965); Joe M. Richardson, *The Negro in the Reconstruction of Florida, 1865–1877* (Tallahassee, 1966); and Alan Conway, *The Reconstruction of Georgia* (Minneapolis, 1966).

In 1938 Horace M. Bond suggested a revision of the history of the Reconstruction in terms of the influence exercised by powerful business interests in "Social and Economic Forces in Alabama Reconstruction," *Journal of Negro History*, XXIII (July, 1938) and *Negro Education in Alabama* (Washington, 1939). See also A. B. Moore, "Railroad Building in Alabama during the Reconstruction," *Journal of Southern History*, I (November, 1935) and James L. Sellers, "The Economic Incidence of the Civil War in the South," *Mississippi Valley Historical Review*, XIV (September, 1927). During the period of re-examination of Reconstruction several general studies have appeared. E. Merton Coulter, *The South During Reconstruction* (Baton Rouge, 1947) reaffirmed the position advanced by the Dunning School. Hodding Carter, *The Angry Scar* (New York, 1959) is a popular account. John Hope Franklin, *Reconstruction After the Civil War* (Chicago, 1961) and Kenneth M. Stampp, *The Era of Reconstruction* (New York, 1965) are revisionist in approach and interpretation.

Among the numerous works dealing with the conflict between the President and Congress and the triumph of Radical Reconstruction is Howard K. Beale, *The Critical Year, A Study of Andrew Johnson and Reconstruction* (New York, 1930). It has been superseded, to a great extent, by Eric L. McKitrick, *Andrew Johnson and Reconstruction* (Chicago, 1960) and LaWanda and John Cox, *Politics, Principle, and Prejudice* (Glencoe, 1963). See also David Donald, *The Politics of Reconstruction* (Baton Rouge, 1965). Also important are Horace E. Flack, *The Adoption of the Fourteenth Amendment* (Baltimore, 1908); Benjamin B. Kendrick, *The Journal of the Joint Committee of Fifteen on Reconstruction* (New York, 1914); Jacobus Ten Broek, *The Anti-Slavery Origins of the Fourteenth Amendment* (Berkeley, 1951); and William Gillette, *The Right to Vote: Politics and the Passage of the Fifteenth Amendment* (Baltimore, 1965). The pioneer study of the Freedmen's Bureau was Paul S. Peirce, *The Freedmen's Bureau, A Chapter in the History of Reconstruction* (Iowa City, 1904). A more recent work is George R. Bentley, *A History of the Freedmen's Bureau*

(Philadelphia, 1955). See also W. E. B. DuBois, "The Freedmen's Bureau," *Atlantic Monthly*, LXXXVII (March, 1901). Additional matters are treated in John Eaton, *Grant, Lincoln and the Freedmen* (New York, 1907). Educational activities are covered in Bond, *The Education of the Negro in the American Social Order*; Holmes, *The Evolution of the Negro College*; Luther P. Jackson, "The Educational Efforts of the Freedmen's Bureau and Freedmen's Aid Societies in South Carolina, 1862–1872," *Journal of Negro History*, VIII (January, 1923); Henry L. Swint, *The Northern Teacher in the South, 1862–1870* (Nashville, 1941); and Willie Lee Rose, *Rehearsal for Reconstruction: The Port Royal Experiment* (Indianapolis, 1964). In addition to the works already cited, the following shed considerable light on certain economic aspects of Reconstruction: Walter L. Fleming, *The Freedmen's Savings Bank* (Chapel Hill, 1927) and Wesley, *Negro Labor in the United States*.

Political currents are discussed in Luther P. Jackson, *Negro Office-Holders in Virginia* (Norfolk, 1945); Samuel D. Smith, *The Negro in Congress, 1870–1901* (Chapel Hill, 1940); Alrutheus A. Taylor, "Negro Congressmen a Generation After," *Journal of Negro History*, VII (April, 1922); G. David Houston, "A Negro Senator," *Journal of Negro History*, VII (July, 1922); William A. Russ, "The Negro and White Disfranchisement during Radical Reconstruction," *Journal of Negro History*, XIX (April, 1934); and R. H. Woody, "Jonathan J. Wright, Associate Justice of the Supreme Court of South Carolina, 1870–1877," *Journal of Negro History*, XVIII (April, 1933). For other aspects see Otis A. Singletary, *Negro Militia and Reconstruction* (Austin, 1957) and James M. McPherson, *The Struggle for Equality: Abolitionists and the Negro in the Civil War and Reconstruction* (Princeton, 1964).

XVIII. Losing the Peace

Many of the titles of the previous chapter provide valuable information on the overthrow of Reconstruction. A fresh and stimulating discussion of the forces behind the overthrow and of the way in which the compromise of 1877 was reached is in C. Vann Woodward, *Reunion and Reaction: The Compromise of 1877 and the End of Reconstruction* (Boston, 1951). For a general view of the plight of the Negro see Rayford W. Logan, *The Negro in American Life and Thought: The Nadir, 1877–1901* (New York, 1954). The Southern Negro is discussed in C. Vann Woodward, *Origins of the New South, 1877–1913* (Baton Rouge, 1951). Two books covering Republican policy are Vincent P. DeSantis, *Republicans Face the Southern Question* (Baltimore, 1959) and Stanley P. Hirshon, *Farewell to the Bloody Shirt* (Bloomington, 1962). Reconstruction and post-Reconstruction violence is treated in many of the above titles. For Klan activities see John C. Lester, *The Ku Klux Klan: Its Origin, Growth, and Disbandment* (New York, 1905); Stanley F. Horn, *Invisible Empire: The Story of the Ku Klux Klan, 1866–1871* (Boston, 1939); and David M. Chalmers, *Hooded Americanism; The First Century of the Ku Klux Klan* (New York, 1965). See also Francis B. Simkins, *The Tillman Movement in South Carolina* (Durham, 1926) and Alfred B. Williams, *Hampton and His Red Shirts* (Charleston, 1935).

The deterioration of the Negro's political position has been treated by many authors. For general treatments see V. O. Key, *Southern Politics*; Paul Lewinson, *Race, Class, and Party*; and William A. Mabry, *Studies in the Disfranchisement of the Negro in the South* (Durham, 1933). At the state level consult Vernon Wharton, *The Negro in Mississippi*; Albert D. Kirwan, *Revolt of the Rednecks: Mississippi Politics, 1876–1925* (Lexington, 1951); Helen G. Edmonds, *The Negro and Fusion Politics in North Carolina* (Chapel Hill, 1951); Frenise A. Logan, *The Negro in North Carolina, 1876–1894* (Chapel Hill, 1964); George Tindall, *South Carolina Negroes, 1877–1900* (Columbia, 1952); and Robert E. Martin, *Negro Disfranchisement in Virginia* (Washington, 1938).

The effect of the decline of the Negro's position on the Negro himself is ably discussed in August Meier, *Negro Thought in America, 1880–1915* (Ann Arbor, 1963). For an articulate Negro's reaction see T. Thomas Fortune, *Black and White: Land, Labor, and Politics in the South* (New York, 1884). The views of a Southern white man, sympathetic to the Negro, are expressed in George Cable, *The Negro Question*, edited by Arlin Turner (New York, 1958).

C. Vann Woodward has discussed the beginnings of segregation in several places. See especially the second revised edition of his *The Strange Career of Jim Crow* (New York, 1965). For other aspects of the beginnings of segregation see Charles E. Wynes, *Race Relations in Virginia, 1870–1902* (Charlottesville, 1961) and John Hope Franklin, "Jim Crow Goes to School: The Genesis of Legal Segregation in Southern Schools," *South Atlantic Quarterly*, LVIII (Spring, 1959). For a little-known sidelight of Negro life see Phillip Durham and Everett L. Jones, *Negro Cowboys* (New York, 1965).

XIX. *Freedom South of the Border*

For a brief discussion of the social, political, and economic problems of the Caribbean islands, see Eric Williams, *The Negro in the Caribbean* (Washington, 1942). Four articles by Charles H. Wesley in the *Journal of Negro History* illuminate several aspects of Negro life in the West Indies. They are: "The Negro in the West Indies," XVII (January, 1932); "The Abolition of Negro Apprenticeship in the British Empire," XXIII (April, 1938); "The Emancipation of the Free Colored Population in the West Indies," XIX (April, 1934); and "The Neglected Period of Emancipation in Great Britain, 1807–1823," XVII (April, 1932). Gardner, *History of Jamaica* is one of the better works on an individual island, but two articles by Ronald V. Sires in the *Journal of Negro History* are valuable supplementary reading: "Negro Labor in Jamaica in the Years Following Emancipation," XXV (October, 1940) and "Sir Henry Barkly and the Labor Problem in Jamaica," XXV (April, 1940). For information on Santo Domingo see Sumner Welles, *Naboth's Vineyard* (New York, 1928) and George W. Brown, "The Origins of Abolition in Santo Domingo," *Journal of Negro History*, VII (October, 1922). In addition to James, *Black Jacobins*, see Harold P. Davis, *Black Democracy* (New York, 1936); James G. Leyburn, *The Haitian People* (New Haven, 1941); and Rayford W. Logan, *Diplomatic Relations of the United States with Haiti, 1776–1891*

(Chapel Hill, 1941) for able discussions of recent problems of the island republic. Mercer Cook's "The Literary Contribution of the French West Indian," *Journal of Negro History*, XXV (October, 1940) contains valuable information on the intellectual history of the French islands.

For mainland developments see Tannenbaum, *Slave and Citizen*; Ramos, *The Negro in Brazil*; Pierson, *Negroes in Brazil*; Mary W. Williams, *The People and Politics of Latin America* (Boston, 1938); and Charles E. Chapman, *Republic Hispanic America* (New York, 1937). Additional works of value in connection with this chapter are listed in the readings for Chapter IX.

XX. Canadian Negroes

William Renwick Riddell has made a significant contribution to understanding slavery in Canada. His works have been published primarily in the *Journal of Negro History*. Several of them are: "Slavery in Canada," V (July, 1920); "Notes on the Slave in Nouvelle France," VIII (July, 1923); "Further Notes on the Slave in Canada," IX (January, 1924); "The Slave in Upper Canada," IV (October, 1919); and "The Baptism of Slaves in Prince Edward Island," VI (July, 1921). The crusade against slavery is treated by Fred Landon in "The Anti-Slavery Society of Canada," *Journal of Negro History*, IV (January, 1919). Landon is the pioneer student of Negro migration into Canada from the United States. Among his articles that have appeared in the *Journal of Negro History* are the following: "Agriculture among the Negro Refugees in Upper Canada," XXI (July, 1936); "The Buxton Settlement in Canada," III (October, 1918); "Canadian Negroes and the John Brown Raid," VI (April, 1921); "Canadian Negroes and the Rebellion of 1837," VII (October, 1922); "Henry Bibb, A Colonizer," V (October, 1920); and "The Negro Migration to Canada after the Passing of the Fugitive Slave Act," V (January, 1920). Works of Fred Landon appearing elsewhere are: "Anthony Burns in Canada," Ontario Historical Society, *Papers and Records*, XXII (1925); "Negro Colonization Schemes in Upper Canada before 1860," Royal Society of Canada, *Transactions*, Third Series, XXIII (1929); and "Social Conditions Among the Negroes in Upper Canada," Ontario Historical Society, *Papers and Records*, XXII (1925). An excellent overall treatment of Negro settlements in Canada is William H. and Jane Pease, *Black Utopia: Negro Communal Experiments in America* (Madison, 1963).

Among the contemporary accounts which give invaluable information concerning the Negro settlements are: Levi Coffin, *Reminiscences* (Cincinnati, 1876); Benjamin Drew, *Northside View of Slavery* (Boston, 1856); Samuel G. Howe, *The Refugees from Slavery in Canada West* (Boston, 1864); Benjamin Lundy, *The Diary of Benjamin Lundy*, edited by Fred Landon (Toronto, 1922); and Austin Steward, *Twenty-Two Years a Slave and Forty Years a Freeman* (Rochester, 1857). See also, Siebert, *Underground Railroad*; Henry A. Tanser, *The Settlement of Negroes in Kent County, Ontario* (Chatham, 1939); and Carter G. Woodson, *A Century of Negro Migration* (Washington, 1918). For discussions of recent developments see Ida C. Greaves, *The Negro in Canada* (Orillia, 1930) ; Robert W. O'Brien, "Victoria's Negro Colonists," *Phylon*, III (First Quarter, 1942) ; and Carl Wittke, *A History of Canada* (New York, 1928).

XXI. Philanthropy and Self-Help

The effect of philanthropy on the development of American education in general receives able treatment in Jesse B. Sears, *Philanthropy in the History of American Higher Education* (Washington, 1922) ; while philanthropic activities among Negroes are discussed in Ullin W. Leavell, *Philanthropy in Negro Education* (Nashville, 1930). For the growth of education among Negroes during the period see Bond, *Education of the Negro in the American Social Order* and Holmes, *Evolution of the Negro College*. J. L. M. Curry, a leader in the program of developing education among Negroes in the South, discusses the problem in *A Brief Sketch of George Peabody*, and *A History of the Peabody Education Fund through Thirty Years* (Cambridge, 1898), and *Difficulties, Complications and Limitations Connected with the Education of the Negro* (Baltimore, 1895). A work that goes beyond these titles and discusses the role of philanthropy in the discrimination against the Negro in education is Louis R. Harlan, *Separate and Unequal* (Chapel Hill, 1958).

The views of Booker T. Washington have been discussed by numerous friends and enemies. His views, as expressed by himself, may be found in the following works: *The Negro in the South; His Economic Progress in Relation to his Moral and Religious Development*, with W. E. B. DuBois (Philadelphia, 1907) ; *Selected Speeches of Booker T. Washington*, edited by E. David Washington (Garden City, 1932) ; and *Up From Slavery; An Autobiography* (Garden City, 1900). See also Emmett J. Scott and Lyman B. Stowe, *Booker T. Washington, Builder of A Civilization* (Garden City, 1916). W. E. B. DuBois, the most relentless critic of Washington, has aired his views in many books and articles. Among them are *The Souls of Black Folk, Essays and Sketches* (Chicago, 1903) and *Dusk of Dawn, An Essay toward the Autobiography of a Race Concept* (New York, 1940). For other discussions of Washington's program, see Merle Curti, *The Social Ideas of American Educators* (New York, 1935) ; Charles S. Johnson, "The Social Philosophy of Booker T. Washington," *Opportunity*, VI (April, 1928) ; and W. Edward Farrison, "Booker T. Washington: A Study in Educational Leadership," *South Atlantic Quarterly*, XLI (July, 1942). Recent studies of Washington include Basil J. Mathews, *Booker T. Washington* (Cambridge, 1948) ; Samuel R. Spencer, Jr., *Booker T. Washington and the Negro's Place in American Life* (Boston, 1955), and August Meier, *Negro Thought in America*. For studies of DuBois, see Francis L. Broderick, *W. E. B. DuBois: Negro Leader in Time of Crisis* (Stanford, 1959) and Elliott M. Rudwick, *W. E. B. DuBois: A Study in Minority Group Leadership* (Philadelphia, 1961).

The problems of Negro labor and other aspects of economic life are treated in Spero and Harris, *The Black Worker* and Wesley, *Negro Labor in the United States*. The status of Negro business enterprises at the turn of the century is discussed in W. E. B. DuBois, *The Negro in Business* (Atlanta, 1899) and Booker T. Washington, *The Negro in*

Business (Boston, 1907). Banking enterprises among Negroes have been carefully analyzed and criticized in Harris, *The Negro as Capitalist*, while another phase of economic life is treated in William J. Trent, *Development of Negro Life Insurance Enterprises* (Philadelphia, 1932).

The Atlanta University Studies, edited by W. E. B. DuBois, are an important source of information concerning the social and cultural development of American Negroes during the period. See, for example, *The College-Bred Negro* (Atlanta, 1900) ; *The Negro Common School* (Atlanta, 1901) ; and *Some Efforts of American Negroes for Their Own Social Betterment* (Atlanta, 1898). For religious developments, see Woodson, *History of the Negro Church* and David M. Reimers, *White Protestantism and the Negro* (New York, 1965). An able analysis of the growth of institutions is in Guy B. Johnson, "Some Factors in the Development of Negro Social Institutions in the United States," *American Journal of Sociology*, XXX (November, 1934). Literary activities of Negroes are carefully traced in Loggins, *The Negro Author*. Journalistic activities receive attention in Penn, *The Afro-American Press and Its Editors* and Detweiler, *The Negro Press in the United States*. For sketches of prominent contemporary Negroes see William J. Simmons, *Men of Mark: Eminent, Progressive, and Rising* (Cleveland, 1887). For general problems see Logan, *The Negro in American Life and Thought*.

XXII. The Negro and American Imperialism

For the growth of American interest in imperialism and the extension of American influence, see Thomas A. Bailey, *Diplomatic History of the American People* (New York, 1940) ; Walter Millis, *The Martial Spirit* (Boston, 1931) ; and Julius W. Pratt, *The Expansionists of 1898* (Baltimore, 1936). There is no exhaustive account of the Negro's part in the Spanish-American War. The following titles are among the better ones available: Edward L. N. Glass, *The History of the Tenth Cavalry, 1866–1901* (Tucson, 1921) ; James M. Guthrie, *Campfires of the Afro-American* (Philadelphia, 1899) ; Edward A. Johnson, *History of Negro Soldiers in the Spanish American War and Other Items of Interest* (Raleigh, 1899) ; Miles V. Lynk, *The Black Troopers, or the Daring Heroism of the Negro Soldiers in the Spanish American War* (Jackson, 1899) ; and *A New Negro for a New Century* (Chicago, 1900).

The emergence of an American imperial policy is discussed in Howard C. Hill, *Roosevelt and the Caribbean* (Chicago, 1927) and Theodore Roosevelt, *Colonial Policies of the United States* (Garden City, 1937). The American administration of Puerto Rico is treated in Pedro Capo-Rodriguez, "Some Historical and Political Aspects of the Government of Porto Rico," *Hispanic American Historical Review*, II (November, 1919) and Bolivar Pagan, *Puerto Rico: The Next State* (Washington, 1942). The acquisition and administration of the Virgin Islands are ably handled in Charles C. Tansill, *The Purchase of the Danish West Indies* (Baltimore, 1932) and Luther H. Evans, *The Virgin Islands, From Naval Base to New Deal* (Ann Arbor, 1945). The relations of the United States and Haiti are given attention in George

W. Brown, "Haiti and the United States," *Journal of Negro History*, VIII (April, 1923) and Logan, *Diplomatic Relations of the United States with Haiti*. See also James A. Padgett, "Diplomats to Haiti and Their Diplomacy," *Journal of Negro History*, XXV (July, 1940). "The Ministers to Liberia and their Diplomacy," *Journal of Negro History*, XXII (January, 1937) by the same author traces the influence of American diplomats on Liberia's history.

XXIII. Dawn of a New Century

The main problems arising during the Roosevelt administration are discussed in H. F. Pringle, *Theodore Roosevelt* (New York, 1931). For a criticism of Roosevelt's policy with regard to the Negro, see Alfred H. Stone, *Studies in the American Race Problem* (New York, 1908). The impact of the city upon the condition of Negroes is treated in Thomas J. Woofter, *Negro Problems in Cities* (Garden City, 1928). For information concerning the problems of Negroes in New York see George E. Haynes, *The Negro at Work in New York City* (New York, 1912); James W. Johnson, *Black Manhattan* (New York, 1930); and Claude McKay, *Harlem: Negro Metropolis* (New York, 1940). Two full-length studies that should be consulted are Gilbert Osofsky, *Harlem: The Making of a Ghetto* (New York, 1966) and Seth M. Scheiner, *Negro Mecca* (New York, 1965). Various aspects of the problems of Negro life in urban centers are discussed in Woodson, *A Century of Negro Migration;* Caroline B. Chapin, "Settlement Work among Colored People," *Annals* of the American Academy of Political and Social Science, XXI (March, 1903) and R. E. Clark, "Negro Home Life and Standards of Living," *Annals* of the American Academy of Political and Social Science, XLIX (September, 1913).

Violence both in the South and North receives special attention in Ray S. Baker, *Following the Color Line* (New York, 1908). For a discussion of the growth of prejudice in a Northern state, see Frank U. Quillen, *The Color Line in Ohio* (Ann Arbor, 1913). Anti-Negro views' are canvassed in I. A. Newby, *Jim Crow's Defense: Anti-Negro Thought in America, 1900–1930* (Baton Rouge, 1965). The status of lynching is the concern of Arthur Raper in *The Tragedy of Lynching* (Chapel Hill, 1933). See also Ida Wells Barnett, "Our Country's Lynching Record," *Survey*, XXIV (January, 1913) and E. B. Reuter, *The American Race Problem* (New York, 1927). The growth of organized protest against violence to Negroes is traced by DuBois in *Dusk of Dawn*. The story of the emergence of the major protest organization is told in Mary W. Ovington, *How the National Association for the Advancement of Colored People Began* (New York, 1914); Robert L. Jack, *History of the National Association for the Advancement of Colored People* (Boston, 1943); and Langston Hughes, *Fight for Freedom: The Story of the NAACP* (New York, 1962). Other service organizations are discussed in L. Hollingsworth Wood, "The Urban League Movement," *Journal of Negro History*, IX (January, 1924) and J. E. Moorland, "The Young Men's Christian Association among Negroes," *Journal of Negro History*, IX (January, 1924). See also Addie Hunton, *William A. Hunton* (New York, 1938). Dilemmas which Negroes faced are discussed in Kelly Miller, *Race Adjustment* (New

York, 190). For a discussion of politics see Nowlin, *The Negro in American National Politics*.

XXIV. In Pursuit of Democracy

The best general account of the Negro in the war is Emmett J. Scott's *The American Negro in the World War* (Washington, 1919). The difficult problems which Negro soldiers faced both at home and abroad are treated in Arthur W. Little, *From Harlem to the Rhine, The Story of New York's Colored Volunteers* (New York, 1936), and Charles H. Williams, *Sidelights on Negro Soldiers* (Boston, 1923). Chester D. Heywood's *Negro Combat Troops in the World War: The Story of the 371st Infantry* (Worcester, 1928) is diminished in importance by the condescending attitude of the author. The difficulties of the ranking Negro officer are told in Abraham Chew, *A Biography of Colonel Charles Young* (Washington, 1923). The efforts to raise the morale of Negro soldiers is described in Addie W. Hunton and Katherine M. Johnson, *Two Colored Women with the American Expeditionary Forces* (New York, 1920). See also Robert R. Moton, *Finding a Way Out* (Garden City, 1921).

The phenomenon of Negro migration during the war is treated in a variety of ways in numerous works. Among the better analyses are the following: Louise V. Kennedy, *The Negro Peasant Turns Cityward* (New York, 1930); Emmett J. Scott, *Negro Migration during the War* (New York, 1920); Ray S. Baker, "The Negro Goes North," *World's Work*, XXXIV (July, 1917); and Henderson Donald, "The Negro Migration, 1916–1918," *Journal of Negro History*, VI (October, 1921). For discussions of the problems of Negro labor see Spero and Harris, *The Black Worker*; Wesley, *Negro Labor in the United States*; and three works by George E. Haynes: "The Effect of War Conditions on Negro Labor," *Proceedings* of the Academy of Political Science, VIII (February, 1919); *The Negro at Work During the World War and During Reconstruction* (Washington, 1921); and *The Trend of the Races* (New York, 1922). An example of wartime violence is extensively treated in Elliott M. Rudwick, *Race Riot at St. Louis, July 2, 1917* (Carbondale, 1964).

The influence of America's attitude toward the Negro on the treaties is discussed by Rayford W. Logan in *The Senate and the Versailles Mandate System* (Washington, 1945). See also George L. Beer, *African Questions at the Paris Peace Conference* (New York, 1923). *Crisis, Afro-American*, and *Pittsburgh Courier* are important sources of information on the conditions among Negroes during the war.

XXV. Democracy Escapes

The violent reaction against Negroes in the post-war period is described in Walter White, *Rope and Faggot, A Biography of Judge Lynch* (New York, 1929); Frank Tannenbaum, *Darker Phases of the South* (New York, 1924); and Moorfield Storey, *Problems of Today* (Boston, 1920). The rise of the new Ku Klux Klan is traced and analyzed in John M. Mecklin, *The Ku Klux Klan: A Study of the American Mind* (New York, 1924) and Walter White, "Reviving the

Ku Klux Klan," *Forum*, LXV (April, 1921). The best account of a race riot during the period of reaction is the study made by the Chicago Commission on Race Relations, *The Negro in Chicago, A Study of Race Relations and A Race Riot* (Chicago, 1922). Several of the post-war riots are discussed as a background to recent developments in Arthur I. Waskow, *From Race Riot to Sit-In: 1919 and the 1960's* (New York, 1966). For the reaction of Negroes, see the collection of articles from Negro newspapers in Robert T. Kerlin, *The Voice of the Negro, 1919* (New York, 1920).

Efforts to find solutions to the problems during the period are discussed in Paul Baker, *Negro-White Adjustment* (New York, 1934) ; Herbert A. Miller, *Races, Nations and Classes* (Philadelphia, 1924) ; and Thomas J. Woofter, *The Basis of Racial Adjustment* (Boston, 1925). Programs which Negroes developed to improve their status are vividly described by James Weldon Johnson in *Along This Way* (New York, 1933). See also Abram L. Harris, "The Negro Problem As Viewed by Negro Leaders," *Current History*, XVIII (June, 1923) and Horace M. Bond, "Negro Leadership Since Washington," *South Atlantic Quarterly*, XXIV (April, 1925). The efforts to secure relief in the courts are described in Bernard Nelson, *The Negro and the Fourteenth Amendment Since 1920* (Washington, 1946) ; Mangum, *The Legal Status of the Negro*; and R. W. Hainsworth, "The Negro and the Texas Primaries," *Journal of Negro History*, XVIII (October, 1933). For information on the Garvey Movement see Amy Jacques-Garvey, *Philosophy and Opinions of Marcus Garvey* (New York, 1923) ; McKay, *Harlem: Negro Metropolis*; Roi Ottley, *New World A-Coming* (New York, 1943) ; and E. David Cronon, *Black Moses: The Story of Marcus Garvey and the Universal Negro Improvement Association* (Madison, 1955). Father Divine's movement is described in John Hoshor, *God in a Rolls Royce* (New York, 1936), a volume which contains stereotype notions of the Negro. For a discussion of the impact of the depression on the Negro see T. Arnold Hill, *The Negro and Economic Reconstruction* (Washington, 1937) ; Myrdal, *An American Dilemma*; and Richard Sterner, *The Negro's Share* (New York, 1943).

XXVI. A Harlem Renaissance

Many of the important works which shed light on the new Negro literary movement were mentioned in the text. In Spero and Harris, *The Black Worker*, important socio-economic aspects of the movement are discussed. The forces which gave rise to the Renaissance are taken up in Rollin L. Hartt, "The New Negro," *Independent*, CV (January 15, 1921), while the difficulties involved in the new movement are the concern of James Weldon Johnson in "The Dilemma of the Negro Author," *American Mercury*, XV (December, 1928). The movement is traced carefully and ably by Langston Hughes in *The Big Sea* (New York, 1940) and by James W. Johnson in two of his works, *Black Manhattan* and *Along This Way*. Every aspect of the movement is analyzed and interpreted in Alain Locke, *The New Negro: An Interpretation* (New York, 1925). Among the many critical studies of the literary aspects of the movement, the following are outstanding· Sterling Brown, *The Negro in American Fiction*; Elizabeth L. Green, *The*

Negro in Contemporary American Literature (Chapel Hill, 1928); J. Saunders Redding, *To Make a Poet Black* (Chapel Hill, 1939); and the works mentioned in the introduction of "Bibliographical Notes;" Frederick W. Bond, *The Negro and the Drama* (Washington, 1940); see also Benjamin Brawley, "The Negro Literary Renaissance," *The Southern Workman*, LVI (April, 1927). Anthologies which furnish satisfactory selections of the Negro writers are Sterling Brown and others, *The Negro Caravan*; V. F. Calverton, *Anthology of American Negro Literature*; James Weldon Johnson, *The Book of American Negro Poetry* (New York, 1922); Arna Bontemps, *American Negro Poetry* (New York, 1963); James Weldon Johnson, *The Book of American Negro Spirituals* (New York, 1925); and James Weldon Johnson, *The Second Book of Negro Spritals* (New York, 1926). For an able discussion of art during the period, see Porter, *Modern Negro Art*.

XXVII. The New Deal

The political regeneration of the Negro constitutes an engrossing story that is told, for one locality, by Harold F. Gosnell, *Negro Politicians, The Rise of Negro Politics in Chicago* (Chicago, 1935). See also Ralph Bunche, "The Negro in the Political Life of the United States," *Journal of Negro Education*, X (July, 1941). The Negro press, especially *Afro-American, Norfolk Journal and Guide, Pittsburgh Courier, Crisis*, and *Opportunity*, are important sources of information concerning political activities among Negroes. Analyses of Negro political activities are made in "The Fortune Quarterly Survey: XIII," *Fortune*, XVIII (July, 1938); James E. Allen, "The Negro and the 1940 Presidential Election," unpublished Master's thesis (Howard University, 1943); and Harold F. Gosnell, "The Negro Vote in Northern Cities," *National Municipal Review*, XXX (May, 1941). For an able description of the rise of the New Deal, see Louis M. Hacker, *A Short History of the New Deal* (New York, 1934). The activities of the Negro advisers are discussed in Laurence J. W. Hayes, *The Negro Federal Government Worker* (Washington, 1941); Ottley, *New World A-Coming*; and William J. Davis, "The Role of the Adviser on Negro Affairs and the Racial Specialist in National Administration, 1933–1940," unpublished Master's thesis (Howard University, 1940).

The relationship of the Negro to the many new government agencies is treated in John P. Davis, "Blue Eagles and Black Workers," *New Republic*, LXXXI (November 14, 1934); Marian T. Wright, "Negro Youth and the Federal Emergency Programs: CCC and NYA," *Journal of Negro Education*, IX (July, 1940); Sterner, *The Negro's Share*; and Hill, *The Negro and Economic Reconstruction*. See also Van Deusen, *The Black Man in White America* and Charles S. Johnson, *The Economic Status of Negroes* (Nashville, 1933). There have been several excellent studies of Negro labor in recent years. Among them are Horace Cayton and George S. Mitchell, *Black Workers and the New Unions* (Chapel Hill, 1939); Charles L. Franklin, *The Negro Labor Unionist of New York* (New York, 1936); Herbert R. Northrup, *Organized Labor and the Negro* (New York, 1944); and Robert C. Weaver, *Negro Labor, A National Problem* (New York, 1946). The story of the growth of a powerful Negro labor union is ably told by B. R. Brazeal in *The Brotherhood of Sleeping Car Porters* (New York, 1946).

XXVIII. Social and Cultural Strivings

Satisfactory general statements concerning recent trends in the education of Negroes may be found in Bond, *Education of the Negro in the American Social Order* and Holmes, *Evolution of the Negro College*. The psychological and social factors involved in separate education are treated in Buell G. Gallagher, *American Caste and the Negro College* (New York, 1938) and Doxey A. Wilkerson, *Special Problems in Negro Education* (Washington, 1939). For discussions of the influence of education on the process of integration, see Charles S. Johnson, editor, *Education and the Cultural Process* (n.p., 1943). The Yearbook issue of the *Journal of Negro Education* deals with some aspects of the problem of Negro education each year. Especially important are the issues for July, 1933, "A Survey of Negro Higher Education," and for July, 1940, "A Critical Survey of the Negro Adolescent and His Education." The inequalities of Negro education receive special attention in Rayford W. Logan, "Educational Segregation in the North," *Journal of Negro Education*, II (January, 1933); Henry J. McGuinn, "The Courts and Equality of Educational Opportunity," *Journal of Negro Education*, VIII (April, 1939); and Leon A. Ransom, "Legal Status of Negro Education under Separate School Systems," *Journal of Negro Education*, VIII (July, 1939). For discussions of the growing interest in provisions for graduate training, see Rufus E. Clement, "Legal Provisions for Graduate and Professional Instruction for Negroes in States Operating Separate School Systems," *Journal of Negro Education*, VII (April, 1939); Oliver C. Cox, Provisions for Graduate Work Among Negroes and the Prospects of a New System," *Journal of Negro Education*, IX (January, 1940); and Fred McCuiston, *Graduate Instruction for Negroes in the United States* (Nashville, 1939).

Material on education and especially on the desegregation of the schools has been exceedingly voluminous in recent years. Virtually every yearbook (Summer) edition of the *Journal of Negro Education* as well as other issues contains material on the subject. *Southern School News* began publication shortly after the 1954 Court decision on desegregating the schools and has valuable information on events and trends. *Integrated Education* is a more recent periodical, but it should be consulted. Herbert Hill and Jack Greenberg, *Citizen's Guide to Desegregation* (Boston, 1955) and Harry Ashmore, *The Negro and the Schools* (Chapel Hill, 1954) provide excellent overall treatments of school desegregation. Specific experiences and examples of school desegregation are presented in Robin Williams and Margaret W. Ryan, *Schools in Transition: Community Experiences in Desegregation* (Chapel Hill, 1954); Omer Carmichael, *The Louisville Story* (New York, 1957); James H. Tipton, *Community in Crisis* (New York, 1953); Wilson and Jane Record, *Little Rock, U.S.A.: Materials for Analysis* (San Francisco, 1960); and James W. Silver, *Mississippi: The Closed Society* (New York, 1964).

682 · BIBLIOGRAPHICAL NOTES

Concerning the problems and achievements of Negroes in various fields, see Harry W. Greene, *Holders of Doctorates among American Negroes* (Boston, 1946); Charles S. Johnson, *The Negro College Graduate* (Chapel Hill, 1938); Carter G. Woodson, *The Negro Professional Man and the Community* (Washington, 1934); G. Franklin Edwards, *The Negro Professional Class* (Glencoe, 1959); and Deitrich C. Reitzes, *Negroes and Medicine* (Cambridge, 1958). Eliza Atkins Gleason has discussed the Negro library as an educative force in *The Southern Negro and the Public Library* (Chicago, 1941).

The Negro's world is exhaustively described in Myrdal, *An American Dilemma*. Shorter, but able descriptions of the Negro community are in Van Deusen's *Black Man in White America*; Davie, *Negroes in America*, and Frazier, *The Negro in the United States*. For a searching, critical analysis of the Negro middle class, see E. Franklin Frazier, *Black Bourgeoisie* (Glencoe, 1957). Important sources of information are Florence Murray, *The Negro Handbook* (New York, 1946); John P. Davis, *The American Negro Reference Book*; and Talcott Parsons and Kenneth Clark, *The Negro American* (Boston, 1966). Special aspects of the Negro's world are discussed in Detweiler, *The Negro Press in the United States*; Mays and Nicholson, *The Negro's Church*; and the Yearbook issue of the *Journal of Negro Education*, VIII (July, 1939), "The Position of the Negro in the American Social Order." Privation and opportunities are discussed in Michael Harrington, *The Other America: Poverty in the United States* (New York, 1962) and Eli Ginzberg, *The Negro Potential* (New York, 1962).

Lives of individual Negroes are presented in Bardolph, *The Negro Vanguard*; Ridgley Torrence, *The Story of John Hope* (New York, 1948); Mary Church Terrell, *A Colored Woman in a White World* (Washington, 1940); Helen Buckler, *Dr. Dan: Pioneer in American Surgery* (Boston, 1954); Roi Ottley, *The Lonely Warrior: The Life and Times of Robert S. Abbott* (Chicago, 1955); Rackham Holt, *George Washington Carver* (Garden City, 1943); Edwin R. Embree, *Thirteen Against the Odds* (New York, 1945); and *The Autobiography of Malcolm X* (New York, 1965). The problem of the relationship between the Negro's Americanization and his African background is discussed in Harold R. Isaacs, *The New World of Negro Americans* (New York, 1963).

The American Youth Commission studies shed considerable light on the problem of adjustment which Negroes in America face. The principal titles are J. H. Atwood and others, *Thus Be Their Destiny* (Washington, 1941); Allison Davis and John Dollard, *Children of Bondage* (Washington, 1940); E. Franklin Frazier, *Negro Youth at the Crossways* (Washington, 1940); Charles S. Johnson, *Growing Up in the Black Belt* (Washington, 1941); Ira DeA. Reid, *In a Minor Key* (Washington, 1940); Robert L. Sutherland, *Color, Class, and Personality* (Washington, 1942); and W. Lloyd Warner and others, *Color and Human Nature* (Washington, 1941). Programs for the improvement of the status of Negroes are discussed in Rayford W. Logan, editor, *What the Negro Wants* (Chapel Hill, 1944); the entire issue of *Survey Graphic*, XXXI (November, 1942), "Color, Unfinished Business of Democracy," and Ralph J. Bunche, "The Programs of Organizations Devoted to the Improvement of the Status of the American Negro,"

Journal of Negro Education, VIII (July, 1939). See also *Crisis, Opportunity, Southern Patriot*, and *New South*, the last two journals being the official publications of the Southern Conference for Human Welfare and the Southern Regional Council respectively. Broader programs for the improvement of intergroup relations are discussed in Alexander Alland and James W. Wise, *The Springfield Plan* (New York, 1945); Theodore Brameld, *Minority Problems in the Public Schools* (New York, 1946); Spencer Brown, *They See for Themselves* (New York, 1945); Rachel Davis Du Bois, *Build Together Americans* (New York, 1945); Hortense Powdermaker, *Probing Our Prejudices* (New York, 1944); Kenneth B. Clark, *Prejudice and Your Child* (Boston, 1955); and George E. Simpson and J. Milton Yinger, *Racial and Cultural Minorities* (New York, 1965).

XXIX. Fighting for the Four Freedoms

Releases of the press sections of the War and Navy Departments and of the Office of War Information provide considerable information on the activities of Negroes both on the home front and on the battlefields during the war. A variety of facts and most of the statistics have been gathered and printed in Murray, *Negro Handbook*. Many excellent pictures of Negroes in the war are provided in John D. Silvera, *The Negro in World War II* (n.p., 1946). A good summary of the military operations is in Roger W. Shugg and H. A. De Weerd, *World War II* (Washington, 1946). For a discussion of the place of the Negro in the military organizations of the United States, see Seymour J. Schoenfeld, *The Negro in the Armed Forces* (Washington, 1945). The definitive work on Negroes in the Army, however, is the volume in the Special Studies Series of the United States Army in World War II: Ulysses Lee, *The Employment of Negro Troops* (Washington, 1966). For discussions of changes in military policy regarding Negroes see Dennis D. Nelson, *The Integration of the Negro into the United States Navy* (New York, 1951) and Lee Nichols, *Breakthrough on the Color Front* (New York, 1954). Walter White, *A Rising Wind* (New York, 1945) is an excellent account of the activities of Negroes on the fighting front.

The Negro press is indispensable in getting a complete picture of Negroes during the war. See also L. D. Reddick, "The Negro in the Navy in World War II," *Journal of Negro History*, XXXII (April, 1947). The problem of integrating Negroes in the war effort is the principal concern of Earl Brown, "American Negroes and the War," Harper's Magazine, CLXXXIV (April, 1942); Earl Brown and George R. Leighton, *The Negro and the War* (New York, 1942); and "The Negro's War," *Fortune*, XXV (June, 1942). Several journals have devoted entire issues to the problem of the impact of the war on Negroes. Among them are: *Survey Graphic*, "Color, Unfinished Business of Democracy," XXX (November, 1942); *Annals* of the American Academy of Political and Social Science, "Minority Peoples in a Nation at War," CCXXIII (September, 1942); *Journal of Negro Education*, "The American Negro in World War I and World War II," XII (Summer, 1943); and two issues of the *Journal of Educational Sociology* with L. D. Reddick as special editor, "The Negro in the North during Wartime," XVIII (January, 1944) and "Race Relations on the Pacific Coast," XIX (November, 1945). The apprehension of Southern whites concerning the American Negro and the war is expressed by John Temple Graves in "The Southern Negro and the War Crisis," *Virginia Quarterly Review*, XVIII (Autumn, 1942).

The part which Negroes played in producing the goods of war has received special attention in the Council for Democracy's *The Negro and Defense* (New York, 1941) ; Weaver, *Negro Labor;* and Northrup, *Organized Labor and the Negro*. Negro morale was the concern of most of the writers, but the following were particularly concerned about it: Horace M. Bond, "Should the Negro Care Who Wins the War?" *Annals* of the American Academy of Political and Social Science, CCXXIII (September, 1942) ; James A. Bayton, "The Psychology of Racial Morale," *Journal of Negro Education*, XI (April, 1942) ; Guion G. Johnson, "The Impact of the War upon the Negro," *Journal of Negro Education*, X (July, 1941) ; and J. Saunders Redding, "A Negro Looks at This War," *American Mercury*, LV (November, 1942).

XXX. *The Post-War Years*

For a discussion of some of the major problems confronting the Negro, see Rayford W. Logan, *The Negro and the Post-War World: A Primer* (Washington, 1945). The several publications of the Truman administration that deal with post-war problems are mentioned in the text. The development of machinery regarding fair employment is discussed in Malcolm Ross, *All Manner of Men* (New York, 1948) ; Louis Rauchames, *Race, Jobs, and Politics* (New York, 1953) ; and Louis Kesselman, *The Social Politics of FEPC* (Chapel Hill, 1948). For trends in housing see Morton Deutsch, *Interracial Housing* (Minneapolis, 1951) and Robert C. Weaver, *The Negro Ghetto* (New York, 1948). Race and radical politics is discussed in Wilson Record, *The Negro and the Communist Party* (Chapel Hill, 1951), while other political matters are covered in Henry L. Moon, *Balance of Power: The Negro Vote* (New York, 1948).

In Howard Zinn, *The Southern Mystique* (New York, 1964) there is a stimulating analysis of the forces in the South that are opposed to change. Carl Rowan, *Go South to Sorrow* (New York, 1957) discusses the South's resistance to social change in a climate that calls for economic change. There are several valuable treatments of Southern reaction to the move to desegregate the schools, including Hodding Carter, *The South Strikes Back* (New York, 1959) and John B. Martin, *The Deep South Says "Never"* (New York, 1957). The Southern position is summarized in William D. Workman, *The Case for the South* (New York, 1960).

The beginnings of the Negro Revolution are discussed in Martin Luther King, *Stride Toward Freedom: The Montgomery Story* (New York, 1958) and Louis Lomax, *The Negro Revolt* (New York, 1962). For a treatment of the Black Muslims as a factor in the growing Negro revolt see C. Eric Lincoln, *The Black Muslims in America* (Boston, 1961) and Essien U. Essien-Udom, *Black Nationalism: A Search for Identity in America* (Chicago, 1962). The work of the United States Commission on Civil Rights is set forth in its publications, including its annual reports, the reports of its state advisory committees, and its hearings.

XXXI. The Negro Revolution

The literature on the militant drive for equality is already beyond the point of easy listing and is growing at a rapid rate. A recent comprehensive bibliography covering the Negro Revolution is Elizabeth Miller, *The Negro in America: A Bibliography*. Several works have appeared in recent years that do not deal with the Revolution specifically but give perspective and background. Among them are Loren Miller, *The Petitioners: The Story of the Supreme Court of the United States and the Negro* (New York, 1966); Milton Konvitz, *A Century of Civil Rights* (New York, 1961); Arna Bontemps, *100 Years of Negro Freedom* (New York, 1961); United States Commission on Civil Rights, *Freedom to the Free* (Washington, 1963); and the lectures at Wayne State University in 1962–1963 to observe the centennial of the Emancipation Proclamation: Arnold M. Rose, editor, *Assuring Freedom to the Free* (Detroit, 1964).

The problems to which the militant movement addressed itself are the main interest of several works. See especially Louis Lomax, *The Negro Revolt*; John P. Roche, *The Quest for the Dream: The Development of Civil Rights and Human Relations in Modern America* (New York, 1963); Charles Silberman, *Crisis in Black and White* (New York, 1964); William J. Brink and Louis Harris, *The Negro Revolution in America* (New York, 1964); and Alan F. Westin, editor, *Freedom Now!: The Civil-Rights Struggle in America* (New York, 1964), which contains many statements written by the leaders themselves. For a more lengthy discussion of the movement by some of the leaders see Kenneth B. Clark, editor, *The Negro Protest* (Boston, 1963). The student protest movement is treated in Howard Zinn, *SNCC: The New Abolitionists* (Boston, 1964).

The experiences of participants in marches, demonstrations, and other forms of protest are covered in the following works: Martin Luther King, *Why We Can't Wait* (New York, 1964); Merrill Proudfoot, *Diary of a Sit-In* (Chapel Hill, 1962); James Peck, *Freedom Ride* (New York, 1962); Nicholas Von Hoffman, *Mississippi Notebook* (New York, 1964); John Ehle, *The Free Men* (New York, 1965); and James W. Silver, *Mississippi: The Closed Society*. See also Arthur I. Waskow, *From Race Riot to Sit-in*. Lorraine Hansberry, *The Movement: Documentary of a Struggle for Equality* (New York, 1964) and Doris E. Saunders, *The Day They Marched* (Chicago, 1963) contain excellent photographs of events in the movement. President Kennedy's role is assessed in Harry Golden, *Mr. Kennedy and the Negroes* (Cleveland, 1964) and Doris Saunders, editor, *The Kennedy Years and the Negro: A Photographic Record* (Chicago, 1964).

Important social and economic problems related to the Negro Revolution are discussed in Talcott Parsons and Kenneth Clark, *The Negro American* and Daniel P. Moynihan, *The Negro Family: The Case for National Action*, and President Lyndon B. Johnson's Commencement Address at Howard University in June, 1965. In Dale L. Hiestand, *Economic Growth and Employment Opportunities for Minorities* (New

York, 1964) ; Paul Bullock, *Merit Employment* (Los Angeles, 1960) ; and Vivian W. Henderson, *The Economic Status of Negroes: In the Nation and in the South* (Atlanta, 1963) there are illuminating discussions of discrimination in industry and the relationship between Negro employment and the national economy. The search for new industrial opportunities for Negroes is discussed in Eli Ginzberg, editor, *The Negro Challenge to the Business Community* (New York, 1964). For other aspects of the problem of equal economic opportunity see Whitney M. Young, *To Be Equal* (New York, 1964) and Nat Hentoff, *The New Equality* (New York, 1964). Kenneth B. Clark, *Dark Ghetto: Dilemmas of Social Power* (New York, 1965) discusses poverty in the inner city and ways of solving the problem.

Ralph Bunche, *A World View of Race* (Washington, 1936) calls attention to the relationship between imperialism, colonialism, and the problem of race. See also Merze Tate, "The War Aims of World War I and World War II and Their Relation to the Darker Peoples of the World," *Journal of Negro Education*, XII (Summer, 1943). In two works W. E. B. DuBois discusses the connection between colonies and world peace: *Color and Democracy* (New York, 1945) and *The World and Africa* (New York, 1947). For discussions of the interest of Negro Americans in Africa see Harold Isaacs, *The New World of Negro Americans;* his *Emergent Americans: A Report on Crossroads Africa* (New York, 1961) ; John A. Davis, editor, *Africa as Seen by American Negroes* (Paris, 1958) ; and articles in *Freedomways* and the *Journal of African History*. Experiences of individual Negro Americans in the quest of identification with Africa are recounted in Eslanda Goode Robeson, *African Journey* (New York, 1945) ; Era Bell Thompson, *Land of My Fathers* (New York, 1954) ; and Richard Wright, *Black Power: A Record of Reactions in a Land of Pathos* (New York, 1954).

Index

Cotton Kingdom, 168, 171–4; slaves in, 186; recovers, 311
Council of Economic Advisers, 642
Council of Federated Organizations, 638
Council of Safety, 327
Council of the Indies, 118
Council on Equal Opportunity, 641
Couvent, Madame, 230
Covarrubias, Miguel, 510
Cowper, William, 155
Cox, Oliver, 558
Craft, Ellen, 252
Craft, William, 252
Craig, A. U., 471
Crandall, Prudence, 248
Cravath, Erastus M., 308
Crawford, Anthony, 454
Creole, 249
Crevecoeur, Hector St. John de, 98
Crichlow, Ernest, 522
Crisis, 476, 487, 502, 505, 605; quoted, 478–9; published, 447; works of Negro poets in, 505; literary contests, 506, 512
Croix de Guerre, awarded to Negro troops, 462–3, 465, 466, 591
Cromwell, Oliver, 137
Croom, J. C., 468
Crow, Lester, 571
Crum, William D., 434–5, 437
Crummell, Alexander, 241
Crusader, quoted, 485
Cuba, 60, 416; slaves imported into, 53, 63, 69, 112; abolishes slavery, 349; economic conditions in, 354–5; education in, 355–6; Spain's treatment of, 417; revolts in, 417; American interest, 417–18; fighting in, 421–4; Negro troops on duty in, 424; Spain loses, 425; Negroes in, 426; *see also* Havana
Cuban Confederation of Labor, 354
Cuffe, Paul, 159, 238
Cullen, Countee, 504, 513
Cumberland Presbyterian Church, 309
Cuney, Waring, 511
Curaçao, 61
Current History, 506
Curry, J. L. M., 384, 392

Daiquiri, 421
Dallas, Texas, Negro population, 620
Dallas Co., Alabama, 638
Dalton, Georgia, 337
Damara, 21
Dancy, John C., 337
Danish West India Company, 68
Danish West Indies, 68, 427–8; *see also* Virgin Islands
Darien, Georgia, 221
Dark Princess, The, 501
Dark Water, 501
Darker Phases of the South, 499
Darlington, South Carolina, 613
Darrow, Clarence, 484, 510
Daughters of Jerusalem, 226
Daughters of the American Revolution, 520
Davey, Gloria, 520
David, 20
David Walker's Appeal, 212, 243, 250, 263
Davids, Tice, 254–5
Davis, A. K., 318
Davis, Allison, 568
Davis, Arthur, 358
Davis, B. O., 577
Davis, B. O., Jr., 587
Davis, Benjamin, 524
Davis, Ellabelle, 520
Davis, Jefferson, 197, 292; denounces North's treatment of Negroes, 274–5; urges impressment of slaves, 287; on enlistment of Negroes, 289; Revels fills Senate seat of, 319
Davis, John, 170
Davis, John W., 524
Davis, Ossie, 518
Davis, Sammy, Jr., 518
Dawn Industrial Institute, 374
Dawson, William (Musician), 519
Dawson, William L. (Congressman), 613–14
Day, Thomas, 224
Dean, William H., 533, 558, 606
DeBerry, W. N., 405–6
Decatur, Stephen, 138
Declaration of Independence, 129, 243; silent on slavery, 130
Dede, Edward, 230
Dee, Ruby, 518
Deep are the Roots, 517
Deerfield, Massachusetts, 110
DeGrasse, John V., 291
Delany, Martin: author, 233; opposes colonization society, 240; supports New World colonization, 240–1; officer in Civil War, 291
Delaware: early slavery in, 98–9; anti-slavery society, 140; Negro population, 145; delegates to Negro convention, 236; during Civil War, 271; Lincoln's plan to emancipate slaves, 280; Negro State college, 389

Salem, Massachusetts, slave trade, 103
Salem, Peter, 131–2
Salt Lake City, Utah, 418
Salvation Army, 596
Samoan Islands, 415
Sampson, Edith, 606
San Antonio X-Ray, 412
San Francisco, California, 571, 645; Negro population, 597, 620; United Nations at, 601–2; Civil Rights protests, 631
San Juan Hill, 421
Sankore, University of, 19
San Martin, Negroes with, 348
Sante Fe, New Mexico, 419
Santiago, 424
Santo Domingo, *see* Dominican Republic
Sao Paulo, 120, 360
Sao Salvador, *see* Banya
Sao, Thome, 119
Savage, Augusta, 522
Savage, W. Sherman, 558
Savannah, Georgia, 84, 221; siege of, 134–5, 137; Negro Baptist church, 162; docks use Negroes, 197; Negro schools, 202, 276–7; Negroes in business, 313–20; Negro collector, 434; Negro population, 436
Savings Bank of the Grand Fountain United Order of True Reformers, 404
Sawyer, George S., quoted, 262
Saxton, Rufus, 274, 277
"Scalawags," 329
Schiefflin, W. J., 449
Schmeling, Max, 574
Schomburg, A. A., 506
School History of the Negro Race . . ., 410
Schools, *see* Colleges; Education; High Schools
Schurz, Carl, quoted, 324, 325
Schuyler, George, 506
Scoble, John, 374
Scott v. Sanford, *see* Dred Scott Decision
Scott, Emmett J.: in World War I, 457–8, 460, 461, 474; investigates race clashes, 460–1; holds conference, 475
Scott, Hazel, 518
Scott, Winfield, 273
Scribner's Magazine, 422
Scruggs, William L., quoted, 357
Seabees, Negro, 588
Seabrook, Whitemarsh B., 262
Seattle, Washington, 597

Secret Information Concerning Black Troops, 468
Segregation, 454; in churches, 200, 227–8; in education, 228–9, 342, 553–5; laws in South, 342; residential, 436, 454, 481; in federal employment, 454; interstate bus, outlawed, 565; in army, 577; laws in the South, 627; de facto, 628, 644
"Seizure of Haiti by the United States . . . , The," 430
Seldes, Gilbert, 200
Selective Service, 458; Negroes under, 455–6, 463–4; Act passed, 455, 576, 580
Seligman, E. R. A., 449
Selling of Joseph, The, 260
Selma, Alabama, 288; march, 638
Senate, 427, 437; Negroes in, 319–20; Ben Tillman in, 339; dishonesty in, 437; committee investigates riot, 442; kills anti-lynching bill, 487; Negro staff members, 614
Senegal River, 12
Sergipe, 120
Services of Colored Americans . . ., 233
Seven Arts, The, 503
Seven Years' War, 51, 53
Seventy Six Association, 327
Sewall, Joseph, 107
Sewall, Samuel, 260
Seward, William H., 269, 427; debates compromise of 1850, 266; discusses emancipation with Lincoln, 282
Shabataka, 8
Shadd, Abraham, 251
Shadrach, 266
Shaler, Nathaniel, 169
Shannon, Fred, 278
Shantung Peninsula, 425
Sharecropping, 398
Shaw, Robert Gould, 291, 293
Shaw University, 550, 552
Shays, Daniel, 141
Shepard, James E., 407, 551
Sherman, Roger, 143
Sherman, Thomas W., 277
Sherman Anti-Trust Act, 433
Shingler, W. P., 292
Shirley, George, 520
Shoofly Regiment, 518
Shortridge, Samuel, 526
Shreveport, Louisiana, 436
Shuffle Along, 508, 509
Sibelius, Jan, 520
Siboney, 421

JOHN HOPE FRANKLIN is Chairman of the Department of History at the University of Chicago. Born in Oklahoma in 1915, he was graduated from Fisk University, of which he is now a trustee, in 1935. Harvard University awarded him the master's degree in 1936 and the doctorate in 1941. Professor Franklin has been a member of the history faculty at Fisk, at St. Augustine's College, at the North Carolina College at Durham, at Howard University, and he was Chairman of the Department of History at Brooklyn College. He has taught as Visiting Professor at Harvard, Wisconsin, and the University of California; he was a Fulbright Professor in Australia and Pitt Professor of American History and Institutions at Cambridge University in England.

Dr. Franklin, a member of Phi Beta Kappa, has held both a Rosenwald Fellowship and a Guggenheim Fellowship. Among his many published works are *The Free Negro in North Carolina, 1790-1860* (1943), *The Militant South, 1800-1860* (1956), *Reconstruction After the Civil War* (1961), and *The Emancipation Proclamation* (1963). He edited, with Isidore Starr, *The Negro in Twentieth Century America*, available in Vintage Books.

VINTAGE HISTORY—AMERICAN

VINTAGE POLITICAL SCIENCE
AND SOCIAL CRITICISM

VINTAGE CRITICISM,
LITERATURE, MUSIC, AND ART

VINTAGE BIOGRAPHY AND AUTOBIOGRAPHY